PAUL SHERIFF *teaches* Visual Basic® 6

201 West 103rd Street,
Indianapolis, Indiana 46290

Paul D. Sheriff

Paul Sheriff Teaches Visual Basic® 6

International Standard Book Number: 0-7897-1898-7

Library of Congress Catalog Card Number: 98-86964

Printed in the United States of America

First Printing: April, 1999

02 7 6

Trademarks

Warning and Disclaimer

Executive Editor
Chris Denny

Acquisitions Editor
Chris Denny

Development Editor
Tony Amico

Managing Editor
Jodi Jensen

Project Editor
Heather Talbot

Copy Editor
Bart Reed

Indexer
Kevin Fulcher

Proofreader
Mona Brown

Technical Editor
Sakhr Youness

Software Development Specialist
Andrea Duvall

Interior Design
Ruth C. Lewis

Cover Design
Mike Freeland

Layout Technicians
Amy Parker
Ayanna Lacey
Heather Hiatt Miller

Contents at a Glance

Table of Contents

Foreword

When ADVISOR MEDIA wants to field its Visual Basic "A-team," Paul Sheriff is the first person called. To present the popular VB technical workshops at ADVISOR DEVCON and to write Visual Basic "how-to" articles in *ACCESS-OFFICE-VB ADVISOR Magazine*, Paul is again the first choice—because he's the best. In recognition of his expertise and leadership in helping colleagues master Visual Basic, Paul has long held the title of *ADVISOR* Contributing Editor.

I've known Paul for several years. In the early '90s, he was an acknowledged master of Clipper, the most sophisticated programming technology of its day. When Paul switched to Windows and chose Visual Basic as his tool, there was no doubt he'd master it, too. Paul did more than master VB, he "got it." This is important.

Many programmers are good, even great, mechanics. They know what goes where, and how it all works. Give a master mechanic a design and it will get built. But where does the design come from? Paul is a visionary architect. He understands the concepts underlying Visual Basic, and he uses this insight to envision, design, and create superior applications.

As you work your way through this comprehensive book, you'll learn how to use Visual Basic—but you'll also be learning the "Paul Sheriff way" to use Visual Basic. I hope you pay attention to the nuances. In any programming environment, there are several ways to do almost anything. What you want to learn is the smart way. That's what Paul explains in these pages. It's wisdom he spent many years acquiring, and you have it in your hands right now.

When you're ready for monthly guidance on VB or you want to learn from Paul, face to face, at DEVCON, come and see us at *ADVISOR*. I look forward to hearing about your Visual Basic programming success.

John L. Hawkins

CEO & Editorial Director

ADVISOR MEDIA, Inc.

`www.advisor.com`

About the Author

Paul D. Sheriff has more than 13 of years experience in programming business applications. Paul is proficient in Visual Basic and is considered one of the leading Visual Basic programmers in the industry. Paul has been very active in the Visual Basic community. He has been the president of the Orange County Visual Basic User Group. He has written more than 40 articles for many different publications and is now a contributing editor to *ADVISOR* magazine, writing many articles on Visual Basic 3, 4, 5, and now 6. Paul also speaks at the Advisor Publications Developer's conferences and at Microsoft Tech-Ed.

Over the years, Paul has been a featured speaker with many different training companies. He has taught Visual Basic and SQL Server all across the country and even all over the world. Paul also has more than 50 training videos on the topics of Visual Basic, SQL Server, and introductory-level computer programming.

In 1991, Paul started Paul D. Sheriff & Associates, Inc., a high-level computer consulting company specializing in high-quality custom software. PDSA, Inc. is a Microsoft solution provider. Since starting PDSA, Inc., Paul and his team have consulted in many different industries, such as aerospace, real estate, medical, and hotel, as well as for the government.

Paul received his MIS degree from California State University, Long Beach, and he supplemented this with specialized courses at McDonnell Douglas as well as outside training courses. Paul taught C language programming for two years at McDonnell Douglas and was one of the highest-rated speakers on the Clipper 5.0 Masters Seminar Series. Paul is now one of the top-rated Visual Basic instructors with Application Developers Training Company (`www.AppDev.com`) and TREK Services (`www.TREKServices.com`).

Paul is the father of two daughters, which keeps him and his wife quite busy. When Paul is not working, he spends a lot of time hiking, motorcycle riding, skiing, and spending time with his dog, Rusty.

Paul D. Sheriff & Associates, Inc. is available for consulting work and onsite training in Visual Basic, SQL Server, and Internet/intranet applications. Contact Paul D. Sheriff & Associates, Inc. at (888) 899-PDSA (toll free) or at (714) 734-9792. Fax: (714) 734-9793. Email: `Psheriff@pdsa.com`.

You can visit the PDSA Web site at `http://www.pdsa.com`.

Acknowledgments

There are many people I need to thank for their continued support over the years. First and foremost, my wife, Ann, for putting up with me at the kitchen table while writing this book. She also had the job of watching over our newborn daughter right when I started writing this book. Second, my parents, for always pushing me to learn, and telling me that I can do anything I want. I would also like to thank everyone at my company, PDSA, Inc., for their help in proofreading and keeping the business going while I wrote this book. I would also like to thank Erik Ruthruff for his help over the past 10 years. Erik, you are responsible for making me a better writer with all the editing you have done on my material over the years.

Tell Us What You Think!

As the reader of this book, *you* are our most important critic and commentator. We value your opinion and want to know what we're doing right, what we could do better, what areas you'd like to see us publish in, and any other words of wisdom you're willing to pass our way.

As an Executive Editor for Que, I welcome your comments. You can fax, email, or write me directly to let me know what you did or didn't like about this book—as well as what we can do to make our books stronger.

Please note that I cannot help you with technical problems related to the topic of this book, and that due to the high volume of mail I receive, I might not be able to reply to every message.

When you write, please be sure to include this book's title and author as well as your name and phone or fax number. I will carefully review your comments and share them with the author and editors who worked on the book.

Fax: 317-581-4666

Email: `feedback@quepublishing.com`

Mail: Executive Editor
Que
201 West 103rd Street
Indianapolis, IN 46290 USA

Introduction

PAUL D. SHERIFF & ASSOCIATES, INC.

High Quality Software & Training.

Courseware Design: Paul D. Sheriff

Technical Editor: Paul D. Sheriff

Printed in the United States of America.

Fundamentals of Visual Basic 6

This book is designed for programmers who have little or no Visual Basic or Windows programming experience. Students will learn the syntax of the Visual Basic language, event-driven programming, and how to put together a complete Visual Basic application. The emphasis in this book is on good coding practices such as industry naming standards, indentation, and code reusability.

Assumptions

To be able to use this book effectively, you should have some previous programming experience. This means you're a programmer in another language, you've taken a class on programming at a local college, or you've read a book on how to become a programmer.

It's assumed that you own a copy of Microsoft Windows 95, Windows 98, or Windows NT 4.0 or later and, of course, that you own a copy of Visual Basic 6 Professional or Enterprise Edition.

Conventions Used in This Book

There are certain typographical conventions that are followed in this book. You'll find exercises for you to perform, bits of source code, and keywords for the Visual Basic language.

Italic font is used to emphasize a term that's being defined.

The following is what you'll see when there's an exercise for you to do. You'll see an exercise head followed by a series of numbered steps and an analysis of what you've just learned:

EXERCISE

A Specific Title Appears Here

1. Insert a disk into the floppy disk drive.
2. Continue working through the steps to complete the exercise.

At the end of each exercise there will be an analysis/summary paragraph.

All sample source code appears in a fixed-pitch font:

```
If bPerform Then
    MsgBox "Please select another option"
End If
```

Sometimes we will refer you to the book's companion Web site. On the Internet, simply type `http://www.mcp.com/product_support`. Then in the Book Information and Downloads text box, enter the ISBN, which is 0-7897-1898-7, and click the Search button.

Introduction to Visual Basic 6

Visual Basic Overview

VISUAL BASIC IS A PROGRAMMING LANGUAGE and development environment that allows you to create programs that run under the Windows operating system (OS). This rich language enables you to develop many different types of applications. You can create programs that interact with databases, interact with the Internet, and even interact with hardware. In this chapter, you'll also learn about the different features and components that make up the Visual Basic programming language and development environment. Along the way you'll learn a little about the Windows operating system, and why developing programs for this environment may be different than what you're used to.

Chapter Objectives

- Learn what Visual Basic is
- Learn the history of the Visual Basic language
- Be able to identify the features of Visual Basic
- Know what compiler options you have with Visual Basic
- Know the different versions of Visual Basic you can purchase
- Be able to identify the different kinds of applications you can create
- Be able to identify the different types of files that make up a Visual Basic application
- Learn how to use Microsoft Windows
- Learn the different parts of a window
- Learn the difference between event-driven and procedural coding

Sample Project File: None

What Is Visual Basic?

Visual Basic is a programming language used to create Windows-based applications. Visual Basic is based on the old BASIC (Beginner's All-Purpose Symbolic Instruction Code) language. What makes it "visual" is that you "paint" your interface, as opposed to using lines and lines of code to describe the interface. Visual Basic makes it very easy to get the user interface portion of your application up and running. Using typical drag-and-drop techniques, common in most Windows applications, you'll find that painting screens is very simple.

Although based on the old BASIC language, Visual Basic has definitely grown up. Hundreds of functions and the latest technological advances have been added to the language to make it an industrial-strength development environment suitable for almost any type of Windows application.

Visual Basic is also proving itself, little by little, as a viable tool for enterprise-wide applications and solutions. This is especially true with the advent of Internet programming and object-oriented programming.

A Visual Basic Application

To create a Visual Basic application, you'll need to learn to take small components and "glue" them together into a complete application. The most common components you'll use are forms, controls, classes, and procedures (see Figure 1.1).

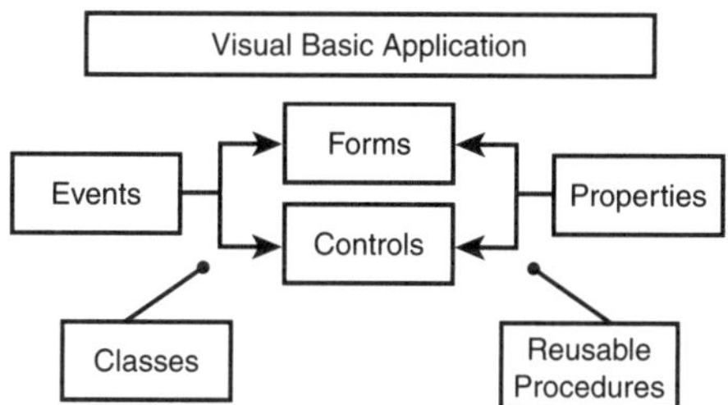

FIGURE 1.1 Visual Basic application components.

Forms are windows upon which you build your user interface, and *controls* are the building blocks of the user interface. Controls, also called *ActiveX Controls*, are interface tools, such as labels, text boxes, and command buttons, that you use to display information to the user, gather information from the user, and respond to user actions. *Classes* are templates from which you can create your own objects at runtime. These reusable class modules aid you in organizing your application into small components that can be built into a complete application. *Procedures* are small routines you write that are callable from anywhere in your application. These routines will perform a function for you that you write once but can call many times.

A very important concept in any Windows programming language is events. An *event* is something that occurs in response to a user interaction with the keyboard or the mouse. Events are messages that the operating system sends to your application. You will write some code to respond to these events and learn more about these in Chapter 5, "Events Happen."

Hierarchy of Visual Basic Applications

As you work with Visual Basic, you'll quickly learn that there's a hierarchy to the components you work with. An *application* is made up of forms, modules, and classes. A form is made up of properties, procedures, events, and controls. Controls are also made up of properties and events. Here's an overview of the basic components that make up a Visual Basic project:

Project

Application Properties

Forms

Properties

Property Procedures

Event Handlers

Other Procedures

Controls

Properties

Event Handlers

Methods

Modules

Procedures

Functions

Classes

Properties

Property Procedures

Public Methods

Private Methods

Three Steps to Creating an Application

No matter which type of application you choose to build, you'll always perform the same steps to create it. If you remember to follow these three steps, your Visual Basic development will go much smoother:

1. Create the interface.
2. Set the properties for the controls.
3. Write the code.

You should always create the visual portion of your application prior to writing any code. If you "paint" your application first and set the properties for each component in your visual presentation, you'll find that you spend less time writing and rewriting code.

History of Visual Basic

Visual Basic developed from the old QuickBasic language that was available under the DOS operating system. QuickBasic is the same language as BASIC, it is just Microsoft's product name for its version of BASIC. Visual Basic started out as the brainchild of Alan Cooper. Cooper developed Visual Basic and then sold the product to Microsoft. Microsoft took the undeveloped product, code-named it "Thunder," and proceeded to create a programming language that would soon become one of the premier development environments in the Windows environment.

Here's the Visual Basic timeline:

- Version 1 is released in May of 1991.
- The Professional Toolkit, a set of custom controls tacked onto Visual Basic, is released in January of 1992.
- A much-improved version 2 is released in October of 1992.
- Version 3 is released in May of 1993. With this release, Visual Basic really comes into its own and becomes a serious development tool.
- Version 4, released in September of 1995, includes object-based programming concepts in the language and makes Visual Basic the premier development language for Windows development.
- Version 5 is released in March of 1997. It includes the ability to create ActiveX controls, which makes it a serious contender to VC++. VC++ is a very low-level language that has typically been used for creating ActiveX controls and other "system-level" programming. Now Visual Basic is able to perform many of these same functions.
- Version 6 is released in August of 1998. It adds many more enhancements to the language, including a number of new wizards to help developers create applications even faster.

Features of Visual Basic

Visual Basic has many features; in fact, it has so many, it's impossible to list them all here. However, the following is a list of some of the more prominent features:

- Visual Basic is a superset of the Visual Basic for Applications (VBA) programming language, which is included with most of the Office products.
- Includes a GUI development environment for developing Windows applications.
- Provides the ability to develop and test applications using an interpretive run function.
- Allows for the creation of p-code and native code EXE files. P-code is a tokenized form of your source code that will be broken down at runtime into machine code. P-code can be stored more efficiently and executed faster than your source code, which is why Visual Basic will create this intermediary form.
- Object-based development is possible using class modules.
- Rapid application development (RAD).
- Allows for the creation of COM components such as ActiveX controls, DLLs, and EXEs.
- Has many Internet development possibilities, including the following:
    - ActiveX documents
    - DHTML applications that help you test browser applications
    - IIS applications that help you build server-based applications
    - Web browser control
    - FTP/HTTP support through a custom control
    - Winsock control
- Has an excellent integrated Help facility and Books Online.
- Includes good debugging facilities.
- Has many wizards that help automate repetitive tasks.

- Can be extended easily through the use of Windows API calls, hundreds of third-party controls and DLLs, and integration with other Windows applications through COM and DCOM.
- Uses many database access methods to get at different types of data.

Visual Basic Advantages

Visual Basic has many advantages over other development languages. Here's a list of some of these advantages:

- Has A shorter learning curve and development time than C/C++, Delphi, and even PowerBuilder.
- Removes the complexities of the Windows API from the programmer.
- Allows for rapid application development.
- Excellent for business applications.
- Used by most of the Office Suite tools as their macro language, with the rest to follow. Other companies as well are starting to support VBA in their products, such as AutoCAD, Visio, CorelDRAW, SAP, and many others.
- Allows you to create ActiveX controls.
- Allows you to reuse third-party controls and components, as well as your own.
- Supplies wizards to help you learn the language as well as to enhance your productivity with the more difficult features of the language.
- Object oriented in nature. It's not a complete OOP language, but it's getting closer.
- Can integrate with the Internet on both the server side and the client side.
- Can create ActiveX Automation servers.
- Integrates with Microsoft Transaction Server.
- Can run servers either on the same machine or remotely on another computer. This allows for true distributed processing.
- Visual Basic has a large community of developers (more than 3 million worldwide according to Microsoft). This means continued support for new developers.

Visual Basic Disadvantages

Although it has many advantages, Visual Basic still has a few disadvantages. Most of these are related to some limitations of Visual Basic in getting at real low-level functionality in hardware and the operating system. The following is a list of some of these disadvantages:

- Runtime distribution requirements are larger than those for C/C++.
- Not as much functionality as C/C++ in getting to features of the OS.

Code Generation Options

There are basically two kinds of programming languages: interpreted and compiled. Visual Basic lets you take advantage of both of these within one environment. This is one of the best features of Visual Basic. An *interpreted language* waits until runtime to translate the source code into machine language. A *compiled language* translates all the source code into machine code, all at one time. The advantage to using an interpreter is quick development time, whereas the advantage to using a compiled language is quick runtime execution.

With Visual Basic, you have the best of both, because Visual Basic has the ability to run interpreted in the development environment but can compile the source into machine code for the final runtime. Visual Basic uses a modified version of an interpreted language called *p-code*. Let's take a look at the differences between a p-code executable and a natively compiled executable.

p-code

Interpreted languages must translate each line of source code into machine language (ones and zeros) each time that line of code is executed. Therefore, if a line is executed 100 times, it's translated 100 times. To write an interpreted language, you simply write the source, and then run it. Examples of interpreted languages are the old traditional GW-Basic and most batch languages.

Compiled languages translate all the source code just once into machine language. To write a compiled application, you typically write the source code, compile and link the program, and then run the program. Examples of compiled languages are COBOL, Fortran, and C.

p-code is a hybrid of interpreted and compiled languages. A compiler compiles the source code, but it does not produce machine language. Instead, it produces a series of symbols for the source code. These symbols make a line of code that has five words into just one or two characters. When you run the program, a p-code interpreter interprets each line of the p-code, turning it into machine language. When p-code is executing, it's faster than interpreted code because there are fewer characters to read; however, it's still slower than compiled code. Visual Basic has the option of generating p-code or generating native code.

Native Code

Visual Basic also has the ability to generate native code EXE files. This can give you some significant enhancements in performance when doing CPU-intensive calculations.

If you have a part of your program that's CPU bound (generating Mandelbrot sets, for example), you can compile that piece into native code. You might also want to write this piece as a C language DLL that you could call from Visual Basic.

Which Option Should You Choose?

When you're running a Windows program, much of the CPU time is used by Windows function calls or calls to external DLLs, not by the source code in your program. A lot of time is also spent waiting on the user to perform the next task, click the next button, or maybe type the next character. Therefore, Visual Basic p-code programs are generally fast enough for most business applications.

Future of Visual Basic

Since the introduction of *Visual Basic for Applications (VBA)*, Microsoft has positioned Visual Basic as the premier general-purpose Windows development tool. It's the glue for assembling software components into software solutions. All the Microsoft Office products now include Visual Basic as their macro/development language. Many third-party companies are licensing VBA so that their customers can program their products. Microsoft has also created a scripting edition of Visual Basic for Internet development both in the browser and on a Web server called VBScript. Visual Basic's main competitors are Powersoft's PowerBuilder, Borland's Delphi, and Microsoft's own Visual C++, Access, and Visual FoxPro. Although these are all fine languages, none enjoys the success or widespread use that the Visual Basic language does.

Versions of Visual Basic

You can purchase three different versions of Visual Basic. The following sections provide an overview of these different versions and explain who might purchase them.

Visual Basic Learning Edition

The Learning Edition is specifically targeted at people who just want to try out the language or educators who want to teach the Visual Basic language to students. This edition comes with a CD-ROM that interactively trains you on the language. This edition comes with a rich set of standard controls and allows you to create standalone EXEs and COM DLLs.

Visual Basic Professional Edition

The Professional Edition is targeted at the individual consultant who just needs to create smaller applications. It comes with all the standard controls but adds many more to the list. In addition, you can use the full ADO object model instead of just ADO data control, as is the case with the Learning Edition. It allows you to create native code EXEs, ActiveX controls, ActiveX documents, and ActiveX EXEs or DLLs. Many additional productivity-enhancing wizards are included in this edition.

Visual Basic Enterprise Edition

The Enterprise Edition comes with all the features of the Professional Edition as well as includes many other tools that help you develop enterprise-wide applications. This edition is targeted at the corporate development shop or a larger consulting shop that creates large applications. In addition to the standard and enhanced controls, the Enterprise Edition also includes the following tools:

- SQL Server 6.5 Developer Edition
- Microsoft Transaction Server
- Visual SourceSafe
- Visual database tools
- Integrated T-SQL Server debugger

Visual Basic Application Types

You can create many different types of applications with Visual Basic. These different types are used when you need to solve a specific problem. Let's look at each of the different types of applications you can build.

Standard EXE

Choose this type of application if you want to create a standalone application that will not need to be run within another application. Most business applications will be of this type but may also include one or more of the following types of applications.

ActiveX EXE

This type of application is generally created to be used by other applications for a particular service or services. These services may run on the same machine or remotely via remote automation or DCOM. These services do not normally provide a visual interface.

ActiveX DLL

This type of application is generally created to be used by other applications for a particular service or services. The DLL must reside on the same machine as the controlling application. It runs within the same process space as the application that calls it. These services do not normally provide a visual interface. The DLL may also be run on another machine that's running Microsoft Transaction Server.

ActiveX Control

This type of application is used to design OCX components that can be used within a variety of applications. These tools will generally show up in a toolbox within a programming environment. They expose properties and/or methods that perform some function for an application.

ActiveX Document DLL

This type of application is developed to be used within the context of another application. It's very similar to an ActiveX EXE and DLL, but it generally provides an interface to the calling application. Being a DLL, it runs in the same process space as the calling application. There is a document (VBD) that goes along with the DLL that needs to be run within a container such as Microsoft Binder or Microsoft Internet Explorer 4.*x* or above.

ActiveX Document EXE

This type of application is developed to be used within the context of another application. It's very similar to an ActiveX EXE and DLL, but it generally provides an interface to the calling application. Because this type of application is an EXE file, it will run in a separate process space than the calling application. There's a document (VBD) that goes along with the DLL that needs to be run within a container such as Microsoft Binder or Microsoft Internet Explorer 4.*x* or above.

IIS Application

An IIS application is one that you create to run under the Internet Information Server. An IIS application is an ActiveX DLL with class modules that are called from an ASP page. Inside of these classes you can write any valid Visual Basic code. This can give you some more functionality that may otherwise be impossible to do in the VBScript language. This type of application can be browser independent. You don't need any specific browser, because all the code runs on the server.

DHTML Application

You're able to create and test Dynamic HTML code snippets that can run under Internet Explorer 4.0 on a client machine. Most Web designers use NotePad, FrontPage, or another tool for creating HTML, and then add Dynamic HTML by hand. Using Visual Basic makes this process easier, because you can use the full Visual Basic language to respond to events on a Web page instead of just code snippets written in VBScript or JScript. You can design the HTML pages and write the code snippets in a DLL that resides on the client machine and interacts with the browser.

Visual Basic Application Components

When you start to create a Visual Basic application, you need to be familiar with the different types of disk files you can store. You can save many different types of files, depending on the type of application you create. The following sections discuss the files that make up the various types of Visual Basic applications you can create.

Projects

A Visual Basic *project* is a collection of forms, controls, references to automation servers, application creation settings, and version information. All these different components reside in separate files, and the project file contains a list of them all. A project file is an ASCII text file with a .VBP (Visual Basic Project) extension. Inside this file you'll find a list of all the files that make up a project. If you combine multiple projects together, you'll create a file with a .VBG extension. This is a list of other VBP files that will be loaded into the Visual Basic design environment at one time.

Forms

A *form* is a window that's displayed on the Windows desktop or inside an MDI form. A form generally has many different controls placed upon it. The form, its controls, and the code associated with the form are all stored together on the disk in a file with an .FRM extension. Any graphical items contained within picture type properties will be stored to an FRX file with the same name as the FRM file. If you have an FRX file, make sure you copy it along with the FRM file if you ever move the file to a new location.

Controls

A *control* is a tool used to display information or retrieve information from the user. Examples of controls are boxes, buttons, graphics, labels, and grids. The toolbox is used to select and then draw controls on a form. Controls come in two forms: standard controls and custom controls. The standard controls are always present in the toolbox. The custom controls are brought into the Visual Basic environment and extend the toolbox. Controls have a file extension of .OCX.

Code Modules

Code, or source code, is written to make controls and forms respond to user interaction. Code is made up of variable declarations, constants, procedure or function declarations, statements, calls to the Windows API, loops, conditional constructs, and so on. Code modules are stored in ASCII text files with a .BAS extension. These are sometimes called *standard modules*.

Class Modules

Class modules allow you to create your own objects. They're the prototype for these objects, defining their properties and methods. Visual Basic allows for the creation of classes complete with properties and methods. There's no inheritance yet, but a substantial benefit can still be gained by using these classes for encapsulation of code. Class modules are stored in files with a .CLS extension.

User Controls

You can build your own custom controls with Visual Basic 6. These custom controls are stored into a CTL file with any graphical elements contained within a CTX file.

Property Pages

Property pages are used within the context of user controls. These pages are used to view and change the properties of user controls in an easy to understand format. These pages are stored in a PAG file.

User Document (ActiveX Document)

User document is a somewhat misleading term. Using Visual Basic, you can design a form or application and give it a .VBD extension. This creates not only the VBD file but also the ActiveX DLL or EXE file needed to display the VBD file. This active document can then be contained within any container application such as Microsoft Binder or Internet Explorer.

IIS Applications

IIS applications are made up of WebClasses and WebItems. A *WebClass* is a DLL that runs under IIS 4.0 and has a set of WebItems, which can be HTML templates and/or classes that send out HTML to the browser. The designers you use with an IIS application store the information in a DSR (text) and DSX (binary) files.

DHTML Applications

A DHTML application has code modules and designers that are stored in DSR and DSX files. You also have HTM or HTML files associated with this type of project. When you compile your project and get ready to distribute it, you have to distribute your HTML and a DLL to the end user.

Resource Files

A resource file allows you to store Windows resources such as strings, bitmaps, cursors, and icons. You can then load these resources on demand. One common use of resources is to store all the strings in the program that represent a given language. Then, by just changing those strings, you can convert the program to another language without having to change the rest of the program. This is a huge benefit for translating and maintaining programs in several languages. The source for a resource file is stored into an RC file. After compiling the RC file, you have an RES file that will be distributed with your application.

Microsoft Windows

Let's now turn our attention to Microsoft Windows itself and how it interacts with Visual Basic applications. Microsoft Windows is a graphical environment where the user interacts with pictures as well as text. This type of graphical interface is easier for users to learn due to standard interface objects (called *controls*). Microsoft Windows comes in a few different "flavors." Each has a graphical interface but may vary as to the different platforms they run on.

Windows allows you to run more than one application at a time, and you can easily transfer data back and forth between those applications. The use of standard interface objects in Windows simplifies learning and using the computer. Once users learn these standard objects (controls), they'll find that these objects are often repeated in many of the applications developed for Windows. When you develop your applications, you should use these standard interface objects.

TIP

A standard user interface simplifies learning a Windows application. You should follow standard conventions when designing your applications.

In Windows, the main user interface tool is a *window*—a rectangular area on the screen that communicates information to the user. The window is used as a "desktop." The user interacts with all windows through the keyboard and the mouse. For a good example of a window, bring up the Windows Explorer. It is possible to create windows that are not rectangular, but you will have to use other tools, or custom controls. Figure 1.2 shows you an example of a standard window.

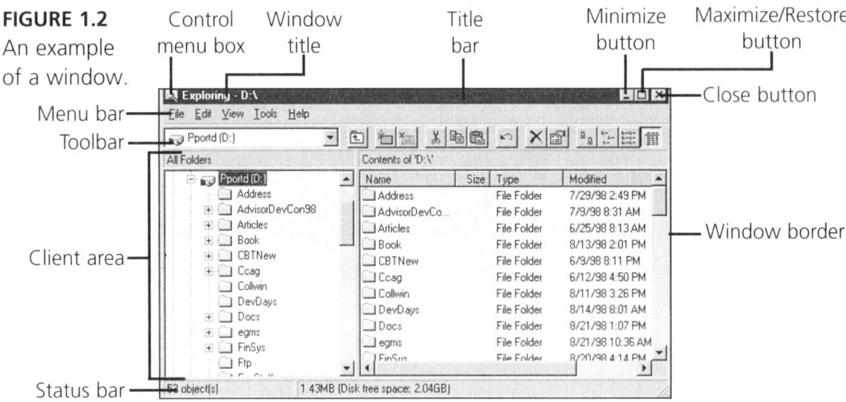

FIGURE 1.2 An example of a window.

Different Elements of a Window

Each window has many common elements. Table 1.1 shows some of the standard features found on each window created by the operating system.

Table 1.1 Elements of a Window

Element	Description
Title bar	Displays the application's name in the center of the top of the window.
Window title	Names the application or document on the title bar.
Menu bar	Lists commands or actions you can select for the window.
Minimize button	Reduces the window to an icon on the desktop.
Maximize button	Enlarges the window to take up the full desktop.
Close button	The button on the upper-right side of window that when clicked will close the window.
Restore button	Restores a maximized or minimized window to its previous size.
Toolbar	Allows fast access to commonly used menu operations using the mouse.

Element	Description
Status bar	Provides status information to the user.
Client area	A work area. This area can change depending on the program being run.
Window border	The outline around a window that sometimes allows for the resizing of the window.
Control menu box	Allows the user to resize, move, maximize, minimize, and close the window. The control menu box is located in the upper-left corner of the window. (Also called the *system menu*.)

Windows 3.*x* and Windows for Workgroups 3.*x*

Microsoft Windows 3.*x* is an operating environment that runs on top of DOS. An Intel computer is required for this operating environment, and DOS must be installed on the computer to run it. Windows 3.*x* uses DOS for all its file handling but handles the mouse, video display, serial ports, and so on itself. Windows 3.*x* is a 16-bit operating environment and cannot be used for running Visual Basic 5 and 6.

NOTE

For 16-bit development, you'll need to use either Visual Basic 3 or Visual Basic 4 (16-bit version). Visual Basic 5 and Visual Basic 6 only run on 32-bit platforms.

Microsoft Windows 95/98

Microsoft Windows 95 and Windows 98 are 32-bit operating systems that do not need DOS for anything (except to boot). These operating systems require an Intel computer to run on. They still use the DOS FAT file system and have many DOS components still contained in them. This makes them backward compatible with old DOS and Microsoft Windows 3.*x* systems. Peer-to-peer networking and client/server networking are built into these operating systems, thus making it easy to hook computers together.

Microsoft Windows NT/2000

Microsoft Windows NT Workstation/Server is a 32-bit operating system that rivals UNIX systems in functionality. Intel computers, as well as several RISC-based systems, can run this operating system. Peer-to-peer networking and client/server networking are built in. You may choose to use the FAT file system or the new NT file system (NTFS). Windows NT and Windows 95/98 will be merged in the next version to a version that will be called Windows 2000.

TIP

Windows 3.*x* is a 16-bit operating system whereas Windows 95/98 and Windows NT are 32-bit operating systems. Fewer 16-bit applications are being developed as the 32-bit operating systems replace older Windows systems.

Throughout this book, when I refer to Windows, I mean any of the 32-bit operating systems, since I won't be covering 16-bit development at all.

Computing Terms

Let's go over a few terms to help you understand computers.

What Is an Operating System?

When you talk about Microsoft Windows, you're talking about a program that runs on a computer. To be able to run something on a computer, you must have a piece of software (a set of instructions to the computer) that tells the computer what to do. This is the role of an operating system (OS)—that is, to control the operation of the hardware of the computer. There are many different operating systems: DOS (Disk Operating System), various mainframe OSs, UNIX, Windows, and many others.

Application Programs

Application programs rely on an operating system to run. Examples of applications are Microsoft Word, Microsoft Excel, and even the Visual Basic development environment. An application will use the OS to handle the low-level interfaces to the computer, such as keyboard input, output to the video display device, and output to the printer. By relying on the OS for this functionality, your job of writing an application program is much easier.

Programming Applications for Windows

Many programmers are coming from DOS-based systems or mainframe/minicomputer systems and are now having to learn how to program for Windows. There are several key differences in the way you code for DOS/mainframes versus how you code for Windows. The main difference you must overcome involves the concept of event-driven versus procedural programming.

Procedural Programming

In procedural programs, the program begins and starts telling the operating system what to do (for example, display a line on the screen or get a keystroke from the user). The program is in control and gives directives to the operating system. The user cannot do anything that the program does not allow. The user must follow the program's flow and cannot deviate from that flow.

In addition, a procedural system usually only allows a single task to be executing at any one time. Therefore, to execute another program one must exit the current program and then start another one. For example, if you're using a word processor in this environment and want to now run a spreadsheet, you need to leave your word processor prior to starting the spreadsheet application.

Event-driven Programming

In an event-driven application, the operating system is in control. Instead of the program telling the operating system what to do, the operating system tells the program what's going on and gives it a chance to respond. It does this through the mechanism of an *event*.

TIP
The operating system is in control in an event-driven system.

Windows is a multitasking operating system. This means that more than one program can be running concurrently. This allows the user to switch from one program to another at any time. You, as an application programmer, will need to think differently about how you write your programs. Instead of writing code to control everything about the environment, such as the keyboard input and waiting for keystrokes, you'll now simply respond to an event that the operating system gives to you. You can no longer force the operating system to stop and wait for your program to complete; you need to be aware that the operating system will give your program a time-slice to run within. This is what is meant by *multitasking*.

Messages

Internally, Windows can be thought of as a message-processing engine. It receives messages and dispatches others. A message can be generated by the user clicking a window or pressing a key on the keyboard. A message can also be generated by such things as the system clock ticking. These messages are dispatched by Windows to the various objects on the system, including your Visual Basic programs.

Events

When a Visual Basic program receives a message, it generates an event. Event-driven programming describes an application that waits for an event and then responds to those events when they happen. Windows continually feeds your program messages that you will handle as events. All windowing operating systems require event-driven programming techniques.

An event can be a mouse click, a key press, mail coming into your mailbox, a fax being received in the background, or a timer/alarm clock going off. An event may even be triggered by your application. Therefore, an event can be something that is generated by a user or something that is generated by the OS.

When you begin to program for the Windows environment, you'll learn about common visual components such as command buttons, text boxes, list boxes, and combo boxes. Users may click a button, type data into a text box, click a list box, or "drop down" a combo box. The component then receives an event, such as a mouse click, and has a chance to respond to the event. An event that is not handled is either discarded or a default action may be taken by the system.

Table 1.2 shows you the events that you may respond to on a command button.

Table 1.2 Examples of Command Button Events

Event Name	Description
`Click`	The button is clicked on with the mouse or keyboard.
`MouseMove`	Occurs when the mouse moves over a command button.

Different objects will have different events that you respond to. Table 1.3 shows you some of the events for a text box. You can see that there are different events you'll respond to.

Table 1.3 Examples of Text Box Events

Event Name	Description
`GotFocus`	The text box receives input focus.
`KeyPress`	A key is pressed.
`LostFocus`	The text box loses input focus.
`Change`	Text changes via user input or code.

Message Queue

Each message that's generated is put into a queue. Windows manages this queue on a first-in, first-out basis. Windows is responsible for dispatching messages to the appropriate object that has focus, or Windows may determine that the message is for another object and give it focus.

Focus

A computer has only a limited set of devices: one keyboard, one screen, one mouse, and a few COM and printer ports that all programs must share. When dealing with data input, Windows gives a visual clue to you about which window has "focus." To show that the keyboard will affect a specified window, Windows changes the title bar of the window. To show that the keyboard can type into a textbox, Windows places a blinking bar in the text box (called the *caret*). There are other indications of focus, depending on the type of window or control. In general, focus usually indicates which window or part of a window the input device will interact with.

Summary

This chapter introduced you to the Visual Basic language. You learned about the different types of applications you can create using Visual Basic. You also learned a little of the history of Visual Basic. In addition, you learned about the Windows operating system. Developing event-driven programs for the Windows environment is very different than developing programs for a procedural environment. Given the wide variety of applications you can create with Visual Basic, it's no wonder Visual Basic is the number one language of choice for developing event-driven Windows applications.

Review Questions

1. Describe the main object used in Visual Basic to build an application.
2. Name three types of applications you can build in Visual Basic.
3. List the three steps to creating a Visual Basic application.
4. What's the biggest advantage to using graphical operating systems?
5. What's the big difference between Windows 3.*x* and Windows 95 or Windows NT?
6. Name three different parts of a window.
7. Give some examples of events.

Getting Started

THIS CHAPTER INTRODUCES YOU TO THE BASICS of creating a Visual Basic application. First, you'll see which options you need to change the first time you use Visual Basic. You'll also learn how to start Visual Basic and build a simple data entry form. In this process, you'll identify which controls are used for input and which controls are used for display. You'll also learn to use properties to change the look and feel of a form.

Chapter Objectives

- Look at how to use the Visual Basic Design Environment
- Learn to create a new project
- Learn how to create and run a form
- Learn to identify a property
- Learn to identify controls
- Learn the common properties of a form
- Find out how to save a project

Sample Project Filename: \Chapter02\GetStarted.vbp

Visual Basic Environment

The Visual Basic design environment is like a mechanic's large, multidrawer toolbox in that it contains everything you need to build a Windows application, just like the mechanic's toolbox gives him everything he needs to build or repair a car. You'll use this environment, known as the *Integrated Development Environment (IDE)*, to build all your Windows applications. You need to learn about the different windows contained within this design environment to become an effective Visual Basic developer. Figure 2.1 shows you many of the different windows you'll see in this development environment.

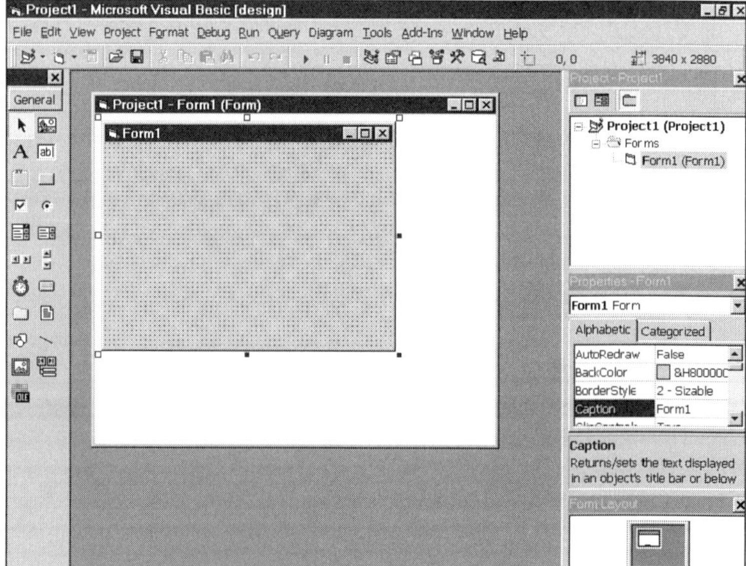

FIGURE 2.1
Visual Basic design environment.

Menu Bar

The menu bar has menus that "drop down" to reveal a list of commands. These menus will perform an operation for you, such as opening or saving a project or formatting your source code. If you think in terms of a mechanic's multidrawer toolbox, this would be like labels on the outside each drawer telling the mechanic which type of tools are contained within each drawer. There are many different menus and drop-down menus you'll need to familiarize yourself with. Let's look at some of the different top-level menus you'll use so that you can learn about the general functionality for each one.

Under the File menu is where you find menus that help you open, save, and print projects. The Edit menu is where you find menus that assist you with editing your source code. The View menu helps you display the different windows in the environment. The Project menu is where you add new windows and set properties for the project you're creating. The Format menu assists you in laying out the controls in your application. The Debug menu is used when you're tracking down bugs or stepping through your source code at runtime. The Run menu starts and stops your application. The Tools menu is where you use many of the wizards that come with Visual Basic. The Add-Ins menu brings up other wizards that come with Visual Basic. The Window menu helps you bring up the different items contained in your project. And, finally, the Help menu assists you in obtaining help on the Visual Basic language and with using the development environment. You'll use most of these menus as you go through this book.

Toolbar

The Visual Basic *toolbar* has icons located horizontally across the top of the Visual Basic Developer Studio window. These tools are shortcuts to the different menu items. The standard toolbar has the most commonly used actions. There are different toolbars that you can "dock" to the Visual Basic development environment. This means that the toolbar will stick to either the top, bottom, left, or right of the IDE, no matter how you size or move the IDE. You'll learn about the Debug, Edit, and Form Editor toolbars in Chapter 18, "IDE and Editor Tips and Tricks."

Toolbox

The Visual Basic *toolbox* is the vertical grouping of controls found on the left side of the visual design screen. These controls are like a mechanic's tools in that they each have a specific function they perform. If you position your mouse over a control and leave it there for about a second, a *ToolTip* will pop up showing you the type of control it is. You'll use this toolbox to grab controls that will make up your user interface. You can add additional controls to this toolbox to get more functionality, just like a mechanic can buy more tools. You'll learn to do this in many of the later chapters.

Form

A *form* is the main object used to create the user interface for an application. Think of a form as a blank canvas that an artist uses to paint a picture. All controls are placed on a form to create a screen that the user will interact with. Think of your local ATM machine that you interact with at the bank to get money. It's a combination of words, pictures, and buttons that you press. This is the "user interface" for the ATM—you're the user, and it's what you interact with. The form window in the Visual Basic development environment contains one form on which you'll draw one screen. You may open as many of these form windows as you have forms in your application. Again, when you think of interacting with the ATM, you deal with many different screens that change based on the operation you're performing. It's your job to design each of the screens your users will interact with.

Project Explorer Window

The *Project Explorer window* displays a list of all the components that make up your application. This hierarchical list will display each of the different component types within a separate folder. You may also toggle this to a normal list box that displays all the components in a standard list. Each time you add a new component to the project, it will show up in the Project Explorer window. To work with a particular component, you simply double-click the component name in the Project Explorer window.

Properties Window

The *Properties window* displays a list of all the design-time properties available to the component that has focus. This list of properties may be different as you select different components on your form. You can view the properties either in an alphabetical or categorized list. When you're just starting to become a Visual Basic developer, it may help you to use the categorized list. However, as you become more familiar with the properties associated with a particular control, you may find that the alphabetical list allows you to move around easier within this window.

Immediate or Debug Window

The *Immediate window* (sometimes called the *Debug window*) is normally only viewed in break mode. Break mode is entered when you're debugging an application. In this window, you can perform math operations, print the values of variables, assign values to variables, and even call procedures. You'll learn more about this window in Chapter 16, "The Debugger."

Form Layout Window

The *Form Layout window* helps you size your form to fit a certain monitor size as well as helps you determine where on the screen the form will be displayed. When you move a form in this window, the `Left` and `Top` properties of the form are automatically set at that location on the screen. In addition, if you're developing on a monitor with the resolution set to 1024×768, you may need to make sure a user with a resolution of 800×600 can still view the form correctly. If you right-click the Form Layout window, you can choose Resolution Guides from the pop-up menu. These guides show you the different resolutions so you can determine whether your form will fit within a given resolution.

Online Help

You can press F1 at any time to receive help on Visual Basic. The online Help system is *context sensitive*—that is, it gives you help on the object that currently has focus in the design mode. The Help system in Visual Basic is actually quite good. You should plan on spending a lot of time in it as you're learning Visual Basic.

From the Help menu, you can search for any topic from a list of suggested topics. You can also access Visual Basic's Books Online. Books Online contains all the printed documentation for Visual Basic in an electronic format. You can jump directly to the Microsoft Web site on the Internet for late-breaking topics and updates to the Visual Basic language.

Visual Basic First-time Setup

Before using Visual Basic for the first time, you should set a few options that will remain constant throughout your development process. In other words, the options presented here will remain in effect after you set them. These options can be set by choosing the Tools, Options menu, which will present the dialog box shown in Figure 2.2. You won't understand all these options at this point, but it's important to start your development the right way. If you don't set these options now, it will be necessary to go back into your project and make changes to every form and module you develop.

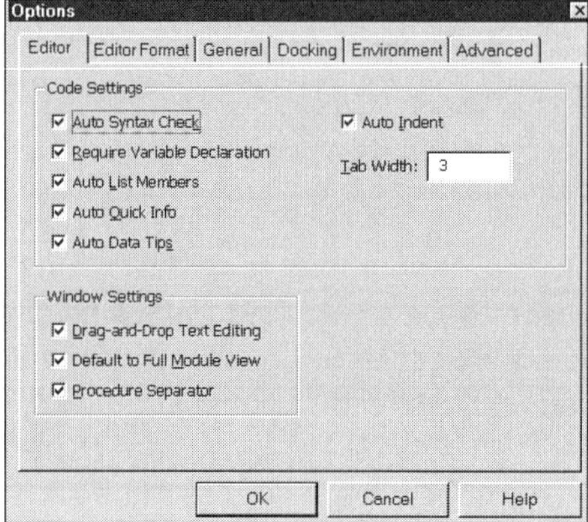

FIGURE 2.2 The Visual Basic Options dialog box.

Editor Tab

The Editor tab is where you control items that affect the editing of code. The following sections detail the options you should check to make sure your environment is consistent from application to application.

Require Variable Declaration

By checking this item, you're specifying that you want all variables to be declared prior to usage in every module/form/class module you create. This is very important in the maintenance and debugging of your code. If this option is not checked, variables may be created on the fly, which means that misspelled variables become a new variable instead of referencing the one you intended. This can be a very hard bug to track down. By checking this option, a statement will be added at the beginning of each of your new modules; Option Explicit. This is what enforces the variable declaration check.

> **NOTE**
> You can (and will need to) add this statement to any modules you created prior to setting this option.

Tab Width

This option is very subjective; however, I prefer the value 3. This means that three spaces will be inserted into the code window whenever the Tab key is pressed. Indention is very important for the readability of code. I find that two spaces are not enough to distinguish the levels sufficiently, whereas anymore than three can sometimes require panning back and forth in the code window if the lines of code get too long. Of course you can always use the line continuation character "_" to break up your lines if they get too long.

General Tab

Under this tab are options that affect the design grid on forms, error trapping, compiling, and other miscellaneous items.

Grid Units: Points

The `Width` and `Height` properties should be set to a multiple of 15 because 15 twips per pixel is a standard measurement for most monitors. In addition, the minimum size of a combo box (a control you'll use quite a bit) is 300 twips. The number 15 will divide into 300 evenly, so this makes lining up controls much easier. My preferred number is 60 for the `Width` and `Height` properties.

WHAT ARE TWIPS?

Throughout Visual Basic, units are generally measured in *twips*. Twip stands for "twentieth of a point." A *point* is a typographical unit of measure that equates to 1/72nd of an inch. Therefore, a twip equates to 1/1440th of an inch. On a printer, 1,440 twips will equate exactly to one inch. However, on the screen, a larger or smaller monitor will change this size. A twip on the screen is only accurate in relation to font sizes. For example, 200 twips will equal the height of a 10-point font (approximately).

Compile on Demand

Visual Basic has an option to defer the compilation of a program until you actually get to that point at runtime. This can help your program get started quicker when you click the Run button. However, it also means that you'll wait until runtime to get any errors that may otherwise be caught by the compiler.

I prefer to leave this option unchecked, because I think you should always perform a full compile on your projects. For some large projects, this means you'll need to wait longer the first time the project is compiled, but subsequent compiles will be very quick.

Environment Tab

The Environment tab is where you'll find options for Visual Basic startup, your project startup, and template information.

When a Program Starts

This option should be set to either Save Changes or Prompt to Save Changes. When your program starts after compiling, you'll be prompted to save any changes made before running it. This ensures that if a fatal error occurs in your program, any changes you have made prior to the fatal error will be saved.

Creating a New Project

The first step in building a standard Visual Basic application is to create the user interface. If you design the user interface first, you'll find that writing the code to go along with the user interface goes much smoother.

When you start up the Visual Basic IDE, you'll be asked to select the type of project you want to develop. Let's begin with a standard EXE application. Once you've selected this option, you now have a blank form ready to accept some controls.

A Sample Program

In this chapter, you'll start putting together an employee information form. Follow along with the exercise in this chapter to learn how to put together the user interface for a Visual Basic application. Figure 2.3 is an example of what this screen looks like.

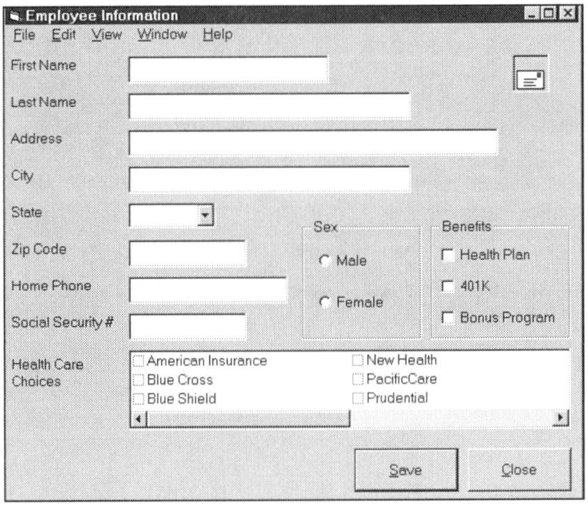

FIGURE 2.3
The Employee Information form.

Example's Filename: Employee10.frm

Forms

Forms are the main building blocks of a Visual Basic application. Forms are windows on which controls are placed. A form is itself a ready-to-run Visual Basic application.

EXERCISE

Creating a New Project

1. Open the Visual Basic design environment and select Standard EXE.
2. You should see a form in the middle of your development environment.
3. Press the F5 key to make this form run as a standard window.
4. Once the form is up and running, you'll see a standard window displayed.
5. You can resize this window using your mouse by grabbing at the sides of the window.
6. You can resize this window using your keyboard by selecting the Move option from the system menu. The system menu can be selected by clicking in the upper-left corner of any window.
7. You can minimize the form on the taskbar or maximize the form to cover the full screen.

8. Once you're done, click the close button in the upper-right corner of the window.
9. After closing the window, you'll be returned to the Visual Basic design environment.

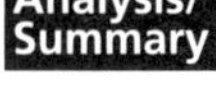

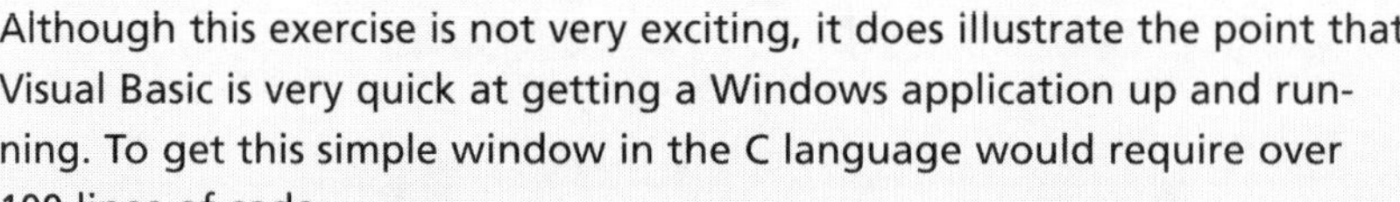

Although this exercise is not very exciting, it does illustrate the point that Visual Basic is very quick at getting a Windows application up and running. To get this simple window in the C language would require over 100 lines of code.

Lifecycle of a Form

When a form is displayed by Visual Basic, it goes through a lifecycle. First, the form is *initialized*, which means any custom properties you may have created or variables in the form are created. Next, the form is *loaded*, which means that all the controls and any other graphical elements on the form are brought into memory. Next the form is displayed on the screen.

After all this has happened, the user may now interact with the form. If the user closes the form, there's a series of steps it goes through to unload itself. First, an event is fired that gives you (the developer) a chance to stop the unloading from happening. Next, an event fires that unloads the graphical part of the form and all the controls on the form. Finally, if the form is released from memory, a termination event fires that releases any custom properties or variables in the form. You'll learn about each of these events in the next couple of chapters.

Properties

Each form is made up of certain characteristics, such as its size, position, name, caption, and color. These characteristics are called *properties*. Properties may be changed either at runtime or design time. Some properties can only be changed at design time, and some only at runtime. It depends on the individual property. Properties are used to give forms a desired look and feel.

Let's change a couple of properties on the form currently displayed in the design environment.

EXERCISE

1. Click once anywhere on the form. This gives the form focus. *Focus* refers to the currently selected object. You'll know whether an object is selected because it will have resizing handles all along the outside border of its window and the title of the window will be highlighted.
2. Go to the Properties window and find the `Caption` property. This property will display the text you type into it in the title bar of the form.
3. Change the `Caption` property to `Employee Information`.
4. Notice that the caption of the form has now changed.
5. Change the `WindowState` property from `0-Normal` to `2-Maximized`. By changing this property, you affect the behavior of the form. When you run the program, the form should now cover the entire screen.
6. Find the `Name` property and change it to `frmEmployee`. This is the name you'll use to refer to this form when you write source code. It's recommended that every form be prefixed with the letters *frm*. In fact, all the controls you add to the form will have prefixes that indicate their control type. This will help you identify the types of controls in your source code without having to look to see what the controls are on the form. You might want to look at the programming standards I have outlined in Appendix A of this book.

NOTE
Some properties are available only at runtime. These properties will not show up in the Properties window. Additionally, some properties are read-only or write-only at runtime. Check the online Help for a description of each property and when it may be set.

As you can see, we have just changed the look of this form by changing the `Caption` property. If you change the `WindowState` property and then run the form, you'll see that the form now covers the entire screen. This is what properties are for—to customize the look or behavior of an object.

Common Form Properties

Forms and controls have many properties. However, not all of them are important or will be used that often. Table 2.1 lists some of the more common properties you may change for a form.

Table 2.1 Common Form Properties

Property	Description
`BorderStyle`	Determines the border style: `0-None`, `1-Fixed Single`, `2-Sizable`, `3-Fixed Dialog`, `4-Fixed ToolWindow`, `5-Sizable ToolWindow`. You'll set this property based on what you're doing with the form. You might use `0` for a splash screen that pops up when your program is first started, or you might use `1` for a typical data entry screen that does not change size. The other values are used for special windows that either change size or may not be sizeable.
`Caption`	This property is displayed in the title bar area of a form. Use it to identify to the user what this form is used for.
`ControlBox`	Set this property to `True` if you want a control box menu to appear when the user clicks the upper-left corner of the form. The default for this is `True`, so just leave the property set this way. However, based on what `BorderStyle` is set to, this value may change.
`KeyPreview`	Set this property to `True` if you want the form to receive all keystrokes prior to the control getting the keystroke. This can be helpful if you need to do something to the keystroke prior to the text going into one of the controls on the form.
`MaxButton`	Displays `True` if you want a maximize button to appear in the upper-right corner of the form.
`MinButton`	Displays `True` if you want a minimize button to appear in the upper-right corner of the form.
`Name`	This is probably the most important property because it specifies the name you'll use to identify this unique form in your source code. You'll need to have a unique name for every form in a project. You should always preface the name of a form with the letters *frm*.
`StartUpPosition`	Determines the location of the form when it's first loaded and displayed: `0-Manual`, `1-Center Owner`, `2-Center Screen`, `3-Windows Default`.

Property	Description
`Visible`	Indicates whether or not the form is visible. You might use this property to temporarily hide a form when it's not being used by the user.
`WindowState`	This property determines the mode in which the form is display. You can set it to `Normal`, which means the form will use the `Top`, `Left`, `Width`, and `Height` properties to calculate the size of the form. You may also choose `Minimized` if you want the form to be minimized on the task bar. Or, you can set it to `Maximized` to have it take up the entire screen area.

EXERCISE

Changing Properties to See Their Effect

1. Set the `BorderStyle` property to `1-Fixed Single`. Now, when you run the form, you'll be unable to size it. You'll typically use this type of form when developing a business application because you'll place controls in certain locations and you won't want the user to resize the form so that the controls can't be seen.
2. Reset the `WindowState` property back to `Normal`.
3. You might want to try changing some of the other properties such as the `MinButton`, `MaxButton`, and `ControlBox` to see the effect this has on the form. After setting these properties, run the project by pressing F5 to see the changes these settings make.

Properties can do a lot to change the look and behavior of a form or control. As you can see from this exercise that just one change can greatly affect how your application is presented.

Naming the Project

When you start creating a Visual Basic application, you should have an idea of what this application will be used for. In this book, you'll create an employee time tracking system. This application can be used for employees to track their time spent working on projects each day.

Now that you have a form started, you should create a name for the project.

EXERCISE

SETTING PROJECT PROPERTIES

1. Select Project, Project1 Properties from the menu.
2. Set the following properties on the General tab:

   Project Name: **EmpInfo**

   Project Description: **Employee Time Tracking System**

   Startup Object: **frmEmployee**
3. Set the following properties on the Make tab:

   Auto Increment: Check this box
4. Under the Version Information Frame, set the Type information:

   Company Name: Enter your company name **(PDSA, Inc.)**

   Legal Copyright: Enter a copyright notice for your company **(Copyright 1998, PDSA, Inc.)**

   Product Name: **Employee Time Tracking**

   Icon: **frmEmployee**

These properties are saved in your VBP file once you save the project. However, before you save this project, let's talk about each of the project properties (see Table 2.2).

The Project Properties Dialog

Let's take a look at the rest of the properties that you can set for your Visual Basic project.

Table 2.2 Project Properties

Project Property	Description
Project Name	This is a unique identifier for this application. It must follow standard variable or procedure naming standards. This means you're not allowed any spaces or special characters in the name.
Project Description	This is a description of the application.
Startup Object	Which form you want to start with when you press the Run button. You may choose a form or create a procedure called `Main` as the startup.

Project Property	Description
Auto Increment	If you check this option, every time you compile the application, Visual Basic will generate a new revision number for you.
Company Name	This is used in the version properties attached to the EXE.
Legal Copyright	This is used in the version properties attached to the EXE.
Product Name	This is used in the version properties attached to the EXE.
Icon	This is the icon you assign to the final EXE that will show up in the folder. You choose a form name that has the `Icon` property set to the particular icon you want to use.

Saving the Project

Now that you've started developing a project, you should save it. It's best not to save your forms and projects in the \VB directory. You should create a separate subdirectory for each project you create. I typically save my projects on a separate drive and directory from my default Visual Basic installation directory.

EXERCISE

Saving a Project

1. Using Explorer, create a folder off the root directory named \Employee.
2. Select File, Save Project from the Visual Basic menu.
3. Select the \Employee folder from the dialog box.
4. When prompted for the name of the form, type in **Employee.frm**.
5. When prompted for the name of the project, type in **Employee.vbp**.

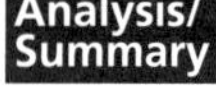

You've now saved the changes you made in two different files. The FRM file contains all the information necessary to create your form. The VBP file contains a list of all the forms that make up your project. In this case, there is just one file—the Employee.frm file.

Summary

In this chapter, you learned how to create a new project using Visual Basic. You learned how to make a form a running application. You then learned to name the project and save that project to disk.

Review Questions

1. What's a form?
2. What's a property?
3. Which property will display the form maximized when it's displayed?
4. Which property will change the title bar of the form?

3

Controls

THIS CHAPTER INTRODUCES YOU TO THE DIFFERENT controls you can place on a form to build a user interface that you can interact with. You'll learn how to build a simple data entry form using label and text box controls. In this process, you'll identify which controls are used for input and which controls are used for display. You'll also learn to use properties to change the look and feel of the controls.

Chapter Objectives

- Learn to identify which controls are used for input
- Become familiar with the controls used for display purposes
- Learn the common properties of all controls
- Find out how to add controls to a form
- Learn the naming standards for controls
- Learn to create menus

Sample Project Filename: \Chapter03\Controls.vbp

Controls

A blank form is not very useful by itself. To jazz up the form you created in the last chapter, you'll now place controls on it. *Controls* are what the user interacts with on a form. For example, label controls display information to the user, and text box controls allow the user to enter information into the form.

I like to think of controls as the building blocks of the user interface of your application. Just like a mechanic uses nuts and bolts to assemble an engine, you'll use controls to build your application. Each control, by itself, is just one piece of the engine. Separately they don't do much, but when you put them together, you have a great application.

Adding Controls to the Form

Controls may be added to a form two ways. The first method is to double-click the control in the toolbox. This places the control in the middle of the form with a default height and width. The second method is to click once on the control in the toolbox and then move your mouse to the position on the form where you want to begin drawing the control. You size the control by clicking and holding the left mouse button down while drawing on the form. You'll repeat this process for each of the controls needed to create your user interface. In this chapter, you'll learn which controls you'll be using for your user interface, but first let's review some basics of control manipulation.

Controls in the Toolbox

At first glance, all the tools in the toolbox may look daunting. Don't let that stop you from trying them out. After awhile you'll learn what each control does. If you move your mouse over each control and hover it there for about half a second, a ToolTip will pop up showing you the name of that control.

When you choose the Standard EXE project, you load all the standard controls Visual Basic includes in its runtime engine. Figure 3.1 shows the standard Visual Basic toolbox.

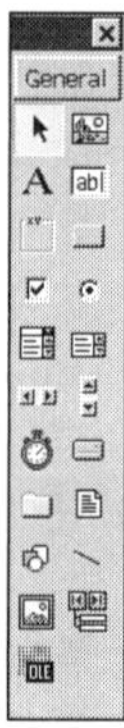

FIGURE 3.1
The Visual Basic toolbox.

Table 3.1 will give a brief description about each of the different controls included as part of the standard package. You'll eventually learn to use each of these; however, in this chapter, you'll just learn about the most commonly used controls.

Table 3.1 Standard Controls

Control	Description
Picture box	Displays a graphical image (BMP, JPEG, GIF, and so on) on a form. This can be used to display a picture of an employee or any other graphical picture.
Label	Displays text on a form that usually precedes another control to describe what that control will do.
Text box	Displays and accepts text from a user. This will be the main mechanism the user has for putting information into your application.

continues

Table 3.1 Continued

Control	Description
Frame	Used to group other controls within a container. You'll find that when you want to group many controls into one logical area on your form, a frame can help you do it.
Command button	Used to perform an action when a user clicks this control. This is the main way the user signifies he or she is finished with your form or wants to have the application perform some process.
Check box	Used to signify a true or false condition. You may use this control to ask the user to choose one, two, or maybe three different options. For example, you may ask the user to choose one or many health care options, one or many bonus plans, or one or many payment options.
Option button	Used as a group of buttons that define mutually exclusive options. You may use these option buttons to have the user choose between one of many items. For example, male or female, short or tall, or high or low.
List box	This control displays a list of items to the user. The user can have the option of choosing one or many items.
Combo box	This control is a combination of a text box and a list box. It can display a set of items in a drop-down list. It can also accept text that the user inputs via the keyboard.
Horizontal scroll	A scroll bar you can use to display a horizontal scrolling option to your user. This is typically used as a volume control for adjusting the sound of your computer's speakers.
Vertical scroll	A scroll bar that you can use to display a vertical scrolling option to your user.
Timer	This tool fires an event to which you can respond every pre-set amount of time measured in milliseconds. You might use this to update a clock within your application.
Drive list box	Used to display a list of disk drives on your system. This can be used when you want the user to choose a particular disk on his or her computer. It's most commonly used in combination with the directory list box and file list box.
Directory list box	Used to display a list of folders for a particular disk drive. This is used to enable the user to select a particular folder from his or her computer's hard disk.

Control	Description
File list box	Used to display a list of files in a particular folder. This is used to enable the user to select a particular file from a specific hard drive and folder.
Shape	Used to draw a rectangle, square, oval, circle, rounded rectangle, or rounded square on a form. This control is not actually used much in a business application but could be used if you're writing a drawing program.
Line	Used to draw lines on your form. I typically use this control to separate groups of controls on my form.
Image	Used to display a graphical image (BMP, JPEG, GIF, and so on) on a form. This control is very similar to a picture control but doesn't use up as much memory. There are also differences in the methods and properties between these two controls.
Data	The data control allows you to retrieve data from a data source and then display that data into the text boxes on a form. This control is now superceded by the ADO data control, which you'll learn about in a later chapter. Therefore, this control should not be used.
OLE	Allows you to insert objects from other applications into your Visual Basic form. For example, you may place a Microsoft Word or Excel object on your form so your users can interact with these applications within your application.

Resizing and Moving Controls

After a control has been added to a form, you can move or resize it by clicking it one time to give it focus. You can then move the control by clicking it anywhere and dragging it with your mouse. You can resize the control by grabbing one of the resizing handles on the sides of the control and moving your mouse while holding down the left button. The resizing handles are the squares on the outside corners of the control, as shown in Figure 3.2.

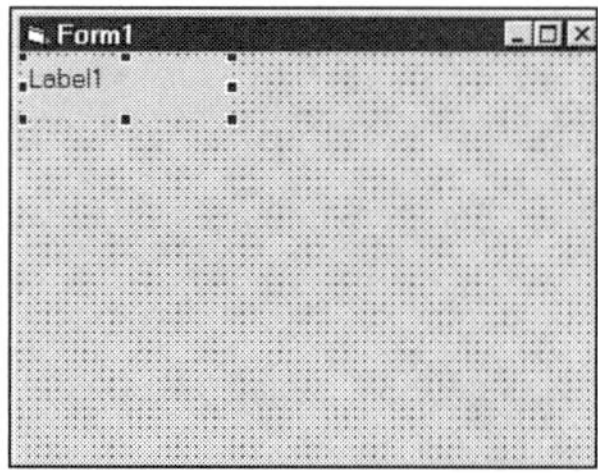

FIGURE 3.2 Resizing handles on a label control.

Properties Common to Forms and Most Controls

Once you start to use forms and controls, you'll find that they have many different properties. However, they also have several properties in common. You'll by no means be setting all of these properties—most of them you leave at their default values. Table 3.2 is a list of those properties you'll find in common among forms and controls.

Table 3.2 Common Form and Control Properties

Property	Description
`BackColor`	This property is used to change the background color of a control or form. If you'll be changing colors, try to use only the system colors. If you hard-code a color into a control, it may conflict with the users' colors they set up in their Control Panel.
`Font`	This property is used to change the appearance of the text of a particular control.
`ForeColor`	This property is used to change the foreground color of a control or form. Use the same care when setting this property as you do with `BackColor`.
`Height`	Indicates the height of the control.
`Left`	Indicates the left-most point of the control.
`Name`	Identifies the name of the control.
`Tag`	Provides a user-definable slot for you to put in whatever text you might want. I might use this for keeping track of the last time a user clicked on a control, or maybe whether the control has been edited.
`Top`	Indicates the top-most point of the control.
`Visible`	Indicates whether the control is visible.
`Width`	Indicates the width of the control.

Now that you've learned about many of the different properties you'll use on forms and controls, let's look at the most commonly used controls.

Label Control

A *label* control is used to display text to the user. This control is typically used to identify input areas directly to the right or below the label. Add some label controls to your `frmEmployee` form that will be used to label text boxes for the Employee Information form.

EXERCISE

DRAWING A LABEL CONTROL

1. Select a label control in the toolbox by clicking once on the control.
2. Draw the label on the form near the top-left corner.
3. Change the `Name` property to `lblLabel`.
4. Change the `Caption` property to `First Name`.
5. Now add the rest of the labels as shown in Figure 3.3.
6. Make the `Name` property on each label control `lblLabel`. You'll be prompted to specify whether you want to create a control array. Answer yes to this prompt.

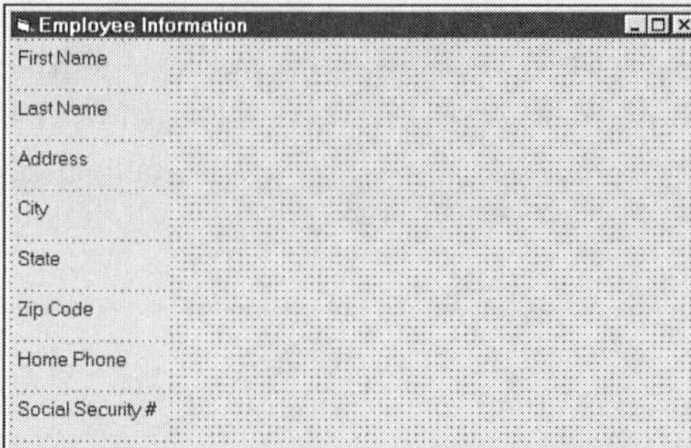

FIGURE 3.3
The Employee Information form with label controls.

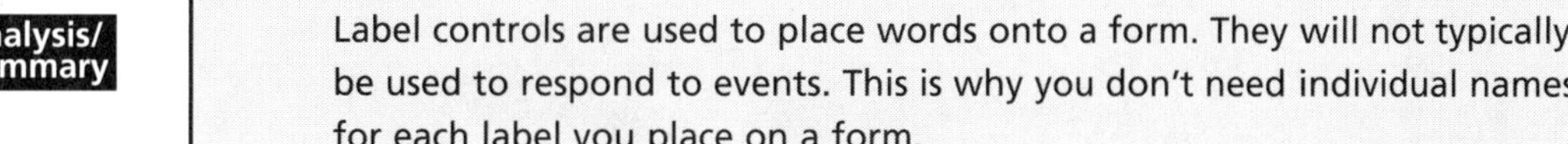

Label controls are used to place words onto a form. They will not typically be used to respond to events. This is why you don't need individual names for each label you place on a form.

Example's Filename: Employee1.frm

Common Label Control Properties

As is the case with from forms, you'll probably never change all the properties of a label control. Table 3.3 lists the properties you'll change most often for the label control.

CONTROL ARRAYS

You created a control array in the preceding exercise. A *control array* is a list of the same type of control, all of which share the same name. You created eight label controls, and each one's name is `lblLabel`. When you answer yes to the prompt to create a control array, Visual Basic automatically sets the `Index` property of each of these controls to a unique value. The Index property plus the name of the control is now how you will be able to distinguish one control from another.

Table 3.3 Common Label Properties

Property	Description
`Alignment`	Set this property to have the text right, left, or centered within the label.
`AutoSize`	After adding the text to the `Caption` property of the label control, you may have to size it manually to get all the text to show. This property will automatically size the control to the height and width of the text that's placed in it.
`BorderStyle`	Displays a border around the label.
`Caption`	Displays text inside of the label.
`Name`	Identifies the name of the control. The standard prefix when naming this type of control is *lbl*.
`Visible`	Indicates whether the control is visible.
`WordWrap`	If set to `True`, this property allows the caption to wrap to another line.

Text Box Control

A text box control is used to retrieve information from the user. Besides the label control, a text box is the tool you'll use most often when designing a Windows application. Now you can add text boxes to the form next to the labels to collect the employee information.

When adding text boxes to your form, try to draw them the same height as the labels. Also, make each box a size that's appropriate to the data you're trying to collect. For example, the Last Name text box should be slightly longer than the First Name text box. When you add text boxes to a form, the `Text` property will automatically be filled in with `Text`*n*. Some programmers set the `Text` property to the same value as the `Name` property, and some just set the `Text` property to a blank string.

EXERCISE

CREATING TEXT BOXES

1. Add text boxes to your form to make it look like Figure 3.4.
2. Create the text boxes with the properties set to the values shown in Table 3.4.

Table 3.4 Text Boxes to Add to the Form

Name	MaxLength
txtFirst	20
txtLast	25
txtAddress	50
txtCity	35
txtState	2
txtZip	10
txtPhone	14
txtSSN	11

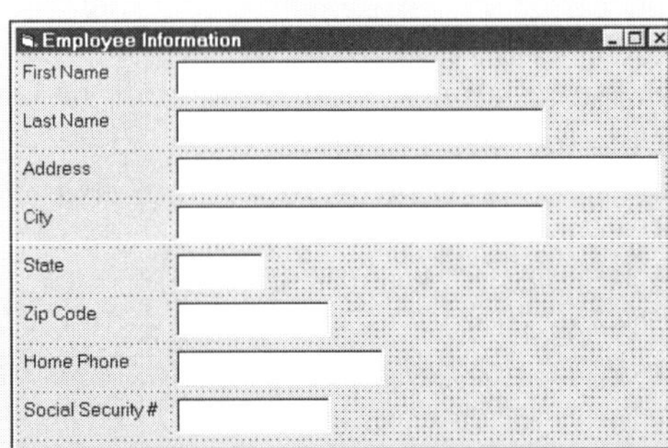

FIGURE 3.4
Text boxes on the Employee Information form.

Text boxes are the main user-interface tool that is used to gather user input. It is very important that you not only name each one individually, but that you also set the `MaxLength` to restrict the user's input to a reasonable size.

Example's Filename: Employee2.frm

Common Text Box Properties

Table 3.5 lists the properties changed most often for the text box control.

Table 3.5 Common Text Box Properties

Property	Description
`Enabled`	When this property is set to `True`, the user may type text into the text box. When it's set to `False`, the user will not be able to type text in the text box or move the cursor into the control. In addition, the control will be grayed. The gray color in Windows typically means a control is not available to be typed into, or clicked upon.
`Locked`	When this property is set to `True`, the user may move the cursor into the control but will be unable to change any of the characters. This allows the user to view all the text by scrolling left and right. The text will not be grayed.

Property	Description
`MaxLength`	Set this property to the maximum number of characters the user will be allowed to type into the text box. If set to `0`, any amount up to 2,048 characters may be input. If the `MultiLine` property is set to `True`, up to about 32KB of text may be input.
`MultiLine`	If this property is set to `True`, the user may scroll the text box up and down but not left and right. If you set this property to `True`, you'll typically set the `ScrollBars` property to allow for a vertical scroll bar. If you don't set this property, the user can still scroll left and right by using the keyboard.
`Name`	Set this property to the name of the control as you want to refer to it in your code. You should always preface the name of the text box with *txt*.
`ScrollBars`	This property may be set to display horizontal or vertical (or both) scroll bars on the text box control. You'll typically use this property when you set the `MultiLine` property to `True`.
`TabIndex`	The `TabIndex` property is set to a number that reflects the order in which you want to have your users tab through all the controls on your form.
`TabStop`	When this property is set to a `True` value, the control gets focus as the user tabs through the controls on your form. If this is set to a `False` value, the control will not get focus. However, the user can still click this control with the mouse to give it focus.
`Text`	This property displays text to the user and is filled with the text the user types in the control.
`ToolTipText`	Set this property to a textual value that you want to have displayed when the user hovers his or her cursor over the text box for a few seconds.
`Visible`	Indicates whether the control is visible.

Command Buttons

A *command button control* is used when you want the user to perform some action on a form. The action may be to close the form, save information on the form, or call another form. The user can click the command button with the mouse or tab to the command button and press the spacebar. Once the command button is clicked, it will generate an event. You can write code in that event to perform an appropriate action. You'll learn how to write code that responds to events in Chapter 5, "Events Happen."

ADDITIONAL NOTES ON THE TEXT BOX

If you want to verify that the user has entered a minimum amount of characters into a text box, you have to write some code to test for this. You would enter this code in either the KeyPress, KeyDown, or KeyUp events. If you want to create a password-type text box, you can set the `PasswordChar` property to an asterisk (*) or to any other character you want. When the user types, only that character will show up in the text box, but the `Text` property will be set to the actual letters the user types in.

Command Button Common Properties

Command button controls have very few properties you need to be concerned with. Table 3.6 is a list of the most commonly changed properties for a command button control.

Table 3.6 Command Button Properties

Property	Description
`Cancel`	When you set this property to a `True` value, it generates its `Click` event when the user presses the Esc key. Only one command button on the form may have this property set to `True`.
`Caption`	Set this property to the text you want to display on the command button. If you place an ampersand (&) before a letter in the caption, you'll create an underscore under that letter. The user can press the Alt key in combination with that letter to have the `Click` event fire for this command button.

Property	Description
`CausesValidation`	When set to `True`, this property causes the `Validate` event on other controls to occur. You might set the `CausesValidation` property to `False` on a command button so that the `Validate` event on the text box does not occur. This way, the command button can call a help routine telling the user what the required input is for a particular text box.
`Default`	Set this property to a `True` value when you want to fire the `Click` event when the user presses the Enter key. Only one command button on the form may have this property set to `True`.
`Enabled`	When this property is set to a `True` value, the user is able to click the button. When it's set to `False`, the user isn't able to click this command button. In addition, the control will be grayed.
`Name`	Set this property to the name you want to use to refer to the command button in your code. You should preface the name of the control with *cmd*.
`Picture`	This property can be set to a bitmap, GIF, or JPEG file if you've set the `Style` property to `1-Graphical`. The picture will be displayed on the command button instead of the text in the `Caption` property.
`Style`	Set this property to `0-Standard` if you want to display text on the command button, or you can set the property to `1-Graphical` if you want to display a picture on the command button.

EXERCISE

Adding Command Buttons to Your Project

1. Increase the size of the form.
2. Add a command button to the Employee Information form that will allow you to close the form when the button is clicked.
3. Set the `Name` property to `cmdClose`.
4. Set the `Caption` property to `&Close`. The ampersand (&) character tells Windows to make the next letter appear underlined.
5. Set the `Cancel` property to `True`.
6. Add another command button. Set it next to the Close button.
7. Set the `Name` property to `cmdSave`.

8. Set the `Caption` property to `&Save`.
9. Set the `Default` property to `True`.
10. The resultant form should look like the one shown in Figure 3.5.

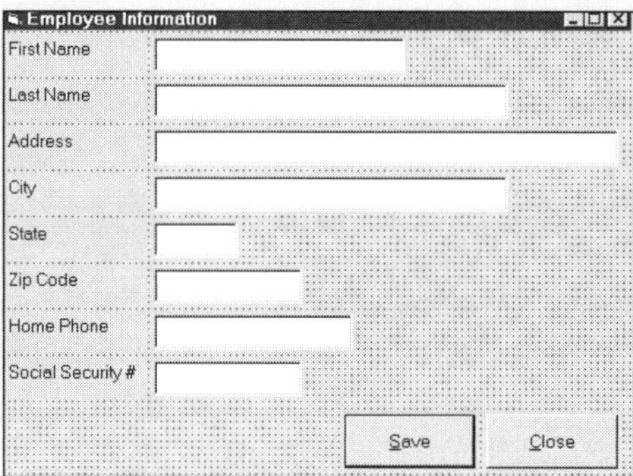

FIGURE 3.5
The Employee Information form with two command buttons.

Command buttons are used to let the user commit changes, undo changes, or any other type of action on a form-level basis. You can set properties to make the command button respond to the Enter key or the Escape key as well as the mouse.

Example's Filename: Employee3.frm

TIP
Now would be a good time to save the project. It's always a good idea to save your work periodically. You never know when the power may go out.

Frames

The frame control is designed to allow you to insert a group of controls into a box and add a caption to describe the purpose of these controls. In the next section, you'll learn about check boxes and option buttons, which typically are used in a group. Any type of control that belongs in a group will fit into a frame control very well.

By putting controls into a frame, you identify them as being a part of a group. The frame control is what is known as a *container control*. A container control is any control that acts as a parent to all the controls within it. This is similar to a form, which has many controls on it, and those controls are all governed by the action of the form.

EXERCISE

Add a Frame Control to Group Controls

1. Add a frame in the lower-right corner of the Employee form.
2. Set the `Name` property to `fraSex`.
3. Set the `Caption` property to `Sex`.
4. Make sure you form looks like the one shown in Figure 3.6.

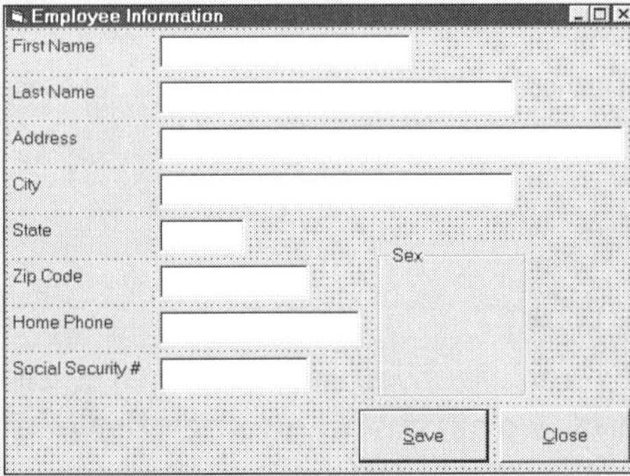

FIGURE 3.6
The Employee Information form with a frame control.

A frame control is typically used to group other controls. Be sure to draw the frame first, give it focus, and then draw the other controls on top of the frame.

Example's Filename: Employee4.frm

Common Frame Properties

You'll change very few properties for the frame control. Table 3.7 lists the properties changed most often for the frame control.

Table 3.7 Common Frame Properties

Property	Description
`Caption`	Set this property to the value you want to display on the top-left side of the frame.
`Enabled`	Set this property to `False` to disable all the controls contained within the frame control.
`Name`	Set this property to the name of the control as you want to refer to it in source code. You should preface the name with the letters *fra*.
`Visible`	When you set this property to `False`, all of the controls within the container will be hidden.

Option Buttons

An *option button*, sometimes called a *radio button*, is used to create mutually exclusive options. For example, if you've created a field named Sex, an employee can only choose one of two options—male or female. When you click one of the option buttons, any other button previously selected in the group will automatically turn off. You can group option buttons by placing each group in separate frames.

EXERCISE

Add Option Buttons for Mutually Exclusive Options

1. Click once on the Sex frame to give it focus. This ensures that the option buttons you're about to add are placed inside of the frame.
2. Grab an option button from the toolbar and draw it on the frame.
3. Set the `Name` property to `optMale`.
4. Set the `Caption` property to `Male`.
5. Copy and paste another control.
6. Click once on the `optMale` option button to give it focus.

7. Press Ctrl+C to copy the control to the Clipboard.
8. Click once on the frame to give it focus.
9. Press Ctrl+V to paste the control on the frame.
10. Answer no when prompted to specify whether you want to create a control array.
11. Set the `Name` property to `optFemale`.
12. Set the `Caption` property to `Female`.
13. The form should now look like the one shown in Figure 3.7.

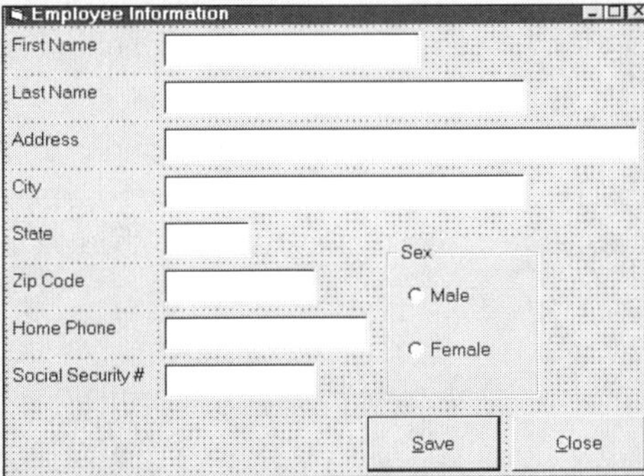

FIGURE 3.7
Option buttons on the Employee Information form.

Option buttons are used for mutually exclusive options. When the user clicks on one button, the others will turn off automatically.

Example's Filename: Employee5.frm

Common Option Button Properties

Table 3.8 lists the properties changed most often for the option button control.

Table 3.8 Common Option Button Properties

Property	Description
`Alignment`	This property can be set to `Left Align` or `Right Align`. This determines on which side of the text the option button will appear.
`Caption`	Set this property to the text that you want to have appear next to the option button.
`Name`	Set this property to the value you want to use to refer to this control in your code. You should preface the name with the letters *opt*.
`Picture`	This property can be set to a bitmap, GIF, or JPEG file if you've set the `Style` property to `1-Graphical`. The picture will be displayed beside the option button instead of the text in the `Caption` property.
`Style`	Set this property to `0-Standard` if you want to display text beside the option button, or you can set the property to `1-Graphical` if you want to display a picture beside the option button.
`Value`	When this property is set to `True`, the option button is selected by default. Only one option button in a group may be set to `True` at one time.

Check Boxes

A *check box* allows the user to select one or more choices from a list of values. These choices are not mutually exclusive like the choices for the option buttons are; instead, you may have multiple values selected at the same time.

EXERCISE

Adding Check Boxes

1. Add another frame next to the Sex frame.
2. Set the Name property to `fraBenefits`.
3. Change the `Caption` property to `Benefits`.

4. Add check boxes as shown in Figure 3.8. (Table 3.9 shows the `Name` and the `Caption` properties you need to set for these check boxes.)

Table 3.9 Check Boxes

Name	Caption
`chkHealth`	`Health Plan`
`chk401k`	`401K`
`chkBonus`	`Bonus Program`

FIGURE 3.8
Check boxes on the Employee Information form.

Check boxes will allow the user to choose one or more options. It is a good idea to group these in a frame as well as option buttons.

Example's Filename: Employee6.frm

Common Check Box Properties

Table 3.10 lists the properties you'll change most often for the check box control.

Table 3.10 Common Check Box Properties

Property	Description
`Alignment`	This property can be set to `Left Align` or `Right Align`. This determines on which side of the text the check box will appear.
`Caption`	Set this property to the text you want to have appear next to the check box.
`Name`	Set this property to the value you want to use to refer to the control in your code. You should preface the name with the letters *chk*.
`Picture`	This property can be set to a bitmap, GIF, or JPEG file if you've set the `Style` property to `1-Graphical`. This picture will be displayed next to the check box instead of the text in the `Caption` property.
`Style`	Set this property to `0-Standard` if you want to display text beside the check box, or you can set the property to `1-Graphical` if you want to display a picture beside the check box.
`Value`	The check box may be set to one of three states: `0-Unchecked` means that no check mark shows up in the check box. A value of `1-Checked` means that this item has been selected and a check mark is visible. `2-Grayed` means that this check box is not available at this time.

Picture Control

A picture control has two different uses: It can be used to display a picture, such as a bitmap, icon, or JPEG or GIF file, and it can be used as a container control like a frame. When used to display a picture, the picture control will load the picture, but the picture will retain its original size—in other words, it will not resize itself to the width and height of the picture control.

When you're using the picture control as a container for other controls, all the controls you place into it will move with the picture control. One of the nice features of using the picture control as a container is that it has an `Align` property. This property allows you to align the control to the top, left, right or bottom of the form. If you move or resize the form, the picture control will move or resize with the form.

EXERCISE

Adding a Picture Box

1. Place a picture box at the top-right corner of the form.
2. Set the `Name` property to `picMail`.
3. Set the `AutoSize` property to `True`.
4. Click on the ellipsis (...) in the `Picture` property to load a file from disk.
5. Select the file MAIL01a.ico in the ..\Visual Basic\Graphics\Icons folder. The form should now look like the one shown in Figure 3.9.

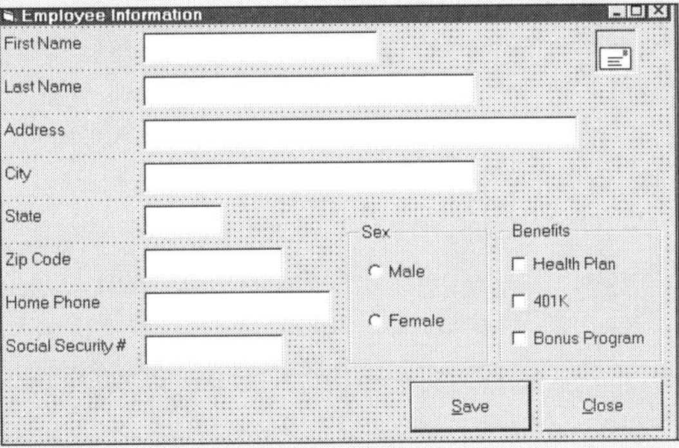

FIGURE 3.9
A picture control on the Employee Information form.

The Picture control can give your applications a nice graphical touch of color. Use it sparingly though, because this control takes up some significant memory and other resources.

Example's Filename: Employee7.frm

Common Picture Control Properties

Table 3.11 lists the properties you'll change most often for the picture control.

Table 3.11 Common Picture Control Properties

Property	Description
`Align`	Set this property to `None`, `Align Top`, `Align Bottom`, `Align Left`, or `Align Right` to make the picture control align or not align to the form.
`AutoSize`	Set this property to `True` if you want to have the picture control automatically adjust its size to the size of the graphic loaded into the control. If this property is set to `False` and the size of the graphic is larger than the size of the picture control, the graphic will be clipped.
`BorderStyle`	Set this property to either `None` or to `Fixed Single`.
`Name`	Set this property to the value you want to use to refer to the control in your code. You should preface the name with the letters *pic*.
`Picture`	This property can be set to a bitmap, GIF, or JPEG file.

Image Control

The image control is a lightweight version of the picture control. Unlike the picture control, the image control does not have an `Align` property. However, this control does have a `Stretch` property that allows the graphic that's placed in it to be stretched to the size of the control. Other than these differences, the image control is essentially the same as the picture control. If all you're doing is displaying a graphic, you should always use an image control. If you need to align controls to the top or bottom of a form, you may want to use a picture control instead.

Summary

In this chapter, you learned how to create a new project using Visual Basic. You learned how to make a form into a running application. You added controls to the form and set properties to change the look and behavior of those controls. Along the way, you learned about the prefixes used to name each of the different controls.

Review Questions

1. Which control is used to display information to the user but doesn't allow the user to change the information?
2. Which control is used to retrieve typed input from the user?
3. Which control allows the user to select only one of a group of choices?
4. Which control allows the user to select one or more of a group of choices?
5. Which controls display many items to the user?

4

Lists and Menus

MANY TIMES IN AN APPLICATION, YOU NEED to display many items to the user. These items may come from a database or may simply be a hard-coded list. You have two basic ways to present this information: You can use a list box or a combo box. In this chapter, you'll learn to use both of these tools. In addition, you'll learn to create a menu system for your forms.

Chapter Objectives

- Learn to use a list box
- Learn to use a combo box
- Learn to create menus
- Learn the naming standards for controls

Sample Project File Name: \Chapter04\ListsMenus.vbp

List Box Control

A list box control provides a list of items you want to display to the user as choices he or she may choose from. For example, you might use a list box to display a complete list of employees or maybe a list of options to the user about the employees. You only use a list box control when you have some substantial real estate on your form. If you're limited on space and want to have multiple items displayed, a combo box will work better. Combo boxes are covered in the next section.

A list box has a `List` property that contains a list of the items to display. These items may be sorted by setting the `Sorted` property to `True`. You can choose to have the user select just one item from the list or have the user select multiple items by setting the `MultiSelect` property to either `Simple` or `Extended`, respectively. You can also set the `Style` property to `Checkbox`.

EXERCISE

Adding a List Box

1. **Add a new label at the bottom of the form. You might need to make the form longer to accommodate this new label and the list box you'll be adding. Set the `Caption` property of the label to `Health Care Choices`.**
2. **Add a list box to the right of this label.**
3. **Set the `Name` property to `lstHealth`.**
4. **Click the `List` property to see a drop-down list.**
5. **Add five or six health care companies to this list. After adding a choice to the `List` property, you need to press Ctrl+Enter to move to the next line.**

6. When you're done, close the list. You'll now see the choices listed in the list box.
7. Run this form so you can see how the list box reacts when you click an item and whether you have to scroll to see more options. Notice that the scrollbar will automatically appear if you have more options than will fit into the area in which you drew the list box. See Figure 4.1.

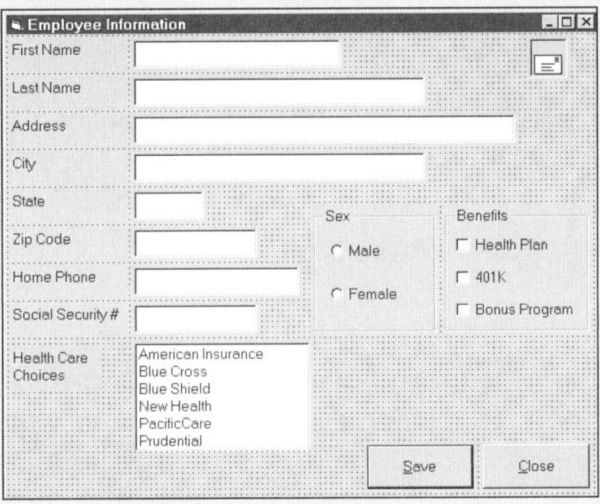

FIGURE 4.1
The list box on the Employee Information form.

Example's Filename: Employee8.frm
A list box will present multiple items to a user to select from. The values can be entered at design time or at runtime.

Multiple Columns

If you have more room horizontally, you might want to have the columns snake across rather than have the user scroll down to see more choices. Set the `Columns` property to a value greater than zero to create snaking columns. Figure 4.2 shows what happens when you set the `Columns` to `1`.

FIGURE 4.2
A list box with multiple columns.

Example's Filename: Employee8.frm

Sorting the List

You can have the list sorted by setting the `Sorted` property to `True`. The sorting in a list box is always in an ascending order. There is no option to have a descending sort.

MultiSelect List Boxes

The normal list box you add to a form allows a user to select just one of the values at a time. You can allow the user to highlight multiple items in the list box by setting the `MultiSelect` property to `1-Simple`. When the list box is set to this value, the user can continue to click items in the list box. Each time he or she clicks a new item, that item will be highlighted. If the user clicks one of the items already highlighted, that item will no longer be highlighted.

EXERCISE

CHANGING THE MULTI-SELECT CAPABILITIES OF A LIST BOX

1. Change the `MultiSelect` property to `1-Simple`.
2. Run the form and try clicking several of the items in the list box.

Setting the `MultiSelect` property to `True` will allow the user to choose multiple items from the list box control.

You can also set the `MultiSelect` property to `2-Extended`. In this case, the list box acts like the Windows Explorer. If you click an item, it will be highlighted. Then, to highlight additional items, you have to hold down the Ctrl key and click. You can also select all items between the first one highlighted and the last one highlighted by holding down the Shift key. One more method is to click and hold your mouse and drag your mouse over the items you want to highlight. Of course you may find this last method a little harder to control.

EXERCISE

Try the Multi-Select Form

1. Change the `MultiSelect` property to `2-Extended`.
2. Run the form and try highlighting items in different ways using the Ctrl and Shift keys.

You can use many different methods to select items in a list box. Find which one works best for you!

You also have the option of setting the `Style` property to `CheckBox`. When this option is selected, a check box will appear next to each item in the list. You toggle a check box by clicking it.

EXERCISE

Using Check Boxes on a List Box to Select Multiple Items

1. Change the `Style` property to `1-Checkbox`.
2. Change the `Columns` property back to `0`.
3. Run the form and select different items by clicking check boxes. You will see an example of what this should look like in Figure 4.3.

An internal list called `Selected` will be set to either a `True` or `False` value to represent which items are selected in the list when any of the preceding methods are used. `Selected` is actually a property that only exists at runtime. It will always have as many items in it as you have in the list itself. You can loop through this `Selected` property and perform processing on each of the selected items.

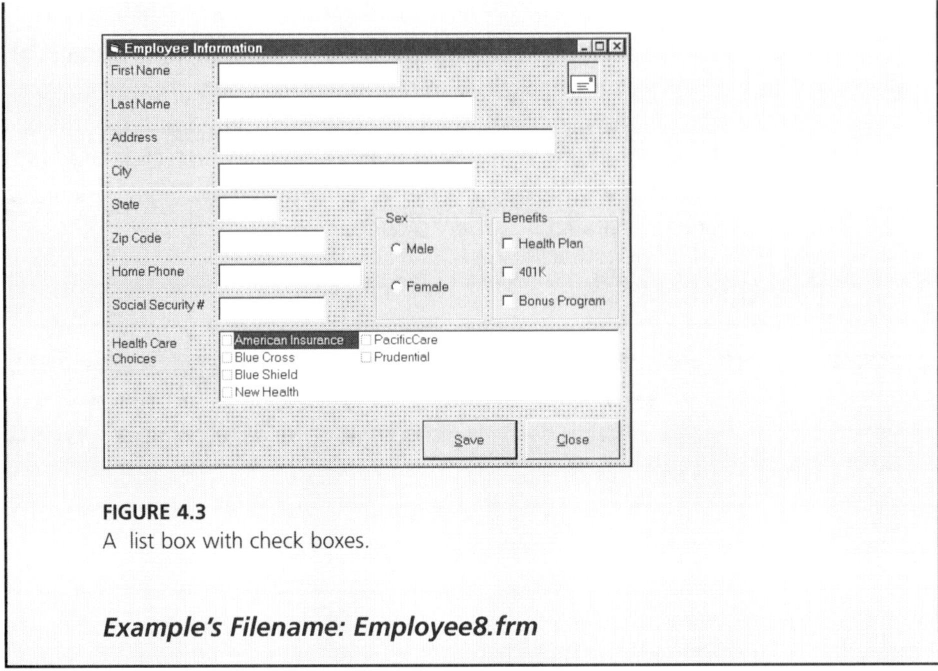

FIGURE 4.3
A list box with check boxes.

Example's Filename: Employee8.frm

The *IntegralHeight* Property

You may notice as you work with the list box that you're not able to stretch the height exactly to where you want. This is because the list box always calculates the number of rows it can display given the state of the current font you've set. It always keeps the height of the control so that it can display only full rows of data without cutting a row in half. If this is a problem for you, you can turn off this behavior. Set the `IntegralHeight` property to `False` and the list box can be stretched to any height you want.

List Box Properties

Table 4.1 lists the properties you'll change most often when working with the list box control.

Table 4.1 List Box Control Properties

Property	Description
`Columns`	The number of snaking columns you want to have displayed in the list box.
`IntegralHeight`	Set this property to `True` if you want to have Visual Basic calculate the height for the control based on the current font size.
`ItemData`	An internal numeric array that parallels the `List` array.
`List`	An array of the values placed in the list box control.
`MultiSelect`	Set this property to `0-None`, `1-Simple`, or `2-Extended`.
`Name`	Set this property to the value you want to use to refer to this control in your code. You should preface the name with the letters *lst* for consistency with accepted industry naming standards.
`SelCount`	A runtime-only property that returns the number of highlighted or selected items in the list.
`Selected`	A runtime-only property that's an array of `True` and `False` values corresponding to the items selected in the list.
`Sorted`	Set this property to `True` to have the items added to the list box to be displayed in a sorted order.
`Style`	Set this property to `0-Standard` or `1-CheckBox`.

Combo Box Control

A combo box is a combination of a text box and a list box. This control is used when you want to present a list of items to the user, but you don't have a lot of real estate on your form. The list portion of this combo box will be dropped down a certain number of rows to show the list to the user.

The combo box control has three different styles that can be set. First, it can be set to `0-DropDown Combo`. With this style, you can either type text into the text portion of the combo box or select a value from the drop-down list.

The second style is `1-Simple`. This style looks like a list box sitting directly underneath a text box. If you select an item in the list, it puts the value into the text box portion. You're also allowed to type text into the text box portion of the combo box. Of course if you choose this style, you will need to extend the height of the combo box to see all the items in the list.

The last style is `2-DropDown List`. This style allows you to select only from the list portion. You're not allowed to type any text in the text portion of the combo box.

No matter which style you use, if you press a key in the text portion of the combo box, it will search for the letter you've typed. It will not perform a drill-down search; however, if you have five items that start with the letter J, for example, you can keep hitting the J key to cycle through all five items.

A good place for this control on the Employee Information form would be in place of the State text box. The user should choose a state from a list instead of typing in the value in a text box. If you make a user type in a value, he or she might type it incorrectly. If the user simply selects a value from a combo box, he or she cannot type it in wrong.

The combo box control has many of the same properties as the list box control—the `Sorted` property, the `List` property, and the `IntegralHeight` property. Remember that a combo box is just a list box with a text box attached to it.

EXERCISE

Adding a Combo Box of State Codes

1. Click the State text box on the Employee Information form to give it focus.
2. Press the Delete key to delete that text box.
3. Add a combo box to the same location where the text box was positioned.
4. Set the `Name` property to `cboState`.
5. Set the style to `2-DropDown List`. You want to use this style for lookup fields, where the user can't add new values to the list.
6. Set the `Sorted` property to `True`.
7. Now you can change the `List` property just like you did for the list box control and add the different state codes. See Figure 4.4 for an example of what this combo box might look like.

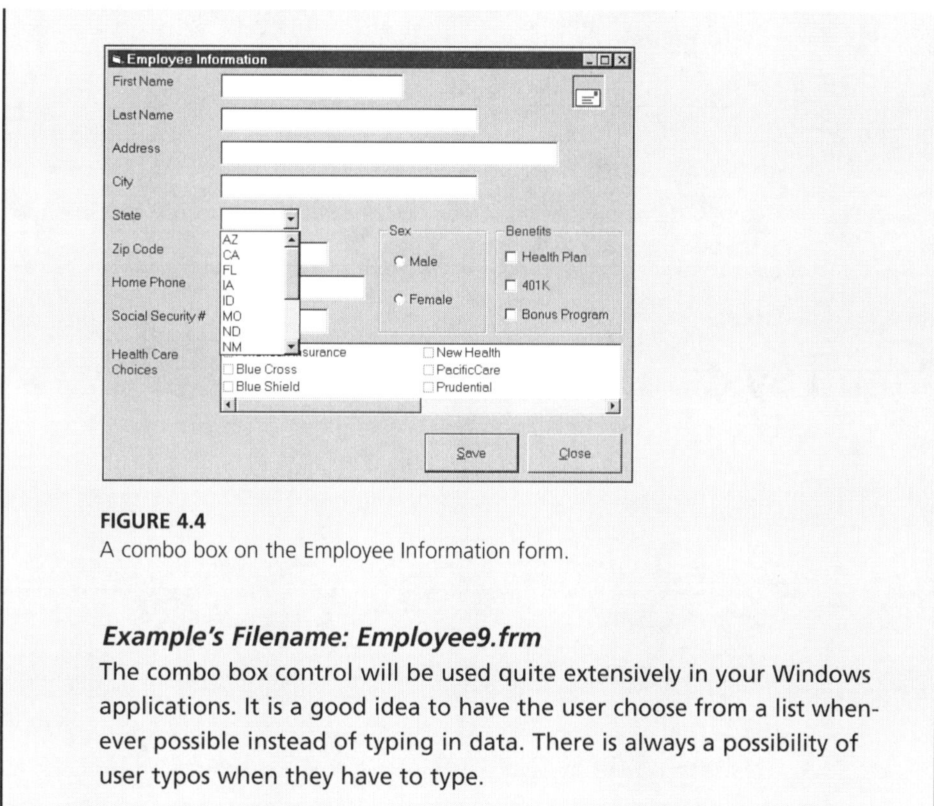

FIGURE 4.4
A combo box on the Employee Information form.

Example's Filename: Employee9.frm

The combo box control will be used quite extensively in your Windows applications. It is a good idea to have the user choose from a list whenever possible instead of typing in data. There is always a possibility of user typos when they have to type.

Combo Box Properties

Table 4.2 lists the properties you'll change most often when working with the combo box control.

Table 4.2 Combo Box Control Properties

Property	Description
`IntegralHeight`	Set this property to `True` if you want Visual Basic to calculate the height for the control based on the current font size.
`ItemData`	An internal numeric array that parallels the `List` array.
`List`	An array of the values placed in the combo box control.
`Name`	Set this property to the value you want to use to refer to this control in your code. You should preface the name with the letters `cbo`.

continues

Table 4.2 Continued

Property	Description
`Sorted`	Set this property to `True` to have the items added to the combo box displayed in a sorted order.
`Style`	Set this property to `0-DropDown Combo`, `1-Simple Combo`, or `2-DropDown List`.

Menu System

Every Windows applications has a menu bar directly under the title of the window. Menus are used to present multiple choices and actions for a user to perform. Menus can be designed for those users who need or prefer to use the keyboard. Menus offer additional functionality to your Visual Basic program, such as context-sensitive menus that pop up when right-clicked with the mouse.

You'll find many standard menu items from one Windows application to another. For example, you'll always find a File menu. Under the File menu, you'll typically find an Exit or Close menu. In most applications, you'll find a Help menu with an About menu item that displays a dialog box containing information about the application.

Menu Standards

Before building menus for your application, look at existing menu designs in other Windows applications. You'll see some standard menu items as well as standard conventions for informing the user of what the menu items can accomplish.

Look at Visual Basic, Word, Excel, PowerPoint, or any other Windows product and observe the different menus. Here are some standard conventions to follow when creating your menus:

- An arrow to the right of a menu item signifies that another menu will display when you click this one. Visual Basic automatically adds an arrow if you create drop-down menus.
- An ellipsis (...) signifies that clicking this menu item brings up a dialog box that asks you for information. Visual Basic will *not* insert ellipses for you. You must put them on the menu item yourself if you'll be calling a dialog box from that menu item.

- A check mark positioned to the left of a menu item is used to inform the user that a certain option is currently in effect. For example, you may use this on a View menu to signify that a toolbar is being displayed.
- You can group menu items under a submenu by putting a separator bar between different menu items. Menu items can be separated by creating a menu item with the caption property set to a hyphen (-). You'll need to create a unique name for each separator bar.
- Menu shortcut keys, sometimes called *access keys*, *hotkeys*, or *accelerator keys*, are shown as a key combination to press without going to the menu item. For example, Ctrl+X is the same as selecting Edit, Cut. The F1 key is the same as choosing Help.
- Each of the top-level menu items has an underlined letter. This tells the user that he or she can press the Alt key in combination with this letter to access the menu items. Underlined letters in drop-down menus indicate that the user can press the key instead of clicking the item with the mouse. To make an underlined letter, precede the letter in the `Caption` property with an ampersand (&) character.

Menu Editor

A menu is created in Visual Basic by selecting a form and then pressing Ctrl+E, by selecting Tools, Menu Editor, or by selecting the Menu Editor icon on the toolbar. The Menu Editor window, shown in Figure 4.5, allows you to put in Windows menu items one by one. This is probably the least visual part of Visual Basic.

FIGURE 4.5 The Menu Editor dialog box.

Each property on the Menu Editor dialog box can be used to set different options for the menu item.

Common Menu Properties

Let's look at the most important properties for this dialog box (see Table 4.3).

Table 4.3 Common Properties for Menu Items

Property	Description
`Caption`	This is the menu item you want to display to the user. Putting an ampersand (&) in front of a letter causes the letter that follows to be underlined. In the top-level menu items, an underlined letter for an option can be selected by pressing Alt + the underlined key or by selecting the menu option with the mouse. On the drop-down menu items, an underlined letter for an option is selected by pressing that letter after the drop-down list is displayed.
`Name`	Set this property to the name you want to use to refer to this menu item in your source code. You should preface this name with the letters *mnu*.
`ShortCut`	This property displays a list of all the different keystroke combinations you can assign to a menu item.
`Checked`	Set this property to `True` if you want to place a check mark next to the menu item.
`WindowList`	Set this property to `True` when you want to create a list of open windows in a Multiple Document Interface (MDI) application. You'll learn to create MDI applications in Chapter 15, "Multiple Document Interface."

EXERCISE

Adding a Menu

1. Bring up your form and press Ctrl+E.
2. Set the `Caption` property to `&File`.
3. Set the `Name` property to `mnuFile`.
4. Click the Next command button to move to the next menu.
5. Set the `Caption` property to `&Open`.

6. Set the `Name` property to `mnuFOpen`. (I always preface menu items on drop-down menus with the first letter of the top-level menu.)
7. Click right-arrow button to indent this menu item. This indentation tells the menu system to create the menu item as a drop-down menu under the File menu item.
8. You can continue this process of indenting until you've created as many menus as you want. See Figure 4.6 for an example.

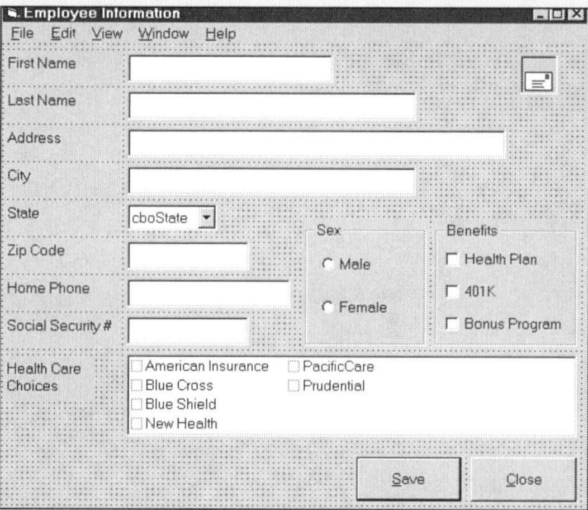

FIGURE 4.6
Menu items on the Employee Information form.

Example's Filename: Employee10.frm

Menus are added using the Menu Editor window. While not very "visual," it does the job.

NOTE
Keep the number of drop-down menu levels to a minimum. Most Windows applications limit the number of menus you have to go through to three or less.

Table 4.4 lists all the menus you might create for the employee form.

Table 4.4 Menu Items for the Employee Information Form

Menu Caption	Menu Name
`&File`	`mnuFile`
`&Employee`	`mnuFEmp`
`    -`	`mnuFSep`
`    E&xit`	`mnuFExit`
`&Edit`	`mnuEdit`
`    Cu&t`	`mnuECut`
`    &Copy`	`mnuECopy`
`    &Paste`	`mnuEPaste`
`&View`	`mnuView`
`    &Toolbar`	`mnuVToolbar`
`    &Status Bar`	`mnuVStatus`
`&Window`	`mnuWindow`
`    Tile &Horizontal`	`mnuWHorizontal`
`    Tile &Vertical`	`mnuWVertical`
`    &Cascade`	`mnuWCascade`
`    &Arrange Icons`	`mnuWArrange`
`&Help`	`mnuHelp`
`    &Help Contents`	`mnuHContents`
`    -`	`mnuHSep`
`    &About...`	`mnuHAbout`

Naming Controls

You'll notice in the preceding examples that prefixes are used to identify the type of objects placed on a form. Certain naming standards are recommended for controls. Table 4.5 shows the recommended prefix and a sample name for objects placed on a form. This list can also be found in the Visual Basic Books Online.

Table 4.5 Naming Standards for Controls

Object	Prefix	Example
Form	frm	frmMail
Check box	chk	chkLanguages
Combo box	cbo	cboStates
Command button	cmd	cmdSave
Data	dat	datMail
Directory list box	dir	dirSource
Drive list box	drv	drvUserDrives
File list box	fil	filSource
Frame	fra	fraCards
Grid	grd	grdPartList
Horizontal scrollbar	hsb	hsbPartList
Image	img	imgIcon
Label	lbl	lblFirstName
Line	lin	linSeparate
List box	lst	lstCountries
Menu	mnu	mnuFile
OLE	ole	oleClient
Option button	opt	optSex
Picture box	pic	picEmployee
Shape	shp	shpRectangle
Text box	txt	txtFirstName
Time	tmr	tmrAlarm
Vertical scrollbar	vsb	vsbPartList

Always use these prefixes in Visual Basic applications. In Appendix A, "VBA Programming Standards," you'll find recommended programming standards for Visual Basic applications. It's strongly suggested that you follow these standards at all times.

Creating an Executable Program

Congratulations, you now have a good start on the Employee Information application. You've just created the user interface, and although this form does not really do anything yet, it's still a great start. In fact, if you're smart, you'll always start by designing the user interface before you write any code. If you do this, you'll find that your Visual Basic programming goes much smoother.

Now, let's create an executable file from the form. You need to learn how to create an EXE that you can distribute to your users, so let's do it now.

EXERCISE

Creating an EXE File

1. Select File, Make Employee.exe from the Visual Basic menu.
2. Be sure to put this EXE file in the same directory as your project file. This is not necessary, but I recommend it for now.
3. Click the OK button.
4. Exit Visual Basic by selecting File, Exit from the menu.
5. Switch over to Windows Explorer.
6. Locate the EMPLOYEE.EXE file and double-click it.
7. Your program should now be running!

Creating an EXE file that can be run in Windows is very simple in Visual Basic. With just a couple of keystrokes you have an application ready to run!

After you stop your program from running by closing the window, go back to Windows Explorer, right-click, and select Properties from the pop-up menu. Under the Version tab, you should find all the properties you created when you set the project properties.

Summary

In this chapter, you learned to use list boxes and combo boxes. A list box is used when you want the user to see many choices at one time, whereas a combo box is for just one selected item. A menu helps an application's user navigate from one form to another, or it can be used to perform selected actions.

Review Questions

1. Which control displays just one item to the user?
2. How can you sort the items in a list or combo box?
3. How do you make a letter in a menu item underlined?

5

Events Happen

ALMOST EVERYTHING YOU DO WITHIN THE WINDOWS environment creates an event. Your forms and controls have the ability to respond to those events via *code snippets* (little bits of procedural code you write). You attach code to each form and control so that these visual elements can perform actions. This chapter introduces you to several events for several controls and shows you how to write the code for each event.

Chapter Objectives

- Learn about the code window
- Learn about form events
- Learn about different events for different controls

Sample Project Filename: \Chapter05\Events.vbp

Code Window

To write code that responds to an event, you first need to double-click one of the controls on your form or the form itself to display a code window. A *code window* is where you type in all the procedures and functions that make your application do something.

EXERCISE

Bringing Up a Code Window

1. Double-click on the form. Be sure not to double-click one of the controls.
2. You should see a code window similar to the one shown in Figure 5.1.

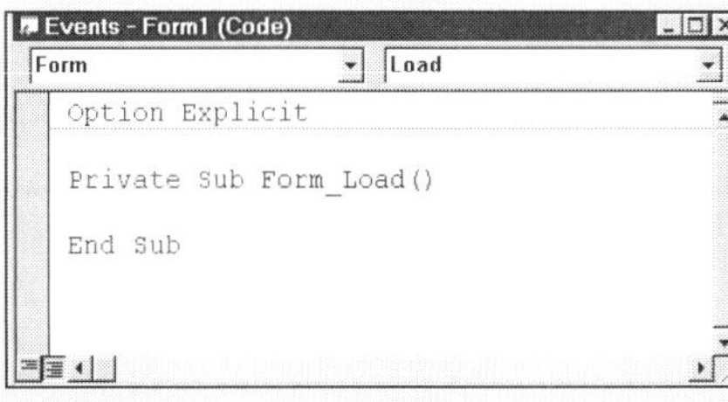

FIGURE 5.1
A code window.

A code window is where you will write all the code for your application.

The code window has several areas of note. The first is the *title bar*, which displays the project name and the module name. Next are the two combo boxes at the top of the window. The one on the left shows you the particular control or object you're writing code for, and the one on the right is the name of the specific event the code is for. The main part of the window is where you write your source code.

This window works just like any source code editor: You can use the Tab key to indent with spaces, the Enter key will add a new line, and so on.

It is *very* important that you always set the `Name` property of a control prior to writing code. If you write the code first and then change the `Name` property of the control, the code is disconnected from the control and deposited into the General section of the form.

> **TIP**
> **Set the `Name` property of all your controls prior to writing source code for them.**

Breakdown of an Event Procedure

Event procedures are bits of code that run when something happens to a form or a control. An event procedure must be defined in a very specific format. In the code window in Figure 5.1, you see a declaration for the `Form_Load()` event procedure. Let's break this down into its constituent parts (see Table 5.1).

Table 5.1 Breakdown of an Event Procedure

Part	Description
`Private Sub`	This declares a new event procedure that's private to this form.
`Form_`	`Form` is a generic name given to every form. Even if the name of the form is `frmCust`, it will still be called `Form_Load()`. This name will change for controls, because it uses the control name followed by an underscore and then the event name.
`Load`	This is the event name that's invoked when the form is loaded by Windows or by your source code.
<blank lines>	In between the first line and `End Sub` is where you'll write your source code.
`End Sub`	This marks the end of the event procedure.

The `Form_Load()` event procedure is normally used to set default values for the form. For example, you can change the position of the form or initialize some of the other properties of the form.

Example's Filename: Employee.frm

EXERCISE

ADDING A *Form_Load()* EVENT PROCEDURE

1. Open the frmEmployee form.
2. Double-click the form.
3. Type in the following code:

```
Private Sub Form_Load ()
    frmEmployee.Top = 1000
    frmEmployee.Left = 500
End Sub
```

The `Form_Load()` event is used to initialize the form to a "good" start state. Setting `Top` and `Left` will move the form to a certain location on the screen. You can set other properties within this event as well.

In this example, you actually change the value of the properties at run-time instead of design time by using the properties window. Try changing the value of these properties to see how the form responds.

How Do You Use Events?

Events are used to run some code that will perform a process based on some user action. An example might be changing the properties of a control, making a form close, closing your entire application, retrieving information from a database, or even displaying a graphic. To cause any of these things to happen, you simply write code that responds to a user action.

Changing Properties at Runtime

As shown earlier, properties can be changed at runtime by using the name of the control and the name of the property in your source code. A dot (.) operator is used to separate the name of the form or control from the property you want to change.

Here are some examples:

```
Form.Caption = "My First Application"
Me.Top = 1000
lblLabel.Caption = "Enter First Name"
txtFirst.Text = "Bill"
```

Common Events

Many events are common from one control or form to another. Let's talk about these common events and what they do before we discuss what each control does specifically (see Table 5.2). It is important to remember that each control has these common events, but each one will have its own particular events as well. For example, you may have five text boxes on a form, and each text box will have these events. Therefore, you can write code to respond differently to the `Click()` event on each text box.

Table 5.2 Common Event Names

Event Name	Description
`Click`	This event occurs when you click a particular control or form.
`DblClick`	This event occurs when you double-click a control or form.
`Change`	This event occurs with a text box and certain other controls whenever the data in the control changes in response to user input or your source code.
`GotFocus`	This event occurs as you move from one control to another. Each control receives this event as you tab from one control to the other. This event happens as you tab into a control.
`LostFocus`	This event occurs as you move from one control to another. Each control receives this event as you tab from one control to the other. This event will fire when you tab out of a control.
`KeyPress`	This event occurs whenever you press a key on a control or form.
`KeyDown`	This event occurs when a key is pressed down on a control or form.
`KeyUp`	This event occurs when a key is released after being pressed down on a control or form.
`MouseDown`	This event occurs when any of the mouse buttons are pressed down on a control or form.
`MouseUp`	This event occurs when the mouse button is released after being pressed down on a control or form.
`MouseMove`	This event occurs when the mouse is moved over a control or form.

The preceding events are just a small sample of the many events that happen for each control. Many controls have very specific events that relate only to how that control works. You'll learn about these generic and specific events in this chapter and in future chapters.

Form Events

A form has many events you can respond to. So far, you've just built one form, and you've pressed the Run button (or F5) to start your program. Visual Basic takes care of the details of displaying this form. Later, you'll write code to display a form, such as this:

```
frmEmployee.Show
```

`Show` is the method that each form has attached to it. A *method* is a bit of internal code for a form or control that performs some action on that object. When the `Show` method is invoked on this form, you're telling the form it should load and display itself. A form knows how to display itself based on the properties you've set in the Property window at design time.

Form_Initialize()

The `Form_Initialize()` event is the first event to occur when you invoke the `Show` method on a form. In this event, no controls are yet loaded into memory, so you can only affect any memory variables. Referencing any controls in this event will cause a runtime error to occur. This event will only occur one time.

Form_Load()

The second event that occurs after the `Show` method is invoked is `Form_Load()`. In this event, the form is loaded into memory. The form isn't displayed yet, but the form and its controls are now loaded. This event will only occur one time.

To place code in the `Form_Load()` event, double-click anywhere on the blank form and add some code. For now, just type in the following code in the code window:

```
Private Sub Form_Load ()
   MsgBox "This is the Form_Load() Event"
End Sub
```

Now just run the form to see a message box appear on the screen. Notice how the message box appears, but the form has not yet been displayed. Also notice that your program has now been frozen until you respond by clicking the OK button on this message box. Once you click this button, your form is displayed.

Common uses of the `Form_Load()` event are to set initial variable values, reposition the form to a certain location, load data from a table into a combo box, or place some default data into certain text boxes. For now, because you haven't added a toolbar or status bar to your form yet, let's disable the menu items under the View menu. Also, let's disable the Save button, because when a form is first loaded, there's nothing to save. Here's how:

```
Private Sub Form_Load()
    mnuVToolbar.Enabled = False
    mnuVStatus.Enabled = False
    cmdSave.Enabled = False
End Sub
```

Notice how you use the name of the control followed by a period and then the name of the property you want to change. This is the standard format for setting properties at runtime and for invoking methods on an object.

Form_Resize()

The `Form_Resize()` event happens whenever a form is resized by the user at runtime or by your source code. For example, the following code causes the **`Resize`** event to fire:

```
Me.Height = Me.Height + 100
```

The `Me` keyword always refers to the current form. By changing the **`Height`** property of the form, you're causing the form to resize itself. This fires the **`Resize()`** event. A common use of the **`Resize()`** event is to shrink or move the controls on the form. You can also use this event to prevent the form from growing too large or shrinking too small.

Form_Activate()

The `Form_Activate()` event occurs after all the other form events have been fired. This event also occurs anytime you give a form focus. If you have several forms open and you move back and forth between each one, each form gets an **`Activate()`** event as you move to it.

Common uses of the **`Activate()`** event are to update a status bar with the current form's name and to enable buttons that were turned off during a **`Deactivate()`** event. Here's an example of the latter use:

```
Private Sub Form_Activate()
    cmdClose.Enabled = True
End Sub
```

I'll typically turn off the buttons on a form when it loses focus. This way, users cannot fire events on a form that they don't intend to fire them on.

Form_Deactivate()

The `Form_Deactivate()` event occurs anytime a form loses focus to another form or application. You might use this event to deactivate buttons on a form so that a user has to give the form focus before clicking its buttons. This might help avoid events firing on one form when the user is currently on another form. Here's an example:

```
Private Sub Form_Deactivate()
   cmdClose.Enabled = False
End Sub
```

Form_QueryUnload()

The `QueryUnload()` event fires when the user attempts to unload the form by clicking the Close button in the upper-right corner. This event may also be fired when you unload a form using the `Unload Me` statement in your Visual Basic code. The `Unload Me` statement is the same as the user closing the form through the Close button or the system menu. In this event, you have the option of canceling the unloading of this form. A common use of this event is to ask the user whether he or she wants to save any changed data prior to closing this form.

Form_Unload()

This is the next-to-last event that occurs before a form is unloaded. You also have the option to cancel the unloading from happening in this event. This event is typically used to restore your Visual Basic application environment to the state it was when the form was first loaded.

Form_Terminate()

The `Form_Terminate()` event is the last event to fire when a form is unloaded. This event is typically used to clean up any form variables that may have been initialized in the `Form_Initialize()` event.

Label Events

There are events associated with label controls; however, in most instances, you will not use them. Labels are generally just used to display data to the user and are not used as an event mechanism. The most common events you may use on labels are the `Change` and `Click()` events.

Text Box Events

You'll probably write a lot of code for text boxes because these are the controls users interact with most often. A lot of the events you will write with text boxes employ data validation, or keeping track of data that has changed. Let's look at some of the more common ones.

The *TextBox_Change()* Event

The `Change()` event is fired when the user types something in the text box. You might write code in this event to enable the Save button because this event signifies that the data has changed on the form.

EXERCISE

ADDING EVENTS TO TEXT BOXES

1. Open the frmEmployee form.
2. Double-click the txtFirst text box and add the following code:

```
Private Sub txtFirst_Change()
    cmdSave.Enabled = True
End Sub
```

The `Change()` event is typically used to determine whether the data in a text box has changed.

This code changes the `cmdSave.Enabled` property to `True` whenever the user changes the text in the txtFirst text box. Of course, you'll need to add this code to every `Change()` event for every text box on the form.

EXERCISE

ADD MORE *Change()* EVENT CODE

1. Add the same code to every `Change()` event for every text box.
2. Run the project and type some data into one of the text boxes. You should see the Save button become enabled with the first key you press.

You should write a `Change()` event for every text box to determine whether any data changes on any text box.

Command Button Events

Command buttons are not very exciting when it comes to events. The event you'll use 99 percent of the time is the `Click()` event.

The *CommandButton_Click()* Event

At this time, your form has two command buttons. Let's write code for each of these command buttons to perform specific actions.

Remember that the Save button becomes enabled whenever you change data in the text boxes. If the user clicks the Save button, you'll need to reset the button when the user saves the data.

EXERCISE

1. Double-click the Save command button and add the following code in the `Click()` event:

```
Private Sub cmdSave_Click() ()
   ' Perform your Save routine here

   cmdSave.Enabled = False
End Sub
```

In this code, you see a line with a single quote (') before it. This signifies a comment in Visual Basic. You'll learn how to save data from a form to a database table in a later chapter. For now, you just need to learn how to use the different events and worry about the details later.

EXERCISE

Add a *Click()* Event to Unload a Form

1. Double-click the Close command button on the form.
2. Add the following code to the `Click()` event:

```
Private Sub cmdClose_Click() ()
   Unload Me
End Sub
```

The `Unload` keyword is a statement that will unload any form. `Me` is a keyword that refers to the current form. You should always use `Me` when referring to the current form, rather than the form name. This way, your code is much more generic and can be copied from one form to another with no changes. This code will cause the `QueryUnload()` and `Unload()` events to fire on a form.

EXERCISE

Try Out the Project

1. Run the project.
2. Change some of the data in one of the text boxes to enable the Save button.
3. `Click()` the Save button to disable it.
4. `Click()` the Close command button to make the form unload.

When you click the Close command button on the last form loaded, the Visual Basic application stops executing because there are no more forms loaded and running. This causes you to return to the Visual Basic design environment.

Frame Events

There are events associated with the frame control; however, in most instances, you will not use them. Frames are generally just used to contain other controls—the user will not interact with the frame that much. The most common event you might use is the `Click()` event.

Option Button Events

Option buttons have one important event you need to write some code for. Just like data being changed in a text box causes the `Change` event fires, if the user clicks an option button, the `Click()` event fires, signifying that the data has changed.

The *OptionButton_Click()* Event

Let's write code in the `Click()` event for an option button that will enable the Save command button.

EXERCISE

ADD *Click()* EVENTS TO OPTION BUTTONS

1. Double-click each of the option buttons in the form and add the following code:

```
Private Sub optMale_Click() ()
   cmdSave.Enabled = True
End Sub

Private Sub optFemale_Click() ()
   cmdSave.Enabled = True
End Sub
```

Each control on your form that changes the data will need to inform the user some data has changed. One commmon technique is to toggle the Enabled property of a command button.

Check Box Events

Check boxes are very much like option buttons. You'll normally respond only to the `Click()` event.

The *CheckBox_Click()* Event

You'll essentially write the same code in a check box `Click()` event that you write in the `Click()` event for an option button.

EXERCISE

Click() EVENTS FOR CHECK BOXES

1. Double-click each of the check boxes in the form and add the following code to enable the Save button.

```
Private Sub chk401k_Click()
   cmdSave.Enabled = True
End Sub
```

```
Private Sub chkBonus_Click()
    cmdSave.Enabled = True
End Sub

Private Sub chkHealth_Click()
    cmdSave.Enabled = True
End Sub
```

Once again, the Click() event of check boxes should enable the Save command button's Enabled property.

Picture Control Events

The picture control can respond to the graphic changing or the user clicking the picture. The most common event will be the user clicking the picture control.

The *Picture_Click()* Event

In the Employee Information form, you created a picture that displays an envelope graphic. This graphic may be used to send some email to an employee. In the `Click()` event, you would write code to send that email. Let's simulate that here by writing the following code:

```
Private Sub picMail_Click()
    ' Send Email here
    frmEMail.Show
End Sub
```

Let's create another form, called frmEmail, and use it to fill in the email information (see Figure 5.2). You can call any form from any other form by simply specifying the name of the form followed by a period and then the **Show** method.

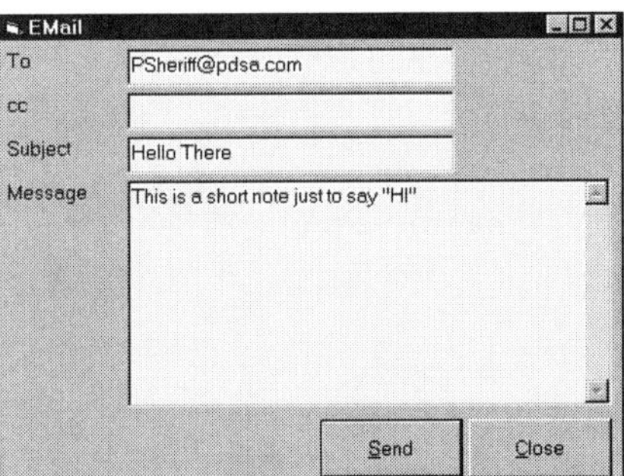

FIGURE 5.2
The Email form.

Example's Filename: Email.frm

Let's create a form that can be used to send email to another employee.

EXERCISE

CREATE AN EMAIL FORM

1. Create a form that looks like Figure 5.2.
2. Add four text boxes as shown.
3. Be sure to set the `MultiLine` property to `True` and the `ScrollBars` property to `2-Vertical` for the Message text box.
4. Add two command buttons as shown.
5. Add the `Unload Me` statement under each of the command buttons.
6. Set the `TabIndex` properties so that the tab order starts with the first text box and continues in order to the last command button.

This exercise gave you an example of how easy it is to put together a form using some of the techniques you have learned in this book so far.

Image Control Events

The image control is exactly like the picture control. You would write the same events for this control as for the picture control.

List Box Events

A list box has many events you can respond to. Most commonly, you'll use the `Click()` event and the `ItemCheck()` event.

The *ListBox_Click()* Event

The `Click()` event occurs whenever the user clicks an item in the list box. You can use this event to retrieve the value of the item clicked. Here's an example:

```
Private Sub lstHealth_Click()
   MsgBox "The Item Selected Is " & _
          lstHealth.List(lstHealth.ListIndex)
End Sub
```

In this code, you'll notice a couple of new items. First, you're using an ampersand (&) character to concatenate a literal string with the value that's returned from the `List()` property of the list box. There's also an underscore at the end of the `MsgBox` line. This is the *line continuation character*, which can be used to continue a line of code on a new line.

The `ListIndex` property is used as an index into the `List()` property array. Whenever the user clicks an item in the list box, the `ListIndex` property is set to the number of the item selected. The `List()` property is an array of the items in the list box. Therefore, you need an index into that array. The `ListIndex` property can be used for this. Figure 5.3 shows you the relationship between the `List()` property and the `ListIndex` property.

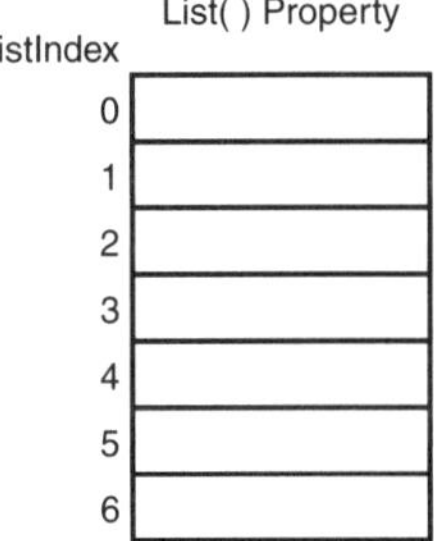

FIGURE 5.3
`List()` and `ListIndex` properties described.

The *ListBox_ItemCheck* Event

The `ItemCheck()` event is fired whenever the list box `Style` property is set to `1-Check Box` and the user clicks the check box of an item. This is different from the `Click()` event, which `Click()` occurs whenever an item is highlighted. The `ItemCheck()` event occurs only when the user clicks the check box area of an item in a list box. Here's an example:

```
Private Sub lstHealth_ItemCheck(Item As Integer)
   MsgBox "The Item Selected Is " & _
          lstHealth.List(Item)
End Sub
```

The `ItemCheck()` method is passed the item number checked. You can use the `Item` parameter as an index into the `List()` array.

Combo Box Events

A combo box has a few events you'll write code for. One of these events depends on the `Style` property of the combo box. If the `Style` property is set to either `0-DropDown Combo` or `1-Simple Combo`, the `Change()` event will fire. If it's set to `2-DropDown List`, the `Change()` event will not fire.

The *ComboBox_Change* Event

The `Change()` event will only fire if the `Style` property is set to `0` or `1`. When the `Style` is set to either of these two values, the combo box can act as either a text box or a drop-down list. If the user types something into the text box portion of the combo box, the `Change` event will fire. You would write code in this event just like for a normal text box.

The *ComboBox_Click()* Event

Whenever the user changes the value in the combo box by clicking an item in the drop-down list, the `Click()` event is fired. You can write code to respond to the user clicking an item in the combo box. For the Employee Information form, you could write code to make the Save button enabled:

```
Private Sub cboState_Click() ()
   cmdSave.Enabled = True
End Sub
```

The *ComboBox_DropDown()* Event

The `DropDown()` event occurs whenever the user opens the drop-down portion of the combo box. This event will only occur when the combo box `Style` property is set to `0-DropDown Combo` or `2-DropDown List`. If the `Style` is set to `1-Simple Combo`, there is no drop-down list; therefore, this event cannot happen. You can use this event to fill the combo box with values only when the user chooses the combo box. This way, you don't have to prefill the combo box with values, which could slow down the loading of the form.

Menu Events

Menus on a form only have one event associated with them—the `Click()` event. No other events are associated with menu items.

The *Menu_Click()* Event

To create code for the `Click()` event, click one of the menu items on your form to display the code window. Let's add code to the form that unloads the form:

EXERCISE

Adding a *Click()* Event to a Menu

1. Open the frmEmployee form.
2. `Click()` the File, Exit menu item.
3. Type in the following code:

```
Private Sub mnuFExit_Click() ()
    Unload Me
End Sub
```

It is a good practice to allow the user a couple of different methods to unload a form. In this exercise you use the `Unload Me` statement in a menu's `Click()` event.

Adding Code to a Top-level Menu

If you have a row of top-level menus, you'll normally have drop-down menus under them. If you do have these drop-down menus, you won't be able to write a `Click()` event for the top-level menus by selecting one and having a code window open up. Instead, you'll need to go into a code window, select the menu name from the Object combo box, and then select the `Click()` event from the Procedure combo box.

This will work for any control. It's not necessary to double-click the object from the form. You can always just select the object and the event you want directly from the code window.

Adding Shortcut Keys

Besides clicking a menu item with your mouse, you can also generate a menu `Click()` event using shortcut keys. To add shortcut keys to your menu items, use the Menu Design window to select the menu item. Go to the Shortcut combo box and click the arrow. You're now shown a list of valid shortcut keys. Select one of these keys; it now becomes a shortcut key that will generate an event.

EXERCISE

Add a Shortcut Key

1. Open the Menu Design window.
2. `Click()` the File, Exit menu item.
3. `Click()` the Shortcut combo box to view the list of available keystrokes.
4. Press the Ctrl+X key combination.
5. `Click()` the OK button to accept this change.
6. Run the project again and press Ctrl+X to invoke the `mnuFExit_Click()` event.

A shortcut key is a great keyboard shortcut for an experienced user.

Summary

In this chapter, you learned how to write code to respond to many different event procedures for some of the basic controls. When a control is double-clicked, a code window appears, allowing you to type in code to respond to an event. There are many different events for each control. However, most of the events are the same for the different controls. This is probably the hardest part of learning the Visual Basic language—that is, learning what each event does.

Review Questions

1. What's the default event for a command button?
2. What's the default event for a text box?
3. What's the default event for an option button?
4. How do you bring up a code window for a particular control?

9

Variables

VARIABLES IN VISUAL BASIC, AS IN ANY programming language, are used to store temporary values in memory. Variables have a name, scope of reference, lifetime, and a data type. The name is used to identify the area in memory where the value is stored. The scope of reference identifies where the variable can be seen and changed. The data type is the kind of data contained in the named memory location.

Chapter Objectives

- Learn the different data types available in Visual Basic
- Learn to declare and name variables
- Determine the scope and lifetime of variables
- Understand variant data types

Sample Project File: \Chapter06\Variables.vbp

What Is a Variable?

A *variable* is a programming term for a value that's stored in your computer program. This value is created by your program and stored somewhere in the memory of your computer. An analogy might be your bank account number for your checking account. This number represents a certain amount of money in your account. You reference that amount of money with this account number. Thus, the account number is like a variable.

Data Types

Remember the game where you put the square peg into the square hole and a round peg into a round hole? You couldn't put the round peg into a square hole. This is similar to the concept of a *data type*. You can only put certain types of values into certain types of variables. It all depends on how you declare the variable.

Variables can store many different types of data. How you declare the variable determines the type of data you can store in it. There are 10 different data types supported by Visual Basic. The numeric data types all have a different range of numbers you can store in them. Make sure you're familiar with the limits of each of these—you don't want a user typing in a number that's greater than the data type you're using, for example. This can be a common source of bugs in an application. Table 6.1 lists some of the data types you can store in a variable. This table is a list of just some of the data types available. Others you'll learn about in later chapters.

Table 6.1 Data Types for Variables

Data Type	Range
`Boolean`	2 bytes. Range: True or False.
`Byte`	1 byte. Range: 0 to 255.
`Date`	8-byte floating point. Range: Jan. 1, 100 to December 31, 9999 and 0:00:00 to 23:59:59.
`Integer` (%)	2 bytes. Range: –32,768 to 32,767.
`Long` (&)	4 bytes. Range: –2,147,483,648 to 2, 147,483,647.
`Single` (!)	4 bytes. Range: –3.402823E38 to 1.401298E-45 for negative values. Range: 1.4011298E-45 to 3.40282E38 for positive values.
`Double` (#)	8 bytes. Range: –1.79769313486232E308 to –4.94065645841247E-324 for negative values; 4.94065645841247E-324 to 1.79769313486232E308 for positive values.
`Currency` (@)	8 bytes. Range: –922,337,203,685,477.5808 to 922,337,203,685,477.5807.
`String` ($)	A string is stored as a Unicode string. This takes 2 bytes per character to store, plus some overhead for a Visual Basic pointer.
`Variant`	A variant can be any of the preceding data types, plus objects, `Null`, and `Empty`. This is the default type for any undeclared variables.

The symbols in parentheses listed after each type are what old Visual Basic programmers used to use to declare a variable as a specific type. This type of nomenclature should not be used anymore and is only presented here in case you come across it in some of the trade journals. Here are some examples:

```
Loop% = 1
Name$ = "John Doe"
Count& = 159999
```

True and False

True and False are used two different ways in Visual Basic. The constants True and False evaluate to –1 and 0, respectively. In Visual Basic, however, any value that is nonzero evaluates to True, and zero evaluate to False. True and False are keywords in Visual Basic. Here's an example:

```
Dim boolPerform As Boolean

boolPerform = True
...
If boolPerform Then
   ...
End If
```

Declaring Variables

There are many ways to declare variables. Although it's not absolutely necessary to declare variables before you use them, every professional Visual Basic programmer will declare them. It is recommended that you check the Require Variable Declaration option in your Visual Basic environment. To set this value, select the Tools, Options menu. Checking this option forces the Option Explicit statement to be added to every module that makes you declare all variables before using them.

How you choose to declare a variable determines the characteristics of that variable, as discussed previously. The Dim statement is most commonly used to declare variables; however, there are other ways to declare variables, as you'll learn later in this chapter:

```
Dim VariableName [As type]
```

When you declare variables, Visual Basic gives each variable a default value. This value will be different for the different data types. For numeric data types, it will always be zero (0). For a string variable, it will be a blank string (""). For a date variable, it will be December 30, 1899 12:00:00AM. Here's an example:

```
Private Sub FormInit()
   Dim intTemp As Integer
   Dim strName As String
End Sub
```

One-line Declarations

Be careful with one-line declarations such as the following:

```
Dim intTemp, intCount As Integer
```

In this code, the variable `intTemp` is not actually given a data type. You may think that because there's an `As Integer` at the end of the line that both variables are declared as an integer type. However, the first variable, `intTemp`, is actually an "untyped" variable. A default data type is given to any untyped variable: the `Variant` data type. You'll learn about variants later in this chapter. If you want to make both of the variables an integer data type, you would change the code to read as follows:

```
Dim intTemp As Integer, intCount As Integer
```

To make your code more readable, you should strive to put each variable declaration on a separate line. This not only looks better but it allows you to put a comment next to each variable describing what that variable does. Here's an example:

```
Dim intTemp As Integer
Dim intCount As Integer
```

Assigning Values to Variables

The equal sign (=) is used to assign a value to a variable you declare. You cannot declare a variable and assign a value to it all in one statement. You must put the assignment on a separate line. Here's some code showing the different data types and how to assign values to them:

```
Dim boolOK As Boolean
Dim bytValue As Byte
Dim dtBegin As Date
Dim dtTime As Date
Dim intLoop As Integer
Dim lngID As Long
Dim sngQty As Single
Dim dblAmount As Double
Dim curPrice As Currency
Dim strName As String

boolOK = True
bytValue = 1
```

```
dtBegin = #9/1/98#
dtTime = #10:10:00 AM#
intLoop = 10
lngID = 100000
sngQty = 2.5
dblAmount = 3.2233
curPrice = 500.65
strName = "Paul"
```

Example's Filename: Vars.bas

All the numeric values are pretty straightforward when you're doing the assignment statements. The `Boolean` value will accept the keyword `True` or `False` as an assignment. The `Date` and `Time` values are denoted with a pound sign (#), and a string value is enclosed by double quotes. You can find this code in the Vars.bas file. Look for the procedure called `VariableAssignment` in the Procedures combo box.

Scope and Lifetime of a Variable

When you declare a variable, you automatically determine a couple of characteristics of that variable. The first is its scope—that is, which procedures can view and change the contents of that variable. The second characteristic is the lifetime of the variable—that is, how long the value stays in memory. Table 6.2 shows the three types of scope a variable can have within a Visual Basic application.

Table 6.2 Scope Definitions

Scope	Description
Global	A variable that can be viewed and changed by any routine within an application.
Module level	A variable that's declared at the top of a form or standard module and can be viewed or changed by any routine within that module.
Local	A variable that's declared within a routine and can only be viewed and changed within that routine.

What Is a Module?

A *module* is a single file that contains one or more routines (procedures or functions) and optionally a user interface (a form). A variable that's declared at the top of one of these modules (outside of any routine) is considered a *module-level variable*. This variable can only be viewed and changed by any routine within this file. This variable will stay in memory, or have a lifetime, as long as that module is in memory.

There are three different types of modules: standard modules (.BAS extension), form modules (.FRM extension), and class modules (.CLS extension). A *standard module* is a global repository for routines and public variables. A *form module* is a Visual Basic form that has a user interface and optionally some public and private variables. A *class module* is a template from which you can create your own objects. A class module can have both private and public variables. You'll learn to use all three throughout this book.

Limiting Your Scope

You should strive to limit the scope as much as possible. Public variables are hard to keep track of, and you never know when some other routine may use that same variable for its own purposes and wipe out the value you were expecting. This can cause a lot of confusion in your programs and may result in your variables' values changing for no apparent reason. Module-level variables are much better, because only the routines in one file may use them. Local variables are the best, because only one routine can view and change them. See Figure 6.1 for a graphical representation of scoping rules. This makes your data very isolated with less chance for corruption.

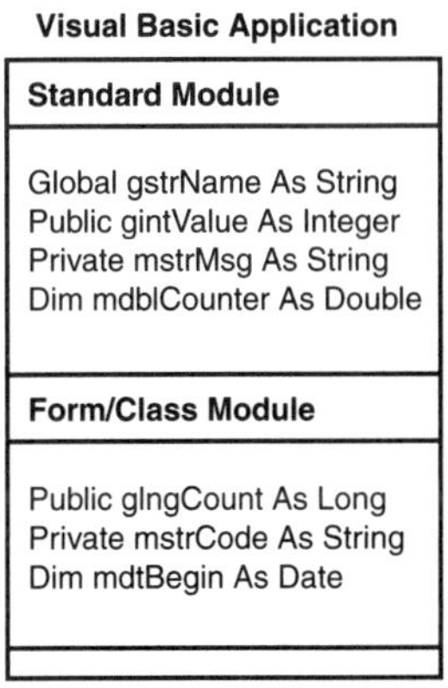

FIGURE 6.1
Scoping rules.

Visual Basic Application

Standard Module
Global gstrName As String Public gintValue As Integer Private mstrMsg As String Dim mdblCounter As Double
Form/Class Module
Public glngCount As Long Private mstrCode As String Dim mdtBegin As Date

TIP

Keep the scope of variables limited and avoid global variables if at all possible.

Rules of Scope

Because there are different locations in which you can declare variables, you need to know where to access the different variables. Table 6.3 shows how and where you declare a variable; it also provides a sample name, the scope, and the lifetime of that variable.

Table 6.3 Declaration of Variables

Declaration	Location	Example	Scope	Lifetime
`Global`	BAS file	`gstrName`	Application	Application
`Public`	BAS file	`gstrName`	Application	Application
`Private`	Module	`mstrName`	Module	Module
`Dim`	Module	`mstrName`	Module	Module
`Public`	Form/class	`FirstName`	Form/Class	Module
`Dim`	Procedure	`strName`	Procedure	Procedure

In this table, you can see that `Global` and `Public` are synonymous when either is declared in a standard module. `Private` and `Dim` are synonymous when either is declared in any type of module. A public variable declared in a module can only be used when it's referenced with that module's name, such as `<modName>.<variableName>`. A `Dim` statement is the only declaration you can use to declare local variables within a procedure.

Public Variables in Standard Modules

Publicly scoped variables must be created in a standard module. To create a standard module, you need to select Project, Add Module from the Visual Basic menu. This inserts a code module into your project. These code modules are where you place all `Public` variables and `Public` procedures (which we'll cover later).

Examples of Variables

The scope of a variable determines which routines are allowed to view or change its value. If you declare a variable in an event procedure using the `Dim` statement, that variable is visible only to that procedure. Furthermore, when the event procedure ends, that variable's value is discarded.

Variables declared with the `Dim` statement are allocated on the stack when the procedure is entered. The *stack* is a temporary area of memory, and the stack that's allocated for a procedure is discarded when the procedure exits, meaning that the contents of all local variables are discarded.

Example's Filename: VarExamples.frm

The form shown in Figure 6.2 will be used to demonstrate the various variable declaration types.

FIGURE 6.2
Examples of variables.

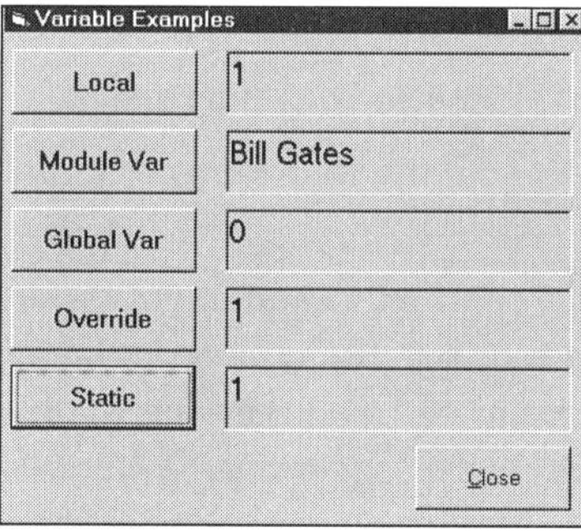

EXERCISE

Load the Sample Project for This Chapter

1. Load the sample project that goes with this chapter.
2. Run the first sample to follow along.

If you load the sample for this chapter it may help you follow the logic for this narration.

Local Variables

Let's first look at local variables that are declared at the top of a procedure. If you click several times on the Local button when the form is running, you'll see that the value stays at 1. The code for this event procedure looks like this:

```
Private Sub cmdLocal_Click ()
   Dim intCount As Integer

   intCount = intCount + 1

   lblLocal.Caption = intCount
End Sub
```

EXERCISE

LOOK AT THE LOCAL COMMAND BUTTON

1. Return to design mode and load the VarExamples.frm file.
2. Double-click the Local command button to view the code.

If you look at the code in this example the following paragraph will be a little easier to follow.

Each time the Local button is clicked, the `Dim` statement causes the `intCount` variable to be reinitialized to 0. Using an assignment statement, the `intCount` variable is incremented by 1 and then the result of this value is placed in the lblLocal label's `Caption` property. Once `End Sub` is executed, the value of `intCount` is released from memory.

Module Variables

If you declare a variable using `Private` or `Dim` in the (General) (Declarations) section of a module, that variable is visible to any procedure contained in that module. No procedures in other modules can view or change a module variable in another module. Prefacing the names of these variables with the letter *m* is a visual clue as to what the scope of the variables is (see Figure 6.3).

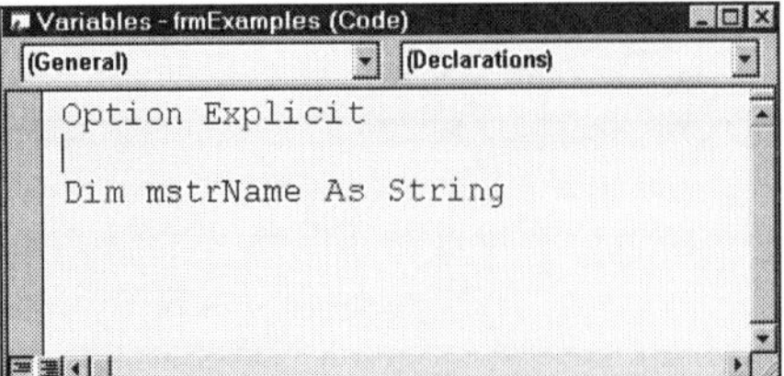

FIGURE 6.3 Example of a module-level variable.

The lifetime of a module variable depends on what type of module created the variable. If the variable is created in a standard module, the variable exists while the application is running. If the module is an FRM file, the variable exists while the form is in memory. The values in a module-level variable remain even if a form is unloaded and reloaded. The only way to release these module-level variables in a form is to set the form equal to the keyword `Nothing`. You'll learn more about `Nothing` in Chapter 21 "The System Objects."

To create a module variable, select either a form or a standard module in the Project Explorer window and then click the View Code button. Select (General) from the Object combo box and (Declarations) from the Procedure combo box. You may now use either the `Private` or `Dim` keyword to declare a variable.

EXERCISE

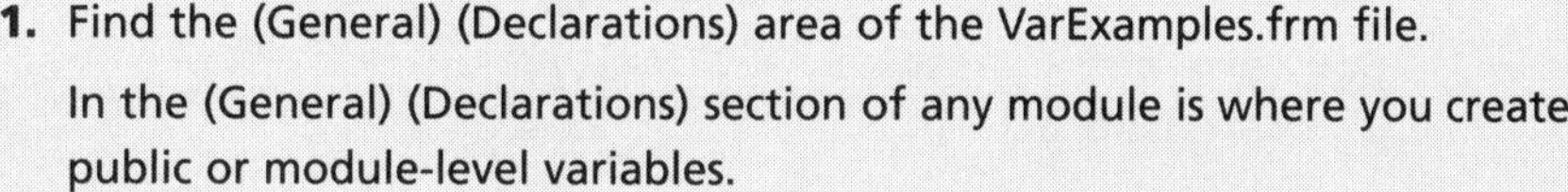

LOCATE THE (GENERAL) (DECLARATIONS) AREA

1. Find the (General) (Declarations) area of the VarExamples.frm file.

In the (General) (Declarations) section of any module is where you create public or module-level variables.

Option Explicit

In the (General) (Declarations) area of all forms (standard and class modules), you'll normally find the statement `Option Explicit`. This statement appears because in the Tools, Options menu, you checked the option Require Variable Declaration. Actually, the Require Variable Declarations check box doesn't do what it says. Instead, it should be called the Insert Option Explicit Statement check box.

The `Option Explicit` statement requires the variable declarations. It tells Visual Basic to make sure all variables are explicitly declared. If the compiler finds any variables that have not been declared, it stops the compile process and informs you of the offending variable name. This option must be in every module in your application. If it's missing from one module, then within that module you are free to declare variables "on-the-fly," thus leading to potential bugs that will be very hard to track down.

TIP

Always use `Option Explicit` and declare your variables as a specific data type. This allows the compiler to catch typos, instead of finding the bug at runtime.

Using a Module Variable

Here's a sample exercise that shows how to use a module-level variable. Let's take a look at this exercise.

In the `Form_Load()` event procedure of VarsExamples.frm you'll see a variable named `mstrName`. It has been assigned the value `Bill Gates`. You cannot give a variable an initial value when you declare it; therefore, the `Form_Load()` procedure is a good place to set module-level variables to a valid starting value:

```
Private Sub Form_Load ()
   mstrName = "Bill Gates"
End Sub
```

Because the `Form_Load()` procedure is part of this module, you can both read and write to the `mstrName` variable. Let's now read and change this value from another event procedure in this module. If you double-click the Module Var command button, you'll see the following code:

```
Private Sub cmdModule_Click ()
   lblModule.Caption = mstrName

   mstrName = "Tom Buttons"
End Sub
```

EXERCISE

Check Out the Module-level Variables Example

1. Run the sample project.
2. Click the Variables command button to run the form VarExamples.frm.
3. Click the Module Var command button twice to see the two values change in the label next to the button.

In the `cmdModule_Click()` event, you retrieve the value from `mstrName` and place it in the `Caption` property of the label. You then change the value of `mstrName` to `Tom Buttons`, so the next time you click this button, the value in the label control will change. If you were to create other event procedures, or even your own user-defined procedures (you'll learn to create these later) within this module, you would be able to read and change the `mstrName` variable from any of them.

Public Variables

A variable declared as `Public` or `Global` within a BAS module will have an application-wide scope. `Public` variables may be changed and retrieved from any form or module in the entire application. A value placed in a `Public` variable will retain its value as long as the program is running. If `Public` variables are prefaced with the letter *g* (for `Global`), you can recognize right away that they have a global scope and will exist as long as the program is running.

EXERCISE

Public Variable Usage

1. Open the Vars.bas file in the sample project by double-clicking it in the Project Explorer window.
2. When you open this file, you'll see the following line of code:

```
Public gintCount As Integer
```

After this declaration has been created, you can use that `Public` variable from anywhere in your program.

EXERCISE

Using Global Variables

1. Double-click the Global command button in the form VarExamples.frm.
2. You should see the following code:

```
Private Sub cmdGlobal_Click ()
    lblGlobal.Caption = gintCount

    gintCount = gintCount + 1
End Sub
```

Each time the Global button is clicked, the `Caption` property of the label is updated to a new value.

EXERCISE

INCREMENTING A GLOBAL VARIABLE

1. Run the sample project.
2. Open the VarExamples.frm form by clicking the Variables command button.
3. Click the Global command button a few times to see the value in the label next to it increment by 1 each time you click.
4. Try closing the form and then running it again to see whether the `Global` variable has retained its value.

Global variables will exist as long as the program is running.

Variables declared with `Public` or `Global` are allocated on the heap, an area of memory that's allocated when the program starts and is discarded when the program ends.

Local Variables Mask Public Variables

If you name a `Local` variable the same name as a module-level or `Public` variable, the `Local` variable name will take precedence within that procedure. This means that you won't be able to access the `Public` variable from within the procedure.

EXERCISE

LOCAL VARIABLES OVERRIDE PUBLIC VARIABLES

1. Stop the project from running.
2. Double-click the Override command button to display the following code:

```
Private Sub cmdGlobalLocal_Click ()
    ' You would normally NOT name
    ' this variable this way
    Dim gintCount As Integer

    gintCount = 1

    lblGlobalLocal.Caption = gintCount
End Sub
```

Notice how the `gintCount` variable is set to 1. This sets the value in the `Local` variable, `gintCount`, not in the `Public` variable.

EXERCISE

RECHECK THE GLOBAL VARIABLE

1. Run this project and increment the `Public` variable several times.
2. Click the Override button. You'll see that the variable `gintCount` is never incremented.
3. Go back and click the Global command button. The value will start incrementing from where you left off last time.

Of course, if you preface your `Public` variables with the letter *g* and your module-level variables with an *m* and you use no prefix for local variables, you'll never have this type of masking going on because you won't have a local variable name that starts with the letter *g*.

\Static Variables

There's another type of declaration you can use for variables. You can declare variables with the keyword `Static` to indicate to Visual Basic that you want to preserve the contents of the variable between function calls. Variables declared with the `Dim` statement lose their value when a procedure ends and are reinitialized the next time the function is called. When you declare a variable with the keyword `Static`, the variable is only initialized once and does *not* lose its value between procedure calls. Variables declared with `Static` are allocated on the heap, an area of memory that's allocated when the program starts and is discarded when the program ends.

EXERCISE

STATIC VARIABLES ARE LOCAL

1. Run the sample project.
2. Click the Variables button.
3. Click the Static command button several times to view the incrementing of the number in the label.
4. Open the VarExamples.frm form in design mode and double-click the Static command button to view the following code:

```
Private Sub cmdStatic_Click ()
   Static intTimesClicked As Integer
```

```
    intTimesClicked = intTimesClicked + 1

    lblStatic.Caption = intTimesClicked
End Sub
```

By using the keyword `Static` to declare the variable, you've created a variable that has a local scope but has a global lifetime.

Fixed-length Strings

When you declare string variables, you normally create a *dynamic* string, which means you can store approximately two billion characters in that string. Visual Basic automatically recalculates the storage requirements for the string as you add or subtract characters. Sometimes, however, you may require a string to have a fixed length. This comes in handy when dealing with fixed-length records in an ASCII text file, for example. You can create a fixed-length string by adding an asterisk (*) operator followed by a numeric value after the declaration of a string variable. Here's an example:

```
Dim strZipCode As String * 10
```

This statement initializes a string variable and fills it automatically with ten character zeros. Character zeros are a special `null` string value. It's not the space character, it's actually a special type of ASCII value.

Once you've created this fixed-length string, it will always stay that size. If you put five characters into this string, the string will still have five character zeros on the end of it. If you attempt to place 15 characters into this string, the last five characters will be truncated.

Implicitly Declared Variables

In Visual Basic, it's not absolutely necessary to explicitly declare variables before you use them. You can simply use a variable name "on-the-fly." Consider the following code:

```
Private Sub cmdOK_Click()
    intLoop = 1

    Print intLoop
End Sub
```

This code simply assigns 1 to a variable named `intLoop`. If this variable does not exist, Visual Basic will create it just before performing the assignment. However, the preceding code will *not* compile if the words `Option Explicit` appear in the (General) (Declarations) section of the module where this code resides.

Example's Filename: Typos.bas

Creating variables on-the-fly has a couple drawbacks. First, the variable will be declared as a `Variant` data type. A variant takes a lot of memory to store. It's best not to use one if you can help it. Second, if you don't declare your variables, a simple typo can create a new variable, where you thought you were using another variable. This can lead to a nasty bug to track down. Therefore, *always* declare your variables prior to using them and be sure `Option Explicit` appears in the (General) (Declarations) section of each module.

EXERCISE

Be Careful with Mistyped Variables

1. Look at the following code and answer the questions that follow:

```
Public Sub CalcValue()
    Dim intVar1 As Integer
    Dim intValue As Integer

    intVar1 = 10
    intValue = 20

    intVar1 = intValue + 50
    intValue = intValue + 10
    intVor1 = intValue - 50

    MsgBox "intVar1 = " & intValue1
    MsgBox "intValue = " & intValue

End Sub
```

2. What is the value of `intVar1`?
3. What is the value of `intValue`?

> If you answered `intVar1` is equal to `-20` and `intValue` is equal to `30`, you're wrong! The reason? The code has a bug. There's a typo in the line that subtracts 50 from `intVar1`. Instead of `intVar1` it's typed as `intVor1` (notice the *o* instead of *a*). If you forget to place `Option Explicit` at the top of the module that has this procedure, the code will run, but it will give you a bad result. If you run the code, it will give you `70` and `30`, which are not the answers you're expecting.

Naming Variables

You must follow certain rules when naming your variables for use in your applications. First, the variable name must begin with a letter. After the beginning letter, the name may contain any combination of letters, numbers, and underscore characters. No punctuation or spaces are allowed in the name. The name can be up to 255 characters but may not be a reserved word. You may use the same name from one procedure to the next, but the variable names must be unique within the same scope. Avoid using one-letter variables because they are hard to understand when you come back to look at your program later. Be careful that you do not use any Visual Basic keywords. These are words that are used in the Visual Basic language and cannot be used as variable names. For a complete list of keywords, look in the Visual Basic Books Online under the Visual Basic Help topic.

Variable Naming Standards

A standard has emerged for naming variables in Visual Basic. It is a variation of the Hungarian Notation used in C language programming. Table 6.4 contains a list of data types and the suggested prefixes you should use when naming your variables. A complete reference may be found in Appendix A of this book.

In this book, you'll see a consistent standard of variable names. You should strive to follow these standards closely in your programming because it will make your programs much easier to read. Here's a condensed list of some general rules to follow when naming variables:

- Make all variable names mixed case—in other words, each word or abbreviation should be capitalized.
- Preface each variable name with the type of data it contains.

Table 6.4 Variable Naming Standards

Data Type	Sample Names	Default Values
Boolean	boolPerform	False
Byte	bytValue	0
Date	dtEntry	December 30, 1899; 12:00:00 AM
Integer	intLoop	0
Long	lngAmount	0
Single	sngAmount	0
Double	dblValue	0
Currency	curChkAmt	0
String	strCompany	""
Variant	vntVar1	Empty

TIP

Always use Hungarian Notation when naming variables. This will make your variable names much more descriptive and will make your programs easier to read. If you are not familiar with Hungarian Notation please refer to Appendix A of this book.

Scope Prefixes

As you saw in the previous examples, the scope of the variable is used as a modifier to the name of the variable. For `Public` variables, you use the letter *g*, which stands for `Global`. The reason for this is because the keyword `Public` was not introduced until Visual Basic 4, and most people had already adopted the standard prefix *g* for the old declaration `Global`.

The prefix *m* is added to the names of all module-level variables declared in the (General) (Declarations) section. No prefix is used for local variables in a procedure.

The *Variant* Data Type

The `Variant` data type allows you to store any type of data in a variable. This variable can change its type at any time. When it does, Visual Basic takes care of all the housekeeping chores. Because it's such a flexible data type, it carries much more overhead (memory and resources) than a normal data type. Therefore, you should only use the `Variant` data type as a last resort.

Variants take up a significant amount of memory compared to normal data types. In addition, they are very slow to retrieve and get values. Because these requirements can slow down your application, you should use normal data types instead of variants whenever possible. Table 6.5 shows you the different data types a variant can store.

Table 6.5 Variant Data Types

Data Type	Description
`Empty`	Declared but not yet initialized.
`Null`	Special data type used with database applications.
`Object`	Special data type that will be covered in Chapters 19–21.
`Integer`	Normal data type.
`Long`	Normal data type.
`Single`	Normal data type.
`Double`	Normal data type.
`Currency`	Normal data type.
`Date`	Normal data type. `Date` and/or `Time` variable.
`String`	Normal data type.
`Boolean`	Normal data type.

As you can see from the table, all the normal data types are accounted for, plus two additional types. The first type, `Empty`, is a special type that's used to initialize the variant when it's declared. Just like an `Integer` data type is initialized to `0` and a string to `""`, a `Variant` data type is initialized to `Empty`. The other type is `Null`. A `Null` is a special value that's returned from a column in a table when no data is stored in that column. Whenever you retrieve data from a table, you need to store that data in a variant first, test it for `Null`, and then convert it into the data type you want.

Let's look at some code to see how to use the `Variant` data type:

```
Dim vntVariable As Variant

vntVariable = 10
...
...
```

```
vntVariable = 5.5
...
...
vntVariable = "Hi There"
```

As you can see in this code snippet, after declaring a variable as a `Variant` data type, you can change it from an `Integer` to a `Single` and then later you can change it to a `String`.

Numeric Strings

When using the `Variant` data type as a string, and the string contains a numeric value such as `10` or `20`, you need to be careful when concatenating two of these types of strings together. Let's look at an example of what happens.

Example's Filename: Variants.frm

The Variants.frm file shows you different results based on how you concatenate two variant strings together. As you can see in Figure 6.4, the first three values differ. Visual Basic has two different methods for concatenating strings together: using a plus sign (+) and using an ampersand (&). Let's take a look at the code for each one of these command buttons to see the difference.

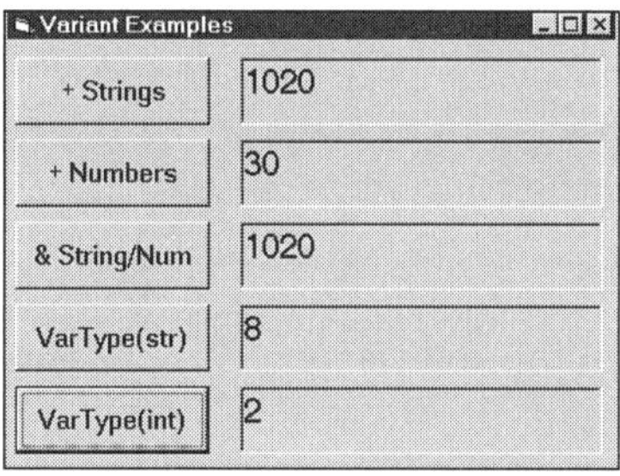

FIGURE 6.4 Variant examples.

EXERCISE

TWO STRING VARIANT VARIABLES

1. **Double-click the + Strings command button to view the following code:**

```
Private Sub cmdStrConcat_Click ()
    Dim vntStr1 As Variant    ' Declared as Variant
    Dim vntStr2 As Variant    ' Declared as Variant

    vntStr1 = "10"             ' Value is a String
```

```
    vntStr2 = "20"            ' Value is a String
    lblStrConcat.Caption = vntStr1 + vntStr2' Value is a String
End Sub
```

2. Note the following output when this code is run:

```
1020
```

In this example, you have two variants, and each one is assigned a string that has a number in it. If you use the plus sign on the two variants, Visual Basic performs string concatenation just like you would expect. However, if one of the variants happens to be a string and the other happens to be numeric, you'll get different results with the same operator.

EXERCISE

String and Numeric with the Ampersand

1. Double-click the + Numbers command button to view the following code:

```
Private Sub cmdVarNumber_Click ()
    Dim vntStr1 As Variant
    Dim vntStr2 As Variant

    vntStr1 = "10"
    vntStr2 = 20
    lblVarNumber.Caption = vntStr1 + vntStr2
End Sub
```

2. Note the following output when this code is run:

```
30
```

In this example, you get a different result—30, an integer number. When you use a plus sign to concatenate two variant data types together, Visual Basic looks at each of the operands and determines whether either one is a numeric variable. If either one is a numeric variable, Visual Basic attempts to convert the other operand to a numeric variable. If it's successful at this conversion, Visual Basic will perform integer arithmetic on the two operands. If it's not successful at the conversion, you'll receive a type mismatch error.

EXERCISE

STRING AND NUMERIC WITH THE PLUS SIGN

1. Double-click the & String/Num command button. In this example, you have to change the plus sign to the ampersand character to concatenate the two values together:

```
Private Sub cmdStrNum_Click ()
    Dim vntStr1 As Variant
    Dim vntStr2 As Variant

    vntStr1 = "10"
    vntStr2 = 20
    lblStrNum.Caption = vntStr1 & vntStr2
End Sub
```

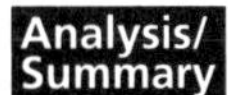

The ampersand tells Visual Basic to use string concatenation if both of the values can be converted to strings. Because you can always convert a numeric value to a string, Visual Basic will be able to perform the concatenation. Therefore, you end up with a concatenated string of "1020" when this example is run.

Concatenating Strings

When performing string concatenation on two variant values, you must take extra care to use the correct operator. You need to know what the data type is for both the operators and choose the appropriate operator.

The standard for most Visual Basic programmers is to always use the ampersand (&) operator when concatenating two strings together. This leaves little ambiguity as to what operation you are actually performing. Of course, this strange behavior between the plus sign and the ampersand only applies to `Variant` variables, so you should not typically have this problem.

Checking the Type of a Variant

To help you determine which operator to use on two different variants, the `VarType()` function is built into the Visual Basic language to enable you to test the data type of the variables in the variants. This function returns a number that corresponds to a constant that you can use to determine the data type. Table 6.6 lists the data types and their corresponding constants.

Table 6.6 Constants for Each *Variant* Data Type

Data Type	VB Constant	`VarType()` Return Value
`Empty`	`vbEmpty`	0
`Null`	`vbNull`	1
`Integer`	`vbInteger`	2
`Long`	`vbLong`	3
`Single`	`vbSingle`	4
`Double`	`vbDouble`	5
`Currency`	`vbCurrency`	6
`Date/Time`	`vbDate`	7
`String`	`vbString`	8
`Object`	`vbObject`	9
`Error`	`vbError`	10
`Boolean`	`vbBoolean`	11
`Variant`	`vbVariant`	12 (only used for arrays of variants)
`DataObject`	`vbDataObject`	13
`Byte`	`vbByte`	17
`Array`	`vbArray`	8192

If you have a `Variant` variable, you can perform the following testing to determine its type:

```
If VarType(mvntVar) = vbBoolean Then
   ...
End If
```

In the example, you can see two different command buttons at the bottom of the Variants.frm form. Under each of these buttons is code that sets the value of a module-level variable named `mvntVar` to a specific data type. The code then uses the `VarType()` function to return the numeric return value.

EXERCISE

1. Double-click the VarType(str) command button to see the following code, which sets the module-level variable `mvntVar` to a `String` data type:

```
Private Sub cmdVarStr_Click ()
    mvntVar = "Hi There"

    lblVarStr.Caption = VarType(mvntVar)
End Sub
```

2. Note the following output when this code is run:

```
8
```

3. Double-click the VarType(int) command button to see the following code, which changes the module-level variable to a numeric data type:

```
Private Sub cmdVarInt_Click ()
    mvntVar = 10

    lblVarInt.Caption = VarType(mvntVar)
End Sub
```

4. Note the following output when this code is run:

```
2
```

Empty Variants

When a variant variable is first declared using `Dim`, `Public`, `Private`, or any other scope, it's initially assigned an `Empty` value. This is a special value that indicates nothing has been assigned to the variable since it was declared. The built-in Visual Basic function `IsEmpty()` returns `True` if the variable contains an `Empty` value and `False` if it does not. Here's an example:

```
Dim vntTemp As Variant
...
If IsEmpty(vntTemp) Then
     vntTemp = "Bill Gates"
End If
```

Summary

Variables are storage locations for values you use in your applications. Variables have data types, scopes, and lifetimes. You can declare public, module-level, and local variables. Also, you should always declare your variables prior to using them. What's more, you should come up with a standard for naming your variables. The `Variant` data type is a heavy-duty variable that requires a lot of overhead and should not be used very often.

Review Questions

1. Name four of the different data types supported by Visual Basic.
2. Declare three local variables using three of the types you listed in the previous question. (Be sure to use the naming standards.)
3. What will the following code display on a form?

```
Dim vntString
vntString = "100"
vntString = vntString + 50
Print vntString
```

Exercises

1. Create a new project.
2. Add a standard module.
3. Add a public variable called `gstrName` as a `String` data type.
4. Add a public variable called `gcurSalary` as a `Currency` data type.
5. Add a text box to Form1 called txtEmployee.
6. Add a text box to Form1 called txtSalary.

7. Add a command button that when clicked moves the data from the text boxes to the global variables. (Note that you'll need to use the `CCur()` function to move the data from the "salary" text box into the global variable and convert the type from string to currency.)
8. Add another command button that when clicked displays the employee name and salary in a message box.

Arrays, Types, and Constants

IN THIS CHAPTER, YOU'LL LEARN to create arrays, user-defined types, and constants. You'll also learn about the built-in constants in Visual Basic. In addition, you'll learn about mathematical and relational operators.

Chapter Objectives

- Learn to declare and manipulate arrays
- Learn about user-defined data types
- Learn about the built-in constants and user-defined constants
- Learn about the different mathematical operators

Sample Project File: \Chapter07\ArraysTypes.vbp

Arrays

An *array* is a group of common elements accessed under a common name. Each element is referenced with a number, called an *index*. Array elements start with zero in Visual Basic (see Figure 7.1).

Index	Array
0	Paul
1	Ken
2	Bill
3	Tom

FIGURE 7.1
An array example.

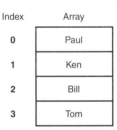

Arrays have the following characteristics:

- Arrays elements start with the number zero (0).
- All elements of the array must have the same data type.
- A variant array may have different data types in each element.
- Arrays may be public, module level (`Private/Dim`), or local in scope.
- Arrays may be a fixed size or dynamically allocated at runtime.

The examples for using arrays are located in Arrays.frm. Let's look at the different examples for this form.

Fixed-size Arrays

An array can be dimensioned to a certain fixed size at declaration time. Public fixed-size arrays may only be declared in a standard module, just as all other `Public` variables. Local and module-level arrays are declared as appropriate. To declare a fixed-size array, you put the number of elements you want inside parentheses following the variable name. Here's an example:

```
Public gastrSSN(3) As String
Public gastrNames(3) As String
Public gacurSalary(3) As Currency
```

This code declares three public array variables that have been declared to hold four elements each, 0 to 3. Two of the arrays can hold `String` variables, whereas the third can only hold `Currency` data. To assign data to each element of the array, you simply specify the array name followed by parentheses and an index number of where you want the value to be placed in the array.

Example's Filename: Arrays.frm

EXERCISE

Look at Some Array Code

1. Double-click the Fixed Size command button to view the following code:

```
Private Sub cmdFixed_Click()
    ' Set SSNs for Employees
    gastrSSN(0) = "555-55-5555"
    gastrSSN(1) = "123-45-6789"
    gastrSSN(2) = "987-65-4321"
    gastrSSN(3) = "333-33-3333"

    ' Set Names for Employees
    gastrNames(0) = "Paul"
    gastrNames(1) = "Ken"
    gastrNames(2) = "Bill"
    gastrNames(3) = "Tom"
```

```
    ' Set Salaries for Employees
    gacurSalary(0) = 100000
    gacurSalary(1) = 150000
    gacurSalary(2) = 60000
    gacurSalary(3) = 90000
    ' Retrieve SSNs, Names & Salaries
    Me.Cls
    Me.Print gastrSSN(0), gastrNames(0), gacurSalary(0)
    Me.Print gastrSSN(1), gastrNames(1), gacurSalary(1)
    Me.Print gastrSSN(2), gastrNames(2), gacurSalary(2)
    Me.Print gastrSSN(3), gastrNames(3), gacurSalary(3)
End Sub
```

Analysis/ Summary

This example assigns employee Social Security numbers to each element of the `gastrSSN` array. Next, employee names are assigned to each element of the `gastrNames` array. Finally, a salary is assigned for each employee to each element of the `gacurSalary` array. Once the values are in the array, the `Me.Cls` command is used to clear the form and then the `Me.Print` method of the form is used to display the values on the form area. The results are shown in Figure 7.2.

FIGURE 7.2
Fixed-size arrays.

It does not matter whether the array was public, module level, or local, the assignment statements and the print statements are all the same. What's important is that the type of data you can put into the array depends on how you declare that array. Arrays can be declared as type `Variant`, which means each element of the array can store a different data type. You'll see an example of this later in the chapter.

Dynamic Arrays

Many times you won't know the number of elements you need in an array until runtime. If this happens, you can create an array with no elements and then redimension that array at runtime to a particular size. Let's create a dynamic module-level array by using the following code:

```
Dim maboolBonus() As Boolean
```

The parentheses with no number between them specifies that this is an array, but it has yet to be given the number of elements. Now, when you click the Dynamic command button, you'll want to redimension the array to 3, which will create an array that can handle four elements:

```
Private Sub cmdDynamic_Click()
   Dim intSize As Integer

   intSize = 3

   ' Redimension the array to the new size
   ReDim maboolBonus(intSize) As Boolean

   maboolBonus(0) = True
   maboolBonus(1) = True
   maboolBonus(2) = False
   maboolBonus(3) = False

   ' Print Bonus Flags
   Me.Cls
   Me.Print maboolBonus(0)
   Me.Print maboolBonus(1)
   Me.Print maboolBonus(2)
   Me.Print maboolBonus(3)
End Sub
```

When you use the `ReDim` statement, Visual Basic completely erases the array and redimensions it to the new size you specify. Notice that you use a variable, `intSize`, to specify the size of the array. You could ask the user to input that value, and then you could place it in the `ReDim` statement.

You may redimension an array variable as many times as you want during the course of a program. However, each time you do, all the values that were in the array before are reinitialized to the default value. In other words, none of the values in the array are preserved.

Preserving Array Contents

Sometimes you might want to preserve the old array contents but just add on a new element. To preserve the contents of the array elements, use the `Preserve` keyword with the `ReDim` statement, like this:

```
Private Sub cmdPreserve_Click()
   ' Preserve any previous values
   ReDim Preserve maboolBonus(4) As Boolean

   ' Add the new value
   maboolBonus(4) = True

   ' Print Bonus Flags
   Me.Cls
   Me.Print maboolBonus(0)
   Me.Print maboolBonus(1)
   Me.Print maboolBonus(2)
   Me.Print maboolBonus(3)
   Me.Print maboolBonus(4)
End Sub
```

When you use the `Preserve` keyword, Visual Basic creates a whole new array in memory to the new size, copies all the values from the old array to the new one, and then deletes the old array. This way, all your old values are preserved, but you've now added room for any new items to the end of the array. Of course, this assumes you have increased the size of the array. You may also decrease the size of the array while still preserving the contents of the array. If you decrease the size, any elements at the end of the array are simply dropped from the new array. Because Visual Basic has to create a new array every time you use the `Preserve` keyword, you want to be judicious in your use of this command—this is a very time-consuming and memory-hungry operation.

Miscellaneous Array Topics

There are many other operations you can perform on arrays. Let's look at some of the different functions and options you have when creating and using arrays.

Setting Array Boundaries

The lower boundary of an array can be changed in one of two ways. First, you can put the `Option Base` statement in the (General) (Declarations) section of a module:

```
Option Base 1
```

`Base` may be set to either 0 or 1. Unless you have some great reason to start the array subscripts at 1, don't use this option. Just leave the subscripts to start at 0, because this is what most Visual Basic programmers expect array subscripts to start with.

You can explicitly state the boundaries of an array right in the declaration of the array using the `To` keyword:

```
Public gaintTypes(1 To 5) As Integer
Private mastrPorts(50 To 100) As String
```

The first statement creates an array of five integers that have indexes from 1 to 5. The second statement creates an array of strings with indexes that range from 50 to 100. Keep in mind that there are 51 elements in this array because the elements begin their numbering at 50.

TIP

It is recommended that unless you need an array to exactly model something in the real world, always use zero as a base. List boxes and other items in Visual Basic use zero as a base, and your code could become confusing if you constantly have to switch between 0 and 1.

The *Array()* Function

If you want to create an array of the type `Variant`, you can declare the array explicitly, as you just learned, or you can use the `Array` function. Consider the following code:

```
Dim vntEmployees As Variant

vntNames = Array("Paul", "Ken", "Bill", "Tom")

Me.Print vntNames(0)
Me.Print vntNames(1)
Me.Print vntNames(2)
Me.Print vntNames(3)
```

This code declares a `Variant` variable that's `Empty`. The `Array` function is then called. It takes all the parameters passed to it, creates an array, and passes that array back the variant. Because a variant can have any value in it, the array that's passed back is perfectly valid in this case. You can now access the array as normal.

The *IsArray()* Function

By looking at the variable name, `vntNames`, in the previous example, you can't tell what kind of data is in the variant variable. However, you can use the `IsArray()` function to determine whether the data in a variant is an array:

```
boolArray = IsArray(vntName)
```

The `IsArray()` function will return `True` if the value in the `vntName` variable is an array. It will return `False` if the value is not an array.

Bounds Checking

Visual Basic will not allow you to overrun an array's boundaries. If you declare an array as a five-element array, you cannot access element 10. If you try to access this element, you'll get a runtime error from Visual Basic. In order to ensure that this does not happen, Visual Basic includes a couple of functions that you can use to get the lower and the upper bounds of an array.

The `LBound()` function will return to you the lower boundary of the array. This is typically set to 0 unless you've used the `Option Base` statement or you've declared the array with the `To` option.

The `UBound()` function will return to you the upper boundary of the array. For example, if you declare the array

```
Dim astrNames(10) As String
```

the `LBound()` function will return 0 and the `UBound()` function will return 10.

Clearing an Array

The `Erase` command in Visual Basic clears out the contents of any array. If you erase a fixed-size array, all the elements in the array will be reinitialized to the default value for that data type. If you erase a dynamic array, the complete array will be released from memory. You then need to redimension the dynamic array back to a new size before you could use it again.

```
Erase astrNames
```

Multidimensional Arrays

A *multidimensional array* is an array that has more than one dimension to it. The most common multidimensional array you'll use is a two-dimensional array. This is like a table with rows and columns. Think of an Excel spreadsheet—this is an excellent example of a two-dimensional array. Visual Basic allows you to create up to 60 dimensions in a array. To create a multidimensional array, you simply specify an index number for each dimension want to create. Here's a typical two-dimensional array declaration:

```
Dim avntEmployees(3, 2) As Variant
```

This example creates four rows and three columns for the array. Remember the previous example that created three different arrays—one for the SSN, one for the name, and one for the salary? Well, with a two-dimensional array, you can combine all of those arrays into one. Let's look at this array to see how you might use it.

Click the Multi-Dimension command button on the Arrays.frm file to view the following code for creating a multidimensional array:

```
Private Sub cmdMulti_Click()
   Const conSSN As Integer = 0
   Const conName As Integer = 1
   Const conSalary As Integer = 2

   ' Create the Array
   Dim avntEmployees(3, 2) As Variant

   avntEmployees(0, conSSN) = "555-55-5555"
   avntEmployees(0, conName) = "Paul"
   avntEmployees(0, conSalary) = 100000

   avntEmployees(1, conSSN) = "123-45-6789"
   avntEmployees(1, conName) = "Ken"
   avntEmployees(1, conSalary) = 150000

   avntEmployees(2, conSSN) = "987-65-4321"
   avntEmployees(2, conName) = "Bill"
   avntEmployees(2, conSalary) = 60000

   avntEmployees(3, conSSN) = "333-33-3333"
   avntEmployees(3, conName) = "Tom"
   avntEmployees(3, conSalary) = 90000

   ' Retrieve SSNs, Names & Salaries
   Me.Cls
   Me.Print avntEmployees(0, conSSN), _
            avntEmployees(0, conName), _
            avntEmployees(0, conSalary)
   Me.Print avntEmployees(1, conSSN), _
            avntEmployees(1, conName), _
            avntEmployees(1, conSalary)
   Me.Print avntEmployees(2, conSSN), _
            avntEmployees(2, conName), _
            avntEmployees(2, conSalary)
```

```
    Me.Print avntEmployees(3, conSSN), _
             avntEmployees(3, conName), _
             avntEmployees(3, conSalary)
End Sub
```

In this example, a 4×3 array is created as a variant. It's created as a variant because you want to put string data and currency data into the same array. Whenever you're creating a multidimensional array, you should create constants for each column. Here, I created three constants to make the code more readable and to make it easier to remember which column I was putting data into. Any time you need to access a multidimensional array, you need to specify all the indexes to get to the particular element you're interested in.

User-defined Types

A *user-defined type* is a complex data type you create that's made of the built-in data types in Visual Basic. You can create a user-defined type to have many elements, where each element is a different data type. If you're familiar with the Pascal programming language, you'll note that a user-defined type is very similar to a *record*. If you're familiar with C Language, you'll note that it's the same concept as a *structure*.

A user-defined type is used in Windows API calls (covered later in this book) and can be used to logically group your data into one variable. However, user-defined types have been replaced by the ability to create class modules. Let's still look at the syntax of user-defined types, because you'll probably use them at one time or another for Windows API calls. Here's the basic syntax:

```
[Private ¦ Public] Type <TypeName>
    <ElementName> [(subscripts)] As DataType
    [<ElementName> [(subscripts)] As DataType]
. . .
End Type
```

Now, here's a practical example using the Employee Information form. Check out the standard module Vars.bas to see the following declaration:

```
Public Type Employee_Type
   strSSN As String
   strFirst As String
   strLast As String
   strStreet As String
   strCity As String
   strState As String
   strZip As String
   curSalary As Currency
   boolBonus As Boolean
End Type
```

As you can see, this data type is now made up of many different string variables, a currency variable, and a Boolean variable. However, each element can only be referenced through a variable declared to be of type `Employee_Type`.

The `Type` declaration, by itself, is just a template of what this data type will look like. To use it, you must declare a `Private` or `Public` variable as `Employee_Type`:

```
Private mtypEmp As Employee_Type
```

After you've created this new variable, you can set the individual elements of this type, just like you set properties for a control or a form:

```
mtypEmp.strFirst = "Bill"
mtypEmp.strLast = "Gates"
mtypEmp.curSalary = 1000000
mtypEmp.boolBonus = True
```

Let's take the Employee Information form you created in a previous chapter and load the data from the form into this structure (see Figure 7.3).

Example's Filename: Employee.frm

In the Save command button, you'll find code that grabs the data from the form and puts it in a module-level variable that's declared as `Employee_Type`. All you're going to do right now is to put the data in and then display some of the data back from the user-defined type variable. Although this is not a real useful example, it does show you the syntax you use when working with a user-defined type:

```
Private Sub cmdSave_Click()
   mtypEmp.strFirst = txtFirst.Text
   mtypEmp.strLast = txtLast.Text
   mtypEmp.strStreet = txtAddress.Text
   mtypEmp.strCity = txtCity.Text
   mtypEmp.strState = cboState.Text
   mtypEmp.strZip = txtZip.Text
   mtypEmp.strSSN = txtSSN.Text
   mtypEmp.boolBonus = chkBonus.Value

   MsgBox "Name = " & mtypEmp.strLast & _
          ", " & mtypEmp.strFirst
End Sub
```

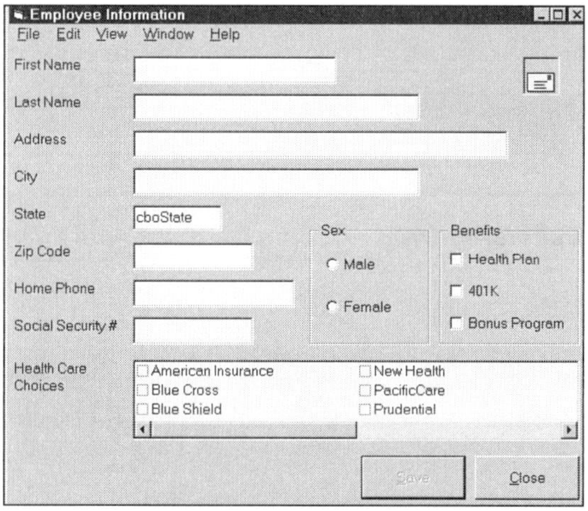

FIGURE 7.3
User-defined type example.

Constants

A *constant* is a value that does not change throughout the life of your program. Constants allow you to assign unmeaningful, "magic" numbers to a mnemonic name that will be much easier to remember. The reason you would create a constant is to avoid "hard-coding" a number in several locations throughout your program. If you were to hard-code a number in several places, what would happen if that number were to change? You would have to remember to go to each of those places and change the number manually. By creating a constant, you can assign the number to a meaningful name in one place in your program and then use that meaningful name everywhere else in your program. Now if you need to change this value, you just change it in the one place, and everywhere it's used in your program will automatically use this new value.

Constants are like variables in that they have scope and a lifetime. They are different from variables in that they may not be changed during the program. Where you declare a constant will determine its scope and lifetime, just like a variable. Let's look at an example of using constants. You can refer to the example form shown in Figure 7.4.

FIGURE 7.4 Example of constants.

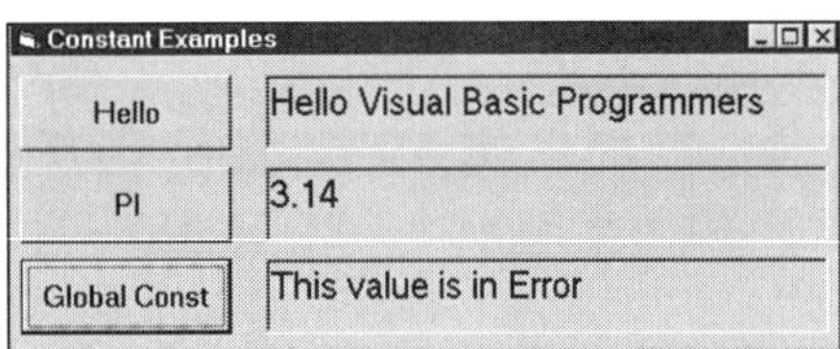

Example's Filename: Constants.frm

Local Constants

The first type of constant we'll look at is a *local* constant declared within an event procedure. This type of constant is not used very often, but it can come in handy in some situations.

EXERCISE

Look at an Example of a Local Constant

1. Double-click the Hello command button to view the following code:

```
Private Sub cmdHello_Click()
   Const conHELLO As String = "Hello Visual Basic Programmers"

   lblHello.Caption = conHELLO

   MsgBox conHELLO
End Sub
```

Instead of the keyword `Dim`, you use the keyword `Const` to declare the constant. You give the constant a name and a data type and then you assign the value to the constant all on the same line. Now whenever you want to use this string in the event procedure, just use the constant `conHELLO`.

Module-level Constants

Next, let's create a module-level constant called `mconPI`. In the (General) (Declarations) section of the Constants.frm file, you'll find the following declaration:

```
Const mconPI As Double = 3.14
```

You can use this constant in any event procedure in this Constants.frm file.

EXERCISE

Using a Module-level Constant

1. Double-click the PI command button to view the following code:

```
Private Sub cmdPI_Click()
   lblPI.Caption = mconPI
End Sub
```

A module-level constant allows you to use a constant value instead of a hard-coded value throughout one form. This will make it easier to read, and easier to change if needed.

Public Constants

The most common type of constants you'll create are public in scope. The reason is that constants are normally used throughout your entire application. To declare a public constant, use code that looks similar to the following:

```
Public Const gconERR_MSG As String = "This value is in Error"
```

You can now use this public constant, `gconERR_MSG`, in any procedure in your entire application.

EXERCISE

Global Constant Example

1. Look in the Vars.bas file to view the aforementioned declaration.
2. Double-click the Global Const command button to view the following code, which uses the public constant:

```
Private Sub cmdConst_Click ()
   lblConst.Caption = gconERR_MSG
End Sub
```

Global constants are the ones you will use most often. These are easy to use all over your application and easy to change.

Built-in Constants

Visual Basic has many other built-in constants that you'll learn about as you use more of the built-in functions in Visual Basic. Many of the custom controls and DLLs you'll use also have their set of built-in constants. Most of the Visual Basic constants start with the prefix *vb*. Other DLLs have their own prefixes.

Mathematical and Relational Operators

Any programming language has a set of symbols that allow you to perform a mathematical or relational operation on two or more operands. These symbols are called *mathematical* and *relational* operators. Visual Basic has a rich set of these operators. Here are some examples:

```
1 + 2
4 - 3
3 < 4
```

Let's look at the list of mathematical operators. The sample form Operators.frm has an example of each of the mathematical operators (see Figure 7.5). Table 7.1 shows you each of the different mathematical operators used in Visual Basic.

FIGURE 7.5
Examples of mathematical operators.

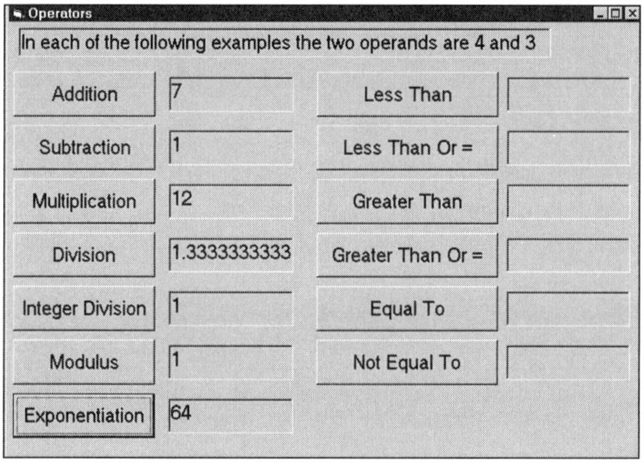

Example's Filename: Operators.frm

Table 7.1 Mathematical Operators

Operator	Description	Example
Addition (+)	Adds two numbers together	`3 + 4 = 7`
Subtraction (-)	Subtracts one number from another number	`4 - 3 = 1`
Multiplication (*)	Multiplies two numbers together	`4 * 3 = 12`
Division (/)	Divides one number by another number	`4 / 3 = 1.3333`
Integer division (\)	Divides one number by another number but truncates the decimal portion of the number	`4 \ 3 = 1`

continues

Table 7.1 Continued

Operator	Description	Example
Modulus (`Mod`)	Divides two numbers and returns just the remainder portion	`4 Mod 3 = 1`
Exponentiation (^)	Raises one number to the power of the second number	`4 ^ 3 = 64`

Relational or Comparison Operators

The relational or comparison operators are used to perform Boolean logic. You'll typically use these operators with an `If` statement, which you'll learn in a later chapter. You can see each of these in the Operators.frm form as well (see Figure 7.6).

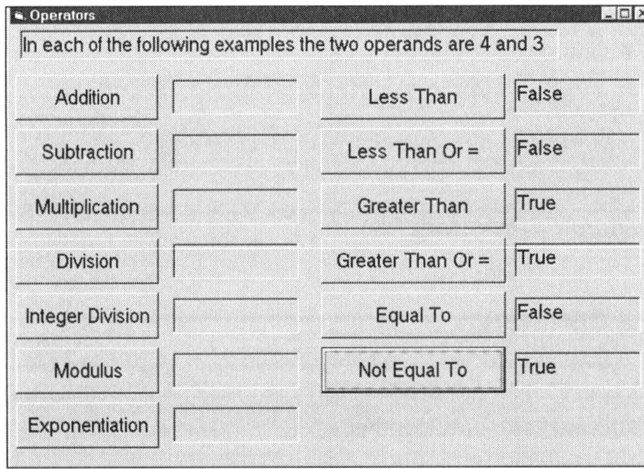

FIGURE 7.6 Examples of relational operators.

Example's Filename: Operators.frm

Table 7.2 is a list of the different relational operators Visual Basic makes available to you. As you can see, you have all the standard operators available in any programming language.

Table 7.2 Relational Operators

Operator	Description	Example
Less than (<)	Is the first operand less than the second?	`4 < 3 = False`
Less than or equal to (<=)	Is the first operand less than or equal to the second?	`4 <= 3 = False`
Greater than (>)	Is the first operand greater than the second?	`4 > 3 = True`
Greater than or equal to (>=)	Is the first than or equal to the second?	`4 >= 3 = True`
Equal to (=)	Is the first operand equal to the second?	`4 = 3 = False`
Not equal to (<>)	Is the first operand not equal to the second?	`4 <> 3 = True`

Order of Precedence

If several operators occur in an expression, each part is evaluated and resolved in a predetermined order known as *operator precedence*. If you place parentheses around any of the expressions, operations within the parentheses are performed first, from the innermost to the outermost parentheses. If there's more than one operator of the same type, they are evaluated in the order they occur, from left to right. Here's a list in the order that an expression with multiple operators would be evaluated:

- Exponentiation (^) and equality (=)
- Not equal (<>)
- Multiplication (*), division(/), and less than (<)
- Integer division (\) and greater than (>)
- Modulus (`Mod`) and less than or equal to (<=)
- Addition (+), subtraction (-), and greater than or equal to (>=)

Summary

Arrays can be used when you need to store many elements under a common name. You have the option using of single- or multidimensional arrays. User-defined types allow you to create your own custom data type based on a combination of the simple data types. Constants are used so that you don't need to hard-code the same values over and over again in your applications. By creating a constant, you make it much easier to change the constant's value later without having to search through your entire application.

Review Questions

1. What will the following code produce?

   ```
   Dim aintValues() As Integer

   ReDim aintValues(1)
   aintValues(0) = 10
   Print aintValues(0)
   ```

   What is displayed by the following code?

   ```
   ReDim aintValues(2)
   aintValues(1) = 20
   Print aintValues(0)
   ```

   What is displayed by the following code?

   ```
   Print aintValues(1)
   ```

2. Declare a constant named `conValue` that holds the value 1.
3. Write a statement that will add 10 to the constant you created in the last question.

Exercises

1. Create a new project.
2. Add a global array to this project.
3. Make this a two-dimensional array that holds timecard information. Have the following elements in the array:

   Date

   Hours worked

   Employee name
4. Create a new form that loads this array in the `Form_Load()` event procedure with some sample data.
5. Create some public constants you can use to reference each of the different subscripts.

Here's another exercise that builds on the previous one:

1. Create a user-defined type of timecard information. Use the same elements as in the previous exercise.
2. Create an array of this user-defined type and load it with some sample data.

8

Conditional Logic and Looping

WHEN WRITING PROGRAMS, YOU OFTEN HAVE to make a decision about which line of code to execute next. If you don't make a decision, all the code in a procedure will simply execute from left to right and top to bottom. Many times you need to execute a different set of code based on some criteria input by the user. Visual Basic helps you perform this type of conditional logic by supplying you with `If` statements and `Select Case` statements. Also, you often need to iterate over a series of steps many times. This type of looping can be accomplished numerous ways with the built-in looping constructs in Visual Basic.

Chapter Objectives

- Learn about the different control structures available in Visual Basic for controlling program flow
- Learn about compiler directives
- Introduce the looping constructs in Visual Basic

Sample Project File: \Chapter08\IfLoops.vbp

If...Then

An `If...Then` statement is used to redirect program flow based on the results of a conditional test. There are two forms of the `If...Then` statement: single line and multiline. You should only use the multiline statement because it's much easier to read.

Here's the single-line syntax:

```
If <Cond> Then <Statement>
```

`<Cond>` can be any expression that evaluates to a `True` or `False` value. `True` is defined as any nonzero number, such as –1, 1, 2, 500, and so on. `False`, on the other hand, is zero (0).

Here's an example:

```
If txtLast.Text = "" Then  MsgBox "Last Name Must be Filled In"
```

If...Then...End If

The multiline form of the `If...Then` statement is terminated with an `End If` statement. You need to use the `End If` statement if you have multiple lines of code in between the `If` and `End If` statements.

Example's Filename: Employee1.frm

Here's the multiline syntax:

```
If <Cond> Then
    <Statement Block 1>
    <Statement Block 2>
    <Statement Block ...>
    <Statement Block n>
End If
```

For an example, look in the Save command button for the following code:

```
Private Sub cmdSave_Click()
   If txtLast.Text = "" Then
      MsgBox "Last Name Must Be Filled In"
   End If
End Sub
```

The *Else* Clause

The `If` statement also allows you to add an `Else` clause you can use to execute a different set of code if the condition evaluates to a `False` condition. Here's an example:

```
Private Sub cmdSave_Click()
   If txtLast.Text = "" Then
      MsgBox "Last Name Must Be Filled In"
   End If
   If optMale.Value = True Then
      MsgBox "Employee is Male"
   Else
      MsgBox "Employee is Female"
   End If
End Sub
```

In this example, the code between `Else` and `End If` is executed if `optMale.Value` is set to `False`.

The *ElseIf* Clause

If you have multiple conditions to check, you can also use the `ElseIf` clause. Each condition is checked until a `True` condition is found. Once the `True` condition is found, the code within the block between the `ElseIf` and the next `ElseIf` or `End If` statement is executed. After executing the block of code, the next line executed will be after the `End If` statement.

Here's the syntax:

```
If <Cond1> Then
     <Statement Block 1>
[ElseIf] <Cond2> Then
     <Statement Block 2>
[Else]
     <Statement Block 3>
End If
```

Here's an example:

```
Private Sub cmdSave_Click()
   If txtLast.Text = "" Then
      MsgBox "Last Name Must Be Filled In"
   End If
   If optMale.Value = True Then
      MsgBox "Employee is Male"
   Else
      MsgBox "Employee is Female"
   End If
   If cboState.Text = "CA" Then
      MsgBox "Employee can sign up for Health Care"
   ElseIf cboState.Text = "AZ" Then
      MsgBox "Employee is eligible for Bonus Programmer"
   ElseIf cboState.Text = "NV" Then
      MsgBox "Employee is eligible for 401k"
   End If
End Sub
```

The *IIf()* Function

The `IIf()` function allows you to combine an `If...Then...Else` statement into one line. The `IIf()` function accepts three parameters. If the first parameter evaluates to a `True` condition, the value of the second parameter is returned. If the first parameter evaluates to a `False` condition, the value of the third parameter is returned.

Here's the syntax:

```
IIF(<Cond1 is True>, <Return Exp1>, <Else Return Exp2>)
```

Here's an example:

```
Dim intTemp As Integer

intTemp = IIf(boolPerform, 1, 0)
```

Here's another example:

```
Dim strLast As String

strLast = IIf(strFirst = "Bill", "Gates", "Whoever")
```

Select Case

A `Select Case` statement is used in place of multiple `If...Then...ElseIf` statements when you're testing the same condition over and over. Your code is more efficient and more readable when you use the `Select Case` construct than multiple `If...Then...ElseIf` statements.

Here's the syntax:

```
Select Case <Expression>
    Case <Expression List 1>
        <Statement Block 1>
    Case <Expression List 2>
        <Statement Block 1>
    Case Else
        <Statement Block>
End Select
```

Example's Filename: Employee2.frm

Here's the first example:

```
Private Sub cmdSave_Click()
   If txtLast.Text = "" Then
      MsgBox "Last Name Must Be Filled In"
   End If
   If optMale.Value = True Then
      MsgBox "Employee is Male"
   Else
      MsgBox "Employee is Female"
   End If
   Select Case cboState.Text
      Case "CA"
         MsgBox "Employee can sign up for Health Care"
      Case "AZ"
         MsgBox "Employee is eligible for Bonus Programmer"
      Case "NV"
         MsgBox "Employee is eligible for 401k"
   End Select
End Sub
```

You can use other forms of the `Select Case` statement. For example, you can use a comma-delimited list when you need to have the same block of code run for different cases. You can also use the `To` operator if you have a range of numbers that will run the same block of code.

Here's the second example:

```
Select Case CCur(txtSalary.Text)
   Case 0 To 40000
      MsgBox "Tax Rate is 15%"
   Case 40001 To 60000
      MsgBox "Tax Rate is 24%"
   Case 60001 To 80000
      MsgBox "Tax Rate is 28%"
   Case 80001 To 10000000
      MsgBox "Tax Rate is 38%"
End Select
```

In this code, the `CCur()` function is used to convert the value in the text box to a currency value.

Here's a third example:

```
Select Case txtCity.Text
   Case "Tustin", "Irvine", "Orange"
      MsgBox "Inform employee of carpool options"
   Case "Mission Viejo", "Newport Beach"
      MsgBox "Inform employee of transportation options"
End Select
```

TIP

When coding `Case` statements, place the most commonly used cases first. This will improve the performance of the `Case` statement.

Compiler Directives

Compiler directives are used when you need to change the way your program is compiled. Compiler directives are `If` statements that direct the compiler as to which code to leave in and which code to take out. For example, you might want to put debugging code in your application, but when you create a final compile, you don't want the debugging code to be there. Also, maybe you want to take out the code for certain features if you're creating a demo version of your product.

Example's Filename: Conditional.frm

#If...Then...#Else...#End If

To create a compiler directive, you use the # symbol in front of the `If` statement. This tells the compiler that the `#If` statement is for it, not for runtime. An example might be to display different languages to a user depending on the compiled version of your code. Here's an example:

```
Private Sub cmdConditional_Click()
   #If cconLANGUAGE = 1 Then
      MsgBox "Good Morning, Mr. Gates"
   #Else
      MsgBox "Guten Morgen, Herr Gates"
   #End If
End Sub
```

When you declare a compiler constant called `cconLANGUAGE` and set that value to `1`, the English edition of the `MsgBox` statement is included in the EXE file. If the value is set to anything else, the German version is included.

Unlike a normal `If` statement, the `#If` statement actually removes the code before it compiles. This leads to reduced EXE size and also prevents compilation errors if the environment does not match the code.

Although not mentioned in the Visual Basic manual, logical operators can be used in the `#If` statement. For example, the following code is perfectly legal:

```
#If cconDEBUGCODE = 1 Or cconDEBUGCODE = 2 Then
   MsgBox "Debugging"
#End If
```

You could also use the conditional compilation feature to turn off your generic error-handling code or maybe call a special error-trapping routine. You'll learn more about error handling in Chapter 17. Here's an example:

```
#If cconERRORSPECIAL = 0 Then
   On Error Goto Load_EH
#Else
   On Error Goto Special_EH
#End If
```

Declaring a Global Compiler Constant

To declare a public compiler constant (one that will be available to your entire application), you need to go to the Tools, Options menu and select the Advanced tab as shown in Figure 8.1.

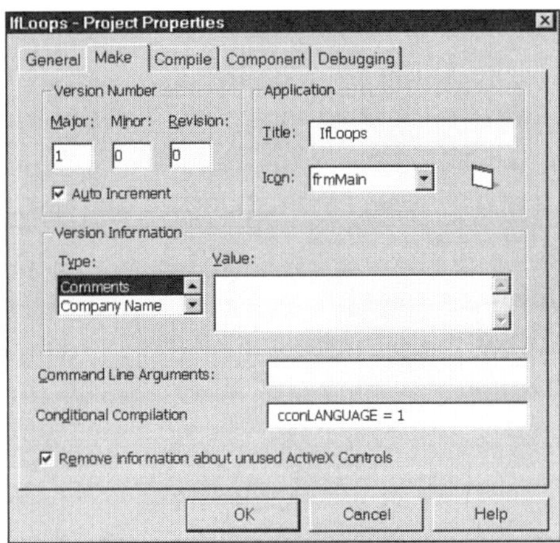

FIGURE 8.1
The Project Properties window.

In the Conditional Compilation text box, enter the constant name, an equal sign, and the value to assign. When you create the constant name, it must follow the naming rules for a Visual Basic variable. The value you assign to the constant can only be a numeric value. You can place multiple values in this text box by separating them with colons (:). Here's an example:

```
cconLANGUAGE = 0 : cconDEBUGCODE = -1
```

Declaring a Module-level Compiler Constant

You can declare compiler constants in the General Declarations section of a module. However, the compiler constants you define here have scope only within that module. Here's an example:

```
' General Declarations Section
Option Explicit

#Const cconLANGUAGE = 0
```

Looping in VB

The ability to iterate over a series of statements is vital in any programming language. For example, you need to loop to retrieve items from a list box, and you need to loop to load items from a database table into a list box. Many other types of looping can occur in your programs. Two types of loop structures are available in Visual Basic: the `Do...Loop` and the `For...Next` loop. The `Do...Loop` construct offers many variations and is typically used if you don't know how many iterations will be performed. The `For...Next` loop is typically used when you know the exact number of iterations to perform on a block of code, see Figure 8.2.

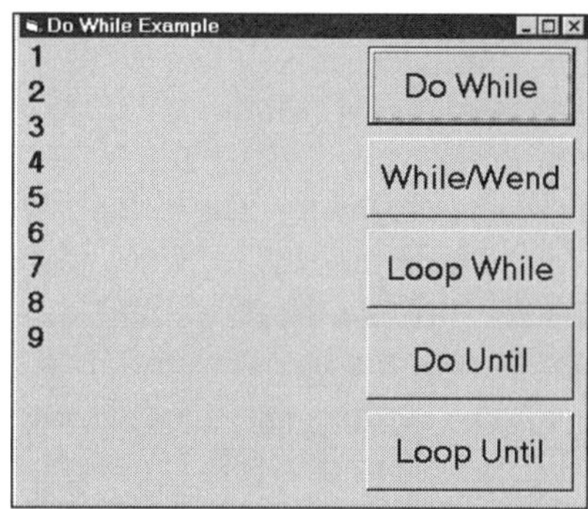

FIGURE 8.2 The *Do While* loop example.

Example's Filename: DoWhile.frm

Do While

The first form of the `Do...Loop` you'll learn about is the `Do While` construct. `Do While` tests a loop condition each time through the loop, and it keeps executing while the test expression is a `True` value. A `Do...Loop` is always terminated with a `Loop` statement. If the condition at the top of the loop is a `True` value, the statements between the `Do` and the `Loop` are executed. It's possible, with this form of loop, that the statements inside the loop may not even be executed. If the condition at the top of the loop evaluates to `False`, none of the statements inside of the block are executed. Here's the syntax:

```
Do While <Cond>
    <Statement Block>
Loop
```

The following example is from the Do While command button:

```
Private Sub cmdDoWhile_Click ()
   Dim intNumber As Integer

   Cls
   intNumber = 1
   Do While intNumber < 10
      Print intNumber
      intNumber = intNumber + 1
   Loop
End Sub
```

While...Wend

The `While...Wend` loop is exactly the same as the `Do While` loop. It's not used too much anymore, but in previous versions of the BASIC language, it was used quite a lot. Therefore, Visual Basic includes this syntax to maintain backward compatibility. This construct is actually not even in the help anymore which means Visual Basic will probably not support it in a future version. Here's the syntax:

```
While <Cond>
    <Statement Block>
Wend
```

The following example is from the While/Wend command button:

```
Private Sub cmdWhileWend_Click ()
   Dim intNumber As Integer

   Cls
   intNumber = 1
   While intNumber < 10
      Print intNumber
      intNumber = intNumber + 1
   Wend
End Sub
```

Loop While

Instead of checking the condition at the top of the loop, as you saw with the **Do While** loop, you can also test the condition at the bottom of the loop. In this example, you'll put the **Do** statement at the top of the loop on a line by itself. You can then have one or many statements. To terminate the loop, you specify **Loop While <Condition>**. As long as the condition evaluates to a **True** value, execution will go back to the top of the loop and execute the statements again. When you use this format of looping, you're guaranteed that the code inside the loop will be executed one time. Here's the syntax:

```
Do
    <Statement Block>
Loop While <Cond>
```

The following example is from the Loop While command button.

```
Private Sub cmdLoopWhile_Click ()
   Dim intNumber As Integer

   Cls
   intNumber = 1
   Do
      Print intNumber
      intNumber = intNumber + 1
   Loop While intNumber < 10
End Sub
```

Do Until

A **Do Until** loop is very similar to the **Do While** loop, except you're executing the loop until a condition becomes **True**. It all depends on what type of logic you need to use to check the loop condition. Here's the syntax:

```
Do Until <Cond>
    <Statement Block>
Loop
```

The following example is from the Do Until command button.

```
Private Sub cmdUntil_Click ()
   Dim intLoop As Integer

   Cls
```

```
    intLoop = 1
    Do Until intLoop = 10
        Print intLoop
        intLoop = intLoop + 1
    Loop
End Sub
```

Loop Until

The `Loop Until` loop checks the condition at the end of the loop instead of the beginning of the loop, just like `Loop While`. The statements inside the loop will always be performed at least once. Here's the syntax:

```
Do
    <Statement Block>
Loop Until <Cond>
```

The following example is from the Loop Until command button.

```
Private Sub cmdLoopUntil_Click ()
    Dim intLoop As Integer

    Cls
    intLoop = 1
    Do
        Print intLoop
        intLoop = intLoop + 1
    Loop Until intLoop = 10
End Sub
```

For...Next

`For...Next` loops are generally used when you know the exact number of iterations that need to be performed. You'll always use a counter variable that automatically increments or decrements as you iterate through the loop. Because you're using a counter, you'll always loop from some start value to some end value. By default, a `For...Next` loop always increments by one every time through the loop. The value used to stop the loop can be a hard-coded number or a variable. See Figure 8.3 for an example of a `For...Next` loop.

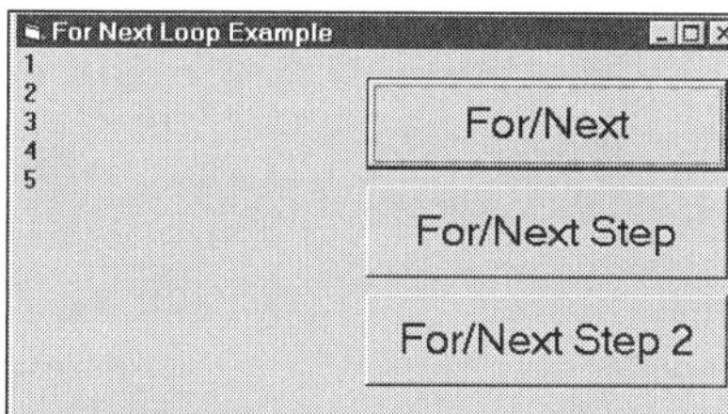

FIGURE 8.3
A *For...Next* loop example.

Example's Filename: ForNext.frm

Here's the syntax:

```
For <Counter> = <Start> To <End> [Step <Inc/Decrement>]
    <Statement Block>
Next [<Counter>]
```

The following example is from the For/Next command button:

```
Private Sub cmdForNext_Click ()
   Dim intLoop As Integer

   Cls
   For intLoop = 1 To 5
      Print intLoop
   Next intLoop
End Sub
```

For...Next Step

The `Step` clause can be added to the `For...Next` loop to specify the increment you want to use for the counter variable. The `Step` clause is listed after the `To` variable and is followed by a numeric value that can be positive or negative. If the number is negative, make sure the start variable is higher than the end variable.

The following example is from the For/Next Step command button:

```
Private Sub cmdForStep_Click ()
   Dim intLoop As Integer

   Cls
   For intLoop = 10 To 1 Step -1
      Print intLoop
   Next intLoop
End Sub
```

This example is from the For/Next Step 2 command button:

```
Private Sub cmdForStep2_Click ()
   Dim intLoop As Integer

   Cls
   For intLoop = 5 To 50 Step 5
      Print intLoop
   Next intLoop
End Sub
```

TIP

Putting the variable name after the `Next` statement is sometimes more efficient and more readable than using `Next` by itself.

The *For...Next* Example

Let's write some code that's very typical in a real-world situation. Remember the email form you created in Chapter 5? Let's add a list box to that form of mailing addresses for people you would send email to. Make this list box a multiselect list box so that you can send email to multiple people. After you make your selections, you can transfer the list of names to the To text box. See Figure 8.4 for an example of what this form should look like.

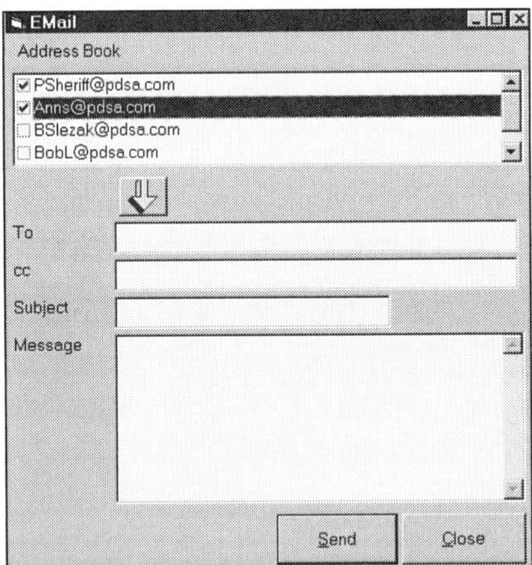

FIGURE 8.4 Email with transfer capability.

Example's Filename: Email.frm

EXERCISE

Add Some Capability to the Email Form

1. Bring up the Email.frm file.
2. Increase the height of the form.
3. Add a label to the form and set the `Name` property to `lblLabel`.
4. Set the `Caption` property to `Address Book`.
5. Add a list box to the form and set the `Name` property to `lstAddresses`.
6. Set the `Style` property to `1-CheckBox`.
7. Add some email addresses to the `List` property of this list box.
8. Add a command button just below the list box.
9. Set the `Name` property to `cmdTransfer`.
10. Set the `Caption` property to nothing.
11. Set the `Style` property to `1-Graphical`
12. Set the `Picture` property to `..\Visual Basic\Icons\Arrows\Arw06dn.ico`.
13. Write the following code for the `Click` event of this command button:

```
Private Sub cmdTransfer_Click()
    Dim intLoop As Integer
    Dim strAddr As String

    With lstAddresses
        For intLoop = 0 To .ListCount - 1
            If .Selected(intLoop) Then
                strAddr = strAddr & .List(intLoop) & "; "
            End If
        Next intLoop
    End With
    txtTo.Text = strAddr
End Sub
```

The preceding code begins by creating two local variables. The `intLoop` variable is used to iterate over the list of items in the list box. The `strAddr` variable is used as a holding area for the addresses that have been selected. Each time through the loop, the `Selected()` property array is checked to see whether the item at the index of the loop is a

True or False value. If it's True, the item is added to the strAddr variable from the List() property at the index of the loop variable. After all the selected items have been retrieved from the list box, the value of the strAddr variable is assigned to the Text property of the txtTo text box. In the above example, I used the With...End With construct. This is used so you don't have to keep typing the list box name over and over again. You can just use the property names with a preceding dot.

Nested Constructs

Any of the conditional logic or looping constructs can be nested within one another. For example, you can have an If statement within a loop, or you can have an If statement in a Case statement. You can have a Do...While loop within a For...Next loop or even inside of a Case statement. You can even have three or more For...Next loops one within another.

Exit For/Exit Do

Sometimes you might need to exit out of a For or Do loop early. You can accomplish this in one of two ways: You can set some value so the condition will drop you out of the loop, or you can use either an Exit For or Exit Do statement. Obviously, Exit For is used when you're in a For...Next loop, and the Exit Do is used when you're in a Do...While loop. The Exit statement only exits from the loop it's coded within. This means that if you have nested loops, you may need multiple Exit statements. Here's an example:

```
For intLoop = 1 To 5
   Print intLoop
   If intLoop = 3 Then
      Exit For
   End If
Next intLoop
```

Exit Sub/Exit Function

Just as you might need to exit a loop early, you might sometimes need to exit a procedure early. To accomplish this, use the Exit Sub or Exit Function statement. Here's an example:

```
Function FormCheck () As Integer
   FormCheck = False

   If Trim$(txtState.Text) = "" Then
      MsgBox "State Code Must Be Filled In"
      txtState.SetFocus
      Exit Function
   ElseIf Trim$(txtCompany.Text) = "" Then
      MsgBox "Company Name Must Be Filled In"
      txtCompany.SetFocus
      Exit Function
   End If

   FormCheck = True
End Function
```

In the preceding `FormCheck()` function, the `FormCheck = True` line has been moved to the bottom of the function. The `FormCheck = False` line is set at the top of the function. If one of the tests fails and you need to exit the function, the `FormCheck = True` line never gets executed.

With...End With

Another construct that will come in handy is the `With...End With` statement. This statement allows you to set multiple properties for one object without specifying the object name over and over again. Take the following code as an example:

```
frmEmployee1.Top = 0
frmEmployee1.Left = 0
frmEmployee1.Caption = "With...End With Example"
frmEmployee1.WindowState = vbMaximized
frmEmployee1.Show
```

Example's Filename: Main.frm

Instead of having to specify the form name, frmEmployee1, over and over again, you can use the following code. Double-click on the `With...End With` command button on Main.frm to see the following code:

```
Private Sub cmdWith_Click()
   With frmEmployee1
      .Top = 0
```

```
            .Left = 0
            .Caption = "With...End With Example"
            .WindowState = vbMaximized
            .Show
        End With
    End Sub
```

As you can see, this code is much more readable than the first version. It also saves the amount of typing you have to do. What's more, a better benefit is that this is more efficient than specifying the same object name over and over again.

Summary

This chapter showed you how to use the different decision structures and looping constructs available in the Visual Basic language. `If` statements and `Select Case` statements allow your program to make decisions as to which code to run. `Do` loops and `For...Next` loops allow you to iterate over many statements a specified amount of time or until some condition becomes true.

Review Questions/Exercises

1. Write an `If` statement that checks to see whether one number is greater than another, and if it is, displays a message box saying "Number 1 is greater than Number 2."
2. Write a `Do...Loop` that loops from 10 to 1. Print each value on the form.
3. Write a `For...Next` loop that loops from 1 to 100 and only prints the value 50 when the loop variable becomes 50.

6

Procedures and Functions

A Visual Basic application is made up of many different components. So far, you've created the user interface, event procedures, variables, arrays, constants, and user-defined types. These components are important, but probably the most important elements in any program are procedures and functions. Procedures and functions are just like the event procedures you already created, except these procedures and functions are not tied to any visual element. Instead, they're just bits of code sitting in a module file waiting to be called from an event procedure or another procedure or function.

Chapter Objectives

- Learn about event procedures and user-defined procedures
- Learn to view all procedures in a project
- Learn about code modules or BAS files
- Learn how to pass arguments to a procedure or function
- Learn to use optional parameters
- Learn about named arguments
- Learn to declare and return data from a function
- Learn about function and procedure naming standards

Sample Project File: \Chapter09\Procedures.vbp

Procedures

Procedures are bits of code that can be used to respond to events, or you can write general procedures that can perform some action. Procedures do not return values to the calling routine. Procedures are identified by the keyword `Sub` in their declaration.

Naming Procedures

You must follow certain rules when naming variables, procedures, and functions. All procedures and functions must begin with a letter. After the first letter, they may contain an combination of letters, numbers, and underscore characters. No other characters are allowed. Procedure names may be up to 255 characters long.

Event/Subprocedures

Event procedures are always declared with the keyword `Sub`, which stands for *subroutine*. A subroutine is a set of statements executed by calling a name where these statements are stored. No value is returned from a subprocedure. The difference between an event procedure and any other subprocedure is that Visual Basic defines the name of the event procedure and what arguments are passed into the procedure. Your own procedures you can name whatever you want and pass any arguments you want.

Scope of Procedures

A procedure may be either private or public. A private procedure can be called only by other procedures within the same form, standard module, or class module. A public procedure can be called from any other procedure outside the module. For code in a standard module, a public procedure is global to the entire application. For code in a form or class module, a public procedure is a method that applies to the object.

Creating a Procedure

To create a procedure, you first need to decide what the procedure will do. Next, you decide what the scope of the procedure will be—private or public. There are a couple of different methods you can use to create a new procedure. First, you must be in a code window in a module. Next, you select Tools, Add Procedures to display a dialog box that prompts you for the name of a procedure or function. Figure 9.1 shows what this dialog box looks like.

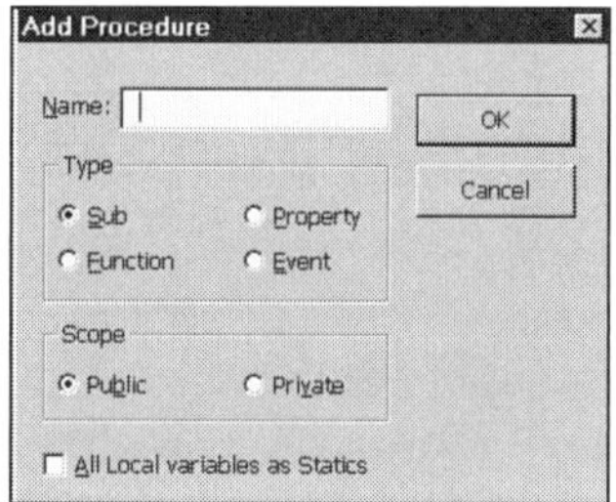

FIGURE 9.1
The Add Procedure dialog box.

In this dialog box, you input the name of a procedure and then select the type of procedure you want to create. You may select either `Sub` or `Function` for this chapter. In later chapters, you'll learn about the other two types. You also select the scope of the procedure—either `Public` or `Private`. After you input the name and click the OK button, you'll see that a stub of the procedure name will be input into the code window. For example, if you input the name `EmployeeDisplay` and click the `Private` scope, you'll see the following stub in the code window:

```
Private Sub EmployeeDisplay ()

End Sub
```

The second method of creating a new procedure is to position your cursor on a blank line in the code window and type in **`Private Sub EmployeeDisplay`** and then press the Enter key. This adds a new procedure into the code window. Now all you have to do is write the code for the `EmployeeDisplay` procedure.

EXERCISE

Write Your Own Procedure

1. Select the Employee Information form and double-click it in the Project Explorer window.
2. Open up a code window for this form.
3. Add the `EmployeeDisplay` procedure using one of the methods described previously.
4. Add the following code in this procedure:

```
Private Sub EmployeeDisplay()
   Dim strName As String

strName = txtLast.Text & ", " & txtFirst.Text

    MsgBox strName
End Sub
```

In this routine, you get the last name from the txtLast text box and the first name from the txtFirst text box. The two values are then concatenated together with a comma in the middle.

Calling Procedures

To call a procedure or function from another procedure or function, you simply put the name of the procedure on a line by itself, like so:

```
EmployeeDisplay
```

In addition, you can put the keyword `Call` in front of the name of the procedure:

```
Call EmployeeDisplay
```

The preferred method is to place the `Call` keyword in front of the call to the procedure. This helps you distinguish that it's a call to a procedure and not just a Visual Basic statement or a function call. Let's now call the `EmployeeDisplay` procedure you just created.

EXERCISE

CALL YOUR OWN PROCEDURE

1. Double-click the Save command button on the Employee Information form.
2. Add the following call to the procedure `EmployeeDisplay`:

```
Private Sub cmdSave_Click()
Call EmployeeDisplay
End Sub
```

It is preferable to use the `Call` keyword when you call your own procedures. This makes the code more readable, and offsets your own procedures from built-in Visual Basic statements.

Sub Main() Procedure

You can start a Visual Basic application using two different methods. First, you can use a form to start your application. This means that the form is loaded first and then it displays itself. The second method is to use a startup procedure. The name of this procedure must be called `Main()`. Figure 9.2 shows you the Project Properties dialog box, which is where you set how you wish to start your project.

FIGURE 9.2
The Project Properties dialog box.

EXERCISE

SET THE STARTUP OBJECT

1. Select Project, EmpInfo Properties from the Visual Basic menu.
2. On the General tab (shown in Figure 9.2), select from the Startup Object combo box either the form or Sub Main. Go ahead and select Sub Main.
3. Create a `Sub Main()` procedure in the BAS file. Be sure to make it a public sub so it can be called by the Visual Basic compiler. If you make it private, Visual Basic can't call it when the EXE starts up.
4. Add the following code to the `Sub Main()` procedure:

```
Public Sub Main ()
   frmEmployee.Show
End Sub
```

Now run the project. The Employee Information form should appear just like before. The only difference is you can now add other code to the `Sub Main()` that can execute before displaying your first form in your application.

It's generally a good idea to begin your applications with `Sub Main()` instead of a startup form. If your first startup form has a lot of controls on it, the form can take quite awhile to load. This will cause a delay in the initial startup of your program.

When you begin with `Sub Main()`, your application starts up right away because there's not a form to load, just a procedure. This means you could add a display of a "splash screen" while you load your Employee Information form. A splash screen does not generally have a lot of controls on it, so it can load quickly. Then, while it's being displayed, you can load other forms. Here's an example of what this type of coding might look like:

```
Public Sub Main()
   Screen.MousePointer = vbHourglass

   ' Display the Splash Screen
   frmSplashScreen.Show
   frmSplashScreen.Refresh

   ' Pre-Load the Employee Form
   Load frmEmployee
```

```
    ' Do any other processing


    ' Now display the Employee Form
    frmEmployee.Show

    Screen.MousePointer = vbDefault
End Sub
```

This code contains some concepts that you haven't learned yet. However, most of them are pretty easy. `Screen.MousePointer` is the object used to set the cursor to an hourglass so that the user knows something is happening. Next, `Show` shows the splash screen and then `Refresh` refreshes the form. The `Refresh` method is used because a form may be partially displayed, but the code will continue on. While the code is continuing, the form will not be fully displayed on the screen. The `Refresh` method forces the screen to paint the form in its entirety before any other code will run. Next, the `Load` command is used to load the Employee Information form. The `Load` command loads all the controls on the form, but it does not display the Employee Information form on the screen. However, when it's finally time to perform the `Show` method on the Employee Information form, the form will display almost instantaneously because the controls are already loaded.

After the Employee Information form is loaded, you can perform any other type of preinitialization of your application, such as connecting to a database, preloading some static data from a table into an array in memory, and reading some values from the Registry. Remember that the user is still seeing the hourglass cursor and looking at the splash screen while all this background processing is occurring. After the Employee Information form is finally shown, the cursor is set back to its default.

TIP

Use the procedure `Sub Main` to start your applications.

Functions

A *function* is simply a procedure that returns one value to the routine that calls it. Functions can be used in expressions such as `intValue = FunctionName()`. This is the primary difference between procedures and functions—the ability to return a value and be used in an expression.

Functions can be written to perform calculations, test values against an internal table, and parse strings. The return value from a function may be any valid data type, an array, a user-defined type, or an object. The same rules for naming procedures also apply to functions. Also, the same rules apply to functions as they do to procedures regarding public and private scope.

Creating a Function

You create a function in the exact same way do a procedure. The primary difference is that instead of `Sub`, you use the keyword `Function`. Of course, you may choose either private or public scope. You also need to give the function a data type that it will return. You do this with the `As` keyword after the name of the function. To specify what the return value will be, you set the name of the function equal to the value you want to return. Here's an example:

```
Private Function EmployeeDisplay() As String
   Dim strEmp As String

   strEmp = "My Last Name is " & txtLast.Text
   strEmp = strEmp & " and my first name is " & txtFirst.Text

   EmployeeDisplay = strEmp
End Function
```

Notice in the function declaration that the `As String` keywords follow the name of the function. This tells the calling routine what type of data to expect from this function. After you create a string, you can return it by putting the name of the function on the left side of the equal side in an assignment statement.

Calling Functions

If you call a function from a procedure or another function, you'll typically place the return value in a variable or pass it onto another procedure or function. Consider the following code:

```
Private Sub cmdDisplay_Click()
   Dim strName As String

   strName = EmployeeDisplay()
   MsgBox strName

   MsgBox EmployeeDisplay()
End Sub
```

This code first calls the `EmployeeDisplay()` function, and the return value goes into the `strName` variable. The `MsgBox` procedure is then called and passed this string variable. Of course, I could have just put the `EmployeeDisplay()` function immediately after the `MsgBox` procedure because it's expecting a string variable, which is exactly what's returned from the `EmployeeDisplay()` function. A function can be called just like a procedure, as shown here:

```
Call EmployeeDisplay()
```

In this case, the return value from the `EmployeeDisplay()` function is simply thrown away. You may be wondering why you would do this? Why not just make this function a procedure? What will be the deciding factor on whether you create a function or a procedure is whether you need to retrieve a value back from the routine.

Parameters and Arguments

If you look at the `MsgBox` procedure that's called to display information in a dialog box on the screen, you'll notice that you always have to give it some string input. This input is called a *parameter*. A parameter is something you pass to a procedure so that it can do something with that value. The `MsgBox` procedure takes the parameter that's passed and displays it in a dialog box on the screen. You can pass parameters to your own procedures as long as you set up the arguments to accept them.

Example's Filename: Employee.frm

> **NOTE**
> When you pass a value to a procedure, it's called a *parameter*. In the declaration of that procedure, the values coming in are called *arguments*.

Defining Arguments in Your Procedures

Procedures and function can accept any type of argument you want. You just need to give the argument a name and a data type, just like you would a local variable. In fact, arguments are just local variables that happen to be declared on the same line as the procedure name. To create a procedure that accepts arguments, you would write the procedure definition as follows:

```
Public Sub EmployeeDisplay(strFirst As String, _
                           strLast As String)
```

```
   Dim strEmp As String

   strEmp = "My Last Name is " & strLast
   strEmp = strEmp & " and my first name is " & strFirst

   EmployeeDisplay = strEmp
End Sub
```

In this version of the `EmployeeDisplay` procedure, the first and last names of the employee are passed in. This makes this procedure much more reusable it's not reliant on the txtFirst and txtLast text boxes being created on the form. Any value from any text boxes can be passed in, no matter what its name is.

Calling Procedures with Parameters

Now that we've made this procedure accept these arguments, we need to call it in a different manner. First, we'll pass each parameter in the order they are declared in the function. Second, we'll separate each parameter with a comma. Because these parameters are declared as strings, the string values must be enclosed in double quotes. We'll use a slightly different syntax when calling a procedure using the `Call` keyword versus not using the `Call` keyword. Here's an example:

```
Private Sub cmdSave_Click()
   EmployeeDisplay "Bill", "Gates"
   Call EmployeeDisplay("Michael", "Gilbert")
End Sub
```

Notice that when the `Call` keyword isn't used, the parameters aren't placed in parentheses. However, if you do use the `Call` keyword, you'll need to add parentheses around the two parameters.

The preceding example uses hard-coded strings as the parameters to the `EmployeeDisplay` procedure. However, you could also pass in the values from the text boxes on the form. Here's how:

```
Private Sub cmdSave_Click()
   EmployeeDisplay txtFirst.Text, txtLast.Text
   Call EmployeeDisplay(txtFirst.Text, txtLast.Text)
End Sub
```

And, of course, you could also assign the values in the text boxes to variables and then pass them to the procedure:

```
Private Sub cmdSave_Click()
   Dim strFirst As String
   Dim strLast As String

   strFirst = txtFirst.Text
   strLast = txtLast.Text

   EmployeeDisplay strFirst, strLast
   Call EmployeeDisplay(strFirst, strLast)
End Sub
```

Parameters in Functions

Functions can also be declared to accept arguments just like procedures. Here's the same `EmployeeDisplay` routine written now as a function that accepts arguments:

```
Public Function EmployeeDisplay(strFirst As String, _
                               strLast As String) As String
   Dim strEmp As String

   strEmp = "My Last Name is " & strLast
   strEmp = strEmp & " and my first name is " & strFirst

   EmployeeDisplay = strEmp
End Function
```

Calling Functions with Parameters

To call this function, you still follow all the old rules. You're just adding the ability to pass in the two parameters.

```
Private Sub cmdSave_Click()
   Dim strName As String

   MsgBox EmployeeDisplay("Bill", "Gates")

   strName = EmployeeDisplay("Michael", "Gilbert")
   MsgBox strName
End Sub
```

Call by Value and Call by Reference

You can use two different methods for passing in parameters to a procedure: call by value and call by reference. There's a big difference between these two methods, as you'll see in this section.

Example's Filename: PassParms.frm and Func.bas

Call by Reference

By default, Visual Basic passes all arguments to procedures "by reference." This means that the routine accepting the parameters can actually change them. As an example, let's take another look at the example that takes the values from the text boxes and assigns them to variables:

```
Private Sub cmdSave_Click()
   Dim strFirst As String
   Dim strLast As String

   strFirst = txtFirst.Text
   strLast = txtLast.Text

   EmployeeDisplay strFirst, strLast
   Call EmployeeDisplay(strFirst, strLast)
End Sub
```

The `strFirst` and `strLast` variables are local to the `cmdSave_Click()` event procedure. This means that no other routine can see or affect these variables, right? Well, not exactly. The `EmployeeDisplay()` procedure can change these variables if the arguments are created by reference. In the `EmployeeDisplay` procedure, the two arguments are declared `As String`. This means that they're being passed in by reference. It's the same as placing the keyword `ByRef` in front of the arguments, as shown here:

```
Public Sub EmployeeDisplay(ByRef strFirst As String, _
                           ByRef strLast As String)
   Dim strEmp As String

   strEmp = "My Last Name is " & strLast
   strEmp = strEmp & " and my first name is " & strFirst

   EmployeeDisplay = strEmp
End Sub
```

In the `EmployeeDisplay` procedure, no changes are made to the arguments `strFirst` and `strLast`. However, in other procedures, you may make changes. Consider the following procedure:

```
Private Sub ProcByRef(ByRef intArg1 As Integer, _
                      ByRef strArg2 As String)
    intArg1 = 20
    strArg2 = "Gates"
End Sub
```

The `ProcByRef` procedure accepts two arguments: an integer called `intArg1` and a string called `strArg2`. Notice that the `ProcByRef` routine does change the values of the arguments. Let's see what happens when we call this procedure and pass in variables as parameters to this procedure:

```
Private Sub cmdReference_Click ()
    Dim intRet As Integer
    Dim strRet As String

    intRet = 10
    strRet = "Bill"

    Call ProcByRef(intRet, strRet)

    Me.Print intRet   ' Prints 20
    Me.Print strRet   ' Prints "Gates"
End Sub
```

The event procedure `cmdReference_Click()` declares two local variables. One is an integer initialized to `10`, and the other is a string initialized to the value `Bill`. These two variables are then passed to the procedure `ProcByRef()`. After the procedure `ProcByRef()` has executed, what's the value of the variables? You can't tell just by looking at the routine. If you look at the procedure definition for `ProcByRef()`, you see that the two parameters are received by reference. This means that the addresses of the parameters passed to the routine are what's actually passed. Therefore, any change made in the `ProcByRef()` procedure to the two arguments is reflected in the calling procedure. In Figure 9.3 you can see lines from both the calling procedure and the called procedure point to the same memory location in the computer. This is because the parameters are being passed by reference.

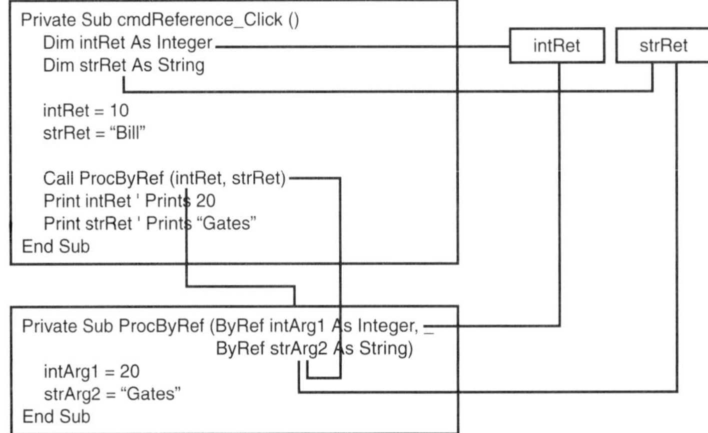

FIGURE 9.3 A call by reference.

Although the keyword `ByRef` is actually optional in front of the declaration of the arguments, I recommend putting it in because it makes the code much clearer to read.

I also recommend avoiding the use of `ByRef` all together, because it's difficult to track down a bug where you're expecting a local variable not to change and it does. You have to spend time walking through each of the procedures called to find out where the local variable is getting changed. This is a terrible waste of time. It's much better to not let procedures change their arguments. This way, you avoid these problems totally.

Of course, there are times when you need to get more than one value back from a function. Because a function can only return one value, you may need to pass a parameter by reference so that you can get two different values back. Consider the following code:

```
Private Sub cmdFuncByRef_Click ()
   Dim intChars As Integer
   Dim strValue As String

   intChars = StringChange(strValue)

   MsgBox strValue
End Sub
```

In this example you may need to change both the string variable, `strValue`, and you may also need to return how many characters were changed by the `StringChange()` function. It does not really matter what the `StringChange()` function does—this is just to illustrate the point that sometimes a `ByRef` call is necessary.

Call by Value

To ensure that a procedure does not change any of the values or parameters passed to it, use the `ByVal` keyword when declaring arguments. When the `ByVal` keyword is used, Visual Basic passes a copy of the value in the variable, not the actual address of where the variable is stored. This way, any changes you make to any of the lower-level arguments will not change the values in the calling procedure. Here's an example:

```
Private Sub cmdValue_Click ()
   Dim intRet As Integer
   Dim strRet As String

   intRet = 10
   strRet = "Bill"

   Call ProcByValue(intRet, strRet)

   Me.Print intRet
   Me.Print strRet
End Sub
```

In the `ProcByValue` procedure, the keyword `ByVal` is placed in front of the declaration of the arguments:

```
Sub ProcByValue (ByVal intArg1 As Integer, _
                 ByVal strArg2 As String)
   intArg1 = 20
   strArg2 = "Gates"
End Sub
```

If you execute the `cmdValue_Click()` event, the arguments do not change, so the values printed are `10` and `Bill`. This format is probably used more often than the call by reference, because most of the time you just need to pass values to another routine without changing the values. In Figure 9.4 the lines for the calling procedure and the called procedure point to different locations in memory. This is what happens when you use the `ByVal` keyword, the values are stored in separate memory locations.

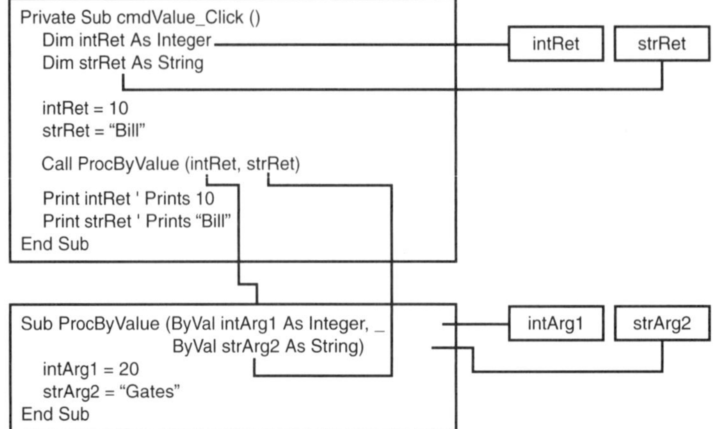

FIGURE 9.4
A call by value.

Optional Arguments

Visual Basic allows you to create optional arguments in the declaration of a procedure. This means you can call the procedure either with or without these parameter. You have two methods for specifying optional arguments. Let's look at both of them.

Optional Variant

You can create an optional variant argument, as shown in the following code. When you use a variant in the declaration and the procedure is called without the parameter, an `Empty` value will be assigned to the variant. You can test for this `Empty` value by using the built-in Visual Basic function `IsMissing()`. Here's a procedure with this type of definition:

```
Public Sub ProcOptionalVar(ByVal intFirst As Integer, _
                           ByVal intSecond As Integer, _
                           Optional vntName As Variant)

   If IsMissing(vntName) Then
      vntName = "Default Name"
   End If

   MsgBox vntName
End Sub
```

Example's Filename: PassParms.frm and Func.bas

In the preceding code, the `vntName` variable is checked within an `If` statement to determine whether it was passed in. If it was not passed in, a default value can be assigned to the missing parameter. Here's an example of how you might call the `ProcOptionalVar()` procedure:

```
Private Sub cmdOptionalVar_Click()
    ' Call with parameter filled in
    Call ProcOptionalVar(1, 3, "Bill Gates")
    ' Call with no 2nd parameter
    Call ProcOptionalVar(2, 5)
End Sub
```

Optional Argument with a Data Type

The second way to declare an optional argument is to give it a data type, just like you would normally. In fact, this is the preferred method, because variants carry a lot of overhead. Here's another procedure that has an optional argument with a data type declared:

```
Public Sub ProcOptional(ByVal intFirst As Integer, _
                        ByVal intSecond As Integer, _
                        Optional intValue As Integer = -1)

    If intValue = -1 Then
        MsgBox "The value was not passed in"
    Else
        MsgBox "The value is " & intValue
    End If

End Sub
```

This example assigns the argument a default value right in the declaration. This way, if the argument does not receive a value, it will be assigned the default value specified. When you declare an argument with a data type, you cannot use the `IsMissing()` function. Instead, you just need to check this value against the default value to see whether they are the same. Obviously, you want to choose a default value that's something that would never be passed into this procedure. Otherwise, you wouldn't know whether it was passed or assigned to the default value.

Named Arguments

When you pass parameters to a procedure, you've had to pass those parameters in the exact order in which they were declared in the procedure. There are two problems with this: First, you may not always remember the order (although the syntax guide pop-up helps with this). Second, it's not very readable later when you're just looking at the call to the procedure. To help solve these problems, you can pass in the parameters using the argument name itself. Here's an example:

```
Private Sub cmdNamed_Click()
   Call ProcOptionalVar(intSecond:=10, _
                        intFirst:=50, _
                        vntName:="A Name")
End Sub
```

Example's Filename: PassParms.frm and Func.bas

Here, you see the call to the `ProcOptionalVar` procedure, where the actual argument names in the call are used. To do this, give the argument name followed by a colon and an equal sign (`:=`) and then the value you want to give to that argument. This helps make the code more readable, and it also allows you to pass in the arguments in any order you want.

Naming Standards

When you start to create your own functions and procedures, you'll want to create a standard for how you name them. Here's a list of some general guidelines to follow:

- Your procedures and functions should always begin with a noun.
- Do not use an underscore in the name. This will help you distinguish between your procedures and Visual Basic event procedures.
- Use standard suffixes such as those shown in Table 9.1.

Table 9.1 Standard Suffixes for Naming Procedures

Suffix	Usage	Example
`Init`	Initializes something only called once	`FormInit`
`Save`	Saves data from a form to a table	`FormSave`

Suffix	Usage	Example
`Get`	Retrieves the value of something on another form	`StatusGet`
`Set`	Sets the value of something on another form	`StatusSet`
`Check`	Checks the data the user typed in	`FormCheck`
`Clear`	Clears the controls on a form to a default state	`FormClear`
`Load`	Loads a combo or list box	`cboStateLoad`
`Kill`	Kills module-level variables	`FormKill`

The reason for this naming standard is to follow the object and event paradigm that has already been set in Visual Basic. Additionally, Visual Basic sorts the procedure names in the Procedure combo box alphabetically. By naming everything with an object name first, all the procedures for one object show up in one place.

Visual Basic events always start with the object name, followed by an underscore, and then the event. The object is a noun, and the event is a verb or action. Follow this naming standard for your own functions.

NOTE
Microsoft formerly used the verb first, followed by the noun. This was the reverse of object-oriented standards as well as Microsoft's own way of naming event procedures. The company has since changed its way of doing this.

Summary

This chapter introduced you to the use of your own custom procedures and functions. You learned to create procedures and functions both with and without arguments. You also learned the difference between `ByVal` and `ByRef`. (Remember to always use `ByVal` unless you need to return more than one value from a function.)

Review Questions

1. True or False? You may use a letter or underscore as the first character for a procedure name.
2. What's the file extension used for code modules?

3. True or False? Global variables are declared in the declarations section of code modules or forms.

4. What will be displayed in the following code?

```
Sub Proc1(intParm As Integer, strValue As String)
intParm = 10
strValue = "Hi There"
End Sub

Dim intTemp As Integer
Dim strName As String
intTemp = 5
strName = "Bill"
Call Proc1(intTemp, strName)
Me.Print intTemp
```

What's displayed in the following code?

```
Me.Print strName
```

5. What will be displayed in the following code?

```
Dim intTemp As Integer
Dim strName As String

intTemp = 5
strName = "Bill"
Call Proc1(intTemp, ByVal strName)
Me.Print intTemp
```

What's displayed in the following code?

```
Me.Print strName
```

What's displayed in the following code?

```
Sub Proc1(ByVal intParm As Integer, strValue As String)
   intParm = 10
   strValue = "Hi There"
End Sub
```

Exercises

1. Create a public function in a BAS module to which you can pass a ZIP code string. This function should verify that the ZIP code is in the proper ZIP code or ZIP+4 format.
2. Create a public function in a BAS module to which you can pass a Social Security number (SSN) string. This function should verify that the SSN is in the proper format: 999-99-9999.
3. Add a Birth Date text box named txtBirthDate to the Employee form.

   Add a Salary text box named txtSalary to the form.

   Create a function in the Employee Information form called `FormCheck()` that returns a Boolean value.

   This function should validate the following information for the fields on the form:

   - The txtLast cannot be empty.
   - The cboState combo box must have a state selected.
   - The ZIP code must be filled in and must be in either a ZIP code or ZIP+4 format.
   - The SSN must be filled in and must be in a valid format.
   - The birth date must be a valid date.
   - The salary field must be numeric.
   - If the Health Plan check box is selected, make sure that at least one item in the Health Care Choices list box has been cheked.

10

Built-in Visual Basic Functions

VISUAL BASIC HAS MANY BUILT-IN FUNCTIONS you can call. These are used to manipulate strings and dates as well as return system information. In this chapter, you'll learn about the different Visual Basic functions and methods that are attached to forms and controls.

Chapter Objectives

- Learn about the built-in Visual Basic functions
- Learn about string functions
- Learn about date functions
- Learn about methods

Sample Project File: \Chapter10\VBFuncs.vbp

Using Built-in Functions

Visual Basic has many built-in functions that are a part of the base language and may be called at any time from your procedures. Table 10.1 is a list of some of the more common ones you'll use. A complete list of functions can be found in the Visual Basic Books Online.

Notice that many of the functions have two forms—with a trailing dollar sign ($) and without. Those with the dollar sign return a value as a `String` data type. Those without it return a value as a variant data type with the `VarType` string.

Table 10.1 Most Commonly Used Built-in Functions

Function(s)	Description
`Chr, Chr$`	Convert an ASCII value to a string
`Asc`	Converts a string to an ASCII value
`Str, Str$`	Convert a number to a string
`Format, Format$`	Convert a number to a formatted string
`Val`	Converts a string to a number
`Date, Date$`	Get current system date
`Now`	Gets current system date and time
`Time, Time$`	Get current system time
`InputBox, InputBox$`	Display an input box and prompt the user for one string
`MsgBox`	Displays a message box
`LCase, LCase$`	Convert a string to lowercase
`UCase, UCase$`	Convert a string to uppercase

Function(s)	Description
`Space, Space$`	Return a string of repeating spaces
`String, String$`	Return a string of repeating characters
`Len`	Returns the length of a string
`InStr`	Determines whether one string is in another string
`Left, Left$`	Return the leftmost portion of a string
`LTrim, LTrim$`	Trim spaces from the left of a string
`Mid, Mid$`	Find a string that's contained within another string
`RTrim, RTrim$`	Trim spaces from the right of a string
`Right, Right$`	Return the rightmost portion of a string
`Trim, Trim$`	Trim spaces from both the left and right of a string
`IsDate`	Is a variant of a `Date` type
`IsNull`	Is a variant of a `Null` value
`IsNumeric`	Is a variant of a numeric value
`Beep`	Sounds a tone

String Functions

Visual Basic has a wealth of string functions you can use. If Visual Basic does not have the function you need, you can typically create it from these functions. Let's look at some of the more commonly used string functions in the example shown in Figure 10.1.

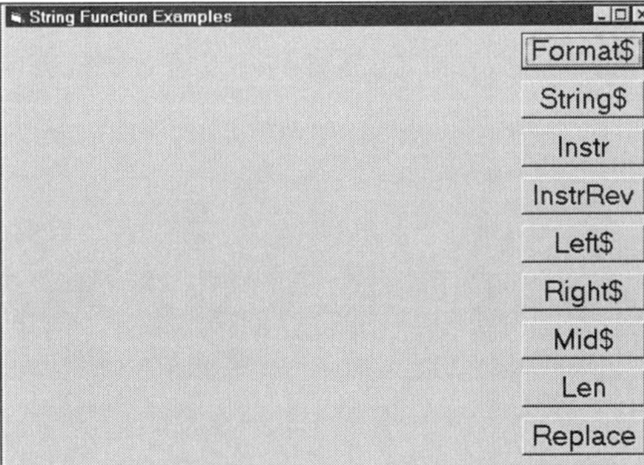

FIGURE 10.1
String function examples.

Example Filename: String.frm

For each of the functions listed in this section, you can click the corresponding button on the form to see the results.

Format$()

`Format$()` returns a string in a specified format. You can pass date, time, number, or string data to this function, along with instructions on how to format the string. This function replaces the `Print Using` statement in older BASIC languages. Here's an example:

```
Private Sub cmdFormat_Click ()
   Me.Cls
   Me.Print Format$(Now, "General Date")
   Me.Print Format$(Now, "Short Date")
   Me.Print
   Me.Print Format$(50, "Currency")
   Me.Print Format$(1250, "Currency")
   Me.Print
   Me.Print Format$(0, "Yes/No")
   Me.Print Format$(1, "Yes/No")
   Me.Print Format$(0, "True/False")
   Me.Print Format$(1, "True/False")
   Me.Print Format$(0, "On/Off")
   Me.Print Format$(1, "On/Off")
End Sub
```

String$()

`String$()` returns a string made up of a specific number of characters. Here's an example:

```
Private Sub cmdString_Click ()
   Me.Cls
   Me.Print String$(20, "*")
   Me.Print String$(5, "#")
   Me.Print String$(30, "-")
End Sub
```

InStr()

`InStr()` returns the location where one string resides in another string. String functions are "one based," not "zero based" like arrays. Here's an example:

```
Private Sub cmdInstr_Click ()
   Dim strName As String
   strName = "Bill Gates"

   Me.Cls
   Me.Print strName
   Me.Print InStr(strName, "G")
   Me.Print InStr(strName, "Gates")
End Sub
```

The first argument you typically pass to the `Instr()` function is the string you wish to search within. The next parameter is the string you wish to search for. This function will return the numeric location of where the 2nd parameter is located within the first.

InStrRev()

`InStrRev()` returns the location where one string resides in another string, but from the end of the string. Here's an example:

```
Private Sub cmdInstrRev_Click()
   Dim strValue As String

   strValue = "Microsoft Visual Basic 6.0"
   Me.Cls
   Me.Print "strValue = " & strValue
   Me.Print "InStr(strValue, ""B"") = " & InStr(strValue, "B")
   Me.Print "InStr(strValue, ""Visual"") = " & _
            InStr(strValue, "Visual")
End Sub
```

Left$()

`Left$()` returns the leftmost number of characters specified in a string. Here's an example:

```
Private Sub cmdLeft_Click ()
   Dim strName As String
   strName = "Bill Gates"
```

```
   Me.Cls
   Me.Print strName
   Me.Print Left$(strName, 4)
   Me.Print Left$(strName, 7)
End Sub
```

The `Left$()` function's first parameter is the string you wish to retrieve the leftmost characters from. The 2nd parameter is how many of those characters you want to retrieve.

Right$()

`Right$()` returns the rightmost number of characters specified in a string. Here's an example:

```
Private Sub cmdRight_Click ()
   Dim strName As String
   strName = "Bill Gates"

   Me.Cls
   Me.Print strName
   Me.Print Right$(strName, 7)
   Me.Print Right$(strName, 10)
End Sub
```

The `Right$()` function's first parameter is the string you wish to retrieve the rightmost characters from. The 2nd parameter is how many of those characters you want to retrieve.

Mid$()

`Mid$()` returns a substring of a specified number of characters within a string. Here's an example:

```
Private Sub cmdMid_Click ()
   Dim strName As String
   strName = "Bill Gates"

   Me.Cls
   Me.Print strName
   Me.Print Mid$(strName, 1, 4)
   Me.Print Mid$(strName, 6, 2)
End Sub
```

The Mid$() function's first parameter is the string you wish to retrieve the some characters from. The 2nd parameter is the character position you wish to start with. The 3rd parameter is how many of the next characters you want to retrieve.

Len()

Len() returns the number of characters in a string. Here's an example:

```
Private Sub cmdLen_Click ()
   Dim strName As String
   strName = "Bill Gates"

   Me.Cls
   Me.Print "strName = " & strName
   Me.Print "Len(strName) = " & Len(strName)
End Sub
```

Replace

The Replace function allows you to substitute one character (or characters) in a string with another character (or characters). Here's an example:

```
Private Sub cmdReplace_Click()
   Dim strValue As String

   strValue = "Microsoft Visual Basic 5.0"
   Me.Cls
   Me.Print "strValue = " & strValue
   MsgBox "Replace(strValue, ""5.0"", ""6.0"") = " _
            & Replace(strValue, "5.0", "6.0")
End Sub
```

The Replace() function will find values in the first parameter that match the 2nd parameter, and replace those characters with the values in the 3rd parameter.

NOTE
The following functions do not have corresponding buttons in the example.

Trim$()

`Trim$()` removes both leading and trailing spaces from a string. Here's an example:

```
Me.Print Trim$("   HI THERE    ")     ' Prints "HI THERE"
```

RTrim$()

`RTrim$()` removes trailing spaces from a string. Here's an example:

```
Me.Print RTrim$("   HI THERE    ")     ' Prints "   HI THERE"
```

LTrim$()

`LTrim$()` removes leading spaces from a string. Here's an example:

```
Me.Print RTrim$("   HI THERE    ")     ' Prints "HI THERE   "
```

Str$()

`Str$()` returns a string from a numeric expression. Here's an example:

```
strNumber = Str$(100)        ' Returns "100"
```

UCase$()

`UCase$()` returns a string in all uppercase letters. Here's an example:

```
Me.Print UCase$("Bill Gates") ' Returns "BILL GATES"
```

LCase$()

`LCase$()` returns a string in all lowercase letters. Here's an example:

```
Me.Print LCase$("BILL GATES") ' Returns "bill gates"
```

Space$()

`Space$()` returns a specified amount of spaces in a string. Here's an example:

```
strSpace = Space$(50)   ' strSpace will be equal to 50 spaces
Me.Print Len(strSpace) ' Prints 50
```

Date Functions

This section looks at some of the most commonly used date functions. Figure 10.2 shows you the example from this chapter that illustrates these functions.

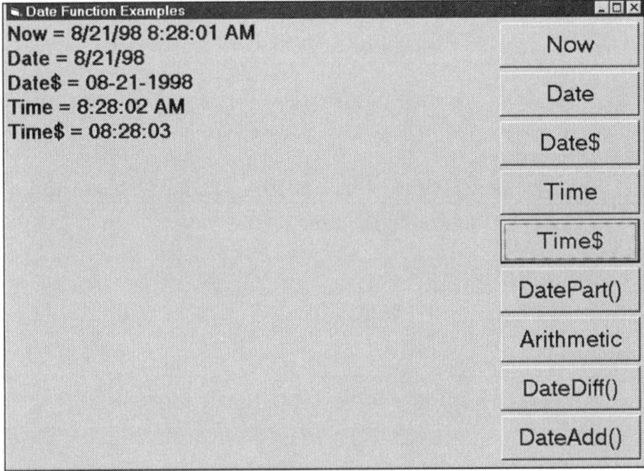

FIGURE 10.2
Date function examples.

Example's Filename: Dates.frm

For each of the functions listed in this section, you can click the corresponding button in the example.

Now

This function returns a variant that's a date/timestamp. It's based on the current system date and time. Here's an example:

```
Private Sub cmdNow_Click ()
   Dim dtDate As Date

   Me.Cls
   ' Get System Date/Time
   dtDate = Now

   Me.Print "Now = " & dtDate
End Sub
```

Date()/Date$()

The Date() function returns a variant of type Date. Date$() returns a ten-character string in the format *mm-dd-yy*. Here's an example:

```
Private Sub cmdDate_Click ()
   Me.Print "Date = " & Date
   Me.Print "Date$ = " & Date$
End Sub
```

Here's the output:

```
3/24/95          ' Gets this from International Settings
                 ' in the control panel
3-24-1995
```

Time()/Time$()

Time$() returns the current system time. Here's an example:

```
sTime = Time$()
```

DatePart()

DatePart() returns the specified part of a date variable. Use it to return the day, year, month, and so on. Here's an example:

```
Private Sub cmdDatePart_Click ()
   Dim dtDate As Date

   Me.Cls
   ' Get System Date/Time
   dtDate = Now

   Me.Print dtDate
   Print
   Me.Print DatePart("m", dtDate)
   Me.Print DatePart("d", dtDate)
   Me.Print DatePart("yyyy", dtDate)
   Me.Print DatePart("q", dtDate)
   Me.Print DatePart("w", dtDate)
End Sub
```

Here's the output:

```
3/24/95

3
24
1995
1
6
```

The first parameter to the `DatePart()` function is a string that specifies which part you want to retrieve. There are many of these different strings you can pass. See the online help for more information. The 2nd parameter to this function is a valid date/time variable.

Date Arithmetic

When you have a variant `Date` type, you can add and subtract any amount of days between two dates. Simply use the plus and minus operators. Here's an example:

```
Private Sub cmdArith_Click ()
   Dim dtDate As Date

   Me.Cls
   ' Get System Date/Time
   dtDate = Now

   Me.Print dtDate
   Print
   Me.Print dtDate + 1
   Me.Print dtDate - 1
End Sub
```

Here's the output:

```
3/24/95

3/25/95
3/23/95
```

DateDiff()

This function returns the specified interval of time between two dates. Here's an example:

```
Private Sub cmdDiff_Click ()
   Dim dtDate1 As Date
   Dim dtDate2 As Date

   Me.Cls
   dtDate1 = #1/1/95#       ' Jan. 1, 1995
   dtDate2 = #3/24/95#      ' Mar. 24, 1995
   Me.Print dtDate1
   Me.Print dtDate2
   Print
   Me.Print DateDiff("d", dtDate1, dtDate2)
   Me.Print DateDiff("w", dtDate1, dtDate2)
   Me.Print DateDiff("m", dtDate1, dtDate2)
End Sub
```

Here's the output:

```
1/1/95
3/24/95

82
11
2
```

The `DateDiff()` function uses the same string arguments as the `DatePart()` function as the first parameter. The next two parameters are the dates you wish to retrieve a difference of.

DateAdd()

`DateAdd()` returns a date after adding or subtracting a specified time interval to another date. Here's an example:

```
Private Sub cmdAdd_Click ()
   Dim dtDate As Date
   Me.Cls
   ' Get System Date/Time
   dtDate = Now
```

```
    Me.Print dtDate
    Print
    Me.Print DateAdd("d", 90, dtDate)
    Me.Print DateAdd("ww", 8, dtDate)
    Me.Print DateAdd("m", 5, dtDate)
    Me.Print DateAdd("m", -6, dtDate)
End Sub
```

Here's the output:

```
3/24/95

6/22/95
5/19/95
8/24/95
9/24/94
```

The `DateAdd()` function uses the same string arguments as the `DatePart()` function as the first parameter. The 2nd parameter is how many units you wish to add to the 3rd parameter.

Conversion Functions

There are many functions used to convert from one data type to another. Figure 10.3 is the form from the example for this chapter.

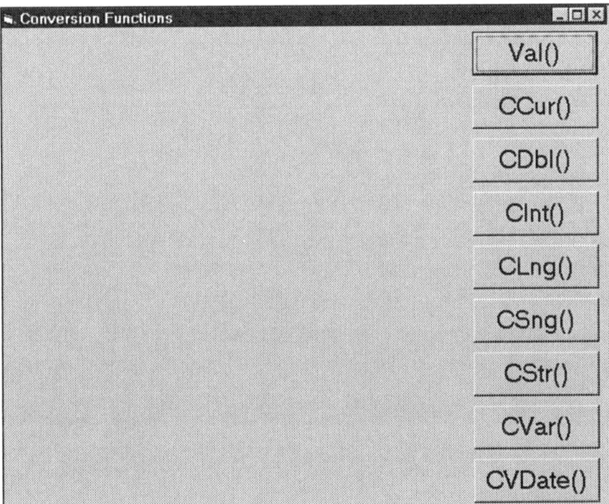

FIGURE 10.3 Conversion functions.

Example's Filename: Conversions.frm

For each of the functions listed in this section, you can click the corresponding button in the example.

Val()

`Val()` returns a numeric value for a string variable. If the converted string contains characters other than numbers, `Val()` converts up to the nonnumeric character. Here's an example:

```
Private Sub cmdVal_Click ()
   Me.Print "Val(""100"")  " & Val("100")

   Me.Print "Val(""10a0"")  " & Val("10a0")

   Me.Print "Val(""a100"")  " & Val("a100")
End Sub
```

Here's the output:

```
100
10
0
```

CCur()

`CCur()` converts any numeric or string expression into a currency value. Here's an example:

```
Private Sub cmdCCur_Click ()
   Dim curAmount As Currency

   curAmount = CCur("5.51")

   Me.Cls
   Me.Print curAmount
End Sub
```

CDbl()

`CDbl()` converts any numeric or string expression into a double value. Here's an example:

```
Private Sub cmdCDbl_Click ()
   Dim dblValue As Double

   dblValue = CDbl("12.99334")

   Me.Cls
   Me.Print dblValue
End Sub
```

CInt()

`CInt()` converts any numeric or string expression into an integer value. Here's an example:

```
Private Sub cmdCInt_Click ()
   Dim intCount As Integer

   intCount = CInt(1555.9)

   Me.Cls
   Me.Print intCount
End Sub
```

Here's the output:

```
1556
```

NOTE
The `CInt()` function does round any decimal portion.

CLng()

`CLng()` converts any numeric or string expression into a long value. Here's an example:

```
Private Sub cmdCLng_Click ()
   Dim lngRet As Long
```

```
    lngRet = CLng("40560")

    Me.Cls
    Me.Print lngRet
End Sub
```

CSng()

CSng() converts any numeric or string expression into a single value. Here's an example:

```
Private Sub cmdCSng_Click ()
    Dim sngValue As Single
    Dim dblValue As Double

    dblValue = 554.5594
    sngValue = CSng(dblValue)

    Me.Cls
    Me.Print "dblValue = 554.5594"
    Me.Print "sngValue = CSng(dDbouble)  " & sngValue
End Sub
```

CStr()

CStr() converts any numeric or string expression into a string value. Here's an example:

```
Private Sub cmdCStr_Click ()
    Dim strInteger As String
    Dim intValue As Integer

    intValue = 1000
    strInteger = CStr(intValue)

    Me.Cls
    Me.Print "intValue = 1000"
    Me.Print "strInteger = CStr(intValue)  " & strInteger
End Sub
```

CVar()

`CVar()` converts any numeric or string expression into a variant value. Here's an example:

```
Private Sub cmdCVDate_Click()
   Dim vntDate As Variant
   Dim strDate As String

   strDate = "4/1/95"
   ' This will create a string variant
   vntDate = CVDate(strDate)

   Me.Cls
   Me.Print "strDate = ""4/1/95"""
   Me.Print "vntDate = CVDate(strDate)  " & vntDate
   Me.Print "VarType(vntDate)  " & VarType(vntDate)
End Sub
```

CDate()

`CDate()` converts a string or string variant into a date type. Here's an example:

```
Private Sub cmdCVDate_Click ()
   Dim dtDate As Date
   Dim strDate As String

   strDate = "4/1/95"
   ' This will create a string variant
   dtDate = CDate(strDate)

   Me.Cls
   Me.Print "strDate = ""4/1/95"""
   Me.Print "dtDate = CVDate(strDate)  " & dtDate
   Me.Print "VarType(dtDate)  " & VarType(dtDate)
End Sub
```

You see the two sets of double quotes in the above code? The reason for this is you need to delimit strings in Visual Basic with double quotes, but if you need to get double quotes in your output on the screen, you will need to use two double quotes to get one in the final output.

Functions to Test Data Types

Sometimes you may need to check the type of data a user has typed into a text box. For example, suppose you're expecting the user to type in a date or some numeric data. Well, a text box control accepts all characters—there's no automatic way to mask the data so that only a certain type of data comes in. Therefore, you may need to check the data to make sure the user input the correct type. You can do this with a couple of functions presented in this section as shown in Figure 10.4.

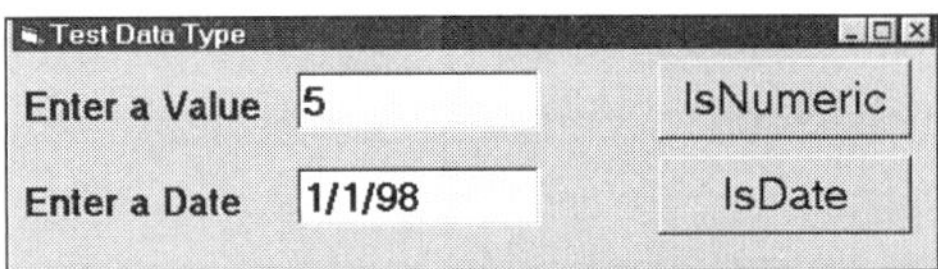

FIGURE 10.4
Test data type example.

Example's Filename: TestDataType.frm

IsNumeric()

The `IsNumeric()` function will return `True` if the value passed to it can be converted to a number. Here's an example:

```
Private Sub cmdIsNumeric_Click()
   If IsNumeric(txtNumeric.Text) Then
      MsgBox "Value is Numeric"
   End If
End Sub
```

IsDate()

`IsDate()` returns `True` if the value passed to it is a valid date. Here's an example:

```
Private Sub cmdIsDate_Click()
   If IsDate(txtDate.Text) Then
      MsgBox "Value is a Date"
   End If
End Sub
```

CAUTION

When `IsDate()` is combined with `CVDate()`, Visual Basic can consider a string such as "334466" as a valid date. Make sure you always check variant and strings with `IsDate()` prior to converting them.

Methods

A *method* is a procedure or function that's a part of an object you use. It's used to perform an action on a particular object. For example, a form is an object that has a `Show` method used to display the form. There's also a `Refresh` method on the form object (as well as on most controls, such as text boxes). Controls are also objects and, as such, have methods. Here are the major differences between methods and procedures:

- You cannot view or modify the code for a method on a Visual Basic object.
- Methods are always bound to an object. You must specify the object name first and then the name of the method.

Examples of Methods

You'll need to learn a few methods for the different objects. Most are self-explanatory. Table 10.2 shows you a list of the different objects and the various methods you can invoke on those objects.

Table 10.2 Common Methods

Method	Applies To	Description
`Me.Cls`	Forms	Clears the graphic or text drawn on a form.
`Hide`	Forms	Used to hide a form without unloading it.
`Line`	Forms	Used to draw a line on the form area.
`Move`	Forms, most controls	Used to move an object from one location to another and, optionally, change the size of the object.
`PaintPicture`	Forms, graphical controls	Used to draw a bitmap or other picture on a form, picture box, image box, or other graphical control.
`PopupMenu`	Forms	Displays a pop-up menu over a form.
`PrintForm`	Forms	Prints the currently displayed image of the form to the default printer.

continues

Table 10.2 Continued

Method	Applies To	Description
`Refresh`	Forms, most controls	Allows you to refresh the contents of an object. `Refresh` can be used when you're in a tight loop and need to have the screen update a progress value.
`SetFocus`	Forms, most controls	Used to set the input focus to a particular control or give a form focus.
`Show`	Forms	Used to load and display a form.
`Zorder`	Forms, most controls	Sets the Z coordinate of a particular object. The Z Order represents which window sits "on top" or "beneath" another window. This property can be used to bring a particular form to the front of the screen or to the back of the screen.

Here are some examples of methods you can use with different controls:

```
frmEmployee.Show              ' Display a form
frmEmployee.Move 0, 0         ' Move a form
txtFirst.SetFocus             ' Set focus to a text box
```

Summary

Visual Basic has many built-in functions for manipulating strings, numeric values, dates, and so on. Using these functions is a lot better than having to write the routines yourself. You also learned about some of the more useful methods built into forms and controls.

Review Questions

1. What's the function that determines whether one string is contained within another string?
2. What's the function that returns the current system date and time?
3. Which function(s) return only the current system date as a string?
4. Which function allows you to add days, months, quarters, and so on from a date?

Dialog Boxes

DIALOG BOXES ARE THOSE WINDOWS you can pop up anytime you need to ask the user for additional information or present some information to the user. Dialog boxes can be created by you, or you can call built-in functions in Visual Basic that present standard Windows dialog boxes. In this chapter, you'll learn to use the `MsgBox` and `InputBox` functions. You'll also learn to use the common dialog control and how to create your own About box.

Chapter Objectives

- Learn the uses of dialog boxes
- Learn the difference between modal and nonmodal operations
- Learn to use the `MsgBox` function
- Learn to use the `InputBox` function
- Learn about the common dialog control
- Learn to build your own About box

Sample Project File: \Chapter11\Dialogs.vbp

Uses of Dialog Boxes

Dialog boxes have two major uses: displaying information to the user and retrieving data from the user. You use dialog boxes almost anytime you use a Windows application. Examples of dialog boxes are the File Open, File Save, and About dialog boxes in typical Windows applications such as Microsoft Word and Microsoft Excel. The File Open and File Save dialog boxes are used to enable the user to open a file and save a file, respectively. These dialog boxes must be completed prior to continuing with the program. The About box is used to convey information to the user. In Visual Basic, the form you use to set project properties is also a dialog box.

Modal Versus Nonmodal

Dialog boxes can be one of two types: modal or nonmodal (modeless). Modal dialog boxes are used when you need the user to respond to some prompt or message before continuing with the program. The user is not able to shift focus to another part of the application until the question is answered and the dialog box is closed. The user may still task-switch to another application running in the Windows environment, he or she just can't do anything in the application in which the modal dialog box is opened.

You've already used a couple different modal dialog boxes in this book. The `InputBox` and `MsgBox` functions are modal. Both of these dialog boxes require the user to respond prior to continuing with the program. These modal dialog boxes are referred to as *application modal*, because only the current application is frozen. *System modal* dialog boxes are possible in Windows, but they're hardly ever used.

An example of a system modal dialog box is a password-protected screensaver. A system modal dialog box doesn't allow the user to do anything else in the Windows environment until he or she responds to it.

Nonmodal dialog boxes are simply forms that are displayed and can be left open. The user is allowed to shift focus to another part of the application. Examples are the toolbox and the Project window in Visual Basic. These boxes stay active while you're working within Visual Basic, and you can go to other parts of the Visual Basic IDE.

MsgBox

`MsgBox` can be used as both a statement and a function. When used as a statement, you present information to the user. This could be used to communicate information about an error that has occurred or an informational message about mail arriving in the inbox.

The `MsgBox` dialog box has five arguments you can pass to it: the message to display to the user, the icon/buttons to display in the dialog box, the title for the dialog box, the Help file's name, and the Help context ID.

```
MsgBox "Press the Enter key to continue..."
MsgBox "Hello World", vbExclamation, "Hello"
```

The second parameter is generally one or more constants that are added together to create both an icon and the buttons on the `message box`. Table 11.1 shows you the constant to use for the different icons.

Table 11.1 Constants for the Second Parameter of the *MsgBox* Statement

Constant	Icon Displayed	Icon
`vbCritical`	Critical message icon	
`vbQuestion`	Warning query icon	
`vbExclamation`	Warning message icon	
`vbInformation`	Information message icon	

Besides the different constants for the icons, you can add to this parameter the constants for the buttons you want to appear. Table 11.2 presents a list of the different constants you can use for the buttons.

Table 11.2 Constants for the Buttons on the *MsgBox*

Button Constant	Description
`vbOkOnly`	Displays the OK button only. This is the default.
`vbOkCancel`	Displays both the OK and Cancel buttons.
`vbYesNo`	Displays the Yes and No buttons.
`vbYesNoCancel`	Displays the Yes, No, and Cancel buttons.
`vbRetryCancel`	Displays the Retry and Cancel buttons.
`vbAbortRetryCancel`	Displays the Abort, Retry, and Cancel buttons.
`vbMsgBoxHelpButton`	Adds the Help button to the `MsgBox`.

You can specify which button is the default button on the message box. This is accomplished by adding to the second parameter one of the `vbDefaultButton`*n* constants. The *n* is the number of the button to set the focus to and can be a value from 1 to 4.

```
intButton = MsgBox("Save Data", vbQuestion + vbYesNo, "Save"
```

You can try out some of the options by loading the sample project for this chapter and clicking the MsgBox command button on the main form to display a sample message box, as shown in Figure 11.1.

Example's Filename: MsgBox.frm

When you click the first command button on the MsgBox.frm sample form, you'll see a message box appear (see Figure 11.1).

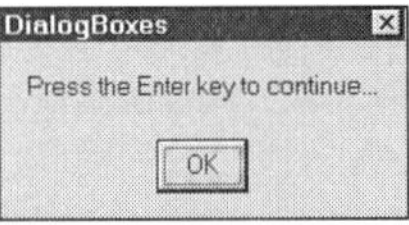

FIGURE 11.1 A simple `MsgBox` example.

You might use this simple type of message box when a long process completes or when you just need to inform the user of some simple information that needs an acknowledgment.

This message box is generated using the following code:

```
Private Sub cmdSimple_Click()
   MsgBox "Press the Enter key to continue..."
End Sub
```

When you click the second command button on the from, you'll see a different message box appear (see Figure 11.2). Adding icons to the message box reinforces what you're trying to get across to the user.

FIGURE 11.2
A MsgBox with the critical icon.

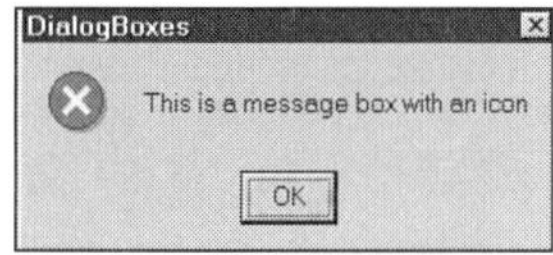

The critical icon is used when a fatal type of error occurs. This message box is generated using the following code:

```
Private Sub cmdIcon_Click()
   MsgBox "This is a message box with an icon", vbCritical
End Sub
```

When you click the third command button on the form, you'll see the message box shown in Figure 11.3. Notice the use of the question mark icon in combination with the buttons that ask the user to respond.

FIGURE 11.3
A MsgBox with Yes and No buttons.

This message box is generated using the following code:

```
Private Sub cmdYesNo_Click()
   If MsgBox("Save the data?", vbQuestion + vbYesNo, _
            "Save") = vbYes Then
      MsgBox "You pressed the Yes button"
   Else
      MsgBox "You pressed the No button"
   End If
End Sub
```

When asking the user a question, you should keep the question short and simple. In the preceding code, `MsgBox` is used as a function call to retrieve the clicked button. You can see that I'm comparing the value returned against the constant `vbYes`. Several constants are used to determine which button has been clicked in a `MsgBox` (see Table 11.3).

Table 11.3 Constants That Tell Which Button Was Clicked

Constant	Description
`vbAbort`	The Abort button was clicked.
`vbCancel`	The Cancel button was clicked.
`vbIgnore`	The Ignore button was clicked.
`vbNo`	The No button was clicked.
`vbOK`	The OK button was clicked.
`vbRetry`	The Retry button was clicked.
`vbYes`	The Yes button was clicked.

If you think the user might need more help with a particular dialog box, you should add a Help context ID and Help file to the parameters you pass to the `MsgBox` dialog box. To add the Help button to the `MsgBox`, use the following code:

```
Private Sub cmdHelp_Click()
   MsgBox "A Critical Error Has Occurred", _
                 vbCritical + vbAbortRetryIgnore _
                 + vbMsgBoxHelpButton, _
                 "Error", App.Path & "\MyHelp.hlp", 5
End Sub
```

When you click the fourth command button in the form, you'll see the message box shown in Figure 11.4.

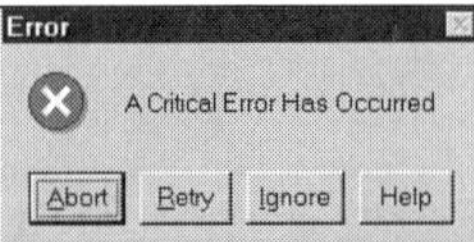

FIGURE 11.4 A message box with a Help button.

When you click the Help button, it retrieves the last two parameters so that it knows which Help file to display and which Help context ID within that Help file to show. The Help context ID is a unique number that corresponds to a particular page in your help file for this application.

InputBox() Function

The `InputBox()` function creates a modal dialog box that can be used to retrieve one piece of information from a user. Instead of having to create your own custom dialog box to ask the user for a piece of information, you can utilize this built-in dialog box.

Example's Filename: InputBox.frm

`InputBox()` enables you to enter a caption, a title, and a default value for the input box, and it even allows you to position the input box to a certain location on the screen. In its simplest form, you can call the `InputBox()` function with just one parameter, as shown in the following code, to have an input box show up like the one in Figure 11.5.

```
Private Sub cmdSimple_Click()
   Dim strName As String

   strName = InputBox("Enter an Employee Name")
   MsgBox "You input " & strName
End Sub
```

In the `cmdSimple_Click()` event, you need to declare a variable, `strName`, to hold the value that will come back from the `InputBox()` function. This string is the value the user types into the text box in the input box. If the user presses the Cancel button, a blank string is returned.

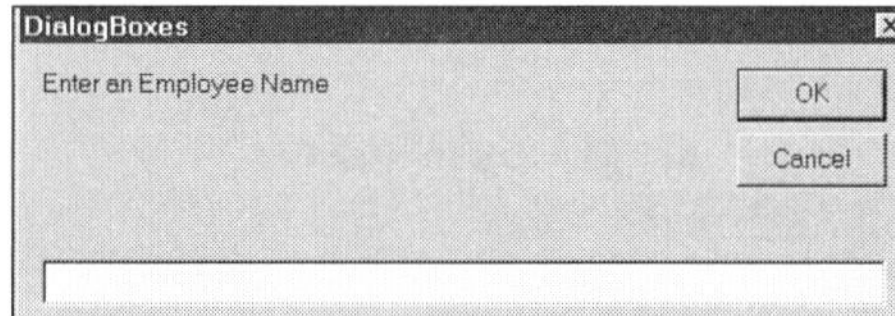

FIGURE 11.5
A simple input box.

Adding a Caption

To add a caption to the `InputBox()` function, you need to add a second parameter with the value you want to place in the title bar of the input box. See Figure 11.6 for an example of an input box with a caption.

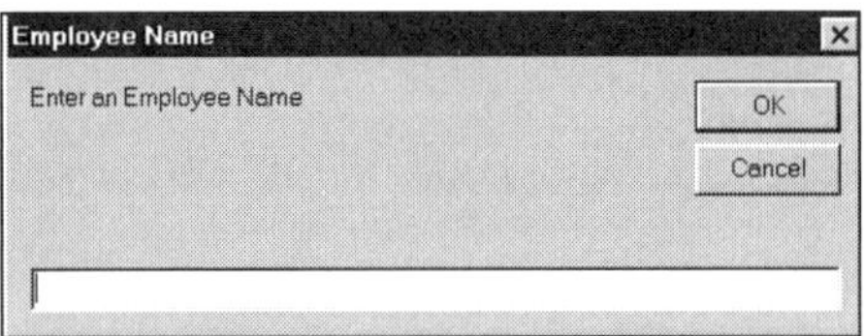

FIGURE 11.6 An input box with a caption.

I recommend that you always pass in the `Caption` parameter, because this will help describe the input box. If you do not pass it in, Visual Basic will just use the EXE name for the caption. Here's the code that generates the input box shown in Figure 11.6:

```
Private Sub cmdCaption_Click()
   Dim strName As String

   strName = InputBox("Enter an Employee Name", _
                      "Employee Name")
   MsgBox "You input " & strName
End Sub
```

Adding a Default Value

You can specify a value that appears in the text box when the input box first appears. Just add the third parameter to the `InputBox()` function, and that value appears in the text box of the input box. Here's an example:

```
Private Sub cmdDefault_Click()
   Dim strName As String

   strName = InputBox("Enter an Employee Name", _
                        "Employee Name", _
                        "Bill Gates")

   MsgBox "You input " & strName
End Sub
```

Using a default value is ideal when you have some data in another location that you want to allow the user to override. This gives the user a starting point from which to change the data.

Positioning the Input Box

Unlike the `MsgBox()` dialog box, you can position an input box by specifying the `Top` and `Left` coordinates as the fourth and fifth parameters. Here's an example:

```
Private Sub cmdPositioned_Click()
   Dim strName As String

   strName = InputBox("Enter an Employee Name", _
                      "Employee Name", _
                      "Bill Gates", _
                      Me.Left + lneSep.X1 + _
                      (Me.Width - Me.ScaleWidth), _
                      Me.Top + lneSep.Y1 + _
                      (Me.Height - Me.ScaleHeight))

   MsgBox "You input " & strName
End Sub
```

In the above example you use the ScaleWidth and ScaleHeight to get just the inside dimensions of the form you are on. These dimensions do not include the title bar, or the borders of the form.

This example lines up the `InputBox()` function with a form and a line control that's located on that form.

Common Dialog Control

One of the benefits of using the Windows operating system is the consistency you see between the different applications you use within Windows. This is due to a common set of dialog boxes included in the Windows dynamic link libraries (DLLs). Because it's a little difficult to call the functions in the DLLs to display these dialog boxes, Visual Basic provides a custom control called the *common dialog control* that acts as a simple interface to these functions, thus making it much easier to use the common dialog boxes within your Visual Basic application. The following dialog boxes can be called from this control:

- File Open
- File Save As
- Color Selection
- Font Select
- Printer Selection and Printer Setup
- Call the WinHelp.exe

The common dialog control is contained in ComDlg32.ocx. This OCX file wraps up the function calls to Commdlg.dll that must be in the Windows\System directory on your computer.

Note that these dialog boxes don't open files, save files, or print anything. Instead, they allow the user to select filenames or fill in printer information. It's up to you to perform the opening of the file, the saving of the file, and the printing. You retrieve the properties from the dialog box and use them to perform a specific operation.

Example's Filename: CommonDlg.frm

Common Properties of the Common Dialog Control

As is the case with most controls, you won't use all the properties of the common dialog control. In fact, the common dialog control has a lot of properties, because it's used for so many different types of dialog boxes. Some properties deal only with the File Open dialog box, and you won't use them if you're calling the Printer Selection dialog box. Table 11.4 shows the properties most often changed and/or retrieved when using the common dialog control.

Table 11.4 Properties of the Common Dialog Control

Property	Description
`CancelError`	If this property is set to `True` and the user clicks the dialog box's Cancel button, the Visual Basic runtime error system is triggered. This allows you to trap when the user clicks the Cancel button instead of having to check to see whether value was filled in.
`Color`	This property is filled in with a number that indicates the color selected by the user from the Color dialog box.

Property	Description
`Copies`	This property is filled in with a number that indicates the number of copies the user selected in the Copies text box in the Printer dialog box.
`DefaultExt`	You set this property prior to calling a File Open or File Save dialog box. This file extension is used to select files. If the user types in a file name without an extension, this extension is added to the file automatically prior to the `FileName` property being filled in.
`DialogTitle`	You can set the window title for the dialog box by filling in this property.
`FileName`	You can set this property to the filename you want to appear as a default when the File Open or File Save dialog box is opened. This property is filled in with the name of the full path and filename after the user selects a file from the dialog box.
`FileTitle`	This property returns the filename without any path.
`Filter`	This property can be filled in with one or more masks to enable the user to select different types of files. For example • Text Files (*.txt) • Access Databases (*.mdb) These filter options appear in a combo box at the bottom of the dialog box. When the user chooses one of these filters, only those files that have the appropriate extension are displayed in the dialog box.
`FilterIndex`	Set this property to the filter in the `Filter` property to use as the default.
`Flags`	This property is set to certain constants, depending on the type of dialog box you're calling. These options help you toggle certain options off and on when using the dialog box. You'll see examples of this property in this chapter.
`InitDir`	Set this property to a valid directory on your system to have a File Open or File Save dialog box display files in that directory.
`Name`	Set this property to the name you want to use for the control. The prefix you'll use is *dlg*.
`PrinterDefault`	Set this property to `True` if you want to have the changes made in the Printer Setup dialog box change the Windows default printer.

File Open/Save Dialog

The File Open dialog box is shown in Figure 11.7. The File Save As dialog box is essentially the same box, except the title reads "Save As."

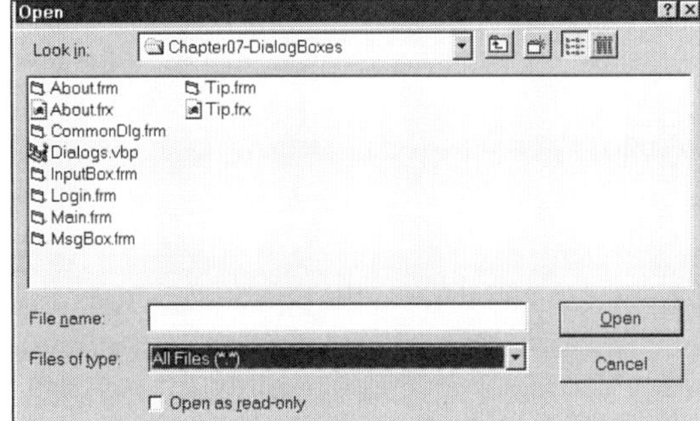

FIGURE 11.7 The File Open dialog box from the common dialog control.

This dialog box is generated by the following code:

```
Private Sub cmdFileOpen_Click()
   Dim strFiles As String

   cdlCommon.InitDir = App.Path

   ' NOTE: Don't put spaces by the Pipe character!
   cdlCommon.Filter = "Access Databases (*.mdb)¦*.mdb¦" & _
                      "INI Files (*.ini)¦*.ini¦" & _
                      "All Files (*.*)¦*.*"

   cdlCommon.Flags =  cdlOFNAllowMultiselect + _
                      cdlOFNLongNames + _
                      cdlOFNExplorer
   cdlCommon.MaxFileSize = 3000

   cdlCommon.ShowOpen

   strFiles = cdlCommon.FileName
   txtFileOpen.Text = strFiles
End Sub
```

To use this sample you need to add the common dialog control from the Project, Components menu and set the Name property to *ctlCommon*.

To display the File Open dialog box, perform the ShowOpen method on the common dialog control. Of course, you'll most likely want to set some additional properties prior to showing the dialog box.

Using the *Filter* Property

To use the Filter property, set the filter to a multipart string delimited with the pipe character (¦). The first part of each filter will start with the words you want to have appear in the Files of Type combo box at the bottom of the File Open dialog box. The second part after the pipe delimiter is the wildcard characters you use to select the files of that particular type. For example, in the preceding code, you would set the filter property as follows:

```
cdlCommon.Filter = "Access Databases (*.mdb)¦*.mdb¦" & _
                   "INI Files (*.ini)¦*.ini¦" & _
                   "All Files (*.*)¦*.*"
```

You can select three different types of files with the dialog box that are opened with this filter set (MDB, INI, and all files). Note that you cannot have any spaces between the pipe character and the other characters.

TIP
Make sure you don't put spaces between the pipe characters in the Filter property.

Setting the Flags

You can use the Flags property to change the way the File Open dialog box works. Table 11.5 lists some of the more common flags.

Table 11.5 Flags You Might Set for the File Open Dialog Box

Flag Constant	Description
cdlOFNAllowMultiSelect	Allows the user to select multiple filenames using the Shift or Ctrl key.
cdlOFNExplorer	Opens an Explorer-like dialog box instead of the old-style Windows dialog box.
cdlOFNFileMustExist	When this flag is set, the file the user is trying to select must already exist.

continues

Table 11.5 Continued

Flag Constant	Description
`cdlOFNLongNames`	If this flag is set, long filenames can be returned from the File Open dialog box.
`cdlOFNPathMustExist`	The path the user types in must exist. If it does not exist, then the user must locate the path manually instead of typing the value in.
`cdlOFNOverwritePrompt`	If you set this option, the File Save As dialog box will generate a message box asking the user whether he or she wants to overwrite an existing file.

When working with the multiple filenames flag, the string returned will contain all the files in one long string, separated by a space character. The name of the path will be the first item listed in this space-delimited string. Here's an example:

```
D:\Train\VB6\intro\samples\Chapter011-DialogBoxes About.frm About.frx
➥ Chapter7.vbp Chapter7.vbw
```

Of course, this can cause problems with long filenames, because they may contain spaces. Therefore, if you choose the multiple filenames option, you should also choose the long filenames flag and the Explorer flag. If you use all these options, you'll no longer get a space-delimited string but rather a `Chr(0)`-delimited string. The `Chr()` function returns a character for an ASCII code that can't be expressed on a keyboard. `Chr(0)` is a common delimiter for strings since the user can't type this on the keyboard.

If you just use the multiple filename and long filename flags without the Explorer flag, you'll still get a space-delimited flag, which won't help you distinguish between the different files.

If you choose to use the multiple filenames option, you'll also need to set the `MaxFileSize` property to the maximum number of bytes you expect to receive. This property can be set from `1` to `32767`. I suggest setting this value to the maximum, because you can't be sure how many files a user might select. This way, you know you'll have enough room to hold all the data the user selects.

Print Dialog

Prior to a report being printed, some information should be gathered from the user concerning how he or she wants to print the report. You can have the user choose those options from the Print dialog box. You can set flags to control which options display on this dialog box. The most common properties the user will select are the printer, the print range (start page and end page), and the number of copies. Figure 11.8 shows a typical Print dialog box.

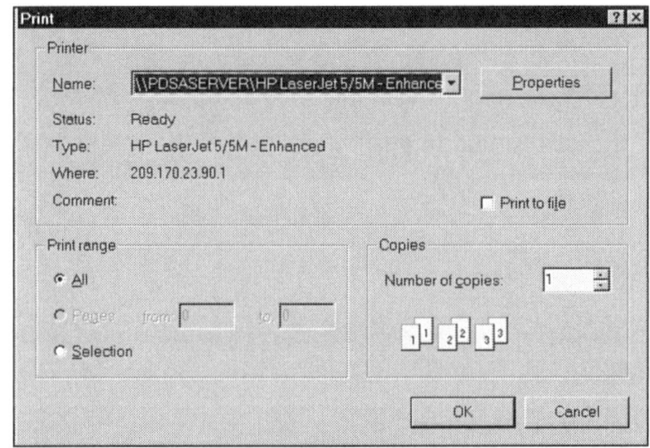

FIGURE 11.8
The Print dialog box.

This dialog box is generated by the following code:

```
Private Sub cmdPrinter_Click()
    ' Reset any flags
    cdlCommon.Flags = 0

    ' Display the Printer Dialog Box
    cdlCommon.ShowPrinter
End Sub
```

It's a good idea to reset the `Flags` property to `0`—this will clear any other values that may have been left over from any previous method calls using the same common dialog. The `ShowPrinter` method displays the Print dialog box.

Flags for the Print Dialog Box

You can set quite a few flags that control the look and feel of the Print dialog box. Table 11.6 lists some of the more common ones.

Table 11.6 Flags for the Print Dialog Box

Flag Constant	Description
`cdlPDAllPages`	This flag sets the state of the All Pages option button.
`cdlPDCollate`	This flag sets the state of the Collate check box.
`cdlPDDisablePrintToFile`	Set this flag to disable the Print to File check box.
`cdlPDHidePrintToFile`	Set this flag to hide the Print to File check box.
`cdlPDNoPageNums`	Set this flag to disable the Pages option button.
`cdlPDPageNums`	Set this flag to enable the Pages option button.
`cdlPDPrintSetup`	Set this flag to call the Print Setup dialog box.
`cdlPDPrintToFile`	Set this flag to enable the Print To File check box.

Print Setup Dialog

Besides setting print options, you may want the user to actually change the default printer. The standard Windows Print Setup Dialog box can be called by the same method used previously, but you must first set the `Flags` property to the constant `cdlPDPrintSetup`. Figure 11.9 shows the Print Setup dialog box.

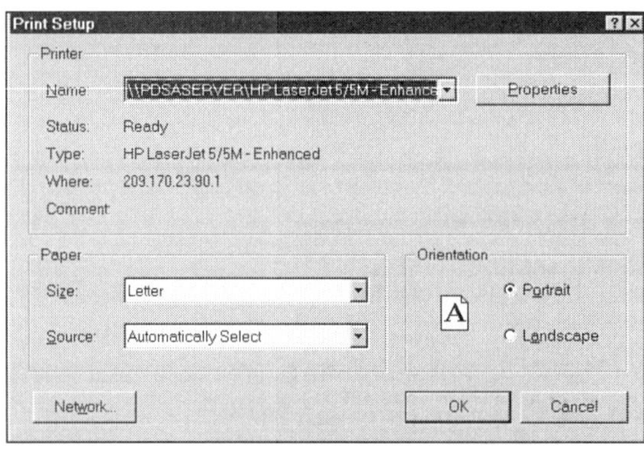

FIGURE 11.9 The Print Setup dialog box.

This dialog box is generated by the following code:

```
Private Sub cmdPrintSetup_Click()
   ' Select the Print Setup Flag
   cdlCommon.Flags = cdlPDPrintSetup

   ' Display the Print Setup Dialog Box
   cdlCommon.ShowPrinter
End Sub
```

Setting the `Flags` property to `cdlPDPrintSetup` causes the Print Setup dialog box to come up instead of the Printer Selection dialog box.

NOTE
This dialog box actually changes your Windows default printer.

Font Dialog Box

The Font dialog box can be used to change fonts for a text box, label, or any control that has a `Font` property. You can invoke this dialog box using the `ShowFont` method of the common dialog control. You might use this dialog when you allow the user to modify the settings of the fonts within a form or within the entire application. Figure 11.10 shows an example of what the Font dialog looks like.

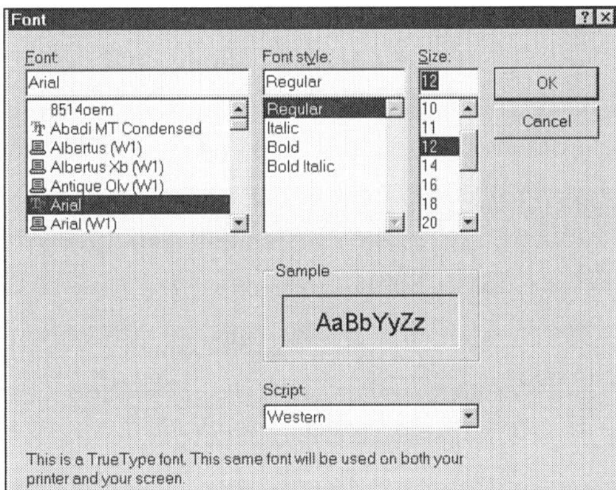

FIGURE 11.10
The Font dialog box.

The Font dialog box is generated with the following code:

```
Private Sub cmdFont_Click()
    ' Select both printer and screen fonts
    cdlCommon.Flags = cdlCFBoth
    ' Display the Font dialog box
    cdlCommon.ShowFont

    ' Get the Font information
    With lblFont
        .FontName = cdlCommon.FontName
        .FontBold = cdlCommon.FontBold
        .FontItalic = cdlCommon.FontItalic
        .FontSize = cdlCommon.FontSize
    End With
End Sub
```

As is the case with the other dialog boxes, no fonts are actually changed when you use this dialog box. Instead, properties are put into the common dialog control. Therefore, after the `ShowFont` method, you need to take the font properties from the dialog control and assign them to the controls you want to change.

Flags for the Font Dialog Box

You can set quite a few flags to control the look and feel of the Font dialog box. Table 11.7 lists some of the more common ones.

Table 11.7 Flags for the Font Dialog Box

Flag Constant	Description
`cdlCFANSIOnly`	When this flag is set, the user cannot select a symbols-only font.
`cdlCFBoth`	When this flag is selected, both printer and screen fonts are displayed in the font selection window.
`cdlCFFixedPitchOnly`	When this flag is selected, only fixed-pitch fonts on the system will be displayed in the font selection window.
`cdlCFLimitSize`	When this flag is set, only font sizes between the `Min` and `Max` properties are displayed.
`cdlCFPrinterFonts`	When this flag is set, only printer fonts are displayed in the font selection window.
`cdlCFScalableOnly`	When this flag is set, only scalable fonts are displayed in the font selection window.
`cdlCFScreenFonts`	When this flag is set, only those fonts that can be used onscreen are displayed in the font selection window.
`cdlCFTTOnly`	When this flag is set, only TrueType fonts are displayed in the font selection window.

Color Dialog Box

Setting colors in your application is not a good idea because users can typically modify their Windows colors using the Control Panel. If you hard-code a color into the `ForeColor` or `BackColor` property of a control and the user has chosen that same exact color from the Control Panel, any text you put into the control will not show up.

However, if you give your users the ability to change colors, they can customize the colors so they don't conflict with their system colors. You can do this by using the Color dialog box, as shown in Figure 11.11.

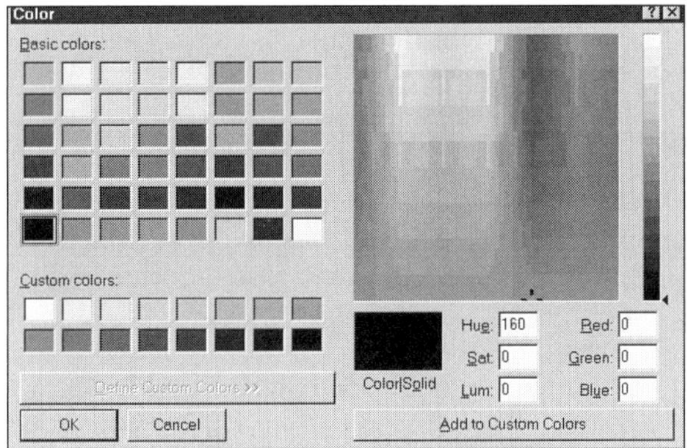

FIGURE 11.11
The Color dialog box.

This Color dialog box is generated by using the following code:

```
Private Sub cmdColor_Click()
    ' Reset the Flags
    cdlCommon.Flags = cdlCCFullOpen

    ' Display the Color dialog box
    cdlCommon.ShowColor

    ' Fill in the background color with
    ' the color from the common dialog
    lblColor.BackColor = cdlCommon.Color
End Sub
```

The `Flags` property is set to `cdlCCFullOpen` so you get the full dialog box. If you don't set this flag, you won't see the custom colors on the right side of the dialog box. The only other `Flag` option you may set is `cdlCCPreventFullOpen`. If you set the `Flag` property to this value, the user won't be allowed to select the Define Custom Colors command button.

Making Your Own Dialog Box

You can make your own dialog box by creating a new form, putting the appropriate controls on it, and then calling the form from a menu or command button. This pop-up form can be displayed either modally or modeless. (A *modal* form is one that must be closed before the rest of the application can continue processing.)

Creating an About Box

Most Windows applications have a standard About box that contains copyright information about the program. These About dialog boxes usually have author information, company information, serial numbers, and sometimes system information, such as the amount of Windows memory.

Let's add an About box to the Employee Information form's menu. If you remember in Chapter 4, "Lists and Menus," you added a Help menu with an About menu under it; we'll call a modal dialog box from this menu.

EXERCISE

Adding an About Dialog Box

1. Bring up the Employee Information form project.
2. Select Project, Add Form from the Visual Basic menu.
3. The Add Form dialog box appears (see Figure 11.12).

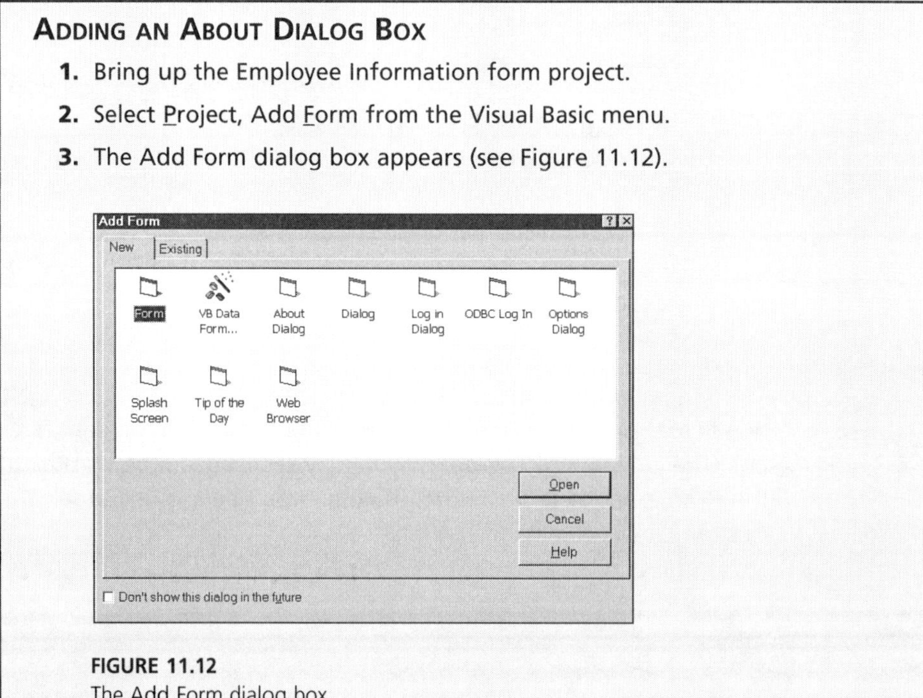

FIGURE 11.12
The Add Form dialog box.

4. Select the standard form About Dialog from this list of templates to add it to the project.
5. After adding this dialog box to the project, you should see a form in your project that looks like the one shown in Figure 11.13.

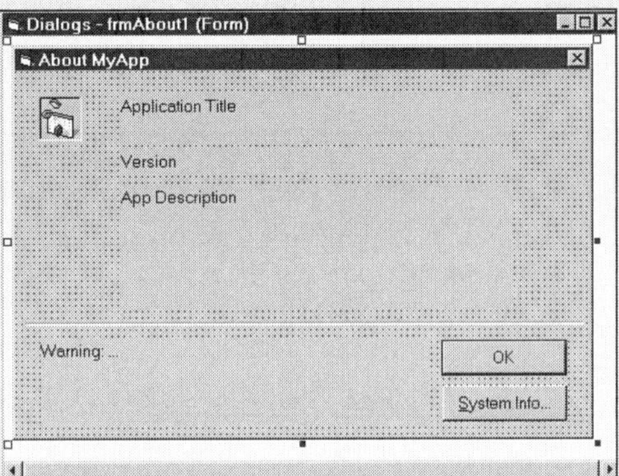

FIGURE 11.13
The standard About Dialog template.

You can see in Figure 11.12 that there are several types of dialog boxes you can add to your project. You use these different dialog boxes as templates, and you can change them once they're added to your project.

The standard About dialog box, shown in Figure 11.13, has several areas you need to fill in at runtime. First is the Application Title label. In the `Form_Load()` event, you'll see the following code that is included with this template:

```
Private Sub Form_Load()
    Me.Caption = "About " & App.Title
    lblVersion.Caption = "Version " & App.Major & _
                         "." & App.Minor & _
                         "." & App.Revision
    lblTitle.Caption = App.Title
End Sub
```

In this `Form_Load()` event, you can see that `"About "` and the application's `Title` property are placed in the `Caption` property. This `Title` property is set in the Project Properties dialog box. The `App` object is an object that receives these different properties when your application starts up. The `App` object also receives the

`Major`, `Minor`, and the `Revision` properties from the Project Properties dialog box as well.

Of course, you need to add text to both the App Description label and the Warning label. You can hard-code this into the `Form_Load()` event, or you could pull the values from data you place in the `FileDescription` and `Comments` properties for the project. So, let's change the `Form_Load()` event a little bit.

EXERCISE

1. Select Project, *<ProjectName>* Properties from the Visual Basic menu.
2. Add some text describing your application to the File Description property in the Make tab under the Version Information frame. See Figure 11.14 for an example of the Project Properties window.
3. Add some text for a typical disclaimer to the Comments property in the Make tab under the Version Information frame. For example, "Warning, this computer program is protected by copyright law and international treaties."
4. Add the following code to the `Form_Load()` event:

```
Private Sub Form_Load()
    Me.Caption = "About " & App.Title
    lblVersion.Caption = "Version " & App.Major & _
                         "." & App.Minor & _
                         "." & App.Revision
    lblTitle.Caption = App.Title
    lblDescription.Caption = App.FileDescription
    lblDisclaimer.Caption = App.Comments
End Sub
```

In the lblDescription and lblDisclaimer label controls, you add the `App.FileDescription` and `App.Comments` properties, respectively. The `App` object is automatically filled with the data you entered into the Project Properties dialog box. You don't need to do anything to set these properties, other than enter them at design time. Visual Basic takes care of loading the data into the `App` object at runtime for you. You'll learn more about the `App` object in a later chapter.

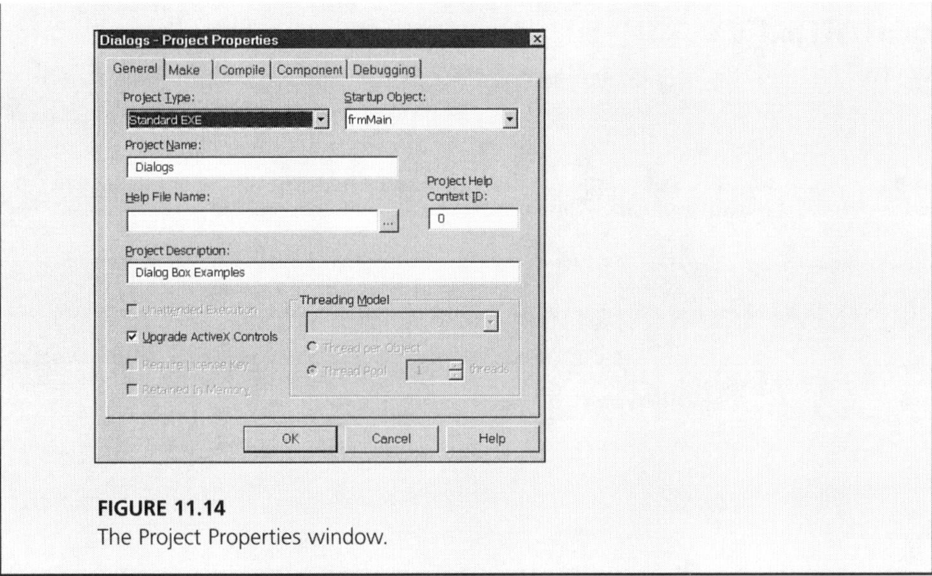

FIGURE 11.14
The Project Properties window.

Next, you need to call this About dialog box from your menu on the Employee Information form.

EXERCISE

Display the About Menu

1. Select the Help, About menu item from the form to bring up a code window:

```
Private Sub mnuHAbout_Click()
    frmAbout.Show vbModal
End Sub
```

Most application programmers display their About forms modally—you should do the same. Passing the argument `vbModal` to the `Show` method tells Visual Basic to not allow any other processing in the application until the form is unloaded.

Summary

In this chapter, you learned about some of the common dialog boxes in Visual Basic. You also learned to use the `MsgBox` and `InputBox` functions. In addition, you learned to use the common dialog control, which can be used to display many Windows common controls. You also learned to use the About form template that comes with Visual Basic.

Review Questions

1. True or False? Once a modal dialog box is displayed, a user may also use other parts of the same application.
2. True or False? The `InputBox()` function allows several values to be input.
3. What's the name of the method that's invoked on a common dialog control to make the Save As dialog box appear?
4. Write some code that modally displays a form called frmModal.

Exercises

1. Add a Tip of the Day dialog box to your application.
2. Add a login dialog box to your application.

12

The ADO Data Control

VISUAL BASIC INCLUDES A CUSTOM CONTROL that allow you to display, edit, and update values in a database with no coding on your part. This control is called the *ADO data control*. Simply adding this data control to your form allows text boxes, labels, and other controls to become "data aware." This means that with just a few steps and no programming, you can display and edit values in a database. There are actually three different flavors of the data control: Jet, ADO, and Remote Data Objects (RDO). In this chapter, you'll learn about the ADO data control because that's the control you'll use for the new projects you create with Visual Basic 6.

Chapter Objectives

- Learn about the different methods for getting at data
- Learn to get data from a Microsoft Access database
- Be able to hook up the data control to data-aware controls
- Be able to create a form that adds, edits, and deletes data from a table

Sample Project File: \Chapter12\ADODataControl.vbp

Getting at Data

You have three primary methods for manipulating data in a database using the Visual Basic language. You can use the Jet engine, the Remote Data Objects, and ADO. Each of these different data access methods has both a data control interface and an object interface. In this chapter, you'll learn about the ADO data control as one of the methods. In future chapters, you'll learn about other methods. Let's start out with an overview of each of the primary methods of data manipulation.

The Jet Engine

The Jet engine is the same engine that powers Microsoft Access. Jet is a very powerful engine for getting at ISAM (Indexed Sequential Access Method) files such as a Jet MDB. An MDB file is an Access database. This is the file extension that is assigned to these Access/Jet database files. It also has the capability to get at database servers that are ODBC (Open Database Connectivity) compliant—for example, SQL Server, Oracle, Sybase, and others. Jet is much more efficient at getting at ISAM-type databases rather than database servers. You should only use Jet if you inherit a legacy application and Jet is already being used. Jet should also only be used if you're only going to use a Jet MDB and will never use a database server.

You have the option of using a Jet data control or the Jet Data Access Objects (DAO) from Visual Basic. The Jet data control uses the Jet DAO objects for all its access—they're just wrapped up into a custom control to make them easier to use. Jet also has a new added feature called *ODBC Direct* to help you speed up the data access to an ODBC data source such as SQL Server. The ODBC Direct layer is actually a component that sits on top of RDO, which you'll learn about in the next section. ODBC Direct was developed to take legacy Visual Basic applications using Jet against an ODBC data source and convert them to a faster data access method. Figure 12.1 shows the different methods you can use with Jet to get at data.

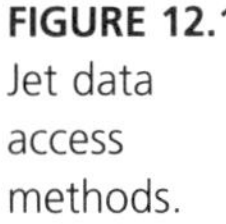

FIGURE 12.1
Jet data access methods.

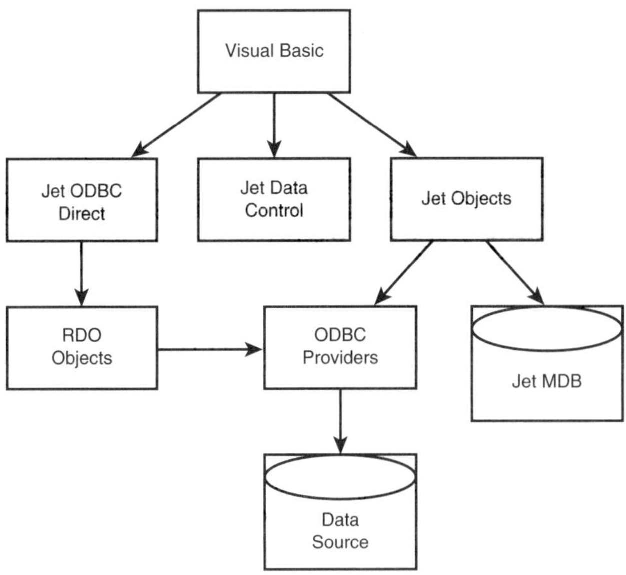

Jet is a technology that will not receive as many updates in the future and is therefore not recommended for new development.

The Remote Data Objects (RDO) Engine

The Remote Data Objects (RDO) access method has a data control interface and objects that can be programmed directly, just like the Jet engine. RDO was specifically designed to manipulate data on an ODBC data source. As such, it's very fast at this type of manipulation against SQL Server, Oracle, or any other database server. However, the performance against an ISAM file system such as a Jet MDB is not very good. Figure 12.2 shows you the different methods of access to a data source you can use with RDO.

RDO is a technology that will be phased out of future versions of Visual Basic and as such should not be used for new development.

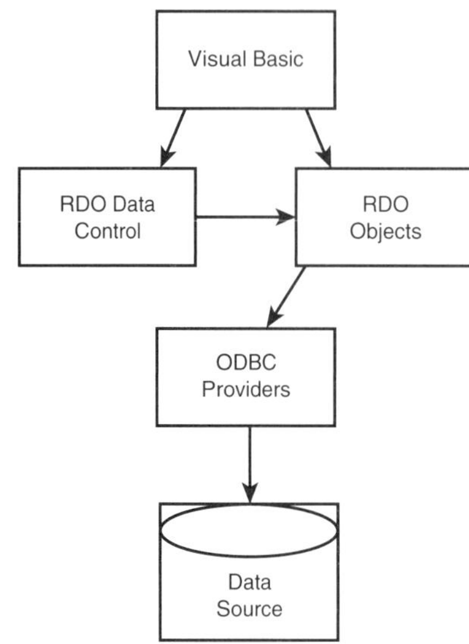

FIGURE 12.2
RDO data access methods.

ActiveX Data Objects

The ActiveX Data Objects (ADO) data control is considered to be the future of data access. It uses a new Universal Data Access method called *OLE DB*, which promises to allow you to access data in a wide variety of formats using a common object model. OLE stands for Object Linking and Embedding. Of course this does not have a lot to do with database access, but this technology just happens to fall under this umbrella. This means that any future development you do should take advantage of ADO and the OLE DB type of access. ADO has comparable features and performance, whether it's used against an ISAM or ODBC database. Figure 12.3 shows the mechanisms behind the ADO objects.

Use ADO for all your new development because this object model will continue to be enhanced in future versions of Visual Basic.

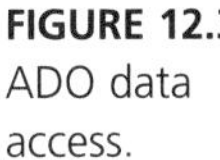

FIGURE 12.3
ADO data access.

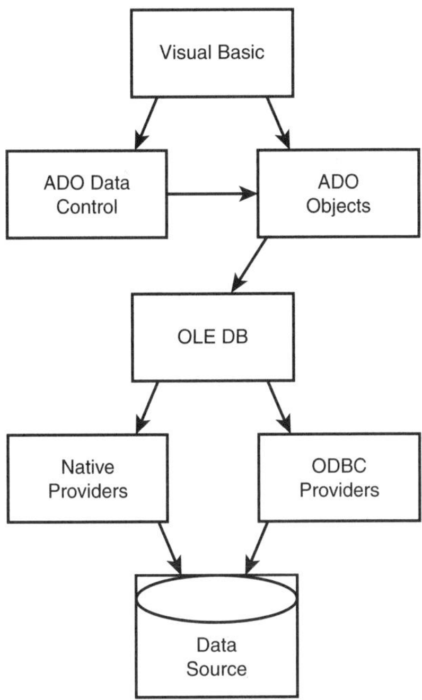

Universal Data Access

UDA is Microsoft's answer to the problem of having to use different access methods for each type of data source you want to get data from. A data source can be a relational database, an Indexed Sequential Access Method (ISAM) file or even a nontraditional data store such as an email server. Universal Data Access is based on an underlying set of Component Object Model (COM) components called OLE DB. Sitting on top of this layer is the ADO object model. Let's look at each of these in turn.

OLE DB

The OLE DB specification consists of a set of OLE interfaces that provide applications with a common access method to data. It does not matter in which format this data is stored—text, XLS, email, MDB, or SQL Server. The interfaces defined in OLE DB will support the capabilities of the Database Management System (DBMS) to retrieve and/or modify data.

OLE DB uses the Component Object Model (COM) as an underlying technology. By utilizing these services, much of the duplication between different data access tools can be eliminated. Also, because COM is a standard that's licensed to standards organizations, it can become a cross-platform standard as other companies jump on the band wagon. This will make your code more portable between different programming environments and tools.

ActiveX Data Objects

ADO is what you'll use from Visual Basic to get at data. You, as a Visual Basic programmer, cannot program the OLE DB layer directly (nor would you want to). This layer is reserved for C++ programmers. Instead, you'll use ADO for all your data manipulation.

ADO is an interface to the OLE DB layer that utilizes a provider to retrieve and update data in a data source. There are a couple of native providers that allow direct access to SQL Server, Oracle, and Microsoft Access MDBs. There is also the Microsoft ODBC provider for OLE DB. This provider allows you to establish a connection to a data source via ODBC. Because ODBC supplies drivers for many different data sources, you can use ADO to manipulate a wide variety of databases.

ADO's primary advantage over other database access methods is its ease of use, high speed, low memory overhead, and small disk footprint. Also, because it's an object-based data access method, it's easy to learn. The learning curve for Jet programmers will be low since ADO uses an object model just like Jet does. While the object model is different, it is still easy to learn.

ADO Features

ADO has several features that make it an ideal object model for building client/server and Web-based applications. Here's a list of some of these features:

- Small object model, which makes it easy to learn.
- Low memory footprint, so more memory is freed up for your application.
- Fast access to a data source.
- Connections can be established on-the-fly, which is great for Web-based applications.
- Different cursor types are supported, including server-side and client-side cursors.

- Support for stored procedures, including input and output parameters and return values.
- Multiple recordsets can be returned.
- Advanced recordset cache management, including number of rows to return and how many rows to cache on the client.
- Asynchronous queries can be used for those queries that take a long time to complete. This allows your users to continue working your application while the database server is processing the data.
- Events will be called to signify that processing is complete or that processing is about to happen. You'll use these events quite a bit because Visual Basic is well designed to interact with events.

Although ADO supports these listed features, you'll need to make sure the underlying OLE DB provider supports each of them as well. Not all providers are created equal, and what one may support, another may not.

ADO Object Hierarchy

Like most COM interfaces, ADO has a hierarchical object model. However, unlike most of the database interfaces out there (such as Jet and RDO), ADO's hierarchy doesn't necessarily need to be followed. You can start at the `Connection` object, or you can start directly with a `Recordset` object—either way, you'll get a connection to the data source. The following is a sampling of the hierarchy contained within ADO.

```
Connection
    Errors -> Error
    Command
        Parameters -> Parameter
    Recordset
    Fields -> Field
```

Referencing ADO

ADO can be used from most programming languages, including Visual Basic, VBA within any of the Microsoft Office products (Microsoft Excel, Microsoft Access, Microsoft PowerPoint, and Microsoft Word), Visual C++, Visual FoxPro, VBScript, and others. To use the ADO objects, you need to set a reference to the Microsoft ActiveX Data Objects 2.0 Library. Once you've referenced this library in your Visual Basic project, all the aforementioned objects can be used.

Service Providers for OLE DB

The service providers are the actual workhorses of the ADO/OLE DB object models. Although ADO and OLE DB provide very generic, consistent interfaces, the service providers are the ones that are customized according to the data source they'll be using. For example, the way the SQL Server service provider retrieves data is completely different than the way the Jet MDB service provider retrieves data.

Native Providers

There are currently three native OLE DB providers that can supply data through OLE DB to ADO. These are for Jet, SQL Server, and Oracle. As mentioned, each works very differently underneath the hood, but the syntax used from a Visual Basic application is exactly the same. Native providers promise to support more features of the data source because they can get at all the features of that data source. In addition, they should also be much faster because there's no intermediate layer such as an ODBC driver.

ODBC Provider

The ODBC provider is simply a wrapper on top of the Open Database Connectivity (ODBC) standard. ODBC is a standard proposed by Microsoft for connecting to various database servers through a common application programming interface (API). It's a standard set of function calls that can be utilized from C, C++, Visual Basic, Delphi, PowerBuilder, and just about any front-end tool. This API allows you to program your source code one time and easily port that application to another database server with little or no coding changes. ODBC is installed with Visual Basic, any of the Microsoft Office products, and with Visual Studio. Most likely, you've ODBC already installed on your system.

You still need to learn about ODBC because there are not that many native providers for OLE DB yet, so you still need to use the ODBC drivers to get at some database servers.

Let's walk through how to create an ODBC data source. (If you're familiar with this process already, feel free to skip ahead to the next section.)

ODBC Setup

Once ODBC has been installed on your system, you can create new data source names (DSNs) using the ODBC Administrator program. Access the ODBC Administrator by clicking the appropriate icon in the Control Panel (see Figure 12.4).

FIGURE 12.4
The ODBC Administrator icon.

After clicking the icon shown in Figure 12.4, you'll be presented with the ODBC Data Sources Administrator (DSA) dialog box shown in Figure 12.5.

> **NOTE**
> You may have a slightly different version than the one I'm presenting in this book, but it should have all the same elements. The ODBC DSA allows you to add, delete, and modify data sources. A data source name is a name you define to point to a particular data source. A data source may be SQL Server, Oracle, or Microsoft Access, for example. You may have one or more ODBC data source names that point to one data source.

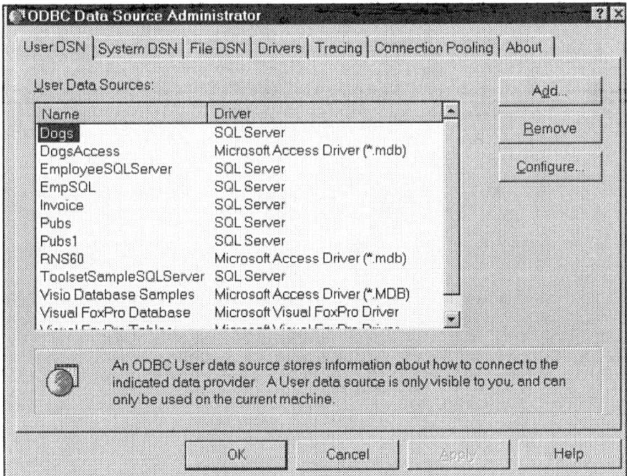

FIGURE 12.5
The ODBC Data Source Administrator.

Once the data source name (DSN) has been added to your system, you can access it from your application. The DSN is any name you want to use. For consistency, it is best to make your DSNs the same for all your users.

A DSN can be created for each user on a particular machine, or it can be created once for every user of a particular machine. To create one DSN for all users on a particular machine, click the System DSN tab and create the DSN there. To create a DSN for one particular user, you create the DSN under the User DSN tab.

Adding a New Microsoft SQL Server Data Source

Let's walk through the steps for setting up a DSN for a Microsoft SQL Server–type database. If you don't have SQL Server, you can skip to the next section, where you'll learn to create a data source name for an Access MDB.

EXERCISE

CONFIGURING AN ODBC DATA SOURCE

1. Bring up the ODBC Data Sources Administrator dialog box from Control Panel.
2. Click the Add button.
3. Select SQL Server from the list of drivers in the dialog box shown in Figure 12.6.
4. Click the Finish button to create the new data source.

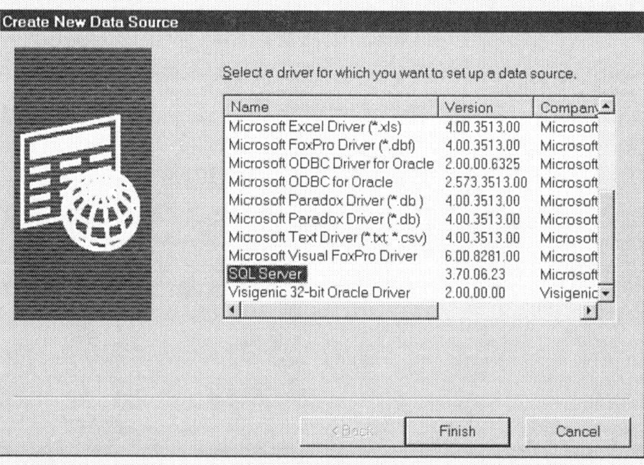

FIGURE 12.6
The Create New Data Source dialog box.

5. If you're using the SQL Server driver version 3.5 or above, you'll be walked through a wizard and asked to fill in various information.
6. If you're using an earlier SQL Server driver, all the information will be on one screen.
7. Table 12.1 lists the fields and values you should fill in. If you can't find a listed field, just ignore it. If there are other fields that are not listed, just ignore them, too. (I'm going to assume you're somewhat familiar with SQL Server. If you are not, there are several good books available on SQL Server configuration options.)

Table 12.1 ODBC DSN Setup for SQL Server

Field	Description
Data Source Name	This is an identifying name that you'll reference from your front-end application. Type in **EmployeeSQL** for this DSN.
Description	This optional field just gives you additional information about what the DSN is used for.
Server	This property determines which SQL Server you want to connect to. You may have several servers on your network, so you need to choose a particular one.
Authenticity ID	Choose the "With SQL Server authentication using a login ID and password entered by the user" option.
Login ID	You need to type in a login ID that has access to the SQL Server. This property will generally be overridden at runtime by the user.
Password	The password for the login ID you entered.
Default Database	Choose the Employee database that comes with this book. If you haven't already installed it, see Appendix E for installation instructions.

An ODBC data source just gives you a variable that you can use to point to this area in memory that contains the information necessary to connect to the database you have chosen.

Each ODBC setup may be different, depending on the data source you're connecting to and the different driver versions. However, you'll always need to specify a data source name. This name is what you'll use to identify the information you just entered in the ODBC Administrator. By putting the information into the ODBC Administrator, you save yourself having to type in all this information in your application program. In addition, you can change the underlying data source but keep the same DSN, and your application should run against this new data source with little or no changes.

Adding a New Microsoft Access Data Source

Let's now create a Microsoft Access database data source. You'll find that the process is very similar but the ODBC driver for Access will ask for different information specific to opening an Access database.

EXERCISE

Create an Access DSN

1. Bring up the ODBC Data Sources Administrator dialog box from the Control Panel.
2. Click the Add button.
3. Select Microsoft Access Driver (*.mdb) from the list of drivers in the dialog box shown in Figure 12.6.
4. Click the Finish button to create the new data source.

Once you click the Finish button, the ODBC Administrator calls a specific function in the appropriate driver to have it configure the data source. Each driver will bring up its appropriate dialog boxes. For the Microsoft Access driver, you'll see the dialog shown in Figure 12.7.

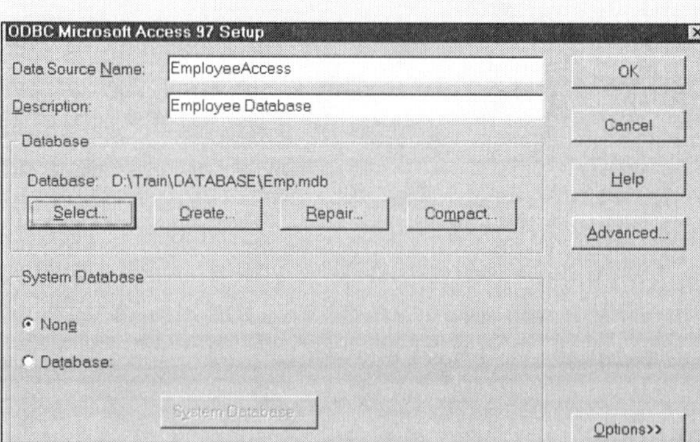

FIGURE 12.7
The ODBC Microsoft Access 97 Setup dialog box.

As you can see, this setup screen differs from the SQL Server driver dialog, because Microsoft Access needs different information than SQL Server. You need to fill in a unique data source name, such as "EmployeeAccess." Next, you need to select the database you want to connect to (for example, D:\Employees\Employees.mdb). If you've created security groups for that particular MDB file, you'll need to click the Database option button under the System Database frame and then click the Database button to choose the particular SYSTEM.MDW file for this MDB. When you're finished, click the OK button to save the DSN.

You now have a DSN created that can be used to connect to the Jet database. You'll use this DSN from ADO to manipulate the data within the Access MDB file.

The ADO Data Control

Now that you have some background about connecting to a database, let's dive in and use the ADO data control. The data control allows you to connect information in a table to the text boxes, check boxes, and other controls on your form. By connecting a data control to the different controls on your form, you're able to view and edit data without writing a line of code. Figure 12.8 shows you what the data control looks like in the toolbox.

To use the ADO data control, select Project, Components from the Visual Basic menu. Select Microsoft ADO Data Control 6.0 (OLEDB) from the list of available components. Once you add this component to your project, a new tool is added to the toolbox (see Figure 12.8).

FIGURE 12.8
The ADO data control in the toolbox.

The data control will build a set of records based on either a table name in your database, a query in your database, or even a SELECT SQL statement. Each column in this set of records is then matched up to each control on your form through properties you set in those controls. If the name of the column in the recordset matches the name of the column in your control, the information from the recordset is moved into your control. Figure 12.9 shows how the data moves to and from the data control to the controls on your form.

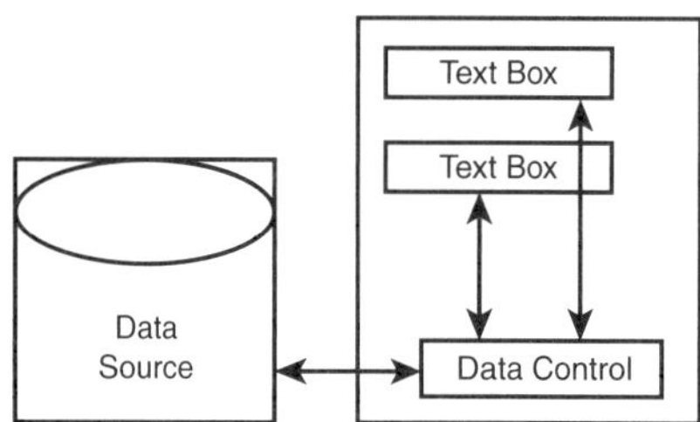

FIGURE 12.9 Data control data movement.

When you place a data control on a form, it's able to interact with text boxes, check boxes, and many other "data-aware" controls. It does this via properties you set on the controls. These controls, once set, inform the data control how to get and set the data they contain.

Moving Through Records with the Data Control

The data control does not look like much at first glance, but it actually gives you a lot of power. After you set just a few properties, the data control can go out to the requested data source and retrieve a set of records. This returned set of records is an ADO Recordset object. You can then move through this set of records by clicking the four record movement areas of this control, as shown in Figure 12.10.

Each time you click one of the record movement buttons, the data control moves to that record in the table. Then the data control retrieves the data from the table and places it in the appropriate controls, based on the properties you set. Before you learn about the properties, let's first look at the concept of a *recordset*.

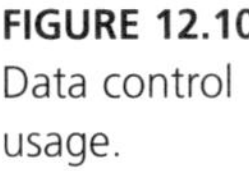

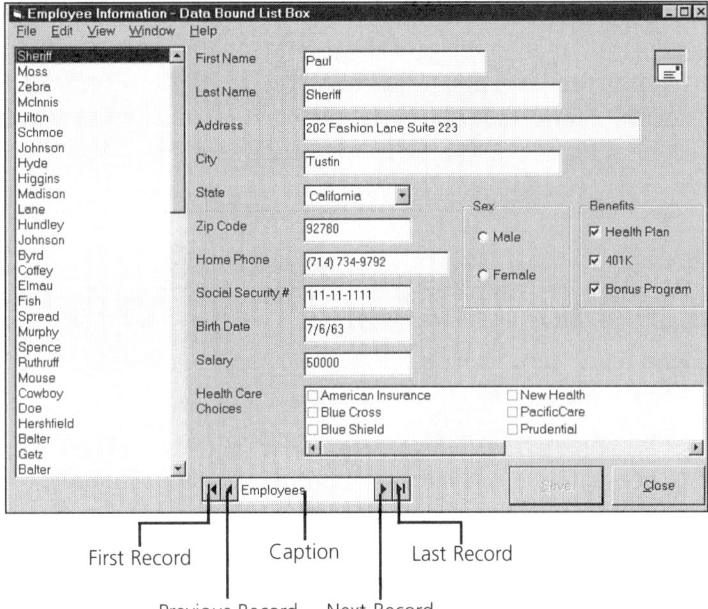

FIGURE 12.10
Data control usage.

Recordsets

You can think of a recordset as an array of records that come from the database. A recordset allows you to move forward and backward through the records. A recordset is also referred to as a *cursor*. As you move through the recordset, it keeps track of which record you're in. You have the ability to move to the next record, to the previous record, and even to the first and last records. When you hit the first record in the recordset, a "phantom" record appears before this record. When you move before the first row and are positioned on this phantom record, you're at the *beginning of file* (BOF). When you hit the last record in the recordset, another "phantom" record appears after the last real record in the set. When you move past the last row and are positioned on this phantom record, you're at the *end of file* (EOF). Figure 12.11 shows a stylized view of a recordset.

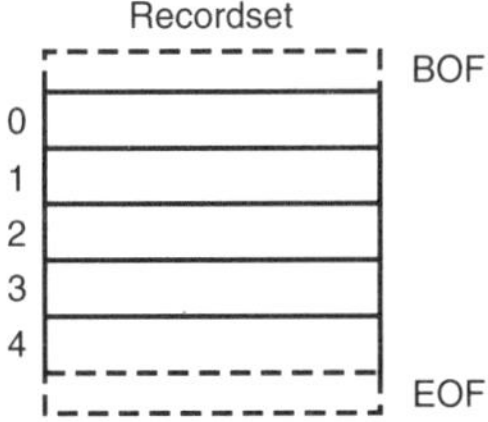

FIGURE 12.11
A recordset is an array of data.

If you've used Microsoft Access, you're familiar with the concept of a *datasheet*. This is a display of all the rows and columns in a particular table. A datasheet is nothing more than a recordset. You know that at the last record is a record that has an asterisk (*) next to it; this is the phantom record, and it's where you can add a new record to the table. Microsoft Access does not show the phantom record before the first record in the table.

EXERCISE

LOOK AT THE EXAMPLE DATABASE

1. Find the Employees.mdb file on the companion Web Site for this book and copy it to a directory on your hard drive somewhere.
2. Open this MDB file in Microsoft Access.
3. Double-click the tblEmployees table to view the datasheet.

In the examples that come with this book, you'll find an Access database called Employees.mdb. This file has many tables in it, one of which is an employee table called *tblEmployees*. In this chapter, you'll connect this employee table up to the employee form you've been building in this book.

Cursor Types

There's a property on the data control that determines the type of cursor you want to use. Which cursor type you choose determines what you can do with the resulting record set. You can use a *forward-only* cursor if all you're using this recordset for is to load a list box one time, and you don't need to use the cursor after this loading. You may also use a *dynamic* cursor if you want to view all changes made to the underlying table, and you want to make changes to the table. This type of cursor is very expensive on both the server and the client. The other type of updatable cursor is called a *keyset*. This type of cursor is not as expensive as a dynamic cursor, but it still allows updates. You'll be able to see other users' changes and deletes, but you won't be able to see records that users add. The last type of cursor is a *static* cursor. This type of cursor is fully scrollable (can move forward and backward) but may not be updatable.

ADO Data Control Properties

There's a standard set of properties you'll set most frequently with the ADO data control. Table 12.2 shows a list of these properties and provides a description of what they do.

Table 12.2 Data Control Properties

Property	Description
`Align`	Aligns the data control to either the top, left, bottom, or right of the form.
`BOFAction`	Set this property to what you want to have happen when the user scrolls the data control to the first record in the recordset. Valid options for this property are to have it stay on the first real record in the recordset or to have it move to the phantom record.
`Caption`	This is the area between the movement buttons that you can use to display the name of the table or even the number or records in the recordset.
`CommandType`	The four different types of commands are Unknown, Text, Table, and Stored Procedure. These are related to the ADO `Command` object, which you'll learn about later.
`ConnectionString`	This connection string is what's used to connect to the data source itself. You can write this yourself or you can pop up a dialog box to have the user fill this in by answering a series of questions. This property can be set at runtime, which you may do if you need to change server names in case one server goes down and you need to switch to another.
`ConnectionTimeOut`	Set this to the number of seconds you want to wait for a connection. The default is 15 seconds. You can set this to any amount or to zero (0) to wait indefinitely. This value is subject to change based on how busy your server is, and even how busy your network is. You may want to make this a value that the user can change in his or her configuration.

continues

Table 12.2 Continued

Property	Description
`CursorLocation`	This property determines where the cursor is located. It can be set to either the client side or server side. If you place the cursor on the client side, you'll get an additional structure on your workstation to handle the movement through the recordset. If you place the cursor on the server side, this information will stay on the server. There are pluses and minuses to both of these methods. If you have the cursor on the workstation, you'll cause more network traffic. If you leave it on the server, your server can become overburdened. There is no easy answer here, so you need to be able to change this as your application warrants.
`EOFAction`	This property determines what happens when you scroll to the last real record in the recordset. You can set it to `0-MoveLast` (the default), or you can set it to `1-EOF` or `2-AddNew`. If set it to `1-EOF`, the user will be left with a blank record on the screen. If it's set to `2-AddNew`, the user can enter a new record and then press any of the other record movement buttons to save that record.
`Mode`	There are many different modes you can set for this database connection. For example, you can open the data source for read-only or exclusive use. See the online help for more information.
`Orientation`	This property allows you to orient the data control vertically or horizontally.
`Password`	This is the password you'll use to log into the data source. This property might not be required, depending on the data source.
`RecordSource`	This property can be filled in with the name of a table or query. It may also be a SQL `SELECT` statement.
`UserName`	This is the login ID you'll use to log into the data source. This property might not be required, depending on the data source.

Using the Data Control

Let's now discuss how to add a data control to the Employee Information form and connect it to the text boxes and check boxes on the form. The idea is to connect a table in a database directly to the text boxes and other controls on your form so you don't have to write a lot of code to be able to interact with the database. After you finish hooking up the text boxes and check boxes, your form should look like the one shown in Figure 12.12 when you run it.

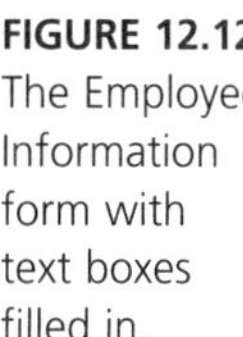

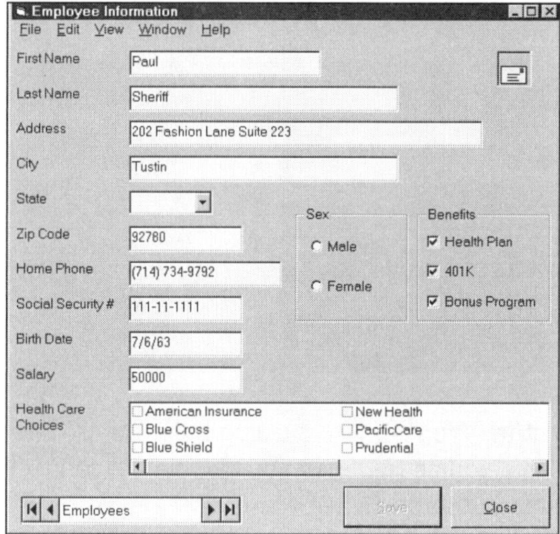

FIGURE 12.12
The Employee Information form with text boxes filled in.

Example's Filename: Employee1.frm

EXERCISE

LOOK AT THE PROPERTY PAGE FOR AN ADO DATA CONTROL

1. Add a data control to your form and set the `Name` property to `datEmployees`.
2. Set the `Caption` property to `Employees`.
3. Click the (Custom) property to bring up the property pages and then read the next section.

The Custom property will bring up the property pages for the ADO Data Control. Using the property pages is much easier than setting individual properties in the Property Window.

Using the Property Pages

The easiest way to configure the ADO data control is through the property pages. After adding a data control to your form, you should click on the (Custom) property to bring up the property pages for this control. See Figure 12.13 for an example of how you might set up a connection for an Access MDB file.

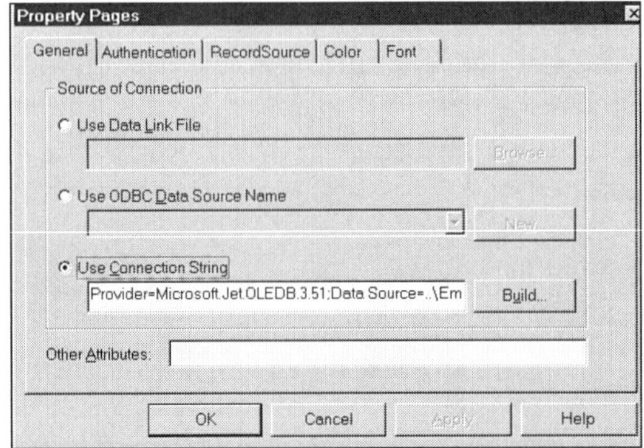

FIGURE 12.13 The property page for the `Connection String` property.

Under the General tab of the Property Pages dialog box, you can select Use Data Link File or Use ODBC Data Source Name, or you can build a connection string by clicking the `Build` command button. When you click the Build command button, you bring up the Data Link Properties dialog box, as shown in Figure 12.14. This dialog box is where you can build the connection string that ADO uses to connect to your data source.

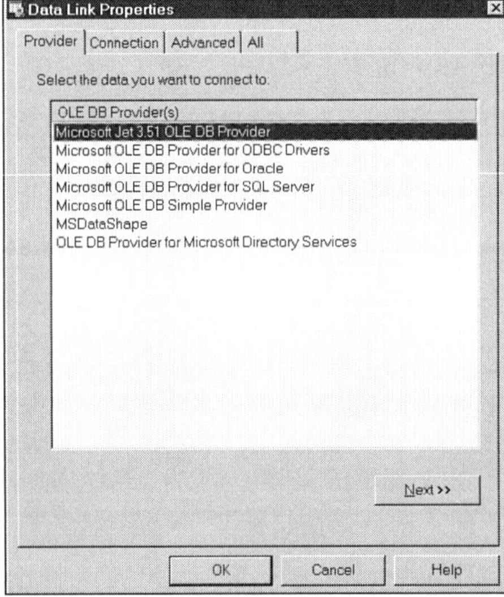

FIGURE 12.14 The Data Link Properties dialog box.

In the Data Link Properties dialog box, you're prompted to select an OLE DB provider. After you select which provider you want, click the Next button to specify connection information, such as the name of an Access database. If you choose the Microsoft Jet 3.51 OLE DB Provider option from the list and then click Next, you'll see the dialog box shown in Figure 12.15. In the Connection tab of this dialog box, select or enter a full path and filename of where your database is located.

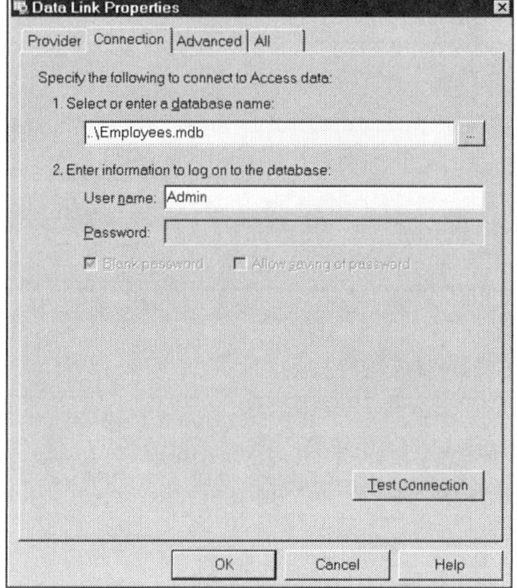

FIGURE 12.15 The Connection tab of the Data Link Properties dialog box.

After configuring this information, you can click the OK button to have the connection string written back to the property page for the ADO data control.

After configuring the data source, you should move to the RecordSource tab of the Property Pages dialog box for the data control and create a `SELECT` statement that retrieves information from the table you want. In Figure 12.16, you can see that the statement `SELECT * FROM tblEmployees` has been entered.

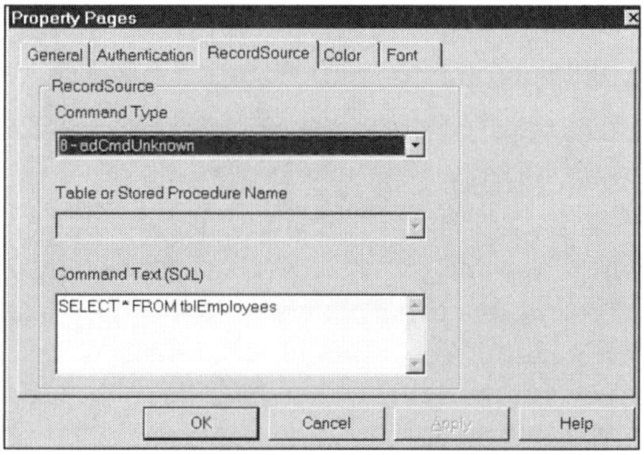

FIGURE 12.16 The property page for the `RecordSource` property.

EXERCISE

Set the SQL String for the RecordSource

1. Set the Command Text (SQL) property on the RecordSource tab in the ADO property page to `SELECT * FROM tblEmployees`.

Setting this property to an SQL string tells the Data Control where to get the information to build the Recordset object.

Setting the Text Boxes to Display Data

Now that you've set the data control to the appropriate data source and SQL statement. It's time to connect the fields in the table to the text boxes on your form. To connect the data in the table to the text boxes and check boxes, follow the steps shown in the next exercise.

EXERCISE

Hook Up the Data Control to Text Boxes

1. Click once on the First Name text box to give it focus.
2. Set the `DataSource` property to `datEmployees`. This is the name of the data control.
3. Click the `DataField` property to give it focus.
4. Click the drop-down arrow next to the property to display a drop-down list of field names.
5. Select the sFirst_nm field from the list.
6. Repeat these steps for each of the text boxes and the check boxes on the form. Just skip any of the other controls for now.

When you're finished, you should be able to run the project and see the data from the employee table. You can click the record movement buttons on the data control to move from one record to another.

Editing Records

You're able to edit any of the data in the text boxes simply by typing into those text boxes. To save the changes you make, click any of the record movement buttons to move to another record. This saves any of the changed data in the text boxes back to the table.

Adding Records

To add a new record to a table using the data control, you need to set the `EOFAction` property to a value other than the default.

EXERCISE

ADDING NEW RECORDS AT RUNTIME

1. Set the `EOFAction` property to `2-adDoAddNew`.
2. Run the project again.
3. Click the Move Last button to move to the last record. Click once on the Move Next button to move to the phantom record. You should now have a blank screen in which to add a new record.
4. Add another employee to this form.
5. Click the Move First button to save the newly added record.
6. Click the Move Last button to see the new record.

The Data Control allows you to add new records on-the-fly just by setting a property.

Summary

Using the ADO data control allows you to create database applications with very little effort. Using just a few properties and some code, you can make a complete add, edit, and delete data entry form. There are many data-aware controls that automatically interact with the data control—just by you setting some properties. Data-bound combo boxes, list boxes, and grid controls further round out your ability to create very nice database interfaces with very little coding.

Review Questions

1. Which property do you click to bring up the property pages for a data control?
2. What two properties must you set on each text box to have the data control automatically fill in field information?
3. Which control would you use if you had to display multiple columns?

13

Data Control Programming

NOW THAT YOU'VE LEARNED TO CREATE data entry forms using the ADO data control, let's program that data control to perform other operations on the data. For example, you may want to have the user cancel changes made to the data, save the data by clicking a command button, validate the data before saving, and be able to delete records. To accomplish all this, you need to write some code in the different events of the data control.

Chapter Objectives

- Create a form that adds, edits, and deletes data from a table
- Validate data
- Retrieve a count of the number of records
- Add your own record movement command buttons

Sample Project File: \Chapter13\DCProgramming.vbp

The *Recordset* Property

When a form loads that has a data control on it, the data control will use the properties that have been set, such as the `Connection` and `RecordSource` properties, to attempt to open a recordset before the `Form_Load` event. If everything is set correctly, a recordset is created and a reference to that recordset is contained in the `Recordset` property of the data control. The `Recordset` property can only be set and read at runtime.

Properties of the *Recordset* Object

Because the recordset is an object, it has properties and methods just like a text box control or a data control, which are also objects. Table 13.1 is a list of the most commonly used properties of the `Recordset` object.

Table 13.1 Properties of the *Recordset* Object

Property	Description
`BOF`	Returns `True` if the cursor is positioned before the first record in the recordset.
`Bookmark`	Returns a value that marks or sets a position in the recordset. This is similar to the primary key of the table—it's a unique value. You can use this value to hold the location of a particular record, move to other records, and then return to the record you marked.
`EditMode`	Returns a value that indicates whether the user is adding, editing, or just browsing the data in a recordset.
`EOF`	Returns `True` if the Cursor is positioned after the last record in the recordset.

Property	Description
`RecordCount`	This property is set to the number of records in the recordset. This property might not be available immediately after opening the data control. All records in the recordset need to be read before this will have a true count of the records. The only reliable way to ensure this is accurate, is to scroll all the way through the records until you hit the EOF.

Check for Beginning and End of File

When you're using the `Recordset` property, you'll be constantly checking to see where you are within the recordset. As you move forward and backward through this cursor, you may eventually hit the beginning or the end of the file. You'll use the `BOF` and `EOF` properties to check for these conditions. Table 13.2 shows the different values that these properties can have, as well as what they mean when taken together.

Table 13.2 *BOF* and *EOF* Properties

BOF Value	EOF Value	Description
`True`	`False`	The record pointer is before the first record in the recordset.
`False`	`True`	The record pointer is after the last record in the recordset.
`True`	`True`	There are no rows at all in the recordset.
`False`	`False`	The current record is valid. However, if you've just deleted the current record and have not moved to a new record, these properties will not be changed, and you're on an invalid record.

Methods of the *Recordset* Object

Using the `Recordset` property of the data control, you can programmatically control the operation of the `Recordset` object to move, add, edit, delete, and validate the data in the recordset. Table 13.3 is a list of the most common methods used with the `Recordset` property to perform these operations.

Table 13.3 Methods of the *Recordset* Object

Method	Description
`AddNew`	Adds a new record to the recordset.
`CancelUpdate`	Cancels a pending `AddNew` or `Edit` method.
`Close`	Closes a recordset.
`Delete`	Deletes the current record.
`Find`	Finds a particular record in a recordset based on a search string. If the record you're searching for doesn't exist, the recordset will be placed at the end of the file.
`MoveFirst`	Moves to the first record in the recordset.
`MoveLast`	Moves to the last record in the recordset.
`MoveNext`	Moves to the next record in the recordset.
`MovePrevious`	Moves to the previous record in the recordset.
`Requery`	Rebuilds the complete recordset by rereading the data from the table in the database. You might do this when there are many users changing data at the same time. This allows you to see the other users' additions and/or changes.
`Update`	Updates the current record with the values in the controls.

Events of the ADO Data Control

The ADO data control has a lot of events that are fired when you perform operations on the data control, the recordset, and even the fields. You need to learn about the different events as well as the order in which those events occur—this will be paramount to you using the data control efficiently. Most of the events you'll learn about in the ADO data control have a "before" and an "after" event. The "before" events start with the word *Will*, and the "after" events end with the word *Complete* in the name of the event (see Table 13.4).

Table 13.4 Events of the ADO Data Control

Event	Description
`EndOfRecordset`	This event fires when you're at the end of the `Recordset` object.
`Error`	This event fires when an error occurs when the user attempts to access the data source or the records in the recordset.

Event	Description
`WillChangeField`	This event happens before a change is made to a field object in the recordset. You can use this event to validate a particular value in one of the fields and even cancel the pending operation.
`FieldChangeComplete`	This event is called after the value of one or more field objects has changed.
`WillMove`	This event fires prior to the user moving to a new record in the recordset.
`MoveComplete`	This event fires after a move has happened in the data control either forward, backward, or to a specific record.
`WillChangeRecord`	This event fires prior to the user changing a record.
`RecordChangeComplete`	This event fires after a record has been changed.
`WillChangeRecordset`	This event fires before a recordset is rebuilt or refreshed from the underlying data source.
`RecordsetChangeComplete`	This event fires after the recordset has been rebuilt or refreshed from the underlying data source.

Order of Events

The order in which these events occur in the ADO data control is very important and is something you must learn. The ADO data control loads even before the form is loaded. First, the `Form_Initialize()` event occurs; then the `WillMove` and `MoveComplete` events occur twice in a row. Lastly, the `Form_Load()` event occurs. In the first example in this chapter, I've placed several `Debug.Print` statements to show the order of the events.

EXERCISE

Look at Events for Data Control

1. Load the sample project for this chapter.
2. Bring up the Immediate window by pressing Ctrl+G.
3. Run the sample project.
4. Click the first command button to run the first sample form.
5. You should see results appear in the Immediate window in the order they occur (see Figure 13.1).

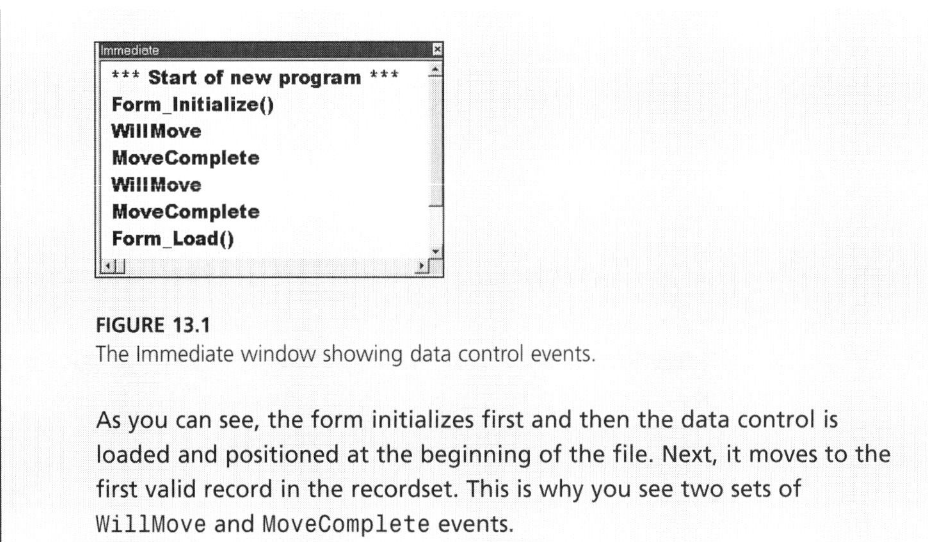

FIGURE 13.1
The Immediate window showing data control events.

Analysis/ Summary

As you can see, the form initializes first and then the data control is loaded and positioned at the beginning of the file. Next, it moves to the first valid record in the recordset. This is why you see two sets of `WillMove` and `MoveComplete` events.

Modifying Data Programmatically

Let's now add the ability to insert records into and delete records from the recordset. Let's also add the ability to cancel any changes made when editing and to cancel the insertion of a new record. Figure 13.2 is an example of what your Employee Information form might look like with the new command buttons for adding, saving, and deleting data.

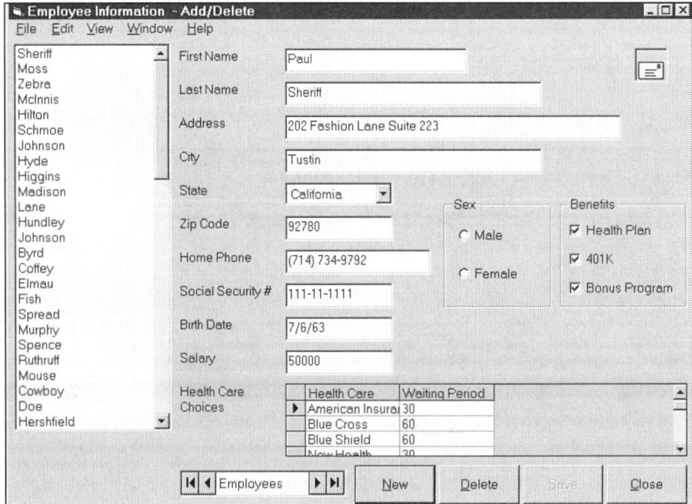

FIGURE 13.2
The command buttons.

Example's Filename: Employee1.frm

EXERCISE

Create Commands for the Data Control

1. Set the `Enabled` property of the Save button to `False`.
2. Add a command button to the Employee Information form and place it next to the Save button.
3. Set the `Name` property to `cmdDelete`.
4. Set the `Caption` property to `&Delete`.
5. Add another command button and place it next to the Delete button.
6. Set the `Name` property to `cmdNew`.
7. Set the `Caption` property to `&New`.
8. You may need to shrink the size of all the command buttons to get them all to fit.

Using command buttons is just one technique of allowing the user to interact with the Data Control. You could also use menus and/or toolbars.

Adding Records

Forcing the user to move to the end of the recordset just to add a new record is not a very good user interface technique. Therefore, let's program the New command button so that the user can add a new record at any time.

EXERCISE

Adding Code to the New Command Button

1. Double-click the New button to bring up a code window.
2. Add the following code to the `Click` event of the New button:

```
Private Sub cmdNew_Click()
    datEmployees.Recordset.AddNew
    txtFirst.SetFocus
End Sub
```

In the Click event of the cmdNew command button, you invoke the AddNew method on the Recordset object of the data control. This actually moves the record pointer to the phantom record in the recordset. By moving to the phantom record, the data control will update the controls bound to it. Because the phantom record is blank, all blank data will display in the controls, which signifies to the user that a new record can be entered. You also set the focus to the txtFirst text box using the SetFocus method.

Saving the Data

Once the buttons have been toggled to their opposite state, about the only thing the user can do is click the Save or Cancel button. You now need to add the code under the Save command button and the Cancel command button to perform their respective actions. Under the `Click` event of the Save button, you'll use the `Update` method of the `Recordset` object to move the data from the controls into the recordset, which will then update the table in the database.

EXERCISE

Adding Code to the Save Button

1. Add the following code under the cmdSave command button by double-clicking on the Save command button.

```
Private Sub cmdSave_Click()
    Dim boolAdding As Boolean

    boolAdding = (datEmployees.Recordset.EditMode = adEditAdd)

    datEmployees.Recordset.Update
    If boolAdding Then
        datEmployees.Recordset.MoveLast
    End If
    Call ToggleButtons
End Sub
```

The first thing you need to check in the Save command button's Click event is to see whether you're in add or edit mode. You can do this by checking the EditMode property of the Recordset object against a constant adEditAdd. You'll use this flag to determine whether you stay on the current row after you update the recordset (as in the case of Edit) or move to the last row in the recordset (as in the case of AddNew).

After updating the recordset with the new record, you need to move to the last row in the recordset if you're adding a new record. All new rows are added to the end of the recordset, so you need to apply the MoveLast method to position yourself on this new record. After you're positioned on the new record, call the ToggleButtons routine to reset the command buttons and the data control back to their normal state. You'll see the code for this ToggleButtons routine later in the chapter.

Detecting Changes in Data

When you want to add the ability to save data programmatically instead of having the data control save it when the user moves off the changed record, you need to start understanding all the Change events that occur when you modify data in the bound controls.

The Change events are those events that occur when you modify data in data-bound controls such as text boxes. This modification can happen either by the user typing a new value into a control or by moving to a new record in the data control. These data-bound controls communicate changes to the ADO data control so that it can fire its events in response to these changes.

If you're just saving the changed record using the Update method of the Recordset object of the data control, a certain event order will occur:

- WillChangeRecord
- WillChangeField
- FieldChangeComplete
- RecordChangeComplete

If you've changed data in the bound controls and then click a button on the data control to move to a new record, a different event order occurs:

- WillMove
- WillChangeField
- FieldChangeComplete

- WillChangeRecord
- RecordChangeComplete
- MoveComplete

If you've used the Jet data control, you'll notice one very important difference between that data control and the ADO data control. When you're using the Jet data control, the `Change` events on the data bound controls occur prior to the `Reposition` event occurring. The `Reposition` event is analogous to the `MoveComplete` event. However, the `MoveComplete` event will happen before the `Change` events for the bound controls occur. This means you need to come up with a different mechanism to determine when a change is triggered in a data-bound control. You need to determine whether the change was made by a user typing or moving the data control to a new record.

A method I use to solve this problem is to move all the values into the `Tag` property of every data-bound control when the user positions to a new record. Then I compare the value in the `Tag` property with what's in the `Text` property to see whether they're different. If the values are different, I know that the user just made the change as opposed to just moving to a new record with the data control.

To accomplish this, I first create a routine to move all the values from the new record into the `Tag` properties. In the `MoveComplete` method, I call a routine I've named `ControlsTagLoad()`:

```
Private Sub datEmployees_MoveComplete(_
            ByVal adReason As ADODB.EventReasonEnum, _
            ByVal pError As ADODB.Error, _
            adStatus As ADODB.EventStatusEnum, _
            ByVal pRecordset As ADODB.Recordset)
   Debug.Print "MoveComplete"

   If pRecordset.EOF Or pRecordset.BOF Then
   Else
      Call ControlsTagLoad(pRecordset)
   End If

End Sub
```

In the MoveComplete event, I check to see whether the user is at the end or beginning of the file. If he or she is not at either end, I call a routine I've named ControlsTagLoad. I pass into this routine the Recordset object that was passed into the MoveComplete event. I use this Recordset object to load the Tag properties:

```
Private Sub ControlsTagLoad(pRecordset As ADODB.Recordset)
   Dim oCtrl As Control

   If pRecordset.EOF Or pRecordset.BOF Then
      For Each oCtrl In Me.Controls
         If TypeOf oCtrl Is TextBox Then
            oCtrl.Tag = ""
         ElseIf TypeOf oCtrl Is CheckBox Then
            oCtrl.Tag = vbUnchecked
         End If
      Next
   Else
      For Each oCtrl In Me.Controls
         If TypeOf oCtrl Is TextBox Then
            oCtrl.Tag = _
        Field2Str(pRecordset(oCtrl.DataField).Value)
         ElseIf TypeOf oCtrl Is CheckBox Then
            oCtrl.Tag = _
        Field2CheckBox(pRecordset(oCtrl.DataField).Value)
         End If
      Next
   End If
End Sub
```

Remember that the normal value properties (Text and Value) have not been set to the new value yet, and the Change event has not yet been fired. In this routine, I load the Tag properties of each data-bound control with the data that's about to be put into the value properties of those controls.

There's also a special case that needs to be taken into account. If the recordset is at EOF or BOF, the user can't access the recordset, so I need to set the Tag property to either a blank string or to the value of vbUnchecked for check boxes. If the user is not at EOF or BOF, I can loop through each of the controls in the Controls collection of the form and check for either a text box or a check box. (You may need to change this routine for each form if you have other types of bound controls on this form.) If the current control is a text box, I then set the `Tag` property of the text box to the value from the `Recordset` object, where the name of the field is equal to the name of the field in the `DataField` property of that text box. I perform the same type of assignment for the check boxes as well.

The *Change* Event

Now that you've synchronized all the data in the value of the data-bound controls, you now need to look at how to toggle the command buttons at the appropriate time in response to a user typing in or moving to a new record.

Let's add code to the `Change` event of the text box controls. This code will help you determine whether the user typed in data or just moved to a new record. In the `Change` event, you need to check to see whether the `Tag` property is equal to the `Text` property. If they are not equal, you know that the user just made a change to the text box. If they're the same, you know that the user just moved from one record to another using the data control:

```
Private Sub txtFirst_Change()
   If txtFirst.Tag <> txtFirst.Text Then
      Call TextChanged
   End If
End Sub
Private Sub txtLast_Change()
   If txtLast.Tag <> txtLast.Text Then
      Call TextChanged
   End If
End Sub
```

EXERCISE

ADD CODE TO THE *CHANGE* EVENTS

1. Add the preceding code to the `Change` event of each text box.

   Analysis/Summary By adding this code to the Change events of each text box you can detect when the user makes changes to the data.

The *TextChanged()* Procedure

The `TextChanged()` procedure, shown in the `Change` events of the text boxes, performs a couple of checks for you. First, it checks to make sure the recordset is on a valid record. If it is on a valid record, the `TextChanged()` procedure then checks to see whether the Save command button has already been toggled to `Enabled`. If it has, you know that the user has made changes and there's no need to call the `ToggleButtons` procedure to toggle the command buttons to become disabled. You'll learn more about the `ToggleButtons` procedure in the next section:

```
Private Sub TextChanged()
   If datEmployees.Recordset.EOF Or _
      datEmployees.Recordset.BOF Then
      ' Do Nothing
   Else
      If Not cmdSave.Enabled Then
         Call ToggleButtons
      End If
   End If
End Sub
```

Toggling the Command Buttons

Once the user enters the edit or add mode, you'll need to turn off the New and Delete buttons so that the user doesn't try to add or delete records while editing data. In addition, you'll need to enable the Save command button so that the user can save the changes just made. You should also disable the data list box and the data control so that the user can't move to a new record until he or she commits or cancels the changes just made. The `ToggleButtons` routine sets the `Enabled` property of each of these controls to the appropriate state.

EXERCISE

ADDING THE *TOGGLEBUTTONS* PROCEDURE

1. Add a general form procedure called `ToggleButtons`, as follows:

```
Private Sub ToggleButtons()
   If cmdClose.Caption = "&Close" Then
      cmdClose.Caption = "&Cancel"
   Else
      cmdClose.Caption = "&Close"
   End If
   cmdSave.Enabled = Not cmdSave.Enabled
   cmdNew.Enabled = Not cmdNew.Enabled
   cmdDelete.Enabled = Not cmdDelete.Enabled
   dlstEmps.Enabled = Not dlstEmps.Enabled
   datEmployees.Enabled = Not datEmployees.Enabled
End Sub
```

In the ToggleButtons routine, you change the Caption of the Close command button to become Cancel. This avoids you having to place another command button on the form just to cancel changes made to the form. In addition, you'll toggle all the Enabled properties the command buttons, the DataList control, and the data control to be the opposite of what they are now. When the user first enters the add or edit mode, this will make sure the user finishes what he or she is doing before performing any other actions. After the user saves the data, you can then call the ToggleButtons routine again. This will turn these controls back to their original state.

Deleting Data

At some point, the user will probably need to delete a record from a table. In order to accomplish this, you need to apply the `Delete` method to the `Recordset` object. The `Delete` method deletes the current row from the underlying base table and from the recordset.

EXERCISE

Add Code to the Delete Command Button

1. Double-click the Delete command button.
2. Add the following code to the `cmdDelete_Click` event:

```
Private Sub cmdDelete_Click()
    Dim intResponse As Integer

    Beep
    intResponse = MsgBox("Delete the current Employee", _
                         vbYesNo + vbQuestion, _
                         "Delete Employee")
    If intResponse = vbYes Then
        datEmployees.Recordset.Delete
        Call DataReposition
    End If
End Sub
```

After a user deletes a record, that record will become invalid in the recordset, so you need to move off that record. The user has the choice of moving forward to the next record, moving backward to the previous record, or maybe moving to the first or last record. The best way to handle this is to create a routine called `DataReposition` to perform this movement. By creating a procedure, you'll be better able to reuse this code in other forms where you need the same functionality.

EXERCISE

Create the Reposition Procedure for the Data Control

1. Create a general form procedure called `DataReposition`.
2. Add the following code:

```
Private Sub DataReposition()
    With datEmployees.Recordset
        .MoveNext
        If .EOF Then
            .MovePrevious
        End If
    End With
End Sub
```

In this routine you perform a `MoveNext` method to move to the record after the one just deleted. After you perform a `MoveNext`, you might hit the end of the file. Therefore, immediately after moving to the next record, you need to check the EOF property. If you've hit the EOF, you should perform a `MovePrevious` method to move to a valid record.

Canceling Changes

If the user clicks the New command button or types a character into a data-bound control by mistake, he or she will need some way to cancel out of that mode without having to close the entire form. As you'll remember, you toggled the `Caption` of the Close command button to Cancel, so in the `Click` event of the cmdClose button, you need to write some code to provide a way to cancel out of the adding or editing of the data.

EXERCISE

ADD CODE TO THE CLOSE COMMAND BUTTON

1. Double-click the Close command button and add the following code:

```
Private Sub cmdClose_Click()
    If cmdClose.Caption = "&Close" Then
        Unload Me
    Else
        datEmployees.Recordset.CancelUpdate
        If datEmployees.Recordset.EditMode <> adEditAdd Then
            datEmployees.Recordset.Move 0
        End If
        Call ToggleButtons
    End If
End Sub
```

In this event procedure, you first need to check to see whether the `Caption` property of the Close command button is equal to `&Close`. If it is, you know that the user has not entered an editing mode and can therefore unload the form. If it's not equal to `&Close`, then the `Caption` must be equal to `&Cancel`, which means you need to cancel the updating of data from happening. You apply the `CancelUpdate` method to the Recordset object of the data control to cancel the AddNew or editing of data from happening. If the recordset is in edit mode, you need to refresh the current record on the form. To do this, check the `EditMode` property of the `Recordset` object to verify that you're not doing an add operation. If this is the case, simply use the `Move` method to move zero records from the current record. This forces the data control to refresh all the controls on the form with the values in the recordset. The last thing to do is to toggle the command buttons back to their original nonediting state by calling `ToggleButtons` one more time.

Validating Data

When the user enters data into the text boxes, you may need to make sure the data is valid before you commit the data to the database. You can use a couple different methods to validate the data. Let's look at how you do this with the ADO data control.

Example's Filename: Employee2.frm

When the user clicks the Save button, you apply the `Update` method to the `Recordset` object of the data control. This method causes a couple events to occur prior to the data being committed to the database. You have the option of stopping the commit from taking place by setting a parameter in one of these events to a certain value. The event that you'll learn about now is called `WillChangeRecord`. This event fires just before the record is about to be changed. The first parameter passed to this event, called `adReason`, tells you the reason why this event is being called. In this case, it's because the `Update` method was invoked. It will also pass in an `adStatus` parameter that you can set to a particular constant to stop the update from happening.

EXERCISE

1. Type in the `WillChangeRecord` event, as shown here, for the `Employee` data control:

```
Private  Sub datEmployees_WillChangeRecord(_
         ByVal adReason As ADODB.EventReasonEnum, _
         ByVal cRecords As Long, _
         adStatus As ADODB.EventStatusEnum, _
         ByVal pRecordset As ADODB.Recordset)
    Dim strErr As String
    Debug.Print "WillChangeRecord"

    If Not datEmployees.Recordset.EOF And _
       Not datEmployees.Recordset.BOF Then
       If Trim$(txtFirst.Text) = "" Then
          strErr = strErr & _
             "First Name must be filled in" & vbCrLf
       End If
       If Trim$(txtLast.Text) = "" Then
          strErr = strErr & _
             "Last Name must be filled in" & vbCrLf
       End If
       If Trim$(txtBirthDate.Text) <> "" Then
          If Not IsDate(txtBirthDate.Text) Then
             strErr = strErr & _
                "Birth Date is not a valid date" & vbCrLf
          End If
       End If
```

```
        If strErr <> "" Then
           MsgBox strErr, vbExclamation, "Data Error"
           mboolError = True
           adStatus = adStatusCancel
        End If
     End If
End Sub
```

In this routine, you should check all the controls on the form that must be filled in with correct data. If any of these are in error, create a string value that lists each error in turn. At the end of the routine, you can check this string to see whether it's filled in. If so, you can display a message box with this error string to inform the user of the problems with the fields on the form. In addition, you might also want to set a module-level variable called `mboolError` to a `True` value to communicate back to the `cmdSave_Click()` event that an error occurred in the data.

You also need to stop the update to the base table from happening. To do this, you set the `adStatus` argument to the constant `adStatusCancel`. This informs the data control to abort the updating of the table.

EXERCISE

DETECTING ERRORS

1. Add a module-level variable called `mboolError` to the (General) (Declarations) section of the Employee Information form.
2. Change the `cmdSave_Click()` event to check for this module-level variable:

```
Private Sub cmdSave_Click()
   Dim boolAdding As Boolean

   mboolError = False
   boolAdding = (datEmployees.Recordset.EditMode = adEditAdd)

   datEmployees.Recordset.Update
   If Not mboolError Then
      If boolAdding Then
         datEmployees.Recordset.MoveLast
      End If
```

```
            Call ToggleButtons
        End If
    End Sub
```

The lines in bold are the lines you need to add to the `cmdSave_Click()` event. First, you need to set the `mboolError` variable to a `False` value. When you call the `Update` method of the data control, the program will trigger events such as the `WillChangeRecord` event, in which you'll set the `mboolError` variable to a `True` value if any of the fields are in error. Then, after the `WillChangeRecord` event has completed, control will pass back to the line after the `Update` method in the `cmdSave_Click()` event. You can check to see whether the `mboolError` variable is still a `False` value. If it is, you know you can go to the new record and toggle the buttons back to a valid value. Otherwise, you do nothing so that the user has to fix whatever fields are in error.

Data Control Error Handling

When dealing with an external database engine, you always have the potential for errors. As such, you need to have some good error handling in your program to account for these errors. The ADO data control has a built-in event that's called when there's an error related to the database or the table and/or fields contained in the data control.

Why Do Errors Happen?

Many things can go wrong when you're using a database. As such, you need to be prepared to handle these errors. Here's a list of things that can go wrong with a database:

- Someone could have deleted the database.
- The network is down and the database is on a shared network drive.
- The database server is down.
- The database is corrupted.
- Someone has the database open for exclusive use.
- Someone has the table open for exclusive use.

These are just some of the reasons you may have an error occur when using a database. If any of these happen, the `Error` event will be triggered in the data control, and it's up to you to take some appropriate action. There are other errors that can occur, and you'll learn to deal with them in Chapter 17, "Error Handling."

Example's Filename: Employee2.frm

Error Event

An `Error` event will be fired when an error is encountered in the data control. The `Error` event is passed an error number, description, and several other parameters. Depending on the database system you're using, the error number may be the same for all errors. This is the case for Access MDB files. In this case, it's better to just display the `Description` parameter. The only other parameter you need to be familiar with is the `fCancelDisplay` parameter. You set this parameter to `True` if you're displaying the error yourself. This tells the data control not to display its error message once the `Error` event is complete. I recommend calling your own error-handling routine from this `Error` event. That way, you can call this procedure from every data control's `Error` event on the form.

EXERCISE

ADD THE *ERROR* EVENT

1. Add the following code to the `Error` event of the datEmployees data control:

```
Private Sub datEmployees_Error(_
        ByVal ErrorNumber As Long, _
        Description As String, _
        ByVal Scode As Long, _
        ByVal Source As String, _
        ByVal HelpFile As String, _
        ByVal HelpContext As Long, _
        fCancelDisplay As Boolean)

    Call DCErrorCheck(ErrorNumber, Description, fCancelDisplay)

End Sub
```

2. Next, add a module-level variable called `mboolLoadError` to the (General) (Declarations) area of this form.
3. Type in the `DCErrorCheck()` procedure, as shown here:

```
Private Sub DCErrorCheck(ByVal ErrorNumber As Long, _
                               Description As String, _
                               fCancelDisplay As Boolean)
    If Not mboolLoadError Then
        MsgBox Description
        mboolLoadError = True
        fCancelDisplay = True
    Else
        fCancelDisplay = True
    End If
End Sub
```

Analysis/ Summary

I wrote the `Error` event of the data control to call a procedure I wrote called `DCErrorCheck()`. In the `DCErrorCheck()` procedure, I check another module-level variable called `mboolLoadError` to determine whether an error has already occurred on another data control. If it has, I simply cancel the display of the error from this data control's `Error` event. This way, if I have three data controls and each one is trying to call a database that's not there, I don't get three error messages that are all the same.

EXERCISE

TEST THE ERROR HANDLING

1. Close down the Visual Basic design environment so that the data controls on the forms will release the Access MDB.
2. Rename the Employees.mdb file to another name.
3. Reload the sample project and run the example to see the error message appear.
4. You could also try opening the database for exclusive use in Access and run the example to see a different error message.
5. Don't forget to rename the database back to Employees.mdb.

You should always test your error handling using different scenarios. For example, what would happen if there were no records in the table?

Unloading the Form on an Error

If the user receives an error when the data control is loading at runtime, there's no reason to bring up the form. As such, let's add code so that the form will unload if an error occurs. Remember the `mboolLoadError` flag you set in the `DCErrorCheck()` procedure? You can use this in the `Form_Activate()` event to determine whether an error occurred when the data control was loading. Because the `Form_Activate()` event is the last event to occur after a form loads, the `mboolLoadError` variable will be set to `True` if an error has occurred. If this flag is set, you might as well unload the form.

EXERCISE

WRITE THE *FORM_ACTIVATE()* EVENT

1. Add the following code to the `Form_Activate()` event:

```
Private Sub Form_Activate()
    If mboolLoadError Then
        Unload Me
    End If
End Sub
```

Summary

Programming the data control's `Recordset` object will help you make a nicer user interface than just the normal data control. Using just a few properties and some code, you can make a complete add, edit, and delete data entry form. Error handling and data validation are important to any data entry form, and you learned how to accomplish these techniques by using the many events of the data control. Adding a `Find` method can add a nice finishing touch to your data entry form.

Review Questions

1. Which event do you use to perform data validation?
2. Which event reports back errors from the data control to your form?
3. Which property can you use to report the current record position?
4. Which method do you use to search for a particular record in the recordset?

14

Additional Data Control Topics

LET'S NOW LEARN ABOUT SOME OF THE ADDITIONAL data-aware controls that you can hook up to the ADO Data Control. You will learn to use the data-aware combo box, list box, and grid. You will also learn to display the number of records in the Recordset, create your own data movement command buttons, and find records in the Recordset.

Chapter Objectives

- Learn to use the data-aware combo box, list box, and grid
- Learn to display the number of records in the Recordset
- Create your own data movement command buttons
- Find records in the Recordset

Sample Project File: \Chapter14\DCTopics.vbp

Other Data-aware Controls

Besides text box and check box controls, other data-aware controls ship with Visual Basic—for example, the data-aware combo box, list box, and grid control can also be manipulated with the data control. These data-aware controls are very robust. Let's try each of these controls to see how they work.

Data-bound Combo Box

The data-bound combo box (DataCombo) is used when you need to load a combo box with a list of values and have that control updated to the value contained in your main table. You have a classic foreign key example within the Employee table, and you have a State ID field that relates to the State table in the same database. All the values in the State ID field must be a part of the State table. Let's add a DataCombo to your form in place of the existing State combo box. However, you'll first need to load a new component to get the DataCombo control into the toolbox.

Example's Filename: DataCombo.frm

EXERCISE

Add the Data List Controls to Your Project

1. Select Project, Components from the Visual Basic menu.
2. Check the Microsoft DataList Controls 6.0 (OLEDB) option from the list and then click the OK button.

There should be two new tools added to your toolbox after selecting this component. One is the data-bound combo box (DataCombo) and the other is the data-bound list box (DataList). Figure 14.1 shows what the DataCombo control looks like in the toolbox.

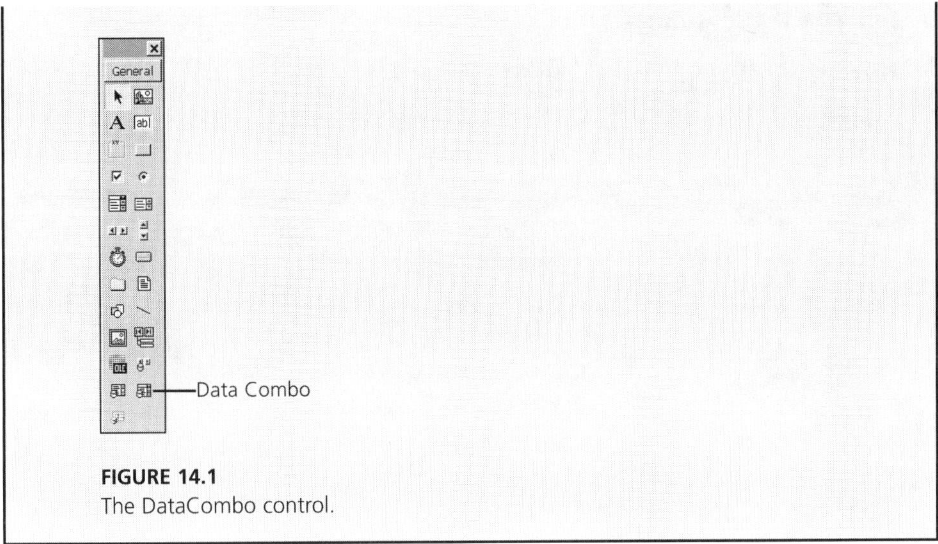

FIGURE 14.1
The DataCombo control.

DataCombo Common Properties

You'll use a few different properties to populate this control versus the standard combo box. The standard combo box control must be populated manually using the `List` property at design time or by invoking the `AddItem` method at runtime. The DataCombo control can be loaded via a connected data control. It can also be used to set the data in a related data control. This is controlled by the properties listed in Table 14.1.

Table 14.1 DataCombo Common Properties

Property	Description
`RowSource`	The name of the data control used to populate the list portion of the combo box. This means you need to add a data control to the form just for loading this combo box. You'll see the appropriate properties on this data control that will load the data into the DataCombo control.
`ListField`	The name of the field in the data control specified by the `RowSource` property used to populate the list portion of the DataCombo control.

continues

Table 14.1 Continued

Property	Description
`DataSource`	The name of the data control used when an update is made to the base table.
`DataField`	The name of the field in the SQL of the `RecordSource` property. This `RecordSource` property is the one located in the data control whose name you specified in the `DataSource` property.
`BoundColumn`	This field should match the field you're using in the `DataField` property, except this is the field that comes from the data control specified in the `RowSource` property.
`MatchEntry`	This field can be set to perform basic matching or extended drill-down–type matching when you're searching for values in the DataCombo control.

Let's now add this control to the Employee Information form.

EXERCISE

Add the DataCombo Box

1. Click once on the State combo box.
2. Press the Delete key to remove this combo box from the form.
3. Add a DataCombo control in the location where the old combo box was located.
4. Add another data control to the Employee Information form.
5. Set the `Name` property to `datStates`.
6. Set the `Caption` property to `States`.
7. Using the property pages like you did previously for the datEmployees data control, set the connection properties to the same database.
8. Set the Command Text (SQL) field on the RecordSource tab to `SELECT * FROM tblStates`.
9. Set the `Visible` property to `False`. This way, the user can't move this data control. This data control will only be used to load the combo box.
10. Click once on the DataCombo control to give it focus.
11. Set the `Name` property to `datcboStates`.

12. Set the `RowSource` property to `datStates`.
13. Set the `ListField` property to `szState_desc`.
14. Run the project at this point and click the DataCombo box to see a list of state codes in the list portion of the control.

Now that you have this combo box loaded with data, you need to synchronize it to the employee data. You want the value in the lState_id field in the Employee table to update the information in the DataCombo control. Also, you want the lState_id in the Employee table to be updated with a new value whenever the user selects a new state from the combo box.

EXERCISE

SET THE PROPERTIES OF THE DATACOMBO BOX

1. Set the `DataSource` property of the datcboStates combo box to `datEmployees`.
2. Set the `DataField` property to `lState_id`.
3. Set the `BoundColumn` property to `lState_id`.
4. Double-click the datcboStates combo box and add a call to the `TextChanged` procedure in the `Click` event.
5. Run the project. You should see the data in the combo box updated as you move to employees in different states. You should also be able to change the data and save that data back to the Employee table.

This is an easy way to present information from a foreign key table to the user. This combo box is loaded and will change as you move through the data.

Data-bound List Box

The data-bound list box (DataList) is used when you want to have a table loaded into a list box automatically by a data control. This cuts down the amount of code you need to write. The DataList control is displayed in the toolbox when you select the Microsoft Data List Controls 6.0 (OLEDB) option from the Components menu. Figure 14.2 shows what this control looks like in the toolbox.

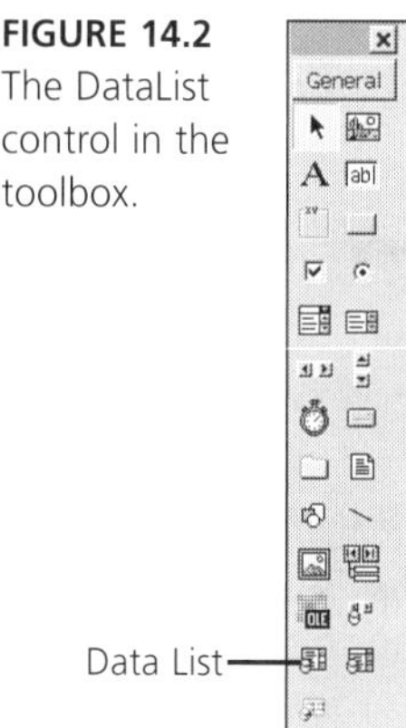

FIGURE 14.2 The DataList control in the toolbox.

DataList Common Properties

You'll use a few different properties to populate this control versus the standard list box control. The standard list box control must be populated manually using the `List` property at design time or by invoking the `AddItem` method at runtime. The DataList control, like the DataCombo control, can be loaded via a connected ADO data control. This is controlled by the properties listed in Table 14.2.

Table 14.2 DataList Common Properties

Property	Description
`RowSource`	The name of the data control used to populate the DataList control. You can create a data control just for loading this list box if you want. Of course, you could just use the same data control for loading the list as you use for the main data of your form.
`ListField`	The name of the field in the data control specified by the `RowSource` property used to populate the DataList control.
`DataSource`	The name of the data control used when an update is made to the base table.
`DataField`	The name of the field in the SQL of the `RecordSource` property. This `RecordSource` property is the one located in the data control whose name you specified in the `DataSource` property.
`BoundColumn`	This field should match the field you're using in the `DataField` property, except this is the field that comes from the data control specified in the `RowSource` property.
`MatchEntry`	This field can be set to perform basic matching or extended drill-down–type matching when you're searching for values in the DataList control.

Let's now add this control to the Employee Information form (see Figure 14.3).

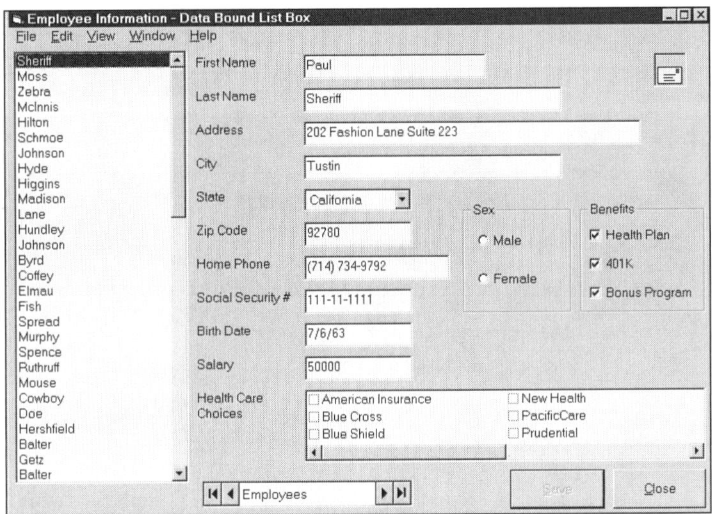

FIGURE 14.3 The DataList control on the Employee Information form.

Example's Filename: DataList.frm

EXERCISE

Add a DataList Control

1. Increase the width of the form to put a DataList control next to all the other controls.
2. Move all the custom controls over to the far right of the screen. You can select all the controls by pressing Ctrl+A; you can then move the controls as a group using your mouse.
3. Draw a DataList control next to the controls on the left side.
4. Set the `Name` property to `dlstEmp`.
5. Set the `DataSource` property to `datEmployees`.
6. Set the `DataField` property to `lEmp_id`.
7. Set the `BoundColumn` property to `lEmp_id`.
8. Set the `RowSource` property to `datEmployees`.
9. Set the `ListField` property to `szLast_nm`.

You should now be able to run this form and see the first item in the list highlighted. You can also move through the records using the command buttons, and the highlight on the list box will move.

Synchronizing the List Box

Of course, what would be even nicer on this screen is the ability to click the DataList control and have the data in the controls update to reflect the current name selected. You can do this with just a few lines of code.

EXERCISE

Add Code to the *MouseUp()* Event of the DataList

1. Double-click the DataList control.
2. Select the `MouseUp()` event from the Procedures combo box.
3. Type in the following code in this event:

```
Private Sub dlstEmp_MouseUp(Button As Integer, _
                            Shift As Integer, _
                            x As Single, _
                            y As Single)
    datEmployees.Recordset.Bookmark = dlstEmp.SelectedItem
End Sub
```

Each time the user clicks an entry in the list box, you need to tell the data control to move to that row. To accomplish this, you can use the `SelectedItem` property of the DataList control, which is a bookmark of the `Recordset` in the data control. As such, you can take this value and give it to the `Bookmark` property of the `Recordset` object of the data control. This forces the data control to move to that record, thereby updating all the bound controls on the form.

Data-bound Grid Control

The data-bound grid control (DataGrid) is a new grid that works with the ADO data control only. It's not the same grid that shipped with Visual Basic 5. Be careful that you select the Microsoft DataGrid Control 6.0 (OLEDB) option and not the Microsoft Data Bound Grid Control 5.0 option, which can be used only with Jet data controls. (Note that you might not have the version 5 grid control if you don't have Visual Basic 5 on your system.)

Grids are great for displaying multiple columns of data that otherwise might not fit in a list box. Also, a list box can't display data in neat columns without using a Windows API call, and even then the data can grow too large for a column and push the next column farther to the right. With a grid, you can have each column display within a specified width, and even have it wrap the text within the column, if you want. Figure 14.4 shows what the DataGrid control looks like in the toolbox.

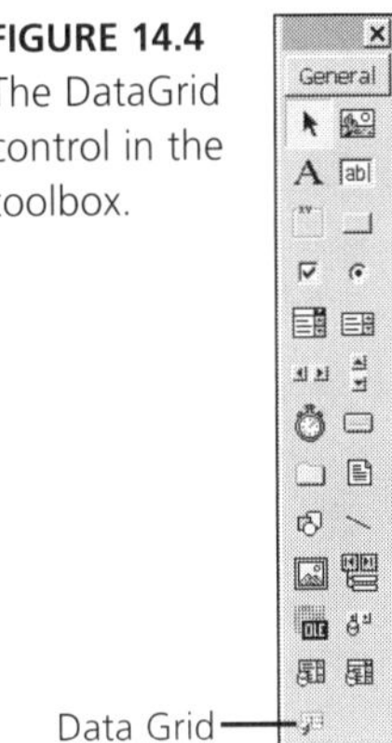

FIGURE 14.4
The DataGrid control in the toolbox.

DataGrid Common Properties

The DataGrid control has a few more properties than the other data-bound controls, and most have to do with controlling the grid's behavior. Table 14.3 shows you the list of the properties you'll most likely use.

Table 14.3 DataGrid Common Properties

Property	Description
`AllowAddNew`	Set this property to `True` if you want to allow the user to go to the last row in the grid to add a new row.
`AllowDelete`	Set this property to `True` if you want to allow the user to highlight a row and press the Delete key to delete a row from the table.
`AllowUpdate`	Set this property to `True` if you want to allow the user to update a row.
`ColumnHeaders`	Set this property to `True` if you want to have headers appear over each column.

Let's replace the list box for the health care choices on the Employee Information form with a DataGrid control that shows two fields from the tblHealthCare table. This table is also located in the Employees.mdb file that comes with the examples. Figure 14.5 shows what the form will look like after you add the DataGrid control.

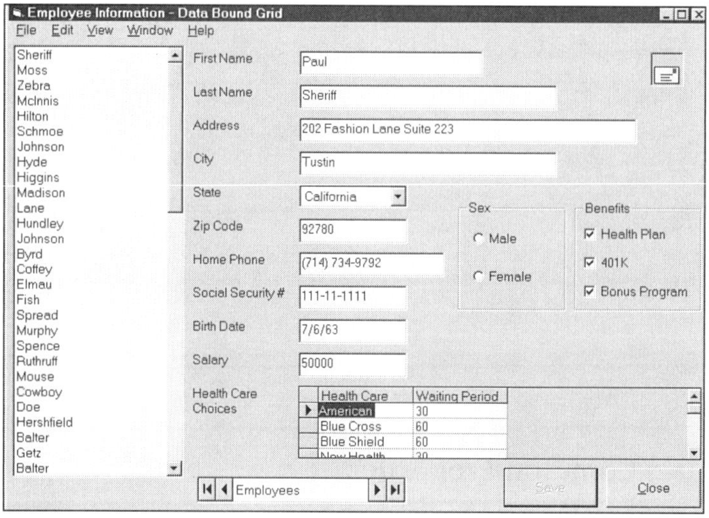

FIGURE 14.5 The DataGrid control on the Employee Information form.

Example's Filename: DataGrid.frm

EXERCISE

USING THE DATAGRID CONTROL

1. Click once on the Health Care Choices list box.
2. Press the Delete key to delete this list box.
3. Remove any code associated with this list box from the code window.
4. Add another data control to the Employee Information form.
5. Set the `Name` property to `datHealth`.
6. Set the `Caption` property to `Health`.
7. Use the property pages to set the connection to the Employees.mdb file, just like you did for the other data controls.
8. Set the `RecordSource` property to `tblHealthCare`.
9. Select Project, Components from the Visual Basic menu.
10. Select the Microsoft Data Grid Control 6.0 (OLEDB) option from the list of components.

11. Draw a DataGrid control on the form where the list box used to be.
12. Set the `Name` property to `dgrdHealth`.
13. Set the `DataSource` property to `datHealth`.
14. Set the `AllowUpdate` to `False`.

Using the DataGrid control is great when you need multiple columns of information to be displayed to the user.

Now you need to assign columns to the grid. To do this, you need to select the (Custom) property to bring up the property pages that allow you to customize the columns.

Property Pages

A *property page* is a customized view of the properties for a control. Property pages are typically used when you have repeating groups of information that you need to set as properties for a control. Using property pages is generally easier than using the simple Properties window in Visual Basic. In the Columns tab of the DataGrid control, you can input all the columns you want to set up for this grid (see Figure 14.6).

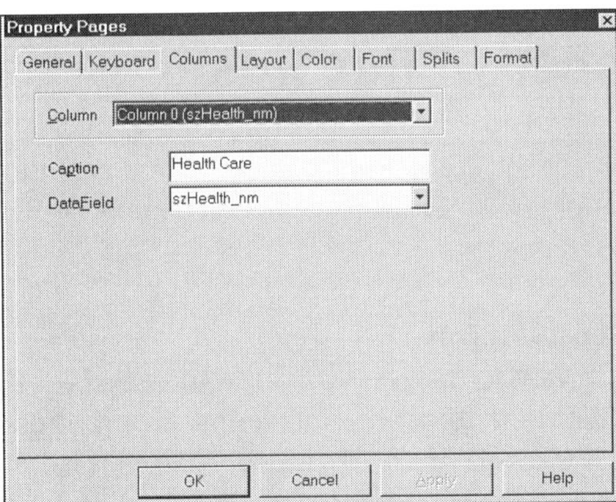

FIGURE 14.6 The Columns tab in the property page for the DataGrid control.

EXERCISE

Set the DataGrid Properties

1. Double-click the (Custom) property to bring up the property pages for the DataGrid control.
2. Click the Columns tab to bring up the dialog box shown in Figure 14.6.
3. Select Column0 from the Column combo box.
4. Assign the `Caption` property a value of `Health Care`.
5. Change the `DataField` property to `szHealth_nm`.
6. Select Column1 from the Column combo box.
7. Assign the `Caption` property a value of `Waiting Period`.
8. Change the `DataField` property to `iWaitingPeriod_amt`.
9. Click OK to save the changes.
10. Now run the project. You should see the health care choices appear in the grid.

You can customize many facets of this grid control, such as the format in which to display data, whether to allow the user to resize the grid at run-time, the ability to add, edit, delete data, and even how the keyboard reacts while the grid has focus.

Displaying the Number of Records

Sometimes you might want to inform the user of how many records are in the table and which record he or she is currently looking at. You can use the `Caption` property of the data control to display this information. Figure 14.7 shows what this might look like.

Example's Filename: RecCount.frm

Of course, you would not want to do this if you have thousands of records, because it does take a lot of time to get the total number of records from the data control. The reason why it takes so much time is you have to force the `Recordset` object to go to the last row in the set. This means it has to read every row, and this can take some time on a slow network or if the table has thousands of records. However, if you have a small amount of records, this might be acceptable.

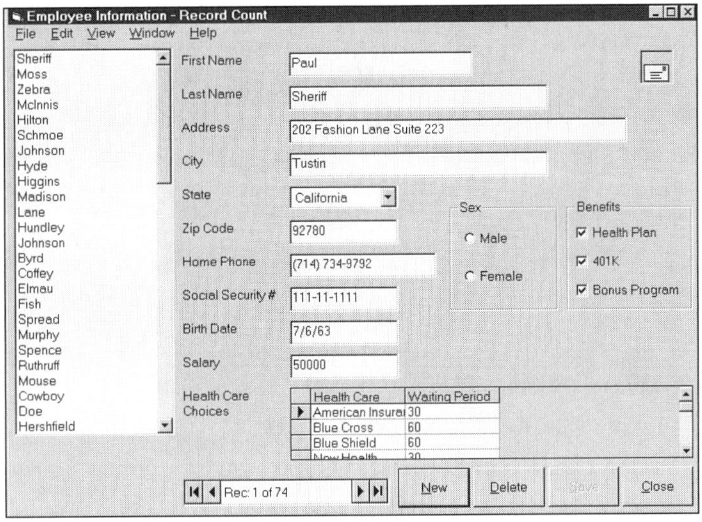

FIGURE 14.7
Displaying the record count.

NOTE
Depending on the OLE DB provider you're using, the data control might report the total number of rows right back to you or sometimes it might require you to go to the last row. To be safe, always go to the last row.

EXERCISE

CHANGE THE *FORM_LOAD()* EVENT

1. Double-click the form and go to the `Form_Load()` event.
2. Add code to have this event to move to the last row in the recordset.
3. Add another line of code to have the data control come back to the first row in the recordset:

```
Private Sub Form_Load()
    Debug.Print "Form_Load()"
    mnuVToolbar.Enabled = False
    mnuVStatus.Enabled = False

    datEmployees.Recordset.MoveLast
    datEmployees.Recordset.MoveFirst
End Sub
```

By moving to the last row in the recordset, you force all the rows to be loaded into the cache. This allows the data control to count the number of rows. Then, of course, you need to reposition yourself back to the first row in the recordset so that you're at the beginning of the set when the form is displayed. Now let's add the code to display the record count in the `Caption` property of the data control.

EXERCISE

WRITE THE *MOVECOMPLETE()* EVENT

1. Double-click the Employees data control.
2. Position to the `MoveComplete` event and add the following code:

```
Private Sub datEmployees_MoveComplete(_
        ByVal adReason As ADODB.EventReasonEnum, _
        ByVal pError As ADODB.Error, _
        adStatus As ADODB.EventStatusEnum, _
        ByVal pRecordset As ADODB.Recordset)
   Debug.Print "MoveComplete"

   If pRecordset.EOF Or pRecordset.BOF Then
   Else
      Call ControlsTagLoad(pRecordset)
      With datEmployees
         .Caption = "Rec: " & _
                    .Recordset.AbsolutePosition & _
                    " of " & _
                    .Recordset.RecordCount
      End With
   End If
End Sub
```

In this code, you use the `AbsolutePosition` property to retrieve the current record number from the `Recordset` property of the data control. You also use the `RecordCount` property of the `Recordset` object to retrieve the total amount of rows in the recordset.

Your Own Record Movement Buttons

Instead of using the data control to move forward and backward through the recordset, some programmers like to create their own command buttons, or maybe even menu items, to perform this movement. You can accomplish this quite easily. The first step is to make the data control invisible and then add your own command buttons with the appropriate graphics. See Figure 14.8 for an example of what these command buttons might look like.

FIGURE 14.8 Record movement command buttons.

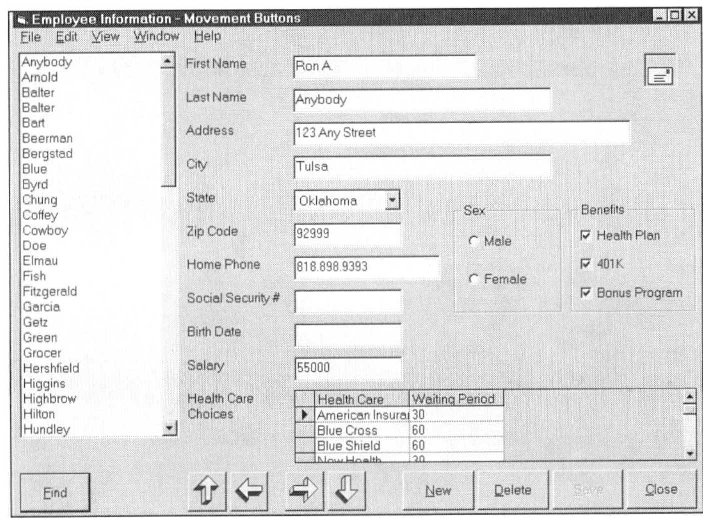

Example's Filename: Movement.frm

Making the Data Control Invisible

Because you're performing all the record movement yourself, you can set the `Visible` property of the Employee data control to `False`. The control remains visible in design mode but does not display when you run the application.

EXERCISE

Hide the Data Control

1. Click once on the data control to give it focus.
2. Set the `Visible` property to `False`.
3. Now move the data control off to one side of the form.

Once the data control is hidden you can now control the movement through the records yourself.

Record Movement Buttons

Now let's add four command buttons where the data control was located. You'll then set a couple of properties to add arrows to each command button.

EXERCISE

ADD RECORD MOVEMENT COMMAND BUTTONS

1. Add four command buttons as shown in Figure 14.8.
2. Set all four command buttons' `Caption` properties to blank.
3. Set all four command buttons' `Style` properties to `1-Graphical`.
4. Set the `Name` and `Picture` property of each as listed in Table 14.4.

Table 14.4 *`Name`* and *`Picture`* Properties

Name	Picture
`cmdFirst`	`<Visual Basic Path>\Graphics\Icons\Arrows\Arw06up.ico`
`cmdPrevious`	`<Visual Basic Path>\Graphics\Icons\Arrows\Arw06lt.ico`
`cmdNext`	`<Visual Basic Path>\Graphics\Icons\Arrows\Arw06rt.ico`
`cmdLast`	`<Visual Basic Path>\Graphics\Icons\Arrows\Arw06dn.ico`

You will find a lot of useful graphics under your default Visual Basic installation path. In Table 14.4 you just substitute the `<Visual Basic Path>` with the location where you installed Visual Basic 6. I use the up arrow for the First record in the Recordset, and the down arrow for the Last record.

Now that you have the user interface drawn, let's add the code to manipulate the recordset of the data control. You need to add code to each of the four command buttons to move to the first and last records, as well as to move forward and backward through the recordset.

EXERCISE

Write Code to Move Through the Recordset

1. Double-click each of the command buttons in turn and add the following code:

```
Private Sub cmdNext_Click()
    With datEmployees.Recordset
        If Not .EOF Then
            .MoveNext
            If .EOF Then
                .MovePrevious
            End If
        End If
    End With
End Sub

Private Sub cmdPrevious_Click()
    With datEmployees.Recordset
        If Not .BOF Then
            .MovePrevious
            If .BOF Then
                .MoveNext
            End If
        End If
    End With
End Sub

Private Sub cmdFirst_Click()
    datEmployees.Recordset.MoveFirst
End Sub

Private Sub cmdLast_Click()
    datEmployees.Recordset.MoveLast
End Sub
```

2. You should also update the `ToggleButtons` routine to turn off these command buttons when you enter an editing mode:

```
Private Sub ToggleButtons()
    If cmdClose.Caption = "&Close" Then
        cmdClose.Caption = "&Cancel"
    Else
        cmdClose.Caption = "&Close"
```

```
    End If
    cmdSave.Enabled = Not cmdSave.Enabled
    cmdNew.Enabled = Not cmdNew.Enabled
    cmdDelete.Enabled = Not cmdDelete.Enabled
    datEmployees.Enabled = Not datEmployees.Enabled
    cmdNext.Enabled = Not cmdNext.Enabled
    cmdPrevious.Enabled = Not cmdPrevious.Enabled
    cmdFirst.Enabled = Not cmdFirst.Enabled
    cmdLast.Enabled = Not cmdLast.Enabled
End Sub
```

The cmdNext and cmdPrevious command buttons have the most code because you need to perform EOF and BOF checks. If you attempt to move to the phantom records, you'll need to move back off of them because you don't want a blank row to display on the screen.

Finding Records

With the current form design, the user either has to move through every record, one by one, to find a particular employee or scroll through the list box. You may want to add a Find command button to the form to allow the user to input a last name in a search operation.

EXERCISE

Add a Find Command Button

1. Add a command button to the form and place it under the list box.
2. Set the `Name` property to `cmdFind`.
3. Set the `Caption` property to `&Find`.
4. Double-click the command button to bring up a code window.
5. Type in the following code:

```
Private Sub cmdFind_Click()
    Dim strLast As String
    Dim vntBookmark As Variant

    strLast = InputBox("Enter Employee Last Name", _
                       "Find Employee")
```

```
    If strLast <> "" Then
        vntBookmark = datEmployees.Recordset.Bookmark
        datEmployees.Recordset.Find _
                 "szLast_nm LIKE '" & strLast & "*'"
        If datEmployees.Recordset.EOF Then
            datEmployees.Recordset.Bookmark = vntBookmark
            MsgBox "Employee Not Found"
        End If
    End If
End Sub
```

After adding the Find command button you need to write some substantial code to find a record in the Recordset. See the discussion below for an explanation.

In the `Find` routine, you need to declare two variables. One to hold the last name the user types into the `InputBox()` function; the second to hold a bookmark from the `Recordset` object. After asking the user to type in a last name in the input box, you need to grab the current bookmark of the `Recordset` object. This bookmark can be used in case the name the user types in does not exist. You'll use this bookmark to go back to the current record.

Next, you use the `Find` method of the `Recordset` object to search where the szLast_nm field in the table is like the name typed in by the user. Add an asterisk after the last name to perform a wildcard search. If the last name is found, the recordset will be positioned to that new record. If it is not found, the recordset will be positioned at the end of the file. If the recordset is at the end of the file, you should set the `Bookmark` property of the `Recordset` object to the value you saved prior to the `Find` method. This will move the recordset back to the record where the user was positioned prior to searching. You should then pop up a message box to inform the user that the name was not found.

One thing that will make the searching for last names of employees easier is to sort the data in the list box. Add an `ORDER BY` clause to the Command Text (SQL) property in the data control property pages. The `SELECT` statement should look like the following in the Command Text property:

```
SELECT * FROM tblEmployees ORDER BY szLast_nm
```

One last thing is to add the Find command button to the `ToggleButtons` routine so that it's disabled when the user enters an "edit" or "add new" mode.

Summary

Using the other data-aware controls that ship with Visual Basic can help you get a nice interface working very quickly. Using the DataCombo and DataList boxes will present lists of data from tables very quickly. For multi-column lists, the DataGrid is an excellent choice. Displaying the number of records that are contained in the Recordset is nice, but you need to be aware of the performance hits you will take. Adding a find routine is a nice way for the user to move directly to a record without sequentially searching through each record.

Review Questions

1. Which property do you set a data control to for populating the list portion of a Data Bound Combo or List Box?
2. Which property do you set with a field name to populate the list portion of a Data Bound Combo or List Box?
3. Which property does the `BoundColumn` property match to: `DataSource` or `RowSource`?
4. What does the `MatchEntry` property do?

15

Multiple Document Interface

THIS CHAPTER INTRODUCES YOU TO THE CONCEPT of Multiple Document Interface (MDI). You'll learn to create an MDI application in Visual Basic as well as why you might want to use this interface. You'll also learn about the child forms contained within the MDI application as well as how to create pop-up, context-sensitive menus.

Chapter Objectives

- Learn to create an MDI application
- Identify the difference between SDI and MDI
- Learn how to create an MDI form
- Learn how to create MDI child forms
- Learn how to create pop-up menus

Sample Project Name: \Chapter15\MDI.vbp

What Is MDI?

MDI is a popular interface in which you can have multiple documents/forms open in one application. Examples of MDI applications are Microsoft Word, Microsoft Excel, Microsoft PowerPoint, and even the Visual Basic integrated development environment. Each of these applications allows you to have multiple documents open, and these documents are all contained within one container form. The container form is also known as the *parent window*. Each document, or form, has its own window but is confined to the boundaries of the parent window. This means that you can't drag the form outside of the parent window.

Single Document Interface

MDI is only one mechanism for creating an application. It's possible to have an application that only has one form. This is an example of a Single Document Interface (SDI) application. Notepad is an example of an SDI. When you're in Notepad, you can only edit and view one file at a time.

You don't have to create your applications in an MDI paradigm. Even if you have multiple forms in your project, you can simply have each one as a separate, standalone form not contained by any parent form. The only drawback to this is that if the user wants to close your application, he or she must close each form individually, or you have to write code to close all the windows when you want to close the entire application.

Uses of MDI

MDI is most commonly used in those applications where the user can have many forms to work on at the same time. Word processor applications (such as Word), spreadsheet applications (such as Excel), and project manager applications (such as Project) are all good candidates for MDI applications. MDI is also handy when you have a large application, and you want to provide one mechanism for closing all of its forms when the user exits the application.

Creating an MDI Form

To create an MDI form, select Project, Add MDI Form. This creates a new form in your project that has different properties than a normal form. You're limited to one MDI form per project. In fact, after adding the MDI form, the Add MDI Form menu item will be grayed out.

You can have as many child forms as you want in your project. *Child forms* are those forms that stay within the MDI container. You may also have as many standard forms in your project as you want.

MDI Icons

Visual Basic displays different icons in the Project window to represent MDI forms, MDI child forms, and standard forms. See Figure 15.1 for an example of the different icons.

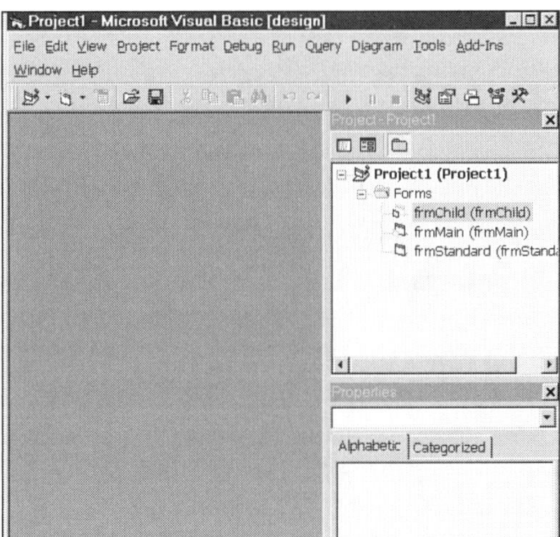

FIGURE 15.1
Icons depict different form types in the Project window.

To understand these icons, refer to Table 15.1 for a list of the form names and the type of forms they represent in the Visual Basic project window.

Table 15.1 Description of Each Form in the Project Window

Form Name	Description
frmMDI	This is the MDI form.
frmChild	This is an MDI child form. It has its `MDIChild` property set to `True`.
frmStandardForm	This is a standard form.

Runtime Features of MDI Child Forms

At runtime, the MDI form and the MDI child forms take on special features. Here's a list of these features:

- All child forms are displayed within the MDI parent's *client* area. (See the following note.)
- Child forms can be moved and resized only within the MDI parent's client area.
- Child forms can be minimized and their icon displayed within the parent's client area.
- Child forms can be maximized within the parent's client area and the caption of the child form appended to the caption of the MDI form.
- If the active child has any menu items, they will replace the MDI form's menu bar. The child menus are not displayed on the child form.
- Windows automatically gives a child form with a sizable border a default size. This size is based on the size of the MDI parent's client area. You can override this by setting the `BorderStyle` property of the child form to `1-Fixed Single`. I recommend that you do this because you don't want users to accidentally cover up the controls you worked so hard to place at a certain location.
- Child forms cannot be displayed modally.
- When you load an MDI child form, the parent is automatically loaded. However, the opposite is not true. If you load a parent form, the children of that form will not be loaded automatically.

- The MDI form can be minimized, and only one icon will be displayed on the desktop representing the MDI form and all of its children.
- If the MDI form is unloaded, all the loaded children are also unloaded.

NOTE
The client area is any usable area on the MDI form that's clear of any toolbars, status bars, or picture controls that may be on the MDI form.

Creating the Employee Tracking System

Let's now create a complete MDI application using the Employee Information form you developed in earlier chapters. To accomplish this, you'll need to perform several steps. First, add an MDI form to the project. Next, set the Employee Information form's `MDIChild` property to `True`. Finally, copy the menus from the Employee Information form to the MDI form.

EXERCISE

Make Your Own MDI Project

1. Open your Employee project.
2. Select Project, Add MDI Form from the Visual Basic menu.
3. Double-click the MDI Form template to add this template to your application.
4. Set the `Name` property of the MDI form to `frmMain`.
5. Set the `Caption` property to `Employee Tracking System`.
6. Set the `WindowState` property to `2-Maximized`.
7. Save the project, naming the MDI form "Main.frm."

It is very easy to create an MDI project. Remember that you are allowed only one MDI form in one application.

Moving Menus

You now need to move the menus from the Employee Information form to the MDI form. Unfortunately, there's no easy way to do this with Visual Basic. You need to open up the MDI form and the Employee Information form in Notepad or WordPad.

EXERCISE

Moving Menus from One Form to Another

1. Open the Employee Information form in Notepad or WordPad. When you look at this form, you'll find a lot of definitions for the different controls contained on the form.
2. Look down quite a ways through these definitions until you find the definition `VB.Menu mnuFile`. This is where your menus begin. Here's an example:

```
Begin VB.Menu mnuFile
      Caption          =   "&File"
      Begin VB.Menu mnuFEmp
         Caption          =   "&Employee"
      End
      Begin VB.Menu mnuFSep1
         Caption          =   "-"
      End
      Begin VB.Menu mnuFExit
         Caption          =   "E&xit"
         Shortcut         =   ^X
      End
   End
   Begin VB.Menu mnuEdit
      Caption          =   "&Edit"
      Begin VB.Menu mnuECut
         Caption          =   "Cu&t"
      End
      Begin VB.Menu mnuECopy
         Caption          =   "&Copy"
      End
      Begin VB.Menu mnuEPaste
         Caption          =   "&Paste"
      End
End
...
...
...
```

This code shows how Visual Basic stores the information for your menus. It's pretty easy to figure out how this information is stored. Visual Basic simply lists the menu name and then indented under that menus into another form is a list of the drop-down menu items.

Now what you need to do is cut all the menus items from the Employee Information form and then open up the MDI form and paste the menu items at the end of the form's control list.

EXERCISE

Paste Me

1. Cut all the menu items out of the Employee Information form.
2. Open the Main.frm file in Notepad or WordPad.
3. Locate the last "End" in the form description and paste in the items just before it.
4. Save both of the form changes you've made and exit from Notepad/WordPad.
5. Reopen your project and display the MDI form.
6. You should see that the menus are now displayed in the MDI form.
7. Click the File menu and then click the Employee menu item.
8. Add the following code:

```
Private Sub mnuFEmp_Click()
    frmEmployee.Show
End Sub
```

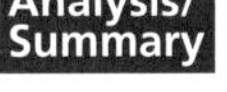

This bit of code allows the main MDI form to display the Employee Information form. You're not quite done yet—there are still some things you need to do to make this a true MDI application.

EXERCISE

Making an MDI Child Form

1. Open the Employee Information form in design mode.
2. Set the `MDIChild` property to `True`. This allows the Employee Information form to act as an MDI child form to the MDI parent.
3. Set the `BorderStyle` property to `1-Fixed Single` so that the MDI form will not automatically resize the Employee Information form when it's displayed.
4. Add a BAS module so that you can add a `Sub Main()` procedure to the application.

5. Set the Name property of the BAS module to modAppCode.
6. Save this module using the name "AppCode.bas."
7. Create a Sub Main() procedure in the BAS file. Be sure to make it public.
8. Move any lines of code that explicitly reference those menus from the Employee Information form to the MDI form.
9. Add the following code to the Sub Main() procedure:

```
Public Sub Main ()
    frmMain.Show
End Sub
```

10. Change the startup object to be the Sub Main() procedure you just added.
11. Select Project, EmpInfo Properties from the Visual Basic menu.
12. On the General tab, select "Sub Main" from the Startup Object combo box.

Now when you run this project, the MDI form will appear. You can then select the Employee menu item from the MDI menu and the Employee Information form will appear. Notice that the Employee Information form now has all the characteristics described for MDI child forms: You can only move it within the MDI parent form, you can minimize it and it will show up on the parent form, and so on. If you close the parent form, the Employee Information form will also be closed. This is probably the best feature—you only need to close one form, and all of the other forms close automatically.

Child Menus in MDI Applications

In the Employee application, you created menus on the MDI parent. Normally, most applications just have one menu. In an MDI application, you need to be very careful when creating menus on forms other than the MDI form. If a child form has a menu, the child's menu is displayed on the MDI form, *not* on the child form. When the child form has the focus, that child's menu replaces the MDI form's menu on the menu bar. If the child does not have a menu, the menu of the MDI form continues to be displayed.

This behavior of overriding the menu on the MDI parent form only applies to MDI child forms. Standard forms that are not MDI child forms maintain separate menus, and these menus will not show up on the MDI parent.

Arranging Child Forms

If your application can have multiple child forms open, you may want to enable the user to arrange them from the Window menu, like you can do in Word or Excel. Visual Basic provides four options: Tile Horizontal, Tile Vertical, Cascade, and Arrange Icons.

`MDIForm` has an `Arrange` method you can pass a constant to that tells the open child forms how to arrange themselves. The following code shows each of these options, which you can attach to the menu items under the Window menu:

```
Private Sub mnuWArrange_Click()
   Me.Arrange vbArrangeIcons
End Sub

Private Sub mnuWCascade_Click()
   Me.Arrange vbCascade
End Sub

Private Sub mnuWHorizontal_Click()
   Me.Arrange vbTileHorizontal
End Sub

Private Sub mnuWVertical_Click()
   Me.Arrange vbTileVertical
End Sub
```

To test this behavior, let's create a blank form that does nothing but allows you to resize it.

EXERCISE

Arranging Child Forms

1. Add a form to your project.
2. Set the `Name` property to `frmChild`.
3. Set the `Caption` property to `Child Form`.
4. Set the `MDIChild` property to `True`.
5. Add a menu to the main MDI form with the `Caption` property set to `&New Child`.

6. Set the Name of this menu item to mnuFileChild.
7. Add the following code to this menu item:

```
Private Sub mnuFileChild_Click()
    Dim frmNew As frmChild

    Set frmNew = New frmChild

    frmNew.Show
End Sub
```

In many Windows applications, you have the ability to open many instances of the same form. For example, in Word, you can have many different documents open; in Excel, you can have many spreadsheets open. Each of these documents are *not* separate forms—they're created from a common template. This is what the preceding code accomplishes.

The New keyword in the line that assigns the form to the object variable frmNew is what informs Visual Basic to make a new instance of the form named frmChild. Think of this form as a photocopy of the original form. All the properties of the frmChild form are duplicated, and a new Form object variable is created. One important point to note is that the frmChild form is never loaded—it's only used to make a copy of itself for these new variables.

You can now use this menu item at runtime to see new instances of the form appear.

EXERCISE

Try Out the Window Menu Items

1. Run this project.
2. Click the New Child menu item three times.
3. You should now have three instances of the child form displayed.
4. Try out each of the menu items under the Window menu.
5. Minimize each of the forms and then move the icons on the parent MDI form to different locations. Now run the Arrange Icons menu item.

As you can see keeping child forms in alignment is actually quite simple in Visual Basic.

Positioning Child Forms

Run the program and display the Employee Information form. Notice that it appears in just one spot on the MDI. If you want to automatically position this form, you can set the `Top` and `Left` properties of the Employee Information form. However, these positions are in relation to the MDI form's *client area* (the area of an MDI form just below the menu and right above the bottom of the form). Therefore, the coordinates 0,0 relate the position immediately under the MDI form's menu.

Centering Forms

Sometimes you may want to center child forms within the parent form. Although there's a `StartUpPosition` property on the forms, when you set the `MDIChild` property to `True`, this property cannot be set to anything other than `Manual`. This means you need to write code to position the form. Here's some code that centers an MDI child form within the main form:

```
Public Sub ChildFormCenter(oForm As Form)
   With oForm
      .Move (frmMain.ScaleWidth / 2) - (.Width / 2), _
            (frmMain.ScaleHeight / 2) - (.Height / 2)
   End With
End Sub
```

This code uses the frmMain form's `ScaleWidth` and `ScaleHeight` properties as the base for where to move the form. The `Scale` properties provide the inside dimensions of the MDI form. The inside dimensions are from the bottom of the menu area of the form to the bottom of the form, minus any border and controls that are aligned to the bottom of the form—in other words, the MDI client area. Calling the `ChildFormCenter()` procedure from the `Form_Load()` event of the Employee Information form will center this form within the parent form.

```
Private Sub Form_Load()
   Call ChildFormCenter(Me)
End Sub
```

NOTE

MDI child forms cannot have their `StartUpPosition` properties set to anything other than `0-Manual`.

Tracking Child Windows

Visual Basic has the capability to keep track of the list of child windows open within the parent MDI form. To create this list, set the `WindowList` property of a menu item to `True`.

EXERCISE

Adding a `WindowList`

1. Open frmMain in design mode.
2. Open the menu design window.
3. Click the Window menu item.
4. Check the `WindowList` property.
5. Run the application. Open a few of the child forms and then click the Window menu to see a list of open forms.

A list of open windows is typical of most MDI applications. Be sure to add this to your MDI applications by setting the `WindowList` property.

Creating Pop-up Menus

In many applications, you can click the right mouse button at certain locations to cause context-sensitive menus to appear. These menus give you the ability to perform certain actions based on where you've clicked.

To create a pop-up menu, you need to create a top-level menu group with its `Visible` property set to `False`. You can create as many subitems as you want under this menu—these are the items that will be displayed on the pop-up menu.

In an MDI application, you need to create the pop-up menus on the main MDI form only. If you don't, any child form menus will replace the MDI form's menu at runtime. This can make things quite a challenge to program; therefore, you should create *all* menus on just the MDI form. This includes all the pop-up menus you'll use throughout your application. If you want to create a pop-up menu on the Employee Information form, you need to reference the menu on the frmMain MDI form.

EXERCISE

CREATING A POP-UP MENU

1. On the frmMain form, add a top-level menu called mnuEmployee.
2. Set the `Visible` property on the mnuEmployee menu to `False`.
3. Add `&New`, `&Save`, `&Delete`, and `&Close` menus under this menu.
4. Go to the Employee Information form and select the `Form_MouseUp()` event.
5. Add the following code:

```
Private Sub Form_MouseUp(Button As Integer, _
                         Shift As Integer, _
                         X As Single, _
                         Y As Single)
    If Button = vbRightButton Then
        PopupMenu frmMain.mnuPopEmp
    End If
End Sub
```

Analysis/ Summary

In this code, you check to see whether the button pressed is the right mouse button by comparing the argument passed to the `MouseUp` event against the constant `vbRightButton`. If they are equal, you invoke the PopupMenu method and pass it the name of a menu. Because you're on the Employee Information form, you need to preface the name of the menu with the MDI form name, frmMain. Now you can run this project and right-click over the Employee Information form to have this pop-up menu displayed.

One thing to notice is that if you position your mouse over a text box, label, or any other control, the code will not fire. That's because you're only trapping the `MouseDown` event for the form. If you want to have the pop-up menu appear over other controls, you need to duplicate this code for every control.

Unloading an MDI Application

To unload an MDI application, you simply need to unload the MDI form. In the File, Exit menu, place the following code:

```
Private Sub mnuFExit_Click()
   Unload Me
End Sub
```

This causes the parent MDI form to unload. When the parent form unloads, any open child forms must also unload. This little bit of code causes everything to be unloaded and your application to be shut down.

Stopping the Unload

If the user starts to edit information on a child form and then attempts to close the MDI parent form, the child form has the ability to stop the parent from unloading while in this edit mode. Of course, it's up to the child form to inform the parent that it cannot close right now. You write this type of code in the child form's `QueryUnload` event. Here's an example:

```
Private Sub Form_QueryUnload(Cancel As Integer, _
                             UnloadMode As Integer)
   If cmdSave.Enabled Then
      MsgBox "Changes on the Employee form " & _
             "have not been saved. Please save " & _
             "prior to unloading application"

      Cancel = True
   End If
End Sub
```

When a form is about to unload, it invokes the form's `QueryUnload` event. Visual Basic passes in a `Cancel` parameter by reference so that you can set this `Cancel` flag to `True` if you want to stop the unloading of the form. In a Chapter 25, "Data Entry with ADO Objects," you'll learn a technique for asking the user whether he or she wants to save the changes prior to unloading the form.

Summary

In this chapter, you learned to build an MDI application using several techniques found in professional Windows applications. You learned to create forms that stay within the boundaries of the MDI form. You also learned to create menus. Whether or not you choose to use the MDI paradigm depends on the complexity of your application and how many forms will be displayed at one time.

Review Questions

1. How many MDI parents are allowed in a Visual Basic program?
2. How do you make a form an MDI child form?
3. Can a child form be displayed modally?
4. On which form should you create pop-up menus?

16

The Debugger

THIS CHAPTER EXAMINES THE BASICS OF THE SOURCE code debugger that's built into the Visual Basic environment. You'll learn about the different modes of Visual Basic, how to step through code, and how to set breakpoints. In addition, you'll learn about the different windows in the Visual Basic environment that give you a lot of information about your running program.

Chapter Objectives

- Learn the three modes of Visual Basic
- Learn to invoke the debugger
- Learn to watch variables and set breakpoints
- Learn to control and view the execution path of your source code in the debugger
- Learn to use the Immediate window

Sample Project File: \Chapter16\Debugging.vbp

Three Modes of Visual Basic

You can work in one of three modes in Visual Basic: design, run, or break. Each mode has a specific function, and knowing which mode you're in is very important.

Let's take a look at the three different modes you'll be working in. First, in design mode you build your user interface and write the source code. Next, in run mode you run your application. Finally, in break mode you can edit code, test variables, reset values, and step through your source code line by line.

You can tell which mode you're in by looking at the Visual Basic title bar. After the name of the project, you'll see "Microsoft Visual Basic" followed by "[design]," "[run]," or "[break]." Get used to looking at the title bar for information on which mode you're currently in, because there are things you can and can't do in each mode.

The Debug Toolbar

If you right-click the toolbar area of the Visual Basic IDE, you can select the Debug toolbar (see Figure 16.1).

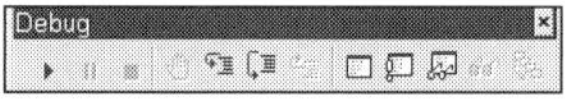

FIGURE 16.1 The Debug toolbar.

From this toolbar, you can run, stop, and pause your application. You can also perform other functions related to debugging your application. From left to right, the tools on the Debug toolbar are as follows:

- Run the project
- Pause the project
- Stop the project
- Toggle breakpoints
- Step into procedure
- Step over procedure
- Step out of procedure
- Locals window
- Immediate window
- Quick watch window
- Call Stack Window

You'll learn more about each of these tools in this chapter.

Invoking the Debugger

To begin your application using the debugger, select Debug, Step Into or Debug, Step Over The Step Into option shows you each line of source code as it runs. This is great when you need to see each line as it executes, test different variables, or even change lines of code.

The Step Over option allows you to run an entire procedure without stepping into that procedure. This is useful when you know a function works, but you don't want to spend the time stepping through it. When you use this option, it executes the procedure and then places you back in break mode immediately after the call to that procedure.

You can invoke the debugger and enter break mode in several ways:

- By pressing Ctrl+Break at runtime
- By placing a `Stop` statement in your code

- By setting a breakpoint
- By pressing F8 to run the program

Example's Filename: Debug1.frm

Exercise

Stepping Through Your Code

1. Select Tools, Options from the Visual Basic menu.
2. Select the Project tab from the Options window.
3. Select the frmDebug1 as the startup form.
4. Click the OK button.
5. Press F8 to begin the process. You should see a code window that looks like the one shown in Figure 16.2.
6. Press F8 to execute the next line of code. Continue to press F8 to execute each subsequent line of code.
7. When you get to a point where a form is displayed, you won't see any more code.

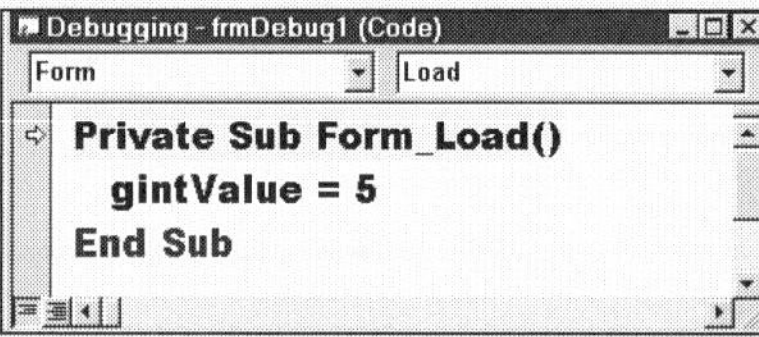

FIGURE 16.2
The frmDebug1 form showing a global variable.

You will use the F8 key quite often as you debug your application.

NOTE
When a form is displayed, your code is no longer running. Instead, Visual Basic is just waiting for an event to happen. If you click one of the controls in which you have written code, you will be placed into break mode after you click.

Now that you know how to start a program in break mode, let's look at all the different things you can do while in break mode.

Quick Watch

If you're in break mode and want to immediately view the contents of a variable in the current procedure, position your cursor on that variable, click the mouse, and then press Shift+F9. Instead of pressing Shift+F9, you can also click the icon that looks like a pair of glasses on the Debug toolbar. You can also select Quick Watch from the Debug menu.

Exercise

View Values in the Quick Watch Window

1. Click the Start command button.
2. Press F8 until you're in the `Proc1` procedure (see Figure 16.3).
3. Press F8 again until you've highlighted the line shown in Figure 16.3.
4. Click your mouse once on the `intTemp` variable.
5. Press Shift+F9 to see the Quick Watch window (see Figure 16.4).

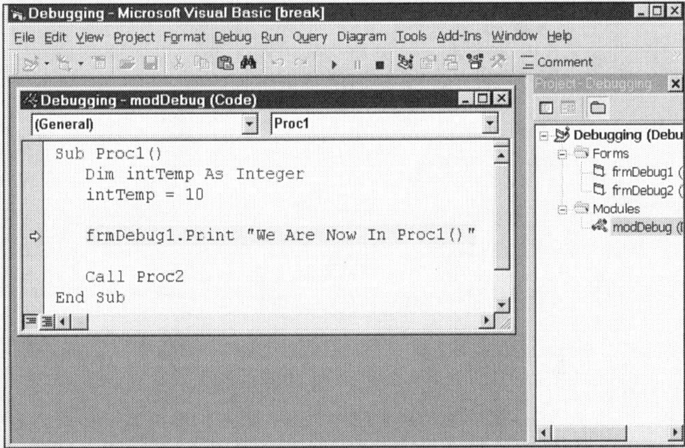

FIGURE 16.3
Proc1 in a code window.

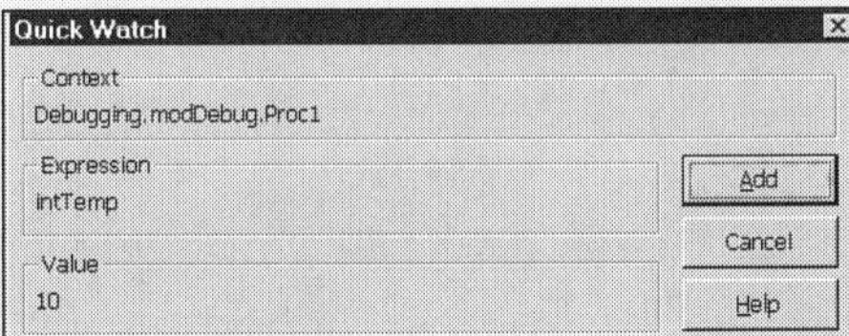

FIGURE 16.4
The Quick Watch window.

The value of `intTemp` is `10`. The Quick Watch window is wonderful for viewing the contents of variables on the fly. Also, you can also just hover your cursor over a variable, and the value of that variable will be displayed in a tooltip.

Setting the Next Statement to Execute

Sometimes when executing a program, you need to skip a section of code or back up and execute the same code again. Visual Basic allows this as long as the line you want to move to is in the current procedure.

Exercise

1. Press F8 to continue executing the program from the previous exercise.
2. Stop when you're in the `Proc2` procedure and your code window looks like the one shown in Figure 16.5.

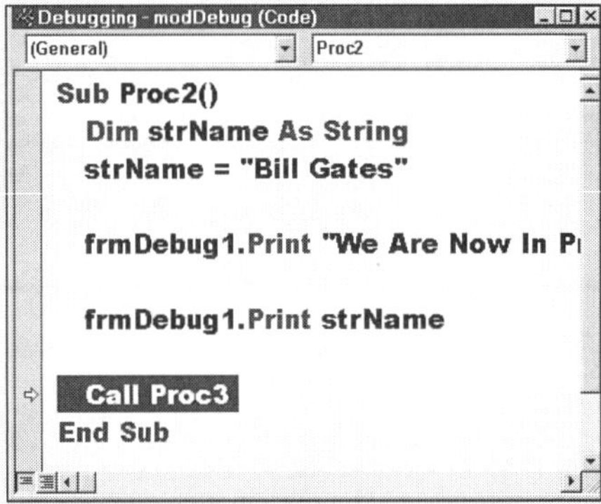

FIGURE 16.5
Calling *Proc3*.

3. At this point, you may want to change some code. Position your cursor to the line that reads `strName = "Bill Gates"`.
4. Change `Bill Gates` to `Tom Buttons`.
5. Force Visual Basic to reexecute the statements in the `Proc2` statement by right-clicking the line you want to reexecute and then selecting Set Next Statement from the pop-up menu.

6. You should now see a boxed line around the line you want to start executing.
7. Press F8 to begin executing these statements again.

Being able to move back and try different statements, and even add code on the fly is a great productivity tool in Visual Basic. You can also set the line to reexecute by selecting Set Next Statement from the Run menu.

The Call Stack Window

While in break mode, Visual Basic allows you to display the list of procedures you've executed to get to your current location. This is very handy when you aren't sure how you got to where you are.

Exercise

Viewing the Call Stack Window

1. Continue executing the program until you're in the `Proc3` procedure.
2. Your screen should look like the one shown in Figure 16.6.

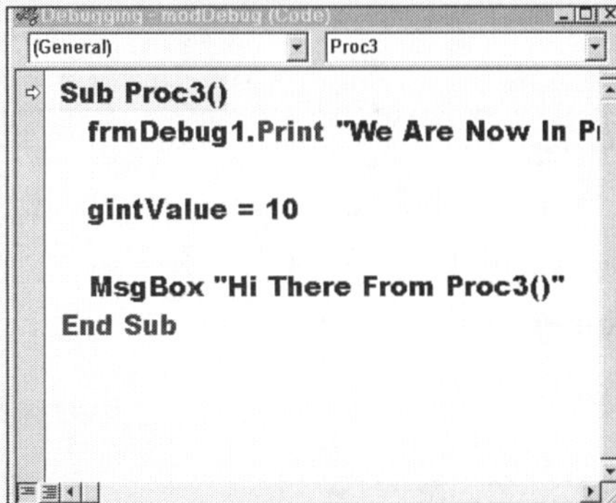

FIGURE 16.6
Getting ready to display the Call Stack Window.

3. Select Tools, Calls, press Ctrl+L, or click the Call Stack button on the toolbar. Any of these actions will display the Call Stack window (see Figure 16.7).

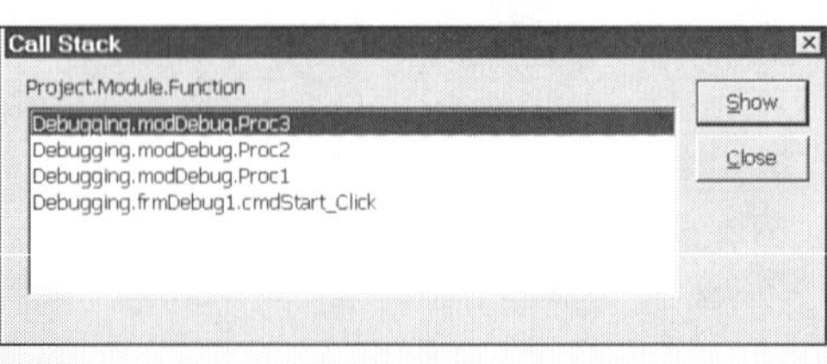

FIGURE 16.7
The Call Stack window.

The topmost value in the list is where you're currently executing code. Each lower item in the list is where you came from.

Setting Breakpoints

Many times when you're testing an application, you don't want to read through every line in your program to arrive at where you think the error is. Therefore, instead of pressing F8 to step into your code from the beginning, you can set a breakpoint in your source code to tell Visual Basic where to stop executing when it reaches this line.

Exercise

Setting Breakpoints

1. Stop the program by selecting Run, End from the menu bar, or by clicking the VCR Stop button on the toolbar.
2. Open up the Debug.bas file and go to the `Proc2` procedure.
3. Click the line that reads `frmDebug1.Print "We Are Now In Proc2()"` (see Figure 16.8).
4. Press F9 to set a breakpoint.
5. Run your program by pressing F5. Click the Start command button to begin running the program. When you reach the breakpoint, Visual Basic will automatically put you in break mode.

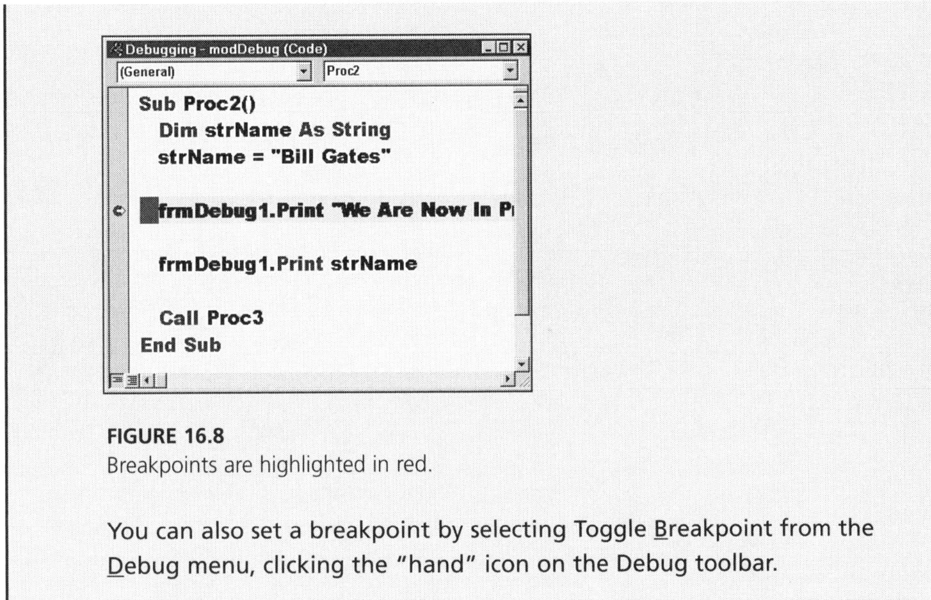

FIGURE 16.8
Breakpoints are highlighted in red.

You can also set a breakpoint by selecting Toggle Breakpoint from the Debug menu, clicking the "hand" icon on the Debug toolbar.

After a breakpoint is set, you can run the application normally. When Visual Basic hits that line, it automatically puts you in break mode. At this point, you can change your code, inspect variables, or do anything else needed to make your application run correctly. Of course there are some changes that may require to you stop the execution of your code. For example, if you change the type of a parameter or variable, or you declare a new variable, you will need to stop execution and reexecute from the beginning of your program.

Breakpoints are cleared after the VBP file is unloaded. There is no way to save breakpoints.

The *Stop* Statement

The `Stop` statement can be placed anywhere in your code where you want execution to stop and want to enter the debug mode. `Stop` is an executable statement and is therefore saved with your code. This is the primary advantage of using the `Stop` statement—it's saved when you leave Visual Basic.

However, you want to make sure you remove these statements prior to making an EXE file. They act just like the `End` statement in an EXE file in that they immediately halt your program. Here's an example:

```
Sub Proc2()
    Dim strName As String
    strName = "Bill Gates"

    frmDebug1.Print "We Are Now In Proc2()"

    Stop

    frmDebug1.Print strName

    Call Proc3
End Sub
```

TIP

Be sure to remove `Stop` statements from your code before making an EXE file, or you can surround the `Stop` statements with conditional compilation (`#if/#endif`) statements so they're not included in the compiled program.

Setting Watch Variables

Many times in an application, you can watch the value inside of a variable or property. Visual Basic lets you specify which variables you want to watch. These are placed in a special Watch pane above the Immediate window.

Exercise

Adding Watch Variables

1. Stop the application.
2. Go to the `Form_Load()` procedure in Debug1.frm.
3. Click the `gintValue` variable and select Debug, Add Watch from the Visual Basic menu. The `gintValue` variable has already been added to the Expression text box.
4. Choose the (All Modules) option from the Modules: combo box in the Context frame shown in Figure 16.9. This tells Visual Basic to watch the variable named `gintValue` through all of the modules.

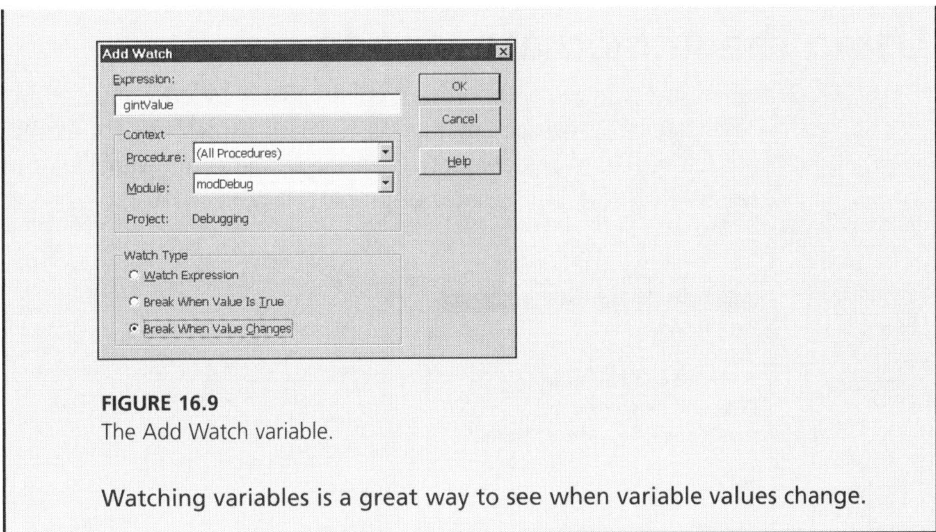

FIGURE 16.9
The Add Watch variable.

Watching variables is a great way to see when variable values change.

Besides just setting a watch variable, you may want to enter an expression in the text box. This allows you to test that expression. Table 16.1 provides an explanation for each of the options you may select in the Add Watch window.

Table 16.1 Watch Types

Option	Description
Expression	This can be any valid Visual Basic expression. It can be a variable name, or you can test to see whether a variable is equal to a certain value.
Context	You can tell Visual Basic which variable to watch—a local, form/module-level, or global variable.
Watch Type	You can determine when to enter break mode by selecting the Break When Value Is True option. For example, enter the following in the Expression text box: `gintValue = 10` Once the value in the variable `gintValue` becomes `10`, Visual Basic automatically puts you in break mode. You can then see the line where this change occurred. You can tell Visual Basic to stop execution anytime the value in a variable changes by selecting the Break When Value Changes option. This is particularly useful for testing which routines change a global or module-level variable.

Using the Immediate Window

In break mode, you can bring up the Immediate window and perform statements. These statements can be any valid Visual Basic expression. For example, you can print the results of an operation, print the contents of a variable or property, and even set the value of a variable or property. Figure 16.10 shows the Immediate window.

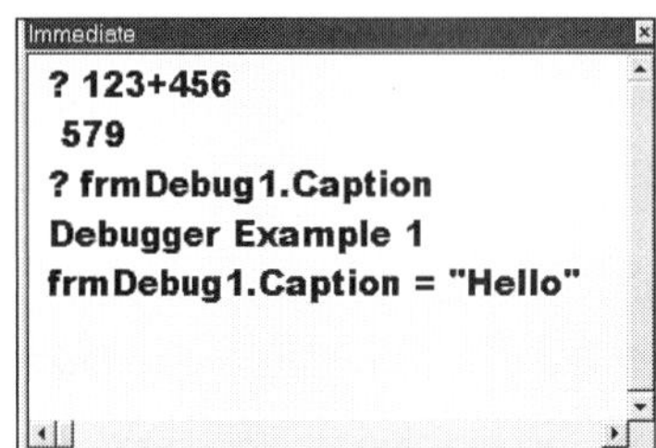
Immediate
? 123+456
579
? frmDebug1.Caption
Debugger Example 1
frmDebug1.Caption = "Hello"

FIGURE 16.10 The Immediate window.

Notice that you can use a question mark (`?`) instead of the keyword `Print`.

Printing to the Immediate Window

Many times during the testing of your application, you may find that when you're stepping through code, it works fine, but when you run the program straight through, it doesn't work. The reason for this is because you can change the way your program runs by using the debugger. Every time you switch from your program to the debugger, you're inadvertently firing events. Because different events fire during this process, they change how your program normally runs. Therefore, instead of using the debugger to test values, you may find it convenient to print these values to the Immediate window.

You can print directly to the Immediate window from within your application by executing the `Debug.Print` method. These values will stay around even when you return back to design mode. It can be useful to see these intermediate values without having to enter break mode and change the execution of your program. Here's an example of using the `Debug.Print` method:

```
Debug.Print "strMyString = " ; strMyString
Debug.Print "I am now executing the Form_Click() procedure"
```

To illustrate these points, an order of events is shown as an example in the Debug2.frm sample form. In this program, you see output in the Immediate window from many of the different events. Here's a listing of some of the more common ones:

```
Private Sub txtName_Click ()
   Debug.Print "txtName_Click"
End Sub

Private Sub txtName_MouseDown (Button As Integer, _
            Shift As Integer,    X As Single, Y As Single)
   Debug.Print "txtName_MouseDown"
End Sub

Private Sub txtName_MouseMove (Button As Integer, _
            Shift As Integer, X As Single, Y As Single)
   Debug.Print "txtName_MouseMove"
End Sub

Private Sub txtName_MouseUp (Button As Integer, _
            Shift As Integer, X As Single, Y As Single)
   Debug.Print "txtName_MouseUp"
End Sub
```

Move your mouse around and click the different controls to see the effects of the events being fired.

Summary

This chapter presented you with the different features of the integrated debugging environment in Visual Basic. This powerful tool helps you track down bugs very easily. By setting breakpoints, inspecting the values of variables, and stepping through your code line by line, you can debug your application much more efficiently.

Review Questions

1. What are the three modes in Visual Basic?
2. Which key marks a line as a breakpoint?
3. Which statement prints values from the Immediate window when the application is in break mode?

4. Which statement allows printing to the Immediate window from within the application?
5. Which statement causes VB to halt execution of your program?

Error Handling

THIS CHAPTER DISCUSSES HOW TO RESPOND to runtime errors in Visual Basic. Runtime errors can occur when files are not available, when a floppy disk is not in the disk drive and you are trying to write to it, when the structure of a table changes, when you attempt to print to a nonexistent printer, and many other external factors. In this chapter, you'll learn the many different methods of handling errors in your code.

Chapter Objectives

- Learn error-handling techniques
- Learn the different methods for handling errors
- Utilize the `Err` object
- Create a generic error handler

Sample Project File: \Chapter17\Errors.vbp

How Visual Basic Handles Error

If Visual Basic detects an error in your program, you'll see a dialog box appear that tells you what the error is and allows you to go into debug mode, end the program, or get help. As you can see from looking at Figure 17.1, this dialog box is not very descriptive, and it won't give the user a clue as to how to handle this error. As a result, you'll probably want to add your own error handling to your applications.

NOTE

Only when you're running from the Visual Basic development environment will you have all the command buttons shown in Figure 17.1. If you've created an EXE file, the only button you have to respond to is the OK button. When you click this button, the Visual Basic program will end very abruptly.

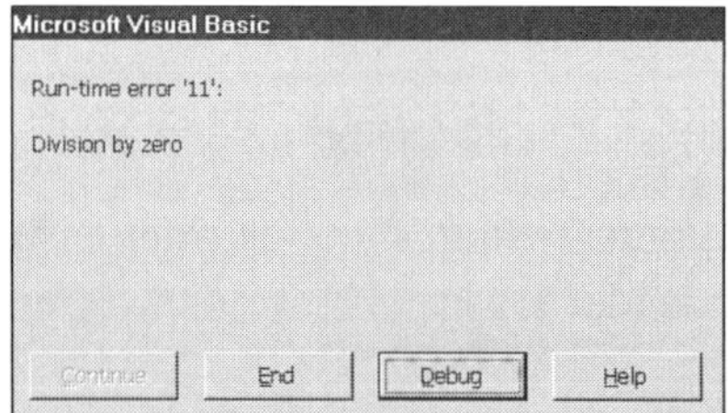

FIGURE 17.1 The Visual Basic error dialog box.

You can see this error dialog box by running the sample project for this chapter and clicking the Divide Error command button and then clicking the VBError command button on the Divide By Zero form.

Error-handling Techniques

At runtime, different things can happen that cause an error condition in your program. For example, a file could get deleted or a database file is unable to be opened for some reason or is not in the location it should be. If this situation isn't handled in your code, your program will bomb. Visual Basic supplies an error-handling method that allows you to trap and deal with these unwanted errors.

To perform error handling in Visual Basic, you must complete three steps:

- Tell Visual Basic what to do if an error occurs
- Write some code that will handle, or fix, the error
- Return back to what you were doing when the error occurred or continue on with the program

On Error GoTo <LabelName>

The statement On Error Go To *<LabelName>* tells Visual Basic that from this point forward in the program, if an error occurs, the program should jump to the label identified. You'll see this form of error handling most often. The label name you use must be within the same procedure.

Example's Filename: Divide.frm

In the form shown in Figure 17.2, three different forms of error handling are demonstrated.

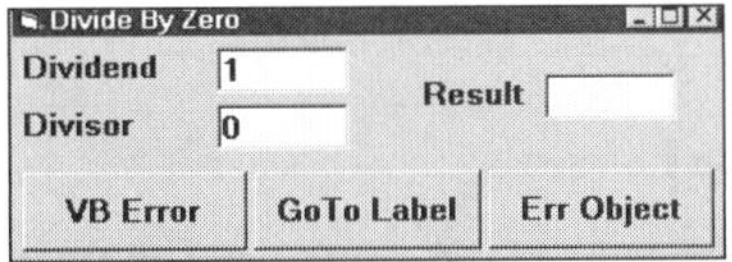

FIGURE 17.2
Error handling techniques.

The first method is to just let Visual Basic handle the error. The second method shows you how to use the On Error GoTo *<LabelName>* option. Let's look at the code under the GoTo Label command button:

```
Private Sub cmdGotoLabel_Click()
    On Error GoTo Error_EH

    Stop
```

```
    txtResult = CInt(txtDividend) / CInt(txtDivisor)

    Exit Sub

Error_EH:
        MsgBox "A divide by error has occurred (value / 0) " & _
                "which means that someone input some bad data into the
program."
    Exit Sub
End Sub
```

Although this is just some sample code that doesn't do a lot, it does demonstrate the common format you'll use in any routine in which you need to handle errors. Your first line of executable code should be an `On Error Goto <LabelName>` statement. This informs Visual Basic that if an error occurs anywhere after the `On Error GoTo` statement, the program should jump to the label named `Error_EH`. This label name must be within the same procedure. There is no global error-handling technique in Visual Basic.

If you attempt to divide by a number by zero, the line of code that does the division will cause an error to occur, in which case Visual Basic starts executing the lines of code after the error label. This example displays a message box telling the user that a divide-by error has occurred. It's not very elegant, but it does show you how the error handling works.

Notice the `Exit Sub` routine right before the `Error_EH` label. This is there in case no error occurs. If you don't put an `Exit Sub` before your label, Visual Basic simply drops right into the error-handling label. Labels are not executable code, they are just place markers.

Statements to Put in an Error Label

In the previous examples, after an error occurs, we simply exit the procedure. There are actually four different statements you can use after an error occurs:

- `Resume Next`
- `Resume [<LabelName>]`
- `Resume`
- `Exit Sub/Exit Function`

You will learn about each of these in this chapter.

The *Err* Object

Visual Basic creates an object that contains error information every time a runtime error is generated. This `Err` object can be used to retrieve information about the type of error that has occurred. The `Err` object contains the properties shown in Table 17.1.

Table 17.1 Properties of the *Err* Object

Property	Description
`Number`	Returns or sets the current error number. After an error is generated, this property contains a unique error number.
`Description`	Returns or sets the description for the error number generated. The description corresponds to the value in the `Number` property.
`HelpContext`	Contains the Visual Basic Help file context ID for the value in the `Number` property.
`HelpFile`	Contains the path and filename of the Visual Basic Help file. You may also place your own Help filename in this property.
`LastDLLError`	This property contains the error code generated from the last call to a DLL.
`Source`	The name of the current Visual Basic project or DLL.

The `Err` object also has two methods that can be invoked, as listed in Table 17.2.

Table 17.2 Methods of the *Err* Object

Method	Description
`Clear`	Clears any information currently contained in the `Error` object.
`Raise`	Raises an error, thus triggering an error to occur in the calling program. You must pass at least the `Number` property as an argument to the `Raise` method. Also, be sure to clear the object prior to invoking the `Raise` method.

In the rest of this chapter, you'll learn how to use this `Err` object.

Err.Number

The `Err.Number` property returns a number associated with the error that occurred. The error numbers are broken up into different categories. If `Err.Number` returns a zero, no error has occurred. You can check for specific errors by comparing the `Err.Number` property against a certain value.

Err.Description

The `Err.Description` property returns a short string describing the last error that occurred. This string can sometimes be used to display a message to the user. However, these messages are generally pretty cryptic. It's my recommendation that you come up with more descriptive error messages.

Let's take a look at an example:

```
Private Sub cmdErrObject_Click()
   On Error GoTo Error_EH

   Stop

   txtResult = CInt(txtDividend) / CInt(txtDivisor)

   Exit Sub

Error_EH:
   If Err.Number = 11 Then
      MsgBox "A Divide By Zero Error Has Occurred"
   Else
      MsgBox Err.Description
   End If
   Err.Clear

   Exit Sub
End Sub
```

In this example, you can see that you can check for a specific `Divide By Zero` error number. If that error number is received, the user has input some bad data. If it's not the error number 11, you should display the `Description` property from the error object so the user can at least get some other error information.

Getting a List of Errors

Sometimes it's not always easy to look up the errors Visual Basic generates. You can press F1 and attempt to look for the error codes Visual Basic has defined. However, I've created a sample program that will generate a list of common Visual Basic errors (see Figure 17.3).

Example's Filename: ListErrors.frm

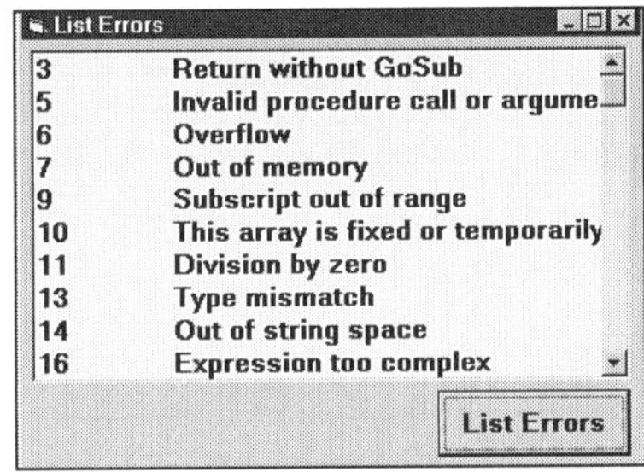

FIGURE 17.3
List of errors.

```
Private Sub cmdErrorList_Click()
   Dim intLoop As Integer

   For intLoop = 1 To 32766
      If Error(intLoop) <> _
         "Application-defined or object-defined error" Then
         lstErrors.AddItem intLoop & vbTab & Error(intLoop)
      End If
   Next intLoop
End Sub
```

This code loops through all the error numbers in the range of 1 to 32,766. This is the valid range of error numbers for Visual Basic. Each time through the loop, the loop number is passed to the `Error()` function. This function returns the description of the error that corresponds to that number. There are other error numbers you may receive from the `Err` object, but these error numbers come from DLL files you've referenced in your application.

The `Error()` function returns either a valid error description or, if the error number you're trying to retrieve is not defined, the string "Application-defined or object-defined error" will be returned. This means that the designers of Visual Basic haven't assigned an error to this particular error number.

On Error Resume Next

Instead of creating a label to jump to when you want to handle errors, you can handle errors right after the line of code where the error has occurred. The statement `On Error Resume Next` tells Visual Basic that if an error occurs, the program should simply skip to the next line of code and bypass the line where the error has occurred. This type of error handling is not the most effective, and it can lead to code that's more difficult to read. However, in some instances, it will come in really handy.

Example's Filename: KillFile.frm

In the form shown in Figure 17.4, you input a filename to delete. If the file exists, it's deleted using the Visual Basic statement `Kill`. If the file does not exist, a trappable error is generated.

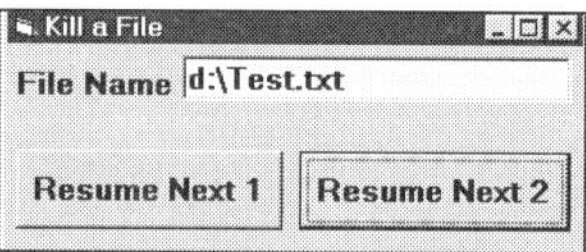

FIGURE 17.4 Some `Resume Next` examples.

The following code shows how you can handle trappable errors:

```
Private Sub cmdResumeNext_Click()
   ' Delete a file, if it exists.
   On Error Resume Next

   Stop

   Kill txtFileKill
   If Err.Number Then
      Debug.Print "File Did Not Exist"
   End If

   Err.Clear
End Sub
```

First, you set up your own error trap by using the `On Error Resume Next` statement. You then attempt the `Kill` statement on the filename in the text box. After the `Kill` statement, you can simply check the `Err.Number` property to see if it's a value other than zero. If it is, you know that the file was not valid and nothing was deleted. This really isn't a problem because if you're trying to delete a file and that file has already been deleted, you don't really need to perform any processing at all. In fact, in a real application, I wouldn't even check the `Err.Number` in this case.

Resume Next in the Error Label

Another method of using the `Resume Next` statement is to use it in the error label itself. Of course, this is not often done, but it is presented here just for completeness:

```
Private Sub cmdResumeNext2_Click()
    ' Delete a file, if it exists.
    On Error GoTo Error_EH

    Stop

    Kill txtFileKill

    Err.Clear

NormalExit:
    Exit Sub

Error_EH:
    Resume Next
End Sub
```

In this code, a normal error trap is set using a label name. Inside of the label, `Resume Next` is called, and it jumps to the line after the line that has the error.

Resume <LabelName>

Sometimes you'll want to just ignore errors or go to a different location when an error occurs. You should be very careful when using this technique, because you could make your code kind of hard to follow. Figure 17.5 shows the sample that will illustrate this technique.

Example's Filename: FileLen.frm

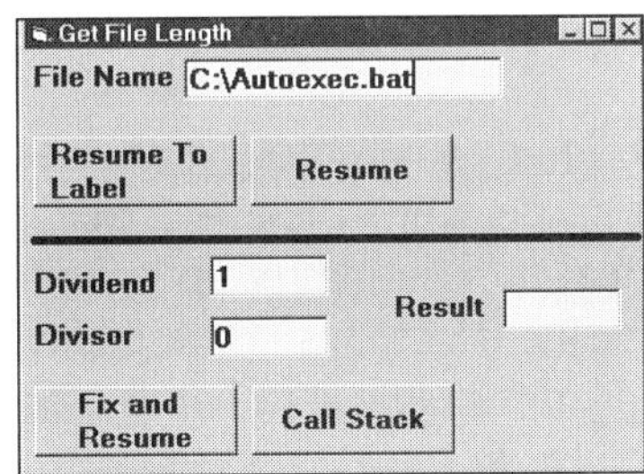

FIGURE 17.5 The Resume to Label and Resume examples.

You'll find that a lot of programmers use two labels in every procedure—one for a normal exit of the function and one for the error label. Here's an example:

```
Private Sub cmdResumeLabel_Click()
   ' Demonstrate the Resume statement.

   On Error GoTo Error_EH

   Stop

   Screen.MousePointer = vbHourglass

   ' Attempt to open a file on Drive A:
   MsgBox "The length of the file is: " & _
          FileLen(txtFileLen)

NormalExit:
   ' Clean up Code
   Screen.MousePointer = vbDefault
   Exit Sub

Error_EH:
   MsgBox "Error Opening File"
   Resume NormalExit
End Sub
```

This technique is great if you have some cleanup code you need to perform when exiting the procedure normally or if you're exiting because of an error. Instead of having to put the cleanup code in two places, you can simply put it in the normal exit label. In this example, I simply reset the `MousePointer` back to a normal cursor instead of the hourglass, which it was set to at the beginning of the procedure. You can view and run the sample code as shown in Figure 17.5 by loading the sample project and try it out.

Resume

In some applications, if an error occurs, you may want to give the user the chance to fix the error. For example, if an error occurs when the user is opening a file on a floppy disk drive, the problem may be that the user has not put the floppy disk in the drive yet. Therefore, you can just ask the user to insert the floppy disk and then try the operation again. Here's the code you would use to handle this situation:

```
Private Sub cmdResume_Click()
   ' Demonstrate the Resume statement.

   On Error GoTo Error_EH

   ' Attempt to open a file on Drive A:
   MsgBox "The length of the file is: " & _
          FileLen(txtFileLen)

NormalExit:
   Exit Sub

Error_EH:
   Select Case Err.Number
      Case 5      ' Invalid parameter.
         If MsgBox( _
            "The floppy disk drive isn't ready. Try again?", _
            vbQuestion + vbYesNo) = vbYes Then
             Resume
         Else
             Resume NormalExit
         End If

      Case Else
         ' Call a generic last-ditch error handler
         Call ErrorHandler

         Resume NormalExit
   End Select
End Sub
```

In this code, you check the `Err.Number` property to see whether it's the error number you're looking for. If it's 5, you know you need to prompt the user to input the floppy disk into the drive. In the `MsgBox()` function, you ask the user whether he or she wants to attempt the operation again. If the answer is Yes, you can perform a `Resume` to retry the operation. If the answer is No, you can simply resume to the normal exit routine. You should always give the user a way to cancel out of the procedure; otherwise, he or she may end up in an endless loop.

Of course using the error numbers themselves is not a very good practice. You should probably declare global constants to define each error that you may encounter.

Fix and Resume

If the user is getting a divide-by-zero error, you can easily remedy this via some simple coding on your part. All you have to do is detect that a divide-by-zero error has occurred by checking the `Err.Number` property to see if it's number 11. If it is, you can inform the user of the problem and prompt the user for a new divisor using the `InputBox()` function. Here's how:

```
Private Sub cmdFixResume_Click()
   On Error GoTo Error_EH

   txtResult = CInt(txtDividend) / CInt(txtDivisor)

   Exit Sub

Error_EH:
   If Err.Number = 11 Then
      MsgBox "A Divide By Zero Error Has Occurred, " & _
             "Please enter a new divisor"
      txtDivisor = InputBox("Enter a Divisor", "Divisor")
      Resume
   Else
      MsgBox Err.Description
   End If
   Err.Clear

   Exit Sub
End Sub
```

After the user inputs the new divisor, you can then perform a `Resume` statement to retry the operation one more time.

Errors in the Call Stack

Let's take a look at what happens when error handling is only used in some but not all procedures in a program. When clicked, the CallStack command button on the FileLen.frm form in the sample project calls three procedures. The first procedure has error handling set, and it immediately calls the `Error2()` procedure, which does not have any error handling. The `Error2()` procedure then calls the `Error3()` procedure, which also does not have any error handling. The `Error3()` procedure then performs a division by zero. When this happens, Visual Basic checks the call stack to find out where the last error trap was created. It will look back to the `Error2()` procedure and find out that there's no error trap in that procedure, so it then goes back to `Error1()`, where it will find an error trap. It then removes `Error3()` and `Error2()` from the call stack and calls the label in the `Error1()` procedure.

The `Error1()` procedure pops up a message box that says "What happened??" It then performs a **`Resume Next`**. Where does this **`Resume Next`** go to? Does it go to the line after the line of code that generated the error in the `Error3()` procedure? No! It can't because `Error3()` is no longer is in memory. Therefore, the only place it can go to is the line after the call to the `Error2()` procedure within the `Error1()` procedure:

```
Public Sub Error1()
   On Error GoTo Error_EH

   Call Error2

   MsgBox "Calculation Complete?"

NormalExit:
   Exit Sub

Error_EH:
   MsgBox "What happened??"
   Resume Next
End Sub

Public Sub Error2()
   ' No error handling in here

   Call Error3

   ' The following line won't happen
   MsgBox "After the call to Error3"
End Sub
```

```
Public Sub Error3()

    ' This line will cause an error
    ' with a zero divisor
    txtResult = CInt(txtDividend) / CInt(txtDivisor)

    MsgBox "Calculation Complete"
End Sub
```

This is why it's very important to put error handling into every procedure that could conceivably generate an error. If you don't do this, you'll never be sure where an error comes from, and this will be a very hard bug to track down.

Turning Error Handling Off

Error-handling routines are disabled automatically as soon as the procedure in which they are executed returns to the calling procedure. To turn error handling off within the same procedure, you can put the following line in your program:

```
On Error Goto 0
```

Creating a Global Error Handler

Obviously, you could end up writing a lot of duplicate code if you attempt to handle the same error in every procedure. So you might want to think about creating a generic error-handling routine. In this routine, you could create a big `Select Case` statement to check for specific errors. It could either attempt to fix them or just give up. You can also choose to display a better dialog box than the normal Visual Basic error dialog box. Figure 17.6 shows an example of a dialog box that gives you a little more information than the normal Visual Basic error dialog box.

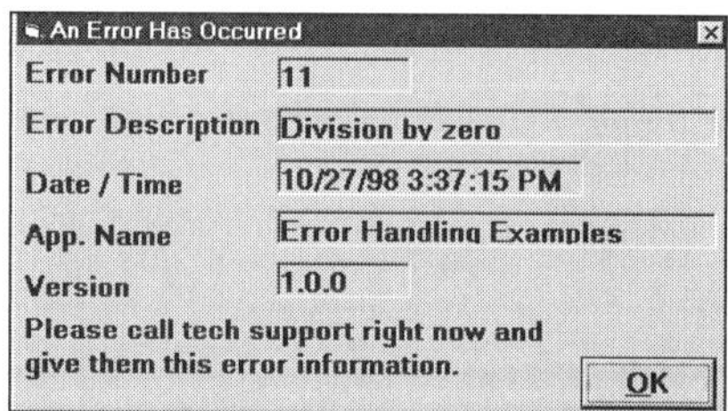

FIGURE 17.6 A generic error form.

Example's Filename: Error.frm

Although this dialog box is a far cry from a good error-handling solution, it at least gives the user a little more information, and it also explains how to handle the problem.

Summary

Error handling is very important in any application. It's very important to include error handling in every procedure that could potentially cause an error. There are many ways to handle errors in a Visual Basic application. It's up to you to choose the best method of error handling. I recommend that you create a global error handler to handle the majority of normal errors. Then you can just add specific code in each procedure that needs it.

Review Questions

1. Write an error statement that causes VB to jump to a label named `FormLoad_EH`.
2. Which statement causes execution to continue at the line following the one where the error occurred?
3. Which object/property returns a string describing the error that just occurred?
4. Write a statement that turns off error handling.

Exercises

If you use the common dialog control and you click the Cancel button on the File Open or File Save As dialog box, a trappable error will occur. Add this type of error handling to a program that traps this error.

18

IDE and Editor Tips and Tricks

When using the Visual Basic Integrated Development Environment (IDE), you have some built-in features that can speed up your development time. This chapter explores some of the tricks you should be familiar with when using Visual Basic.

Chapter Objectives

- Learn to use the Visual Basic Editor
- Learn to move around the IDE efficiently
- Learn some form-editing tips and tricks

Sample Project File: Any Project

Using the Code Editor

The Visual Basic code editor is pretty well stocked with hot keys and tricks that help you when writing your code. The following sections discuss some of the features you'll probably use quite often while writing code in the Visual Basic code editor.

Find Text

You can search for text anywhere in a current procedure, a current module, and in any module in an entire project. From any code window, you can select the Edit, Find menu or you can press Ctrl+F to bring up the Find dialog box, as shown in Figure 18.1. If you highlight a piece of text in your code window and then select the Find dialog box, that text will be automatically added to the Find What combo box.

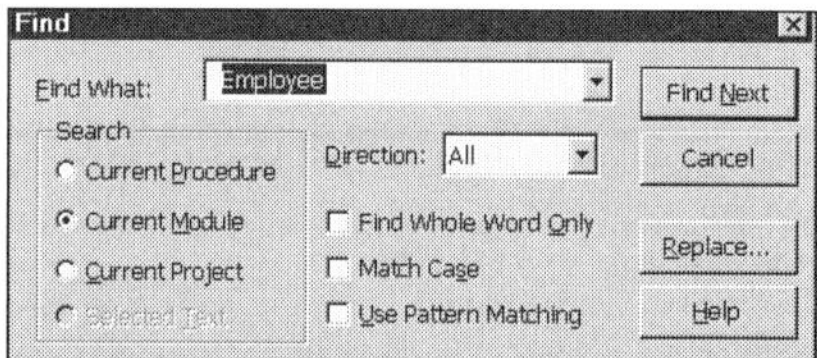

FIGURE 18.1 The Find dialog box.

This dialog box allows you to enter some text in the Find What field and then click the Find Next command button to find the next location in your code that matches the string. You can leave this dialog box open and keep clicking the Find Next command button to find the subsequent occurrences of the string. You can also close the Find dialog box and then press F3 to perform the Find Next operation over and over again.

You also have other options for finding a particular string in your source code. You can choose to search only within the current procedure, search within the current module, or search across all the modules in the entire project. In addition, you can find a whole word that matches the string you input, you can perform a case-sensitive search, and you can put in wildcards such as "*" and "?" to perform pattern matching. The wildcard characters are the same as what you use to find a file in Explorer. For example, if you input `str*`, the Find dialog box searches for any word that begins with the letters *str*. Also, you can use `?` as a placeholder for one character. Therefore, if you input `?str`, the Find dialog box searches for any word that contains any letter followed by the letters *str*.

Search and Replace

Many times when you're programming, you need to replace a certain string of text with something different (for example, changing a variable from one name to another). This can be done in the Replace dialog box. To bring up the Replace dialog box, you can select Edit, Replace from the Visual Basic menu, press Ctrl+H from within a code window, or click the Replace command button in the Find window. Figure 18.2 shows you an example of the Replace dialog box.

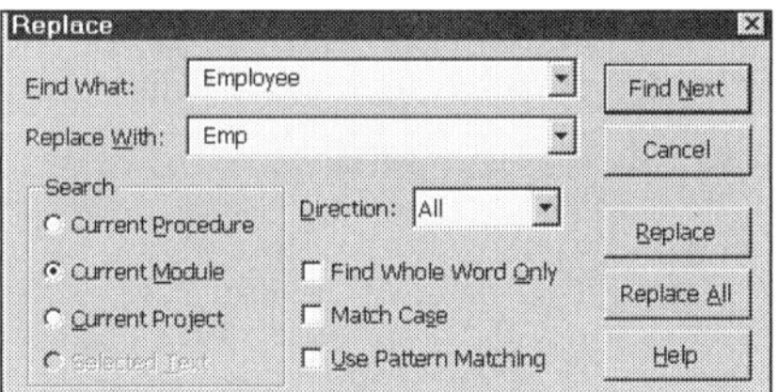

FIGURE 18.2
The Replace dialog box.

This dialog box is essentially the same as the Find dialog box, but it allows you to replace a certain piece of text with a different piece of text at a time by using the Replace button. You can also find the next occurrence of the Find What text by clicking the Find Next button. If you want to replace all the values within the scope specified, you can click the Replace All button.

Editing with a Split Screen

Just below the Object and Proc bar in the code window, you can see a thin line. If you grab this line with your mouse, you can drag it down until there are two panes in the edit window. This is very useful if you need to look at module-level variables at the same time you're editing some code in another part of the module. Figure 18.3 shows an example of this.

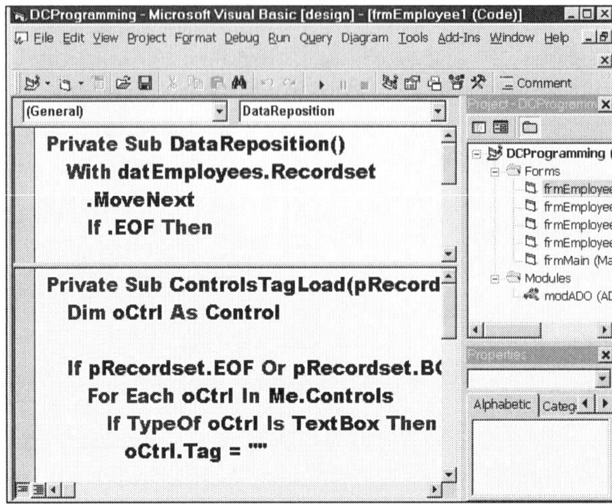

FIGURE 18.3 Split-screen editing.

Moving to the Next/Previous Procedure

You can use a few different methods to move to the next or previous procedure for the current module when you're in procedure view. You can press any of the following keys to move up through the list of procedures:

- Ctrl+up arrow
- Ctrl+Page Up
- Page Up

Also, you can use any of the following keys to move down through the list of procedures:

- Ctrl+down arrow
- Ctrl+Page Down
- Page Down

Jumping to a Procedure Definition

If you're looking at a code module that calls a procedure or function, you can move your cursor to that procedure/function call and press Shift+F2, select Procedure Definition from the View menu, or right-click the procedure name in the call and select Definition from the pop-up menu. This displays the procedure definition in the code window.

Using a Block Indent

If you want to indent a group of lines in the editor, highlight the block of text with your mouse or use the Shift and arrow keys. Next, press the Tab key to execute the move. The entire block moves to the right by the amount specified in your Tab Stop Width setting. Press Shift+Tab to move the entire block back to the left. You can also select Indent or Outdent from the Edit menu.

To align a group of lines, press Shift+Tab until they're all flush against the left margin; then press Tab until they're properly indented.

Using a Block Comment

Sometimes you need to comment out a block of code. To do this, you can manually place a single quote before each line. However, the Edit toolbar presents an easier method. Select View, Toolbars, Edit from the Visual Basic menu. This displays the Edit toolbar, as shown in Figure 18.4. From here you can select the Comment Block and UnComment Block icons.

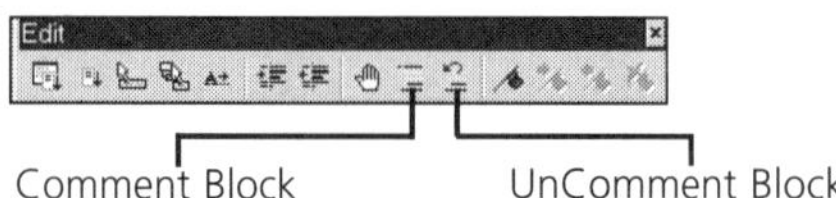

FIGURE 18.4 The Edit toolbar.

Now you can simply highlight a group of lines and click the Comment Block icon, or you can click the UnComment Block icon to toggle between commented code and uncommented code.

Viewing All Properties/Procedures

From any code window, you can press F2 to display the Object Browser. Here's where you can view all the object properties and procedures (methods) for all the objects in your project. The Object Browser also allows you to select which library of objects to view. You can view any of the loaded libraries (DLLs or OCXs) in your Visual Basic design environment. Besides properties and methods, you can also see any defined constants.

Using Full Module View

You can toggle the view of the editor to display either one procedure/function at a time or all procedures/functions. To do so, select Options from the Tools menu and then select the Editor tab and check or uncheck the Full Module View check box.

You can optionally have a line to separate the procedures by checking the Procedure Separator check box.

You can find a toggle for this option on every code window in the lower-left corner, as shown in Figure 18.5.

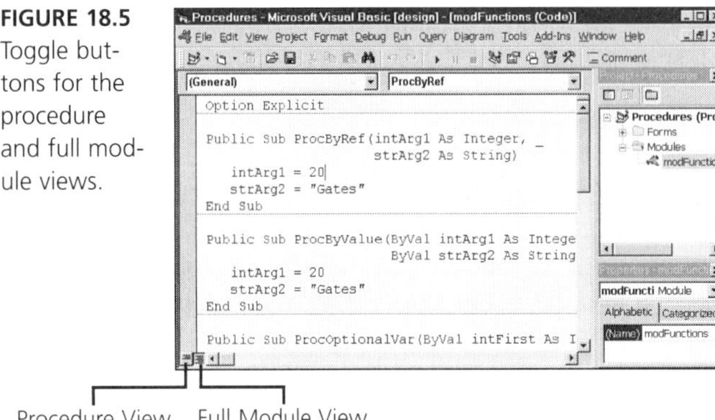

FIGURE 18.5 Toggle buttons for the procedure and full module views.

Tabbing Between Windows

To move quickly between the various open windows (forms, classes, modules) in your Visual Basic session, press Ctrl+Tab to iterate forward and Shift+Ctrl+Tab to iterate backward. This keeps your hands on the keyboard instead of having to use the mouse to select a specific window.

Creating New Procedures and Functions Quickly

There are two ways to create a new procedure or function. You can select Tools, Add Procedure from the Visual Basic menu, or you can move your cursor to the first line or last blank line in a code window and type **`Sub`** or **`Function`**. Next, you type the name of the procedure or function and press the Enter key. You may optionally include the `Public` or `Private` scope keywords and parameters.

Using Bookmarks

While editing a large project, you may find yourself bouncing around from procedure to procedure in different modules. If this is the case, you may want to quickly get back to a specific line of code. You can use the Bookmarks icon on the Edit toolbar to set a bookmark. Position your cursor on a line of code and press the Toggle Bookmark icon (see Figure 18.6).

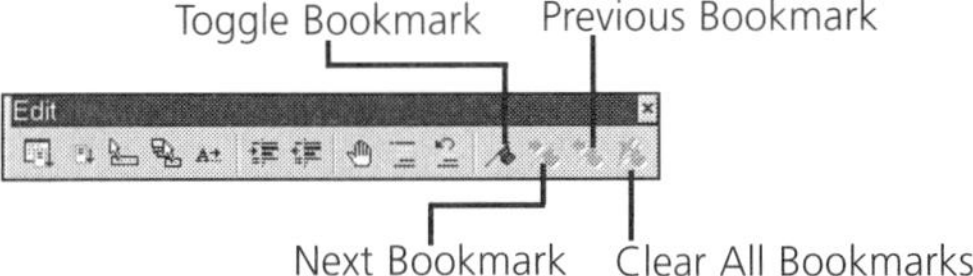

FIGURE 18.6
Bookmark icons on the Edit toolbar.

You can continue placing as many bookmarks as you want in a project. You can then use the Next and Previous Bookmark icons to move from one to the other. Note that you cannot save bookmarks. When you close the Visual Basic development environment, all the bookmarks will be erased.

Form Editing Tips and Tricks

As is the case when using the code window, you have some tips and tricks available to help speed up your development time when creating your user interface.

Setting the *Font* Property

If you set the `Font` property on a form prior to adding controls to the form, all the controls you add will inherit the font style for that form. This speeds up the process of making the fonts the same for all of your controls.

Setting the *TabIndex* Property

The `TabIndex` property is used to set the order in which the Tab key moves from one field to the next on a form. The lowest number is where the cursor starts on a form. Numbering continues sequentially until the last control is reached.

The easiest way to set the `TabIndex` property is to start with the control that's to be the last one in the tab order. Click this control and go to the Property window. Place a zero in `TabIndex` and press Enter. Now click the next-to-last control and enter zero. Continue this process until you finish with the first control.

Visual Basic automatically renumbers the `TabIndex` property if you enter a value for one control that already exists for another control. It assumes you want the current control to come before the previous one, so it renumbers all other controls starting with one greater than the value you just entered.

Marking Groups of Controls

To mark a group of controls at one time, place your mouse over the top-left corner of the form, press and hold down the left mouse button while dragging it until all controls are contained within the outline displayed. When you let go of the mouse button, all the controls are marked. You can also use the Shift or Ctrl key in combination with the left mouse click to individually mark controls.

After highlighting all the controls you want in the selection, look at the Properties window to see a list of properties that these controls have in common. For example, you can set the `Height` property and `Left` property for all these controls to one value. You can also highlight these controls and press the Del key to delete them from the form.

Another way to select all the controls on a form is to press the Ctrl+A key combination.

Marking Groups of Controls on a Container

To mark a group of controls inside a container control, click the container control to give it focus and then press and hold down the Ctrl key. Next, click and hold down the left mouse button and drag the cursor to outline all the controls within the container control. It's very important that you give the container control focus prior to selecting all the controls in it.

Using a Property Window Trick

You can press Ctrl+Shift+<*letter*> to move quickly to any property you want to change. For example, if you're positioned on the `Caption` property and you want to move to the `Width` property, press Ctrl+Shift+W to go to this property. If there are more properties with the same letter you can keep pressing Ctrl+Shift+<*letter*> to move to each new property.

Using Toggle Properties

Many properties, such as the Align property, allow you to select from an enumerated list of values. You can choose these values from a drop-down combo box. You can also double-click the property name itself to toggle the values from one to the other. You can also press the number or letter of the value and the property value will be updated in the Property Window.

Creating More Than One Control

If you hold down the Ctrl key while selecting a control from the toolbox, you can draw more than one control without having to reselect the control each time. Press the Esc key or select another control to return to a normal cursor.

Moving and Sizing Controls

Often you need to move one or more controls from one location to another. You have a couple ways you can accomplish this. First, you need to give the control focus or select multiple controls using the techniques described earlier. Next, you can move these controls with the mouse to the new location. The alternate method is to hold down the Ctrl key while using your arrow keys to move the controls one grid unit in any direction.

Controls may be sized by using the Shift key in combination with any of the arrow keys. If you want to increase the height of a control, use the Shift key with the up-arrow key. If you want decrease the width of a control, use the Shift key with the left-arrow key.

Formatting Controls

Lining up controls in a graphical environment can be a difficult process. Having the grid on the form really helps this process, but sometimes you need to line up several controls on a common grid line. Under the Format menu, you'll find many menu items that can help you to align and size controls on a particular grid and to a particular control.

In general, you'll use these formatting menu options on groups of controls. When you highlight a group of controls, one of the controls will be the "controller." This control will have its sizing handles in a different color from the rest. When you're applying any of the formatting options, this control will be the one that all the other controls get the sizing/formatting options from. The following headings are the names of the Format menu items. Letís go through each of these.

Align

This menu option allows you to align selected objects with each other using the object selected as the alignment reference. Table 18.1 shows you the different alignment commands used.

Table 18.1 Alignment Options in the Format Menu

Alignment	Description
Lefts	Puts the leftmost edges in line with the last selected object
Centers	Puts the centers in line with the last selected object
Rights	Puts the rightmost edges in line with the last selected object
Tops	Puts the tops in line with the last selected object
Middles	Puts the middles in line with the last selected object
Bottoms	Puts the bottoms in line with the last selected object
To Grid	Snaps the top-left corner of the selected objects to the closest grid

Make Same Size

Using the object selected as a reference, this menu option makes the other selected objects the same size (see Table 18.2).

Table 18.2 Sizing Options in the Format Menu

Sizing	Description
Width	Adjusts the width
Height	Adjusts the height
Both	Adjusts both the width and the height

Horizontal Spacing

The commands under this menu option change the horizontal spacing between selected objects (see Table 18.3).

Table 18.3 Horizontal Spacing Options Under the Format Menu

Spacing	Description
Make Equal	Makes the spacing between the selected objects equal, using the outermost objects as endpoints
Increase	Increases the horizontal spacing by one grid unit, based on the object with focus

Spacing	Description
Decrease	Decreases the horizontal spacing by one grid unit, based on the object with focus
Remove	Removes the horizontal spacing so that the objects are aligned with their edges touching, based on the object with focus

Vertical Spacing

The commands under this menu option change the vertical spacing between selected objects (see Table 18.4).

Table 18.4 Vertical Spacing Options Under the Format Menu

Spacing	Description
Make Equal	Makes the spacing between the selected objects equal, using the top and bottom objects as the endpoints
Increase	Increases the vertical spacing by one grid, based on the object with focus
Decrease	Decreases the vertical spacing by one grid, based on the object with focus
Remove	Removes the vertical spacing so that the objects' borders are touching, based on the object with focus

NOTE

If using the Vertical/Horizontal Spacing command does not produce the results you want, try to manually rearrange some of the objects and repeat the command.

Center in Form

The commands in this menu item center the selected objects on the central axes of the form (see Table 18.5).

Table 18.5 Centering Options Under the Format Menu

Centering	Description
Horizontally	Aligns the middles of the selected objects to a horizontal line in the middle of the form
Vertically	Aligns the centers of the selected objects to a vertical line in the center of the form

Order

The commands in this menu item change the order of the selected objects on a form (see Table 18.6).

Table 18.6 Ordering Options Under the Format Menu

Order	Description
Bring to Front	Moves the selected objects to the front of all other objects on a form
Send to Back	Moves the selected objects behind all other objects on a form

Lock Controls

From the Format menu, you can choose the Lock Controls menu item. When you select this, all the controls on a particular form are locked down. This means that any attempt to move the controls will be unsuccessful until the controls are unlocked. This is very useful after you've finished precisely lining up controls and now need to click the controls to add code. This way, you cannot inadvertently move the controls.

Changing the IDE

You'll find many items in the Tools, Options menu you can use to change how the IDE works.

Docking

By default, all the toolboxes are docked to the sides of the Visual Basic IDE. This can be changed by selecting Tools, Options from the Visual Basic menu and then under the Docking tab unchecking which toolboxes you don't want docked.

SDI Development Environment

Before Visual Basic 4, the IDE used to consist of individual free-floating windows. If you want to go back to this style of IDE, you can select the SDI Development Environment option from the Advanced tab of the Tools, Options menu item.

Toolbars

The toolbars that appear below the menus in the IDE can be docked on the top, left, right, or bottom. You simply drag and drop them to where you want them located.

The four basic toolbars are Standard, Edit, Form, and Debug. They each have icons that relate to the different functions you perform when in their respective modes. You can display as many of these toolbars as you want at one time.

Customizing Toolbars

You can customize any of the existing toolbars in the Visual Basic environment. Select View, Toolbars, Customize from the Visual Basic menu bar to bring up the Customize dialog box, as shown in Figure 18.7.

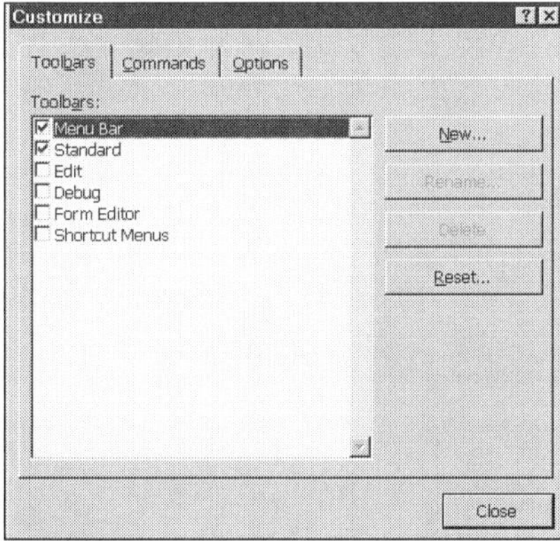

FIGURE 18.7 The Customize dialog box.

From the Toolbars tab, you have the option of selecting a toolbar so that it appears within the development environment, adding a new toolbar that you can then add icons to, or resetting a toolbar back to its normal state. If you choose the Commands tab, you'll see a screen like the one shown in Figure 18.8. From here, you can drag and drop commands from the list box on the right to any of the displayed toolbars in the Visual Basic Design Environment.

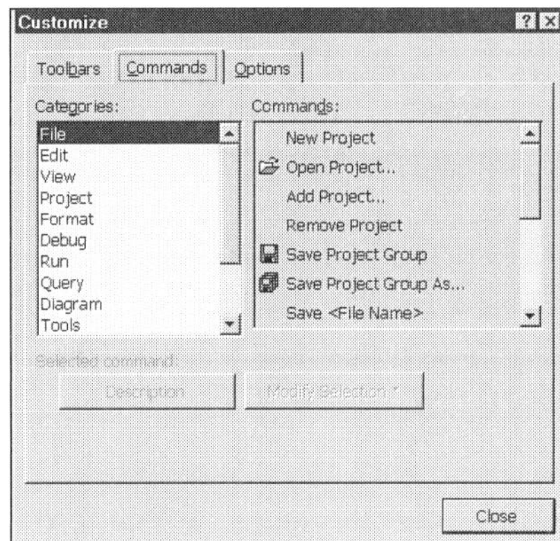

FIGURE 18.8 The Commands tab on the Customize dialog box.

Add-Ins

Visual Basic ships with many different utilities that are included under the Add-Ins menu. If you select the Add-Ins, Add-Ins Manager menu item, you'll see a list of items similar to the list shown in Figure 18.9.

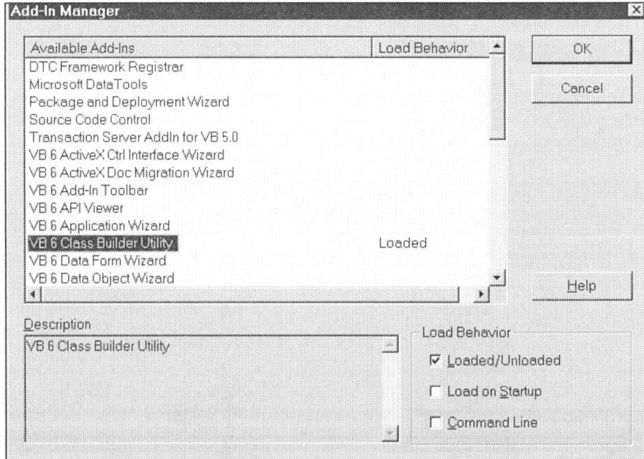

FIGURE 18.9 The Add-In Manager dialog box.

All the items that start with VB6 were installed with the Visual Basic 6 development environment. These add-ins are used to help you develop your application. Table 18.7 briefly describes each add-in in this list.

Table 18.7 Add-ins in Visual Basic 6

Add-in	Description
VB6 ActiveX Ctrl Interface Wizard	This add-in comes in handy when you're creating ActiveX controls. It helps you add properties, events, and methods to your ActiveX controls.
VB6 ActiveX Doc Migration Wizard	If you have an existing Visual Basic application that you want to run under a browser, try using this add-in to help you migrate this application to an ActiveX document. Although it doesn't work very well on any normal application, it works fine for a simple demo.
VB6 API Viewer	This API viewer is the same one that appears under the Microsoft Visual Studio 6.0 Tools folder.
VB6 Application Wizard	This add-in gives you a good start on developing a full MDI, SDI, or Explorer-like application.
VB6 Class Builder Utility	If you'll be building a lot of class modules, you'll definitely need to use this utility to help you build all the properties and methods.
VB6 Data Form Wizard	If you'll be creating data entry forms with bound controls, this wizard will help you build those forms just by selecting a table in your database.
VB6 Data Object Wizard	For three-tier applications, you might utilize this tool to build classes that interact with a database.
VB6 Property Page Wizard	When you're building ActiveX controls, this tool helps you build a property page for your custom properties.
VB6 Resource Editor	If you'll be creating any multilingual applications, a resource file is needed to hold all the strings that appear in the labels and messages. The Resource Editor add-in will help you build a file for all of these messages.

continues

Table 18.7 Continued

Add-in	Description
VB6 Template Manager	When you select this add-in, three new menus items are added to the Tools menu. All three add items to the currently displayed form in the design mode. First, you can have templates of menus that can be added. Second, you can have templates of code snippets that you can add to a form or module. Third, you can have control sets, complete with code, that you can add to a form.
VB6 Wizard Manager	If you want to build a wizard like the ones you see in Microsoft products, this add-in will help you manage the design of the different forms that make up the wizard.

You'll learn about these various add-in throughout this book.

Toolbox Tricks

The Visual Basic 6 toolbox that has the custom controls on it can be changed to a different width, and you can create additional tabs. As you add and subtract the custom controls via the Project, Components menu, you'll see that your toolbox can grow quite large. In fact, as you add more controls to the toolbox, it can grow so large that you won't be able to see all the controls. At this point, you'll need to grab the right edge of the toolbox to increase the width of the toolbox.

Of course, if you add too many controls, then your toolbox takes up the whole width of your design environment. In this case, you might want to break up your toolbox into different tabs in addition to the General tab on the toolbox.

EXERCISE

CREATE TABS ON THE TOOLBOX

1. Right-click the toolbox.
2. Select Add Tab from the context-sensitive menu.
3. Fill in a new tab name. For example, you may want to put all grid- and list-type controls under a new tab named Lists.

After you've created this new tab, you can just drag and drop controls from the General tab to this tab.

Creating Templates

When you select Project, Add Form or any of the "Add" menu items, you're typically presented with a Template dialog box that asks you for the kind of template you want to add. You're allowed to add to this list of templates. Under the default folder for your Visual Basic 6 installation, you'll find the \Template folder. Under this folder, you'll find different folders for each of the different types of items you can add to a project. For example, there's the \Forms folder for different form templates and the \Classes folder for different class templates. If you design a form that you want to use in all your projects, you can simply copy that form to the \Forms folder, and it will then appear in the Template dialog box when you select Project, Add Form from the Visual Basic menu bar.

Summary

There are many keystrokes and mouse tricks you can use in the development environment. These tips and tricks should help you in your development efforts. I gathered this list from techniques I use and my employees use in our shop. For more information on keystrokes you can use in the IDE, check the Visual Basic Books Online.

Review Questions

1. What's the hot key combination that brings up the Find dialog box?
2. What's the hot key combination that brings up the Replace dialog box?
3. Which property sets the tab order of controls on a form?
4. Why would you use a bookmark?
5. What's an add-in?

Exercises

1. Try some of the Format menu items on your forms.
2. Add the Comment and UnComment buttons to your Standard toolbar.

Intermediate Visual Basic 6

19

Object-based Programming

VISUAL BASIC 4 INTRODUCED THE ABILITY TO CREATE classes, thus opening the door for object-based programming. This chapter discusses the object-based programming (OBP) paradigm and how it has been implemented in Visual Basic. You'll become conversant with the terminology that's utilized when talking about OBP. You'll also create your own class modules, learn how to make a form an object, and see a real example of a class that you'll be able to use in your applications.

Chapter Objectives

- Learn object-oriented terminology
- Learn to create class modules
- Learn to create some reusable classes

Sample Filename: None

Defining Object-based Programming

Object-based programming (OBP) is a method of software design and construction. It's the next logical progression from structured programming, and it improves your code reusability and maintainability.

Object-based programming and object-oriented programming (OOP) are very similar, but Visual Basic is not an object-oriented language. Instead, it has an object-like syntax and can deal with objects that you create or ones that have already been created. In this chapter, I use the term OOP to refer to both object-oriented and object-based programming.

Object-based programming is simply a method of designing individual software components (classes) with associated behaviors (methods) and data (properties) and then piecing these components together to create a complete application.

Objects are designed and implemented as individual units that accomplish a specific task, or tasks, independent of any other objects or code within an application. OOP languages were designed with a windowing environment in mind. The complexities of dealing with windows makes the OOP paradigm almost a necessity.

OOP Terminology

When moving to any new software development method, such as OOP, you must learn some new terms. These terms may seem strange at first, but I think you'll find that most of them relate to concepts you've probably already implemented in your existing applications. Let's take a look at each of the new terms.

Class

A *class* is a template or blueprint for how an object will look and behave at runtime. The class contains all the methods and properties (code and data) for an instance of an object. Think of a class as a cookie cutter. This cookie cutter can be used to make as many cookies as you want. All the cookies will look exactly alike immediately after you cut them.

Object

An *object* is an instance of a class. An object is a physical entity that you can interact with at runtime. An object is defined as being of the type `ClassName`. For example, you declare a string or integer variable like this:

```
Dim strName As String
Dim intLoop As Integer
```

You declare an object variable in pretty much the same manner:

```
Dim oEmployee As Employee
```

The variable `oEmployee` is the object you use at runtime, just as you would use a variable named `strName`. The important point is that you would not use `Employee` at runtime, just like you would not use `String` as a variable in your program.

Differences Between Classes and Objects

There's a lot of confusion and misuse of the terms *class* and *object*. The two are very different from each other, but they are often used interchangeably. Once again, a *class* is a template. A template is a blueprint from which objects are made. An *object* is a physical entity that exists in memory. Each object is based on a class template.

When learning the difference between a class and an object, you might find it helpful to go back to the cookie cutter example. You know those metal (or plastic) things you stick into cookie dough. The cookie cutter can be used to create several cookies (objects). Each individual cookie is an object. However, you would not eat the metal template!

Each cookie can have different properties set on it. For example, the first cookie you create might have its `PowderedSugar` property set to `True`, whereas the second cookie might have its `ColoredSprinkle` property set to `True`. Although these objects were created from the same class, they are separate, distinct entities in memory, and each can have different properties set.

TIP

Classes are templates, whereas objects are the actual physical entities.

Properties are only one piece of a class. The other part consists of methods that can be performed. Going back to the cookie example, the `Cookie` class can have several methods, such as `Bake` and `Eat` (`Eat` being the most prevalent).

Now we need to relate this to the classes and objects you're already familiar with in Visual Basic. Let's think about forms and text boxes. Each form you create in a project can have different properties set; however, they are all derived from the same form class. Same with text boxes—they're also derived from the same class, but each one has different properties. You're already familiar with classes and objects. Now all you need to do is learn what to use them for and how to create your own in Visual Basic.

Instantiation

Instantiation is the act of creating an object based on a class. In Visual Basic terms, this is the process of declaring the object and then using it in your program. When you instantiate an object in Visual Basic, it takes up memory and possibly resources in the system. If a class is a cookie cutter and the object is a cookie, then the process of creating the cookie based on the cookie cutter is *instantiation*.

In Visual Basic, an object is instantiated when the first property or method is called, or when you create a new instance of that class. Take the following code example:

```
Sub TestObject ()
   Dim oEmp As Employee

   Set oEmp = New Employee   ' Creates object here

   oEmp.FirstName = "Bill"
End Sub
```

The object is instantiated on the line where the `New` keyword is used.

Properties

The concept of *properties* should not be new to you at this point. You' ve used properties to affect the look or behavior of a particular form or control. Properties simply hold the data about the particular object. These properties are defined by the class to be used by each individual object instantiated by that class.

Properties may be either public or private. Public properties are those that are exposed for use by other objects or code in an application. For example, a form object has `Top`, `Left`, `Width`, and `Height` properties. These public properties can be changed from the Properties window of Visual Basic.

Private properties are used only internally by the object itself. Internally, a form may hold other data, such as the window style and the parent who owns the window. This is data that you cannot see or change but is still part of the form class.

Here are some examples of public properties:

```
frmEmployee.Top = 10
txtFirstName.Text = "Bill"
```

Methods

Methods are procedures or functions defined by a class. These snippets of code can only be invoked through a corresponding object that's created as that type of class. Methods are typically used to change something about the object or tell the object to perform some action. Let's use an example from some built-in objects in Visual Basic. Here's an example:

```
frmEmployee.Move 100, 100
```

This line of code moves the frmEmployee form to a specified location on the screen. The `Move` method is part of the `Window` class, upon which a Visual Basic form is based. Some programmer wrote source code to make a form object move. Another example would be to use the common dialog control, like this:

```
dlgCommon.ShowOpen
```

In this example, you're telling an object to perform some action on itself. The message you're sending to this object is to show its Open dialog box. The common dialog control knows how to perform this action. In fact, if you were to look at the `ShowOpen` method, you would see that all it does is perform some Windows API calls, which you could actually do yourself from Visual Basic. The big difference here is that you simply need to remember one method instead of all the parameters and declarations needed to make the Windows API calls.

Encapsulation

Encapsulation is another word for *data hiding*. The concept of data hiding has been around since the beginning of programming. Most programmers strive to create "black-box routines," which are passed some data, perform some operation, and maybe pass something back. You don't know how the routine performs the operation, you only know that the data you receive is correct. In other words, the functionality has been encapsulated in this routine. In OOP, you encapsulate properties (data) and methods (subroutines) into a single class file.

Polymorphism

Literally translated from Greek, *polymorphism* means *multifaceted* or *many faced*. What this means in the programming world is that similar classes can contain properties and methods of the same name, but they have different behaviors. For example, two objects of different class types may have `Paint` methods, but what they paint is different for each object. Here's another example: You have a `Customer` object and an `Invoice` object, and each has a `Print` method. Obviously, the `Print` method does different things for the `Customer` object than it does for the `Invoice` object.

Most likely, you've already used polymorphism and you may not have even realized it. If you create two forms, you have created two separate classes. When you display each form, you use the method `Show`. This method is implemented in each form, but it displays each form differently because each form is designed differently.

OOP purists would argue that to truly have polymorphism, you must have inheritance. Because Visual Basic implements "interfaces" and not "inheritance," they would be right. However, polymorphism can still exist, just by defining a standard set of properties and methods that are used across all your own objects.

Constructors

A *constructor* is a procedure that's automatically invoked when an object is first instantiated. Constructors contain code to perform an object's initialization. Each class created in Visual Basic has a `Class_Initialize()` procedure as its constructor.

The best example of a constructor involves what happens when you insert a new form into a project. The form appears in the design environment with a default size, border style, colors, and so on. This does not happen by magic—some programmer wrote the constructor event for a form class that initializes all the properties for that form object.

Consider an example of a class module that opens a handle to a file on disk. To do this, it must ask the operating system for the file handle. The operating system allocates that file handle in memory and passes it to Visual Basic. If you forget to release that file handle, you've stolen resources from the operating system. In the `Class_Initialize` procedure, you grab the file handle, and in the *destructor*, you release that file handle.

TIP
Use constructors to initialize the data for an object.

Destructors

A *destructor* is a procedure that's automatically invoked when an object is destroyed. Destructors contain code that performs an object's cleanup. Each class created in Visual Basic has a `Class_Terminate()` routine as its destructor.

When you remove a form from a Visual Basic project, all the memory and resources allocated to that form when it was created must now be "deallocated." Again, a programmer had to write all the code to perform this deallocation when a form object is destroyed by Visual Basic.

Let's take the example of an object that uses a file handle. You write the code to make sure that the file handle is closed and released back to the operating system before that reference to the object goes out of scope. The code to close the file handle is most likely contained within the destructor of that class.

This is very similar to how the Data control works. If you place a Data control on a form it will open a recordset object for you. You don't need to ever close that recordset because the Data control does this for you. When the Data control is released from memory it calls the destructor method on the Recordset object which will close and release that object for you.

TIP
Use `Class_Terminate()` to close file handles or perform other cleanup for an object.

Object-based Coding Versus Procedural Coding

There's are big differences between procedural coding and object-oriented coding. The biggest one is how you deal with data in both methodologies. In the object-oriented paradigm, the data is passed in once to the object repository (properties) and then all routines (methods) work on this data without having to pass the data to each method. With procedural code, the data has to be passed to each function individually or be made global. Either way, you leave yourself wide open to mistakes. In procedural coding, you'll generally see longer parameter lists than in object-oriented programming.

Procedural Data Usage

As an example of procedural coding, think of how you would have to draw a form if forms were not objects. Remember that a form has many properties in its properties sheet. To accomplish this using procedural coding, you have to pass all the properties as parameters to a procedure to tell the form how to draw itself. Here's an example:

```
Call DisplayEmpForm(1, 1, 1025, 2045, _
        1, 1, 0, &H000000, &HF00000, "Sans Serif", _
        True, False, etc., etc., etc.)
```

In the `DisplayEmpForm` procedure call, you can see each of the different "properties" is being passed as a data value. There are several problems with this scenario. First, you must remember what each parameter is and what position to pass it in. Second, the line of source code is very long. Third, there's no way to initialize the function so the data values are initialized (constructor). Fourth, if you want to change, add, or delete any parameters, you'll break every line of code that calls this function (unless you can set up optional parameters). As you can see, there are a lot of problems with the traditional approach to programming applications.

OOP's Data Usage

A form is an object that set defaults for most of its properties in its constructor event. You only have to change the properties you need to override and then invoke a method to display the form:

```
frmEmployee.Top = 10
frmEmployee.Left = 10
frmEmployee.Show
```

The object takes care of all the details internally concerning how to display itself. Additionally, if you need to add more functionality, you simply add a new property and set a default for it in the constructor. This does not break any existing code, but any object that needs this new property may now use it. Also, if this new property adds something to the interface of the object, every object now gets this new change without any other source code changes!

Function/Method Naming

Another advantage of OOP is *polymorphism* (the ability for each object to have the same method names but perform different actions based on those methods). For example, an Employee form is different from a TimeSheet form, but each has a

`Show` method and a `PrintForm` method. The Employee form is displayed differently and printed differently from the TimeSheet form, but each one has the same method names.

In a procedural language, you would have to come up with different names for each of the functions to show or print a screen, such as `EmpShow`, `EmpPrint`, `TimeSheetShow`, and `TimeSheetPrint`. For us as programmers, this makes it more difficult to remember all these function names. It also makes it more difficult to keep coming up with new names that are unique for each new form added to the application.

Staying Consistent

It's very important to stay consistent in the naming of your methods. If you've defined one verb (`Show`) as the method used to display an object, all your objects should always use the same verb. If you teach all your programmers to use this one verb, they only need to memorize one word.

As we all know, different people can use different verbs to describe the same action. One programmer may create an object and call the method to display this object `Show`. Another programmer may create another object and call the method to display this object `Display`. Yet another creates another object and calls the method to display the object `Draw`. All three verbs mean the same thing, but each object now has a completely different interface. For new programmers trying to use these objects, they now have to look up the method used to display a particular object.

Another advantage to this consistency is that you can create a collection of objects in an application that you need to iterate over and invoke a method. If the method to invoke has the same name across all objects, you only need one line of code to accomplish this. Here's an example:

```
Dim oObject As Object
For Each oObject In colOfObjects
   oObject.Show
Next
```

If the objects didn't have a consistent interface, the following code would have to be written:

```
Dim oObject As Object
For Each oObject In colOfObjects
   If TypeOf oObject is Employee
```

```
      oObject.Show
   ElseIf TypeOf oObject is TimeSheet
      oObject.Display
   ElseIf TypeOf oObject is EmpType
      oObject.Draw
   End If
Next
```

Not only is this code more difficult to read, it's also much slower to execute because Visual Basic is forced to perform type checking against each of the different types of objects.

Converting to Object-based Programming

The hardest part of learning object programming is not the terminology or writing code. You can learn the new words, and writing code you've probably been doing for years. What's not so easy is deciding what should be a class and what should not. To help you make the decision, you can follow a few methods to identify objects.

Converting Existing Projects

The first method involves looking at an existing Visual Basic projects that was developed procedurally. Find some global variables that all have some relationship to one another. Then find those functions that use those global variables. Chances are that the global variables can become properties of a class, and the public procedures that operate upon those global variables can become the methods.

Replacing User-defined Types

Another method also looks at an existing project. If you've ever used user-defined types, you'll know that these are very similar to objects. The only difference is that the user-defined type is just the data (properties). You then need to find the functions that utilize this user-defined type, and you should be able to combine both of these items into one class.

Making Form Properties

The last method of determining what should be a class involves looking at global variables that are just used to pass information from one form to another. If you have this situation, you can now make properties on forms so that you can pass data from one form to another.

Simple Object-based Design

To find classes in a project, you first need to analyze what you need that application to accomplish. If you're creating a business application, such as an employee time-tracking system, you can identify the following items in the real world:

- Employees
- Employee types
- Timesheets

You'll also find that the following actions need to be performed:

- Employees are input to the system.
- An employee's information is printed.
- Employees are assigned a type.
- Employee types are input to the system.
- Timesheet information is input to the system.

In this example, you've identified the objects—`Employees`, `EmployeeTypes`, and `TimeSheets`—and you've identified some actions (methods)—`Employees.Input`, `Employees.Print`, `EmployeeTypes.Input`, and `EmployeeTypes.Print`. Now you simply need to identify all the attributes (data or properties) for each object. For the `Employees` object, you have the following properties:

- First Name
- Last Name
- Employee ID
- Address
- City
- State
- ZIP Code
- Salary

You can make properties for each of these items in the `Employees` object. You would then identify the properties for each of the other objects in your system.

As you can see, object-oriented design involves looking at things in the real world and modeling them in terms of objects, actions, and data (or classes, methods, and properties). There are several tools available on the market that can help you create a design document using a Unified Modeling Language (UML). These tools let you create pictures that will model the entities you are trying to automate in your program. In some cases these tools allow you to even generate the classes for your application.

Other Examples of Classes

Many classes are reusable in many different business applications. These classes don't really model things in the real world so much as they deal with computer-related items used in software development. Here are some reusable classes that you'll see built in this book and that can be used in your own applications:

- INI file class
- Registry class
- TextStream class

The reason for creating these classes is to abstract and encapsulate the data and methods into easy-to-use routines. This makes performing operations on these type of processes easier to do for beginning programmers, and it lets advanced programmers focus on more critical areas of the application.

Advantages of OOP

Now that you've learned the terminology of OOP and how to apply it in Visual Basic, let's look at some of the advantages of using this methodology. You've already been exposed to most of these advantages; they're reiterated here so you'll *really* learn them.

Encapsulation

In any programming language, you should strive to make black-box functions. These routines should perform tasks for you, without you knowing how they actually did the work. This is called *encapsulation*. Unfortunately, not all black-box routines are totally self-contained. They often rely on global variables or other routines.

By defining the exposure of the properties and methods of a class, the developer can define the safe behavior of the object without relying on external sources.

Polymorphism

Different classes can contain methods and properties of the same name. As such, working with these different objects becomes very easy. You no longer need to memorize the different calls for each object; instead, you can always make the same call, just to different objects. For example, two classes, `clsEllipse` and `clsSquare`, may both have `Paint` methods, but calling each one's `Paint` method causes different and obvious results. From a design point of view, the application that uses these objects is not concerned about how or what the objects paint, it just wants them to paint. Because the methods have the same name, the interface to both objects is very easy to use and remember.

Testing

Because classes define discrete, encapsulated behavior, it's easier to test the class as a whole than it is to test the system as a whole. The term *unit testing* fits better with object-oriented programming than with any other programming method. This is not to say that "system" testing is not required. It's just easier to test the robustness of a class than it is a set of unrelated code that may have to be called in a specific sequence.

Code Reusability

Because classes should be designed as self-contained units, they can be shared between projects very easily. All the data as well as the routines that operate on that data are encapsulated in the class definition; therefore, name conflicts with other routines and variables isn't a concern. Adding an existing class to a project is as simple as adding the appropriate CLS file.

Disadvantages of OOP

Of course, not all of OOP is nice and rosy. Like any programming method, it does have its drawbacks. Let's discuss some of the disadvantages to OOP.

The Learning Curve

The learning curve to understanding and creating robust classes is not small. Most of us have had the procedural method of development ingrained in us since we first started programming. Do not underestimate the time it's going to take to modify your current way of thinking. It's very easy to create classes, but it's not so easy to create truly robust, reusable classes. In addition, the design process for OOP is much different than the procedural, top-down design that you may have learned. Of course, if you're brand new to programming, this type of programming method might actually come to you a lot easier.

Performance

Unfortunately, the performance of some object-based programming languages suffer somewhat. With Visual Basic, you may find a 10 to 20% speed reduction when using objects as opposed to functions. However, with a little bit of optimization, such as using `With...End With`, and caching properties in local variables, most of this performance hit can be reduced. With today's faster computers, this is not as much of an issue as it once was.

Not Everything Is an Object

The biggest mistake most developers make when learning OOP is to try to make everything a class. Not every task fits well in the object-oriented paradigm. You'll still write a lot of code that's *not* object oriented. You need to be able to identify those tasks that are appropriate to encapsulate as objects and those that are not.

For example, if you have some functions that perform string manipulation, and these functions do not rely on any global variables, just leave them as functions. You need to look at a function to see whether it just uses parameters passed to it and simply returns one value. If so, it's probably best to leave this as a simple function than to create a class.

TIP

Don't try to make everything in your application an object.

Summary

This chapter introduced you to the terminology used in object-oriented programming (OOP). Learning OOP is not hard, it just takes a little different thinking on your part. Although there are a lot of terms, most of them are concepts you already know about. OOP has both advantages and disadvantages; however, the advantages far outweigh the disadvantages.

Review Questions

1. What is polymorphism?
2. What does *instantiate mean*?

20

Creating Class Modules

Now that you understand the terminology of OOP, let's apply those concepts to Visual Basic. In this chapter, you'll create your own class modules, learn how to make a form an object, and see a real example of a class that you'll be able to use in your applications.

Chapter Objectives

- Learn to create class modules
- Learn to create some reusable classes
- Learn to set default properties

Example's Filename: \Chapter20\OOP.vbp

Visual Basic Class Modules

Visual Basic CLS files contain all the properties and methods for your classes. Classes can be created in two different ways in Visual Basic: You can select Project, Add Class Module from the Visual Basic menu, or you can select the Class Builder Utility from the Add-Ins menu.

Once you create a CLS file, you need to identify what types of internal data you need to hold in the class. You create `Private` variables in the General Declarations area of the class module to hold this data. Then you need to decide which properties you want to give read access and which properties you want to give write access.

You can decide which private data to give read and write access by using `Property Get` and `Property Let` procedures in your class. A `Property Get` procedure is like a function that returns information about a `Private` variable. A `Property Let` is like a procedure you can use to set information in a `Private` variable. There's also the `Property Set` procedure, which can be used to pass in an object reference to your class.

Creating a Simple Class

The first class you'll build will track information about an employee. You'll create a class called `Employee` that contains the properties `EmpID`, `FirstName`, `LastName`, and `Salary`. To build this class, use the steps outlined in the following exercise.

EXERCISE

Creating a Class Module

1. Create a new project using the Standard EXE template.
2. Insert a CLS file by selecting Project, Add Class Module.

3. Select a new class when prompted.
4. Press F4 to bring up the Properties window if it's not already docked in the design environment.
5. Set the `Name` property to `Employee`. Just ignore the other properties for now.
6. Add four `Private` data variables to the CLS file in the General Declarations area by typing in the following code:

```
Option Explicit

Private mlngEmpID As Long
Private mstrFirstName As String
Private mstrLastName As String
Private mcurSalary As Currency
```

Because you've created these variables as private module-level variables, no other routines outside of this class module will be able to read and write to these private variables. Obviously, one of the reasons to create an object is to allow other modules the ability to read and write to the properties of that object.

Reading Properties

After creating the private variables, you need to allow other modules in the project to read this private data. To accomplish this, you add multiple `Property Get` procedures to the class module.

EXERCISE

ADDING *PROPERTY GET* PROCEDURES

1. Add the following `Property Get` procedures to the `Employee` class:

```
Property Get EmpID() As Long
   EmpID = mlngEmpID
End Property

Property Get FirstName() As String
   FirstName = mstrFirstName
End Property
```

```
Property Get LastName() As String
    LastName = mstrLastName
End Property

Property Get Salary() As Currency
    Salary = mcurSalary
End Property
```

A `Property Get` procedure is just like a function because it returns a value to the calling procedure. To return a value from a function, you need to set the function name equal to the value to return. The preceding code returns the value of the private variables from each of the `Property Get` procedures by assigning the appropriate private variable the name of the `Property Get` procedure.

TIP

A `Property Get` procedure is like a function that returns a value.

Class Initialization

When an object is created from a class, all the private variables are initialized to the default value appropriate for that data type. If you create a private `String` variable, it will be initialized to a blank string. If you create a private `Integer` variable, it will be initialized to `0`. In the preceding example, you created a private `Currency` variable, so the default value for this variable will be `0`. To initialize this variable to a different value, you need to initialize it in the `Class_Initialize` event for the class.

To write the initialization code, select the left combo box from the class module window and open it so you can view the `Class` object. Select the `Class` object, and you'll see that the right combo box now contains the `Initialize` event. Visual Basic will automatically place `Sub Class_Initialize()` into the module.

EXERCISE

ADD A *CLASS_INITIALIZE()* EVENT

1. Add the following code to the Class_Initialize event:

```
Private Sub Class_Initialize()
    mlngEmpID = 1
    mcurSalary = 25000
End Sub
```

Now when you create an instance of this class, the mlngEmpID variable will be initialized to 1 and the mcurSalary variable will be initialized to 25000. To test this, let's use the form created by Visual Basic when you first entered the Visual Basic design environment. Follow the steps in the next exercise to create a form that uses the Employee class.

EXERCISE

USING YOUR NEW CLASS MODULE

1. Add a command button to the default form that was created when you entered the new project.
2. Set the Name property to cmdDisplay.
3. Set the Caption property to Display.
4. Double-click this command button.
5. Add the following code to this command button:

```
Private Sub cmdDisplay_Click()
    Dim oEmp As Employee

    Set oEmp = New Employee

    MsgBox oEmp.Salary
End Sub
```

When you click the command button at runtime, the Class_Initialize() event will be fired just prior to the call to the Property Get procedure for Salary(). This means the mcurSalary variable will be initialized to the value 25000. When you use the Salary property attached to the Employee object, the Property Get routine will be fired. The value in the mcurSalary variable is returned and passed to the MsgBox statement to be displayed on the screen.

Writing to Properties

Besides just reading values from private data values in an object, you'll also want to write information into these private data values. For this you need to create a `Property Let` procedure. A `Property Let` procedure is a subroutine that accepts one argument—the value to set. The `Property Let` procedure should have the same name as the `Property Get` procedure. Let's add the appropriate `Property Let` routines to this class.

EXERCISE

ADDING *PROPERTY LET* PROCEDURES

1. Add the following `Property Let` procedures to the `Employee` class:

```
Property Let EmpID(ByVal lngEmpID As Long)
   mlngEmpID = lngEmpID
End Property

Property Let FirstName(ByVal strValue As String)
   mstrFirstName = strValue
End Property

Property Let LastName(ByVal strValue As String)
   mstrLastName = strValue
End Property

Property Let Salary(ByVal curSalary As Currency)
   mcurSalary = curSalary
End Property
```

The `Property Let` code for `FirstName` is fired when you set a value in the `FirstName` property, the `Property Let` code for `LastName` is fired when you set a value in the `LastName` property, and so on.

TIP

A `Property Let` procedure always has one parameter that's passed to it. The parameter is not required to be passed by value, but it's a good practice. Be aware that passing a parameter by value is much safer than passing it by reference. The parameter's type must be the same data type as the return value from the `Property Get` procedure of the same name.

EXERCISE

TRY OUT THE *PROPERTY LET*

1. Modify the code in the `cmdDisplay_Click()` event of the command button to set the `FirstName` and `LastName` properties as shown in the following code:

```
Private Sub cmdDisplay_Click()
    Dim oEmp As Employee

    Set oEmp = New Employee

    oEmp.FirstName = "Bill"
    oEmp.LastName = "Gates"

    MsgBox oEmp.LastName & ", " & oEmp.FirstName
End Sub
```

Visual Basic looks at the line of code that contains the call to a property of one of your objects to decide whether it should call `Property Get` or `Property Let`. If the property name is on the right side of an expression, it invokes `Property Get`. If the property name is on the left side of an expression, it invokes `Property Let`.

TIP

A `Property Let` procedure is like a Sub procedure that does *not* return a value.

Creating *Property Get* and *Property Let* Procedures

Instead of typing in the `Property Get` and `Property Let` procedures by hand, you can have the Visual Basic design environment create them for you. When you choose the Tools, Add Procedure menu item, you'll be prompted for a procedure name, as well as what type of procedure you want to create. Type in a name and then select a property procedure type. When you click the OK button, the two procedures are generated in the CLS module you have currently selected in the design environment. No code is generated in the procedures, but the two stubs are created for you.

Many programmers ask why they need to create `Property Get` and `Property Let` procedures. They argue that it's possible to simply create a `Public` variable that you can read and write to directly in the class. Although this is true, there are a couple of reasons why you might not want to do this. The biggest reason is that you want to control which properties are read-only, write-only, or both. Additionally, if you need to set other properties when one property is set, this can only be accomplished within a procedure. Another reason is that if you want to change the data type of a property, a procedure will let you perform the conversion, whereas a `Public` variable will not. One other reason is that you can always add data validation code to a `Property Let` procedure. If you have just a Public variable, you can't do this.

TIP
Always use property procedures to expose properties to external routines.

The Class Builder Utility

The Class Builder utility is an add-in to the Visual Basic design environment. It allows you to create new classes, add properties to those classes, and then save the class information back to the Visual Basic design environment. It writes all of the necessary code for create class modules for your application.

To use the Class Builder utility, select Add-Ins, Add-In Manager from the Visual Basic menu. Check the box located next to the Class Builder Utility option and then click the OK button. Now, under the Add-Ins menu, you'll find a menu for the Class Builder utility. Click this menu item, to display the form shown in Figure 20.1.

You can now add a new class to the project or change an existing class just by using this interface. The Class Builder utility can build default `Property Get` and `Property Let` procedures for you if you want. It also allows you to build one class based on the properties of another class. It doesn't allow inheritance—it only copies the appropriate properties and methods from the other class into the new class.

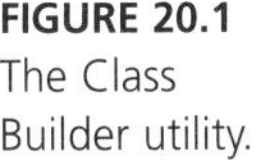

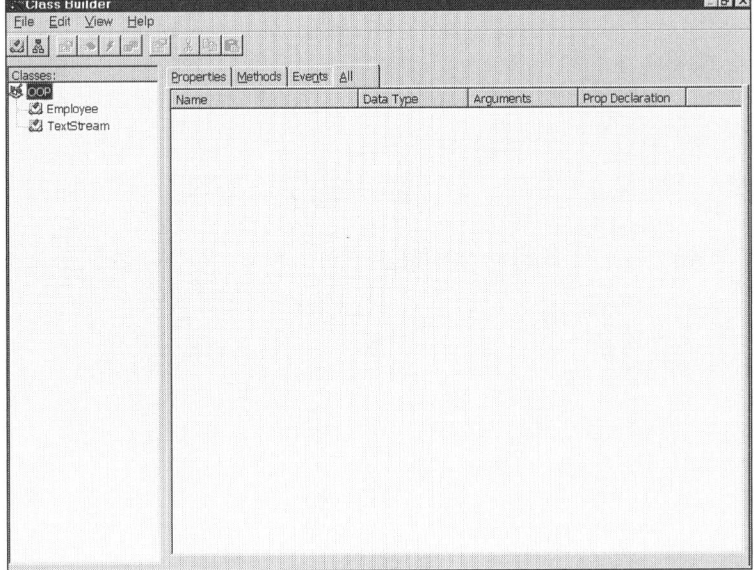

FIGURE 20.1
The Class Builder utility.

Methods

A *method* of a class is a `Public Sub` or `Public Function` created in the CLS file. A method is simply a subroutine or function that you would normally see in a BAS file, but instead it's tied to the object. These methods generally perform some operation on the data contained within the class. They may or may not return a value from the object. This will be determined by whether you write a sub or a function for the method name.

Let's write a method for the `Employee` class that returns a string showing the employee's name in a last name, first name format. To accomplish this, you need to create a new `Public Sub` called `EmployeeName` in the CLS file.

EXERCISE

Creating a Method

1. Create a new `Public Sub` in the `Employee` class module, as shown in the following code:

```
Public Sub EmployeeName()
    Dim strMsg As String

    strMsg = "Employee Name: " & mstrLastName & _
```

```
                    ", " & mstrFirstName & vbCrLf

    MsgBox strMsg
End Sub
```

Although this method doesn't perform anything very useful, it does get across the point that a method is simply Visual Basic code that operates on data within the class and returns that data in some other format. From the command button on the form, you can invoke this method with the following code:

```
Private Sub cmdDisplay_Click()
    Dim oEmp As Employee

    Set oEmp = New Employee

    oEmp.FirstName = "Bill"
    oEmp.LastName = "Gates"

    Call oEmp.EmployeeName
End Sub
```

As you can see, this simplifies the code quite a bit from the previous version, where you had to put the formatting within the command button. Now you can just call a method and it will perform the formatting for you.

Form Objects

Forms are classes! What this means is that you can have properties and methods attached to a form. Actually, forms have always been classes, but prior to Visual Basic 4, it was impossible to get at the underlying architecture to change anything. Now you can treat forms just like any other user-defined class you create.

Creating Form Properties

To create a property on a form, you simply create a `Private` variable in the General Declarations section and then create `Property Get` and `Property Let` procedures, just like you did in the CLS files. Of course, the big question is why would you want to do this? The main reason is to get rid of global variables.

In Visual Basic 3, there were only a couple of ways to pass information from one form to another. None of these were very efficient, and none were encapsulated. One technique was to create a label on the form to be called and pass in the data to the `Caption` property of the form. This worked, but had the side effect of loading the form prior to setting the data on the form. If you needed to use that data in the `Form_Load()` event, it was too late.

Another method was to have the called form reference back to the calling form's controls to grab some pieces of data. This also worked, but now if you wanted to use this one form in another project, it had a link to another form, which you would also have to bring into the project.

Yet another technique was to create some global variables, set them, then perform a `Show` on the form. This also has some drawbacks in that you were now tied to global variables that were in yet another BAS module that you had to bring into your other project if you wanted to reuse the form. Global variables also have a nasty habit of being changed when you least expect it, thereby causing all sorts of unpredictable results in your application.

Starting with Visual Basic 4, you can now create properties on a form, pass the data to that form, and then use that data in the `Form_Load()` event. The reason this can be done is because setting properties on a form does not load the form—it only sets up its data. Now you can copy the form to any other project, and it doesn't rely on any external forms or BAS files.

Example's Filenames: EmpType.frm and Emps.frm

To illustrate this technique, let's create a form for the Employee Types table from which you can select an employee type (see Figure 20.2).

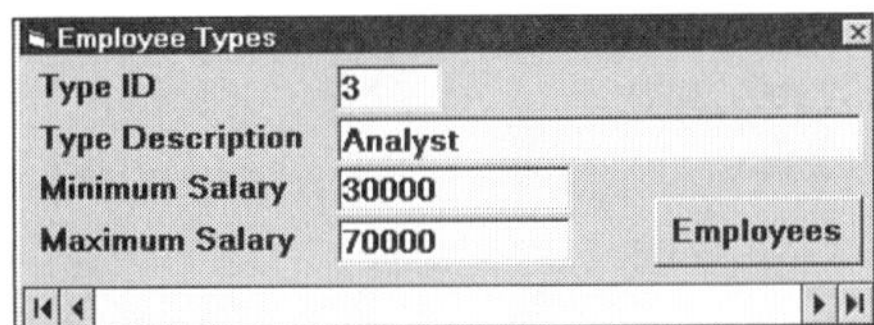

FIGURE 20.2
The Employee Types form.

From here, you should be able to pass the employee type to the Employee form and have it just select those employees that match the type. Here's the code:

```
Private Sub cmdEmployee_Click()
   With frmEmployee
      .EmpTypeID = CLng(Val(Trim$(txtTypeID)))
      .Show
   End With
End Sub
```

In this code, you can see that a property called `EmpTypeID` is being set on the Employee form prior to displaying the form. Setting the properties on the Employee form does not load the form. When the `Show` method is invoked, this property will already be set with the data from the txtTypeID text box on the Employee Types form.

TIP
Use property procedures within forms to pass data from one form to another.

Property Procedures in the Employee Form

In the Employee form, a `Property Let` procedure is created to allow any form or routine to set `EmpTypeID` prior to calling the Employee form:

```
Private mlngEmpTypeID As Long

Property Get EmpTypeID() As Long
   EmpTypeID = mlngEmpTypeID
End Property

Property Let EmpTypeID(ByVal lngValue As Long)
   mlngEmpTypeID = lngValue
End Property
```

These two property procedures hide the actual data value stored in the class. You can use this `Private` data value anywhere within the Employee form. Other forms must use the `Public` interface routines defined using the `Property Get/Let` procedures.

Now in the `Form_Load()` event for this form, you can use the `mlngEmpTypeID` variable to change the `RecordSource` property of a data control:

```
Private Sub Form_Load()
   Dim strSQL As String

   If mlngEmpTypeID <> -1 Then
      strSQL = "SELECT * FROM tblEmployees "
      strSQL = strSQL & " WHERE lEmpType_id = " & _
                        mlngEmpTypeID
      adatEmployees.RecordSource = strSQL
      adatEmployees.Refresh
   End If
End Sub
```

In this code, you check `mlngEmpTypeID` to see whether it's equal to `-1`. If it isn't, you know that the property has been set from another form. The reason you know this is because in the `Form_Initialize()` event, you set the `mlngEmpTypeID` to `-1`:

```
Private Sub Form_Initialize()
   mlngEmpTypeID = -1
End Sub
```

Because the `Form_Initialize()` event happens before any property is set, the value will always be initialized to `-1`. Then, if you call the `Property Let` procedure, you override the value with the employee type ID you pass in.

The *TextStream* Class

Let's now build a class that helps you read and write information in an ASCII text file. This class will encapsulate some of the low-level file I/O statements of Visual Basic so they can have a more object-oriented flavor. It can be a real pain dealing with all the file handles and different methods of opening files, as well as just reading from and writing to ASCII files. To eliminate some of the drudgery, this file I/O class handles the details for you, so all you need to do is set some properties and invoke some methods. This class module has already been built and is available in the sample project for this chapter.

I've modeled this example after the `TextStream` class, which is part of the `FileSystem` objects that come with Visual Basic for Applications. Table 20.1 presents the `Private` variables you'll declare in the General Declarations section of the `TextStream` class.

Table 20.1 *Private* Variables of the *TextStream* Class

Variables	Description
`mintHandle`	The file handle that's retrieved from the operating system. This is a private data item that will not be made public.
`mstrFileName`	The filename you want to read data from or write data to.
`mintOpenMode`	The mode in which you want to open the file. You can choose to open a file for appending data or for reading data. You'll specify this by using an enumerated constant.
`mintFormat`	You can choose the format for opening the file. This property does not actually work in this example—it's just here for compatibility with the real `TextStream` object in the `FileSystem` objects.
`mboolEOF`	This property return `True` when you hit the end of the file.

Table 20.2 lists the `Public` properties that will be exposed to the outside world by the `TextStream` class.

Table 20.2 *Public* Properties of the `TextStream` Class

Property	Description
`AtEndOfStream`	This method returns `True` when you're at the end of the file.
`FileName`	The filename you want to read data from or write data to.
`FileTooBig`	Returns `True` if the file is greater than 32KB in length.

Table 20.3 lists the methods that will be implemented in the `TextStream` class.

Table 20.3 Methods of the *TextStream* Class

Method	Description
`CloseFile`	Closes the file when you're through with it. This method is also called from the `Class_Terminate()` event.
`OpenTextFile`	Opens a file for reading or appending. You'll pass in the filename and the mode for opening the file.
`ReadLine`	Reads a line of data from the text file up to but not including the carriage return and linefeed characters.
`WriteLine`	Writes a line of data to the text file with a carrigage return and line feed placed onto the end of the line.

Let's look at the how you would use the `TextStream` class in an application. I've left out a lot of the error handling just to keep the examples short and understandable; however, in a production application, you would want to have the appropriate error handling in all of these routines.

Writing to a File Using the *TextStream* Class

You'll start out by learning how to write information from a text box into a text file. The form shown in Figure 20.3 has a text box in which you can type some text. It also has a text box that accepts a filename to write information into. After you've entered this text, the Write button can be clicked to put the information into the appropriate text file.

Example's Filename: FileWrite.frm

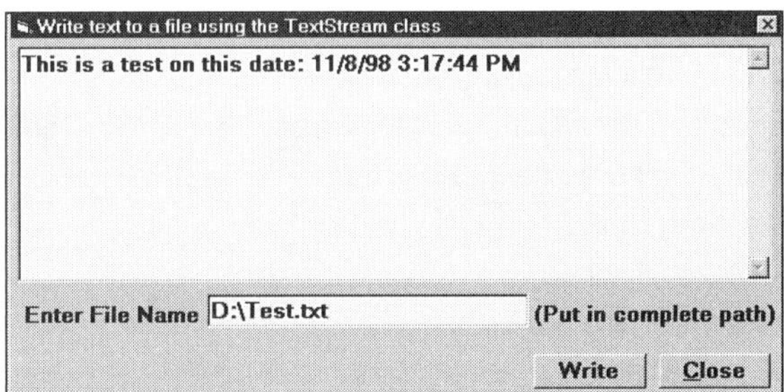

FIGURE 20.3 Writing to a text file using the `Text Stream` class.

In the Write command button, you begin by dimming a variable named `oFile` as a `TextStream` class. This instantiates a new object based on the `TextStream` class. You can now use the properties and methods of this object to write the data to the text file. Here's the code:

```
Private Sub cmdWrite_Click()
   Dim oFile As TextStream
   Dim boolRet As Boolean

   Set oFile = New TextStream

   With oFile
      If .OpenTextFile(txtFile.Text, ForAppending) Then
         Call .WriteLine(txtEdit)
      Else
         MsgBox "Error opening text file"
      End If

      .CloseFile
   End With
   Set oFile = Nothing
End Sub
```

The `OpenTextFile()` method is passed in the name of the file and the mode in which to open the file. If the file does not exist, it will be created. If there's an error in creating the file, a `False` value will be returned from the method, and you can then perform appropriate error handling. After the file is open, call the `WriteLine()` method, passing in the text that you want to store in the file.

Let's take a look at the `OpenTextFile()` method to see how it works:

```
Public Function OpenTextFile(strFile As String, _
        Optional intOpenMode As TSOpenMode = ForReading, _
        Optional intFormat As TSFormat = TristateTrue) _
            As Boolean
   If strFile <> "" Then
      mstrFileName = strFile
      mboolEOF = False
      mintOpenMode = intOpenMode
      mintFormat = intFormat

      If intOpenMode = ForReading Then
```

```
            Open mstrFileName For Input As #mintHandle
         Else
            Open mstrFileName For Output As #mintHandle
         End If

         OpenTextFile = True
      Else
         OpenTextFile = False
      End If
   End Function
```

In the `OpenTextFile()` method, you first set your module-level variables with the argument values that were passed in. Next, you check the mode to see whether you'll be opening the file for reading or appending. If you're opening the file for reading, you'll use the `For Input` option of the `Open` statement. If you're opening the file for appending or writing, you'll use the `For Output` or For Append option of the `Open` statement.

The *Class_Initialize()* Event

Prior to opening a text file with the low-level file I/O commands in Visual Basic, you must first retrieve a file handle from the operating system. This is accomplished with the `FreeFile` statement. This statement is located in the `Class_Initialize()` event of the `TextStream` class:

```
Private Sub Class_Initialize()
      mintHandle = FreeFile
End Sub
```

Each time a new instance of the `TextStream` class is instantiated, a new file handle will be retrieved from the operating system.

Adding Data to the Text File

After the text file is opened, the `WriteLine()` method is used to write the data to the text file. The `WriteLine()` method takes whatever data is passed into it as an argument and appends that data to the file:

```
Public Function WriteLine(_
      Optional strWrite As String = vbCrLf) As Boolean

   If mintHandle <> 0 Then
```

```
      Print #mintHandle, strWrite & vbCrLf
      WriteLine = True
   End If

End Function
```

You can see that you use the `Print` statement with the file handle number you retrieved from the `Class_Initialize()` event. `Print` is a built-in statement in Visual Basic that's used to write information to a file.

Closing the File

Once the write process is finished, the file should be closed. The sample `TextStream` class implements a `CloseFile()` method to close the file handle:

```
Public Function CloseFile() As Boolean
   ' Valid File Handle ?
   If mintHandle <> 0 Then
      Close #mintHandle

      mintHandle = 0

      CloseFile = True
   Else
      CloseFile = False
   End If
End Function
```

The `CloseFile()` method first checks the file handle to see whether it's valid. Any number other than 0 is a valid file handle. `CloseFile()` then calls the `Close` statement to close the particular file handle stored in the object. It also sets the file handle to 0; this way, if any other methods are called after the file is closed, no errors will occur. In every method of this class, the file handle is checked to see whether it's valid prior to performing any operation on the file.

Reading from a Text File

Now that you've seen how to write information into a file, let's look at how to read information out of a file. You still use the `TextStream` class to accomplish this, but you simply use other methods of the class for reading the file.

Example's Filename: FileRead.frm

In the form shown in Figure 20.4, you'll select a file to read using the file controls.

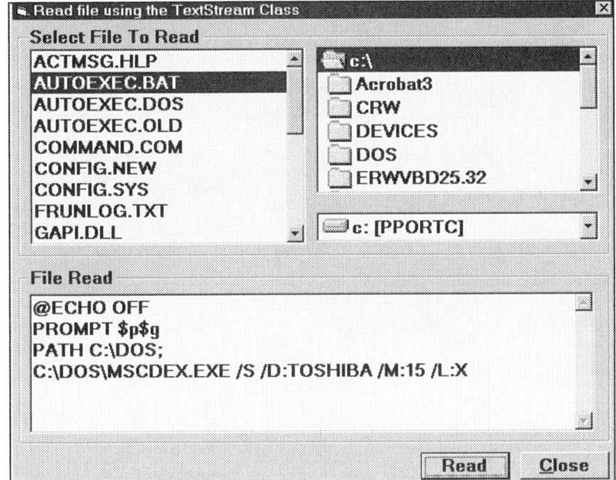

FIGURE 20.4
Reading information from a file.

Once the file is highlighted in the Select File to Read list box, you click the Read command button. In the `Click` event of the Read button is where you'll open the file and read in each line until you hit the end of the file:

```
Private Sub cmdRead_Click()
    Dim oFile As TextStream
    Dim strValue As String
    Dim strFileName As String

    Screen.MousePointer = vbHourglass

    strFileName = GetFileName()

    Set oFile = New TextStream
    With oFile
        .FileName = strFileName
        ' Check For File Too Big - 32K limit on text boxes
        If .FileTooBig Then
            Beep
            Screen.MousePointer = vbDefault
            MsgBox "File Too Big To Read", , "File Open Error"
        Else
```

```
            If .OpenTextFile(strFileName, ForReading) Then
               Do Until .AtEndOfStream
                  strValue = strValue & .ReadLine & vbCrLf
               Loop
               .CloseFile
               txtEdit.Text = strValue
            End If
         End If
      End With
      Set oFile = Nothing

      Screen.MousePointer = vbDefault
   End Sub
```

After declaring a `TextStream` object, you first get the filename from a function called `GetFileName()`. This is a general function that retrieves the path and filename from the directory and file list box controls. Next, you fill in the `FileName` property of the `TextStream` object so you can call the `FileTooBig` property. This property returns `True` if the file is larger than 32KB.

Next, you open the file by passing the filename and the constant `ForReading` to the `OpenTextFile()` method. If the file is opened correctly, you can loop through it until you hit the end of the input stream. Each time through the loop, you'll invoke the `ReadLine()` method to return the line of information just read. Notice that you concatenate onto each line a `CRLF`. This is because the `ReadLine` method does not read the `CRLF` pair.

The *FileTooBig* Property

Prior to reading in the data from the file, you should first check to see whether the file is small enough to be put into a text file. In the `cmdRead_Click()` event, the `FileTooBig` property is queried to see whether the file chosen can fit into a text box. Assuming a text box is limited to 32KB, you can create the `FileTooBig` property as follows:

```
Property Get FileTooBig() As Boolean
   If FileLen(mstrFileName) > 32768 Then
      FileTooBig = True
   Else
      FileTooBig = False
   End If
End Property
```

Although this appears to the outside world as a property of the class, the class itself does not hold a private variable about the file being too big. The `Property Get` procedure simply calculates this every time it's called and returns a `True` or `False` value. This property could just as easily have been implemented as a method of the class, but the point was to show you how to use a property for something other than just retrieving private data from the class.

TIP

`Property Get` and `Property Let` procedures can perform any Visual Basic code, just like any function and sub.

The *Class_Terminate* Event

Whenever an object goes out of scope, a destructor function for that object is called. In Visual Basic, this is called the `Class_Terminate()` event. This procedure fires when an object is either set equal to `Nothing` or goes out of scope (as is the case with a local object).

NOTE

Clicking the End button or terminating your application with the End statement does not fire the `Terminate` event for any user-defined objects.

The `Class_Terminate()` event is the destructor in Visual Basic that's called when an object is destroyed. In the sample `TextStream` class, a file handle is opened when the class is first instantiated. To ensure that this file handle gets closed, you should call the `CloseFile()` method. However, programmers sometimes will get lazy and forget to call the `CloseFile()` method. In the `Class_Terminate()` event of the `TextStream` class, you can call the `CloseFile()` method for them to ensure that it does get called.

Here's the code for the `Class_Terminate()` event in the `TextStream` class:

```
Private Sub Class_Terminate()
   Dim boolRet As Boolean

   boolRet = CloseFile()
End Sub
```

In this event, the `CloseFile()` method is called to make sure that if the file handle is open, it is closed. A class can always call one of its own methods, instead of having to duplicate code from one method to another.

To try this out, remove the call to the `CloseFile()` method from the `cmdRead_Click()` event and then step through this event procedure to see what happens as you step through the `End Sub` of that event.

Warning About Global Objects

When you declare global objects, you must be careful to explicitly release them prior to shutting down your application. If you use the Visual Basic `End` statement, your global objects' `Class_Terminate()` events will *not* be fired. If you let your last form unload by itself, the `Class_Terminate()` event will be fired. However, it's always a good practice to explicitly set all global objects equal to `Nothing` prior to closing your application.

> **TIP**
> **Set all global objects equal to `Nothing` prior to terminating your application.**

To test this, create a form, a BAS file, and a class with a `Class_Terminate()` event in it. Use the `End` statement to kill the application. You won't see the `Class_Terminate()` event fire.

Default Methods and Properties

Most of the controls you use in your Visual Basic projects have a default property. This means that you don't need to specify the name of the procedure when using the object. For example, the following two lines of code are equivalent:

```
MsgBox txtFirstName.Text
MsgBox txtFirstName
```

There is a trade-off when using the default property—it's less readable, but it involves a little less typing. It used to be that not using the property was more efficient, but that has gone away starting with Visual Basic 5. Therefore, it's really just a style issue now of whether you want to use it.

To create a default method or property, you need to set the procedure ID of that method or property to become the default. To do this, select Tools, Procedure Attributes from the Visual Basic menu. You should see a form that looks like the one shown in Figure 20.5.

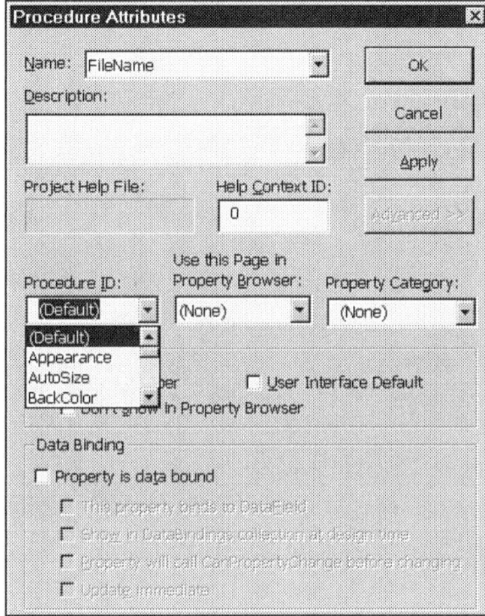

FIGURE 20.5
The Procedure Attributes dialog box.

Click the Advanced command button to display the bottom portion of this dialog box. Next, select the (Default) option from the Procedure ID combo box.

Summary

In this chapter, you learned to create classes in Visual Basic. You saw how wrapping up Visual Basic functionality into a class module (the `TextStream` class) can make the programming of the constructs much easier. You also saw how to potentially eliminate global variables from your application by making properties on forms.

Review Questions

1. How do you expose `Private` variables from a class?
2. How do you create a default property?
3. How do you create a method?

Exercises

1. Create an `EmpType` class. Create the following properties:

   `TypeID` (Long)
   `TypeDesc` (String)
   `MinSalary` (Currency)
   `MaxSalary` (Currency)

2. Create a method that displays these properties in a message box.

21

System Objects

THIS CHAPTER DISCUSSES HOW VISUAL BASIC works with system objects and instances of objects. You'll learn how to use the built-in system objects to get information about the runtime environment, control the printer, manipulate fonts, and exploit various tips and tricks. You'll also learn to create multiple instances of the same form as well as determine a particular object's type at runtime.

Chapter Objectives

- Learn about Object types
- Learn how to determine an object's type
- Learn how to use the built-in System objects
- Create multiple instances of forms

Sample Project File: \Chapter21\SystemObject.vbp

What Is an Object?

An *object* is a complex data type that's made up of properties and methods. Forms and controls are examples of objects. These entities have properties you can set to change their appearance or make them behave a certain way. Methods tell an object to perform some action. You can declare and use variables in your code that represent objects. An object is a reference to an area in memory (that is, a pointer). This pointer can point to a screen object or an object in memory somewhere. These object variables allow you to manipulate forms, controls, system objects, references to ActiveX objects, and so on.

You should already be familiar with objects; you use them every time you develop a Visual Basic application. Forms are objects, and controls are objects. You set the `Top` or `Left` property of a form to make that form display in a certain location. You can invoke the form's `Show` method to make it display on the screen. You create controls by dragging them from the toolbox onto a form. You then change the controls' properties to make them look and act a certain way. Now you'll learn a little about some of the other objects in the Visual Basic environment that you can manipulate.

Object Types

Every control in the Visual Basic toolbox has a specific class name. This class name will vary according to the type of control and the manufacturer of that control. This unique name is known as a specific object type. Table 21.1 shows a list of the specific object types or class names that come with the Professional Edition of Visual Basic.

Table 21.1 Class Names for the Common Controls

CheckBox	Frame	OptionButton
ComboBox	Grid	OLE
CommandButton	HScrollBar	PictureBox
CommonDialog	Image	Shape
Data	Label	TextBox
DirListBox	Line	Timer
DriveListBox	ListBox	VScrollBar
FileListBox	Menu	

In addition to each of the built-in Visual Basic controls, every third-party control you buy must have a unique control name. To find out the name of a specific control, click once on the control and bring up the Properties window. Notice in the Control combo box on the Properties window that the control's name is listed in bold. Next to that name is the class name of the control. (See Figure 21.1 for an example.)

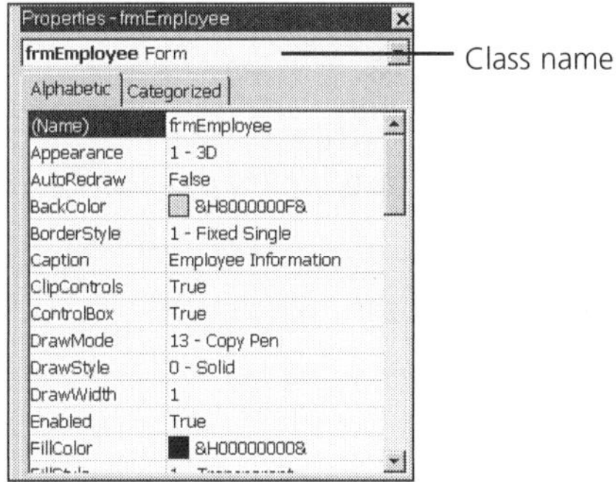

FIGURE 21.1 Properties window showing the properties of a `Form` class.

Generic Object Types

Now that you've learned about the specific object variables, let's look at the generic object types. There are four types of generic object variables you can use when passing objects from one place to another in your application. The following is a list of these generic object types:

- `Form`
- `Control`
- `MDIForm`
- `Object`

Generic object variables can refer to any form or any control on a form in your application. If you don't know the type of control that will be passed to a procedure, you need to use the generic `Control` keyword as the parameter type. If you write a procedure that affects forms in your application, you need to use the `Form` keyword as the parameter type.

Form and Control Objects

Besides the specific data types such as Integer, Double, and String, Visual Basic also allows you to declare and/or use variables that refer to particular visual objects in your application, such as forms and controls.

Forms can be identified and classified by the following:

- The `Name` property of that particular form. This is actually a new kind of class.
- The class to which it belongs (in this case, `Form`, which is the generic object type).

Controls can be identified and classified by the following:

- The `Name` property of that particular control.
- The class to which it belongs (in this case, `Control`, which is the generic object type).
- The specific object type that refers to the type of control, such as `TextBox` or `ComboBox`.

What Do We Do with These Objects?

The reason for learning about these objects is so that you can write more generic code. For example, you may want to accomplish the following with these objects:

- Center any form in your application
- Load a combo box or load a list box with one procedure

Centering Forms

Many times in an application, you want to center a form (or forms) within the total screen area. Although there's a property you can use to do this, you can also write code, as shown here:

```
Sub FormCenter(frmCurrent As Form)
   Dim intLeft As Integer
   Dim intTop As Integer

   intLeft = (Screen.Width / 2) _
            - (frmCurrent.Width / 2)
   intTop = (Screen.Height / 2) _
            - (frmCurrent.Height / 2)
   frmCurrent.Move intLeft, intTop
End Sub
```

Passing Controls to Procedures

Besides passing forms to a generic procedure, you can also pass controls to procedures or functions. This is useful when you have routines that can operate on the same types of controls, such as list boxes and combo boxes.

Example's Filename: ObjPassObj.frm

Both of the controls on the form shown in Figure 21.2 need to be filled with state names.

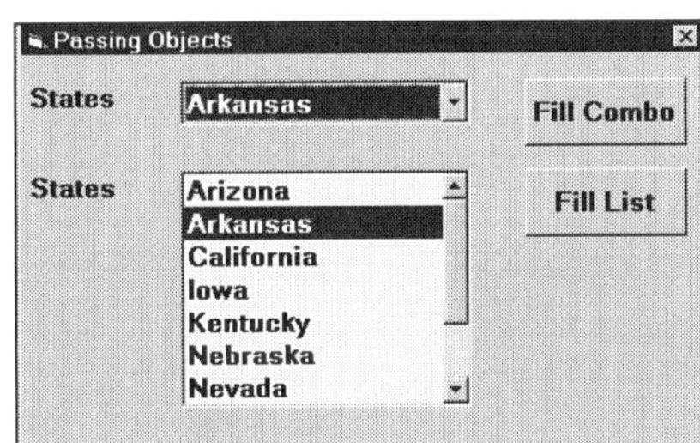

FIGURE 21.2 Passing objects to procedures.

Instead of writing two separate procedures—one to load the combo box and one to load the list box—you can write one generic routine that loads either control. Here's the code written in each of the `Click` events of the command buttons on the sample form:

```
Private Sub cmdCombo_Click ()
   Call StateLoad(cboStates)
End Sub

Private Sub cmdList_Click ()
   Call StateLoad(lstStates)
End Sub
```

The routine to load either the combo box or list box is very simple for this illustration. The `StateLoad()` procedure accepts any type of control as the name `ctlStates`. The `ctlStates` argument is then used to add items to the list with some hard-coded values:

```
Public Sub StateLoad(ctlStates As Control)
   With ctlStates
      .Clear

      .AddItem "Iowa"
      .AddItem "California"
      .AddItem "Arizona"
      .AddItem "Nevada"
      .AddItem "Arkansas"
      .AddItem "Washington"
      .AddItem "Texas"
      .AddItem "Nebraska"
      .AddItem "Utah"
      .AddItem "Kentucky"
   End With
End Sub
```

Although, literally, any type of control could be passed to this procedure, the only controls that would work are list boxes and combo boxes or any type of control that has an `AddItem` method. If a text box was passed to this routine, it would bomb as soon as the `Clear` method was invoked. Therefore it is a good idea to check the type of object in the procedure before using that object.

Determining an Object's Type

In the previous example, I mentioned that if you pass a text box to the `StateLoad()` routine, you get an error because a text box doesn't have a `Clear` routine. Therefore, you should add a test to this procedure to see whether the right type of control was passed in. To accomplish this, you use the `TypeOf` operator. Let's rewrite the `StateLoad()` procedure you just wrote to make sure that only combo boxes and list boxes are used by this procedure:

```
Public Sub StateLoad(ctlStates As Control)
    If TypeOf ctlStates Is ListBox Then
        ' Do Nothing
    ElseIf TypeOf ctlStates Is ComboBox Then
        ' Do Nothing
    Else
        Exit Sub
    End If
    With ctlStates
        .Clear

        .AddItem "Iowa"
        .AddItem "California"
        .AddItem "Arizona"
        .AddItem "Nevada"
        .AddItem "Arkansas"
        .AddItem "Washington"
        .AddItem "Texas"
        .AddItem "Nebraska"
        .AddItem "Utah"
        .AddItem "Kentucky"
    End With
End Sub
```

When to Use Generic Versus Specific Object Types

Although it's tempting to use generic variables when passing arguments to procedures, there is a drawback to this. Visual Basic is forced to use *late binding* when a generic object variable is used. What this means is that Visual Basic has to wait until runtime to determine the type of object that's actually passed to the procedure. This is expensive in terms of performance. Visual Basic must resolve the reference to its internal table every time a method or property is accessed in this generic object.

This slows your application down because Visual Basic has to do some significant processing to lookup these methods and properties.

One more disadvantage to using generic objects is that there's no compile-time checking done on the arguments passed to these routines. Suppose you were to write a procedure that accepts a `String` variable as a parameter. If you try to call this procedure and pass an `Integer` type, you'll receive an error message from the compiler. If the compiler did not perform this type checking, you would have to wait until runtime to get this error. This is exactly what happens with generic object variables. Therefore, you won't receive an error until you hit the line of code where the method is called and the object you passed does not support that method. This can slow your development down in that you need to thoroughly test your application for these types of bugs—you won't get any help from the compiler.

Objects Are Passed by Reference

The code fragment that passed the combo and list box to the state loading routine illustrates an important point about object variables—they're always passed by reference to procedures. This means a pointer to the actual window is passed to procedures. This allows you to change the object's properties in the procedure, and those changes will display on the interface. In fact, there is no way to pass an object variable by value.

System Objects

Visual Basic exposes five global system objects that allow you to query and manipulate your application environment at runtime. These five objects are global and are available anywhere from within your Visual Basic application. Table 21.2 lists the different system objects.

Table 21.2 System Objects

Object	Description
`App`	Allows you to query and set information that's specific to your application.
`Clipboard`	Allows you to retrieve and place information into the Windows Clipboard.
`Debug`	Allows you to print to the Debug window. (This option is not available in your final EXE program.)
`Printer`	Allows you to send text and graphics to the printer.

Object	Description
`Screen`	Allows you to query and set screen-related data in your application. For example, you can set the mouse pointer as well as query the height and width of your screen. You can also determine which form and control currently has focus.

Rules When Using System Objects

System objects are global. This means you do not declare them or pass them to any procedure or function—you simply use them wherever you need them. System objects are only available at runtime. There are no design time properties or methods that can be set.

The *App* Object

The App object provides you with some great information about your running application. The App object only has properties—there are no methods associated with this object. The App object is filled in automatically by Visual Basic right when your program loads. Most of the information comes from the Project, Properties menu, which you set at design time. Table 21.3 lists the important properties of the App object.

Table 21.3 Properties of the *App* Object

Property	Description
`Comments`	This property comes from the Comments value you set in the Project, Properties menu.
`CompanyName`	This property comes from the Company Name value you set in the Project, Properties menu.
`EXEName`	This property is filled in with whatever the EXE filename is for your application.
`HelpFile`	This property comes from the Help File Name value you set in the Project, Properties menu.
`LegalCopyright`	This property comes from the Legal Copyright value you set in the Project, Properties menu.

continues

Table 21.3 Continued

Property	Description
`LegalTrademark`	This property comes from the Legal Trademark value you set in the Project, Properties menu.
`Major`	This property comes from the Major version number value you set in the Project, Properties menu.
`Minor`	This property comes from the Minor version number value you set in the Project, Properties menu.
`Path`	This property is filled in with the path of where the EXE file loaded when your application started.
`PrevInstance`	This property returns `True` at runtime if there's another instance of this application running in the Windows environment. You can use this property to stop another instance of the same application from loading.
`ProductName`	This property comes from the Product Name value you set in the Project, Properties menu.
`Revision`	This property comes from the Revision Version Number value you set in the Project, Properties menu.
`TaskVisible`	This property has a `True` value in it if the program is visible in the task bar of the operating system.
`Title`	This property comes from the Title value you set in the Project, Properties menu.

You can use these properties at runtime to determine the current path where your EXE started (`App.Path`). You can also find out the name of the EXE file (`App.EXEName`). You'll mostly use this object to display the appropriate properties in an About form. Figure 21.3 shows you some of the different properties used to make an About form. All these properties come from the `App` object.

Example's Filename: ObjApp.frm

The information contained on this form is all obtained through properties of the `App` object. In the `Form_Load()` event of this form, a routine is called that fills in each of the text boxes on the form with the information from the `App` object. This routine is listed here:

```
Private Sub Form_Load()
   txtProduct = App.ProductName
   txtVersion = App.Major & "." & _
```

```
                    App.Minor & "." & _
                    App.Revision
    txtCompany = App.CompanyName
    txtCopyRight = App.LegalCopyright
    txtTradeMark = App.LegalTrademarks
    txtTitle = App.Title
    txtEXEName = App.Path & "\" & App.EXEName
    txtFileDesc = App.FileDescription
    txtComments = App.Comments
End Sub
```

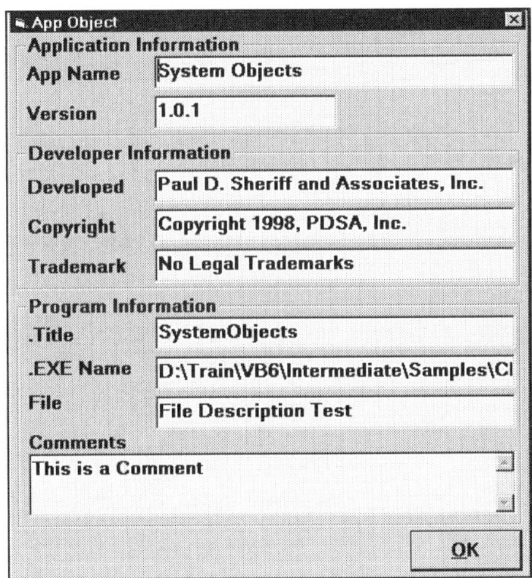

FIGURE 21.3 Samples of the App object properties.

Filling in the Application Information

To fill in the App object with information such as the LegalCopyright and LegalTrademark information, you need to select Project, <Project> Properties from the Visual Basic design menu. Next, select the Make tab to set the properties, as shown in Figure 21.4.

All this information is stored in the project file for your application. When you create an executable file, this information is burned into the header area of the EXE file, where it can be read by the Visual Basic runtime engine for inclusion in the App object.

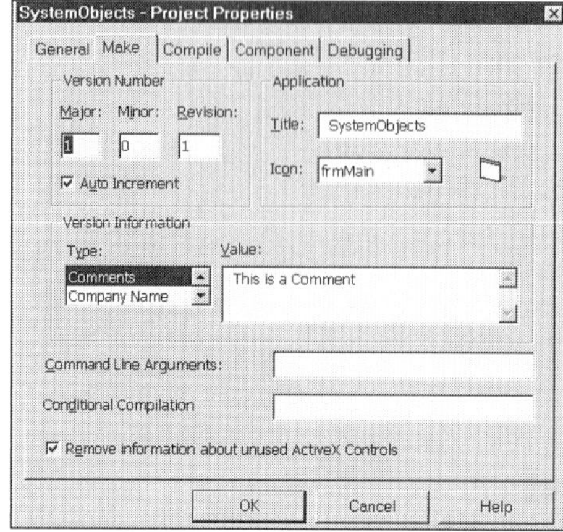

FIGURE 21.4 The Project Properties window.

Checking for a Previous Instance

You can use the `PrevInstance` property of the `App` object to determine whether the program should be loaded. In most cases, you'll not want your user to have multiple copies of your program loaded. To accomplish this, use code like the following in the `Sub Main()` of your application:

```
Sub Main()
   If App.PrevInstance Then
      AppActivate "System Objects"
      End
   Else
      frmMain.Show
   End If
End Sub
```

This code checks the `App.PrevInstance` property; if it returns a `True` value, the `AppActivate` command is called and passed in the title of the main form for the application. Windows will task switch over to that application; then this current instance of your program is ended.

The *Screen* Object

The `Screen` object provides you with information about the currently active screen elements. You can query this object to obtain the handle of the active form and the active control on that form. You'll also use this to set your mouse pointer to different cursor styles. All the different screen fonts available on your system can be queried through the `Screen` object. Table 21.4 lists the most important properties of this system object.

Example's Filename: ObjScreen.frm

Table 21.4 Screen Object Properties

Property	Description
`ActiveForm`	This property is dynamically changed at runtime whenever you move from one form to another. This property will hold a reference to the currently active form in your application.
`ActiveControl`	This property is dynamically changed at runtime to return a pointer to the control on the active form that has focus. This is very useful for performing a copy and paste routine from a toolbar, for example.
`FontCount`	This property returns the number of fonts installed on your computer.
`Fonts`	This property is an array of all the available font names installed on your computer.
`Height`	This property returns the total height of your screen area in a unit of measure called *twips*. (Twips will be explained in the next section.)
`MousePointer`	You can set this property to one of several constants to change how the mouse pointer looks in your application. For example, you use this to change the mouse pointer to an hourglass if the application is performing an operation that might take awhile.
`TwipsPerPixelX`	This property returns the number of twips per pixel on the horizontal axis.
`TwipsPerPixelY`	This property returns the number of twips per pixel on the vertical axis.
`Width`	This property returns the total width of your screen area in a unit of measure called *twips*. (Twips will be explained in the next section.)

Twips

Visual Basic uses a unit of measure called *twips*. There are 1,440 twips per inch. Twips are used because this unit of measure will not change, regardless of what kind of monitor your application is run on. To determine what the resolution of your monitor is, you can run the following code:

```
Private Sub cmdXY_Click()
   With Screen
```

```
        ' X = Width
        ' Y = Height
        lblXY = .Width & "/" & .Height

        ' Calculate Pixel Width/Height of Monitor
        lblTwips = .TwipsPerPixelX & "/" & .TwipsPerPixelY

        ' Calculate the resolution of the screen
        lblRes = .Width / .TwipsPerPixelX & "/" & _
                 .Height / .TwipsPerPixelY
    End With
End Sub
```

On a screen running in 800×600 resolution, you should see that the `Width` and `Height` properties are `12000` and `9000`, respectively. The value `12000` is the number of twips for the horizontal axis (X), and the value `9000` is the number of twips for the vertical axis (Y). The amount of twips per pixel for the X axis is 15, and the amount of twips per pixel for the Y axis is also 15. Dividing the `Width` property by the `TwipsPerPixelX` property gives you the horizontal resolution of your screen. Dividing the `Height` property by the `TwipsPerPixelY` property gives you the vertical resolution of your screen.

Displaying Screen Fonts

You have many available fonts to choose from in the Windows environment. There are also several third-party add-on fonts you can purchase. If you want to give the user a choice of fonts he or she can use in your system, you need to enable the user to retrieve this list from the Windows environment.

Using the `Screen` object, you can query this list of font names in the system. The following code shows how to retrieve the available screen fonts in your system:

```
Private Sub cmdFonts_Click()
    Dim intLoop As Integer

    With Screen
        ' Display Font Count
        lblFontCount = .FontCount

        ' Load list box with all screen fonts
        lstFonts.Clear
```

```
            For intLoop = 0 To .FontCount - 1
                lstFonts.AddItem .Fonts(intLoop)
            Next intLoop
        End With
    End Sub
```

Using the `FontCount` property, you can determine how many fonts are installed on a particular machine. You can then use the `Fonts` property to add each individual font to the list box.

Changing the Mouse Pointer

When performing a long operation, you'll need to inform the user that something is happening. One of the most common methods is to change the mouse pointer to an hourglass icon. You can accomplish this by setting the `MousePointer` property of the `Screen` object. Here's some sample code showing the use of the built-in constants for setting the appropriate cursor:

```
Screen.MousePointer = vbHourglass
...
...
Screen.MousePointer = vbDefault
```

You have 17 different cursors available to you in the Visual Basic environment. Table 21.5 shows you the different settings and the constants that should be used to set each one.

Table 21.5 Cursor Types

Value to Set	Description	Constant Name
0	Default	vbDefault
1	Arrow	vbArrow
2	Cross hair	vbCrosshair
3	I-beam	vbIbeam
4	Icon	vbIconPointer
5	Sizing	vbSizePointer
6	Sizing (NE, SW)	vbSizeNESW
7	Sizing (N, S)	vbSizeNS

continues

Table 21.5 Continued

Value to Set	Description	Constant Name
8	Sizing (NW, SE)	vbSizeNWSE
9	Sizing (W, E)	vbSizeWE
10	Up arrow	vbUpArrow
11	Hourglass	vbHourglass
12	No drop	vbNoDrop
13	Arrow and hourglass	vbArrowHourglass
14	Arrow and question mark	vbArrowQuestion
15	Size all	vbSizeAll
99	Custom icon specified by the `MouseIcon` property	VbCustom

The last cursor type, `99`, is used in combination with the `MouseIcon` property. If you set this type, you must have the `MouseIcon` property filled in with the name of a valid cursor file or an icon (ICO) file.

The *Clipboard* Object

One of the many benefits of the Windows environment is the ability to move text, graphics, and other objects from one application to another. This is normally accomplished via a mechanism called the *Clipboard*. The Clipboard is an area of memory that's a temporary holding area for any valid Windows object.

Normally, you move items from your application to the Clipboard by pressing the Ctrl+C key combination. You can then move to another application, or even stay in the same one, and press Ctrl+V to retrieve that information from the Clipboard.

Visual Basic also takes advantage of this behavior. From any text box, you can highlight an area of text you have typed in and use these key combinations to copy and paste information. For example, you can highlight any part of a name in one text box, press Ctrl+C, and move to another text box and press Ctrl+V to put the text there. This functionality is built into VB and requires no programming on your part (see Figure 21.5).

Example's Filename: ObjClip.frm

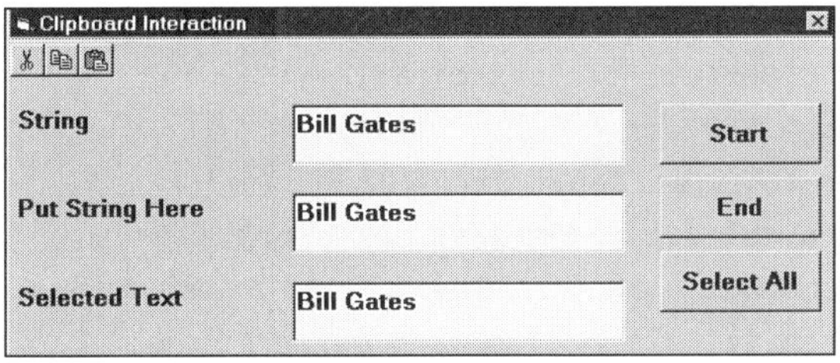

FIGURE 21.5
Example from this chapter's sample project to interact with the Clipboard.

Selecting Text

Many times you'll want to control how the user selects text. For example, to perform a copy-and-paste operation, the user must first highlight all the text to be copied with the mouse. However, there may be times when you want to have that text highlighted automatically. You can set certain properties in text boxes that allow you to control the selection of text. These properties are `SelStart`, `SelLength`, and `SelText`.

The `SelStart` property controls where the cursor is placed in the text box. It also marks the beginning of a block of text you want to mark. If you set `SelStart` to `0`, the cursor is placed at the position prior to the first character in the text box. If you set it to the length of the string in the text box, it's positioned at the character after the string in the text box.

The `SelLength` property controls how many characters are marked after the start of the block. For example, if you set `SelStart` to `0` and `SelLength` to `5`, the first six characters will be highlighted and can be copied to the Clipboard with the Ctrl+C key combination.

The `SelText` property contains the text that's highlighted using the `SelStart` and `SelLength` properties. You can read and write to this property at runtime.

Moving Text to the Clipboard

Once you have the text highlighted, you can then use the `Clipboard` object to transfer data to and from the Windows Clipboard. The three methods used most often are `Clear()`, `SetText()`, and `GetText()`. The `Clear` method empties the Clipboard. The `SetText` method transfers data to the Clipboard. The `GetText` method retrieves data from the Clipboard. Here's some code that illustrates these methods:

```
Private Sub tlbTools_ButtonClick(ByVal Button As _
                                        ComctlLib.Button)
```

```
        If Button.Key = "Cut" Then
            Clipboard.SetText txtString1.SelText
            txtString1.SelText = ""
        ElseIf Button.Key = "Copy" Then
            Clipboard.SetText txtString1.SelText
        ElseIf Button.Key = "Paste" Then
            txtString2.SelText = Clipboard.GetText
        End If
    End Sub
```

When one of the buttons on the toolbar control is clicked, you first need to figure out which button was clicked and then you can write the code to interact with the `Clipboard` object. If the user clicks the "cut" button, you want to grab the selected text from the `SelText` property of the text box and pass that as a parameter to the `Clipboard.SetText` method. You then need to clear the `SelText` property of the text box, because the "cut" button was clicked. The code is the same for a copy operation, except you don't clear the `SelText` property. For a paste operation, you call the `GetText` method of the `Clipboard` object and put the value returned into the `SelText` property of another text box. This is a hard-coded example, so let's now look at one that's a little more generic.

The *Screen.ActiveControl* Property

In the `Screen` object are two properties that are pointers to other objects in your application: `ActiveForm` and `ActiveControl`. These two properties are constantly updated as you open forms, close forms, and click from one form (or control) to another. These objects are useful for creating generic routines that always act upon the currently active form or control.

As an example, suppose you want to allow cut, copy, and paste operations from any text box control on any form. Let's look at the example shown in Figure 21.6.

Example's Filename: ObjControl.frm

FIGURE 21.6 An `Active Control` example.

When the user highlights some text in a text box, he or she should be able to press one of the controls on the toolbar to have that text copied to, cut to, or pasted from the Clipboard. Here's the code in the toolbar that makes sure the user can only perform these operations from a text box control:

```
Private Sub tlbTools_ButtonClick(ByVal Button As _
                                    ComctlLib.Button)
    If TypeOf Screen.ActiveControl Is TextBox Then
        If Button.Key = "Cut" Then
            Clipboard.SetText Screen.ActiveControl.SelText
            Screen.ActiveControl.Text = ""
        ElseIf Button.Key = "Copy" Then
            Clipboard.SetText Screen.ActiveControl.SelText
        ElseIf Button.Key = "Paste" Then
            Screen.ActiveControl.SelText = Clipboard.GetText
        End If
    End If
End Sub
```

Notice the use of the `TypeOf` operator in this code. The `TypeOf` operator is used to determine the type of control. If it's a text box, you can run the code you learned about in the previous section.

Creating New Forms at Runtime

In many Windows applications, you have the ability to open many instances of the same form. For example, in Word, you may have many different documents open, or in Excel, you can have many spreadsheets open. Each of these documents are *not* separate forms—they are just instances of one particular `Form` object.

Let's program the same type of functionality using the Employee Information form. Figure 21.7 shows you a list box filled with employees. If you select one, you can click on the Edit button to display the full information for that employee. Once you click the Edit button, the screen shown in Figure 21.8 will be displayed.

Example's Filename: EmpList.frm

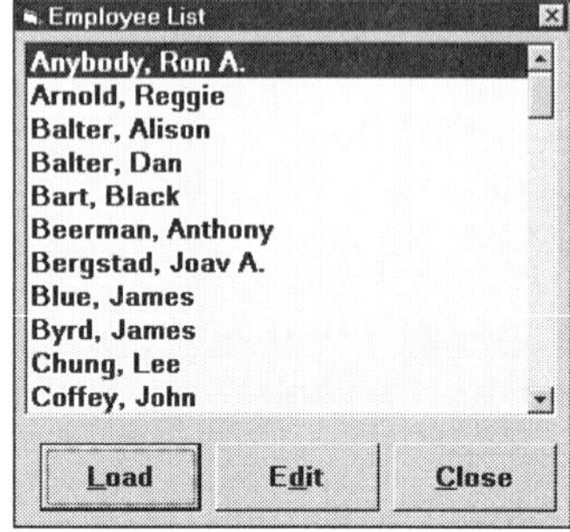

FIGURE 21.7 A list of employees that can be clicked on for editing.

Example's Filename: Emps.frm

FIGURE 21.8 The Employee Information form.

Employee Information
Employee ID 101
First Name Ron A.
Last Name Anybody
Address 123 Any Street
City Tulsa
State OK
Zip Code 92999
Close

Inside the Edit button on the Employee List form, you would expect the code to look something like this:

```
Sub cmdEdit_Click ()
   ' Display the Employee Form
   frmEmployee.Show
End Sub
```

If you click the first employee and execute this code, the form displays with that employee's information in it. However, if you come back to the list box, click another employee, and execute this code again, you simply redisplay the same screen with the old employee information. This is because Visual Basic determines that this form is already loaded and displayed, and it will simply give this form focus. The `Form_Load()` event does not occur again, and that's where the text boxes for the form are initialized with the appropriate data:

```
Private Sub Form_Load()

   Call FormShow

End Sub
```

The Form_Load() event calls the routine FormShow() to get the data from the Employee table:

```
Private Sub FormShow()
   Dim oRS As Recordset
   Dim strSQL As String

   ' Build SQL for loading list box
   strSQL = "SELECT * "
   strSQL = strSQL & "FROM tblEmployees "
   strSQL = strSQL & "WHERE lEmp_id = " & mlngEmpID

   Set oRS = New Recordset

   oRS.Open strSQL, ConnectString(), _
            adOpenForwardOnly, adLockReadOnly
   With oRS
      txtEmpID = mlngEmpID
      txtFirst = !sFirst_nm & ""
      txtLast = !szLast_nm & ""
      txtAddress = !szStreet1_ad & ""
      txtCity = !szCity_nm & ""
      txtState = !sState_cd & ""
      txtZip = !sZip_cd & ""
   End With
End Sub
```

In the code above you can see the SQL statement that will retrieve on unique rows from the employee table based on the employee ID. When you open the Recordset, you pass in the SQL string as well as a connection string. Instead of coding this string right here, I call a function, named ConnectString(), that returns this string to the Open method.

Let's code the Edit button so that a new instance of the Employee form is loaded for each Click event. This way, each form can display a different employee:

```
Private Sub cmdEdit_Click()
   Dim frmNewEmp As frmEmployee

   Set frmNewEmp = New frmEmployee
```

```
        frmNewEmp.EmpID = lstNames.ItemData(lstNames.ListIndex)

        frmNewEmp.Show
    End Sub
```

The `New` keyword in the line that assigns the form to the object variable, `frmNewEmp`, is what informs Visual Basic to make a new instance of the form frmEmployee. This form has an `EmpID` property that's used by the Employee Information form to retrieve the particular employee selected from the list.

All the properties of the frmEmployee form are duplicated, and a new `Form` object variable is created. You may only use the `New` keyword with specific form variables, not generic form variables, generic controls, or specific control variables.

One important point to note is that the frmEmployee form is never loaded, it's only used to make a copy of itself for these new variables. You must use the variable `frmNewEmp` in this procedure to reference that form. If you attempt to reference frmEmployee, you'll load the original form, which is different than the frmNewEmp form.

Summary

Object variables are used to write generic, general-purpose code that can be used by multiple applications. This is a very powerful capability, enabling programmers to reuse forms, controls, and code. The `Set` statement is always used to assign object pointers as well as to destroy the memory used by object variables (this is done by setting the variables to `Nothing`). Multiple copies of the same form can be created at runtime by using the `New` keyword.

Review Questions

1. Name three generic object types.
2. Describe the function of the `New` keyword.
3. Which type of object is more efficient to use—generic or specific? Why?

Collections

Collections are very common in the Visual Basic language. You can think of collections as arrays on steroids. They do everything arrays do, and more. You can access global collections and even create your collections. In this chapter, you'll learn how to manipulate VB's built-in collections and how to create your own collections.

Chapter Objectives

- Learn how to use the `Forms` collection
- Learn how to manipulate the `Controls` collection
- Learn how to build your own collections
- Learn how to wrap your collections into a collection class

Sample Project File: \Chapter22\Collections.vbp

What Is a Collection?

As mentioned earlier, a *collection* is basically an array on steroids. Collections are different than arrays, but they act very much the same in that you have lists of items grouped under a common name. Collections are a lot more powerful than arrays, however, in that they have properties and methods attached to them. These properties and methods allow you to add new items very easily, delete items, and even insert items into a specific location. All these characteristics, plus a few more, make collections a lot easier to utilize than arrays.

Visual Basic allows for a few different types of collections—those that Visual Basic creates automatically, those that you create yourself, and those that are created as a part of ActiveX controls.

Examples of Built-in Collections

Visual Basic maintains a global collection of all the forms that have been loaded at runtime in a collection called `Forms`. Visual Basic also maintains a collection of all the loaded controls for each active form in a collection called `Controls`. There's also a `Printers` collection that reports to you all the printers connected to your system. You'll learn to manipulate these built-in collections first; later you'll learn to create your own collections.

Characteristics of the Built-in Collections

Collections have several attributes that you need to be aware of to use. Let's learn about some of these:

- The Visual Basic collections are never declared because they're global.
- You never pass the built-in collections to a procedure because they're global and don't have to be passed.

- You don't apply the **UBound** and **LBound** functions to collections like you do with arrays.
- Collections are zero based, so their Index starts at zero (0).
- Collections have a **Count** property that tells you how many elements the collection contains.

The *Forms* Collection

The Forms collection is global, so you can refer to it anywhere in your program. The Forms collection only contains those forms that are currently loaded at runtime. You might have 10 forms in your project file, but if only four of them are loaded and/or displayed on the screen, then only those four are contained in the Forms collection. The order of the forms in the collection is arbitrary and changes as forms are loaded and unloaded.

Forms is a Visual Basic reserved word. This means you cannot declare a variable with this name. To loop through all the loaded forms in an application, you can use the following code:

```
Dim intLoop As Integer

For intLoop = 0 to Forms.Count - 1
   Forms(intLoop).BackColor = 255
Next
```

For Each...Next

The For Each...Next construct also allows you to iterate through a collection of objects. You should get used to using this construct because it's much more efficient than the previously shown loop:

```
Dim frmAny As Form

For Each...frmAny In Forms
   frmAny.BackColor = 255
Next
```

The For...Each loop works through an enumeration method that's attached to every collection. This enumeration method keeps track of which object in the collection was just accessed, and it returns the next object the next time through the loop. In the preceding code, a variable is declared as a Form data type. Each time through the loop, the next form pointer in the collection is returned and assigned to the `frmAny` variable. Another advantage of the `For...Each` construct is that you do not need to know how many items there are in the collection.

Keeping Track of Form Instances

If you use the technique of creating forms using the `New` keyword, you'll need to start keeping track of which forms are open. For example, if you create multiple instances of an employee form, then how do you know which form contains which employee?

What's more, you cannot reference any of these "created" forms by their names, because they all have the same name. You need to come up with a method for referencing each individual form. One way is to use the `Forms` collection.

Example's Filenames: EmpList.frm and Employee.frm

In the sample project for this chapter, you'll find two forms that allow you to select an employee from a list and then display that employee's details in an employee form. You can keep that employee's form open while you click yet another employee in the list and display that employee's information in another instance of the Employee Information form. When you start to open multiple instances of forms, you'll need a method of tracking which forms are open. In addition, you'll need to detect whether you've already opened a detail form for an employee. If you have that detail form open, you don't want to open another one—you just want to select it.

Let's look at a method for keeping track of which form goes with which employee. When you open a new Employee Information form, you'll store the employee ID into the `Tag` property of the employee form. Here's some code from the Edit button on the EmpList.frm form:

```
Private Sub cmdEdit_Click()
   Dim frmNew As frmEmployee
   Dim lngEmpID As Long

   If lstNames.ListIndex <> -1 Then
      lngEmpID = lstNames.ItemData(lstNames.ListIndex)
      If Not FormFind(lngEmpID) Then
         ' Create new instance of the form
         Set frmNew = New frmEmployee
```

```
            ' Set Form Property
            frmNew.EmpID = lngEmpID

            ' Display New Instance of the Customer Form
            frmNew.Show

            ' Set Tag Property for Searching
            frmNew.Tag = lngEmpID
        End If
    End If
End Sub
```

This code dims a pointer to the frmEmployee form. It then grabs the employee ID from the `ItemData()` property of the list box and stores it in a local variable. Next, it passes that local variable to the `FormFind()` function, which returns a `True` value if it finds the Employee Information form already open for this particular employee ID. If it does not find this employee form, a `False` value is returned. In this case, it creates a new instance of the form and stores the employee ID in the `EmpID` property on the frmEmployee form instance. Next, it shows the Employee Information form. Finally, it stores the employee ID in the `Tag` property of the Employee Information form. This `Tag` property value is used to find the employee form in the `Forms` collection. This occurs in the `FormFind()` function shown here:

```
Private Function FormFind(lngEmpID As Long) As Boolean
    Dim frmAny As Form

    FormFind = False
    For Each frmAny In Forms
        If IsNumeric(frmAny.Tag) Then
            If CInt(Val(frmAny.Tag)) = lngEmpID Then
                frmAny.SetFocus
                FormFind = True
            End If
        End If
    Next frmAny
End Function
```

The `FormFind()` function loops through the `Forms` collection using a `For...Each` loop. It checks the form reference each time through the loop to see whether the `Tag` property has a numeric value in it. If it does, the value in the `Tag` property is compared against the value passed to this function. If a match is found, the focus is set to that form and a `True` value is returned from the `FormFind()` function.

NOTE
You can also use the form's EmpID property instead of the Tag property, but then you need to check to see whether the form was a form that is of the type frmEmployee. The benefit of the Tag property is that it's already built into the form, so you don't need to do any additional checking.

Checking for Instances of Forms

If you need to check to see whether a particular instance of a form is loaded, you can use the Forms collection:

```
Public Function IsFormLoaded(ByVal strName As String) _
        As Boolean
    Dim oForm As Form
    Dim boolReturn As Boolean

    For Each oForm In Forms
        If oForm.Name = strName Then
            boolReturn = True
        End If
    Next

    IsFormLoaded = boolReturn
End Function
```

The *Controls* Collection

The Controls collection is a part of every form at runtime. It refers to all the loaded controls on a form. You can use this collection to your advantage to perform field validation on controls.

Example's Filename: Employee.frm
In the Employee.frm form, the user is required to enter an employee ID and first and last names in the appropriate fields. If these values are not entered, you need to inform the user that they are required. There are many techniques for showing the user which fields need to be filled in. For example, you can change the background color of the text box or of the label next to the text box. Of course, if the

user has changed the colors on his or her computer to the same color, this change won't be visible. A better method is to fill in these text boxes with the word *<Required>* in italics. This way, the user will immediately see which values need to be filled in (see Figure 22.1).

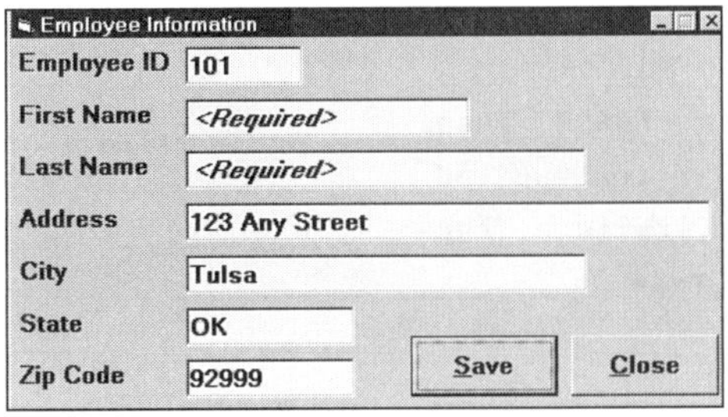

FIGURE 22.1
The `Controls` collection example.

To accomplish this, you need to place the following code in the `Click` event of the cmdSave command button shown in Figure 22.1:

```
Private Sub cmdSave_Click()
   If FormCheck() Then
      Call FormSave
   End If
End Sub
```

The `Click` event in the cmdSave button calls the `FormCheck()` procedure to perform the validation on the Employee Information form. If the appropriate fields are not filled in, the `FormCheck()` function fills them in with *<Required>*. Here's the code for the `FormCheck()` function:

```
Private Function FormCheck() As Boolean
   Dim boolFlag As Boolean
   Dim ctlAny As Control

   txtEmpID.Tag = ""
   txtFirst.Tag = ""
   txtLast.Tag = ""

   If Trim$(txtEmpID) = "" Then
      txtEmpID.Tag = "ERROR"
   End If
   If Trim$(txtFirst) = "" Then
      txtFirst.Tag = "ERROR"
```

```
    End If
    If Trim$(txtLast) = "" Then
       txtLast.Tag = "ERROR"
    End If
    ' Check the Tag property in all controls
    boolFlag = False
    For Each ctlAny In Me.Controls
       If ctlAny.Tag = "ERROR" Then
          ctlAny.Text = conRequired
          ctlAny.Font.Italic = True
          boolFlag = True
       End If
    Next ctlAny

    If boolFlag Then
       MsgBox "The Fields Marked " & _
              conRequired & _
              " Must Be Filled In or Corrected"
    Else
       FormCheck = True
    End If
End Function
```

The `FormCheck()` function first clears all the `Tag` properties of the fields to be checked. It then checks each of the text boxes to see whether they have been filled in. If they have not, it changes the `Tag` property of the text box to `"ERROR"`. After it has checked all the appropriate fields, it loops through the `Controls` collection on the current form. Each time through the loop, it checks the `Tag` property of the current control to see whether it's equal to `"ERROR"`. If it is equal to this value, the `Text` property of this text box is set to `"<Required>"`.

You should set up a constant in the General Declarations section called `conRequired`. This constant should have the value `"<Required>"` contained in it:

```
Private Const conRequired = "<Required>"
```

The reason for this is because you'll use this constant in another location in this form. This way, if you want to change the text, you only need to change it in one location. After the code has looped through all the controls, it can then pop up a message box telling the user he or she needs to fill in all the text boxes marked with *<Required>*.

Of course, you also need to take away the value `"<Required>"` when the user gives the text box focus. You can do this in the `GotFocus()` event of each of the text boxes. Write the `GotFocus()` event for each text box like this:

```
Private Sub txtFirst_GotFocus()
   If txtFirst.Text = conRequired Then
      txtFirst.Text = ""
      txtFirst.Font.Italic = False
   End If
End Sub
```

If the user is tabbing into a text box with the *<Required>* text set, you just need to erase the text and reset the italic font to `False` so when the user types data in, it will be in a normal font.

The *Printer* Collection

The `Printer` collection returns to you all the available printers connected to your computer. You can loop through this collection, just like any other collection, by using the `For Each...Next` statement:

```
Private Sub cmdCol2_Click()
   Dim sMsg As String
   Dim prt As Printer

   For Each prt In Printers
      sMsg = sMsg & "Port   = " & prt.Port & _
                  vbCrLf & _
                  "Device = " & prt.DeviceName & _
                  vbCrLf
   Next prt

   MsgBox sMsg
End Sub
```

Each time through the `Printers` collection, you receive a `Printer` object. You can then access the properties of this `Printer` object and grab the `Port` and `DeviceName` properties, which allow you to see the port and the name of the printer connected to the system. These are just a few of the properties available for the `Printer` object.

The *Collection* Class

Once you start creating class modules, you'll begin to use these classes over and over again in your Visual Basic applications. For those classes that are used several times in one application, it can be tricky keeping track of all their instances. One mechanism that can simplify this process is the `Collection` class.

The `Collection` class is a generic class you can use to hold a collection of your own objects. The `Collection` class allows you to add members to its internal array. It also allows you to retrieve those members later. What's more, you can delete members from this collection and you don't have to worry about moving the other members around to fill in any holes in the collection. The `Collection` object will automatically reshuffle everything as appropriate to make sure there are no empty entries in the collection.

With all of this shuffling around of members, it becomes pretty clear that you can't really use an index number to get to an element. As a result, the `Collection` class implements a property called `Key` that's assigned to each element as you add objects to the collection. The `Key` property is what you use to retrieve an object. The `Key` property must be unique among all of the members you add to this collection.

If you want to access elements with an index number, you can. Just make sure you don't store the index number in a global variable because things move around in the collection and this index number might change.

The `Collection` class only has one property, which is described in Table 22.1.

Table 22.1 Property of the *Collection* Class

Property	Description
`Count`	Returns the total number of items in the collection.

The `Collection` class has three methods, as shown in Table 22.2, you can use to add, retrieve, and delete members from the collection.

Table 22.2 Methods of the *Collection* Class

Method	Description
Add	Adds one item to the `Collection` class. You pass to the `Add` method an object you want to add. You can optionally pass a `Key` value to assign to the `Key` property of this element that uniquely identifies this object. You can also pass a parameter specifying which element you want to insert this object before or after.
`Item`	When you call the `Item` method, you pass in a `Key` value or an index number of the element you want to return an object pointer for. If the `Item` method detects a numeric value passed to it, it searches for the element using the `Index` number. If the item method detects a string value passed to it, it searches for the element using the `Key` value.
`Remove`	The `Remove` method eliminates an element from the collection. You need to pass to the `Remove` method the `Key` or the index number of the element to remove.

Using the *Collection* Class

Let's now look at an example of using the `Collection` class in a real-world situation. Remember the `Employee` class you created in an earlier chapter? You'll now create an example that adds one or many instances of the `Employee` class to a collection (see Figure 22.2).

Example's Filename: Emp1.frm

FIGURE 22.2 The `Collection` Class—Example 1.

In the example shown in Figure 22.2, the user must enter an employee ID, first name, last name, and salary for the employee to be added to the **Employee** object, which is then stored in a module-level collection. This module-level collection is called **mcolEmps** and is declared in the General Declarations area of the form:

```
Dim mcolEmps As Collection
```

You need to declare a new instance of this collection in the **Form_Load()** event, as shown here:

```
Private Sub Form_Load()
   txtEmpID = 1
   txtFirst = "Bill"
   txtLast = "Gates"
   txtSalary = "1000000"

   Set mcolEmps = New Collection
End Sub
```

You can now enter data in the employee form and click the Add command button to add that employee information to the module-level collection:

```
Private Sub cmdAdd_Click()
   Dim oEmp As Employee

   Set oEmp = New Employee
   With oEmp
      .EmpID = CLng(txtEmpID)
      .FirstName = txtFirst
      .LastName = txtLast
      .Salary = CCur(txtSalary)
   End With

   ' Add New Object to Module Level Collection
   mcolEmps.Add oEmp, CStr(oEmp.EmpID)
End Sub
```

The first steps here are to create a new **Employee** object and then add the information from the text boxes to the appropriate properties of the **Employee** object. Next, the **Add** method of the **Collection** object is invoked and passed the **Employee** object, along with the string value of the employee ID. The employee ID must be converted to a string to create a **Key**, because the **Key** property only accepts a string value. Because all employees have unique employee IDs, this is an acceptable key for the collection.

After you've added several `Employee` objects to the employee collection, you can now retrieve one of those objects. To do this, you fill in the text box in the Search For Employee frame. After filling in a unique key value, click the Display command button. The code for the `Click` event of this command button is presented here:

```
Private Sub cmdDisplay_Click()
   Dim oEmp As Employee

   ' Retrieve Search Criteria from Collection
   Set oEmp = mcolEmps.Item(txtSearch)

   ' Display the Employee Name
   oEmp.EmployeeName
End Sub
```

If you type the value `1` in the text box, this value is passed as a parameter to the `Item()` method of the `Collection` object. Because this is a string value, the `Item` method searches through the `Key` properties in the collection to find the element that matches this key. If the element is found, a reference to the object in the collection is returned to the `oEmp` variable. Because this is pointing to a valid `Employee` object, you can now invoke any of the methods on the `Employee` class (such as the `EmployeeName` method, for example). If the element is not found, a trappable error occurs. Therefore, it's a good idea to add some error handling any time you're using the `Item` method.

Problems with Public Collections

Although the preceding implementation seems to work fine, there are some problems with it. The problem with the `Collection` class is that you're allowed to put any object into each element. This means that an `Employee` object could be in the first element, and a form reference could be in the second element. This is not a problem as long as you know what you're doing, but the idea of a collection is that it stores objects that are all of the same type. By storing objects that are all of the same type, you can iterate over the collection and perform a group operation on each element in the collection. If you store two different object types, you'll receive an error if you try to store an element in an object variable that's expecting a different object type.

Example's Filename: Emp2.frm

To illustrate this problem, check out the sample Emp2.frm form (see Figure 22.3).

FIGURE 22.3 This version of the `Collection` class will introduce a potential problem.

When you click the Add Problem command button, you add an `Employee` object and a `Form` object to the module-level `Collection` object. Then, when you click the Display command button, you receive an error retrieving the `Form` object. Here's the code for the Add Problem command button:

```
Private Sub cmdAdd_Click()
   Dim oEmp As Employee

   Set oEmp = New Employee
   With oEmp
      .EmpID = CLng(txtEmpID)
      .FirstName = txtFirst
      .LastName = txtLast
      .Salary = CCur(txtSalary)
   End With

   ' Add New Object to Module Level Collection
   mcolEmps.Add oEmp, CStr(oEmp.EmpID)

   ' Add the current form object to
   ' the Module Level Collection
   mcolEmps.Add Me, "99"
End Sub
```

This code first adds an instance of the `Employee` object, and then it adds a reference to the current form and assigns the key value `99` to that form in the collection. Both are entered into the collection with no problem; however, when you attempt to retrieve the element that has the key `99`, you'll receive an error. Here's the code for the Display command button:

```
Private Sub cmdDisplay_Click()
   Dim oEmp As Employee

   ' Retrieve Search Criteria from Collection
   ' To generate the error set the txtSearch = '99'
   Set oEmp = mcolEmps.Item(txtSearch)

   ' Display the Employee Name
   oEmp.EmployeeName
End Sub
```

If you enter **99** in the txtSearch text box, you'll receive a Type Mismatch error from Visual Basic when you attempt to perform the `Item()` method on the `Collection` object. This is because it's trying to put a `Form` object in a pointer that's declared to hold an `Employee` object.

> **TIP**
> Be careful using the `Collection` object in your code because you can store any type of object within it. This could cause problems at runtime.

Create Your Own *Collection* Class

You can easily solve the problem of using a generic `Collection` class by just not using it. You can create your own "collection" class by wrapping the `Collection` class into your own class module. You'll need to create an `Employees` class (notice the letter *s* on the end of `Employees`) that duplicates the methods of the `Collection` class, but in this case, the **Add** method only accepts employee information, not any type of object.

Example's Filename: Emp3.frm

In the sample project shown in Figure 22.4, you'll find an `Employee` class and an `Employees` class.

FIGURE 22.4 Creating your own `Collection` class.

In the Employees class, you'll find a Collection class declared in the General Declarations area of the class module:

```
Private mcolEmps As Collection
```

Of course, you'll need to create a new instance of this Collection class. This you can do in the Class_Initialize() event, like this:

```
Private Sub Class_Initialize()
   Set mcolEmps = New Collection
End Sub
```

You'll find an Add method in this class, but it does not accept objects. Instead, it only accepts EmployeeID, FirstName, LastName, and Salary values. This forces you to pass in employee data only, not just any data type you want:

```
Public Function Add(ByVal EmpID As Long, _
                     ByVal FirstName As String, _
                     ByVal LastName As String, _
                     ByVal Salary As Currency) As Employee

   Dim oEmp As Employee

   Set oEmp = New Employee
   ' Load Properties of New Class
   With oEmp
      .EmpID = EmpID
      .FirstName = FirstName
      .LastName = LastName
      .Salary = Salary
   End With

   ' Add To Private Collection
   mcolEmps.Add oEmp, CStr(EmpID)

   Set Add = oEmp
End Function
```

In the Add method, you create a new Employee object, fill in the properties from the arguments passed to this method, and then add the Employee object to the private collection in this class. It's customary to return the newly created Employee object from the Add method, so that's what you should do in your Add method as well.

The next method you need to create is the `Item()` method. This method needs to accept a variant argument because you can pass either a numeric value or a string value to the `Item()` method of the `Collection` class:

```
Public Function Item(vntValue As Variant) As Employee
   Dim oEmp As Employee

   On Error Resume Next

   Set oEmp = mcolEmps.Item(vntValue)
   If oEmp Is Nothing Then
      Set Item = Nothing
   Else
      Set Item = oEmp
   End If
End Function
```

This method is very simple to write. First, let's set an error trap to ignore any errors that may occur when you attempt to access the `Item` method. This way, you can just check the `Employee` object after the `Item` method executes to see whether you have anything in the `Employee` object. If it's `Nothing`, you know that you didn't find the object. Otherwise, a valid `Employee` object is returned from this `Item` method.

You also need a `Count` property in your `Employees` class. This property just needs to return the `Count` property in the private collection in your `Employees` class:

```
Property Get Count() As Integer
   Count = mcolEmps.Count
End Property
```

The last method you need to implement is the `Remove()` method. This method also needs to accept a variant argument because either an index number or a `Key` string can be passed to the `Remove` method of the `Collection` class:

```
Public Sub Remove(ByVal vntValue As Variant)
   mcolEmps.Remove vntValue
End Sub
```

Using the *Employees* Class

In the sample form, you'll see a declaration of the `Employees` class in the General Declarations area:

```
Dim moEmps As Employees
```

In the `Form_Load()` event, you need to create a new instance of this `Employees` class:

```
Private Sub Form_Load()
   txtEmpID = 1
   txtFirst = "Bill"
   txtLast = "Gates"
   txtSalary = 1000000

   Set moEmps = New Employees
End Sub
```

Next, look in the Add command button's `Click` event to see how to use this `Employees` collection class:

```
Private Sub cmdAdd_Click()
   ' Add information to the Employees class
   moEmps.Add EmpID:=CLng(txtEmpID), _
              FirstName:=txtFirst, _
              Salary:=CCur(txtSalary), _
              LastName:=txtLast

End Sub
```

This code uses the module-level `Employees` object to add the information from the form into the class. In this example, the `Add` method is called using the named arguments to make it clear which values are being passed.

Next, you can retrieve a particular `Employee` object by filling a value into the txtSearch text box and clicking the Display command button:

```
Private Sub cmdDisplay_Click()
   Dim oEmp As Employee

   If moEmps.Count > 0 Then
      ' Retrieve Search Criteria from Collection
      Set oEmp = moEmps.Item(txtSearch)
```

```
            If oEmp Is Nothing Then
                MsgBox "Employee ID Not Found"
            Else
                ' Display the Employee Name
                oEmp.EmployeeName
            End If
        Else
            MsgBox "No Employees Have Been Added"
        End If
    End Sub
```

In the code for the `Click` event, you'll see that you need to dim an `Employee` object. Don't dim a new `Employee` object, just dim a pointer to an existing object. Remember that the objects already exist in the collection—you're just retrieving a pointer to one of those objects.

After declaring the `Employee` object, make sure there are actually employees in the `Employees` class by checking the `Count` property. If there are employees, go ahead and call the `Item` method, passing in the value in the text box txtSearch. After the call to the `Item` method, you should check to see whether the `oEmp` variable is equal to `Nothing`. If it is, you know that the employee you were looking for was not found. If the employee was found, you can invoke the `EmployeeName` method on the returned `Employee` object to display that employee. This is now a very robust implementation for using collections.

Adding Iteration

By default, any collection class you create does not support the ability to iterate through the collection using the `For Each...Next` construct. You can add this ability, but you must set a special "magic number" in the procedure attributes dialog box.

Example's Filename: Emp4.frm

Consider the example shown in Figure 22.5, where there are two command buttons that have two different methods for looping through the values contained in the `Employees` collection class.

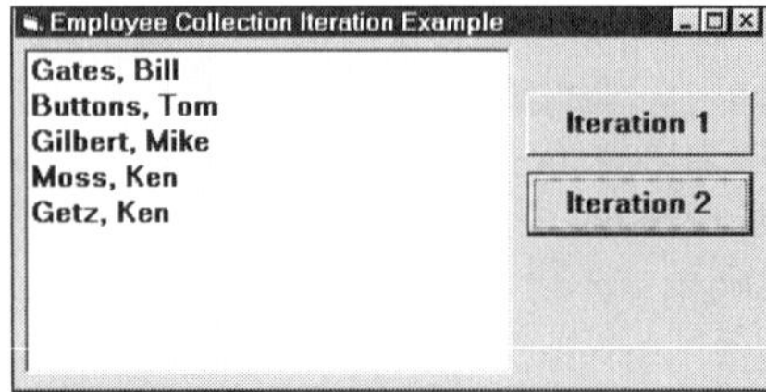

FIGURE 22.5
An employee iteration example.

First, in the `Form_Load()` event, you need to call a routine that loads some `Employee` classes into the module-level `Employees` collection:

```
Private Sub EmpLoad()
   ' Add information to the Employees class
   moEmps.Add EmpID:=1, _
              FirstName:="Bill", _
              LastName:="Gates", _
              Salary:=1000000

   moEmps.Add EmpID:=2, _
              FirstName:="Tom", _
              LastName:="Buttons", _
              Salary:=100000

   moEmps.Add EmpID:=3, _
              FirstName:="Mike", _
              LastName:="Gilbert", _
              Salary:=100000

   moEmps.Add EmpID:=4, _
              FirstName:="Ken", _
              LastName:="Moss", _
              Salary:=100000

   moEmps.Add EmpID:=5, _
              FirstName:="Ken", _
              LastName:="Getz", _
              Salary:=100000
End Sub
```

Next, you can iterate through this collection of employees and load them into the list box using the code underneath the Iteration 1 command button:

```
Private Sub cmdIterate1_Click()
   Dim intLoop As Integer

   lstNames.Clear
   For intLoop = 1 To moEmps.Count
      ' Note, the Item method has
      ' been set to the Default
      lstNames.AddItem moEmps(intLoop).LastName & ", " & _
                       moEmps(intLoop).FirstName
   Next
End Sub
```

You can see that this code loops through the `Employees` collection from `1` to the `Count` value of the number of `Employee` objects in the collection. The `Collection` class always numbers its members starting with 1 instead of 0, just like arrays in Visual Basic do. Notice that for this code to work, you have set the `Item` method in the `Employees` collection to be the default method. This option is set by going into the Tools, Procedure Attributes menu option and choosing the (Default) option from the Procedure ID combo box. (I've tried to match this `Employee` collection to what the normal collection does, and the `Item` method is the default for `Collection` classes.)

Adding the *_NewEnum* Method

Before you can use the `For...Each Next` construct, you need to add a method to the `Employees` collection class that returns a special data type called `IUnknown`. This data type is a COM object that's required to return an object from an iterator operator. There's also a special method attached to the `Collection` class that's hidden: It's called `_NewEnum`. This method is responsible for returning an object from the collection and maintaining which object is the next one to return. Add the following code to your `Collection` classes to use the `For...Each Next` construct to iterate through your collections:

```
Public Function Iterate() As IUnknown
    Set Iterate = mcolEmps.[_NewEnum]
End Function
```

After you've added this method to your `Employee` collection class, you need to perform one more step. Go to the Tools, Procedure Attributes menu item and select the `Iterate()` function from the drop-down list of names. Click the Advanced command button, and in the Procedure ID drop-down list, type in the value **–4**, as shown in Figure 22.6.

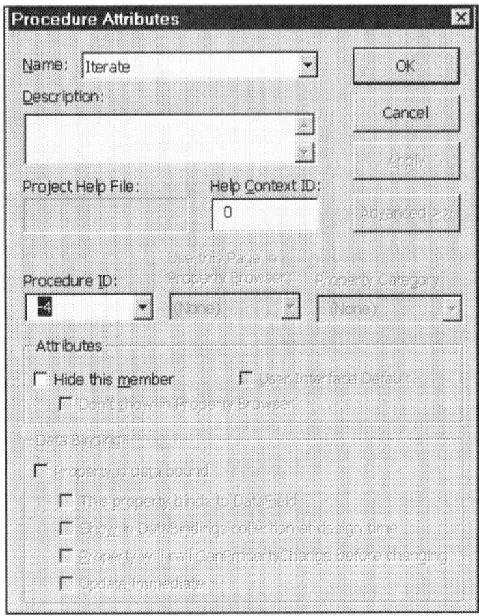

FIGURE 22.6 The Procedure Attributes dialog box.

This value is a special identifier that tells COM that this procedure ID is the iteration function that needs to be able to return the objects one by one from the collection. Now, via the Iterate 2 command button on the sample form, you can iterate through the collection using the `For...Each Next` construct:

```
Private Sub cmdIterate2_Click()
   Dim oEmp As Employee

   lstNames.Clear
   For Each oEmp In moEmps
      lstNames.AddItem oEmp.LastName & ", " & _
                        oEmp.FirstName
   Next
End Sub
```

Summary

There are many different types of collections you can use in Visual Basic. You can use the built-in collections, such as the `Forms`, `Controls`, and `Printers`, and you have the ability to create your own collections using the `Collection` class. It is highly recommended that you create a "collection" class instead of dealing with a generic `Collection` class object.

Review Questions

1. What are the built-in collections in Visual Basic?
2. How might collections help you in developing an application?
3. List the properties of the `Collection` object.
4. What are the methods of the `Collection` object?
5. Why should you build a class that encapsulates the `Collection` object?

Exercises

1. Create a collection class for the `EmpType` class you created in an earlier chapter.
2. Create a form that allows you to input employee type information into the `EmpType` collection class.
3. Enter a few employee types into the collection class.
4. Add a list box to this form and loop through your collection class to populate the employee type description in the collection class.

23

Tips and Tricks

THIS CHAPTER PRESENTS MANY DIFFERENT TIPS and tricks for using forms and controls at runtime. You'll learn to control keystrokes as they are entered into text boxes, to use the `LostFocus()` and the new `Validate()` events, and to use the `DataFormat` property for bound controls. You'll also learn the advantages and disadvantages of buying and using third-party controls. Finally, I present some of the new functions available in the Visual Basic 6 language.

Chapter Objectives

- Learn to control user input
- Learn to use the standard controls for validation
- Learn about formatted input
- Learn about third-party controls
- Learn the new functions in Visual Basic 6

Sample Project File: \Chapter23\Tips.vbp

Handling Keystrokes

Regardless of the type of validation routines you use after the user has entered data, sometimes it's desirable to validate the keystrokes as the user enters them. Although there's a custom control called the Masked Edit control that allows you to set the format for valid characters, it's sometimes better to trap the keystrokes yourself. Let's look at how to handle keystrokes for a text box control (see Figure 23.1).

Example's Filename: Keystrokes.frm

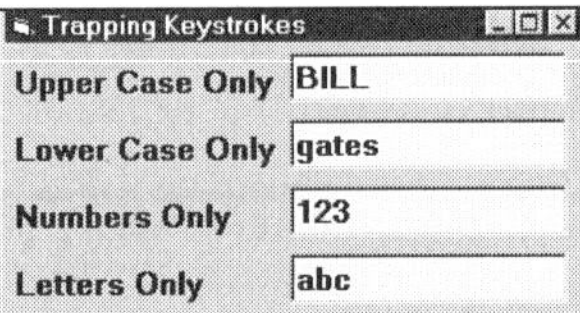

FIGURE 23.1 Trapping keystrokes in a sample form.

Uppercase Input

To make all characters uppercase in a text box or other input control, all you need to do is add one line of code to the `KeyPress` event. The `KeyPress` event is passed the key that's pressed prior to that key being entered into the text box. The keystroke is passed in as an ASCII character value. This means you need to convert it to a normal character using the `Chr$()` function and then apply the `UCase$()` function to the result. Next, you need to convert it back to ASCII code using the `Asc()` function. The resulting ASCII code is then assigned back to the `KeyAscii` argument. Because the `KeyAscii` argument is passed by reference, any changes to this key value will be placed into the text box:

```
Private Sub txtUpper_KeyPress(KeyAscii As Integer)
    KeyAscii = Asc(UCase$(Chr$(KeyAscii)))
End Sub
```

The only problem with the `KeyPress` event is that every keystroke is trapped by this routine. This is a lot of extra work for the program, and it can slow down the input process somewhat. An alternate method is to convert everything to uppercase once the user tabs out of the text box. For that, you can use code like the following:

```
Sub txtUpper_LostFocus()
   txtUpper.Text = UCase$(txtUpper.Text)
End Sub
```

Although the user must wait until he or she tabs out of the field to see the results converted to uppercase, the end result is the same. The `LostFocus()` can also be fired when the user clicks to another control with the mouse.

Lowercase Input

As is the case with the uppercase input example, you only need one line of code placed into the `KeyPress` event of a text box to covert every key pressed to lowercase. In this example, you use the `LCase$()` function to perform the keystroke conversion:

```
Private Sub txtLower_KeyPress(KeyAscii As Integer)
   KeyAscii = Asc(LCase$(Chr$(KeyAscii)))
End Sub
```

Input Numbers Only

Sometimes you might want to have the user only input numeric values into a text box. You use the `KeyPress` event for this type of validation as well. Here's an example:

```
Private Sub txtNumbers_KeyPress(KeyAscii As Integer)
   Select Case KeyAscii
      Case vbKeyDelete      ' Delete Key
      Case vbKeyBack        ' Backspace Key
      Case 48 To 57         ' Number 0-9
      Case Else
```

```
            Beep
            KeyAscii = 0        ' Cancels the keystroke
    End Select
End Sub
```

Of course, you would probably want to place this code in a generic function that you can call from any text box in which you want to trap for numeric input only.

Input Characters Only

To restrict a text box to the characters *A* to *Z* and *a* to *z*, use the following code in the KeyPress event of the text box:

```
Private Sub txtLetters_KeyPress(KeyAscii As Integer)
    Select Case KeyAscii
        Case vbKeyDelete        ' Delete Key
        Case vbKeyBack          ' Backspace Key
        Case 65 To 90           ' Upper Case Chars
        Case 97 To 122          ' Lower Case Chars
        Case Else
            Beep
            KeyAscii = 0        ' Cancels keystroke
    End Select
End Sub
```

As in the previous example, you should create a generic routine that you can call to perform the trap for these keystrokes.

Limiting Characters

To limit the number of input characters, set the number for the MaxLength property to the total number of characters the user can enter. In a data-bound text box, if you do not set this property and then allow the user to enter too many characters, an error might occur when the value back is placed in a table in the database.

Validating Data

Sometimes you need to get immediate feedback of invalid data when the user attempts to leave a field. To accomplish this, you can use the LostFocus() event in a text box.

In the `LostFocus()` event, you check to see whether a text box has been filled in by checking the `Text` property. Be sure to trim the `Text` property, using the `Trim$()` function, in case the user has entered all spaces. Next, give the user a message indicating that the field must be filled in. After the message is displayed, you want to set the focus back to the text box, because the cursor has already moved to the next field.

Deadly Embrace and the *LostFocus()* Event

Placing code in the `LostFocus()` event for a single text box is generally not a problem. However, when you're checking multiple text boxes to see whether they are empty, you can run into some big problems.

Example's Filename: TextBoxes.frm

Consider the following code that's placed in the first two text boxes on the sample form shown in Figure 23.2.

```
Private Sub txtFirst_LostFocus()
    If Trim$(txtFirst.Text) = "" Then
        MsgBox "First Name Field Must Be Filled In"
        txtFirst.SetFocus
    End If
End Sub

Private Sub txtLast_LostFocus()
    If Trim$(txtLast.Text) = "" Then
        MsgBox "Last Name Field Must Be Filled In"
        txtLast.SetFocus
    End If
End Sub
```

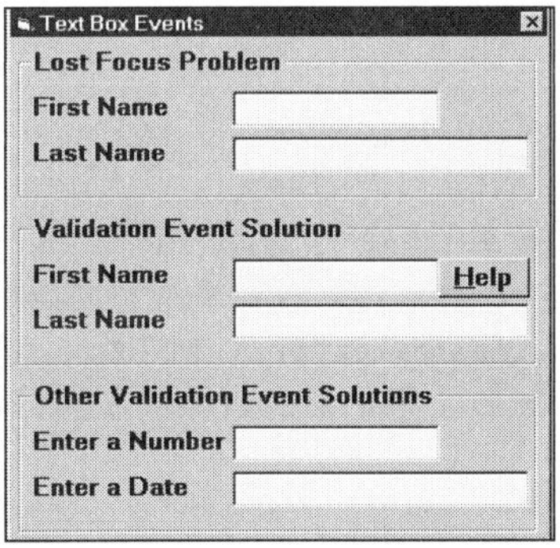

FIGURE 23.2 Validation events using a sample form.

The problem here is that after you press the Tab key, the next field in the tab order receives focus. This means that next text box has fired its `GotFocus()` event and that control now has the input focus. After this occurs, the `LostFocus()` event for the previous text box fires. In the code for the `LostFocus()` on the original text box, you invoke the `SetFocus` method to set focus back to the original text box. In the text box that now has focus, however, you have the same type of code in its `LostFocus()` event. This means it will lose focus as soon as you perform the `SetFocus` event on the original text box. However, focus has then gone to the original text box, which means that the `LostFocus()` event will now fire on the other control, which then sets focus back to itself. Well, as you can see, you are now in an infinite loop. This is known as a *deadly embrace*, a computer science term used when two objects are fighting for a single resource (in this case, the input focus).

To break out of the deadly embrace when using the Visual Basic design environment, press Ctrl+Break to enter break mode. If you have this code in a compiled EXE file, you'll need to bring up Task Manager to end the task.

The *Validate* Event

To avoid the problem with the `LostFocus()` event, Microsoft has added a new event called `Validate` that allows you to check the value in a text box or other control prior to it losing the focus. The `Validate` event can be used to perform any type of validation you require. You can use it to check for blank data, to see whether a minimum number of characters have been input, to make sure only numbers are input, and even to verify that a valid date has been entered.

The `Validate` event is passed in a `Cancel` argument that you can set to a `True` value if you want to cancel the `LostFocus` event. If you set this argument to `False`, the `LostFocus` will occur normally. Within the `Validate` event, you write any type of code needed to ensure you have valid data. For example, the following code checks to see whether a first name field is filled in with any data and that the user has input at least three characters:

```
Private Sub txtFirstValidate_Validate(Cancel As Boolean)
   If Trim$(txtFirstValidate.Text) = "" Then
      MsgBox "First Name Field Must Be Filled In"
      Cancel = True
   ElseIf Len(Trim$(txtFirstValidate.Text)) < 3 Then
      MsgBox "You must enter more than 2 letters"
      Cancel = True
```

```
    End If
    Debug.Print "Validate"
End Sub
```

NOTE
The `Validate` event will not fire if the user closes the form from the control menu.

The *CausesValidation* Property

The problem with the `Validate` event is that you might have a command button on your form that's used to enable the user to get help for the screen. If the user can't leave the field he or she is on because of the `Validate` event, then the help is not accessible. In this case, you need to set the `CausesValidation` property on the command button to a `False` value. When the user moves to this button, you can display the help, and the `Validate` event will not fire for the control. After the user has viewed the help and he or she tries to move to another control, the `Validate` event will fire on the control where the user came from. If the user moves directly back to the other control, the `Validate` event will not fire until he or she tries to move off the control normally.

Control Tricks

Let's now look at some tricks you can use with some of the standard controls. Some things are not readily apparent, and you need to be aware of them.

ToolTips on Controls

Almost every control has a `ToolTipText` property. If you fill this in with some text, that text will appear when the user hovers the mouse over that control. This can be a great help to a user who does not really understand what type of input should go into a particular control.

Finding a Value in a Combo Box

Often you'll have a combo box with a few hundred items in it. If you need to find a value very quickly, there are a few different techniques that you can use. In this chapter, you'll learn two methods; in a later chapter, you'll learn yet another method.

Example's Filename: Combo.frm

In this example, you will find a combo box loaded with state codes (see Figure 23.3).

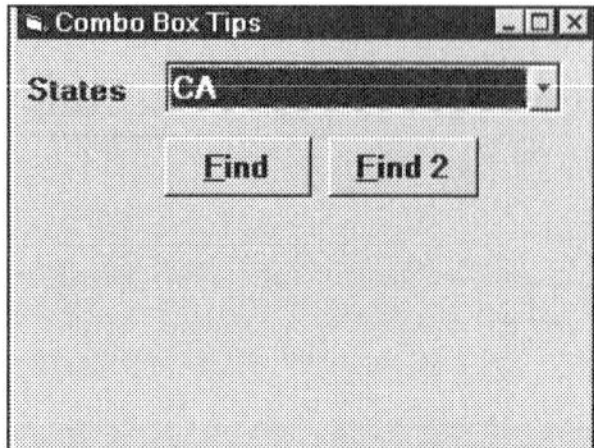

FIGURE 23.3 The Combo Box Tips form.

There are two command buttons that each prompt for a state code to find. The first method uses a loop to find a value:

```
Private Sub StateFind(ByVal strState As String)
   Dim intLoop As Integer
   Dim intPos As Integer

   intPos = -1
   For intLoop = 0 To cboStates.ListCount - 1
      If cboStates.List(intLoop) = strState Then
         intPos = intLoop
         intLoop = cboStates.ListCount
      End If
   Next intLoop

   cboStates.ListIndex = intPos
End Sub
```

The `StateFind()` routine loops through the combo box from `0` to the value of `ListCount - 1`. As it loops through the values, it compares each value in the `List()` property with the value passed in as an argument. If it finds a match, it sets the `intPos` variable to the looping variable. It then drops out of the loop and sets the `ListIndex` property of the combo box to the value in the `intPos` variable. If the value is not found, the `ListIndex` property is set to `-1`, which causes the combo box have no value selected.

The Second Method for Finding Values in Combo Boxes

Another technique for finding a value in a combo box is to set the `Text` property to the value you're seeking. This forces the combo box to be positioned to that value. The problem with this technique is that if the value is not found, a trappable run-time error is generated. Because the error is trappable, you need to check to see whether an error is generated. If it is, you set the `ListIndex` property to `-1` to force the combo box to have no value selected:

```
Private Sub StateFind2(ByVal strState As String)
    On Error Resume Next
    cboStates.Text = strState
    If Err.Number Then
        cboStates.ListIndex = -1
    End If
End Sub
```

The *ComboBox_Click* Event

When you click a combo box to drop down the list portion, the `Click` event is fired. This is great when the user selects a new value in the list, but if the user doesn't change the value, the `Click` event is still fired. If you've written code within the `Click` event to enable a Save button, it will be fired whether or not a change is made. Here's an example:

```
Private Sub cboStates_Click ()
    cmdSave.Enabled = True
End Sub
```

Instead, you need to detect whether the value has been changed in the combo box. To accomplish this, you need to write code in the `GotFocus()` event as well as the `Click` event. In the `GotFocus()` event, you grab the value in the `Text` property and copy it into the `Tag` property, like this:

```
Private Sub cboStates_GotFocus()
    cboStates.Tag = cboStates.Text
End Sub
```

Then you change the `Click` event so that you compare the `Tag` property against the `Text` property. If they are different, you enable the Save button and copy the `Text` property back into the `Tag` property:

```
Private Sub cboStates_Click()
   If cboStates.Tag <> cboStates.Text Then
      cmdSave.Enabled = True
      cboStates.Tag = cboStates.Text
   End If
End Sub
```

This solves the problem of the user just clicking to open the list but not actually changing the value in the combo box.

The *DataFormat* Property

If you want to format the data coming from a data control, you can use the new `DataFormat` property on the text boxes. When you click the `DataFormat` property, a dialog box appears that allows you to choose what type of formatting you want to apply to the data. (See Figures 23.4 and 23.5 for examples of two of these formatting options.)

Example's Filename: DataFormat.frm

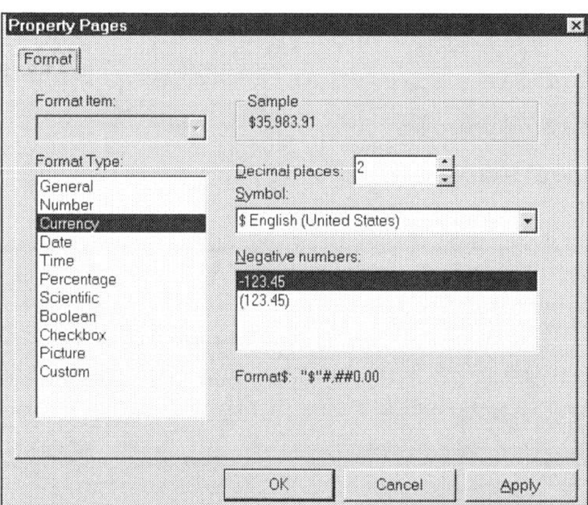

FIGURE 23.4 The `DataFormat` property's currency formats.

When you choose the currency format, you can change the number of decimal places, the symbol type to use, and how to display negative numbers.

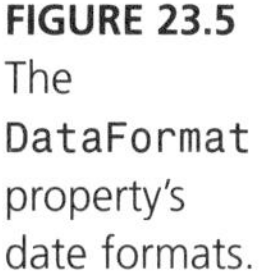

FIGURE 23.5
The `DataFormat` property's date formats.

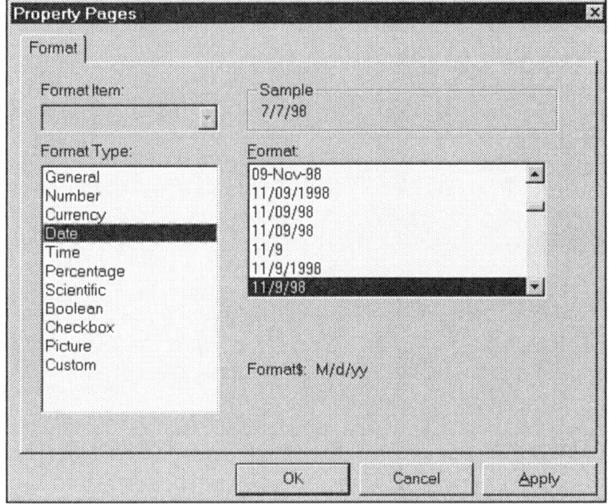

For date formats, you're allowed to choose many different options. Simply select the format in which you want to display the date.

There are many other format types, as you can see in the Format Type list box in Figure 23.5. Each one has a different format value that you can select on the right side of this dialog box. Some even allow you to enter your own custom format.

The *TabIndex* Property and the Label Control

You may have noticed that a label control has a `TabIndex` property. Yet, a label control cannot receive focus. Why is this? Well, the answer is that you can place an ampersand (`&`) character in front of one of the characters in the label's `Caption` property to make that character underlined. When you press Alt+<*letter*>, focus automatically goes to the control that has the next highest `TabIndex` property.

In Figure 23.6, you can see that the *C* in City is underscored. If the `TabIndex` for that label is `6`, and the text box, txtCity, has the `TabIndex` value `7`, when you press Alt+C, focus will jump to the txtCity text box. This is used to help people who like to use the keyboard to jump from one part of the form to another without having to use the mouse.

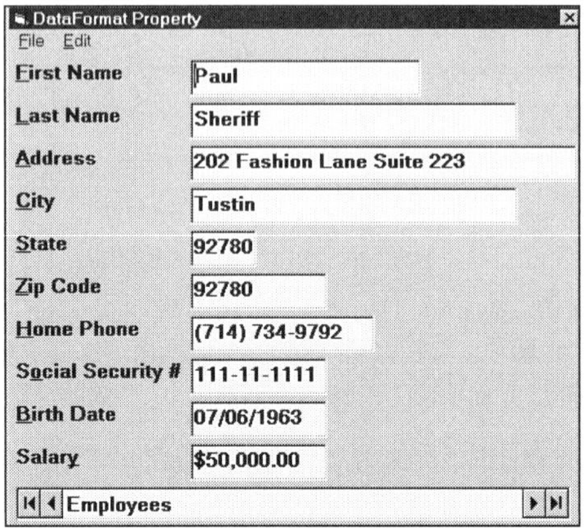

FIGURE 23.6 The `TabIndex` property used with label controls.

Third-Party Controls

Many third-party controls are available in the market today that help you format data, create editable grids, display complete scheduling systems, and perform many other functions. Many of these are good, robust controls; however, you should note that there are both advantages and disadvantages to using them.

Advantages to Using Third-Party Controls

Here's a list of some of the advantages to using third-party controls:

- They're usually pretty easy to use.
- They're generally quick to get up and running in your application.
- You don't need to learn complicated programming techniques.

Disadvantages to Using Third-Party Controls

Here's a list of some of the disadvantages to using third-party controls:

- You don't own the source code, so if you need to make changes to the control, you're dependent on the vendor for these changes.
- If you need any technical support, you might have to wait awhile, or you might have to pay a lot more money.
- If you discover a bug in the control, you're again at the mercy of the vendor to fix the problem in a timely manner. However, what the vendor considers *timely* might not be the same as your definition.

- If a new version of Visual Basic comes out that breaks the custom control, you have to wait for the vendor to upgrade it before you can use the new version of Visual Basic.

Additional Functions in Visual Basic

The Visual Basic language has so many functions that it's impractical to cover them all here. However, the following sections cover a few that you should be aware of. First, let's look at the `Format*()` functions that are introduced in Visual Basic 6.

FormatCurrency()

`FormatCurrency()` is very similar to the `Format()` function using the `Currency` named format. However, you can do a lot more with the `FormatCurrency()` function than you can with the `Format()` function.

Here's the syntax for `FormatCurrency()`:

```
FormatCurrency(Expression [,NumDigitsAfterDecimal
                 [,IncludeLeadingDigit
                 [,UseParensForNegativeNumbers
                 [,GroupDigits]]]])
```

Here's some sample output:

```
FormatCurrency(100) = $100.00
FormatCurrency(100,4) = $100.0000
FormatCurrency(.1,-1,vbFalse) = $.10
FormatCurrency(.1,-1,vbFalse) = $0.10
FormatCurrency(-100,-1, , vbFalse) = -$100.00
FormatCurrency(-100,-1, , vbUseDefault) = ($100.00)
FormatCurrency(1,100,-1, , ,vbFalse) = $1100.00
FormatCurrency(1,100,-1, , , vbUseDefault) = $1,100.00
```

The first parameter is the value you want to use for the currency value. The second parameter is the number of decimal places to use. You can pass `-1` to use the default, as specified in your windows regional settings. The third parameter can be set to one of the tri-state values (`vbFalse`, `vbTrue`, or `vbUseDefault`) to specify the use a leading zero in front of a fractional value. If you specify `vbFalse`, a leading zero is not used; if you specify `vbTrue`, a leading zero is always used. Finally, if you specify `vbUseDefault`, the value specified in the regional settings of your

Control Panel is used. The fourth parameter is another tri-state value that determines whether to use parentheses to signify a negative value. The fifth parameter is a tri-state value specifying the use of grouping values for values over 1,000. A *grouping value* is a comma (,) or a decimal (.) or any other value that's specified in your regional settings in Control Panel.

FormatDateTime()

If you need to have a date returned in different formats, you can use the `FormatDateTime()` function. There are five different constants you can pass to this function to format the output of the date/time value. The constants are shown in the following output:

```
FormatDateTime(Now, [Constant])

vbGeneralDate = 10/26/98 7:38:07 PM
vbLongDate = Monday, October 26, 1998
vbLongTime = 7:38:07 PM
vbShortDate = 10/26/98
vbShortTime = 19:38
```

You only pass two parameters to this function—the date expression and the constant specifying the type of date or time you want to output.

FormatNumber()

`FormatNumber()` is exactly like the `FormatCurrency()` function, without the currency symbol. All the parameters are exactly the same:

```
FormatNumber(100) = 100.00
FormatNumber(100,4) = 100.0000
FormatNumber(.1,-1,vbFalse) = .10
FormatNumber(.1,-1,vbFalse) = 0.10
FormatNumber(-100,-1, , vbFalse) = (100.00)
FormatNumber(-100,-1, , vbUseDefault) = -100.00
FormatNumber(1,100,-1, , ,vbFalse) = 1100.00
FormatNumber(1,100,-1, , , vbUseDefault) = 1,100.00
```

FormatPercent()

The `FormatPercent()` function returns a fractional value in a percentage format. This is ideal for those situations where you need to display a percentage value—such as on top of a progress bar, for example:

```
FormatPercent(10/60) = 16.6667%
FormatPercent(1/3,-1,vbFalse) = 33.33%
FormatPercent(1/3,-1,vbFalse) = 33.33%
FormatPercent(-1 / -2,-1, , vbFalse) = 50.00%
FormatPercent(-1 / -2,-1, , vbUseDefault) = 50.00%
FormatPercent(.11,-1, , ,vbFalse) = 11.00%
FormatPercent(.11,-1, , , vbUseDefault) = 11.00%
```

Round()

The `Round()` function is very *unique*, shall we say? It doesn't work exactly like you might think it would. For example, I was always taught that if a value is .4 or below, you round down to the next lowest whole number, whereas if a value is .5 or above, you round to next higher whole number. Let's take a look at some sample output to see how Visual Basic performs rounding.

```
Round(1.4) = 1
Round(1.5) = 2
Round(1.6) = 2

Round(2.4) = 2
Round(2.5) = 2
Round(2.6) = 3
```

As you can see, when you pass `1.5` to the `Round()` function, it rounds up. When you pass `2.5` to the `Round()` function, it rounds down. Visual Basic always rounds up numbers that are even and rounds down numbers that are odd. Although most people call this a bug, the folks at Microsoft call it a feature, claiming that if you perform a lot of rounding, statistically this will give you more accurate results. Yeah, right! Of course, you can always go back to your seventh grade math book and write your own function to get a "real" rounding function.

StrReverse()

This function takes any string and reverses all the letters. About the only use I can think of for this function is as a part of an encryption routine for a password. You can pass in the password to this function, reverse the password, and then continue to apply other algorithms to encrypt the password into a nonreadable format. Here are some examples:

```
StrReverse("PDSA, Inc.") = .cnI ,ASDP
StrReverse("mom") = mom
StrReverse("dad") = dad
```

MonthName()

If you need to get a month name for a particular number from 1 to 12, you can pass that numeric value to the `MonthName()` function to have it return the month name. Here are some examples:

```
MonthName(Month(Now)) = October
MonthName(2) = February
MonthName(2, True) = Feb
```

If you pass a `True` value as the second parameter, the `MonthName()` function will abbreviate the month name that's returned.

WeekdayName()

The `WeekdayName` function returns the day of the week for a value between 1 and 7. You can use the `DatePart()` function to extract the weekday from a date value. If you pass `True` as the second parameter, the `WeekdayName` function abbreviates the name of the weekday returned. You may pass in a constant as the third parameter to specify the starting day of the week. Therefore, if you only want to calculate work days, you can pass in the constant `vbMonday` as the third parameter. Here are some examples:

```
WeekdayName(DatePart("w", Now)) = Monday
WeekdayName(2) = Monday
WeekdayName(2, True) = Mon
WeekdayName(2, False, vbMonday) = Tuesday
WeekdayName(2, True, vbMonday) = Tue
```

Summary

Restricting user input in text boxes is as simple as adding a little bit of code to the `KeyPress` event or using the `Validate()` event. Values changing in a combo box can cause you problems if you're not aware that the `Click` event fires every time a combo box is clicked. The `DataFormat` property helps you apply formatting to values coming from a data control that will be placed in text box controls.

Review Questions

1. Which event do you use to restrict user input in text boxes?
2. Which function do you use to force uppercase letters?
3. What's the problem with the `LostFocus()` event?
4. What does the `CausesValidation` property do?
5. Which function do you use to display a currency value?
6. Which function do you use to display a date value?

24

ActiveX Data Objects

IN THIS CHAPTER, YOU'LL LEARN THE BASICS of using ActiveX Data Objects (ADO). These are the objects that underlie the ADO data control. You'll learn to create different types of connection strings as well as how to use the `Connection` object and the `Recordset` object. You'll also see how to use a basic `Command` object.

Chapter Objectives

- Learn to use the basic ADO object model
- Learn to use the `Connection` object
- Learn to use the `Recordset` object
- Learn `Command` object usage

Sample Project File: \Chapter24\ADO.vbp

The *Connection* Object

The `Connection` object is the highest object in ADO. If you plan on opening multiple `Recordset` objects in your application, it's best that you open a connection first and then pass that connection to each recordset. This one connection can then be used over and over again instead of having to make a new connection each time. Although it isn't necessary to create a `Connection` object, doing so helps speed up access and cut down on the amount of resources used on both the client and the server.

Properties of the *Connection* Object

A lot of properties are associated with the `Connection` object. Not all of them are useful for understanding the basics of ADO, so Table 24.1 only covers those that are applicable right now.

Table 24.1 ADO *Connection* Object Properties

Property	Description
`CommandTimeout`	How long ADO will wait for a command to execute a stored procedure or other SQL action statement like `INSERT`, `UPDATE`, `DELETE`. The default is 30 seconds, but this can be set to any number of seconds or to 0 to wait indefinitely.
`ConnectionString`	A string of connection information that's used to connect to a data source. This varies with each provider you use. An ODBC provider's connection string is very different than an OLE DB connection string. You'll see examples of how to set this in this chapter.

Property	Description
`ConnectionTimeout`	How long ADO waits for a connection to the data source to open. The default is 15 seconds, but this can be set to any number of seconds or to 0 to wait indefinitely. You might have to change this value based on how busy your server is or how busy your network is.
`CursorLocation`	This property determines where the cursor is located. It can be set to either the client side or the server side. If you place the cursor on the client side, you get an additional structure on your workstation to handle the movement through the recordset. If you place the cursor on the server side, this information stays on the server. There are pluses and minuses to both of these methods. If you have the cursor on the workstation, you cause more network traffic. If you leave it on the server, your server can become overburdened. There's no easy answer here—you need to be able to change this as your application warrants. (Note that the No Cursor option is no longer supported.)
`DefaultDatabase`	This property might not be supported by all providers. If supplied, it tells the provider which database to connect to after connecting to the data source.
`Mode`	You can set many different modes for this database connection. You can open the data source for read-only or exclusive use, as well as many other modes. (See the online help for more information.)
`Provider`	This property returns the name of the provider that the connection is using to connect to the data source. You can also set this property to connect to a particular provider.
`State`	This property returns a status code to tell you the state the `Connection` object is currently in. The valid values are `Closed`, `Open`, `Connecting`, `Executing`, and `Fetching`. Constants are defined for each of these states that you can compare against the state of the object.
`Version`	This property returns the version number of ADO being used. This might be used if you have a feature that's available in only one version of ADO. You could check this to see whether the user has the correct version before the feature is used.

Methods of the *Connection* Object

The `Connection` object has a lot of methods, but, once again, not all of them are important. Table 24.2 lists the most commonly used methods.

Table 24.2 Methods of the *Connection* Object

Method Name	Description
`Close`	This method closes an open connection.
`Execute`	Use this method to execute a stored procedure or any SQL action statement such as an `INSERT`, `UPDATE`, and `DELETE`.
`Open`	After you have set the `ConnectionString` property, you call this method to open a connection to the data source.

Creating a *Connection* Object

You'll generally create one public `Connection` object that can be used throughout your application. You should only need one connection for a typical database application. There may be times when you need to open a second connection, but they should be kept to a minimum. Remember that connections are a scarce resource on a database server and should be opened only as necessary. Let's create a public `Connection` object in a BAS module.

Exercise

Creating an ADO Project

1. In your employee project, you'll need to reference the Microsoft ActiveX Data Objects 2.0 Library from the Project, References menu.
2. Add a BAS module to your employee project.
3. Set the `Name` property to `modADO`.
4. In the General Declarations section, add the following line of code:

```
Public goConn As New ADODB.Connection
```

This line of code creates a public variable called `goConn` that you'll use throughout this application to create recordsets. Now, let's create a routine that opens a connection to a data source. You can use a few different types of connection strings to open a data source. It all depends on the data source you want to open. You can use an ODBC connection string if you're using the ODBC provider; otherwise, you use the OLE DB connection string to specify the provider you want.

Example's Filename: Ado.bas

Here's a function named `DataOpen()` that opens a connection to a data source. You can call this from the `Form_Load()` of your first form or from `Sub Main()`:

```
Public Function DataOpen(oConn As Connection) As Boolean
   On Error GoTo Open_EH

   oConn.CursorLocation = adUseClient

   ' Set the connection string by calling
   ' a function.
   oConn.ConnectionString = ConnectString()

   ' Set the mode of the connection
   oConn.Mode = adModeReadWrite

   ' Open the Connection
   oConn.Open

   DataOpen = True

   Exit Function

Open_EH:
   Call ErrorHandler(goConn)
   DataOpen = False
   Exit Function
End Function
```

After setting the `CursorLocation`, `ConnectionString`, and `Mode` properties, you need to use the `Open` method to open a connection to the data source. You should always use error handling when attempting to open a connection to a database—the database might not be available, the network might be down, or 20 million other things could be wrong that can trigger an error when you're attempting to open a connection to the database.

Creating a Connection String

Notice that the `ConnectionString` property of the `Connection` object is set by calling a function. This function, `ConnectString()`, returns a valid ADO connection string. There are many forms this connection string can take. Here, it's broken out into a function so that each form can be explained:

```
Public Function ConnectString() As String
   ' SQL Server using an ODBC Data Source
   'ConnectString = "DSN=EmployeeSQLServer;" & _
   '                 "UID=sa;PWD=;" & _
   '                 "DATABASE=Employees"


   ' SQL Server using OLE DB Provider
   'ConnectString = "Provider         = sqloledb;" & _
   '                 "Data Source      = (local);" & _
   '                 "Initial Catalog = Employees;" & _
   '                 "User Id          = sa;" & _
   '                 "Password         = ; "

   ' Jet MDB
   ConnectString = "Provider=Microsoft.Jet.OLEDB.3.51" & _
          ";Data Source=" & App.Path & "\..\Employees.mdb"
End Function
```

In this code, you can see three different versions of a connection string. The first one is used to connect to an ODBC data source. The DSN is the name of the data source you created in the ODBC Administrator. To use this version of the connection string, you need to create a DSN called `EmployeeSQLServer`. This needs to point to a SQL Server with a database on that server called Employees.

The second connection string also points to the same SQL Server, but it uses the new OLE DB provider string syntax. The provider for SQL Server is called *sqloledb*. The data source is the name of the NT server that's used for SQL Server, and the initial catalog is the name of the database within SQL Server.

The third version of the connection string is used to connect to a Jet MDB file. All you need is the provider value "Microsoft.Jet.OLEDB.3.51" and then the data source needs to list the full path and filename of the MDB file you want to connect to.

The *Recordset* Object

The `Recordset` object is what does most of the work with data. You use the `Recordset` object to retrieve sets of data and to modify that data. The syntax for retrieving and manipulating data using the `Recordset` object in ADO will be very familiar to any programmer who has used the Jet engine.

Properties of the *Recordset* Object

There are many properties that you can both read from and write to with the `Recordset` object. However, only a few are really important for you to learn. If you've already learned about the `Recordset` object when using the ADO data control, most of the properties listed in Table 24.3 will be a review for you.

Table 24.3 Properties of the *Recordset* Object

Property	Description
`AbsolutePosition`	This property is not supported by all OLE DB providers, but if it's available, it reports back the "row" number of where the current record is in the recordset.
`ActiveConnection`	This property returns the `Connection` object used to open the recordset.
`BOF`	Returns `True` if the cursor is positioned before the first record in the recordset.
`Bookmark`	Returns a value that marks or sets a position in the recordset. This is similar to the primary key of the table; it's a unique value. You can use this value to hold the location of a particular record, move to other records, and then return to the record you marked.
`EditMode`	Returns a value that indicates whether the user is adding, editing, or just browsing the data in a recordset.
`EOF`	Returns `True` if the cursor is positioned after the last record in the recordset.
`RecordCount`	This property is set to the number of records in the recordset. This property might not be available immediately after you open the recordset. All records in the recordset need to be read before this will have a true count of the records. The only reliable way to ensure this is to scroll all the way through the records until you hit the EOF.

continues

Table 24.3 Continued

Property	Description
`CursorType`	The cursor type you want to use for the recordset. This is discussed in more detail a little later in this chapter.
`LockType`	The locking mechanism you want to use if you're editing records in the recordset. This is discussed in more detail a little later in this chapter.
`MaxRecords`	The maximum number of records to return after you open a recordset. You may use this when testing what would otherwise be a very large recordset. For example, if you need to loop through a table that has one million rows, you could set this property to 200, and you'll simulate processing all the rows, even though just 200 are returned.
`Source`	In this property, you fill in a value that's used to create the `Recordset` object. This value can be a stored procedure name, a table name, or a SQL `SELECT` statement. This value can also be an ADO `Command` object. You'll learn more about the ADO `Command` object later in this chapter.
`State`	This property returns the current state of the recordset: It can be `Open`, `Closed`, `Fetching`, `Connecting`, or `Executing`. You would use this if you weren't sure whether a recordset was open. Also, if the recordset is closed, you may need to open it.

Methods of the *Recordset* Object

Like the properties of the `Recordset` object, only some of the methods are really useful, so Table 24.4 only lists those needed for learning the basics of ADO.

Table 24.4 Methods of the *Recordset* Object

Method Name	Description
`AddNew`	Adds a new record to the recordset and the cursor is positioned to that record. All new records are added to the end of the recordset.
`CancelUpdate`	Cancels a pending write operation to the recordset if you've either modified the columns in the buffer or issued an `AddNew` method. You cannot call this method if you haven't performed either of these operations. If you've already called an `Update` method, this method will generate a trappable error.

Method Name	Description
`Clone`	This method can be used to create a copy of the recordset into another `Recordset` object. You might use this if you need to move through the same records in the recordset but at different locations.
`Close`	Closes an open recordset.
`Delete`	Deletes the current record in the recordset.
`Find`	Finds a particular record in a recordset based on a search string. If the record you're searching for doesn't exist, the recordset will be placed at the end of the file.
`Move`	Moves a certain number of records from the current record. You can pass either a positive or negative number to this method to move forward or backward.
`MoveFirst`	Moves to the first record in the recordset.
`MoveLast`	Moves to the last record in the recordset.
`MoveNext`	Moves to the next record in the recordset.
`MovePrevious`	Moves to the previous record in the recordset.
`Open`	Opens a recordset based on a SQL statement, a table name, a stored procedure name, or a `Command` object.
`Requery`	Rebuilds the complete recordset by rereading the data from the table in the database using the same command originally used to open the recordset. You might do this when many users are changing data at the same time. This allows you to see other users' additions and/or changes.
`Resync`	This method also rebuilds a recordset, but it only refreshes records based on the criteria you set in the `Filter` property.
`Save`	This method saves the contents of the recordset to a disk file. You can later reopen that disk file by passing in the same filename to the `Open` method.
`Update`	This method updates the current record with the values in the controls.

Recordset Types

The `Open` method of the `Recordset` object supports different types of cursors to be opened. First, let's look at the full syntax of the `Open` method:

```
oRS.Open Source, ActiveConnection, _
        CursorType, LockType, Options
```

Here's a list of definitions of each of the bolded parameters in the syntax above.

- **`oRS`** is a `Recordset` object you've declared.
- **`Source`** can be a `Command` object, a SQL string, or the name of a file.
- **`ActiveConnection`** is either an active `Connection` object or a connection string.
- **`CursorType`** is a constant that determines the type of cursor that you want to open. The following are the valid cursor types:
  - `adOpenForwardOnly`. This is the default type of cursor opened if you don't pass in the cursor type. You use this type of cursor if all you want to do is to make one pass through the data. For example, if all you need to do is to load a list or combo box, use this type of cursor. This is a fast cursor, and it should be used as much as possible.
  - `adOpenDynamic`. A *dynamic* cursor is one in which, once it's opened, you can scroll forward or backward through the data, edit the data, add new rows, or delete any row in the table. In addition, you can see any other users' additions, edits, and deletions of the data pointed to by this cursor. Because it has so much functionality, this cursor has more overhead than any other cursor type.
  - `adOpenKeyset`. This is similar to the dynamic type of cursor, but you won't see other users' additions, just other users' edits and deletions.
  - `adOpenStatic`. This is a snapshot of the set of data at the time it is read. It can be updated, but any changes made by other users will not be visible.
- **`LockType`** is a constant that determines what type of locking (concurrency) you want to use for the recordset. It can be one of the following constants:
  - `adLockReadOnly`. This is the default lock type for a forward-only cursor. When this is set, you're only allowed to read data—no editing can occur on a recordset created with this type of locking mechanism.
  - `adLockPessimistic`. When this type of locking is set, the data source may lock records immediately when editing starts on the data. This sometimes means right when the data is read from the data source. This can cause a lot of unnecessary locking for long periods of time. Not all data sources support this type of locking. If a data source does not support this type of locking, the driver will generally choose another lock type.

  - `adLockOptimistic`. This is the most common type of locking employed by database management systems. When this type of locking is set, the data source only locks a record when an **`Update`** method is performed on an ADO recordset. Then the data is written, the lock is released. This results in a lot less time spent with locks on the data.
  - `adLockBatchOptimistic`. This is used for *batch optimistic* cursors, typically associated with remote data. This will not be covered in this book.
- **`Options`** is a constant that determines how the provider should evaluate the `Source` argument if it's something other than a `Command` object. The following are some of the definitions of these options:
  - `adCmdText`. The `Source` property is a SQL statement.
  - `adCmdTable` and `adCmdTableDirect`. The `Source` property is a table name.
  - `adCmdStoredProc`. The `Source` property is a stored procedure name.
  - `adCmdUnknown`. The `Source` property is an unknown type. In this case, the driver figures out the type and performs the appropriate action. Of course, this takes longer, so you should avoid this option.

Opening a Forward-Only Recordset

You can use several methods to create a recordset that reads data. You'll see a couple of examples of how to do this in this chapter. Let's look at some code that shows how to open different types of recordsets with different options.

Example's Filename: Recordsets.frm

```
Private Sub cmdForward_Click()
    Dim oRS As Recordset
    Dim strSQL As String

    strSQL = "SELECT "
    strSQL = strSQL & "szLast_nm, "
    strSQL = strSQL & "sFirst_nm "
    strSQL = strSQL & "FROM tblEmployees "

    Set oRS = New Recordset
```

```
    oRS.Open strSQL, goConn, _
            adOpenForwardOnly, _
            adLockReadOnly, _
            adCmdText

    lstNames.Clear
    Do Until oRS.EOF
       lstNames.AddItem oRS!szLast_nm & _
                      ", " & oRS("sFirst_nm")

       oRS.MoveNext
    Loop
    oRS.Close
End Sub
```

In the `Click` event of the ForwardOnly command button, you dim an ADO recordset. You then create a SQL `SELECT` statement so you can pass that to the `Open` method of the `Recordset` object. You then use the `New` keyword to create a new instance of the `Recordset` class. You now pass to the `Open` method the SQL string, the global `Connection` object you created in `Sub Main()`, the cursor type, the lock type, and the option that tells the `Open` method what the source is (in this case, a SQL statement).

After opening the recordset, you loop through it until you hit the end of the file. Each time through the loop, you can grab data from the recordset by specifying the name of the `Recordset` object, followed by the bang operator (`!`), followed by the field name:

```
oRS!szLast_nm
```

You can also retrieve data from a specific field by enclosing the field name in quotes and passing that to the `Recordset` object:

```
oRS("sFirst_nm")
```

Opening a Connection and Recordset Together

In the previous example, you passed the public `Connection` object you created to the `Recordset` object as the second parameter. If you want to open another connection for a particular recordset, you can just pass a connection string as the second parameter. Here's how:

```
Private Sub cmdConnect_Click()
   Dim oRS As Recordset
   Dim strSQL As String

   strSQL = "SELECT "
   strSQL = strSQL & "szLast_nm, "
   strSQL = strSQL & "sFirst_nm "
   strSQL = strSQL & "FROM tblEmployees "

   Set oRS = New Recordset
   oRS.Open strSQL, _
            ConnectString(), _
            adOpenForwardOnly, _
            adLockReadOnly, _
            adCmdText

   lstNames.Clear
   Do Until oRS.EOF
      lstNames.AddItem oRS("szLast_nm") & _
                       ", " & oRS("sFirst_nm")

      oRS.MoveNext
   Loop
   oRS.Close
End Sub
```

In this `Open` method, you pass in a string value as the second parameter instead of specifying a `Connection` object. When you do this, you tell the `Recordset` object to open a new connection when it generates this resultset.

Error Handling

Error handling in ADO is very similar to error handling in Jet and RDO. The `Connection` object contains an `Errors` collection that contains one or many `Error` objects. If a data access error occurs, these `Error` objects are generated and placed in the connection's `Errors` collection. The `Error` object contains several properties that give you a description of the error that has occurred.

The *Error* Object

When an error occurs, an `Error` object is generated and several properties are filled in. Here's a list of some of the `Error` object's properties that are filled in:

- The `Description` property is filled in with a description of the error that's returned from the provider.
- The `NativeError` property contains the error number reported from the data source itself. This number can be different for every database system.
- The `Number` property is a unique number that identifies the error. This number is ADO specific and will not change between database systems.
- The `Source` property contains the name of the service provider, the name of the table, the SQL statement, or the name of the object that generated the error.
- The `SQLState` property is a five-character string that conforms to the ANSI SQL standards and is generally reported back from the underlying ODBC driver or OLE DB provider.

Error Reporting

Here's a simple example of an error handler you can call from any function that uses ADO. You should always pass in the `Connection` object to this procedure because you can't rely on having just one connection. For example, if you open a `Recordset` object with a connection string, you need to pass in the `ActiveConnection` property to the `ErrorHandler()` procedure.

```
Call ErrorHandler(oRS.ActiveConnection)
```

However, if you're using a global `Connection` object, you need to pass that object to the `ErrorHandler()` procedure.

```
Call ErrorHandler(goConn)
```

Example's Filenames: Error.frm and ADO.bas

```
Public Sub ErrorHandler(oConn As Connection)
   Dim oErr As Error
   Dim strMsg As String

   For Each oErr In oConn.Errors
      strMsg = strMsg & _
```

```
                "Error #: " & _
                oErr.Number & vbCrLf
        strMsg = strMsg & _
                "Description: " & _
                oErr.Description & vbCrLf
        strMsg = strMsg & _
                "Source: " & _
                oErr.Source & vbCrLf
        strMsg = strMsg & _
                "SQL State: " & _
                oErr.SQLState & vbCrLf
        strMsg = strMsg & _
                "Native Error: " & _
                oErr.NativeError & vbCrLf
        strMsg = strMsg & vbCrLf
    Next

    MsgBox strMsg
End Sub
```

The Error.frm file has an example of using the error handler. In the example are misspelled columns that, when submitted to the `Open` method of the `Recordset` object, generate an error. The current version of the Jet OLE DB provider does not give you very descriptive error messages right now. By the time you read this, however, this may have changed. To see a good example of some error messages, use either the SQL Server or Oracle provider:

```
Private Sub cmdTestErr_Click()
    Dim oRS As Recordset
    Dim strSQL As String

    On Error GoTo Error_EH

    ' MISPELLED Column Names
    strSQL = "SELECT "
    strSQL = strSQL & "sLast_nm, "
    strSQL = strSQL & "szFirst_nm "
    strSQL = strSQL & "FROM tblEmployees "
```

```
      Set oRS = New Recordset
      oRS.Open strSQL, ConnectString(), _
               adOpenForwardOnly, adLockReadOnly
      oRS.Close

      Exit Sub

   Error_EH:
      Call ErrorHandler(oRS.ActiveConnection)

      Exit Sub
   End Sub
```

Figure 24.1 shows some sample output from this error-handling routine when you use the SQL Server OLE DB provider. Notice the description and the source properties.

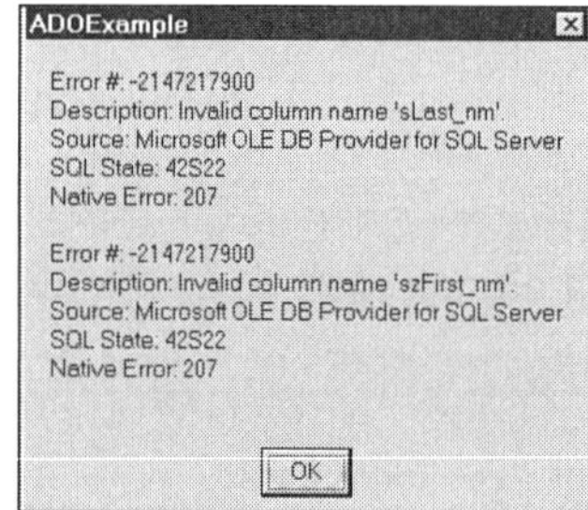

FIGURE 24.1
Example of an error.

Command Objects

A `Command` object is a holder for a specific query that you want to execute against a data source. You can predefine the SQL and any parameters for that SQL, and then replace the parameters at runtime to execute the same SQL statement over and over again without having to redo the SQL statement each time.

Reasons to Use a *Command* Object

Here's a list of reasons why you would want to use a `Command` object:

- You can pass in parameters and receive output parameters from a stored procedure.
- You can reexecute the query with just an `Execute` command.

- You execute the same query on different connections.
- You can create prepared statements that are optimized and saved on the database server while the connection is active. This can help speed up execution of SQL statements that are frequently repeated in an application.
- You can use it to execute an action query such as `INSERT`, `UPDATE`, or `DELETE`.

Example's Filename: Command.frm

```
Private Sub cmdCommand1_Click()
    Dim oCmd As Command
    Dim oRS As Recordset
    Dim strSQL As String

    strSQL = "SELECT "
    strSQL = strSQL & "szLast_nm, "
    strSQL = strSQL & "sFirst_nm "
    strSQL = strSQL & "FROM tblEmployees "

    Set oRS = New Recordset
    With oRS
        .CursorType = adOpenForwardOnly
        .LockType = adLockReadOnly
    End With

    Set oCmd = New Command
    With oCmd
        .CommandText = strSQL
        .CommandType = adCmdText
        .ActiveConnection = ConnectString()
        Set oRS = .Execute
    End With

    lstNames.Clear
    Do Until oRS.EOF
        lstNames.AddItem oRS("szLast_nm") & _
                          ", " & oRS("sFirst_nm")
        oRS.MoveNext
    Loop
```

```
    oRS.Close

    ' Now Use the Command object again
    With oRS
       .CursorType = adOpenKeyset
       .LockType = adLockPessimistic
    End With
    With oCmd
       Set .ActiveConnection = goConn
       Set oRS = .Execute
    End With

    lstNames.Clear
    Do Until oRS.EOF
       lstNames.AddItem oRS("szLast_nm") & _
                        ", " & oRS("sFirst_nm")
       oRS.MoveNext
    Loop
    oRS.Close

    Set oCmd = Nothing
    Set oRS = Nothing
End Sub
```

In this code, you create a `Recordset` object and a `Command` object. First, you set up the cursor types and lock types for the `Recordset` object. Next, you create the `Command` object and fill in the `CommandText` property with the SQL statement. You should set the `CommandType` to tell it that this is a SQL statement in the `CommandText` property. This helps with optimization—the `Command` object does not have to figure out what's in the `CommandText` property. You next set the `ActiveConnection` property to either a connect string or a `Connection` object. Once you've set all these parameters, you just need to perform the `Execute` method on the `Command` object to have it return a recordset.

Summary

ActiveX Data Objects (ADO) is a very easy object model to learn because it doesn't have that many objects. With just a `Recordset` object, a SQL string, and a connection string, you can start accessing data. You can create a global `Connection` object to help with performance, and a `Command` object enables you to reuse the same statement over and over again very easily.

ADO is the future of data access for Microsoft. As such, you should start using this technology for your new applications. You'll see Jet and RDO phased out as ADO gains more features and is used more and more in the Visual Basic and VBA world.

Review Questions

1. Do you need a `Connection` object to establish a connection?
2. Name two different types of cursors ADO supports.
3. What are the properties of the ADO `Error` object?
4. Why would you use a `Command` object?

Exercise

1. Create a program that loads the employee types from the tblEmpTypes table into a list box.

Data Entry with ADO Objects

IN THIS CHAPTER, YOU'LL CREATE A DATA entry form using the ActiveX Data Objects (ADO). You'll find that you need to write a little more code than when you use a data control, but the speed and flexibility you get are well worth it.

Chapter Objectives

- Create a data entry form without a data control
- Learn to add, edit, and delete records

Sample Project File: \Chapter25\DataEntry.vbp

Creating a New ADO Project

In this chapter, you'll learn to create the Employee Information form using just ADO objects instead of the data control. To do this, let's create a new project and then copy the form you already created using the data control into this new project.

Exercise

Creating a Data Entry Form

1. Create a new project in Visual Basic.
2. Set the appropriate properties for this new project.
3. Save this project to a new directory.
4. Copy the old Employee Information form with the data control on it to the new directory.
5. Add this form to the project. Note that you may receive some errors when you load the form. This is normal because you haven't added the data controls to this new project.
6. Open up the code window for the form.
7. Delete all the old code in the code window.
8. Bring up the form in design mode.
9. Delete all the old data controls.
10. Click once on the data list control to give it focus.
11. Press the Delete key to delete this control.
12. Click once on the data combo control to give it focus.
13. Press the Delete key to delete this control.
14. Click once on the data grid control to give it focus.
15. Press the Delete key to delete this control.
16. Select Project, References from the Visual Basic menu.

17. Check the Microsoft ActiveX Data Objects 2.0 Library option.
18. Click the OK button.

You have now started the process of getting rid of all the data aware controls, so you can add regular controls and program those using ADO.

Sub Main()

Create a `Sub Main()` procedure to open a global `Connection` object prior to opening the data entry form. This increases the performance of the application when creating recordsets, because it doesn't need to open a connection every time. Of course you are now using up more resources in the database server if you are using one. If you are just using an Access database, then there is no great amount of overhead.

```
Public Sub Main()
   Dim boolPerform As Boolean

   Screen.MousePointer = vbHourglass

   ' Open the Database Engine
   boolPerform = DataOpen(goConn)

   If boolPerform Then
      frmEmployee.Show
   End If

   Screen.MousePointer = vbDefault
End Sub
```

Now that you have a `Connection` object established, you can create as many `Recordset` objects from that connection as you want.

TIP

Create a public `Connection` object to speed up the creation of `Recordset` objects.

Building the Data Entry Form

You're now ready to build a form that looks like the form you just destroyed, but this one will contain normal controls instead of the data controls. Figure 25.1 shows an example of the form you'll create.

Example's Filename: frmEmployee.frm

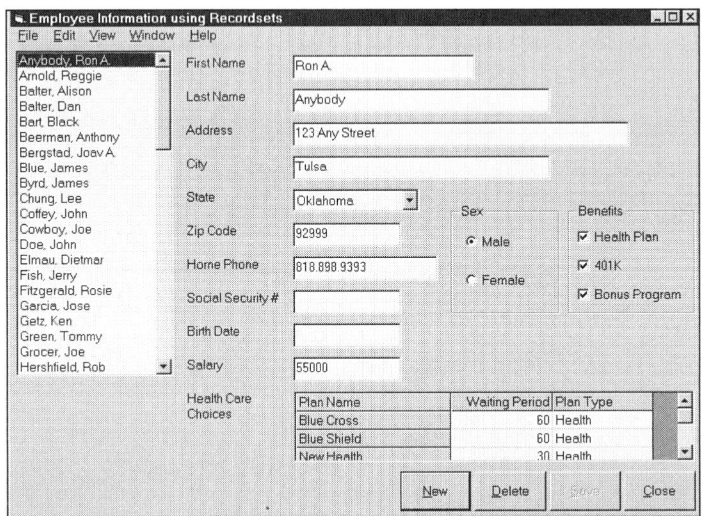

FIGURE 25.1 The ADO objects data entry form.

EXERCISE

Adding Normal Controls to the Form

1. Add a normal list box control to the location where the data list control was located.
2. Set the `Name` property to `lstNames`.
3. Set the `Sorted` property to `True`.
4. Add a combo box control to the location where the data combo control was located.
5. Set the `Name` property to `cboStates`.
6. Set the `Style` property to `2-DropDown List`.
7. Set the `Sorted` property to `True`.
8. Add a flex grid control to where the data grid control was located.
9. Set the `Name` property to `grdHealthCare`.

You now have the Employee Information form back to looking the way you want—now let's learn how to program it.

Now that you have added normal controls where you once had data aware controls, you will now be ready to program these.

Setting Up the Form

Now that you have the screen redesigned, let's add code to get the form to work with ADO objects.

EXERCISE

Adding a Recordset Object

1. Add a module-level `Recordset` object to this form.
2. Add code to the `Form_Load()` event, as shown here:

```
Dim moRS As Recordset

Private Sub Form_Load()
   Set moRS = New Recordset

   Call StateLoad

   Call HealthCareLoad

   Call ListLoad
End Sub
```

In the `Form_Load()` event, you create a new instance of the module-level recordset, call a procedure to load state codes into the State combo box, call a procedure to load the health care plans into the Health Care Choices grid, and load the Employee list box. Each of these routines load the appropriate controls with the appropriate data. The code you'll write to load combo boxes, grids, and list boxes are all very similar.

EXERCISE

Add Some Stubs for Routines You Need to Write

1. Go ahead and add each of the procedure names shown in the `Form_Load()` event to the form:

```
Private Sub StateLoad()

End Sub
Private Sub HealthCareLoad()

End Sub
Private Sub ListLoad()

End Sub
```

These stubs of routines will be programmed to load each of the normal controls.

Now that you've added the stubs to this form, you'll learn how to load up the main list box with employee names.

Loading the List Box

The `ListLoad()` procedure is a general form procedure that loads all the employee names from the tblEmployees table into the list box. The source code is shown here:

```
Private Sub ListLoad()
   Dim oRS As Recordset
   Dim strSQL As String

   strSQL = "SELECT lEmp_id, "
   strSQL = strSQL & "szLast_nm, "
   strSQL = strSQL & "sFirst_nm "
   strSQL = strSQL & "FROM tblEmployees "

   Set oRS = New Recordset
   oRS.Open strSQL, goConn, _
            adOpenForwardOnly, _
            adLockReadOnly
```

```
        lstNames.Clear
        Do Until oRS.EOF
           With lstNames
              .AddItem Trim$(oRS("szLast_nm")) & ", " & _
                       Trim$(oRS("sFirst_nm"))
              .ItemData(.NewIndex) = oRS("lEmp_id")
           End With

           oRS.MoveNext
        Loop
        oRS.Close

        If lstNames.ListCount Then
           lstNames.ListIndex = 0
        End If
     End Sub
```

As you can see, this code is almost exactly the same as the code you just learned about in the last section. Notice that you're loading the last name and first name into the `List()` property with the `AddItem` method, and you're loading the employee ID into the `ItemData()` property at the same location. The only difference in this routine is that at the end of the procedure, you force the list box to highlight the first employee in the list by setting the `ListIndex` property to `0`. When this property is set, it's just like clicking the list box—the `Click` event will fire for this list box.

Displaying an Employee

Once a `Click` event occurs on the Employee list box, you need to display the data for the selected employee in the controls to the right of the list box. You want to display the employee's first name, last name, street address, and so on. Let's write the code for the `lstNames_Click()` event:

```
Private Sub lstNames_Click()
   If lstNames.ListIndex <> -1 Then
      If FormFind() Then
         Call FormShow
      End If
   End If
End Sub
```

When the `Click` event is received by the list box, you should always ensure that a valid element is highlighted by checking whether the `ListIndex` property is set to something other than `-1`. If you remember, a `-1` value in the `ListIndex` property signifies that nothing is highlighted in the list box. If the user has selected a valid value in the list box, the `FormFind()` function is called. If this routine returns a `True` value, the employee highlighted was found in the database, and now the `FormShow` procedure can be called to load the data for that employee into the appropriate controls. You'll now learn how to build the `FormFind()` and `FormShow()` routines.

The *FormFind()* Function

The `FormFind()` function takes the value from the `ItemData()` property and uses it to build a `SELECT` statement that locates the particular employee that matches the value. You need to build a full `SELECT` statement with all the columns you want to use on the form. You also need to add a `WHERE` clause with the value in the `ItemData()` property:

```
Private Function FormFind() As Boolean
   Dim strSQL As String

   strSQL = "SELECT lEmp_id, "
   strSQL = strSQL & "sFirst_nm , "
   strSQL = strSQL & "szLast_nm, "
   strSQL = strSQL & "szCity_nm, "
   strSQL = strSQL & "szStreet1_ad, "
   strSQL = strSQL & "sState_cd, "
   strSQL = strSQL & "lState_id, "
   strSQL = strSQL & "sZip_cd, "
   strSQL = strSQL & "sPhone_no, "
   strSQL = strSQL & "szEMail_ad, "
   strSQL = strSQL & "sSex_type , "
   strSQL = strSQL & "lEmpType_id, "
   strSQL = strSQL & "sSSN_tx, "
   strSQL = strSQL & "dtBirth_dt, "
   strSQL = strSQL & "cSalary_amt, "
   strSQL = strSQL & "dtStart_dt, "
   strSQL = strSQL & "dtEnd_dt, "
   strSQL = strSQL & "boolActive_fl, "
   strSQL = strSQL & "boolHealth_fl, "
```

```
    strSQL = strSQL & "bool401k_fl, "
    strSQL = strSQL & "boolBonus_fl, "
    strSQL = strSQL & "iConcurrency_id, "
    strSQL = strSQL & "dtLastUpdate_dt, "
    strSQL = strSQL & "sLastUpdate_id "
    strSQL = strSQL & "FROM tblEmployees "
    strSQL = strSQL & "WHERE lEmp_id = " & _
                        lstNames.ItemData(lstNames.ListIndex)

    If moRS.State = adStateOpen Then
       moRS.Close
    End If

    moRS.Open strSQL, goConn, _
              adOpenKeyset, adLockPessimistic, adCmdText

    If moRS.EOF Then
       FormFind = False
    Else
       FormFind = True
    End If
End Function
```

The `FormFind()` function uses the module-level recordset you created in the `Form_Load()` event. It builds the `SELECT` statement with the `WHERE` clause, as shown in the following code:

```
strSQL = strSQL & "WHERE lEmp_id = " & _
                    lstNames.ItemData(lstNames.ListIndex)
```

The value in the `ItemData()` property is retrieved and concatenated onto the SQL statement to find the particular employee selected. Then the `WHERE` clause loads a one-row recordset that's used to display the employee data in the appropriate controls on the right side of the form. This one-row recordset is opened as a keyset type to allow for the editing of this employee data. Once the module-level recordset has been opened with this one employee record, it's now time to call the `FormShow` procedure to display the employee data.

The *FormShow* Procedure

The FormShow procedure is very simple. It just takes the data directly from the module-level recordset and moves it into the text boxes:

```
Private Sub FormShow()
   mboolShow = True

   With moRS
      txtFirst = Field2Str(!sFirst_nm)
      txtLast = Field2Str(!szLast_nm)
      txtAddress = Field2Str(!szStreet1_ad)
      txtCity = Field2Str(!szCity_nm)
      Call ListFindItem(cboStates, Field2Long(!lState_id))
      txtZip = Field2Str(!sZip_cd)
      txtPhone = Field2Str(!sPhone_no)
      txtSSN = Field2Str(!sSSN_tx)
      txtBirthDate = Field2Str(!dtBirth_dt)
      txtSalary = Field2Str(!cSalary_amt)
      If !sSex_Type = "M" Then
         optMale.Value = True
      Else
         optFemale.Value = True
      End If
      chkHealth.Value = Field2CheckBox(!boolHealth_fl)
      chk401k.Value = Field2CheckBox(!bool401k_fl)
      chkBonus.Value = Field2CheckBox(!boolBonus_fl)
   End With

   mboolShow = False
End Sub
```

In the FormShow procedure is another module-level variable called mboolShow that you set to a True value. This variable is used to stop the Change events in the text boxes from firing when you load the data from the recordset into the text boxes.

A couple other routines are used to convert possible Null values into blank strings so that they can be loaded into the text boxes. Whenever you retrieve data from a field in a database, you need to check to see whether it is Null. If it is, you have to convert it into a valid value prior to loading it into a control. Now, let's look at the Field2Str() function.

The *Field2Str()* Function

The `Field2Str()` function accepts a variant value (which is what's returned from an ADO recordset). `Variant` is the only data type that accepts a `Null` value, so it must be used as the argument in this function. You'll use the `IsNull()` function to test to see whether the value is `Null`. If it is, a valid blank string (`""`) is returned back to the calling procedure. If the value is not `Null`, the value is then trimmed and returned back to the calling procedure. Here's the code:

```
Public Function Field2Str(vntField As Variant) As String
    If IsNull(vntField) Then
        Field2Str = ""
    Else
        Field2Str = Trim$(CStr(vntField))
    End If
End Function
```

The reason for using the `Trim()` function is that not all providers will trim the data coming back from the database. For example, if the field is defined as 50 characters in the table, but the data in the field is only 20 characters, some providers return 20 characters and others return 50 characters, using 30 padded spaces after the 20 characters.

The *ListFindItem()* Procedure

The `ListFindItem()` procedure is used to search for a value in the `ItemData()` property in a combo or list box. When the state codes are loaded into the State combo box, the descriptions of the states are placed in the `List()` property and the state IDs are placed in the `ItemData()` property. Therefore, when you retrieve the state ID from the employee table, you need to find that state ID in the State combo box by looping through and comparing what's in the `ItemData()` property with the value you pass to the `ListFindItem()` procedure. Here's the code:

```
Public Sub ListFindItem(ctlAny As Control, lngValue As Long)
    Dim intLoop As Integer
    Dim boolFound As Boolean

    For intLoop = 0 To ctlAny.ListCount - 1
        If ctlAny.ItemData(intLoop) = lngValue Then
            ctlAny.ListIndex = intLoop
            boolFound = True
            intLoop = ctlAny.ListCount
```

```
      End If
   Next

   If Not boolFound Then
      ctlAny.ListIndex = -1
   End If
End Sub
```

The two arguments you pass to this procedure are the combo box or list box and the long integer you want to find in the `ItemData()` property. If you find the data when you're looping through the loop, you need to set the `ListIndex` property to the location in the combo or list box.

The *Field2CheckBox()* Function

As with the `Field2Str()` function, you need to check a field value with the `Field2CheckBox()` function to see whether it's `Null`; if it is, you need to change the value to something appropriate for check box `Value` property:

```
Public Function Field2CheckBox(vntField As Variant) As Integer
   If IsNull(vntField) Then
      Field2CheckBox = vbUnchecked
   Else
      Field2CheckBox = IIf(vntField, vbChecked, vbUnchecked)
   End If
End Function
```

This function returns either the `vbUnchecked` constant or the `vbChecked` constant. Notice the use of the `IIF()` function. This function returns the second parameter if the first parameter evaluates to a `True` condition or the third parameter if the first parameter evaluates to a `False` condition. A nice advantage to this routine is that you can use any numeric data type to store the `Value` property of a check box—it doesn't need to be a Yes/No type of field (which not all databases support).

Adding Data

To add a new employee to the database, the user needs to click the New command button. In this button you'll write code to clear all the controls so that the user has blank space in which to add a new employee:

```
Private Sub cmdNew_Click()
   mboolAdding = True
```

```
    Call FormClear
    txtFirst.SetFocus
End Sub
```

In this routine, you set a module-level variable, `mboolAdding`, to a `True` value. This is used when the data is saved so that you know to invoke an `AddNew` method on the `Recordset` object. Next, you'll call a routine called `FormClear`.

The *FormClear* Procedure

This routine simply clears all the text boxes to a blank value, all the check boxes to an unchecked value, and all the combo boxes to an unselected value. Here's the code:

```
Private Sub FormClear()
    txtFirst = ""
    txtLast = ""
    txtAddress = ""
    txtCity = ""
    cboStates.ListIndex = -1
    txtZip = ""
    txtPhone = ""
    txtSSN = ""
    txtBirthDate = ""
    txtSalary = ""
    optMale.Value = True
    chkHealth.Value = vbUnchecked
    chk401k.Value = vbUnchecked
    chkBonus.Value = vbUnchecked
End Sub
```

Saving the Data with the *FormSave* Procedure

After the user has entered the new data into the controls, he or she will then need to click the Save command button to save the new data. In this button, you call a routine named `FormSave` to store the data back into the recordset and then update the database. Here's the code:

```
Private Sub FormSave()
    Dim strName As String
```

```
    On Error GoTo Error_EH

    If mboolAdding Then
       moRS.AddNew
    End If

    ' Store the controls to the recordset
    Call FieldsSave

    moRS.Update

    If mboolAdding Then
       mboolAdding = False
       strName = Trim$(txtLast) & ", " & Trim$(txtFirst)
       ' Reload list box
       Call ListLoad

       lstNames.Text = strName
    Else
       ' Update List Box
       With lstNames
          .List(.ListIndex) = txtLast & ", " & _
                                txtFirst
       End With
    End If

    Call ToggleButtons

    Exit Sub

Error_EH:
    Call ErrorHandler(moRS.ActiveConnection)
    Exit Sub
End Sub
```

The `FormSave` procedure accomplishes a lot of tasks. First, it checks the module level variable `mboolAdding` to see whether the `AddNew` method needs to be called. The `AddNew` method informs ADO that it needs to create a new record in the table. Next, a procedure called `FieldsSave()` is called to move the data from the controls into the module-level recordset. After the data has been stored in the recordset, the `Update` method is invoked to save the data back to the database.

Next, the `mboolAdding` variable is checked to see whether the new employee needs to be added to the list box. Because ADO currently has a problem retrieving the value generated by the `AutoNumber` or `IDENTITY` type fields, it's best to just reload the list box. However, you should position the list box to the new employee you just added. To do this, you need to save the last name and first name from the text boxes into a string variable and then use it to set the `Text` property of the list box immediately after the list box is reloaded. This positions the list box to the new employee record just added.

Let's take a look at the `FieldsSave` procedure. Here, you'll see functions that are the opposite of the functions that converted the data on the way out of the recordset. For example, the `Str2Field()` function is the opposite of the `Field2Str()` function. In the `Str2Field()` function, the text box is checked to see whether the value is blank. If it is, the value that's returned from the `Str2Field()` function is a `Null` value. Here's the code:

```
Private Sub FieldsSave()
   With moRS
      !sFirst_nm = Str2Field(txtFirst)
      !szLast_nm = Str2Field(txtLast)
      !szStreet1_ad = Str2Field(txtAddress)
      !szCity_nm = Str2Field(txtCity)
      !lState_id = cboStates.ItemData(cboStates.ListIndex)
      !sZip_cd = Str2Field(txtZip)
      !sPhone_no = Str2Field(txtPhone)
      !sSSN_tx = Str2Field(txtSSN)
      !dtBirth_dt = Date2Field(txtBirthDate)
      !cSalary_amt = Str2Field(txtSalary)
      If optMale.Value Then
         !sSex_Type = "M"
      Else
         !sSex_Type = "F"
      End If
      !boolHealth_fl = (chkHealth.Value = vbChecked)
      !bool401k_fl = (chk401k.Value = vbChecked)
      !boolBonus_fl = (chkBonus.Value = vbChecked)
   End With
End Sub
```

Editing Data

To edit the data on the form, the user simply needs to type in any of the text boxes, change the value in the combo box, or change a value in an option button or check box. Of course, you need to have code under each of these controls to detect when their values change. You need code in the `Change()` events of the text boxes and in the `Click` events of the combo boxes, option buttons, and check boxes. Here's the code you should place in each of these controls:

```
Private Sub txtLast_Change()
   Call TextChanged
End Sub
```

The procedure `TextChanged` is responsible for toggling command buttons and setting up for the editing of data. Of course, if the buttons have already been toggled, this needs to be detected also.

Detecting That Data Has Changed

The `TextChanged` procedure is actually very simple to code:

```
Private Sub TextChanged()
   If Not mboolShow Then
      If Not cmdSave.Enabled Then
         Call ToggleButtons
      End If
   End If
End Sub
```

In this routine, you first check the `mboolShow` variable to see whether it's a `True` value. If it is a `True` value, you know that the values are changing because the `FormShow` procedure is updating the text boxes to a new employee record. In this case, you don't want to toggle any buttons. If the variable is a `False` value, you need to check the cmdSave command button's `Enabled` property to see whether it's `False`. If it is `False`, you know that you haven't already toggled the buttons and that you should toggle them so that the New and Delete command buttons are disabled and the Save command button is enabled. In addition, you should toggle the `Caption` property of the Close command button to `"&Cancel"` so that the user has the option of canceling the changes he or she just made. Let's take a look at the `ToggleButtons` procedure:

```
Private Sub ToggleButtons()
   If cmdClose.Caption = "&Close" Then
```

```
        cmdClose.Caption = "&Cancel"
    Else
        cmdClose.Caption = "&Close"
    End If
    cmdSave.Enabled = Not cmdSave.Enabled
    cmdNew.Enabled = Not cmdNew.Enabled
    cmdDelete.Enabled = Not cmdDelete.Enabled
    lstNames.Enabled = Not lstNames.Enabled
End Sub
```

You should also disable the list box so that the user can't click another employee while in the middle of editing or adding an employee record.

Deleting Data

To delete an employee record, the user needs to click the Delete command button. The `Click` event of the command button displays a message box asking the user to verify whether he or she really wants to delete this employee's data. Here's the code:

```
Private Sub cmdDelete_Click()
    Dim intResponse As Integer
    Dim intIndex As Integer

    Beep
    intResponse = MsgBox("Delete the current Employee", _
                         vbYesNo + vbQuestion, _
                         "Delete Employee")
    If intResponse = vbYes Then
        intIndex = lstNames.ListIndex
        moRS.Delete
        lstNames.RemoveItem intIndex
        intResponse = ListReposition(lstNames, intIndex)
        If intResponse = -1 Then
            Call Form_Activate
        Else
            lstNames.ListIndex = intResponse
        End If
    End If
End Sub
```

If the user clicks Yes in the message box, you need to delete the record from the database using the `Delete` method on the `Recordset` object. Of course, you need to delete the value from the list box also. To do this, store the `ListIndex` property as an integer value. After the `Delete` method is invoked, remove the employee data from the list box by invoking the `RemoveItem` method and passing in the integer variable.

Now, you have another problem. The data is still displayed in the controls for the employee just deleted, but there's no value highlighted in the list box. You need to highlight a value in the list box, but which value do you highlight? You could just move to the beginning of the list, or you could move forward to the next value in the list or backward to the previous value in the list. The problem is that if the user is deleting a value in the middle of the list, moving to the first value might position the user somewhere he or she doesn't want to be. Also, if the user deletes the last item in the list, he or she can't move forward, and if the user deletes the first item in the list, he or she can't move backward. This is why you need to call a function that determines where in the list to move.

The `ListReposition` function takes care of figuring out where you should position the list box after a deletion. You simply pass in the list box reference and the current position just deleted, and this function returns a value you can use to set the `ListIndex` property to a new value. However, if the user deletes the last value in the list box, this function will return `-1`, in which case you'll call `Form_Activate`. This will be explained in a later section, but let's first take a look at the `ListReposition` function:

```
Public Function ListReposition(lstCtrl As Control, _
                               intIndex As Integer) As Integer
   If lstCtrl.ListCount = 0 Then
      ListReposition = -1
   Else
      intIndex = intIndex + 1

      If intIndex >= lstCtrl.ListCount - 1 Then
         ListReposition = lstCtrl.ListCount - 1
      Else
         intIndex = intIndex - 1
         If intIndex <= 0 Then
            ListReposition = 0
         Else
            ListReposition = intIndex
```

```
            End If
         End If
      End If
   End Function
```

The `ListReposition` function first checks to see whether the list box is empty. If it is, a `-1` value is returned from this function. Next, it checks the value passed in to see where it is in relation to the end of the list. It first adds 1 to the current position and then compares that value with the end of the list. If it hits the end of the list, it returns the last index in the list. If it does not hit the end of the list, it moves backward by one and returns that value. However, if this number goes before the first number in the list, a `0` value is returned, which is the first element in the list. Anyway you go, you'll end up with the value just prior to the one deleted as the value that will be highlighted in the list box.

Handling an Empty Recordset

Now let's turn our attention to what happens if there are no records in the employee table or if the user has just deleted the last row in the table. In either case, the `Form_Activate()` event will be called. If the user has just come into the form and the `ListLoad()` procedure does not load any data, the next event to be called after the `Form_Load()` event is the `Form_Activate()` event. Similarly, if the user deletes the last row and the `ListReposition()` function returns `-1`, the `cmdDelete_Click` event also calls the `Form_Activate()` event. Here's the code:

```
Private Sub Form_Activate()
   Dim intResponse As Integer

   If lstNames.ListCount = 0 Then
      intResponse = MsgBox( _
                     "No Employees, " & _
                     "do you wish to add some?", _
                     vbYesNo + vbQuestion, _
                     "Add Records")
      If intResponse = vbYes Then
         Call cmdNew_Click
      Else
         Unload Me
      End If
   End If
End Sub
```

In the `Form_Activate()` event, all you have to do is check the `ListCount` property of the list box. If the count is equal to `0`, you know that there are no employees in the table. In this case, you display a message box asking the user whether he or she wants to add some employees. If the user clicks Yes, you can invoke the `cmdNew_Click()` event to put the user into Add mode. If the user clicks No, you can unload the form.

Summary

Creating a data entry form using ADO instead of the data control takes a little more code, but it's a little easier to follow the flow as opposed to all the different events you have to write code for when using the data control. Also, you have total control over how everything works instead of being locked into the data control paradigm.

Review Questions

1. What do you use the `ItemData` property for?
2. How do you delete a row using ADO?

Exercises

1. Create a program that loads the employee types from the tblEmpTypes table into a list box.
2. Add the capability to click an employee type and display the appropriate fields on the right side of the list box.
3. Add the capability to add/edit/delete employee types.

Wizards

THIS CHAPTER PRESENTS THE DATA FORM WIZARD and the Application Wizard. You'll learn how to create data entry forms that interact with a database table using the Data Form Wizard. You'll also see how to create a complete application template using the Application Wizard.

Chapter Objectives

- Learn to use the Data Form Wizard
- Learn to use the Application Wizard

Sample Project File: \Chapter26\Wizards.vbp

Data Form Wizard

The Data Form Wizard allows you to specify the name of a table in either an Access MDB database or in a remote database connected through an ODBC data source and generate a data entry form from that table's information. You have the ability to generate forms that use the following formats:

- Single-record data control style
- Data-bound grid format
- Master and detail records
- Microsoft Hierarchical FlexGrid
- Graph format

This tool is available in both the Professional and Enterprise Editions of Visual Basic. To use it, you need to select it from the Add-Ins, Add-In Manager menu item.

The Data Form Wizard asks you a series of questions about the table you want to get information from, which fields from that table you want to use, the type of data entry form you want to create, and whether you want data modification buttons as well as data navigation buttons on the form. Let's look at each of the forms the Data Form Wizard presents to you when you start this process.

The Introduction form, shown in Figure 26.1, prompts you for any previously created profiles. A *profile* is created after you've run the Data Form Wizard one time and have chosen a series of options. You can save all these options into a profile. This is a great idea if you're going to create a lot of screens that are similar in look and feel.

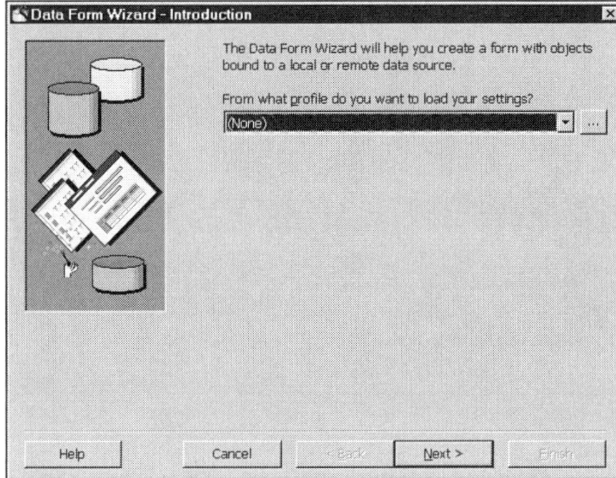

FIGURE 26.1
The Data Form Wizard's Introduction form.

In the Database Type form, shown in Figure 26.2, you need to select which type of database system you want to use for creating the data access form. If you're using an Access database, select the Access option. If you're using an ODBC data source such as SQL Server or Oracle, you should select the Remote(ODBC) option.

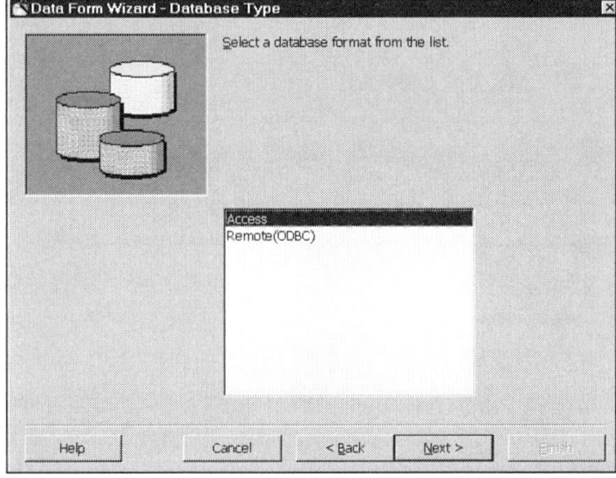

FIGURE 26.2
The Data Form Wizard's Database Type form.

The Connect Information form, shown in Figure 26.3, is displayed if you choose the Remote(ODBC) option on the Database Type form. In this form, you need to have a DSN, a user ID, a password, and a database name. You need to have created a DSN prior to running this wizard in order for that DSN to be displayed in the drop-down combo box.

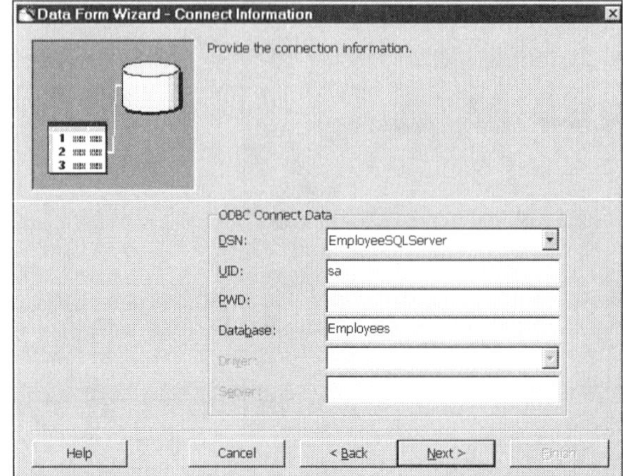

FIGURE 26.3 The Data Form Wizard's Connect Information form.

If you chose the Access option from the Database Type form, you'll see the Database form shown in Figure 26.4. In this form, you need to fill in the full path and filename of the Access database from which you want to select a table or query to build your data access form. You have the option of displaying tables and/or queries on one of the next screens. Just select the appropriate record source from the check boxes on the bottom of this form.

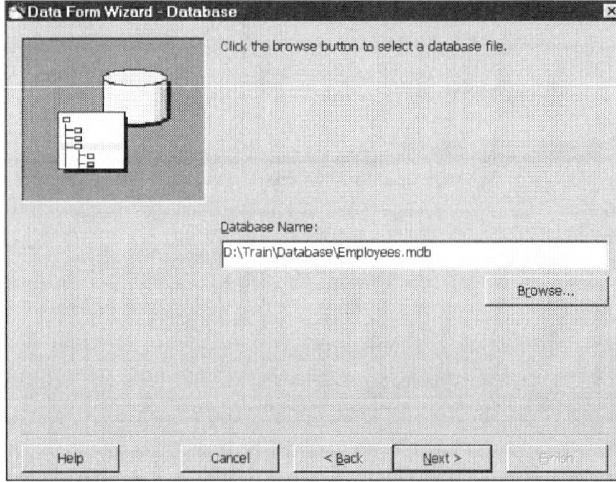

FIGURE 26.4 The Data Form Wizard's Database form.

The next form in the wizard, shown in Figure 26.5, asks you to determine the type of form you want to create. You first fill in the name of the form you'll be creating. Next, you select the type of form to create. Table 26.1 explains the different types of form layouts you can choose.

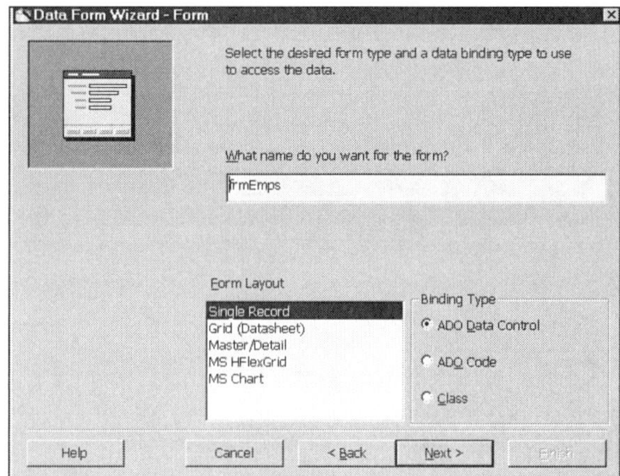

FIGURE 26.5
The Data Form Wizard's Form form.

Table 26.1 Form Layout Options

Form Layout	Description
Single Record	This type of form is just like a normal data control setup. You have labels and text boxes with a data control on a form.
Grid (Datasheet)	This form adds a DataGrid control to a form and connects it to a data control to display and edit the data.
Master/Detail	Use this type of form when two tables have a parent/child relationship. It creates labels and text boxes on the top of the form for the parent data and creates a DataGrid control on the bottom to show the related child information.
MS HFlexGrid	When you choose this option, you're prompted with a couple of different form templates that allow you to choose the style of the grid you want to display. You can have the data displayed normally, or you can have it grouped together based on repeating groups. You can even modify which columns are displayed before other columns using drag-and-drop techniques right within the wizard.
MS Chart	This form type allows you to create a chart of the data in one of your tables. You're presented with several additional forms from which you choose the data fields for the X and Y axes, the titles and legends for the chart, and the type of chart you want to use.

In this step you can also choose the type of binding you want to do with the data. You can choose to create an ADO Data Control, use ADO code, or create a class.

Regardless of which type of form you choose to create, you'll be prompted for the record source for the form (see Figure 26.6). You need to choose a particular table, query or view to use as the data source for your form. Once you've chosen the table, you then need to add the fields you want on the form by moving them from the left list box to the list box on the right. You also have the option to sort the data by a particular column.

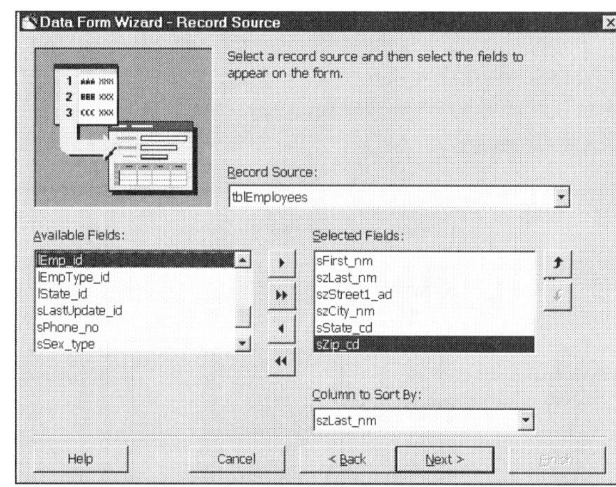

FIGURE 26.6 Data Form Wizard's Record Source form.

At this point, you may be prompted for additional information if you've chosen the MS HFlexGrid form layout or the MS Chart form layout (see Figure 26.7).

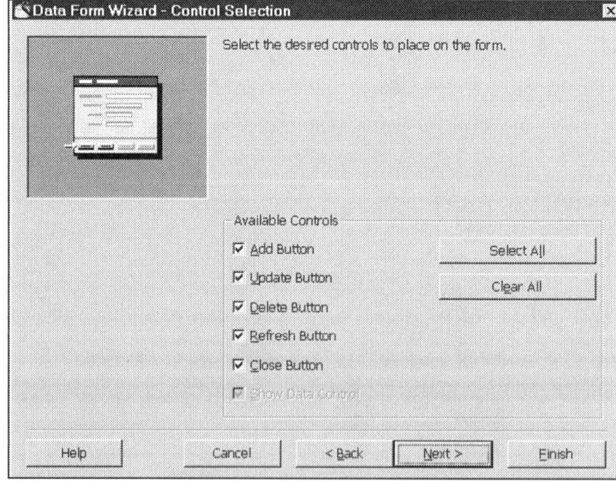

FIGURE 26.7 Data Form Wizard's Control Selection form.

The Control Selection form, shown in Figure 26.7, allows you to choose buttons to add to the form. You have options for adding Add, Update, Delete, Refresh, and Close buttons. If you don't want the user to be able to add and edit the data, uncheck the Add and Update button options.

On the final screen, shown in Figure 26.8, you can press the Finish button to have the wizard create the data access form based on the information you've provided. You also have the option to save the settings you created on this pass through the wizard to a profile name. If you click the button with the ellipsis (...), you'll be given a File Save As dialog box to save the options you chose in this session to a file on disk.

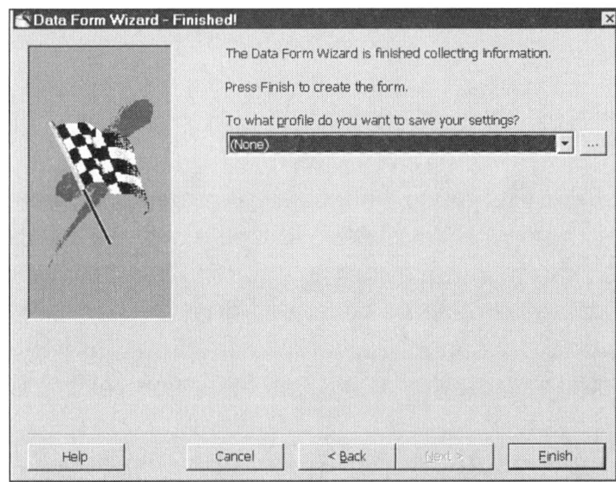

FIGURE 26.8 Data Form Wizard's Finished form.

Examples

In the sample directory for this chapter, I've created several examples using the Data Form Wizard. Table 26.2 outlines each of these examples.

Table 26.2 Examples for the Data Form Wizard

Form Name	Description
frmDFEmpsADOCode	Uses the single-record layout with the ADO Code binding type.
frmDFEmpsChart	Uses the MS Chart option.
frmDFEmpsClass	Uses the single-record layout with the Class binding type.

continues

Table 26.2 Continued

Form Name	Description
frmDFEmpsDC	Uses the single-record layout with the ADO Data Control binding type.
frmDFEmpsDGrid	Uses the grid (DataSheet) layout with the ADO Data Control binding type.
frmDFEmpsHGrid	Uses the MS HFlexGrid layout with the ADO Data Control binding type.
frmDFEmpsMD	Uses the master/detail layout with the ADO Data Control binding type.
frmEmpDC	Uses the single-record layout with the ADO Data Control binding type.

You should load each one of these sample forms just to see what they look like and how they act.

Application Wizard

The Application Wizard assists you in creating a complete application. It uses several of the templates that come with Visual Basic to create MDI, SDI, and Explorer-like application shells. You can then use a shell as a starting point for your own application. Although some of the code that's generated from the Application Wizard leaves a lot to be desired, it's a good way to get started on a user interface. This tool is available in both the Professional and Enterprise Editions of Visual Basic.

Sample Project: \Chapter19\AppWizardGeneration\Employees.vbp

The Introduction form, shown in Figure 26.9, prompts you for any previously created profiles. A *profile* is created after you've run the Application Wizard one time and have chosen a series of options. You can save all these options into a profile. This is a great idea if you're going to create applications that are similar in look and feel.

For this example, we'll walk through creating an MDI-type application.

The Application Wizard has the capability to create applications based on the MDI model, as shown in Figure 26.10. This model has one parent form under which all other forms are child forms. The Application Wizard automatically creates the parent with all the standard MDI menus, provides the ability to create child forms at runtime, and offers several other options based on settings you select in the next few forms.

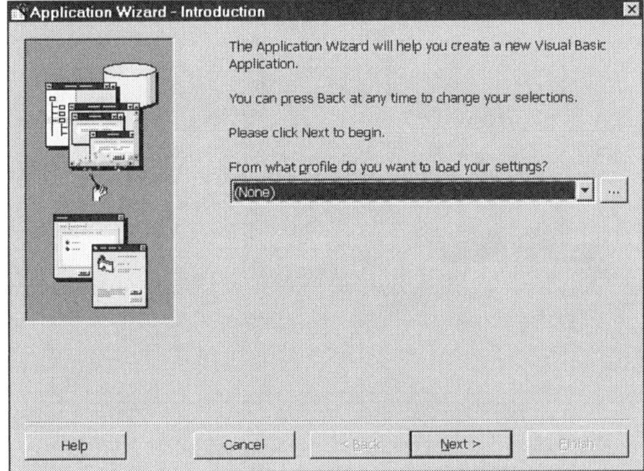

FIGURE 26.9 The Application Wizard's Introduction form.

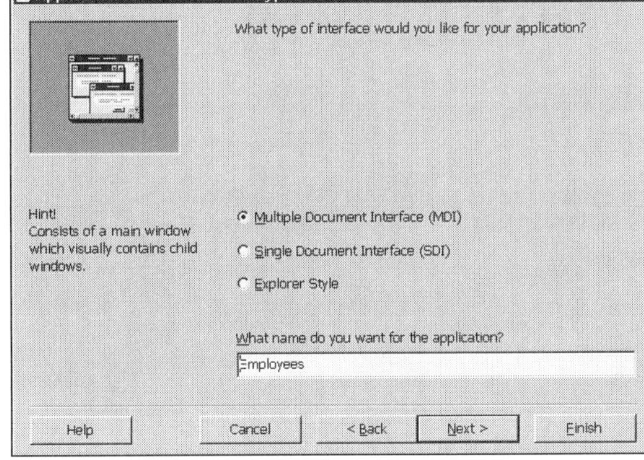

FIGURE 26.10 The Application Wizard's Interface Type form.

The Menus form, shown in Figure 26.11, allows you to select your top-level menus and one level of submenus. You can move these menus around, add separator bars, and remove and add new menus, just by using the different icons to the right of each of the menu lists.

The Customize Toolbar form, shown in Figure 26.12, is similar to the Menus form—here, you can choose which icons you want to add to your toolbar on your main MDI form. You can add and remove buttons as you want. The icons along the top represent your toolbar. The list on the left represents all the icons you can add to your toolbar. The list on the right shows icons you've chosen for your toolbar.

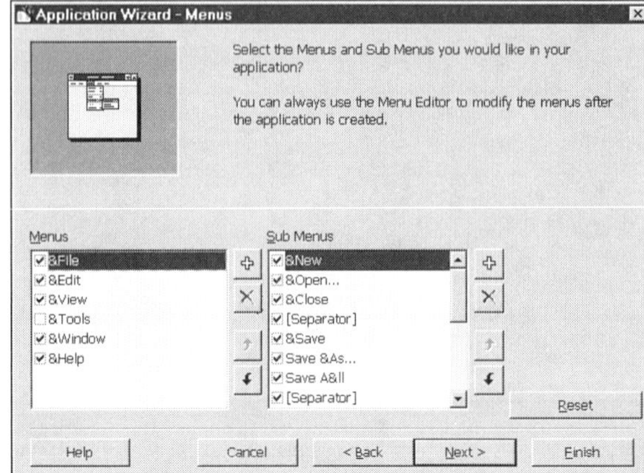

FIGURE 26.11 The Application Wizard's Menus form.

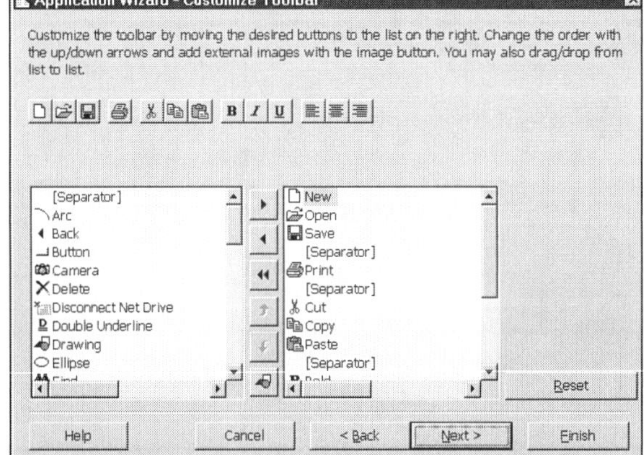

FIGURE 26.12 The Application Wizard's Customize Toolbar form.

If you're writing a multilingual application, you'll want the ability to change all the captions and strings in your application to different languages. A resource file enables you to accomplish this. From the form shown in Figure 26.13 you will be asked if you want use a resource file. A *resource file* is a replaceable file that has a list of all the strings used in your application. You can replace this file at runtime and use function calls in your application to display all the strings for message boxes, captions, and so on in the appropriate language. In addition to strings, a resource file may also hold pictures and other objects.

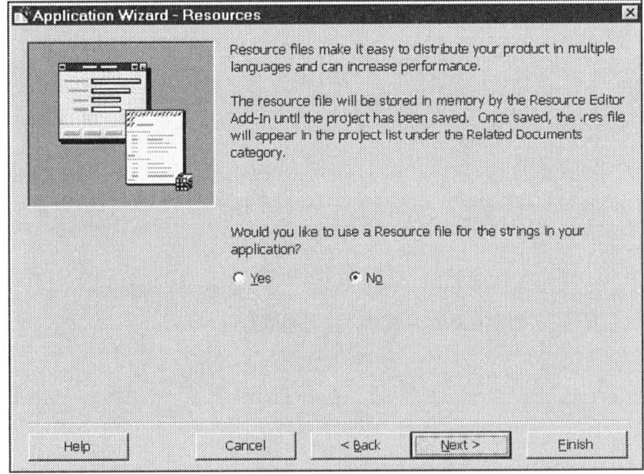

FIGURE 26.13 The Application Wizard's Resources form.

The Application Wizard has the capability to add a browser form to your application. It uses the standard Internet Explorer 4.0 Browser control for this browser form. This allows you to customize which sites your user can visit. This is great for a corporate application where you don't want the users to visit every site on the Internet. Instead, you can create a combo box of approved sites and allow users to get to only these sites through your application. Figure 26.14 will ask you to add a browser, and if you do, where you want to have the browser connect when the form is shown.

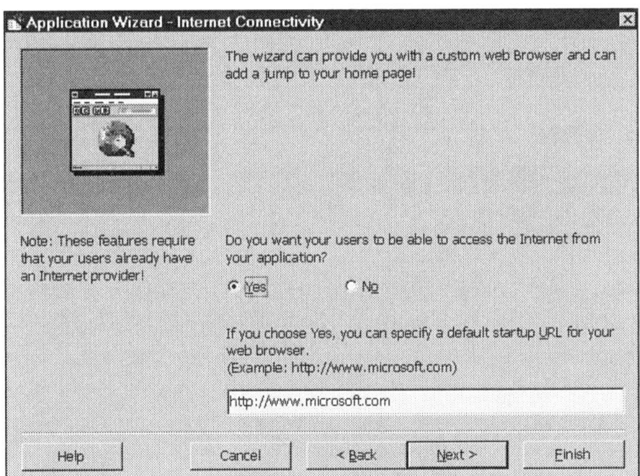

FIGURE 26.14 The Application Wizard's Internet Connectivity form.

You can add many different forms to your application by selecting from the list on the Standard Forms form, shown in Figure 26.15. Besides selecting any of the forms listed with the check boxes, you can also include form templates. *Form templates* are form files you've placed in the \Template folder under your Visual Basic installation directory. Visual Basic places several templates in this location for you, but you can add your own. These forms can then be added to your application via the Application Wizard.

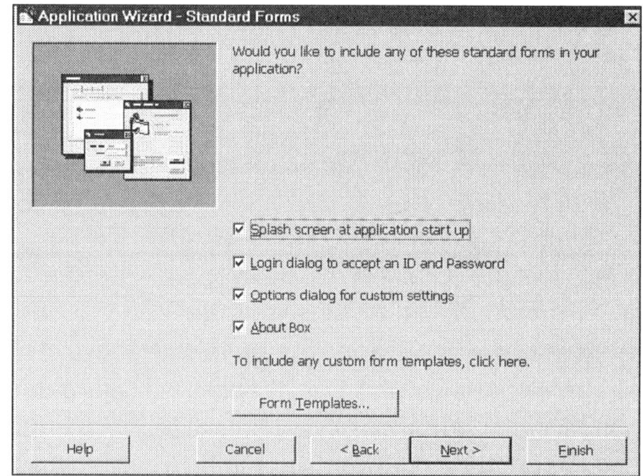

FIGURE 26.15 The Application Wizard's Standard Forms form.

The wizard's next form (Data Access Forms) allows you to call the Data Form Wizard to create as many data access forms as you want. Once these forms are created, they're added to the list box. After the Application Wizard finishes with all its other option forms, it adds them to your project.

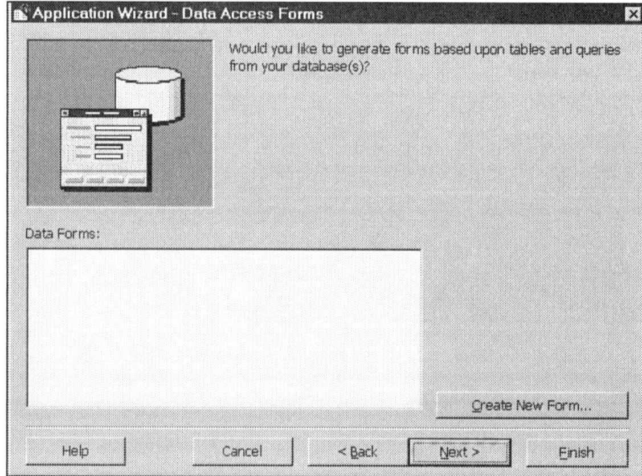

FIGURE 26.16 The Application Wizard's Data Access Forms form.

Figure 26.17 shows the final screen in the Application Wizard. From here you can save all the options you chose in this wizard to a profile. This profile can then be used the next time you run the wizard.

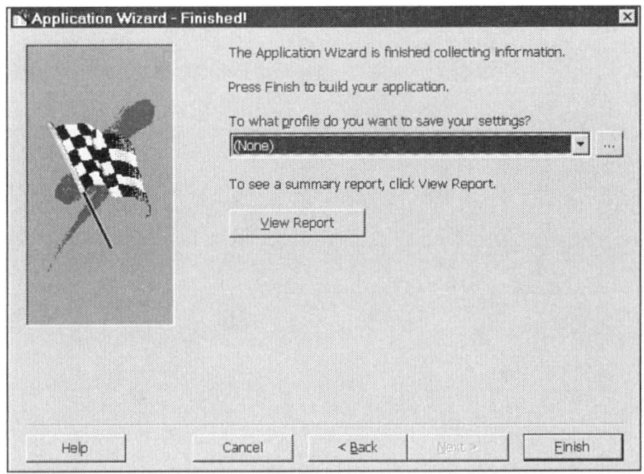

FIGURE 26.17 The Application Wizard's Finished form.

Summary

Using the Data Form Wizard is a great way to get a head start on a typical data entry form for your users. It helps you build several different types of data entry forms that connect with a database. The Application Wizard can help you create an entire template as a starting point for your application.

Review Questions

1. The Data Form Wizard only creates one type of data entry form. True or False?
2. The Application Wizard generates a complete application for you. True or False?

Exercises

1. Create a data entry form based on the tblStates table.
2. Create a data entry form that displays a combo box of state codes. Each time a state code is selected, load a list box with employees for the selected state.

27

Visual Database Tools

THIS CHAPTER GIVES YOU AN OVERVIEW OF THE database tools that come with Visual Basic 6. Some of these tools are available only in the Enterprise Edition, and some are also available in the Professional Edition. You'll learn to use the Data View window and the Data Environment Designer to modify your database schema and retrieve information from your database. These two tools together are worth the cost of upgrading to Visual Basic 6 from a previous version.

Chapter Objectives

- Learn about the different database tools available in Visual Basic
- Learn to use the Data View window
- Learn to use the Data Environment Designer
- Learn to use the Query Builder
- Learn to use the SQL Editor
- Learn to use the Visual Data Manager

Sample Project File: \Chapter27\VisualTools.vbp

Visual Database Tools Overview

In the Microsoft Visual Basic Books Online, you'll see references to the *Microsoft Visual Database Tools*. These are only a few different tools; however, they each have multiple parts to them, and sometimes in the documentation they're called different things. Here's an overview of the different tools and how you can get to them:

- *Data Environment Designer*. This tool is used to create design-time `Connection` and `Command` objects that you can execute at runtime. It encapsulates all the typical connection information and the SQL you need to create runtime resultsets.

  Select Project, Add Data Environment to add the Data Environment Designer to your project.

- *The Data View window*. This tool is a view into your database. You can use it to view tables, stored procedures, views, and triggers. Several other tools are typically used from this window, including the Source Code Editor (also called the *SQL Editor*) and the Query Design Window.

  Select View, Data View Window to open up this tool.

- *UserConnection Designer*. This tool has been superceded by the Data Environment Designer.

- *Visual Data Manager*. This program, sometimes called *VisData*, is a program that allows you to manipulate a database. It's actually written in Visual Basic, and the source code comes with the examples in the \Samples directory with the Enterprise Edition of Visual Basic.

  Select this tool from the Add-Ins, Visual Data Manager menu item.

Data Environment Designer

The Data Environment Designer is a design-time tool that allows you to create connections to a database. These connections can be used at design time to bind controls on forms to the tables/columns in the designer. You can also use these connections at design time to bind tables/columns to the Microsoft Data Report Designer. These connections are also used at runtime to create `Recordset` and `Command` objects. The `Command` objects can run stored procedures or SQL statements and return recordsets, or they can run SQL action queries. This tool is available in both the Professional and Enterprise Editions of Visual Basic.

To add a Data Environment Designer to your project, select Project, Add Data Environment from the Visual Basic menu. This brings up the designer shown in Figure 27.1.

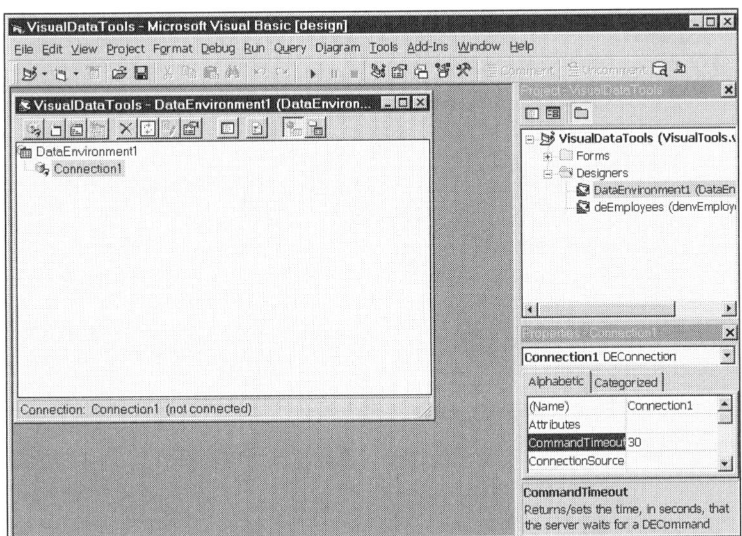

FIGURE 27.1 The Data Environment Designer.

Once you have the Data Environment Designer in your project, you can name the data environment and then set the properties for the connection that has automatically been added to this data environment. You must have at least one `Connection` object for your data environment. A data environment, by itself, does nothing—it's the connection that you use to get at your database.

EXERCISE

Use a Data Environment to Connect to a Database

1. Select Project, Add Data Environment from the Visual Basic menu.
2. Click DataEnvironment1.
3. Set the `Name` property to `deEmployee` in the Properties window.
4. Click Connection1.
5. Set the `Name` property to `cnEmp` in the Properties window.
6. Right-click the `cnEmp` object and choose Properties from the menu.
7. You'll now see a dialog box called Data Link Properties from which you can choose a provider and create a connection to a database (see Figure 27.2).
8. Select either Microsoft Jet 3.51 OLE DB Provider or Microsoft OLE DB Provider for ODBC Drivers and then click the Connection tab.

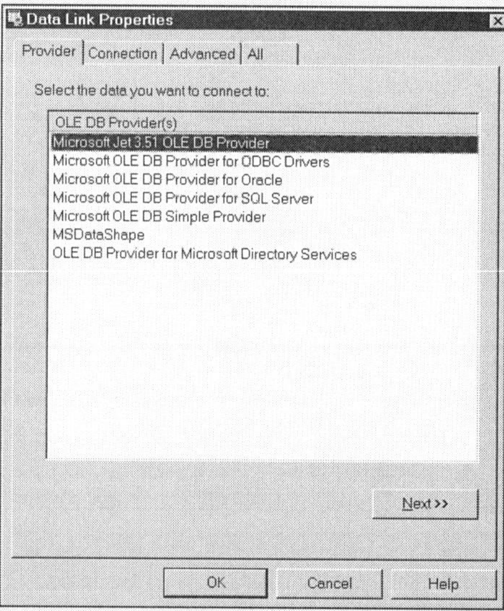

FIGURE 27.2
The Data Link Properties dialog box.

You have created a new data environment and linked that to an Access database. You will now be able to use that data environment instead of creating an ADO connection and Recordset.

Connecting to Microsoft Access

If you'll be using the Employees.mdb file that comes with this book, choose the Microsoft Jet 3.51 OLE DB Provider option. If you've upsized the Employees sample database to SQL Server, choose the Microsoft OLE DB Provider for SQL Server option. If you've upsized the Employees sample database to Oracle, choose the Microsoft OLE DB Provider for Oracle option. See Figure 27.3 for an example of the Microsoft Jet 3.51 OLE DB Provider Data Link Properties dialog box.

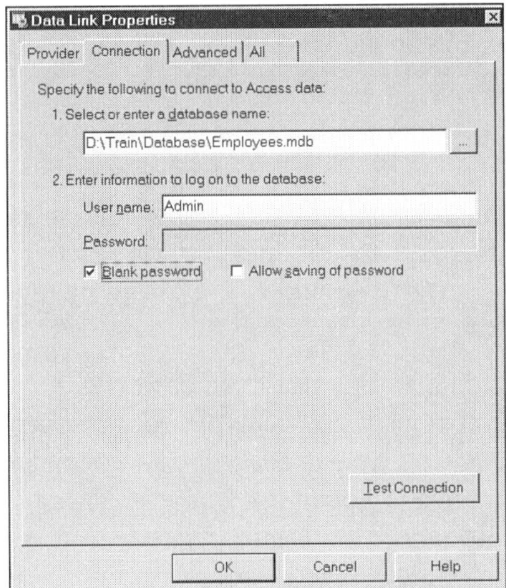

FIGURE 27.3 The Data Link Properties dialog box using the Microsoft Jet 3.51 OLE DB provider.

In the Data Link Properties dialog for the Jet OLE DB provider, you need to specify the full path and filename of an MDB file to connect to. If the database is secured, you need to put in a user name and a password. If it isn't secured, you can just use Admin as the user name. This is all you need to fill in on this screen. At this point, just click the OK button to close the Data Link Properties dialog box.

EXERCISE

ADD A PATH TO THE CONNECTION

1. On the Connection tab of the Data Link Properties dialog box, fill in the full path of where you installed the examples for this book and use **Employees.mdb** as the database name.
2. Fill in **Admin** as the user name.
3. Click the OK button to save this connection information.

For an Access database you need a full path and filename. For other data sources you will need other information such as a server name, database name, and maybe even some network parameters.

Adding Commands

To really do anything with the data environment object, you need to add `Command` objects to the connection. `Command` objects are like views into the data. They allow you to retrieve recordsets for use in bound data forms or you can use them instead of stand-alone ADO recordsets.

You can create a `Command` object that's based on a table, a stored procedure, a view, or a synonym, or you can type in your own SQL `SELECT` statement. You can use the SQL Builder to assist you in writing your SQL statement. `Command` objects can be built automatically by dragging and dropping a table name from the Data View window into the Data Environment window. You'll learn more about the Data View window in the next section.

To add a new command in the data environment, you can either right-click the connection and choose the Add Command menu item, or you can select the Add Command icon from the toolbar. Once you've added a new command, click it and set the `Name` property. Next, you need to open the Properties dialog box for the `Command` object and select the source of the data. Figure 27.4 shows you what the Properties dialog box looks like for a `Command` object.

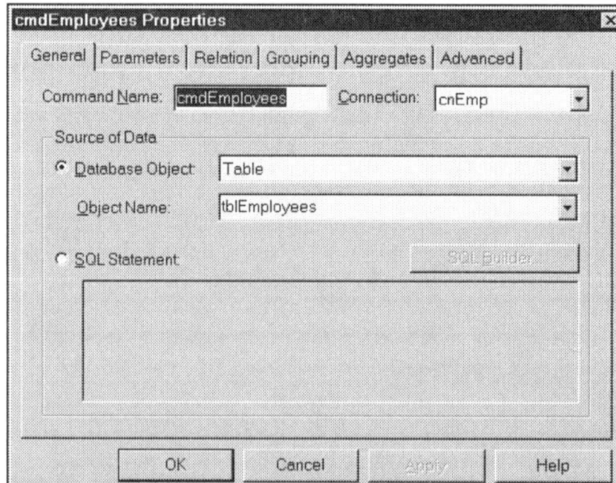

FIGURE 27.4
A `Command` Object's properties.

EXERCISE

Add a Command Object to the Data Environment

1. Add a new `Command` object to the connection you created earlier.
2. Set the `Name` property to `cmdEmployees`.
3. Click the Properties icon to bring up the `Command` object's properties.
4. Click the Database Object drop-down combo box and select Table.
5. Select the tblEmployees table from the Object Name drop-down combo box. Note that the Microsoft OLE DB provider for SQL Server may not allow you to access the Object Name combo box. This usually happens if you've installed a previous version of ADO and did not uninstall it prior to installing Visual Basic 6. You may have to type in the name of the table yourself. If this is the case, type in **tblEmployees** in this combo box.
6. Click the OK button to save this `Command` object.
7. You should now see a plus sign next to the `Command` object you created in the Data Environment window.
8. Click this plus sign to see a list of all the fields in this table.

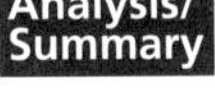

You now have created a command object that can be used as a data source to any data-aware control.

Setting Field Properties

After you've created the `Command` object, you can now set properties for each of the fields in it. If you set the `Caption` property in the Field Properties dialog box as shown in Figure 27.5, you can drag and drop the `Command` object onto a form and all the labels and text boxes will be automatically created, ready to be bound to the data environment.

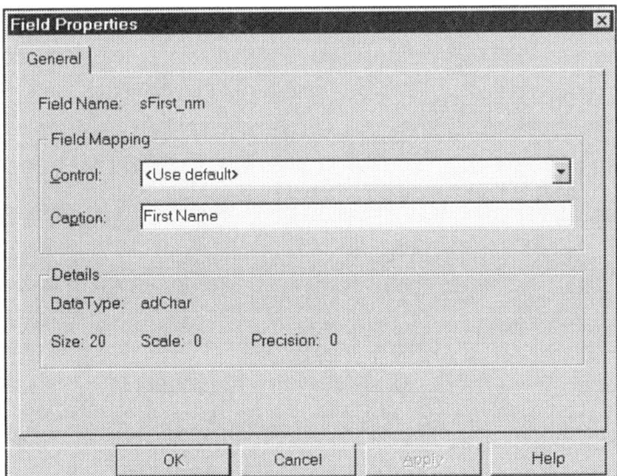

FIGURE 27.5
The Field Properties dialog box.

EXERCISE

Setting Captions for Each Field

1. Click each field in the `Command` object, right-click and select the Properties menu.
2. Set the `Caption` property to a nice descriptive name for each field.

Setting the `Caption` property will generate nice label names if you drag and drop this command object onto a form.

Using the *Connection* and *Command* Objects at Runtime

Now that you have a **Connection** object and a **Command** object, you can use these objects in your source code. About the only things you can do with the Connection object are open it, close it, and execute a SQL **INSERT**, **UPDATE**, or **DELETE** statement. However, when you add a **Command** object, the data environment will automatically build a recordset based on that **Command** object. Here are two different methods for opening the **Connection** object that's attached to the data environment and using the **Command** object to fetch some data:

```
Private Sub cmdTest_Click()
   denvEmployees.cnEmp.Open

   ' Do some processing
   With denvEmployees.rscmdEmployee
      .Open
      Do Until .EOF
         Debug.Print .Fields("szLast_nm")
         .MoveNext
      Loop
      .Close
   End With

   denvEmployees.cnEmp.Close
End Sub
```

In this code, you simply reference the data environment name, followed by the `Connection` object name, and then invoke the `Open` method on the `Connection` object. You then use the `Command` object as a property of the data environment to loop through all the last-name fields in the recordset. Notice that the data environment automatically creates a *rs<CmdObjectName>* property for you.

In the next example, you can create a new data environment object from the existing data environment object. This might be used if you needed to have two different connections to the same database:

```
Private Sub cmdTest_Click()
   Dim deEmp As New denvEmployee

   deEmp.cnEmp.Open

   ' Do some processing
   With deEmp.rscmdEmployee
      .Open
      Do Until .EOF
         Debug.Print .Fields("szLast_nm")
         .MoveNext
      Loop
      .Close
   End With

   deEmp.cnEmp.Close
End Sub
```

In this code, you create a new instance of the data environment `denvEmployee`. This creates a new instance of the `Connection` object within that environment. You then apply the `Open` method to the new connection, and you now have a second connection to the data source.

Connecting to SQL Server

If you want to use SQL Server, you'll get a different Connection tab in the Data Link Properties dialog box. In fact, every provider has a slightly different Connection tab because they each require different information to connect to their server. Figure 27.6 shows you the Connection tab for Microsoft SQL Server.

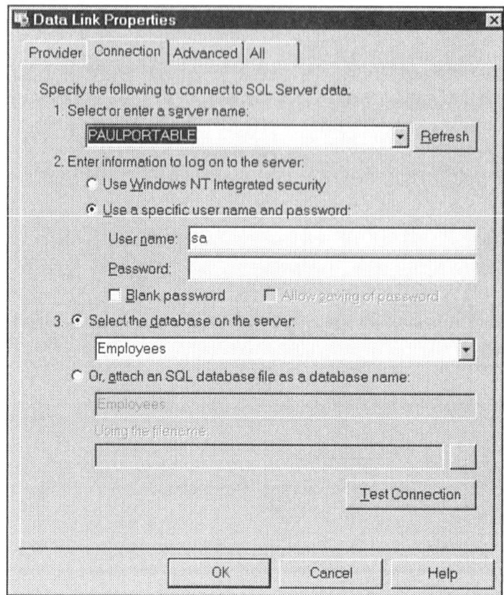

FIGURE 27.6 The Data Link Properties dialog box using the Microsoft OLE DB provider for SQL Server.

On this particular Connection tab, you need to fill in a server name, specify whether you're using Windows NT Integrated Security or standard security to connect to SQL Server, and choose a database from the server.

EXERCISE

UPSIZING TO A SQL SERVER DATABASE

1. Upsize the Employees.mdb file to SQL Server if you have not already done so. For instructions on upsizing this file to SQL Server, refer to Appendix E, "Sample Code Installation Instructions."
2. Fill in the name of your server where SQL Server is located.
3. Choose either Windows NT Integrated Security or fill in a user name and password.
4. Select or fill in the name of the database—most likely, the database is named *Employee*.
5. Click the OK button to save this connection information.

Creating a connection to an Access database or to SQL Server or to Oracle is really different. However, as long as the database structure is the same, these changes will not affect your forms in the least.

Creating Data-bound Forms

Once you've created a data environment and `Connection` and `Command` objects, you're ready to connect your `Command` object to a form that can be used for data entry. All you need to do is to add an ADO data control to your project, drag and drop the `Command` object you created onto a blank form, add the ADO data control to the form, and then write one line of code. I know it sounds too easy, but believe me, it is that easy!

EXERCISE

Binding Command Objects to a Form

1. Add a new form to your project by selecting Project, Add Form from the Visual Basic menu.
2. Add an ADO data control by selecting Project, Components from the Visual Basic menu.
3. Select the Microsoft ADO Data Control 6.0 (OLEDB) option from the list of components.
4. Grab that data control from the toolbox and place it on the new form.
5. Set the `Name` property of the data control to `adcEmp`.
6. Set the `Caption` property to `Employees`.
7. Position your form within the Visual Basic design environment so that you can see both the form and the Data Environment window.
8. Drag the `Command` object `cmdEmployees` onto the form.
9. You should now see the Visual Basic design environment adding labels and text boxes to the form.
10. When this process is complete, you need to set the recordset for the `Command` object to the `Recordset` property of the ADO data control.
11. Double-click the form to bring up the `Form_Load()` event. Write the following line of code in the `Load` event:

```
Private Sub Form_Load()
    Set adcEmp.Recordset = deEmployees.rscmdEmployees
End Sub
```

It is very easy to create a form that displays data. Using the command objects, you can just drag and drop onto a form and write one line of code!

When you add a `Command` object to a connection of the data environment object, you automatically create a property that's a reference to the underlying recordset associated with that `Command` object. The name of the recordset will always be prefaced with the letters *rs*, followed by the name of the `Command` object. All you have to do is set the `Recordset` property of the ADO data control to the recordset in the data environment. You should now be able to run this form and scroll through the records.

Data View Window

The Data View window provides a way for you to look into any database to view and update the objects in that database. You can create tables, indexes, stored procedures, and triggers, as well as Oracle synonyms, functions, and packages within this window. You can use the Data View window instead of switching back and forth between Visual Basic and an external database tool. The Data View window is a great tool and is actually easier to use for certain operations than SQL Enterprise Manager. You're only allowed to view objects in an Access MDB file, but you can add, modify, and delete objects in either SQL Server or Oracle.

This tool is available in both the Professional and Enterprise Editions from the Visual Basic toolbar (see Figure 27.7).

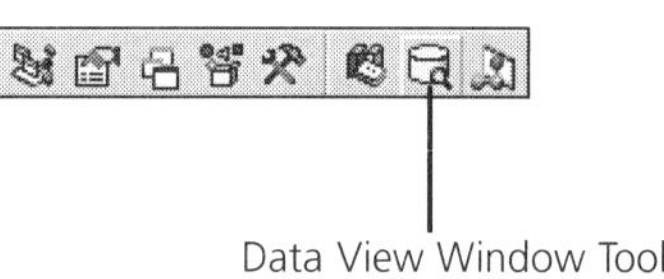

FIGURE 27.7 The Visual Basic toolbar with the Data View window Tool icon.

You can also get to the Data View window from the View, Data View Window menu item. The Data View window is shown in Figure 27.8.

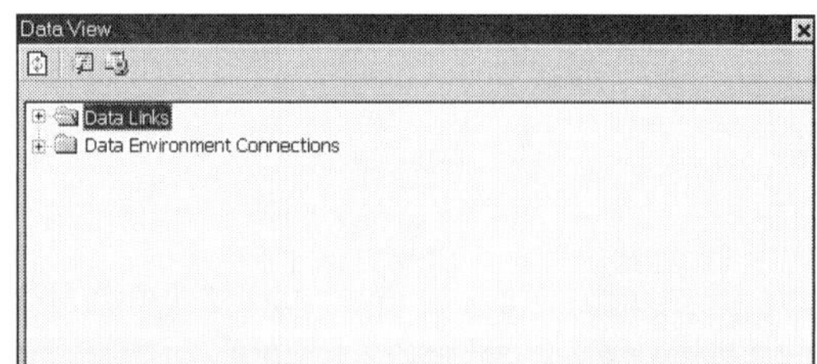

FIGURE 27.8 The Data View window.

Creating a Data Link

Click the third icon from the left to add a new data link to your Visual Basic environment. Once you create a new data link, that link will be around whenever you open the Data View window in Visual Basic. The Data View window keeps any links you create between projects—it's not limited to one project like the data environment is.

EXERCISE

ADD A NEW DATA LINK

1. Open the Data View window.
2. Click the Add a New Data Link icon or right-click the Data Links folder and select the Add a New Data Link menu item.

Once you have a data link, you can use this to view many of the objects in your SQL Server or Oracle database.

When you're using a Jet MDB, you won't be able to add, edit, or delete any of the objects within that database. Figure 27.9 shows you what a connection to a Jet MDB looks like. This limitation might be removed in the future, but for now, you just can't perform these operations. You'll only be allowed to modify objects if you're connected to Microsoft SQL Server or to an Oracle database.

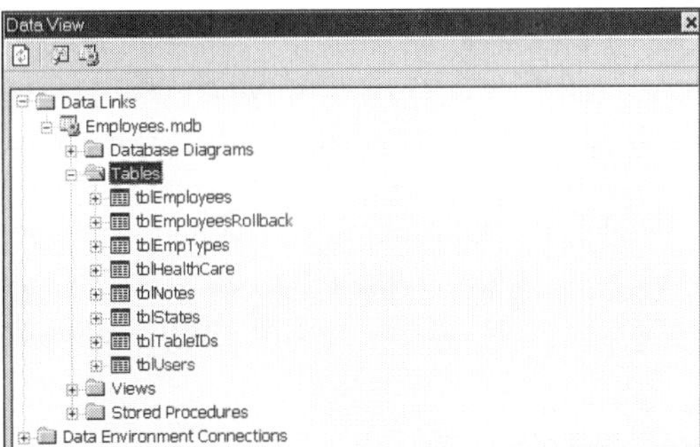

FIGURE 27.9
The Data View window with a connection to a Jet MDB.

Using the Data Link with a Jet MDB

Once you've opened a connection to a Jet MDB, you can now open a list of tables. Click the plus sign (+) next to the Tables folder. This expands the folder into a list of tables in the database. If you double-click one of these tables, the Data View window will open a data sheet for you from which you can view, add, edit, and delete data in this table.

If you expand one of the tables, you can view the list of fields that make up that table. You can then double-click one of the fields for a list of that field's properties, such as the data type, length, owner, and so on. See Figure 27.10 for an example.

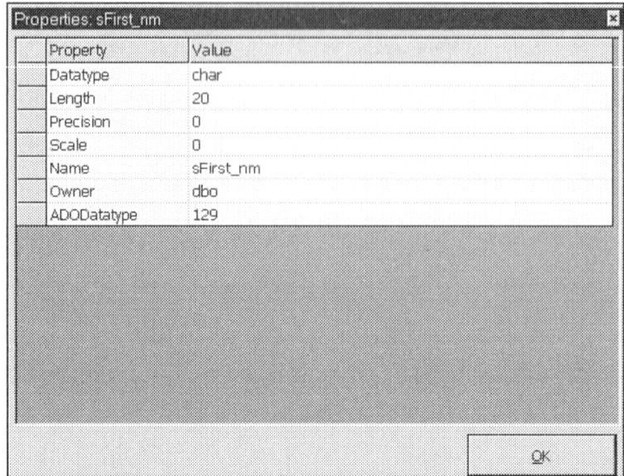

FIGURE 27.10 The field properties for a Jet MDB.

The field properties are lookup only—you can't modify any of the tables, fields, or queries in the Access MDB from the Data View window.

Using a SQL Server Data Link

When you create a data link to SQL Server, you have more options than what you have with an Access MDB. You can create and modify tables, create and edit views, and create and view stored procedures.

To modify a table, right-click the table and select the Design menu. This displays the Design Table window, shown in Figure 27.11, from which you can add fields, change field names, and even drop in fields. One of the nice features of the Design Table window is that when you save the changes you make to the table, it shows you the SQL code it's submitting to the database to make these changes. This will help you learn SQL. You can even save these changes to a text file, which is excellent if later you need to make these same changes to a production database.

The Query Design Window

If you've created views in SQL Server or Oracle or if you want to create new views in SQL Server or Oracle, you can click the Views folder in the Data View window. If you have existing views, they'll show up under this folder. To add a new view, right-click the Views folder and select the New View menu item. This Query Design window is available in the Enterprise Edition only.

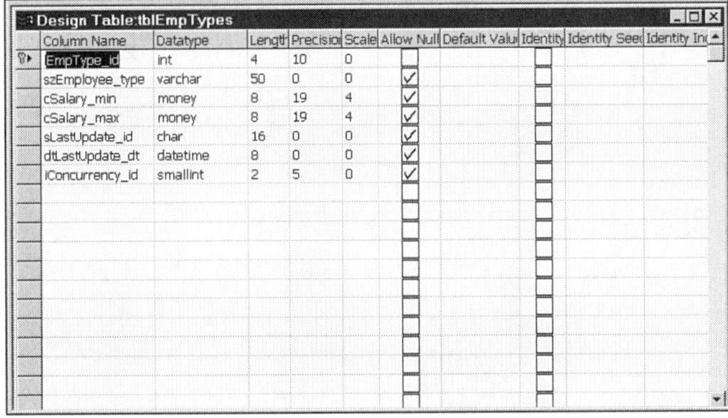

FIGURE 27.11
The Design Table window.

You can create a new view by selecting the table you want to create the view from and dragging it to the Query Design window. Note that you might need to expand the Fields list for the table prior to dragging it to the Query Design window. You can also set relationships by dragging and dropping from one table to another (most relationships will be set automatically if you've created all the appropriate foreign key relationships in your schema).

You'll design most of your queries by dragging and dropping tables from the Data Links window into the Query Design window. After you have the tables in the window, you can set relationships between the tables and select the columns you want to display in this view. Once you've completed the view, you simply close the Query Design window. You'll then be prompted to save the view and input a view name. See Figure 27.12 for an example of a view displayed in the Query Design window.

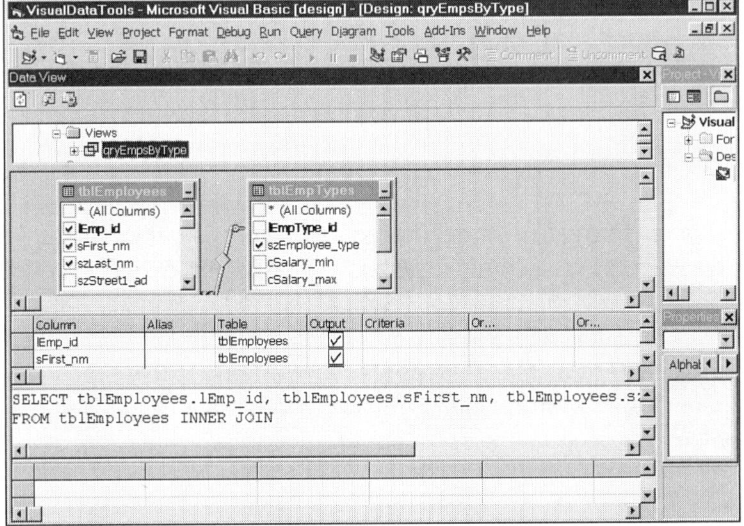

FIGURE 27.12
The Query Design window.

EXERCISE

Build a Query

1. Click the View folder and then right-click to display the menu. Select the New View menu item.
2. Expand the Tables folder to display tables.
3. Grab the tblEmployees table and drop it into the Query Design window.
4. Grab the tblEmpTypes table and drop it into the Query Design window.
5. Set a relationship between the lEmpType_id field in the tblEmployees table and the lEmpType_id field in the tblEmpTypes table by dragging the lEmpType_id field in the tblEmployees table to the lEmpType_id field in the tblEmpTypes table.
6. Click sFirst_nm and szLast_nm in the tblEmployees table.
7. Click szEmployees_type in the tblEmpTypes table.
8. You now have a query complete with an inner join set between the two tables.
9. Click the close button in the upper-right corner of the form.
10. Respond by clicking Yes when asked to save the view.
11. Type in **qryEmpTypes** when prompted for a name for the view.

After saving the view, you should now be able to double-click the view to display a data sheet. (Note that this will only work if you're using the ODBC provider.)

SQL Editor for Stored Procedures and Triggers

When you're displaying the information in the Data View window, you have the option of viewing stored procedures. You can view the columns in the stored procedure as well. If you double-click the stored procedure, you can bring up the SQL Editor window for the stored procedure. It's in this window that you use the appropriate syntax to create a stored procedure on your target database. The SQL Editor is available only in the Enterprise Edition of Visual Basic. From within the SQL Editor window, you have the option of saving the stored procedure to the database, saving it to a local text file, or printing the stored procedure. Again, the option of saving to a local text file makes it easy for you to transfer this stored procedure to another SQL Server in the future. If you are using SQL Server, you can perform the following exercise.

EXERCISE

Create a New Stored Procedure

1. Click the Stored Procedures folder.
2. Right-click and select the New Stored Procedure menu item.
3. In the SQL Editor window, type in the following code:

```
Create Procedure procEmpSalary
As
SELECT szLast_nm, sFirst_nm,
       szEmployee_type, cSalary_amt
FROM tblEmployees
INNER JOIN tblEmpTypes
ON tblEmployees.lEmpType_id =
   tblEmpTypes.lEmpType_id
```

Analysis/Summary

This syntax is for a SQL Server stored procedure that performs a join on the tblEmployees and tblEmpTypes tables and returns a resultset.

As you can see in Figures 27.13 and 27.14, the SQL Editor window is essentially the same for both stored procedures and triggers. This makes sense because a trigger is really just a special kind of stored procedure.

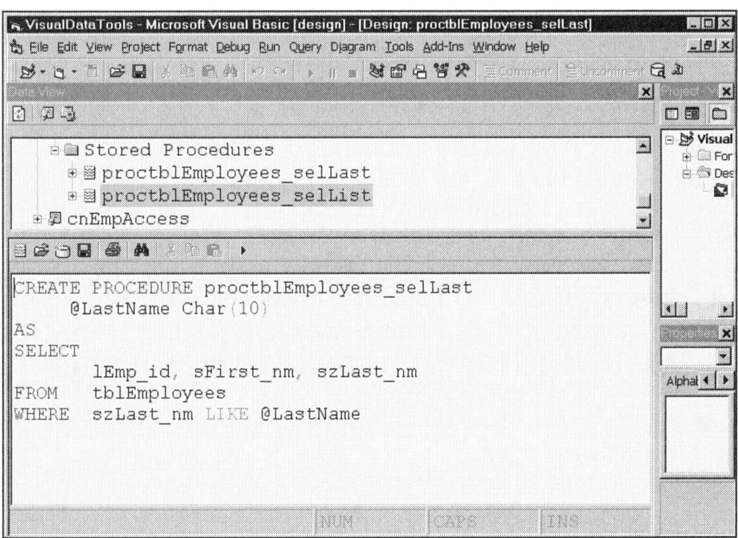

FIGURE 27.13 The SQL Editor window with a stored procedure.

The figures show a different stored procedure than the one you created above, this is just so you can see different examples.

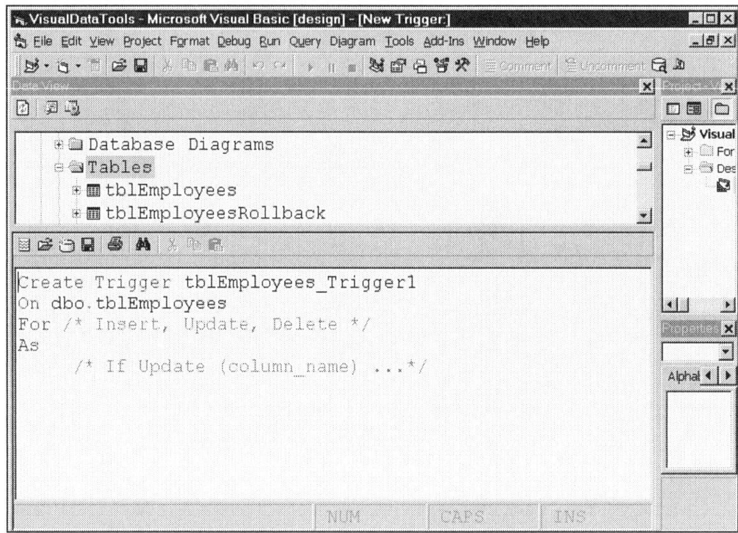

FIGURE 27.14 The SQL Editor Window with a trigger.

The Database Diagram Window

The Database Diagram window allows you to create a view of the tables in your database. You can also create a diagram of the relationships between your tables (see Figure 27.15). You can modify the tables in the Database Diagram Window as well as create separate views of your database.

For example, you can have all the tables that relate to one subsystem on one diagram, and all the other tables for a different subsystem on another diagram. The Database Diagram window is available only in the Enterprise Edition of Visual Basic.

To create a database diagram, you need to select the Database Diagrams folder in the Data View window. You can then right-click to add a new diagram. Then, it's a simple matter of dragging and dropping existing tables from the Tables folder into the diagram, or you can create brand new tables right on the diagram. Database diagrams can only be created for SQL Server and Oracle databases.

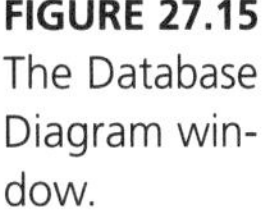

FIGURE 27.15
The Database Diagram window.

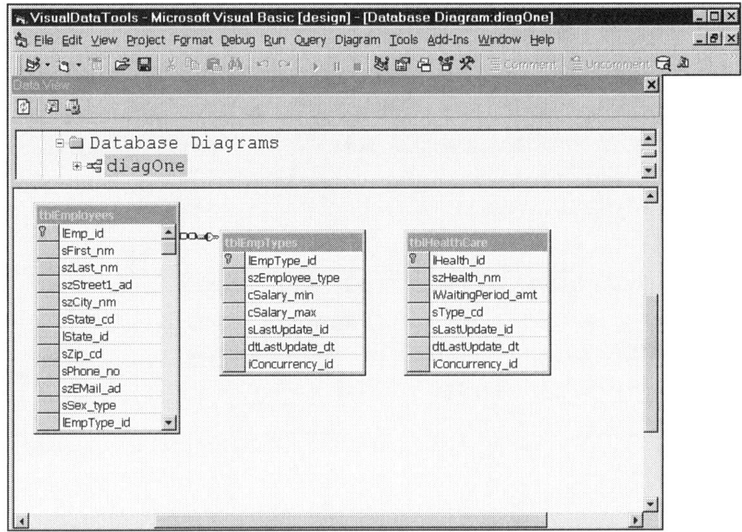

EXERCISE

Create a New Database Diagram

1. Click the Database Diagrams folder.
2. Right-click and select the New Diagram menu item.
3. Expand the Tables folder.
4. Drag and drop tables from the Tables folder to the new database diagram.
5. You can create relationships by choosing a field in one table and dragging and dropping it to the related table. If you're familiar with the Microsoft Access Relationships window, you'll find the Database Diagram window very easy to use.

When you're done, you can save this diagram with a name that will show up under the Database Diagrams folder. You can create as many diagrams as you want, and you can have the same tables in different diagrams. When you save the database diagram, it adds the relationship information you created back to the database. For example, if you add a foreign key reference from one table to another, the database diagram will alter the base table with that information.

Visual Data Manager

Visual Data Manager is an add-in that's actually written in Visual Basic. You can get the complete source code from the Samples directory. This tool is really intended for manipulating the database schemas of ISAM file systems, such as Microsoft Access databases. See Figure 27.16 for an example of what Visual Data Manager (or *VisData*) looks like.

FIGURE 27.16
The Visual Data Manager.

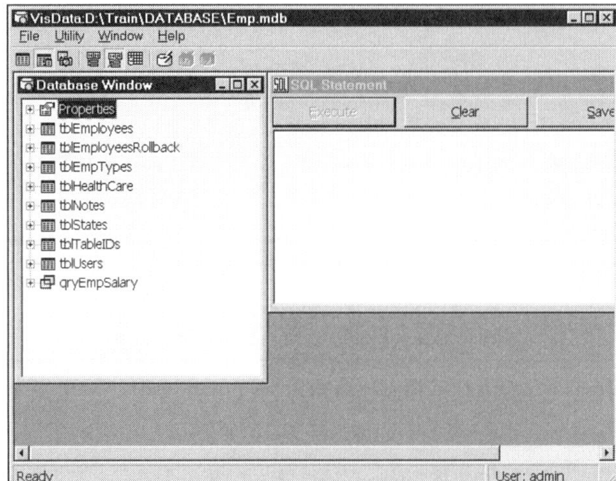

Although this tool does not have all the functionality of Microsoft Access, it's great for making quick modifications to the schema of a Jet database. You can run queries and view all the rows and columns in a table. The results can be displayed in a form created on-the-fly that allows you to add, edit, and delete the data.

Summary

This chapter introduced you to many of the different visual database tools available in Visual Basic 6, Professional and Enterprise Editions. The Data Environment Designer and the Data View window are excellent tools for managing your data, both at runtime and design time. The Data View window is an excellent database manager that allows you to modify database objects. The Data Environment Designer helps you create `Command` objects at design time that can be called very easily at runtime.

Review Questions

1. The Data Environment Designer can only be used at design time. True or False?
2. What is a `Command` object?
3. Will the Data View window show you queries in an Access MDB?
4. Can you modify the objects in an Access MDB with the Data View window?

Exercise

Write the code that opens a data environment `Connection` at runtime.

1. Write the code that opens a data environment `Connection` at runtime.

Using the Windows API

DO YOU WANT TO ADD FLEXIBILITY AND POWER TO YOUR applications? Of course you do—everyone does. You can add a lot to your programs if you take just a little time to understand the Windows API. The Windows API is probably the least understood and most underutilized tool by Visual Basic programmers. C programmers use it all the time. That's why C programmers tend to be excellent Visual Basic programmers. This chapter helps you to understand the inner workings of Windows and teaches you how to find the tools you need to make your applications stand out in the crowd. What's more, you can learn to do all this without using a lot of expensive third-party controls that can drag in a lot of unnecessary overhead.

Chapter Objectives

- Understand how to take advantage of the functions in Windows
- Learn where to find more information on the Windows API
- Learn to declare and call API functions
- Learn some tips for extending Visual Basic
- Build a class that returns system information

Sample Project File: \Chapter28\WindowsAPI.vbp

What Is the Windows API?

The Windows API (application programming interface) is a set of over 1,000 functions that can be used from Visual Basic or any language that can be programmed under Windows 95 or Windows NT. One of the reasons Windows programming has gotten the reputation of being hard to learn is due to the vast amount of functions you need to learn just to get started. Visual Basic uses many of these functions, but it makes them easier to learn by wrapping them into the BASIC language. Windows itself uses most of these functions to perform all its services.

Although there are many API functions you can call, only some of them are really useful. Some are already duplicated within Visual Basic features, and others cannot be called from Visual Basic due to incompatibilities. In this chapter, you'll learn some of the most useful API calls.

Uses of the Windows API

The Windows API is normally used with the C and C++ languages. After all, Visual Basic is supposed to shield us from the complexities of programming for Windows. However, there are times when Visual Basic just can't do certain things. Also, for performance reasons, you might want to use a routine that's built into the Windows environment. Here are some reasons why you might want to use the Windows API:

- To manipulate the system Registry
- To retrieve system information, such as memory and operating system information

- To search for entries in a combo or list box
- To change the style of a window
- To find out the drive types that are on a computer

You'll learn how to do most of these things in this chapter, but first, let's start with some basics.

Windows Components

Three DLLs (Dynamic Link Libraries) are the main components that make up the 32-bit operating systems (Windows 95/98 and Windows NT). A DLL is a library of routines that can be called from almost any programming language. They are dynamic in that they can be loaded and unloaded as you need them. Table 28.1 lists each of these DLLs and their roles within the operating systems.

Table 28.1 Windows Components

Filename	Description
User32.dll	This DLL controls the menuing system, the user interface components, and most of the other visual components in Windows.
Kernel32.dll	This DLL is in charge of the management of memory and various resources when a Windows application is being used.
GDI32.dll	This DLL controls all the painting of graphical elements, performing graphics-based calculations, and other drawing duties.

ANSI Versus Unicode

Unicode is a character set standard developed by the International Standards Organization (ISO) to overcome the 256-character limitation of the ANSI and Extended ASCII character sets used in the older 16-bit versions of Windows. Both the ANSI and Extended ASCII standards use only one byte to express characters in a computer. This limits the total number of unique characters to 256. Unicode uses two bytes per character, thus allowing 65,536 distinct characters. Currently, there are about 34,000 mapped characters in this set. This includes all the characters and alphabets used in the world today, including several antiquated languages such as Sanskrit and Egyptian hieroglyphs. Unicode also includes representations for punctuation marks, mathematical symbols, and dingbats fonts. This leaves substantial room for future expansion, so when the aliens finally land, you can add their language to your application.

Because Visual Basic is a 32-bit application, it uses Unicode for all its string manipulation. This can lead to problems with some of the older Windows API calls that still use the ANSI string characters. Fortunately, Visual Basic includes a function called `StrConv()` to perform conversions between Unicode and ANSI. You can use this function when working with the Windows API.

Sources for Windows API Information

If I were you, I would immediately invest in one book for learning Windows API calls—*Visual Basic Programmer's Guide to the Win32API*, by Daniel Appleman (see Appendix A, "VBA Programming Standards," for more information). This book is considered by most Visual Basic programmers to be the bible for using the Windows API with Visual Basic. It explains how to use most of the Windows API calls that are useful with Visual Basic, and it also explains which ones cannot be used.

Many other reference manuals for the Windows API are available; however, most of them are geared towards C language programmers. If you're a member of the Microsoft Developers Network, you'll have the complete Windows SDK at your fingertips on the CD-ROMs you receive every quarter. However, this won't do you much good unless you know what you're looking for and know about the C language. In this chapter, I explain the basics of how to use the Windows API calls. With this introduction and Appleman's book, you'll be ready to dive right in and create some great Windows applications.

Declaring API Functions to Visual Basic

Prior to using any of the Windows API functions, you must declare your intention to use them to Visual Basic. You can use all the functions in Visual Basic without any declarations because they're built into the Visual Basic language. For any external function that Visual Basic does not know about, you'll need to tell Visual Basic what it's name is, which DLL it resides in, what parameters it expects, and what return type, if any, it returns. You accomplish this using the `Declare` statement. The following is an example of how you might declare a couple of API calls to Visual Basic:

```
Declare Function GetWinFlags Lib "Kernel" () As Long
Declare Sub UpdateWindow Lib "User" (ByVal hWnd As Integer)
```

The declaration of a `Sub` is used for those routines that do not return a value. The declaration of a `Function` is used for those API calls that do return a value. There are only a few API calls that do not return a value, so you'll declare most of them as functions.

Declarations of API calls can be either `Public` or `Private` when declared in the General Declarations section of a BAS module. You may also declare API calls in a class module or form module, but the declarations in these files must be `Private`.

API Text Viewer Utility

You don't need to look up the declarations of API calls and type all the declarations in yourself—instead, you can use a utility that's supplied with Visual Basic. Under the Add-ins, Add-In Manager, you'll find the utility called VB6 API Viewer, which you can load into the Add-Ins menu. When you select the API Text Viewer utility, you'll see a screen similar to the one shown in Figure 28.1. To load in the declarations, you must select File, Load Text File from the API Text Viewer menu. Choose the Win32api.txt file from the list of files presented. If you're prompted to convert the file to a database, go ahead and choose that option—this will speed up the loading of the declarations substantially.

Now that you have the API Text Viewer and the declarations loaded, you can find the declaration you want, double-click it, and have it placed in the text box on the bottom of the screen. Once you have one or more declarations loaded into the text box, click the Copy button to copy all the declarations into the Clipboard. Once there, you can switch to your Visual Basic program and paste the declarations into a BAS module.

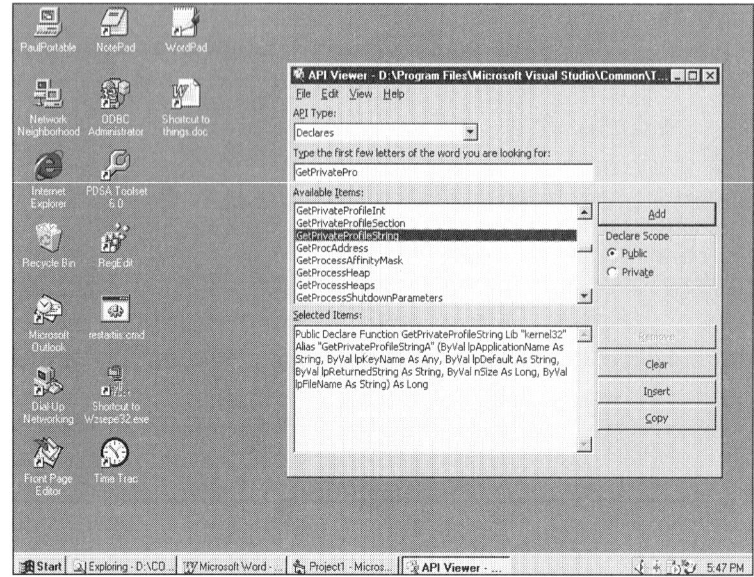

FIGURE 28.1 The API Text Viewer.

Calling API Functions

After you have a declaration in your program, you can now execute that function just like any other function in Visual Basic. Visual Basic takes care of loading the DLL, passing your parameters to the routine, and returning any values back. When calling API functions, you can pass parameters by value or by reference, just like in Visual Basic. However, note that when you're using string parameters, the `ByVal` keyword has a different meaning.

Call by Reference Versus Call by Value

When passing parameters to an API function, you must take care to ensure that you pass the correct data type and value. Some API functions want just a copy of the data (a call by value), whereas others actually want the pointer to the variable in memory (a call by reference). You can look at the declarations to determine whether the function wants a copy of the data or a pointer. If you see the `ByVal` keyword in front of a numeric parameter, it means the function is expecting a copy of the data. For string parameters, however, it's completely different. A Visual Basic string is really a pointer to another area of memory where the string is actually located. Because this is different than a C language string, the `ByVal` keyword must do some translation.

Passing String Parameters

The ByVal keyword tells Visual Basic to convert its String data type into a string that a C language function can read. This format is essentially a character array with a Null terminator on the end of the string. Therefore, Visual Basic reads its pointer, goes to that area of memory where the string is located, and passes the memory address of where the string is located to the function in the DLL. Because most of the Windows API is written in C, you'll most likely always see the ByVal keyword present before any string parameter in a Declare statement.

As mentioned earlier, a Visual Basic string's base address is not actually where the string is located. Instead, it's a certain amount of bytes that Visual Basic uses internally to determine where the string is located, the size of the string, and other information. If you attempt to pass this data to a C language program, the C language program would simply use whatever data was in these bytes instead of looking at the actual string. The only time you would pass a parameter without the ByVal keyword is if the C language function were written for use with the Visual Basic language.

If you forget the ByVal keyword, and the C language function is going to put some data into the string, the C language routine will overwrite memory that's reserved for Visual Basic plus anything else that happens to be located next to it in memory. This is one of the most common causes of fatal application errors.

Another problem with passing strings to a C language function can occur when the Visual Basic string is not allocated enough space to hold whatever data the C language function is going to put into the string. If you dim a string variable, Visual Basic does not set aside any space for this string other than the bytes it needs to manage the variable. The C language does not handle strings dynamically like Visual Basic does. It simply uses character arrays and pointers to add characters to this array. The C language will point to the base address of a character array and then start adding characters to the array until it's done. If the character array is not allocated to enough elements to handle all the data, the C language just continues to write information into the adjacent memory space. It does not care that there may already be other data in that space. Because this is the case, you need to make sure you allocate enough space to the Visual Basic string prior to passing it to the C language function that will put characters into the string. Take the following code fragment, for example:

```
Declare Sub ConvertString _
        Lib "MyLib.dll" (strString As String) As String

Dim strName As String
```

```
strName = "Bill"

ConvertString(strName)    ' Changes strName to "Microsoft"
Print strName       ' You have added 5 characters to strName
```

The `ConvertString()` routine changes the variable `strName` to the string `"Microsoft"`. By doing so, it overwrites five characters somewhere in memory and possibly corrupts another memory location. This is one of the most common causes of fatal application errors. To avoid this type of thing from happening, you must find out the largest string that could be put into the parameter and declare your string to that size prior to calling the routine. For example, if the `ConvertString()` routine can return a 100-byte string, you would perform the following:

```
strName = Space$(100)     ' Create a 100 byte string
ConvertString(strName)
```

By preallocating the space, you ensure that C will not overwrite any other memory area except what is used by this string.

The *SendMessage* API Function

The first example of a Windows API call you'll learn about involves the `SendMessage()` API. This is a very versatile API function, and you'll probably use it more than any other function. `SendMessage()` is used to tell a specific control to perform some operation on itself. You do this by sending a message through Windows to the window you're interested in controlling. The message is received by the control like an event in Visual Basic. The control then responds to this message and performs the appropriate action. Let's look at several examples of using the `SendMessage()` API.

Finding a String in a List Box

If you have a large amount of items in a list or combo box and you want to find a certain string contained in that list, you would normally have to loop through each item, comparing each item to the string you want to find. This process can take quite a while, especially if the list is very large. Using `SendMessage()`, you don't have to write a loop; instead, you can have the list box use some built-in routines to perform the searching for you.

Example's Filename: ApiFind.frm

In the example shown in Figure 28.2, you can search for a state code in a list box full of state codes. Click the Search button to invoke the `Click` event. Here's the code:

```
Private Sub cmdSearch_Click()
   Dim strSearch As String
   Dim lngPos As Long

   strSearch = InputBox$("Enter String To Find:", "Search")

   With lstStates
      If strSearch = "" Then
         .ListIndex = 0
      Else
         lngPos = SendMessage(.hwnd, _
                              LB_FINDSTRING, _
                              -1, _
                              ByVal strSearch)
         If lngPos >= 0 Then
            .ListIndex = lngPos
         End If
      End If
   End With
End Sub
```

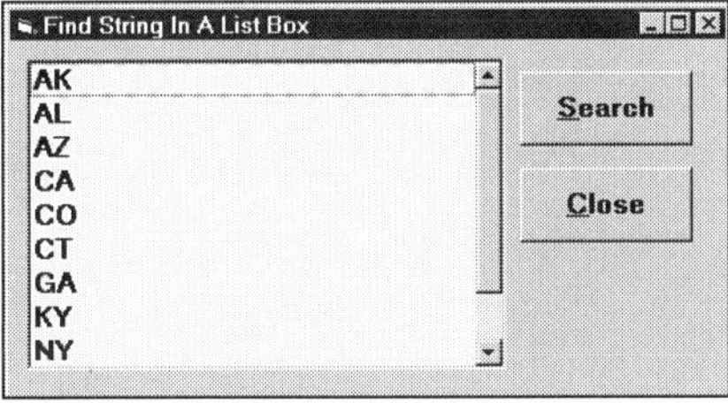

FIGURE 28.2 Finding a string in a list box using `SendMessage()`.

The `SendMessage()` API always expects a handle to a window as the first parameter. A handle is a long integer that uniquely identifies a window within the Windows environment. Almost every control you use with Visual Basic is a window, and these controls have an `hWnd` (handle to a window) property you can use for this parameter. The next parameter is the specific message you want to send to the control. In this case, it's a constant value that you'll also retrieve from the API Text Viewer.

The constant will differ depending on the control to which you're sending the message and what you want that control to do. The last two parameters will also differ depending on the control and the specific message you're sending. In this case, the `-1` value tells the list box to begin `LB_FINDSTRING` at the beginning of the list. The last parameter tells the list box what to find. This string parameter must be prefaced by the `ByVal` keyword.

You can also use very similar code to search for a value in a combo box. However, the second parameter would be `CB_FINDSTRING` instead of `LB_FINDSTRING`.

If you were to write your own searching routine in Visual Basic, it would look like the following:

```
Sub ListSearch (ctrName As Control, strFindStr As String)
   'Search For String
   Dim intLoop As Integer
   Dim strValue As String

   For intLoop = 0 To ctrName.ListCount - 1
      strValue = ctrName.List(intLoop)
      If Trim$(UCase$(strValue)) = _
         Trim$(UCase$(strFindStr)) Then
         ctrName.ListIndex = intLoop
         intLoop = ctrName.ListCount     ' Force Exit From Loop
      Else
         ctrName.ListIndex = -1
      End If
   Next intLoop
End Sub
```

TIP

It's much more efficient to use the `SendMessage()` API to search for a value in a list box than to write your own code in Visual Basic.

Tab Stops in a List Box

The standard list box that comes with Visual Basic does not have a property that allows you to create columns in the list box. However, using the Windows API call `SendMessage()`, you can add tab stops to a list box. This comes in really handy when you're using a proportional font that would otherwise make it impossible to line up columns of data.

Example's Filename: ApiTab.frm

In the example shown in Figure 28.3, one tab stop is defined. The left edge of the list box is not considered a tab. Where the state name begins is where the first tab stop is located. To create a tab stop, you'll once again call the `SendMessage()` function:

```
Private Sub Form_Load()
   Dim lngRet As Long

   lngRet = SendMessage(lstStates.hwnd, _
                        LB_SETTABSTOPS, _
                        1, _
                        40&)

   Call StateLoad
End Sub
```

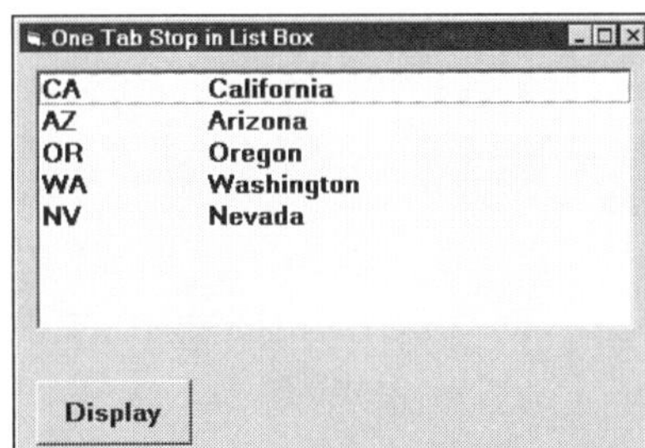

FIGURE 28.3
A single tab stop in a list box.

The `SendMessage()` function once again receives a window handle from the list box. Next, it needs to be passed the constant `LB_SETTABSTOPS` to tell the list box to set one or more tab stops. The third parameter is the number of tab stops you want (in this case, one). Finally, you pass the location for the tab stop.

This is where things get a little more complicated. The fourth parameter, this time, uses a unit of measure called *dialog units*. A dialog unit is the average character width for a given font. To calculate where this will place the tab stop, you can generally divide this number by four. Therefore, the number 40 gives you about 10 average character widths from the left. If you look closely, this just about matches up to the example shown in Figure 28.3.

When you're loading the list box, you simply need to separate each column in the list box with a tab (`vbTab`) character. Therefore, the routine to load the states into the list box looks like this:

```
Private Sub StateLoad()
   With lstStates
      .AddItem "CA" & vbTab & "California"
      .AddItem "AZ" & vbTab & "Arizona"
      .AddItem "OR" & vbTab & "Oregon"
      .AddItem "WA" & vbTab & "Washington"
      .AddItem "NV" & vbTab & "Nevada"
   End With
End Sub
```

Using the `vbTab` constant tells the list box that the text will be placed after the first tab stop. The `vbTab` constant evaluates to `Chr$(9)`.

When you select an item from a list box that contains tabs, you'll retrieve the data with the tab contained in the text field. This means that if you want to get the data in a particular column, you'll need to parse out the tabs to get to the particular data you want. Figure 28.4 shows what the data might look like when it's returned from the `Text` property of the list box.

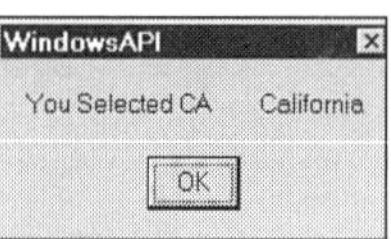

FIGURE 28.4 Data returned from a tabbed list box.

Multiple Tab Stops

Sometimes you may want to have multiple columns of data, similar to a grid control. You can create multiple tab stops in a list box using the same `SendMessage()` function. In Figure 28.5, three tab stops are created in the list box.

Example's Filename: ApiTabs.frm

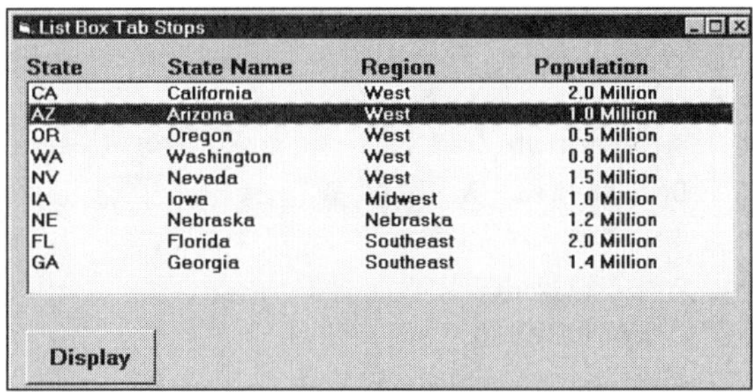

FIGURE 28.5 Multiple tab stops in a list box.

To create multiple tab stops for a list box, you use an array of `Long` data types as the fourth parameter to the `SendMessage()` function. Look at the following code for an example of creating multiple tab stops:

```
Private Sub Form_Load()
   Dim lngRet As Long
   Dim aTabs(2) As Long

   aTabs(0) = 48
   aTabs(1) = 116
   aTabs(2) = 186

   lngRet = SendMessage(lstStates.hwnd, _
                        LB_SETTABSTOPS, _
                        3, _
                        aTabs(0))

   Call StateLoad
End Sub
```

In this code, an array of three longs are created and then the appropriate dialog units are set into each element of the array. Next, `SendMessage()` is called with the third parameter, which is set to the number of tab stops (`3`). The fourth parameter is the first element of the array. The array is passed by reference to the C language routine. The first element is the address of where the array starts in memory. C can now just walk through all three elements by adding four bytes to the base address for each element in the array.

The code for loading the list box contains several tabs in the `AddItem` method. Here's the `StateLoad` procedure for loading the list box:

```
Private Sub StateLoad()
   With lstStates
      .AddItem "CA" & vbTab & _
               "California" & vbTab & _
               "West" & vbTab & _
               "2.0 Million"
      .AddItem "AZ" & vbTab & _
               "Arizona" & vbTab & _
               "West" & vbTab & _
               "1.0 Million"
      .AddItem "OR" & vbTab & _
               "Oregon" & vbTab & _
               "West" & vbTab & _
               "0.5 Million"
      .AddItem "WA" & vbTab & _
               "Washington" & vbTab & _
               "West" & vbTab & _
               "0.8 Million"
      .AddItem "NV" & vbTab & _
               "Nevada" & vbTab & _
               "West" & vbTab & _
               "1.5 Million"
      .AddItem "IA" & vbTab & _
               "Iowa" & vbTab & _
               "Midwest" & vbTab & _
               "1.0 Million"
      .AddItem "NE" & vbTab & _
               "Nebraska" & vbTab & _
               "Nebraska" & vbTab & _
               "1.2 Million"
      .AddItem "FL" & vbTab & _
               "Florida" & vbTab & _
               "Southeast" & vbTab & _
               "2.0 Million"
      .AddItem "GA" & vbTab & _
               "Georgia" & vbTab & _
               "Southeast" & vbTab & _
               "1.4 Million"
```

```
    End With
End Sub
```

Limiting Characters in a Combo Box

If you have a combo box with the `Style` property set to `0 - Dropdown Combo`, you might want to limit the number of characters the user can type into the text box portion of the combo box. The combo box control does not have a `MaxLength` property like the text box control; therefore, you'll need to use the `SendMessage()` API call.

Example's Filename: ApiCombo.frm

In the example shown in Figure 28.6, you have a list of state codes in the combo box. You want to allow the users to enter additional state codes, so you need to limit them to two characters. The following code shows you the call you use to accomplish this:

```
Private Sub Form_Load()
    Dim lngRet As Long

    ' Limit the text portion of
    ' the combo box to 2 characters
    lngRet = SendMessage(cboStates.hwnd, _
                         CB_LIMITTEXT, _
                         2, _
                         0&)

    Call StateLoad
End Sub
```

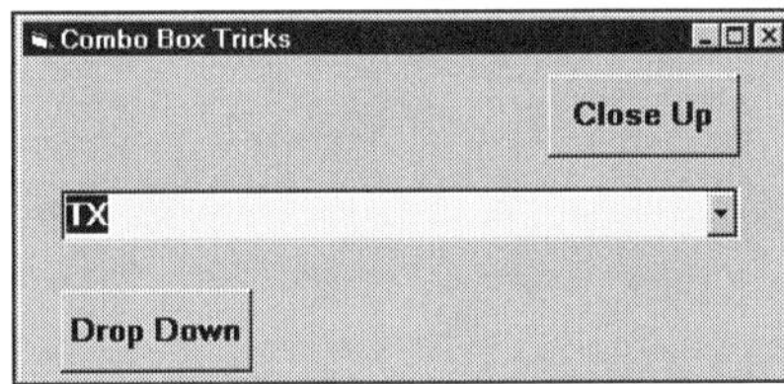

FIGURE 28.6
Limiting characters in a combo box.

The first parameter, as usual, is the window handle to the combo box. The second parameter is a constant value that tells the combo box which method it needs to invoke. In this case, it's the constant `CB_LIMITTEXT`. The third parameter specifies the number of characters to use as the limit for the text portion of the combo box. The fourth parameter is unused; therefore, a long zero (`0`) is passed. The `&` after the parameter informs Visual Basic to make this a long value when it's passed to the `SendMessage()` function.

Changing the List Portion of a Combo Box

A combo box is made up of a text box and a list box. The list portion drops down when the user clicks the down-arrow button on the right side of the combo box. Sometimes you might want to have the combo box list already "dropped down" when you open a form or when the user tabs to that control. This can also be accomplished with the `SendMessage()` function:

```
Private Sub cmdDrop_Click()
   Dim lngRet As Long

   ' Drop down the list portion
   ' of the combo box
   lngRet = SendMessage(cboStates.hwnd, _
                        CB_SHOWDROPDOWN, _
                        1, _
                        0&)

End Sub
```

The third parameter should be set to a nonzero value to make the combo box drop down its list. Similarly, you can close the list portion programmatically by passing a zero value as the third parameter:

```
Private Sub cmdCloseUp_Click()
   Dim lngRet As Long

   ' Close up the list portion
   ' of the combo box
   lngRet = SendMessage(cboStates.hwnd, _
                        CB_SHOWDROPDOWN, _
                        0, _
                        0&)
End Sub
```

The *GetDriveType* Function

If you're writing an application that pulls some of its data from a CD-ROM drive, you can ask the user to fill in the drive letter of the CD-ROM or you can potentially retrieve that information yourself using the `GetDriveType()` function. Of course, if the user has more than one CD-ROM drive, you have to ask which one contains the CD-ROM you're looking for. Alternatively, you could just go look for a certain file on each of the CD-ROM drives until you find the right one.

The `GetDriveType()` function returns a long value you use to compare against one of five constants to determine the type of the disk drive. Table 28.2 lists the constants and what each one means.

Table 28.2 Drive Type Constants

Constant	Description
DRIVE_REMOVABLE	The disk is removable media, such as a floppy disk drive.
DRIVE_FIXED	The disk is a hard disk on the machine.
DRIVE_NETWORK	The disk is a network or remote drive.
DRIVE_CD_ROM	The disk is a CD-ROM.
DRIVE_UNKNOWN	The disk type cannot be determined or is not present.

Example's Filename: ApiDrive.frm

In the sample form shown in Figure 28.7, a combo box is loaded with the letters A through Z. When you select one of the letters from the combo box, the `Click` event calls the `GetDriveType()` function to determine which type of disk drive the letter represents. Here's the code:

```
Private Sub cboDrive_Click()
    Dim lngType As Long

    ' Call the GetDriveType function
    ' to Retrieve the drive type
    lngType = GetDriveType(cboDrive.Text & ":\")
    Select Case lngType
        Case DRIVE_REMOVABLE
            txtDriveType = "Drive is Removable Media"
```

```
            Case DRIVE_FIXED
               txtDriveType = "Hard Disk Drive"
            Case DRIVE_REMOTE
               txtDriveType = "Network or Remote Drive"
            Case DRIVE_CD_ROM
               txtDriveType = "CD-ROM Drive"
            Case Else
               txtDriveType = "Unknown Type or Drive Does Not Exist"
         End Select
      End Sub
```

FIGURE 28.7 Retrieving the type of disk drive for any drive letter.

The `GetDriveType()` function expects you to pass a string value from A to Z with a colon (:) and backslash (\) added to it. This function returns a long value that represents the type of drive selected. The long value that's returned is then compared against the list of defined constants that determine the type of drive.

Retrieving System Resources

In most Windows applications, an About box is provided that describes the application. Sometimes the About box contains system information about the particular machine and the Windows environment. This system information may include the processor type, the total memory, and even the different types of memory available. Other times, the About box only describes the application, and a System Info command button is supplied. If this System Info command button is clicked, a separate utility is called to display the system information.

System Information Utility

The Microsoft System Information utility, shown in Figure 28.8, is a common file that's typically installed with the Microsoft Office applications. The name of this executable is MSINFO32.EXE; you can search your hard drive for this utility. You can write your application so that this utility is called from your own command button, or you can write the appropriate API calls to duplicate this information.

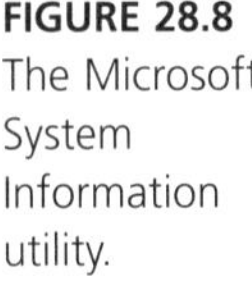

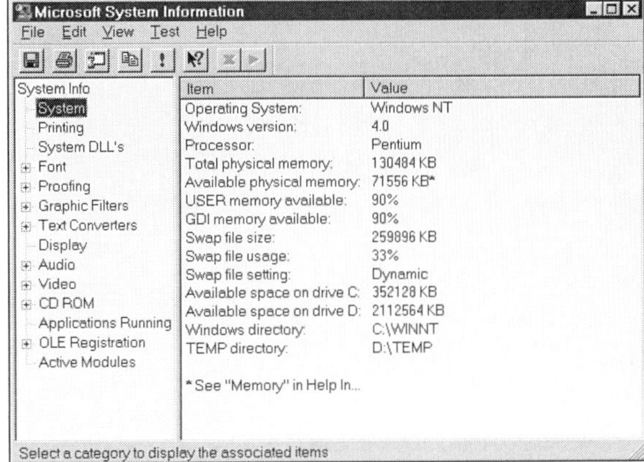

FIGURE 28.8
The Microsoft System Information utility.

The About Form

It's very easy to create your own custom About form to use in any application to display system information. Of course, you have to make about a half-dozen API calls, but it can be done. In fact, this presents an ideal situation where you can use a class module to wrap up all the API calls for retrieving system information. The About form shown in Figure 28.9 will give you an idea of the different types of system information you can retrieve via API calls.

Example's Filename: ApiAbout.frm

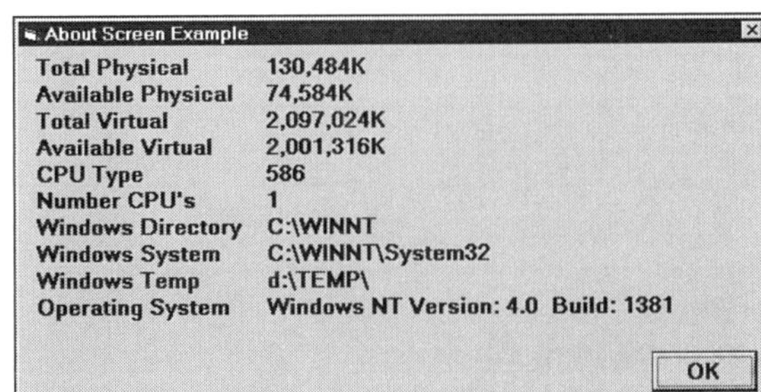

FIGURE 28.9
An About form showing system information.

The About form shown in Figure 28.9 has a private procedure called `SysInfoGet()` that displays all the information shown on the form. Here's the code:

```
Private Sub SysInfoGet()
    Dim oSysInfo As New clsSystemInfo
```

```
        With oSysInfo
            ' Get memory information.
            lblTotPhys = FormatK(.TotalPhysical)
            lblAvailPhys = FormatK(.AvailPhysical)
            lblTotVirtual = FormatK(.TotalVirtual)
            lblAvailVirtual = FormatK(.AvailVirtual)

            ' Get processor information.
            lblNumberOrfProcessors = .NumCPU
            lblCPUType = .CPUType

            ' Get path information.
            lblWindowsDir = .WinDir
            lblSystemDir = .WinSysDir
            lblTempDir = .WinTempDir

            ' Get OS Information
            lblOS = .OperatingSystem
        End With
    End Sub
```

As you can see, this code looks very simple. This is because all of the functionality is hidden in a class module called `clsSystemInfo`. This class module retrieves the system information in each call to each property. Also, note the function called `FormatK()`. This function formats the total amount of memory into a value expressed in kilobytes (1,024 bytes):

```
Private Function FormatK(ByVal lngValue As Long) As String
    FormatK = Format(Fix(lngValue / 1024), _
                     "###,###") & "K"
End Function
```

Now, let's take a look at the System Information class.

The System Information Class

Instead of coding all these Windows API calls in the front-end application, you can encapsulate these calls in a class. The `clsSystemInfo` class has many declarations of Windows API calls, user-defined types, and constants that are used to fill in all the properties of the class. Here's the code:

```
Private  Declare Function GetWindowsDirectory Lib "kernel32" _
         Alias "GetWindowsDirectoryA" (ByVal lpBuffer As String, _
         ByVal nSize As Long) As Long
Private  Declare Function GetSystemDirectory Lib "kernel32" _
         Alias "GetSystemDirectoryA" (ByVal lpBuffer As String, _
         ByVal nSize As Long) As Long
Private  Declare Function GetVersionEx Lib "kernel32" _
         Alias "GetVersionExA" (lpVersionInformation As OSVERSION
➥INFO) As Long
Private  Declare Function GetTempPath Lib "kernel32" _
         Alias "GetTempPathA" (ByVal nBufferLength As Long, _
         ByVal lpBuffer As String) As Long
Private Declare Sub GetSystemInfo Lib "kernel32" (lpSystemInfo As
➥SYSTEM_INFO)
Private Declare Sub GlobalMemoryStatus Lib "kernel32" (lpBuffer As
➥MEMORYSTATUS)

Private Type MEMORYSTATUS
   dwLength As Long
   dwMemoryLoad As Long
   dwTotalPhys As Long
   dwAvailPhys As Long
   dwTotalPageFile As Long
   dwAvailPageFile As Long
   dwTotalVirtual As Long
   dwAvailVirtual As Long
End Type

Private Type OSVERSIONINFO
   dwOSVersionInfoSize As Long
   dwMajorVersion As Long
   dwMinorVersion As Long
   dwBuildNumber As Long
   dwPlatformId As Long
   strReserved As String * 128
End Type

Private Type SYSTEM_INFO
   dwOemID As Long
   dwPageSize As Long
```

```
    lpMinimumApplicationAddress As Long
    lpMaximumApplicationAddress As Long
    dwActiveProcessorMask As Long
    dwNumberOfProcessors As Long
    dwProcessorType As Long
    dwAllocationGranularity As Long
    dwReserved As Long
End Type

Private Const VER_PLATFORM_WIN32_NT = 2
Private Const VER_PLATFORM_WIN32_WINDOWS = 1

' Number of seconds between
' refresh of system information
Const MAX_INTERVAL As Integer = 30
' Max buffer size for Path information
Const MAX_PATH As Integer = 255

' Keeps track of the number of
' seconds elapsed since the
' last access of the properties
' in this class
Dim mdblTimer As Double

' Application Information
Private mstrExeName As String
Private mstrAppName As String

' Windows Directory Information
Private mstrWinDir As String
Private mstrWinSysDir As String
Private mstrWinTempDir As String

' Operating System
Private mstrOS As String
Private mlngMemoryLoad As Long
Private mlngTotalPhysical As Long
Private mlngAvailPhysical As Long
Private mlngTotalVirtual As Long
```

```
Private mlngAvailVirtual As Long
Private mlngCPUType As Long
Private mlngNumCPU As Long
```

This code retrieves three types of information for filling in the properties of the System Information class—the operating system information, the memory and system information, and the Windows directory information. In each of the `Property Get` procedures of this class, you'll find a call to a private method that's responsible for filling in all the properties.

Retrieving the Operating System Version

The `OperatingSystem` property makes a call to a private method called `OSystemGet()`:

```
Property Get OperatingSystem() As String

   Call OSystemGet
   OperatingSystem = mstrOS

End Property
```

The `OSystemGet()` method fills in the module level variable `mstrOS`.

The *OSystemGet()* Method

To retrieve the name of the operating system your application is currently running on, you use the `GetVersionEx()` Windows API call. This function call fills in the `OSVERSIONINFO` user-defined type:

```
Private Sub OSystemGet()
   Dim typOS As OSVERSIONINFO
   Dim lngWord As Long

   typOS.dwOSVersionInfoSize = 148
   lngWord = GetVersionEx(typOS)

   If typOS.dwPlatformId = VER_PLATFORM_WIN32_WINDOWS Then
      mstrOS = "Windows 95/98"
   ElseIf typOS.dwPlatformId = VER_PLATFORM_WIN32_NT Then
      mstrOS = "Windows NT"
   End If
```

```
    ' Get Version Information
    mstrOS = mstrOS & " Version: " & _
                      typOS.dwMajorVersion & "." & _
                      typOS.dwMinorVersion & _
                      "  Build: " & _
                      (typOS.dwBuildNumber And &HFFFF&)

End Sub
```

Not only can you retrieve the version of the operating system your application is running on, but you can also retrieve the version number, the build number, and the platform ID.

Memory and CPU Properties

To retrieve memory and CPU information, you need to make two different API calls. These calls are in the `GetSysInfo()` method. Each `Property Get` procedure calls the `GetSysInfo()` method. Here's the code:

```
Public Property Get TotalPhysical() As Long
   Call GetSysInfo
   TotalPhysical = mlngTotalPhysical
End Property

Public Property Get TotalVirtual() As Long
   Call GetSysInfo
   TotalVirtual = mlngTotalVirtual
End Property

Public Property Get AvailVirtual() As Long
   Call GetSysInfo
   AvailVirtual = mlngAvailVirtual
End Property

Public Property Get AvailPhysical() As Long
   Call GetSysInfo
   AvailPhysical = mlngAvailPhysical
End Property

Public Property Get CPUType() As Long
   Call GetSysInfo
```

```
    CPUType = mlngCPUType
End Property

Public Property Get NumCPU() As Long
    Call GetSysInfo
    NumCPU = mlngNumCPU
End Property
```

The *GetSysInfo()* Method

To retrieve all the memory and system information, you need to make two different Windows API calls. Both calls rely on user-defined types that are passed in by reference and are returned with system information. The two calls are `GlobalMemoryStatus()` and `GetSystemInfo()`:

```
Private Sub GetSysInfo()
    Dim typMS As MEMORYSTATUS
    Dim typSI As SYSTEM_INFO

    ' If the current system information is not current,
    ' requery the system for it.
    If Not IsInfoCurrent() Then
        ' Get the global memory status information.
        typMS.dwLength = Len(typMS)
        Call GlobalMemoryStatus(typMS)
        mlngMemoryLoad = typMS.dwMemoryLoad
        mlngTotalPhysical = typMS.dwTotalPhys
        mlngAvailPhysical = typMS.dwAvailPhys
        mlngTotalVirtual = typMS.dwTotalVirtual
        mlngAvailVirtual = typMS.dwAvailVirtual

        ' Get the system information.
        Call GetSystemInfo(typSI)
        mlngNumCPU = typSI.dwNumberOrfProcessors
        mlngCPUType = typSI.dwProcessorType

        ' Get Windows Directory Information
        Call WinDirInfo
```

```
        ' Get Operating System
        Call OSystemGet
    End If
End Sub
```

The MEMORYSTATUS user-defined type is passed to the GlobalMemoryStatus() function and filled in with memory information. The SYSTEM_INFO user-defined type is passed to the GetSystemInfo() function to retrieve information on the number of processors and processor types.

The Windows Directory Properties

You can also retrieve the directory where Windows is installed as well as the Windows\System directory and the directory to which your TEMP variable is set. Three properties call the WinDirInfo() method to get this information. You can use these properties, for example, to find a particular DLL that you know must reside in the Windows or Windows\System directory. Also, you might need to create a temporary file for your application, and the best place to create this file is where the user has set the location of his or her Temp directory. Here's the code:

```
Public Property Get WinDir() As String
    Call WinDirInfo
    WinDir = mstrWinDir
End Property

Public Property Get WinSysDir() As String
    Call WinDirInfo
    WinSysDir = mstrWinSysDir
End Property

Public Property Get WinTempDir() As String
    Call WinDirInfo
    WinTempDir = mstrWinTempDir
End Property
```

Notice that the WinDirInfo() method is called in each of the Property Get procedures. This ensures that the information is up-to-date when it's retrieved. However, in the WinDirInfo() method, you can see that the actual routines are only called once. Because this information does not change, there's no need to keep making these Windows API calls.

The Windows Directory Information

Information for the Windows directory, the Windows\System directory, and the temporary directory is retrieved via the `GetWindowsDirectory()`, `GetWindowsSystemDirectory()`, and `GetTempPath()` API calls, respectively. A method named `WinDirInfo()` is created to retrieve this information and fill in the properties of the system information class. Here's the code:

```
Private Sub WinDirInfo()
    Dim strBuffer As String
    Dim lngLen As Long

    If mstrWinDir = "" Then
        ' Get the path information (windows, system, and temp).
        strBuffer = Space(MAX_PATH)
        lngLen = GetWindowsDirectory(strBuffer, MAX_PATH)
        mstrWinDir = Left(strBuffer, lngLen)

        strBuffer = Space(MAX_PATH)
        lngLen = GetSystemDirectory(strBuffer, MAX_PATH)
        mstrWinSysDir = Left(strBuffer, lngLen)

        strBuffer = Space(MAX_PATH)
        lngLen = GetTempPath(MAX_PATH, strBuffer)
        mstrWinTempDir = Left(strBuffer, lngLen)
    End If
End Sub
```

Summary

In this chapter, you learned how to use the `Declare` statement to tell Visual Basic that you'll be using a function contained in an external DLL. Using the Windows API, you can perform many tricks with list boxes and combo boxes. You can also retrieve system information about your operating system. These Windows API functions are very powerful and can make your applications do many things that you would normally have to buy third-party tools for. This alone can be worth the investment of your time in understanding and using these Windows API calls.

Review Questions

1. Which function can be used to search for a string in a combo or list box?
2. Which DLL contains the function to determine the Windows platform you're running on?
3. Which function returns the Windows\System directory?

Exercises

1. Create a tabbed list box that displays an employee's first name and last name.
2. Create a routine that searches for an entry in a combo box.
3. Create a routine that identifies all the disk drive types on your system and fills a list box with this information.

29

Storing User Information

IN JUST ABOUT EVERY APPLICATION I'VE EVER developed, I've had to store information about the "state" of the application when the user closes it. Then I have to restore that information the next time the user comes back in. Over the years, there have been many techniques I've used to store this information. Sometimes the information has been stored in tables in a database, sometimes in an `INI` file, and sometimes in the system Registry. Many people say not to use `INI` files anymore because they're passe. Well, I think you need to use whatever mechanism works for you. In this chapter, you'll learn to use both `INI` files and the system Registry. In fact, you'll build two identical class modules using both these methods so that you can switch back and forth between them at any time.

Chapter Objectives

- Learn to read and write `INI` files
- Create an `INI` class
- Learn about the system Registry
- Learn to use the Registry API calls
- Learn to use `GetSetting` and `SaveSetting`
- Create a Registry class

Sample Project File: \Chapter29\UserStorage.vbp

INI Files

An *INI file* is simply a text file with a predefined structure. The structure is very simple, so retrieving information from it is very easy. An INI file has one or more "sections" defined by square brackets (`[]`) around a user-defined name. Next, you'll see a defined key name, an equal sign (=), and then a value for that key. Here's an example:

```
; UserStorage.ini
[Database]
Path=D:\Database\
File=Employee.mdb
JetMDB=-1
OnServer=0
Version=1.1.1

[Env]
Toolbar=-1
StatusBar=0
Menus=-1
```

In this listing, `[Database]` is a section, `Path=` is a key name, and "D:\Database\" is the value for the `Path` key. To retrieve and write this information, you need to use some API calls. Let's look at each one, in turn, in the first example (see Figure 29.1).

Example's Filename: INI.frm

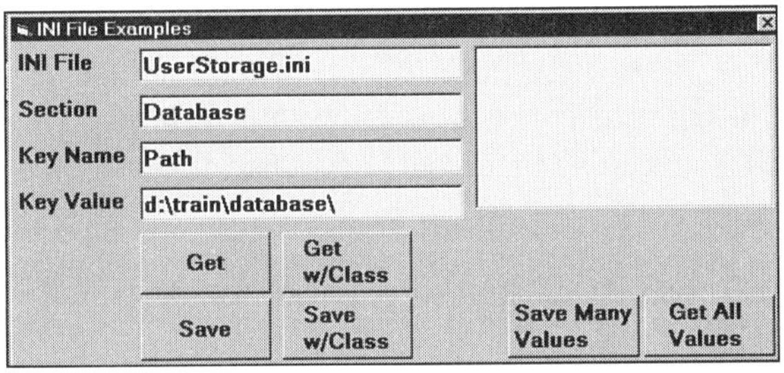

FIGURE 29.1
INI file examples.

GetPrivateProfileString

The first API call you'll use is `GetPrivateProfileString()`. This function retrieves a key value from a given section and key name. To use this function, you need to declare a buffer area to receive the value you're retrieving. Also, notice that you must assign the values of the text boxes to actual string variables, because you cannot pass the contents of a text box to a Windows API call. Here's an example using `GetPrivateProfileString()`:

```
Private Sub cmdGet_Click()
   Dim lngRet As Long
   Dim strIni As String
   Dim strSection As String
   Dim strKeyName As String
   Dim strKeyValue As String

   strIni = Trim$(txtConfig)
   strSection = Trim$(txtSection)
   strKeyName = Trim$(txtKeyName)

   strKeyValue = Space(255)
   lngRet = GetPrivateProfileString( _
                     strSection, _
                     strKeyName, _
                     "", _
                     strKeyValue, _
                     Len(strKeyValue), _
                     strIni)

   txtKeyValue = Left$(strKeyValue, lngRet)
End Sub
```

The INI filename is passed as the last parameter to the function. This must be a fully qualified path and filename, or the INI file must reside in the Windows directory. The `GetPrivateProfileString()` function returns the length of the data it finds. Therefore, you need to use the `Left$()` function to chop off the rest of the spaces after the data.

WritePrivateProfileString

If you need to write data into an INI file, you can call the `WritePrivateProfileString()` function. Once again, you need to store the contents of the text boxes into string variables and then pass those values to the `WritePrivateProfileString()` function. Here's the code:

```
Private Sub cmdSave_Click()
   Dim lngRet As Long
   Dim strIni As String
   Dim strSection As String
   Dim strKeyName As String
   Dim strKeyValue As String

   strIni = Trim$(txtConfig)
   strSection = Trim$(txtSection)
   strKeyName = Trim$(txtKeyName)
   strKeyValue = Trim$(txtKeyValue)

   lngRet = WritePrivateProfileString( _
                      strSection, _
                      strKeyName, _
                      strKeyValue, _
                      strIni)

End Sub
```

Retrieving All Settings

You can also retrieve all key names and values under a given section with the API call `GetPrivateProfileSection()`. You'll use this API call after you've wrapped the INI file information into a class module, later in this chapter.

INI Class

Let's now build a class module that makes using the API calls easier. As you saw in the previous examples, when you're storing or retrieving data from the same section, you have to repeat the INI filename and section name as well as reallocate the buffer space every time. This can be quite a bit of work. Instead, let's wrap up this functionality in a class.

Example's Filename: INI.cls

Properties of the *INI* Class

Table 29.1 shows you the public properties of this `INI` class as well as the private variable each property relates to inside of the class.

Table 29.1 Properties of the *INI* Class

Public Property	Private Variable	Description
`ConfigName`	`mstrConfigName`	The name of the `INI` file
`SectionName`	`mstrSection`	The name of the section to retrieve data from or set data to
`KeyName`	`mstrKeyName`	The name of the key to read from or write to
`KeyValue`	`mstrKeyValue`	The value to write to the `INI` file

Public Methods of the *INI* Class

Besides the properties of the `INI` class, you have methods that allow you to read and write to the `INI` file. Table 29.2 lists each of the method names and provides a description of each.

Table 29.2 Methods of the *INI* Class

Method Name	Description
`KeyGet`	Retrieves information from the `INI` file and returns it as a string value
`KeySave`	Saves information back to the `INI` file

continues

Table 29.2 Continued

Method Name	Description
`Exists`	Returns a `True` value if the key name exists underneath a specified section
`SectionGet`	Retrieves all the key names and key values from a specified section and returns them in a `Variant` array

Class Initialization

When you create an instance of the `INI` class, the `Class_Initialize()` event automatically sets the `ConfigName` property to the name of the EXE file for your project. For example, if your project name is *Emps*, the INI name will be *Emps.ini*. `Class_Initialize()` looks for the INI file in the same directory where the EXE is located. This avoids you having to pass in the INI filename to the class. Of course, you can always pass this information in if you want to store the INI file in another location. Here's the `Class_Initialize()` event for the `INI` class:

```
Private Sub Class_Initialize()
   mstrConfigName = App.Path & "\" & _
                    App.EXEName & ".ini"
End Sub
```

Using the *INI* Class to Get Data

If you click the Get W/Class command button in the sample form, you'll see that information can be retrieved from the `INI` file. The `Click` event for this command button instantiates an instance of the `INI` class. Set the values from the text boxes and then invoke the `KeyGet()` method to retrieve the data. Here's the code:

```
Private Sub cmdGetClass_Click()
   Dim oIni As INI

   Set oIni = New INI
   With oIni
      .ConfigName = Trim$(txtConfig)
      .Section = Trim$(txtSection)
      .KeyName = Trim$(txtKeyName)
      txtKeyValue = .KeyGet
   End With
```

```
    '***************************************
    '* Alternate Method
    '***************************************
    'With oIni
    '    txtKeyValue = .KeyGet(txtSection, _
                               txtKeyName, _
                               "")
    'End With

    Set oIni = Nothing
End Sub
```

Notice that at the end of this routine I have commented out an alternate way to get data—by passing all the relevant information directly to the `KeyGet()` method.

The *KeyGet()* Method in the *INI* Class

The `KeyGet()` method in the `INI` class accepts optional arguments for the section name, the key name, and the default value (in case you don't find the value you're after). Notice that each of the optional arguments has a default value. You can check each of the arguments against their default values to see whether any have been passed into the method. If any have been passed in, you override the module-level variable that corresponds to the argument. After all the module-level variables are set, you fill the `mstrKeyValue` variable to contain 255 spaces. You then call the `GetPrivateProfileString()` function to retrieve the information from the INI file. Here's the code:

```
Public Function KeyGet( _
                Optional strSection As String = "NA", _
                Optional strKeyName As String = "NA", _
                Optional strDefault As String = "") _
                As String
    Dim lngRet As Long

    ' Fill in properties
    If strSection <> "NA" Then
       mstrSection = strSection
    End If
    If strKeyName <> "NA" Then
       mstrKeyName = strKeyName
    End If
```

```
   mstrDefault = strDefault

   ' Get Value
   mstrKeyValue = Space(MAX_VALUE)
   lngRet = GetPrivateProfileString( _
                        mstrSection, _
                        mstrKeyName, _
                        mstrDefault, _
                        mstrKeyValue, _
                        MAX_VALUE, _
                        mstrConfigName)
   If lngRet > 0 Then
      mstrKeyValue = Left$(mstrKeyValue, lngRet)
   Else
      mstrKeyValue = ""
   End If

   KeyGet = mstrKeyValue
End Function
```

Using the *INI* Class to Save Data

If you fill in the Key Value text box with a different value and then click the Save W/Class command button in the sample form, you'll see that information can be saved back to the `INI` file. The `Click` event for this command button instantiates an instance of the `INI` class. Set the values from the text boxes and then invoke the `KeySave()` method to retrieve the data. Here's the code:

```
Private Sub cmdSaveClass_Click()
   Dim oIni As INI

   Set oIni = New INI
   With oIni
      .ConfigName = Trim$(txtConfig)
      .Section = Trim$(txtSection)
      .KeyName = Trim$(txtKeyName)
      .KeyValue = Trim$(txtKeyValue)
      .KeySave
   End With
```

```
    '***************************************
    '* Alternate Method
    '***************************************
    'With oIni
    '    .KeySave txtKeyValue, _
    '             txtSection, _
    '             txtKeyName
    'End With

    Set oIni = Nothing
End Sub
```

Notice that at the end of this routine I have commented out an alternate way to store data by passing all the relevant information directly to the `KeySave()` method.

Using the *INI* Class to Save Many Values

If you click the Save Many Values command button, you'll save many hard-coded values to the `INI` file under the section specified in the Section text box. Here's the code:

```
Private Sub cmdSaveMany_Click()
    Dim oIni As INI

    Set oIni = New INI
    With oIni
        .ConfigName = Trim$(txtConfig)
        .Section = Trim$(txtSection)
        .KeySave strKeyValue:="Employee.mdb", _
                 strKeyName:="File"
        .KeySave strKeyValue:="-1", _
                 strKeyName:="JetMDB"
        .KeySave strKeyValue:="0", _
                 strKeyName:="OnServer"
        .KeySave strKeyValue:="1.1.1", _
                 strKeyName:="Version"
    End With

    Set oIni = Nothing
End Sub
```

In this routine, you see a lot of calls to the `KeySave()` method. Also, notice the use of named arguments.

The *KeySave()* Method in the *INI* Class

The `KeySave()` method is very similar to the `KeyGet()` method in that it receives optional arguments and assigns them to the appropriate module-level variables. Then, the `WritePrivateProfileString()` function is called. Here's the code:

```
Public  Sub KeySave(Optional strKeyValue As String = "NA", _
                   Optional strSection As String = "NA", _
                   Optional strKeyName As String = "NA")
   Dim lngRet As Long

   ' Fill in properties
   If strSection <> "NA" Then
      mstrSection = strSection
   End If
   If strKeyName <> "NA" Then
      mstrKeyName = strKeyName
   End If
   If strKeyValue <> "NA" Then
      mstrKeyValue = strKeyValue
   End If

   lngRet = WritePrivateProfileString(mstrSection, _
                                      mstrKeyName, _
                                      mstrKeyValue, _
                                      mstrConfigName)
End Sub
```

Using the *INI* Class to Get a Section's Values

Sometimes you might want to retrieve all the key names and key values from one section in an `INI` file. In this case, you can call the `SectionGet()` method in the `INI` class to have it return a `Variant` array of all the `KeyName=KeyValue` pairs of data. Here's the code:

```
Private Sub cmdAllSettings_Click()
   Dim oIni As INI
   Dim astrKeys As Variant
   Dim intLoop As Integer
```

```
    Set oIni = New INI

    With oIni
        .ConfigName = Trim$(txtConfig)
        .Section = Trim$(txtSection)
        astrKeys = .SectionGet
    End With

    lstKeys.Clear
    For intLoop = 0 To UBound(astrKeys)
        lstKeys.AddItem astrKeys(intLoop)
    Next

    Set oIni = Nothing
End Sub
```

The *SectionGet()* Method in the *INI* Class

The `SectionGet()` method accepts an optional argument of which section to get keys from. Because you'll be retrieving many values, the `strBuffer` variable is filled with 2,048 spaces prior to the call to `GetPrivateProfileSection()`.

The value that's filled into the `strBuffer` variable is a `Chr(0)`-delimited string with all the `KeyName=KeyValue` pairs in between. Here's an example:

```
Path=D:\Train\Database¦File=Employees.mdb
```

The vertical bar (¦) in this line of code represents `Chr(0)`. Therefore, once you have this string in memory, you need to create a `Variant` array of each of the keyed pairs. You can do this with the new `Split()` function in Visual Basic 6. Pass the string and the delimiter to the `Split()` function, and it returns to you a `Variant` array. Each value in between the delimiters is an element of that array. Here's an example:

```
Public Function SectionGet( _
                Optional strSection As String = "") _
                As Variant
    Dim lngRet As Long
    Dim strBuffer As String

    If strSection <> "" Then
        mstrSection = strSection
    End If
```

```
        If mstrSection <> "" Then
            strBuffer = Space(2048)

            lngRet = GetPrivateProfileSection( _
                                 mstrSection, _
                                 strBuffer, _
                                 Len(strBuffer), _
                                 mstrConfigName)
            If lngRet > 0 Then
                strBuffer = Left$(strBuffer, lngRet)
                SectionGet = Split(strBuffer, Chr$(0))
            Else
                SectionGet = Array()
            End If
        End If
    End Function
```

Using this `INI` class should save you quite a bit of time, as opposed to using the Windows API calls. In addition, if you ever want to change how you get at the information, all you need to do is to change the internals of each of the methods. You don't need to change your front-end application at all.

The System Registry

The System Registry plays the same role as `INI` files—it stores application information. The Registry is a hierarchical database of information that's represented by root keys (sometimes called *hives*), keys, and subkeys. This is very similar to the directory structure that DOS uses.

The Registry holds a lot of information about your machine configuration and about most of the applications that have been installed on your computer. In Windows 3.1, very little information is stored in the Registry because most of the information is stored in `INI` files. In Windows 95, a combination of `INI` files and Registry entries are used. In Windows NT, almost all the information about the system is stored in the Registry. As you can see, as you move to the more robust operating systems, the Registry becomes increasingly important.

Table 29.3 shows the root keys in Windows NT 4.0. These root keys are very similar under Windows 95 and Windows 98.

Table 29.3 Root Keys in the Registry

Root Keys	Description
HKEY_CLASSES_ROOT	This key stores information about registered objects and classes on your system. The associations used in Windows Explorer are kept in this key.
HKEY_CURRENT_USER	This key relates to the current user who is logged into the machine. It stores information such as the printers connected to the machine, the network drives defined by the user, international settings, Control Panel settings, and even software installed for the current user only.
HKEY_LOCAL_MACHINE	This key is a very critical root key because it contains all the information about the hardware installed on the machine. If this information is inadvertently changed, it could cause the machine to stop working. All software information installed on this machine is also registered in this key.
HKEY_USERS	This key holds information about all users on the machine. It holds the default information for creating new users.
HKEY_CURRENT_CONFIG	This key stores general system configuration information about the current software and hardware installed on the system.
HKEY_DYN_DATA	This key holds data that changes as the system runs. None of the data in this key actually needs to be stored when the system shuts down, but it's used internally by other processes. This key is used to hold performance information about Windows.

To edit the System Registry, you can use a tool called the Registry Editor (REGEDIT.EXE). This tool is not installed under any program group; instead, it's an EXE file in your root Windows directory. You should create a shortcut to this tool so that you can use it to view and modify the Registry directly. Figure 29.2 shows what the Registry Editor looks like.

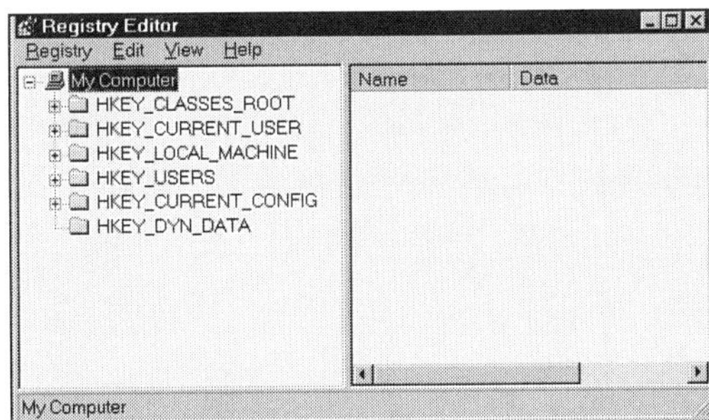

FIGURE 29.2
The Registry Editor.

Manipulating the Registry

You can use Windows API calls to manipulate the System Registry, or you can use built-in Visual Basic functions. Using API calls, you're allowed to manipulate any area of the Registry. However, you're only allowed to manipulate one area of the Registry when you use the built-in Visual Basic functions. Let's look at using the Windows API calls first.

Using Windows API calls, let's modify the only area in the Registry that can be modified by the built-in Visual Basic functions. This area is in `HKEY_CURRENT_USER\Software\VB and VBA Program Settings`. Here, you'll create one or many keys, as needed for each application. For example, the following code shows you a key called `\UserStorage`. Under this key is another key called `\Database`, with a key called `Path` and a value of "d:\train\database":

```
HKEY_CURRENT_USER
    \Software
        \VB and VBA Program Settings
            \UserStorage
                \Database
                    \Path=d:\train\database
```

Example's Filename: Registry.frm

If you click the Get command button shown in Figure 29.3, you'll run code that retrieves information from this area of the Registry. Of course, if you haven't saved anything to this key in the Registry, you won't receive any values back. When you run this example for the first time, click the Save command button to save data to the key first.

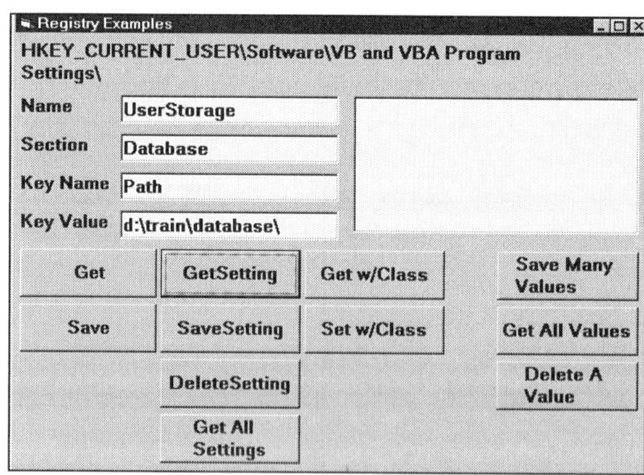

FIGURE 29.3 An application that reads from and writes to the Registry.

Retrieving Data Using API Calls

In the `Click` event of the cmdGet command button, you'll see a lot of code. Using the Windows API calls to manipulate the Registry is not a lot of fun because it takes a lot of work. Don't worry, though, because you'll learn to use the built-in Visual Basic functions to simplify this code quite a bit. You need to know how to use these API calls, however, because you might need to access another area of the Registry at some point. Here's the code:

```
Private Sub cmdReg_Click()
   Dim lngStatus As Long
   Dim lngKey As Long
   Dim strKey As String
   Dim bytBuf(MAX_BYTES) As Byte
   Dim lngType As Long
   Dim vntValue As Variant

   ' This is the key you wish to retrieve
   strKey = "Software" & _
            "\VB and VBA Program Settings" & _
            "\" & txtConfig & _
            "\" & txtSection

   ' Attempt to open the registry key.
   lngStatus = RegOpenKeyEx(ByVal HKEY_CURRENT_USER, _
                            ByVal strKey, _
                            ByVal 0, _
                            ByVal KEY_READ, _
                            lngKey)

   If lngStatus = ERROR_SUCCESS Then
      strKey = txtKeyName
      ' Now try to read the value
      lngStatus = RegQueryValueEx(ByVal lngKey, _
                                  ByVal strKey, _
                                  ByVal 0, _
                                  lngType, _
                                  bytBuf(0), _
                                  MAX_BYTES)
```

```
            ' If success, convert the byte array
            ' to a Unicode string.
            If lngStatus = ERROR_SUCCESS Then
               vntValue = bytBuf
               txtKeyValue = StrConv(vntValue, vbUnicode)
            Else
               txtKeyValue = "Error Reading Value"
            End If
         Else
            txtKeyValue = "Error Opening Key"
         End If
         ' Close the Key
         lngStatus = RegCloseKey(lngKey)

      End Sub
```

To begin using these Windows API calls, you need to create a string variable with the full key of where you want to get to in the Registry. You open this key using the `RegOpenKeyEx()` function. This function returns a status flag that indicates whether the key was opened successfully. It also fills in the `lngKey` variable by reference with a handle to the key.

Once the key is open, you can then retrieve a value from that key by using the key name in the `RegQueryValueEx()` function. Because all the data is stored in the Registry in ANSI character format, you need to pass in a `Byte` array and have the Registry functions fill it in. After the value is placed into the `Byte` array, you use the `StrConv()` function to convert the `Byte` array to a Visual Basic string. Finally, you must close the key using the `RegCloseKey()` function.

Saving Data Using API Calls

You'll now learn to save information to the Registry using the Windows API calls. You'll open a key in the same manner as you did for the `Get` routine. To save a value to a key, use the `RegSetValueEX()` function:

```
Private Sub cmdRegSet_Click()
   Dim lngStatus As Long
   Dim lngKey As Long
   Dim strKey As String
   Dim strValue As String
```

```
    ' This is the key you wish to set
    strKey = "Software" & _
             "\VB and VBA Program Settings" & _
             "\Invoice\DataSource"

    ' Attempt to open the registry key.
    lngStatus = RegOpenKeyEx(ByVal HKEY_CURRENT_USER, _
                             ByVal strKey, _
                             ByVal 0, _
                             ByVal KEY_ALL_ACCESS, _
                             lngKey)

    If lngStatus = ERROR_SUCCESS Then
       strKey = "DataLoc"
       strValue = txtValue
       lngStatus = RegSetValueEx(ByVal lngKey, _
                                 ByVal strKey, _
                                 ByVal 0, _
                                 ByVal REG_SZ, _
                                 ByVal strValue, _
                                 Len(strValue))
       If lngStatus <> ERROR_SUCCESS Then
          txtValue = "Error Setting Value"
       End If
    Else
       MsgBox "Error Opening Key"
    End If
    ' Close the Key
    lngStatus = RegCloseKey(lngKey)
End Sub
```

Saving information to the Registry is almost exactly the same as retrieving information from the Registry. You need to open a key, get a handle, and then use that handle with the `RegSetValueEX()` function. When you're done, you need to close the key so that resources are released.

Built-in Visual Basic Functions

Instead of using the Windows API calls, you can just use Visual Basic's built-in functions to manipulate the area in the Registry in the `HKEY_CURRENT_USER\Software\VB and VBA Program Settings` key:

```
HKEY_CURRENT_USER
    \Software
        \VB and VBA Program Settings
            \ConfigName
                \Section
                    \KeyName
```

The functions you'll use to manipulate this area of the Registry are `GetSetting`, `SaveSetting`, `DeleteSetting`, and `GetAllSettings`.

GetSetting

The `GetSetting()` function returns a single data value to you when you pass in the `ConfigName`, `Section`, and `KeyName` values for where you want to get the data. Look in the `Click` of the GetSetting command button to see the following code:

```
Private Sub cmdGetSetting_Click()

   txtKeyValue = GetSetting(txtConfig, _
                            txtSection, _
                            txtKeyName, _
                            "Can't Find Entry")
End Sub
```

The last parameter of the `GetSetting()` function is a default value in case the entry you're requesting can't be found.

SaveSetting

`SaveSetting` places a single data value in the Registry at the location specified by the `ConfigName`, `Section`, and `KeyName` values. Look at the code in the SaveSetting command button to see the following code:

```
Private Sub cmdSaveSetting_Click()

   SaveSetting txtConfig, _
               txtSection, _
```

```
                  txtKeyName, _
                  txtKeyValue
End Sub
```

DeleteSetting

You can delete a single key value using the `DeleteSetting` statement. Look at the code in the DeleteSetting command button to see the following code:

```
Private Sub cmdDeleteSetting_Click()
   DeleteSetting txtConfig, _
                 txtSection, _
                 txtKeyName
End Sub
```

GetAllSettings

You can retrieve all the settings in a particular section using the `GetAllSettings()` function. This function returns a `Variant` array if any values are returned. Look in the GetAllSettings command button to see the following code:

```
Private Sub cmdGetAllSettings_Click()
   Dim astrKeys As Variant
   Dim intLoop As Integer

   astrKeys = GetAllSettings(txtConfig, _
                             txtSection)
   lstKeys.Clear
   If Not IsEmpty(astrKeys) Then
      For intLoop = LBound(astrKeys) To UBound(astrKeys)
         lstKeys.AddItem astrKeys(intLoop, 0) & _
                    "=" & astrKeys(intLoop, 1)
      Next
   End If
End Sub
```

In the `Click` event of this command button, the `GetAllSettings()` function is called. It returns a `Variant` array to the `astrKeys` variable. This function checks to see whether the array is empty. If it's not empty, the function loops from the lower bound of the array to the upper bound. Each time through the loop, it retrieves the key name from element 0 of this two-dimensional array and the key value from element 1 of this array.

The *Registry* Class

Let's now wrap up the built-in Visual Basic functions in a class named `Registry` so that you don't need to repeat the `ConfigName` and `SectionName` values every time you want to retrieve a different key under the same area.

Example's Filename: Registry.cls

Properties of the *Registry* Class

Table 29.4 shows a list of each of the public properties this class exposes. It also shows you a reference to the internal variables used in the Registry.cls file. Notice that the property names are exactly the same as those for the INI class.

Table 29.4 Properties of the *Registry* Class

Public Name	Private Variable	Description
`ConfigName`	`mstrConfig`	Used to set the configuration name under the VB and VBA Program Settings key
`Section`	`mstrSection`	The section name that will be stored as a part of the configuration
`KeyName`	`mstrKeyName`	The key under the section
`KeyValue`	`mstrKeyValue`	The value to assign to this key name

Public Methods of the *Registry* Class

The method names of the `Registry` class are exactly the same as the methods for the `INI` class. This is so you can switch between the `INI` and `Registry` classes very easily. All you need to do is change the class name from `INI` to `Registry`. Table 29.5 lists the methods and a brief description of each.

Table 29.5 Methods of the *Registry* Class

Method Name	Description
`KeyGet`	Retrieves information from the Registry and returns it as a string value
`KeySave`	Saves information back to the Registry

Method Name	Description
`Exists`	Returns a `True` value if the key name exists underneath a specified section
`SectionGet`	Retrieves all the key names and key values from a specified section and returns them in a `Variant` array
`Delete`	Deletes a specified key name in the Registry along with its value

Class Initialization

When you create an instance of the `Registry` class, the `Class_Initialize()` event automatically sets the `ConfigName` property to the name of the EXE file for your project. If your project name is *Emps*, the entry in the Registry will be `Emps`. This avoids you having to pass in this information to the class. Here's the `Class_Initialize()` event for the `Registry` class:

```
Private Sub Class_Initialize()
   mstrConfigName = App.EXEName
End Sub
```

Using the *Registry* Class to Get Data

If you click the Get W/Class command button in the sample form, you'll see that information can be retrieved from the Registry. The `Click` event for this command button instantiates an instance of the `Registry` class. Set the values from the text boxes and then invoke the `KeyGet()` method to retrieve the data:

```
Private Sub cmdRegClassGet_Click()
   Dim oReg As Registry

   Set oReg = New Registry
   With oReg
      .ConfigName = txtConfig
      .Section = txtSection
      .KeyName = txtKeyName
      txtKeyValue = .KeyGet
   End With

   '****************************************
   '* Alternate Method
   '****************************************
```

```
   'With oReg
   '   txtKeyValue = .KeyGet(txtSection, _
                             txtKeyName, _
                             "")
   'End With

   Set oReg = Nothing
End Sub
```

Notice that at the end of this routine I have commented out an alternate way to get data—by passing all the relevant information directly to the `KeyGet()` method.

This code should look very familiar to you—it's exactly the same as the code in the INI example, except for the name of the class.

The *KeyGet()* Method of the *Registry* Class

The `KeyGet()` method in the `Registry` class accepts optional arguments for the section name, the key name, and the default value (in case you don't find the value you're after). Notice that each of the optional arguments has a default value. You can check each of the arguments against their default values to see whether any have been passed into the method. If any have been passed in, you need to override the module-level variable that corresponds to the argument. After all the module-level variables are set, you then call the `GetSetting()` method to return the data value back to the `mstrKeyValue` variable. Here's the code:

```
Public Function KeyGet( _
                Optional strSection As String = "NA", _
                Optional strKeyName As String = "NA", _
                Optional strDefault As String = "") _
                As String

   ' Fill in properties
   If strSection <> "NA" Then
      mstrSection = strSection
   End If
   If strKeyName <> "NA" Then
      mstrKeyName = strKeyName
   End If
   mstrDefault = strDefault
```

```
   ' Get Value From Registry
   mstrKeyValue = GetSetting(mstrConfigName, _
                             mstrSection, _
                             mstrKeyName, _
                             strDefault)

   KeyGet = mstrKeyValue
End Function
```

Using the *Registry* Class to Save Data

When you fill in the Key Value text box with a different value and then click the Save W/Class command button in the sample form, you save the data back to the Registry. The `Click` event for this command button instantiates an instance of the `Registry` class. Set the values from the text boxes and then invoke the `KeySave()` method to retrieve the data:

```
Private Sub cmdRegClassSet_Click()
   Dim oReg As Registry

   Set oReg = New Registry
   With oReg
      .ConfigName = txtConfig
      .Section = txtSection
      .KeyName = txtKeyName
      .KeyValue = Trim$(txtKeyValue)
      .KeySave
   End With

   '****************************************
   '* Alternate Method
   '****************************************
   'With oReg
   '   .KeySave txtKeyValue, _
   '            txtSection, _
   '            txtKeyName
   'End With

   Set oReg = Nothing
End Sub
```

Notice that at the end of this routine I have commented out an alternate way to store data—by passing all the relevant information directly to the `KeySave()` method.

Using the *Registry* Class to Save Many Values

If you click the Save Many Values command button, you'll save many hard-coded values to the Registry under the section specified in the Section text box. Here's the code:

```
Private Sub cmdSetMany_Click()
   Dim oReg As Registry

   Set oReg = New Registry
   With oReg
      .ConfigName = txtConfig
      .Section = txtSection
      .KeySave strKeyValue:="Employee.mdb", _
               strKeyName:="File"
      .KeySave strKeyValue:="-1", _
               strKeyName:="JetMDB"
      .KeySave strKeyValue:="0", _
               strKeyName:="OnServer"
      .KeySave strKeyValue:="1.1.1", _
               strKeyName:="Version"
   End With

   Set oReg = Nothing
End Sub
```

In this routine, you see a lot of calls to the `KeySave()` method. Also, notice the use of named arguments.

The *KeySave()* Method of the *Registry* Class

The `KeySave()` method is very similar to the `KeyGet()` method in that it receives optional arguments and assigns them to the appropriate module-level variables. Then, the `SaveSetting` statement is called to write the information. Here's the code:

```
Public Sub KeySave( _
          Optional strKeyValue As String = "NA", _
```

```
        Optional strSection As String = "NA", _
        Optional strKeyName As String = "NA")

   ' Fill in properties
   If strSection <> "NA" Then
      mstrSection = strSection
   End If
   If strKeyName <> "NA" Then
      mstrKeyName = strKeyName
   End If
   If strKeyValue <> "NA" Then
      mstrKeyValue = strKeyValue
   End If

   SaveSetting mstrConfigName, _
               mstrSection, _
               mstrKeyName, _
               mstrKeyValue
End Sub
```

Using the *Registry* Class to Get a Section's Values

Sometimes you might want to retrieve all the key names and key values from one section in the Registry. You can call the `SectionGet()` method in the `Registry` class to have it return a `String` array of all the `KeyName=KeyValue` pairs of data. If you click the Get All Values command button on the sample form, you'll see the `SectionGet()` method in use:

```
Private Sub cmdGetSection_Click()
   Dim oReg As Registry
   Dim astrKeys()As Variant
   Dim intLoop As Integer

   Set oReg = New Registry

   With oReg
      .ConfigName = txtConfig
      .Section = txtSection
      astrKeys = .SectionGet
   End With
```

```
      lstKeys.Clear
      For intLoop = LBound(astrKeys) To UBound(astrKeys)
         lstKeys.AddItem astrKeys(intLoop)
      Next

      Set oReg = Nothing
   End Sub
```

In this code, you need to declare an array of variants. The `ConfigName` and `Section` properties of the `Registry` class are then filled in. When the `SectionGet()` method is called, it returns a `Variant` array of strings. The code then loops through this array and loads the keys and values into a list box.

The *SectionGet()* Method in the *Registry* Class

The `SectionGet()` method accepts an optional argument of which section to get keys from. This method creates a `Variant` array that returns a two-dimensional array from the `GetAllSettings()` function. Instead of having a two-dimensional array returned, I like to have a single-dimensional array returned with the keyed pair in each element. Therefore, after retrieving the array from the `GetAllSettings()` function, I loop through the array and convert it to a single-dimensional array by concatenating the value in the first element with an equal sign and the value in the second element. Here's an example:

```
   Public Function SectionGet( _
                   Optional strSection As String = "") _
                   As Variant()
      Dim lngRet As Long
      Dim astrAll As Variant
      Dim astrKeys() As String
      Dim intLoop As Integer

      If strSection <> "" Then
         mstrSection = strSection
      End If

      If mstrSection <> "" Then
         astrAll = GetAllSettings(mstrConfigName, mstrSection)
         If Not IsEmpty(astrAll) Then
```

```
            ReDim astrKeys(UBound(astrAll)) As String
            ' Convert to one-dimensional array
            For intLoop = LBound(astrAll) To UBound(astrAll)
               astrKeys(intLoop) = astrAll(intLoop, 0) & _
                                   "=" & astrAll(intLoop, 1)
            Next
            SectionGet = astrKeys
         Else
            SectionGet = Array()
         End If
      End If
   End Function
```

Summary

Both INI files and the Registry are extremely useful for storing application information. I recommend that you store the name and path information to your database in either of these locations. You could also store information such as the last user who logged into the machine, whether the toolbar or status bar is visible, and even paths to other files your application uses. To do all this, you can use Windows API calls as well as built-in Visual Basic functions, but better yet, you can use a class module to read and write data in either of these storage locations.

Review Questions

1. How do you create an INI file?
2. Which function retrieves data from an INI file?
3. What type of database is the System Registry?
4. Which built-in function gets data from the Registry?
5. Which built-in function writes data to the Registry?
6. If you had to store data for multiple users to get at, which location would you use—an INI file or the Registry?

Exercises

1. Add either the `INI` class or the `Registry` class to your employee project.
2. Save the data for the last employee accessed when you leave the form.
3. Restore the list box to that employee when you enter the form the next time.

30

ActiveX Controls: Part 1

Visual Basic has many different custom controls you can use when developing your user interface. You'll find that many of these are the same controls used within other Windows applications. These applications all use the same DLL and/or OCX files contained within Windows itself. These controls need to be loaded into your project's toolbox because they're not part of the standard controls. In this chapter, you'll learn how to present information using tabs, up/down controls, progress bars, and many other control formats.

Chapter Objectives

- Learn about the many different Windows common controls
- Learn to use the controls new to Visual Basic 6

Sample Project Files: \Chapter30\ControlsPart1.vbp

Windows Controls in Visual Basic

Several OCX files come with the Professional and Enterprise Editions of Visual Basic. In this chapter, you'll learn about the standard Windows common controls. Table 30.1 lists some of the controls you'll learn about in this chapter.

Table 30.1 Windows Common Controls

Component Description	OCX Name	Controls
Microsoft Windows Common Controls 6.0	MSCOMCTL.OCX	TabStrip, Toolbar, StatusBar, ProgressBar, TreeView, ListView, ImageList, Slider, and ImageCombo
Microsoft Windows Common Controls-2 6.0	MSCOMCT2.OCX	Animation, UpDown, MonthView, DTPicker, and FlatScrollbar
Microsoft Windows Common Controls-3 6.0	COMCT332.OCX	Coolbar
Microsoft Tabbed Dialog Control	TABCTL32.OCX	SSTab

To load these controls into your design environment, select Project, Components from the Visual Basic menu. Next, find the name of the component in the list shown in Table 30.1. Also, when you distribute your application at runtime, you'll need to make sure you include these OCX files in your setup program.

The ImageList Control

The ImageList control allows you to store a group of images into a repository from which you can select these images at runtime. Each image (BMP, ICO, JPG, or other graphic file type) is stored as a part of an object created by the ImageList control. An ImageList control is a collection of these `ListImage` objects. Each `ListImage` object can contain a bitmap (BMP), an icon (ICO), a GIF, a DIB, a CUR, or a JPG file.

Each `ListImage` object can be identified by its `Index` or `Key` property. The ImageList control does not show up at runtime; instead, it's used by other controls that display the images contained in the collection of objects within the ImageList control.

Using the ImageList

To set up the ImageList control at design time, select it from the toolbox and place it on a form. Don't worry about the size or where this control is located—it will not show up on the form at runtime. To start adding pictures, click once on the control; then from the Properties windows, click the `Custom` property. This displays the property page for this control. Now you can begin adding pictures to the control.

Select the Images tab and click Insert Picture to add some graphics to this control. You'll find some graphics supplied by Visual Basic if you've chosen the Custom option and selected Graphics from the setup. If you haven't chosen this option, you might want to run the Visual Basic setup again and install the graphics because there are many that you'll find useful.

Example's Filename: ImageList.frm

In the sample form shown Figure 30.1, you'll see a couple of arrows that allow you to loop through all the images in the ImageList control on this form.

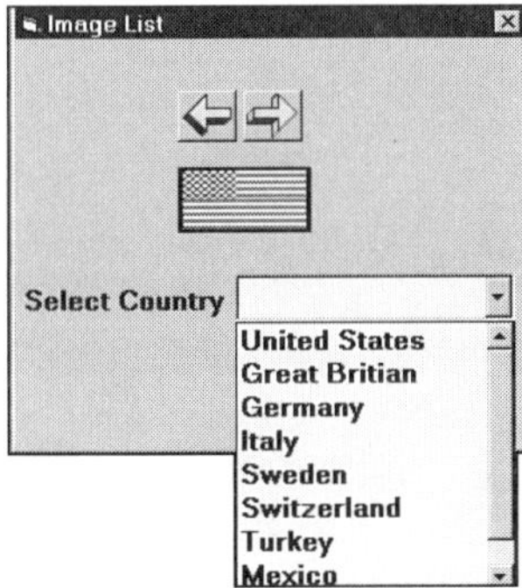

FIGURE 30.1
The ImageList control example.

If you double-click the `Custom` property in the Properties window of the ImageList control, you'll see a form similar to the one shown in Figure 30.2.

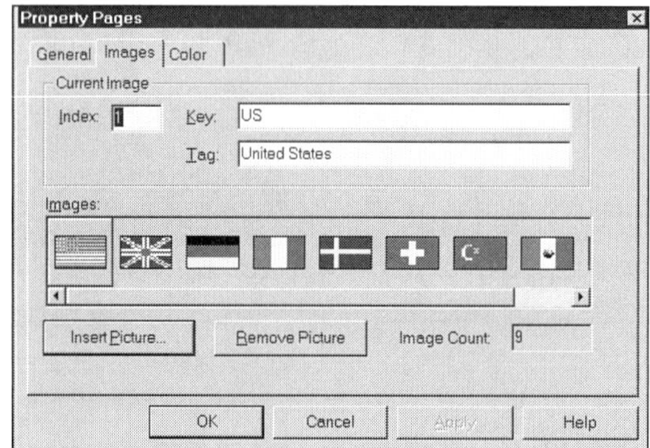

FIGURE 30.2 The property pages of the ImageList control.

In Figure 30.2, you can see that I've loaded flag images of several countries. I set the `Key` property of each picture in the ImageList to a unique value and created a description of each image in their respective `Tag` properties. Also, you'll see the following code in each of the command buttons that loop through the images:

```
Private Sub cmdNext_Click()
   Set imgFlag.Picture = _
       ilsFlags.ListImages(mintIndex).Picture
   mintIndex = mintIndex + 1
   If mintIndex > ilsFlags.ListImages.Count Then
      mintIndex = 1
   End If
End Sub

Private Sub cmdPrev_Click()
   Set imgFlag.Picture = _
       ilsFlags.ListImages(mintIndex).Picture
   mintIndex = mintIndex - 1
   If mintIndex = 0 Then
      mintIndex = ilsFlags.ListImages.Count
   End If
End Sub
```

In each of the `Click` events for these command buttons, you'll see that a module-level variable is used to increment and decrement through the `ListImages()` collection. Each time through the collection, the `Picture` property of the current `ListImage` object is grabbed and its value is placed in the ImageList control's `Picture` property.

Loading the Combo Box with Image Names

In the combo box for this form, you'll find a list of flag names. To load this list, you use the `Tag` property of each `ListImage` object in the ImageList control. Next, you add the `Key` property to the `List()` array of the combo box. This is used to select a flag image from the ImageList when you select an entry in the combo box. Here's the code:

```
Private Sub Form_Load()
   Dim intLoop As Integer
   Dim oImage As ListImage

   For Each oImage In ilsFlags.ListImages
      With cboCountries
         .AddItem oImage.Tag & _
                  Space(50) & vbTab & _
                  oImage.Key
      End With
   Next

   ' Initialize Index
   mintIndex = 1

   ' Display first item
   Call cmdNext_Click
End Sub
```

In the `Form_Load()` event, you loop through each image in the `ListImages` collection. Each time through, you add to the combo box the description of the image from the `Tab` property. In addition, you add 50 spaces, a tab character, and the `Key` property of the image. This way, you have the `Key` property available when you select an item from the combo box, but it's spaced so far to the right that it doesn't show up in the drop-down list.

Now, when you select an item from the combo box, you can retrieve the `Key` property from the combo box. Below is some code you'll write for the `Click()` event of the combo box:

```
Private Sub cboCountries_Click()
   Dim strKey As String

   If cboCountries.ListIndex <> -1 Then
      strKey = Mid$(cboCountries, _
                    InStr(cboCountries, vbTab) + 1)
      Set imgFlag.Picture = _
            ilsFlags.ListImages(strKey).Picture
   End If
End Sub
```

In the `Click` event of the combo box, you retrieve the `Key` value by parsing the `Text` property of the combo box and looking for the tab character. When you find it, you grab the value after that tab character; this is the `Key` value you use to retrieve the picture from the `ListImages` collection.

Toolbar

A common interface in a Windows applications is a toolbar. A toolbar generally resides at the top of a form, just below a menu bar. The toolbar has several icons that allow the user to perform common commands in the application with the click of a mouse. This can sometimes save the user many keystrokes. Windows 95/98 and Windows NT provide a standard toolbar control you can use in your Visual Basic applications. The toolbar control is a part of the Microsoft Windows common controls.

The toolbar control relies on a collection of `Button` objects that you define. You'll create one `Button` object for each button you want displayed on your toolbar. The `Button` object may have a text description or an icon, or both. `Button` objects can be created at runtime, or they can be created at design time using the toolbar property sheet.

Toolbar Common Properties

Let's take a look at the most commonly used properties for the toolbar control. In Table 30.2, you'll find a list of these properties and a description of each.

Table 30.2 Toolbar Common Properties

Property	Description
`AllowCustomize`	If this property is set to a `True` value, the user can double-click the toolbar at runtime to invoke the Customize Toolbar dialog box. This allows the user to customize the toolbar by adding and subtracting buttons from it. To enable the user to do this, you must set up different buttons that can be customized as well as provide the ability to save and restore the custom toolbar.
`BorderStyle`	I typically set this property to `1-Fixed Single` instead of `0-None` to give the toolbar some definition when placed on a form.
`ButtonHeight`	This property determines the height of the buttons at runtime. This property is generally set to the correct value automatically when you set the `ImageList` property to a valid ImageList control. Remember that an ImageList control only contains images of a certain size, so the buttons can only be a certain height.
`ButtonWidth`	This property determines the width of the buttons at runtime. Like `ButtonHeight`, this property should be automatically set by the toolbar.
`Buttons`	This property returns a reference to the `Buttons` collection on the toolbar. Each item in this collection is a `Button` object. See the next section for a description of `Button` objects.
`ImageList`	Set this property to a valid ImageList control. This ImageList control must be on the same form as the toolbar control to be set at design time. You can also set this property at runtime. You'll learn how to do this later in the chapter.
`ShowTips`	Set this property to `True` to be able to display each of the `Button` objects' `ToolTipText` properties.
`Wrappable`	Set this property to `True` if you want to have the `Button` objects wrap to another line when the user resizes the form to a width that will not allow the toolbar to display on one line.

Button Objects

Because the toolbar is made up of a collection of `Button` objects, let's take a look at the common properties for the `Button` object. Table 30.3 explains each of the properties you'll be setting for your `Button` objects.

Table 30.3 Common Properties of the *Button* Objects

Property	Description
`Index`	The index number of where in the `Buttons` collection this `Button` object is located.
`Caption`	The caption to display at the bottom of the button. This property can be used in combination with the `Image` property to display a button that has both a caption and an image. Typically, you find this on a 32×32 pixel button, not on the smaller 16×16 pixel buttons.
`Description`	This description of the button is displayed in the Customize toolbox at runtime. This helps the user determine which buttons to get rid of or add to the toolbar.
`Key`	This is a unique value for the selected `Button` object. It must be unique within the total collection of `Buttons` for this toolbar. You should use the `Key` property to reference a particular button, as opposed to using the `Index` property, because you might move buttons around in the toolbar, which affects the `Index` property but not the `Key` property.
`Value`	This represents the state of the `Button` object at runtime. It can either be `tbrUnPressed` or `tbrPressed` to represent whether the user has selected this button.
`Style`	There are six different styles of buttons you can select. See the next section for a description of each style of button.
`ToolTipText`	Set this property to the value you want to have displayed when the user hovers his or her cursor over this button.
`Image`	This property is either the `Index` number or the `Key` value of a particular image in the ImageList control, which is set in the `ImageList` property of the toolbar.
`Tag`	This property can be used for anything you want.
`MixedState`	This property returns a `True` or `False` value, or it can be set to `True` or `False` if a button is in an indeterminate state. For example, if you've created a button group of Bold, Italic, and Underline buttons, and you highlight a piece of text that contains bold text, italic text, and normal text, then the Bold and Italic buttons would be set to `MixedState` because there are three different types of formatting applied to the selected text.

Styles of Buttons

You can apply six different styles to a button. Table 30.4 lists each of the different styles and gives an explanation of how each one reacts at runtime.

Table 30.4 Button Object *Style* Property Settings

Style	Description
`0-tbrDefault`	This is a normal button that, when pressed, will simply depress, fire the `ButtonClick` event on the toolbar, and then return to normal "unpressed" state. Use this for any action that just needs to be performed and is then complete.
`1-tbrCheck`	This button acts like a toggle. When you click the button, it stays pressed. You can then click the button again to return it to an "unpressed" state.
`2-tbrButtonGroup`	You can create button groups by inserting a separator button (see the next style) and then adding two or more buttons to the toolbar, followed by another separator. When buttons are grouped, they act like option buttons. When you press one button to be selected, the other button in the group will become unselected.
`3-Separator`	This style is used to place some blank space in between buttons. This is used to group common buttons together or to create a button group. The size is determined by the toolbar itself and is approximately one-third the size of a normal button.
`4-PlaceHolder`	This button is like a separator except it's used to place another control on top of the toolbar. If you add a placeholder button, you'll set the `Width` property of this `Button` object to the width you want for the size of the control you place on top of this placeholder. You might use this to place a combo box on the toolbar, like Microsoft Word does with its selection of fonts and styles. If you use this type of button, you need to write code to handle the resizing of the toolbar at runtime. See the online Help for an example of the code you might write.
`5-DropDown`	If you choose this style of button, you can insert `ButtonMenu` objects. A button menu is a menu that's dropped down from a button when clicked. Only one level of menus is allowed. You can then click any of these button menus to invoke the `ButtonMenuClick` event on the toolbar.

An Example of a Toolbar

To create a toolbar, you need to have an ImageList control from which you can create each button. After adding a ListImage control to the form, you need to assign all the images that you want to use on your toolbar. Make sure you assign all of them prior to adding buttons to the toolbar, because once you've assigned the `ImageList` property on the toolbar, you can't change the ImageList control. This means you have to redo your entire toolbar if you want to add just one more icon.

Look at the sample project for this chapter. You'll find an ImageList control and a toolbar control already created. Click the ImageList control, select `Custom` from the Properties window, and view the images that have been added to this control. Next, click the toolbar control and select the `Custom` property to view all the buttons on the Buttons tab of the property page.

Example's Filename: Toolbar.frm

In Figure 30.3, you can see each of the different types of button styles. Run this example and click each of the different buttons to see what it does. To make a button respond and perform an action, you need to write code in the `ButtonClick` event:

```
Private Sub tbrMain_ButtonClick(ByVal Button As Button)
   Select Case Button.Key
      Case "NewRecord"
         MsgBox "Add a new record here"
      Case "SaveRecord"
         MsgBox "Save changes here"
      Case "DeleteRecord"
         MsgBox "Delete a record here"
      Case "UndoRecord"
         MsgBox "Undo changes to a particular record"
      Case "Copy"
         MsgBox "Copy code goes here"
      Case "Cut"
         MsgBox "Cut code goes here"
      Case "Paste"
         MsgBox "Paste code goes here"
      Case "Exit"
         Unload Me
   End Select
End Sub
```

Although this code does not do a lot, it does show you how to use the `Button` object that's passed to this `ButtonClick` event to determine which button was pressed. In this example, you use the `Key` property to determine which button was pressed.

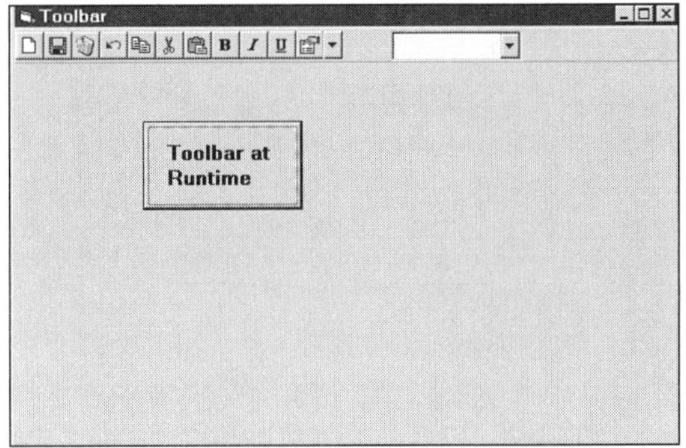

FIGURE 30.3 An example of a toolbar.

Customizing the Toolbar at Runtime

Double-clicking on the toolbar at runtime invokes the Customize Toolbar dialog box, shown in Figure 30.4. This dialog box allows the user to change the order of the buttons on the toolbar, delete buttons, or reset the toolbar to the default state.

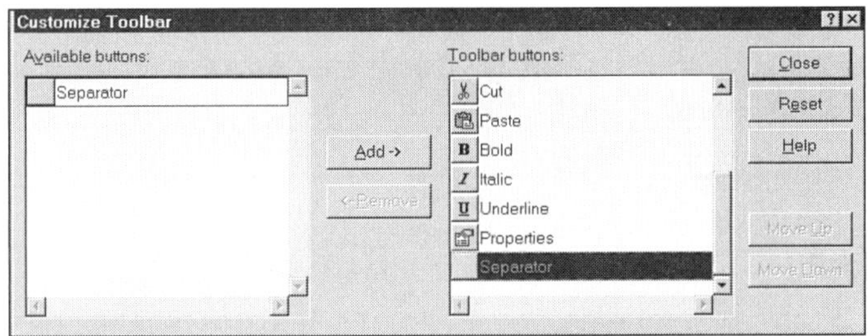

FIGURE 30.4 The Customize Toolbar dialog box.

The Customize Toolbar dialog box allows you to select from any of the available buttons on the left side of the form and add them to the toolbar buttons on the right side of the form. You can move selected buttons up or down, and you can even remove buttons from the toolbar. When you close this dialog box, a `Change` event fires on the toolbar, allowing you to save the changes you make to the Registry. To disable the Customize Toolbar dialog box, set the `AllowCustomize` property of the toolbar control to `False`.

Saving Toolbar Customizations at Runtime

Once the `Change` event fires from the user changing the toolbar via the Customize Toolbar dialog box, the `SaveToolbar` method can be invoked. Here's some code I typically use to store the toolbars for each user:

```
Private Sub tbrMain_Change()
   If Not mboolRestore Then
      tbrMain.SaveToolbar "Toolbars-" & App.EXEName & _
                          "\" & Me.Name, _
                          App.EXEName, _
                          "MainToolbar"
   End If
End Sub
```

In the `Change` event of the toolbar, you invoke the `SaveToolbar` method. You should pass in three parameters that uniquely identify a particular area in the Registry where the toolbars will be stored. All the toolbar information is stored under the `HKEY_CURRENT_USER` key in the Registry.

To emphasize that this entry is for toolbars, you might want to come up with a prefix such as "Toolbars-", followed by the executable name. You then need to determine whether you'll just be saving one toolbar for your application or several. If you have a lot of toolbars for different forms, you might want to add on the form's name in a subkey under `Toolbars`. This is what the second parameter is used for in the `SaveToolbar` method. The last parameter is for the subkey that will actually store the toolbar information. If you use these parameters for the `SaveToolbar` method, you can store as many toolbars for one application as you want.

Restoring Toolbar Customizations at Runtime

To restore a toolbar at runtime, you invoke the `RestoreToolbar` method on the toolbar during the `Form_Activate` event. You must use this method in the `Form_Activate` event and not in the `Form_Load()` event, because the toolbar is not initialized yet. In addition, you must invoke the `Refresh` method on the form after performing a `Show` method. This forces the toolbar to refresh itself, because it has a tendency not to refresh itself after a `RestoreToolbar` method. Here's the code you use in the `Form_Activate` event:

```
Private Sub Form_Activate()
   ' Restore Toolbar
   mboolRestore = True
```

```
    tbrMain.RestoreToolbar "Toolbars-" & App.EXEName, _
                           Me.Name, _
                           "MainToolbar"
    mboolRestore = False
End Sub
```

Notice the use of the module-level Boolean variable `mboolRestore` in this event as well as in the `tbrMain_Change()` event. When you perform a `RestoreToolbar` method, it causes the `Change()` event of the toolbar to fire. Therefore, by setting the `mboolRestore` variable to `True`, you can test to see whether this variable is set when the `tbrMain_Change()` event fires. If it is, you can bypass the `SaveToolbar` method.

Invoking Customization with Code

You can open the Customize Toolbar dialog box by invoking the `Customize` method on the toolbar. You might choose to invoke this command yourself instead of having the user double-click on the toolbar. For example, you might want to create a menu item that performs customization, or you might want them to use the right mouse button to invoke the customization. Here's the code:

```
Private Sub tbrMain_MouseUp(Button As Integer, _
          Shift As Integer, x As Single, y As Single)
    If Button = vbRightButton Then
        tbrMain.Customize
    End If
End Sub
```

Creating Toolbars at Runtime

Once you've assigned the `ImageList` property of the toolbar control, you'll be unable to change the ImageList control without losing all the icons on the toolbar. This means you can't add or delete any images. Because things will change over time, this is not very realistic, and you'll need to modify the ImageList control. As a result, you'll probably want to build your toolbars at runtime. Let's look at another example that shows you how to build toolbars at runtime.

Example's Filename: ToolbarRuntime.frm

FIGURE 30.5 A toolbar built at runtime.

On this form, you won't find an ImageList control, and at design time, the toolbar will look empty. You're going to pass in the ImageList control from the previous form. In most of the applications I develop, I want to have just one central repository for all my toolbar images. As a result, I end up passing an ImageList control from my main MDI form to all the child forms that need one. You can accomplish this by using a `Property Set` procedure and a module-level variable on each form that needs an ImageList. Here's an example:

```
Private milsList As ImageList

Property Set PImageList(ilsList As ImageList)
   Set milsList = ilsList
End Property
```

By using a `Property Set` procedure, you can pass an ImageList control form one form to another:

```
Private Sub cmdToolRun_Click()
   With frmToolbarRunTime
      Set .PImageList = ilsList
      .Show
   End With
End Sub
```

Assuming you have an ImageList control called `ilsList` on the form from which this code is invoked, you can set the `PImageList` property on the form where you need the ImageList control to go. The sample that goes with this chapter is not an MDI application; this is just something you might want to do in your applications.

After you've set this property and invoke the `Show` method on the form, the code in the `Form_Load` event sets the toolbar's `ImageList` property to the module-level reference to the ImageList control:

```
Private Sub Form_Load()
   Set tbrMain.ImageList = milsList

   Call ToolBarCreate
End Sub
```

Next, a routine named `ToolBarCreate` is called to build the `Button` objects for this toolbar:

```
Private Sub ToolBarCreate()
   Dim oBtn As Button

   With tbrMain
      Set oBtn = .Buttons.Add(, "NewRecord", "", _
                             tbrDefault, "NewRecord")
      oBtn.ToolTipText = "New"
      Set oBtn = .Buttons.Add(, "SaveRecord", , _
                             , "SaveRecord")
      oBtn.ToolTipText = "Save"
      Set oBtn = .Buttons.Add(, "DeleteRecord", , _
                             , "DeleteRecord")
      oBtn.ToolTipText = "Delete"
      Set oBtn = .Buttons.Add(, "UndoRecord", , _
                             , "Undo")
      oBtn.ToolTipText = "Undo"

      Set oBtn = .Buttons.Add(, , _
                             , tbrSeparator)

      Set oBtn = .Buttons.Add(, "Exit", , _
                             , "Exit")
      oBtn.ToolTipText = "Exit"

   End With
End Sub
```

To add buttons on the toolbar, you invoke the `Add` method on the `Buttons` collection of the toolbar. The first parameter is the `Index` number. Because you'll generally not use this, you can just skip this parameter. The second parameter is the `Key` value to call this button. The third parameter is the caption, if any, for this particular button. The fourth parameter is the style for this button. You can use any of the constants for this parameter, or you may leave it blank for the default button style. The last parameter is the `Key` or `Index` property of the image in the ImageList you want to use for this button.

The `Add` method passes back a reference to the `Button` object that was just created. As you can see in the preceding routine, this value is placed in the `oBtn` variable that's declared as a `Button` object. You can then use this reference to set any of the other properties that are not exposed as parameters to the `Add` method. For example, you can set the `ToolTipText` property to a value that's appropriate for the button.

Of course, you still need to write code in the `ButtonClick` event for the toolbar to have it respond to each of these buttons. You write this code as you did earlier:

```
Private Sub tbrMain_ButtonClick(ByVal Button As Button)
   Select Case Button.Key
      Case "NewRecord"
         MsgBox "Add a new record here"
      Case "SaveRecord"
         MsgBox "Save changes here"
      Case "DeleteRecord"
         MsgBox "Delete a record here"
      Case "UndoRecord"
         MsgBox "Undo changes to a particular record"
      Case "Exit"
         Unload Me
   End Select
End Sub
```

Coolbar

The Coolbar control is used to contain bands of other controls. Each band can only contain one other control (see Figure 30.6). You'll typically use a container control on each band, such as a picture control or a toolbar. There's not a lot of functionality—such as methods or events—that you need to program on the Coolbar; instead, you just set a few properties and write all the code on the contained control.

Example's Filename: Coolbar.frm

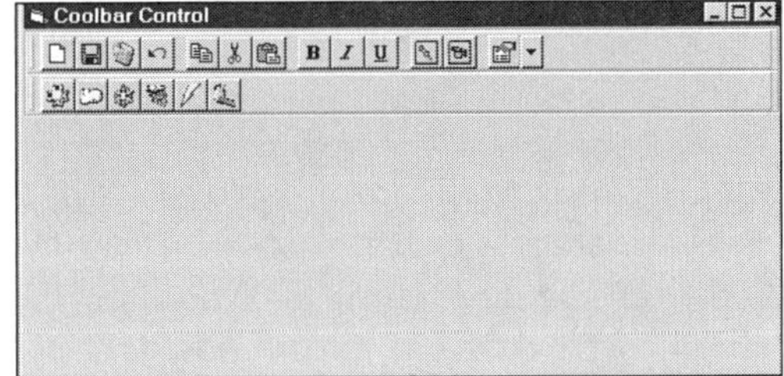

FIGURE 30.6
A Coolbar control.

Common Properties of the Coolbar Control

Table 30.5 lists the properties most commonly used with the Coolbar control and provides a description of each.

Table 30.5 Common Properties of the Coolbar Control

Property	Description
`Align`	Specifies where you want the Coolbar aligned. You can align it to the top, right, left, or bottom of the form on which it's placed.
`BandBorders`	Set this property to `True` if you want to have a slight border in between each of the different bands you create. I recommend that you set this a `True` value because it makes the control look better.
`FixedOrder`	Set this property to `True` to allow the user to move the bands around at runtime. Set this property to `False` if you want to keep the bands in the location where you set them and not let the user move them around.
`Orientation`	You can set this property to `Horizontal` or `Vertical`. Obviously, if you're setting the `Align` property to either `Left` or `Right`, you need to set this property to `Vertical`, whereas if you set the `Align` property to either `Top` or `Bottom`, you set this property to `Horizontal`.
`VariantHeight`	Set this property to `True` to allow each band to be a unique height. I recommend that this property be set to `False` because you typically don't want to have different control and/or picture heights on different toolbars.
`Bands`	This is the collection of `Band` objects. You can add or remove bands from this collection at runtime. You might do this if you want the user to be able to create and add his or her own toolbars to new bands on the Coolbar control.

continues

Table 30.5 Continued

Property	Description
`RowCount`	This property returns the number of rows displayed in the Coolbar at runtime. Remember that this is probably not the number of bands, because more than one band can be displayed on a row. If you want to retrieve the number of bands visible, you can look at the `BandsCount` property.

If you look at the sample project, you will see an example of two toolbars that have been combined onto a Coolbar control. If you want to look at the properties of the Coolbar, be sure to click on the Coolbar and not one of the two Toolbar controls. You can also try moving one of the Toolbars around at runtime to see how you can line them up, or even change their positions on the Coolbar control.

Status Bar

Most MDI applications display status bars at the bottom of their main forms. Status bars are commonly used to display information about programs. For example, in Microsoft Word, the status bar is used to display the current page, current section, number of pages in the document, the current line and column, and information on the state of the Insert key on the keyboard (insert or overwrite mode). Figure 30.7 shows you an example of a status bar control.

Example's Filename: StatusBar.frm

FIGURE 30.7
A status bar control.

A status bar is made up of one or many `Panel` objects. Each `Panel` object can display text or a predefined status that comes from Windows itself. In most of the applications I create, I use the left panel to display the caption of the current form, the middle panel to display the person who is currently logged into the application, and the right panel to display the name of the current form. Tech support can use this information if a user calls with a bug. Tech support can ask the user what the form name is in the lower-right side of the screen when the bug occurs. This uniquely identifies the form where the bug is.

The *Style* Property of the Status Bar *Panel* Object

You can use many styles of panels on a status bar control. Table 30.6 lists the different style values and provides a description of each.

Table 30.6 *Style* Property Values of the *Panel* Object

Style	Description
`0 - sbrText`	Displays text and/or a bitmap in the panel.
`1 - sbrCaps`	The letters *CAPS* will be displayed in bold font in the panel when the Caps Lock key is enabled. The letters will be dimmed in the panel when the key is disabled.
`2 - sbrNum`	The letters *NUM* will be displayed in bold font in the panel when the Num Lock key is enabled. The letters will be dimmed in the panel when the key is disabled.
`3 - sbrIns`	The letters *INS* will be displayed in bold font in the panel when the Insert key is enabled. The letters will be dimmed in the panel when the key is disabled.
`4 - sbrScrl`	The letters *SCRL* will be displayed in bold font in the panel when the Scroll Lock key is enabled. The letters will be dimmed in the panel when the key is disabled.
`5 - sbrTime`	Displays the current time in the panel in the system time format setting.
`6 - sbrDate`	Displays the current date in the panel in the system date format setting.
`7 - sbrKana`	The letters *KANA* will be displayed in bold font in the panel when the Scroll Lock key is enabled. The letters will be dimmed in the panel when the key is disabled.

Setting Panel Values at Runtime

At runtime, you need to fill in with text any `Panel` object you define by setting the `Style` property to `1-sbrText`. Here's some sample code of how you write to the `Text` property of each individual `Panel` object in the `Panels` collection:

```
Private Sub Form_Load()
   With sbrMain.Panels
      .Item("Msg").Text = Me.Caption
      .Item("Login").Text = "PSheriff"
      .Item("Name").Text = Me.Name
   End With
End Sub
```

In the `Form_Load()` event, you reference the `Panels` collection of the status bar named `sbrMain`. On this status bar are three panels with the `Key` properties set to `Msg`, `Login`, and `Name`, respectively. You can set the `Text` property of each one by referencing the `Item` method with the `Key` value of the panel you want to add some data to.

ImageCombo

The ImageCombo control is like the standard combo box in that it displays a list of items. However, in the ImageCombo control, you can specify both a picture and some text for each item. In addition, you're allowed to indent any item to create a hierarchical view of the items.

Example's Filename: ImageCombo.frm

In the example shown in Figure 30.8 are two top-level items: Computer Items and Earth Items. Under each of these top-level items, you can see a list of items that is slightly indented under the top-level item.

FIGURE 30.8 An ImageCombo control example.

Common Properties of the ImageCombo Control

The ImageCombo control has few properties other than the standard ones that are worth mentioning. Table 30.7 lists those properties you'll likely be setting for the ImageCombo control.

Table 30.7 Common Properties of the ImageCombo Control

Property	Description
`ImageList`	Set this property to the name of a valid ImageList control on the same form as the ImageCombo control. Unlike with the toolbar control, you can add to the ImageList control that's tied to this control. Because everything is created at runtime, there's no problem with adding other items.
`ComboItems`	This runtime property exposes the collection of `ComboItem` objects to you. Each item in the list is a `ComboItem` object. You might use this property to loop through the collection and perform some action against each item in the list.
`SelectedItem`	This property returns the currently selected `ComboItem` object to you.

Loading the *ComboItems* Collection

To load the ImageCombo control, you use the `Add` method of the `ComboItems` collection. When you add a top-level item, you don't specify an indentation level; for all other items, though, you will specify an indentation level. Here's an example:

```
Private Sub ComboLoad()
   With icboItems
      ' Load Computer Items
      .ComboItems.Add , "Computer", _
                        "Computer Items", _
                        "PC"
      .ComboItems.Add , "DiskDrive", _
                        "Disk Drives", _
                        "DiskDrive", _
                        , 3
      .ComboItems.Add , "FloppyDrive", _
                        "Floppy Drives", _
```

```
                            "Floppy", _
                            , 3
        .ComboItems.Add , "Monitor", _
                            "Monitors", _
                            "Monitor", _
                            , 3
        .ComboItems.Add , "CDROM", _
                            "CD Rom Drives", _
                            "CDRom", _
                            , 3
        .ComboItems.Add , "Keyboard", _
                            "Keyboards", _
                            "Keyboard", _
                            , 3

        ' Earth Elements
        .ComboItems.Add , "Earth", "Earth Items", "Earth"
        .ComboItems.Add , "Sun", "Sunshine", "Sun", , 3
        .ComboItems.Add , "Rain", "Rain", "Rain", , 3
        .ComboItems.Add , "Snow", "Snow", "Snow", , 3
        .ComboItems.Add , "Lightning", "Lightning", _
                            "Lightning", , 3
        .ComboItems.Add , "Clouds", "Clouds", "Clouds", , 3

        ' Highlight the first item
        .ComboItems.Item(1).Selected = True
    End With
End Sub
```

The `Add` method's first parameter is the `Index` property of this particular item. You should probably not set this one because you want to use the `Key` value instead. The `Key` value is passed in as the second parameter. The third parameter is the text you want to add to the `ComboItem` object. This is what's displayed in the list box next to the image. The fourth parameter is the `Key` value of the image in the ImageList you want to assign to this `ComboItem` object. The fifth parameter is the `Key` value of another image that you might want to use when an item is selected in the ImageCombo control. The last parameter is the number of indents you want to use. In this particular code, a value of `3` is passed. Each indentation level is approximately 10 pixels. Therefore, each `ComboItem` object is indented about 30 pixels to the right of the top-level item.

Summary

You can use many different controls to spruce up your user interface. These controls are not part of the built-in standard Visual Basic controls; you will add them through the Components dialog. They are very easy to use, and with just a little code, you can manipulate them to perform the way you want them to.

Review Questions

1. Which control would you use to store a repository of images?
2. Which control lets you display status messages to the user?
3. Which control gives you a hierarchical view of data using pictures and text?

Exercises

1. Create an MDI form and place a toolbar and a status bar on the form.
2. Have your MDI form call another form. Build a toolbar at runtime on this form.

ActiveX Controls: Part 2

THERE ARE SO MANY CONTROLS AVAILABLE IN Visual Basic that sometimes it's hard to know what each one does. In the last chapter, you learned about only some of the controls available in Visual Basic. In this chapter, you'll learn about many other controls that can help you spruce up your user interface.

Chapter Objectives

- Learn to use the DateTimePicker control
- See how the MonthView control works
- Understand the usage of the Progress bar
- Learn to use the Slider control
- See where to use the UpDown control
- Break up your forms using the TabStrip control
- Learn the differences between the TabStrip and the SSTab control

Sample Project Files: \Chapter31\ControlsPart2.vbp

DateTimePicker Control

Retrieving a date from a user is something almost every application needs to perform. Of course, your application will need to be able to verify that the date is correct. Also, what if the user needs to input a future date? For this, some sort of pop-up calendar would be a great idea for a Windows application. However, who wants to program something like this? Well, the folks at Microsoft have provided this for us in the DateTimePicker control.

The DateTimePicker control has many different formats and styles you can use to input and display the date. In this section, you'll learn about the different formats you can apply to the DateTimePicker control.

The DateTimePicker looks like a combo box with the `Style` property set to `0` (see Figure 31.1). You can type a date directly into the text portion of this control. When you click the down-arrow button to the right of the text, you'll see a drop-down calendar appear just below the text from which you can select a date. When you click any date in the drop-down calendar, that date will appear in the text portion of the DateTimePicker control.

Example's Filename: DateTimePicker.frm

FIGURE 31.1
The DateTime Picker control with different formats.

Common Properties of the DateTimePicker Control

The DateTimePicker control has a lot of properties. Some are used at design time, but the majority you'll use at runtime. Table 31.1 presents a list of the most commonly used design-time properties and a description of what each of those properties can be used for.

Table 31.1 Common Properties of the DateTimePicker Control

Property	Description
`CustomFormat`	This property can be set to a series of format characters that you can put together in a certain order to make the control display the date in the format you want. See the online help for the complete list of format characters you can use.
`Format`	This property can be set to one of four values. See the section, "The `Format` Property," for more information on this property.
`MaxDate`	If you set this property, the user will be forced to select a date less than or equal to the specified date.
`MinDate`	If you set this property, the user will be forced to select a date greater than or equal to the specified date.
`UpDown`	Set this property to `True` if you want the user to use the UpDown arrow to the right of the control to increment any of the parts of the date (month, day, and year).
`Value`	This property reports back the date the user inputs or selects from the drop-down calendar. Also, you can use this property to set a default date on the control at design time.

Runtime Properties of the DateTimePicker Control

Because the DateTimePicker control is used to select dates at runtime, you'll be manipulating many properties at runtime to retrieve date data. Using these runtime properties, you can retrieve any portion of the date that's contained in the DateTimePicker control. Table 31.2 gives you a list of the properties that retrieve the different parts of the date selected.

Table 31.2 Runtime Properties of the DateTimePicker Control

Runtime Property	Description
`Day`	Returns the day as a two-digit number.
`Month`	Returns the month as a two-digit number. Predefined constants are also available for each month—`mvwJanuary`, `mvwFebruary`, and so on.
`Year`	Returns the year as a four-digit number.
`Hour`	Returns the hour as a two-digit number.
`Minute`	Returns the minute as a two-digit number.
`Second`	Returns the seconds as a two-digit number.
`DayOfWeek`	Returns the day of the week as a one-digit number. Predefined constants for each day of the week are built into Visual Basic. For example, `mvwSunday`, `mvwMonday`, `mvwTuesday`, and so on.

The *Format* Property

The `Format` property is used to display and input dates in a set of predefined formats. Besides inputting date formats, you're also allowed to input times. You can even display both a date and a time by using a custom format.

Table 31.3 gives you a list of what the predefined values are for the `Format` property. You can also see an example of what each predefined format will make the control look like at runtime.

Table 31.3 ***Format*** **Property Values**

Value	Example
`0-dtpLongDate`	Saturday, January 01, 2000
`1-dtpShortDate`	1/1/00
`3-dtpTime`	12:00:00 AM
`4-dtpCustom`	When you choose this format, you'll need to fill in the `CustomFormat` property using special format characters. See the next section for examples of using the `CustomFormat` property.

Using the *CustomFormat* Property

Several format characters are available that you can use to create a special date format. For example, a single uppercase *M* represents the month, and a single lowercase *d* represents the day. If you use two of the format characters together, any single digit will be preceded with a leading zero. For example, `d` would display `1`, whereas `dd` would display `01`. Table 31.4 shows you a few ways you can use the `CustomFormat` property and provides examples of how each date will look at runtime.

Table 31.4 ***CustomFormat*** **Property Values**

Value	Example
`M/dd/yyy (dddd)`	1/01/2000 (Saturday)
`M/d/yy`	1/1/00
`MMM, d Year: yyy`	Jan, 1 Year: 2000

Check the online help for more information on the `CustomFormat` property.

Callback Formats

One of the other "custom" format characters you can use is the `X` character. When you use this custom format, two events are called that you can use to write some data back into the DateTimePicker control. As an example, you might fill in the `CustomFormat` property with this string:

```
MMM ddd yyy (XXXXX)
```

Here, you want to put the current quarter into the location where the `X` characters are located. Therefore, if the date is Jan. 1, 2000, you want the string to be displayed in the DateTimePicker control like this:

```
Jan Sat 2000 (Qtr 1)
```

To accomplish this, you need to run the control and have it fire the `FormatSize` event. This event is only called one time and is used to return the largest size of the format you're going to return into the location where the `X` characters are in the `CustomFormat` property. In this case, you know that you'll return five characters (`QTR 1`). Therefore, you would write the `FormatSize()` event as follows:

```
Private Sub DTPicker6_FormatSize(_
            ByVal CallbackField As String, _
            Size As Integer)
   Size = 5
End Sub
```

The `FormatSize()` event accepts an argument called `CallbackField`. This is the field with the `X` characters in it. This event also passes in a `Size` argument by reference. You set this `Size` argument to the size of the data that will be placed into the `CallbackField` argument.

After the `FormatSize` event is called once, every time you change to a new date, the `Format()` event will be called again. This is where you change the `FormattedString` argument that's passed in. This `FormattedString` argument is then placed into the DateTimePicker control at the location where the `X` characters were located. Here's an example:

```
Private Sub DTPicker6_Format(_
            ByVal CallbackField As String, _
            FormattedString As String)
   Select Case Month(DTPicker6.Value)
      Case 1, 2, 3
         FormattedString = "Qtr 1"
      Case 4, 5, 6
         FormattedString = "Qtr 2"
      Case 7, 8, 9
         FormattedString = "Qtr 3"
      Case 10, 11, 12
         FormattedString = "Qtr 4"

   End Select
End Sub
```

As you can see in this code, you're returning a value that represents which quarter you're in. The total size of the string is five characters. This is why you set the `Size` argument in the `FormatSize` event to `5`.

The *CallBackKeyDown* Event

Besides these two events that are called when you have a custom format defined with the `X` character, another event is also fired—`CallBackKeyDown`. This event is fired whenever a key is pressed when the DateTimePicker control has focus and has a `CustomFormat` property with the `X` format character in it. You can use this event to respond to user keystrokes. In the following code, you'll see an example that allows the user to press the letter *J* to toggle between January, June, and July without having to bring up the calendar and jump to those months:

```
Private Sub DTPicker7_CallbackKeyDown(_
            ByVal KeyCode As Integer, _
            ByVal Shift As Integer, _
            ByVal CallbackField As String, _
            CallbackDate As Date)
    Dim strDayYear As String

    strDayYear = DTPicker7.Day & "/" & DTPicker7.Year
    Select Case UCase$(Chr(KeyCode))
        Case "J"
            If Month(DTPicker7.Value) = 1 Then
                CallbackDate = CDate("06/" & strDayYear)
            ElseIf Month(DTPicker7.Value) = 6 Then
                CallbackDate = CDate("07/" & strDayYear)
            Else
                CallbackDate = CDate("01/" & strDayYear)
            End If
        Case "F"
            CallbackDate = CDate("02/" & strDayYear)
        Case "M"
            If Month(DTPicker7.Value) = 3 Then
                CallbackDate = CDate("05/" & strDayYear)
            Else
                CallbackDate = CDate("03/" & strDayYear)
            End If
        Case "A"
```

```
            If Month(DTPicker7.Value) = 4 Then
               CallbackDate = CDate("08/" & strDayYear)
            Else
               CallbackDate = CDate("04/" & strDayYear)
            End If
         Case "S"
            CallbackDate = CDate("09/" & strDayYear)
         Case "O"
            CallbackDate = CDate("10/" & strDayYear)
         Case "N"
            CallbackDate = CDate("11/" & strDayYear)
         Case "D"
            CallbackDate = CDate("12/" & strDayYear)

      End Select
      Debug.Print Now
   End Sub
```

Using the `Day`, `Year`, and `Month` properties, you can figure out which month is currently selected. You then use that month and the key that was pressed to calculate the next month to return back in the `CallbackDate` argument. Once you return the value in the `CallbackDate` argument, this value is placed in the `Value` property, which then causes the `Format` event to fire. Here, you can return `MonthName` into the location of the `X` characters in the `CustomFormat` property. Here's the code:

```
Private Sub DTPicker7_Format(_
            ByVal CallbackField As String, _
            FormattedString As String)
   FormattedString = MonthName(Month(DTPicker7.Value))
End Sub
```

Of course, the `FormatSize` event will also be called. Here's the code for that event, just to be complete:

```
Private Sub DTPicker7_FormatSize(_
            ByVal CallbackField As String, _
            Size As Integer)
   Size = 9
End Sub
```

The MonthView Control

The drop-down calendar portion of the DateTimePicker control is actually another custom control called the MonthView control (see Figure 31.2). When you use this control as a separate control, it has many properties that allow you to select a range of dates and display multiple months at one time.

Example's Filename: MonthView.frm

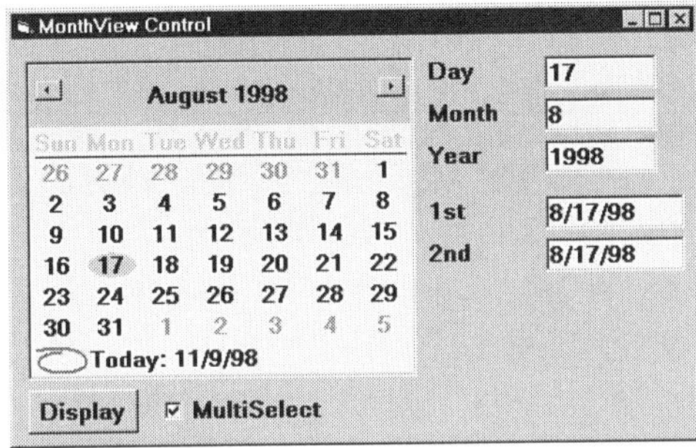

FIGURE 31.2 A MonthView control example.

Common Properties of the MonthView Control

You'll use many properties with the MonthView control. In addition to all the run-time properties of the DateTimePicker control you learned about earlier, the MonthView control also has many unique properties, as listed in Table 31.5.

Table 31.5 Unique Properties of the MonthView Control

Property	Description
`MonthColumns`	Use this property to display multiple month views side by side. The first column displays one month, the next month is displayed in the next column, and so on.
`MonthRows`	This property can be used to display multiple month views up and down. The one on top is the first month, the one below is the next month, and so on.
`MultiSelect`	Set this property to `True` if you want to allow the user to select multiple dates from the MonthView control.
`MaxSelCount`	If you've set the `MultiSelect` property to a `True` value, this property will specify the maximum number of days the user can select by highlighting them in the MonthView control.

continues

Table 31.5 Continued

Property	Description
`ShowToday`	Set this property to `True` if you want to display the area at the bottom of the MonthView control that allows the user to always return to the current date.
`ShowWeekNumber`	Set this property to `True` if you want to display the week number next to each week in the MonthView control. This is the number of weeks since the start of the calendar year.
`StartOfWeek`	You can set this property to any day of the week that you want to appear in the leftmost column in the MonthView control. For example, if you want to have Monday as the leftmost day, you would set this property to the constant `mvwMonday`.
`SelEnd`	This property returns the first date the user selected in a multiple-date selection.
`SelStart`	This property returns the last date the user selected in a multiple-date selection.
`Week`	This is the week number since the start of the calendar year.

Events of the MonthView Control

The MonthView control has many events you can respond to when the user interacts with it. Table 31.6 gives you an idea of what some of these events are and what you might do with them.

Table 31.6 Events of the MonthView Control

Event Name	Description
`DateClick`	This event is fired whenever the user clicks a date. You might use this to update a screen full of employee interviews for a given date.
`DateDblClick`	This event is fired whenever the user double-clicks a date. You might use this to bring up a data entry form for entering a new employee interview for that date.

Event Name	Description
GetDayBold	This event is fired whenever the user moves to a new range of dates. This event passes in the starting date displayed, a count of how many days are displayed, and a Boolean array of False values that you can set to True if you want a date to be made bold on the calendar. You might use this to give the user an at-a-glance view of which days have employee interviews scheduled.
SelChange	This event occurs whenever the user selects a new date or a new range of dates. You might use this to update the caption of the form on which this control resides with the date(s) selected.

The Progress Bar Control

A progress bar control is used as a feedback mechanism to inform a user that a process is taking place. Although it's not the most accurate control, it does provide a good visual clue that something is happening in your application. Figure 31.3 shows examples of two different progress bars. The top bar has the typical "box" look, whereas the bottom progress bar uses the new "smooth scrolling" effect. You would use a progress bar whenever there's a lot of data to go through and the operation the user is performing will take awhile.

Example's Filename: Progress.frm

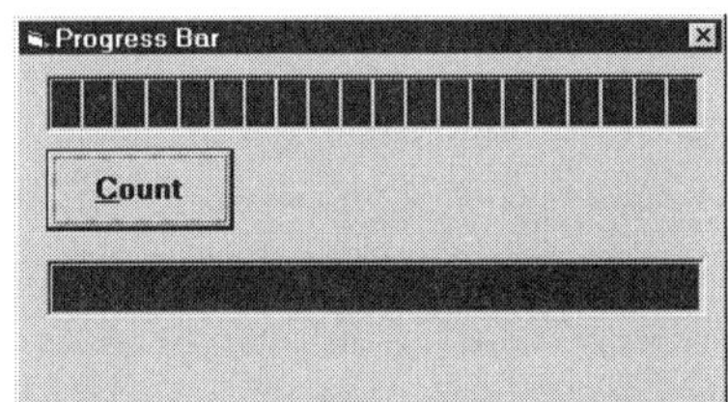

FIGURE 31.3
A progress bar example.

The progress bar control determines how many blocks to put up, depending on the height and the width of the control. All you have to do is to fill in the `Min`, `Max`, and `Value` properties, and the control calculates the amount of blocks to display. In general, it's best if the width of the control is at least twelve times the height of the control.

If you're calculating the percentage complete of a process, you need to set the `Min` property to `0` and the `Max` property to `100`. You then need to know how many total operations you're doing and which operation you're currently on. You'll then calculate a percentage and set this number in the `Value` property of the progress bar.

If you're looping through a set of records, you may want to find out how many records you have in the set; then you can set the `Value` property to the record number you're currently on. In either scenario, it's up to you to set the `Value` property as well as the `Min` and `Max` properties appropriately.

Let's look at the example for this chapter. When the user clicks the command button, the percentage complete displays as the code loops through a set of employee records. Nothing is done to the records, the code just loops through them. In fact, so that the progress bars won't move too fast, a `Delay` procedure is added that pauses for a few CPU cycles before moving to the next record in the set. Here's the code:

```
Private Sub cmdCount_Click()
   Dim oRS As Recordset
   Dim intCount As Integer
   Dim intLoop As Integer
   Dim intPercent As Integer
   Dim strSQL As String

   Screen.MousePointer = vbHourglass

   ' Retrieve Record Count
   intCount = RecCountGet()

   Set oRS = New Recordset
   strSQL = "SELECT lEmp_id FROM tblEmployees"
   oRS.Open strSQL, _
            ConnectString(), _
            adOpenForwardOnly

   If Not oRS.EOF Then
      pbrSmooth.Min = 0
      pbrSmooth.Max = 100
      pbrCount.Min = 0
      pbrCount.Max = 100
```

```
            intLoop = 1
            Do Until oRS.EOF
                intPercent = CInt((intLoop / intCount) * 100)
                pbrCount.Value = intPercent
                pbrSmooth.Value = intPercent

                Call Delay

                intLoop = intLoop + 1
                oRS.MoveNext
            Loop
            pbrCount.Value = pbrCount.Max
            pbrSmooth.Value = pbrSmooth.Max
        End If
        oRS.Close
        Screen.MousePointer = vbDefault

        MsgBox "Done Counting Employees"
    End Sub
```

This routine first gets the total number of records to loop through. The function `RecCountGet()` is called to return this number. In this function, a `SELECT COUNT(*) FROM tblEmployees` is performed to retrieve the total number of records. You could also use the `MoveLast` method and the `RecordCount` property after opening the recordset, but `SELECT COUNT()` is much more efficient; besides, not all OLE DB providers support the `RecordCount` property, so `SELECT COUNT()` will always work regardless of which provider you're using.

Each time through the loop, the percentage is calculated by dividing the count by the looping variable and multiplying by 100. This value is then placed in the `Value` property of each progress bar. In the second progress bar, the `Scrolling` property is set to `1-SmoothScrolling` to get the smooth bar effect.

The Slider Control

The slider control is typically used to allow the user to change a volume setting or increment a value by a small amount (see Figure 31.4).

Example's Filename: Slider.frm

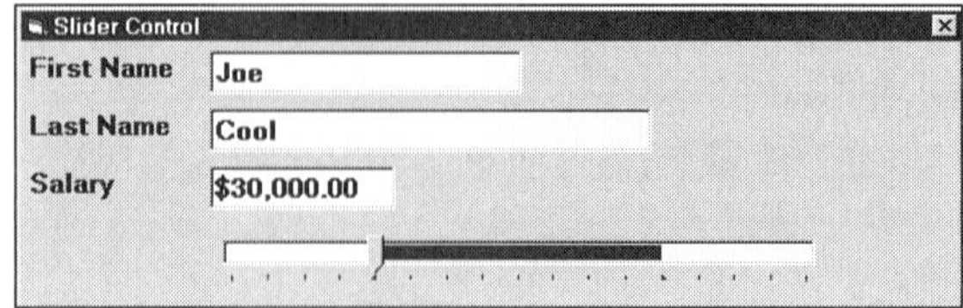

FIGURE 31.4 The slider control example.

Common Properties of the Slider Control

The slider control has several properties that are different from the standard set of properties for controls. Table 31.7 lists these properties.

Table 31.7 Common Properties of the Slider Control

Property	Description
`Min`	Set this property to the minimum value you want to have as a starting value when the user selects the leftmost tick mark of the slider control.
`Max`	Set this property to the maximum value you want to have as an ending value when the user selects the rightmost tick mark of the slider control.
`SelectRange`	Set this property to `True` if you want to display a highlighted range of values within the slider control. If you set this property, you need to set the `SelStart` and `SelLength` properties to valid values within the `Min` and `Max` properties.
`SelStart`	Set this property to a value that's greater than the `Min` property to signify where you want the selection range to start.
`SelLength`	Set this property to a value that's no greater than the `Max` property to signify where you want the selection range to end.
`SmallChange`	Set this property to a value that determines how to increment or decrement the `Value` property when the user grabs the slider and moves it either left or right.
`LargeChange`	Set this property to a value that determines how to increment or decrement the Value property when the user clicks anywhere on the slider control.
`TickFrequency`	Set this property to a value that specifies where to place a tick mark on the slider.

Property	Description
TextPosition	Set this property to a value that signifies where the tooltip text is displayed. It can appear above or below for a horizontal slider or on the left or right for a vertical slider.
ToolTipText	The text to display when the user's cursor hovers over the slider control.
Value	The value the slider is currently set to.

Using the Slider Control at Runtime

In the Slider sample form, the slider is used to control an employee's salary. When the user moves the slider to affect the salary, the text box is updated. What's more, if the user types a value into the text box, the slider control is updated. First, the `Form_Load()` event sets a default value for the salary:

```
Private Sub Form_Load()
   txtSalary.Text = Format("30000", "Currency")
   Call txtSalary_LostFocus
End Sub
```

After the `Text` property of the text box is set, the `LostFocus` event of the text box is called:

```
Private Sub txtSalary_LostFocus()
   sldSalary.Value = CCur(txtSalary.Text)
End Sub
```

When the user moves out of the text box, the slider control is updated to the new value entered in the text box by setting the `Value` property of the slider from the `Text` property of the text box. The `Validate` event is used to make sure a valid numeric value is entered into the text box:

```
Private Sub txtSalary_Validate(Cancel As Boolean)
   If CCur(txtSalary.Text) < sldSalary.Min Then
      Beep
      Cancel = True
   End If
   If CCur(txtSalary.Text) > sldSalary.Max Then
      Beep
      Cancel = True
   End If
End Sub
```

In the `Scroll` event of the slider control, you can grab the current `Value` property from the slider and use that value to update the text box as the slider moves back and forth. Here's how:

```
Private Sub sldSalary_Scroll()
   txtSalary.Text = Format(sldSalary.Value, "Currency")
End Sub
```

The UpDown Control

The UpDown control is used to increment or decrement the value in another control to a new value (see Figure 31.5). You can use this control to increment any type of value you want. You can use it for numeric values, date values, and so on. When you use this control to change numeric values, no code is required. However, for any other type of value, you need to write a little bit of code.

Example's Filename: UpDown.frm

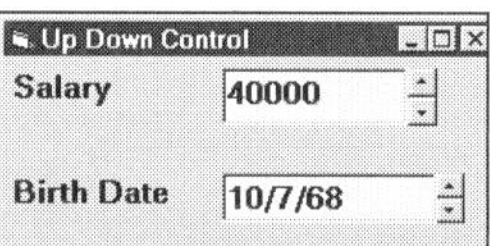

FIGURE 31.5 The UpDown control example.

Common Properties of the UpDown Control

Table 31.8 shows the most commonly set properties for the UpDown control.

Table 31.8 Common Properties of the UpDown Control

Property	Description
`AutoBuddy`	Set this property to `True` in the Properties window if you want it to fill in the `BuddyControl` and `BuddyProperty` properties with the control that has its `TabIndex` property set to one less than this control. For example, if you have a text box next to the UpDown control, and the UpDown control has the value `10` in the `TabIndex` property, set the `TabIndex` property of the text box to the value `9`. Then, set the `AutoBuddy` property to `True` to fill in the `BuddyControl` and `BuddyProperty` properties automatically.
`BuddyControl`	This identifies the name of the control that's the "buddy" to the UpDown control.

Property	Description
`BuddyProperty`	This identifies the name of the property to affect when the up or down arrow is clicked.
`SyncBuddy`	You must set this property to `True` to have the control automatically affect the `BuddyControl` property.
`Increment`	This is the amount you want to use to increment or decrement the value in the `BuddyControl` property.
`Orientation`	You can have the UpDown control display either an up/down arrow or a left/right arrow.

Using the UpDown Control

In the example, the Salary text box has no code because it uses a numeric value. You use the `AutoBuddy` feature of the UpDown control to have the UpDown control affect the salary in the text box.

For the Birth Date text box, you need to write a little code to have the UpDown control affect the date in that text box:

```
Private Sub updDate_DownClick()
   If IsDate(txtBirthDate.Text) Then
      txtBirthDate.Text = CDate(txtBirthDate.Text) - _
                          updDate.Increment
   End If
End Sub
```

When the user clicks the down arrow, the `DownClick` event occurs. This event checks to see whether the `Text` property contains a valid date. If it does, it converts the value in the `Text` property to a date and decrements that value by the value in the `Increment` property of the UpDown control.

When the user clicks the up arrow, the `UpClick` event occurs. The same steps are performed in this event, except it *increments* the value by the value in the `Increment` property of the UpDown control. Here's the code:

```
Private Sub updDate_UpClick()
   If IsDate(txtBirthDate.Text) Then
      txtBirthDate.Text = CDate(txtBirthDate.Text) + _
                          updDate.Increment
   End If
End Sub
```

The TabStrip

The TabStrip control is used when you have many controls that need to be placed on one form but are limited by the available real estate. A tab strip control is shown in Figure 31.6.

Example's Filename: TabStrip.frm

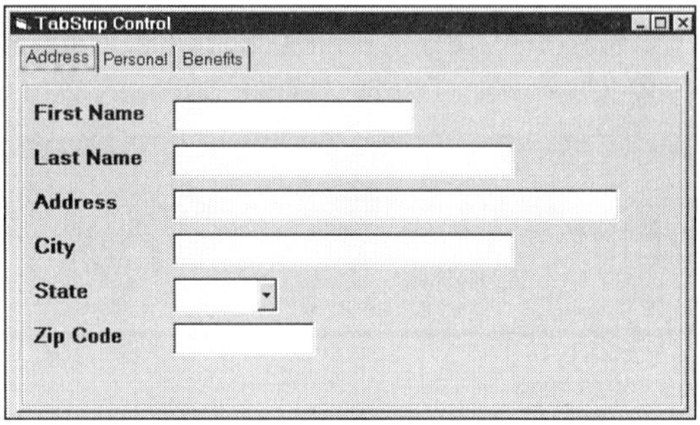

FIGURE 31.6 The TabStrip control example.

Each time you click one of the tabs, a new set of controls is displayed.

Common Properties of the TabStrip Control

The TabStrip control does not have that many properties you'll need to be concerned with. Table 31.9 lists the most important properties of the TabStrip control.

Table 31.9 Common Properties of the TabStrip Control

Property	Description
`Placement`	This property determines where the tabs are to appear. You can set the tabs on the top, bottom, left, or right.
`Separators`	This property determines whether a separator line is displayed when the `Style` property of the control is set to `tabButton` or `tabFlatButton`.
`Style`	This property determines the different styles you can set on the TabStrip control. You can choose normal tabs, button-type tabs, or flat button tabs. Try setting this property to each of the different styles to see the effect it has on the appearance of this control.

Using a Container Control

To use the TabStrip control, you need to place several containers on it. You can then place controls on top of the containers. It's up to you to manipulate the appropriate container when the corresponding tab is clicked. For example, if you have three tabs, you need three container controls. When you click the first tab, you need to make the first container control visible and the other two containers invisible. A good container control to use is the frame control, because you can specify whether to use a border, and it has a little less overhead than a picture control.

When you create the container controls, make sure to place them in a control array and set the `Index` property of each container to `1` through the number of tabs you have on the TabStrip control. Also, make sure you use each container so that it corresponds to the number of the tab. For example, in the example, I created the `fraEmp(1)` control to be the one that holds the controls for the first tab. The second frame, `fraEmp(2)`, houses the controls for the second tab, and so on.

Lining Up the Containers

You should make sure that all the container controls are lined up at runtime. In this example, you use three frame controls as containers. In the `Form_Load()` procedure, you first make all the frames invisible, except for the first one you want to display. Next, you need to line up all the frames to the same location by using the `ClientLeft`, `ClientTop`, `ClientWidth`, and `ClientHeight` properties of the TabStrip control. These properties are automatically set by the control for just the purpose of positioning the container controls:

```
Private Sub Form_Load()
    ' Start with 1st Frame Visible
    fraEmp(1).Visible = True
    fraEmp(2).Visible = False
    fraEmp(3).Visible = False
    With tabEmployee
        fraEmp(1).Move .ClientLeft, .ClientTop, _
                       .ClientWidth, .ClientHeight
        fraEmp(2).Move .ClientLeft, .ClientTop, _
                       .ClientWidth, .ClientHeight
        fraEmp(3).Move .ClientLeft, .ClientTop, _
                       .ClientWidth, .ClientHeight
    End With
End Sub
```

Changing Tabs

When the user clicks a new tab, you need to make one frame invisible and the others invisible. In the `Click` event for the TabStrip control, you need to write the code that does this. First, you check to see whether the tab clicked is the current one. You do this by checking the `Visible` property of the current frame, as specified by the `tabEmployee.SelectedItem.Index` property:

```
Private Sub tabEmployee_Click()
   Dim intIndex As Integer

   intIndex = tabEmployee.SelectedItem.Index

   If Not fraEmp(intndex).Visible Then
      fraEmp(1).Visible = False
      fraEmp(2).Visible = False
      fraEmp(3).Visible = False
      fraEmp(intIndex).Visible = True
   End If
End Sub
```

After you've made all the frames invisible, you set the `Visible` property of the clicked tab to `True`. If you have a lot of tabs, you might want to write a loop instead of listing each of the frames individually.

TIP

When you're laying out all these frame controls on top of each other, they can get kind of difficult to work with. If you right-click the topmost frame control, you can select the Send To Back menu item on the pop-up menu to send this frame behind the other frames on the tab. This will help you move among the different frames more easily.

The SSTab Control

This control is easier to use at design time than the TabStrip control, because it allows you to place controls on each tab. In other words, instead of having to create container controls, you can just move from tab to tab placing controls on each at design time. An example of the SSTab control is shown in Figure 31.7.

Example's Filename: SSTab.frm

FIGURE 31.7
An SSTab control example.

Common Properties of the SSTab Control

Table 31.10 provides a list and description of the common properties of the SSTab control.

Table 31.10 Common Properties of the SSTab Control

Property	Description
`Tab`	The number of the tab that has focus.
`TabCaption`	You pass in a tab number to this property to have it return the caption of that particular tab.
`TabEnabled`	You pass in a tab number to this property to have it return the value of the `Enabled` property of that particular tab.
`TabOrientation`	Use this property to set where you want the tabs to appear. You can set this to the top, bottom, left, or right.
`TabPicture`	You pass in the tab number to this property to have it return or set a picture to appear on the left side of the tab.
`Tabs`	The total number of tabs for the control.
`TabsPerRow`	The number of tabs to display per each row of tabs.
`TabVisible`	Returns a `True` value if the tab is visible. You can set this property to a `False` value to hide a particular tab.
`Rows`	The total number of tab rows visible.
`WordWrap`	Set this property to `True` to have the caption of a particular tab wrap to another line.

When you use this control, you won't need any code at runtime to manipulate the containers, because each tab is its own container and will display any controls placed on it.

Summary

The DateTimePicker and MonthView controls are great when you need to add date-handling capabilities to your applications. The progress bar can help inform your user that processing is occurring during a long operation. Tab controls help you get more information into less real-estate.

Review Questions

1. Which control(s) can you use to select a date?
2. Which tab control is easier to use?

Exercise

1. On the form you created in the exercise in the last chapter, add a tab control. On the first tab of the form, place a DateTimePicker control. Place an UpDown control next to this control and have it increment and decrement the date in the DateTimePicker control. On the second tab, add a MonthView control.

32

Drag and Drop

IT'S PRETTY NEAT TO BE ABLE TO DRAG AND DROP a group of data from one location to another within an application. For example, you can highlight a piece of text in Word or in the Visual Basic code editor and drag it to a new location. In this chapter, you'll learn how to add this drag-and-drop capability to your Visual Basic applications. Although drag and drop may not be appropriate for every screen, adding it in a few key places can really jazz up your application.

Chapter Objectives

- Learn to utilize drag and drop
- Learn how to change the drag icon
- Learn to drag and drop between different controls
- Learn to utilize a control array
- Learn to use the ImageList control

Sample Project File: \Chapter32\DragDrop.vbp

Drag and Drop Defined

Drag and drop is becoming very popular in Windows applications today. Visual Basic includes features that allow you to add this functionality to your application relatively easily. Drag and drop can be an automatic operation, or you can manually code it to happen. This means you can let Visual Basic do some of the work, or you can manually control the entire process.

Dragging is the action of clicking and holding down the mouse button over a control and then moving that control to a new location. *Dropping* occurs when the mouse button is released and the control or data is moved to a new location.

A Sample Application

If you load the sample project for this chapter and run the last example by clicking the Final Example command button, you'll see the form shown in Figure 32.1.

Example's Filename: Drag5.frm

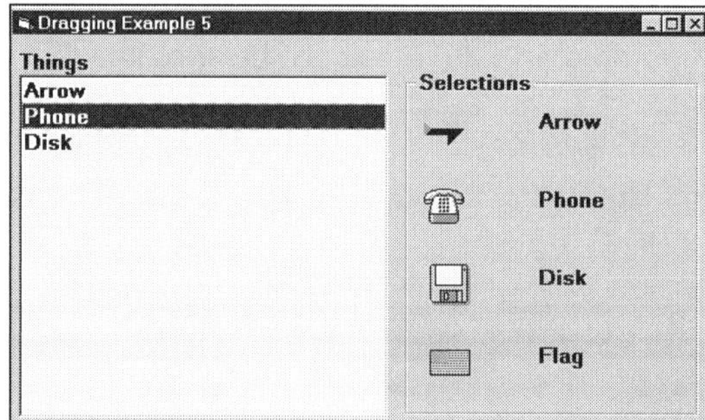

FIGURE 32.1 The final example of drag and drop.

In this example, you can drag the icons on the right side of the form onto the list box to have the words located next to those icons loaded into the list box. This is a fairly sophisticated example, but you'll learn to build this by the time you finish reading the chapter. Of course, you must learn to walk before you can run, so let's first start with a fairly simple example.

Automatic Drag and Drop

Visual Basic allows you to set the `DragMode` property of most controls to `1 - Automatic`. This allows you to click and hold the mouse over the control and then move the mouse. A gray outline will appear signifying that you're in drag mode. When you release the mouse, the outline goes away, but the control stays at the same location where it was before. Let's try this out.

EXERCISE

Using Automatic Drag and Drop

1. Start a new project in Visual Basic.
2. Add a label control to the default form.
3. Set the Name property to `lblDrag`.
4. Set the `BorderStyle` property to `1 - Fixed Single` just so you can see the label a little better.
5. Set the `Caption` property to `Drag Me`.
6. Set the `DragMode` property to `1 - Automatic`.
7. Run the project.
8. Click and hold down the left mouse button over the label.
9. Drag your mouse around the form to see the outline of the label appear.

As you can see by the above exercise, it is very easy to get drag and drop to work.

Well, that was a drag! Okay, okay, bad pun. Let's now have it actually do something. Let's add the ability to drop the control somewhere.

Moving the Control

To have the control actually move somewhere, you need to add code to the DragDrop() event of the form. Because you're dragging this control over the form, you need to have the form move the control.

EXERCISE

ADD THE *DragDrop()* EVENT

1. Double-click the form.
2. Find the DragDrop() event from the Procedures combo box.
3. Add the following code to the Form_DragDrop() event:

```
Sub Form_DragDrop (Source As Control, x As Single, _
                      y As Single)
    Source.Move x, y
End Sub
```

The DragDrop() event will receive a pointer to the control that's being moved over the form. It will also be passed in the current X and Y coordinates of the mouse on the form. By using the Move method on the control being dragged, you can move this control to the location of the mouse on the form.

Once the DragDrop() event is triggered by releasing the mouse, you call the Move method on the control to place that control's Top and Left properties to where the mouse is located. Of course, if you grab the control right in the middle, it will look a little funny when you drop it because the control moves to the exact mouse location—it will look as if the control "jumps" around, and it won't be a smooth operation. However, about the best you can do is to center the control at the mouse location.

EXERCISE

CENTERING THE CONTROL

1. Add the following code to center the control in the middle of the mouse location:

```
Sub Form_DragDrop (Source As Control, x As Single, _
                      y As Single)
    Source.Move (x - Source.Width / 2), _
                (y - Source.Height / 2)
End Sub
```

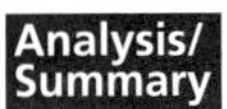

By centering the control where the mouse is, it looks a little better since the control won't jump around the screen as much.

For a completed example of this, you can look at the sample file Drag1.frm, as shown in Figure 32.2.

Example's Filename: Drag1.frm

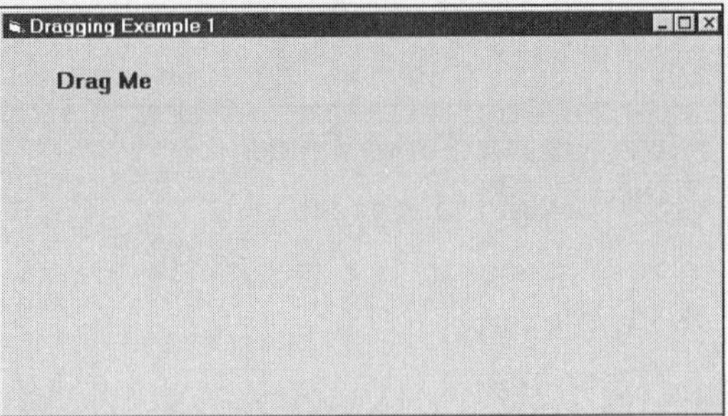

FIGURE 32.2
The first example of drag and drop.

Changing the Drag Icon

Most applications have a nice icon that displays when you start dragging a particular control or data. Just by setting the `DragIcon` property, you can add this functionality to your drag-and-drop operation.

EXERCISE

ADD A *DRAGICON*

1. Go back to design mode on the form.
2. Click the label control one time to give it focus.
3. In the Properties window for the label control, double-click the `DragIcon` property.
4. Locate the Bullseye.ico file in the folder for this chapter. Click the OK button on the Open dialog box to set this property.
5. Run the application again and see what happens when you start to drag the label around the form.

It is nice to give the user a good visual clue that the control is now moving by setting the `DragIcon` property.

No Dropping Here

Have you ever tried to drag a control over someplace it does not want to go? When this happens, you generally see the icon for the international "no" symbol—a circle with a line through it. If you want to use this functionality in your application, you need to add code to change the icon when the control is in a location where it shouldn't be dropped. You do this by adding code to the `DragOver()` events of the items in which you don't want to allow the drop operation to occur.

EXERCISE

Add a Text Box to the Drag Form

1. Go back to Visual Basic design mode.
2. Add a text box to your form so that it looks like the one shown in Figure 32.3.
3. Set the `Name` property to `txtNoDrop`.
4. Set the `Text` property to `Can't Drop On Me`.

In the next sample, you will not allow the Label control to drop on this text box you just added to this form.

Example's Filename: Drag2.frm

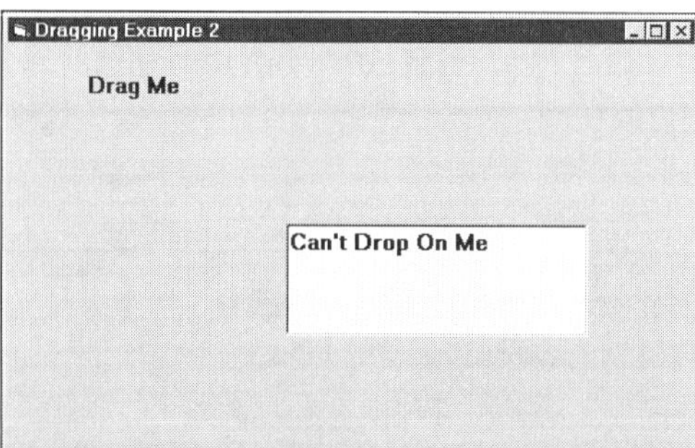

FIGURE 32.3
Can't drop on me.

Time to Save Your Work

Before you begin more work on this example, let's save the project you've created so far in a completely new folder.

EXERCISE

SAVE YOUR WORK!

1. Create a new folder and save all your changes into this folder.
2. Copy all the *.ICO files in the example's folder for this chapter to this new folder you created.

   It is a good idea to save all your work periodically. Be sure to keep the .ICO files in the same directory where your project is located.

The *DragOver()* Event

Before you actually start coding the `DragOver()` event, you need to learn a little about it. First, this event is fired whenever a control is dragged over another control. The `DragOver()` event is passed through four parameters: the control, the X and Y coordinates, and the state of the operation. The `State` argument can be one of three possible values, as listed in Table 32.1.

Table 32.1 Values of the *State* Argument in the *DragOver()* Event

Value	Description	Visual Basic Constant
0	The control being dragged is entering this object for the first time.	`vbEnter`
1	The control being dragged is leaving the object.	`vbLeave`
2	The control being dragged is still over the object.	`vbOver`

Each time the control is moved over the form or any other control on the form, the `DragOver()` event is fired. For when the `State` argument is `vbEnter` or `vbOver`, you can write some code to change the `DragIcon` property of the control to the "no drop" icon. When the `State` argument becomes `vbLeave`, you need to set the `DragIcon` back to the original value. You'll use the `LoadPicture()` function to load the Trffc14.ico file for the "no drop" icon. The `LoadPicture()` function allows you to load any graphic file off of a disk and place that graphic into one of the picture type properties of any form or control. This is one of the files you just copied into your new folder. You'll use the Bullseye.ico file for the normal drag icon.

Of course, because the `DragOver` event is called repeatedly as the mouse is dragged over the control, you need to set a flag to inform the `DragOver` event that the `DragIcon` property has already been changed to the "no drop" icon. For this, you can use a module-level variable.

EXERCISE

Stopping the Drop of a Control

1. Add a module-level variable to this form called `mboolFlag` as a Boolean data type.
2. In the `Form_Load()` event, set this variable to `True`:

```
Sub Form_Load()
    mboolFlag = True
End Sub
```

3. Double-click on the txtNoDrop text box.
4. Locate the `DragOver()` event in the Procedures combo Box.
5. Add the following code:

```
Sub txtNoDrop_DragOver (Source As Control, X As Single, _
                        Y As Single, State As Integer)
    If mboolFlag Then
        If State = vbEnter Or State = vbOver Then
            Source.DragIcon = LoadPicture("trffc14.ico")
            mboolFlag = False
        End If
    Else
        If State = vbLeave Then
            Source.DragIcon = LoadPicture("bullseye.ico")
            mboolFlag = True
        End If
    End If
End Sub
```

Every time the dragged control enters the text box, the `DragIcon` property of the control being dragged is changed. You use the `LoadPicture()` function to load a new icon into the property. You then set a module-level variable `mboolFlag` to indicate that you've already loaded the icon. By setting this flag, you won't keep loading the icon over and over again as this event keeps firing. For when the control moves out of the text box, you need to put the icon back to the original using the LoadPicture() function once again. Of course, you need to set the mboolFlag variable to True again.

You have one remaining problem with this code. If you drop the control on the text box anyway, the DragIcon property will still be set to the "no drop" icon. You need to change the icon back to the original drag icon.

EXERCISE

RESET THE *DRAGICON* AFTER DROPPING

1. Double-click the txtNoDrop text box and select the DragDrop() event.
2. Add the following code to this event:

```
Private Sub txtNoDrop_DragDrop(Source As Control, _
                               x As Single, y As Single)
    Source.DragIcon = LoadPicture("bullseye.ico")
    mboolFlag = True
End Sub
```

It is very important that you reset the DragIcon property after dropping on a control that does not accept drops. The next time the user starts to drag the control, you want it to be back to the normal DragIcon they started with. For a completed example that shows you the DragOver event's State argument, see the Drag3.frm, as shown in Figure 32.4.

Example's Filename: Drag3.frm

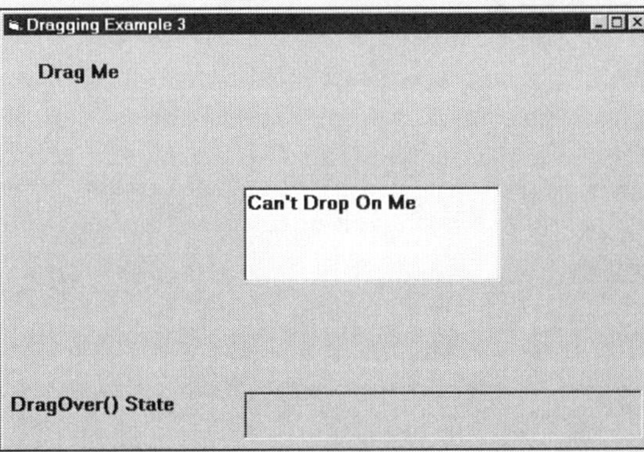

FIGURE 32.4
Run this example to see the DragOver event's State argument.

Manual Drag and Drop

Let's now look at controls for which you can't use the automatic type of drag and drop. These are controls, such as the list and combo boxes, that need to have a `Click` event occur. If you have the automatic mode set, you can't select an item on the list box. Let's build a drag-and-drop form that uses the manual mode of drag and drop, as shown in Figure 32.5.

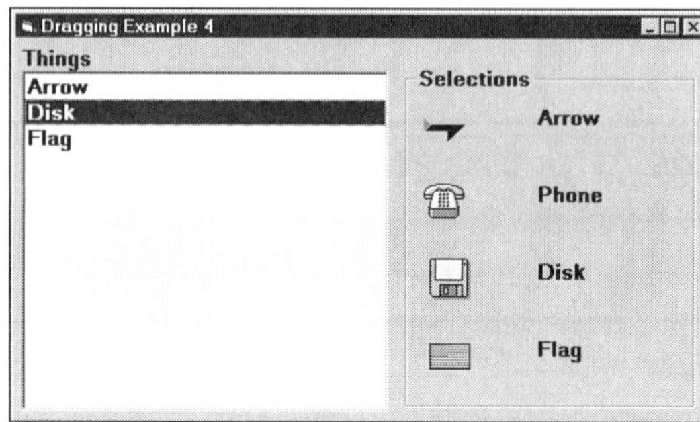

FIGURE 32.5 An example of a manual drag-and-drop form.

EXERCISE

An Example Using List Boxes

1. Create a new form.
2. Set the `Name` property of this form to `frmDragManual`.
3. Add a list box to the form.
4. Set the `Name` property to `lstThings`.
5. Add an image control next to the list box.
6. Set the `Name` property to `imaArrow`.
7. Set the `DragMode` property to `1 - Automatic`.
8. Set the `Tag` property to `Arrow`.
9. Set the `DragIcon` and the `Picture` properties to the arw02rt.ico file located in the example's folder for this chapter.
10. Add another image control directly underneath the arrow image control.
11. Set the `Name` property to `imaPhone`.
12. Set the `DragMode` property to `1 - Automatic`.
13. Set the `Tag` property to `Phone`.

14. Set the `DragIcon` and the `Picture` properties to the Phone01.ico file located in the example's folder for this chapter.
15. Add another image control directly underneath the phone image control.
16. Set the `Name` property to `imaDisk`.
17. Set the `DragMode` property to `1 - Automatic`.
18. Set the `Tag` property to `Disk`.
19. Set the `DragIcon` and the `Picture` properties to the Disk06.ico file located in the example's folder for this chapter.
20. Add another image control directly underneath the disk image control.
21. Set the `Name` property to `imaFlag`.
22. Set the `DragMode` property to `1 - Automatic`.
23. Set the `Tag` property to `Flag`.
24. Set the `DragIcon` and the `Picture` properties to the flgusa02.ico file located in the example's folder for this chapter.
25. Be sure to set the Start Up Object option in the Project, Properties menu to this new form.

You set the `Tag` property of each of the image controls so that you can use these strings when you drop the controls onto the list box. You grab the `Tag` property's value in the `DragDrop` event of the list box. `Tag` is not used by Visual Basic, so you can use it for things like this.

EXERCISE

CHECKING THE *DRAGDROP* FOR A VALID CONTROL

1. Double-click the list box.
2. Select the `DragDrop` event from the Procedures combo box.
3. Add the following code to the event:

```
Sub lstThings_DragDrop (Source As Control, X As Single, _
                       Y As Single)
   If TypeOf Source Is Image Then
      lstThings.AddItem Source.Tag
   End If
End Sub
```

Remember that the `Source` argument is a reference to the image control being dropping on the list box. Therefore, the `Tag` property you set in the image control is used as the parameter to the `AddItem` method of the list box when the control is dropped. You should always use the `TypeOf` operator to make sure the user is attempting to drop the appropriate type of control. For example, if you had a label control on the form as well as the image controls, you might not get a valid `Tag` property to load into the list box.

Removing Items from the List Box

You've seen how to add items to the list box. Let's now look at how to take items out of the list box. In this case, you set one icon on the list box for the drag operation. However, when the user drags the list box over the appropriate image control, you want to signify to the user that this is the image control that he or she can drop it on. This is accomplished by changing the `DragIcon` property when the user is over the appropriate image control.

EXERCISE

Loading the *DragIcon* at Runtime

1. Set the `DragIcon` property of the list box to the Folder05.ico file located in the example's folder for this chapter.
2. Make sure the `DragMode` property of the list box is set to `0 - Manual`.
3. Double-click the list box.
4. Select the `MouseDown` event from the Procedures combo box.
5. Add the following code to the `MouseDown` event:

```
Private Sub lstThings_MouseDown(Button As Integer, _
             Shift As Integer, X As Single, Y As Single)
    lstThings.DragIcon = _
            LoadPicture("folder05.ico")
    lstThings.Drag vbBeginDrag
End Sub
```

In the `MouseDown` event, you need to reset the `DragIcon` property so that you don't need to reset it when the user drops the item on the appropriate ImageList control. This just saves a little code in each `DragDrop` event of the image controls. You then need to invoke the `Drag` method on the list box by passing the constant `vbBeginDrag` to signify that the list box is to go into drag mode.

Now you need to write the code that will change the `DragIcon` property of the list box to a hand dropping a piece of paper when the user is over the image control that matches the item in the list box. You'll write this code in the `DragOver()` event of each of the ImageList controls.

EXERCISE

CHANGE THE *DRAGICON* AS YOU MOVE AROUND THE FORM

1. Double-click the imaArrow image control.
2. Select the `DragOver` event from the Procedures combo box.
3. Add the following code to the `DragOver` event:

```
Sub imaArrow_DragOver (Source As Control, X As Single, _
        Y As Single, State As Integer)
    If TypeOf Source Is ListBox Then
        If Source.Text = imaArrow.Tag Then
            If State = vbEnter Then
                Source.DragIcon = LoadPicture("drop1pg.ico")
            ElseIf State = vbLeave Then
                Source.DragIcon = LoadPicture("Folder05.ico")
            End If
        End If
    End If
End Sub
```

In this event, you first check to make sure that the source control being dragged over the image control is a list box. Remember that the user might be dragging the other image controls around, and you don't want to change the icon if you don't have to. Next, you compare the `Text` property of the list box control to see whether it matches the value in the imaArrow `Tag` property. You then use code very similar to what you did before for the "no drop" text box.

To actually allow the user to drop the item from the list box on the image, you need to check whether the source control is a list box and whether the `Text` property of the source (the list box) is equal to the same value in the `Tag` property of the image control. If they're the same, you know the item can be dropped in the image control, which then removes the item from the list box.

EXERCISE

Remove Items from the List Box

1. Double-click on the imaArrow image control.
2. Select the `DragDrop` event from the Procedures combo box.
3. Add the following code to this event:

```
Sub imaArrow_DragDrop (Source As Control, X As Single, _
                       Y As Single)
    If TypeOf Source Is ListBox Then
        If Source.Text = imaArrow.Tag Then
            Source.RemoveItem Source.ListIndex
        End If
    End If
End Sub
```

You now need to repeat these steps for each of the other image controls on the form. Of course, this results in a lot of duplicate code; instead, you could use a control array, which is our next topic of discussion. To see the completed sample form, check out Drag4.frm in the sample project for this chapter.

Example's Filename: Drag4.frm

Simplifying Drag and Drop

The example you just created has a lot of duplicate code because you repeat the `DragOver` and the `DragDrop` events for each of the image controls. One way to simplify this is to create a control array out of the image controls on the form. Another problem with the preceding code is that you're loading the icon files from disk each time you want to use them. This is not very efficient. Instead, you should store these images in an ImageList control and retrieve the pictures from there.

EXERCISE

ADD ICONS TO AN *IMAGELIST* CONTROL

1. Select Project, Components from the Visual Basic menu.
2. Select the Microsoft Windows Common Controls 6.0 option from the list of components.
3. Add an ImageList control to your project.
4. Set the `Name` property to `imlList`.
5. Click the `Custom` property to bring up the property pages for the ImageList control.
6. Add the Folder05.ico file to the ImageList control.
7. Set the `Key` property for this image to `Folder`.
8. Add the Drop1pg.ico file to the ImageList control.
9. Set the `Key` property for this image to `DropPage`.

Now that you have the ImageList control loaded, let's convert the image controls into a control array.

EXERCISE

CREATE A CONTROL ARRAY OF IMAGE CONTROLS

1. Click the imaArrow image control.
2. Change the `Name` property of the imaArrow image control to `imaPicture`.
3. Click the imaPhone image control.
4. Change the `Name` property of the imaPhone image control to `imaPicture`.
5. When asked whether you want to create a control array, click the Yes button.
6. Click the imaDisk image control.
7. Change the `Name` property of the imaDisk image control to `imaPicture`.
8. Click the imaFlag image control.
9. Change the `Name` property of the imaFlag image control to `imaPicture`.
10. Delete any of the old code for the old image control names.

11. Add the following code for the `DragOver` event for the new imaPicture control:

```
Private Sub imaPicture_DragOver(Index As Integer, _
               Source As Control, x As Single, _
               y As Single, State As Integer)
   If TypeOf Source Is ListBox Then
      If Source.Text = imaPicture(Index).Tag Then
         If State = vbEnter Then
            Source.DragIcon = _
               imlList.ListImages("DropPage").Picture
         ElseIf State = vbLeave Then
            Source.DragIcon = _
               imlList.ListImages("Folder").Picture
         End If
      End If
   End If
End Sub
```

In this code, a new argument is passed to the `DragOver` event—the `Index` property of the control you just dragged over. You now need to use that index to compare the `Text` property in the list box against the `Tag` property of the image control. Now, you can also set the `DragIcon` property by retrieving the `Picture` property of the `ListImages` collection where the `Key` property is `DropPage` or `Folder`, depending on whether you're leaving the control or not. You can also change the `MouseDown` event to pull the "folder" picture when resetting the `DragIcon` property, as shown in the following source code:

```
Private Sub lstThings_MouseDown(Button As Integer, _
            Shift As Integer, x As Single, y As Single)
   lstThings.DragIcon = imlList.ListImages("Folder").Picture
   lstThings.Drag vbBeginDrag
End Sub
```

Drop and Remove

When you're positioned over the correct image control and you let go of the mouse button, the **`DragDrop`** event is fired on the image control. You can now remove the item from the list box. You need to add the following code to replace the code you deleted for the old controls. Notice, again, that you use the **`Index`** argument that's passed in:

```
Sub imaPicture_DragDrop (Index As Integer, _
        Source As Control, X As Single, Y As Single)
    If TypeOf Source Is ListBox Then
        If Source.Text = imaPicture(Index).Tag Then
            Source.RemoveItem Source.ListIndex
        End If
    End If
End Sub
```

To see this example completed, just load the sample project for this chapter and take a look at Drag5.frm (see Figure 32.6).

Example's Filename: Drag5.frm

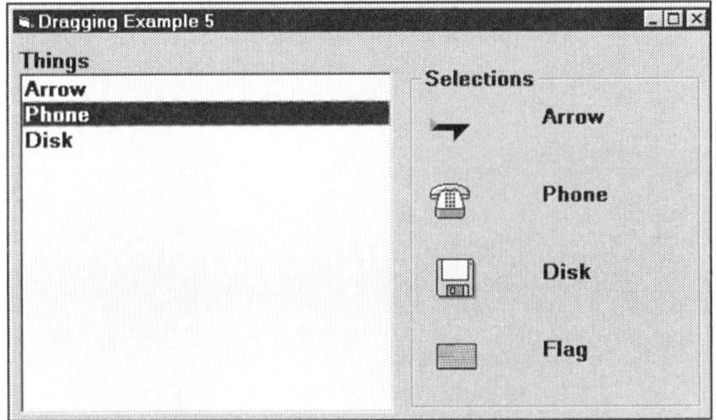

FIGURE 32.6 The final example of drag and drop.

Summary

Drag and drop can add a nice alternative to the pure-keyboard approach for your users. It also makes your application conform to the Windows standard. For many controls, you can choose automatic mode, but for others, you need to program using the manual mode. Also, using an ImageList control is a great way to store the icons you might use for your drag-and-drop operations.

Review Questions

1. Which property sets the icon to use for the dragging operation?
2. Which property do you set to make the drag operation automatic?
3. Which event is fired when a control is dragged over another one?
4. What are the three states the `DragOver()` event can receive?

33

Optimization

At some point, your users ask for a little more speed from your application, or you may decide you want to cut down the size of the EXE to make it a little easier to distribute. In this chapter, you'll learn techniques for speeding up your applications and cutting down the size of your EXEs. Be aware that optimizing under Windows is tenuous at best. Because Windows gives time slices to each application, what runs fast one time may run slower another time. This chapter gives you a sample application you can use to plug in your routines to test which version of a particular routine runs faster.

Chapter Objectives

- Learn some speed optimization tricks
- Learn to time code to see which version runs faster
- Learn some size optimization tricks

Sample Project File: \Chapter33\Optimization.vbp

Speed Optimization Tricks

Optimizing for speed is probably the most important thing you can do for your applications. Because a graphical user interface such as Windows will always be a little slower than a text-based application, the more tricks you can use to speed up your program, the better your users will like it. In this chapter, you'll load the sample project and run each of the tests to see whether the premises you thought were true are really valid assumptions.

Example's Filename: Speed.frm

In each of the examples run, you'll see a routine that creates an instance of a `TimerCompare` class. This class uses the `timeGetTime()` Windows API call to perform measurements in milliseconds. It tracks two sets of times—one for the "slow" method and one for the "fast" method. You should always perform what you think will be the "slow" method first and then perform the "fast" method. Each time, you invoke the `Start`*n* method, perform the process, and then invoke the `Quit`*n* method. After both processes have run, check the `Percent` property in the `TimerCompare` object to have it return the percentage difference between the two times. Here's the code for the sample application:

```
Private Sub LongVSVariant()
   Dim lngLoop As Long
   Dim vntValue As Variant
   Dim lngValue As Long
   Dim oTimer As TimerCompare

   ' Create new Timer object
   Set oTimer = New TimerCompare
   ' Start timer for "Slow" method
   oTimer.Start1
   ' Perform the "Slow" method
```

```
    For lngLoop = 0 To conRepeats
        vntValue = vntValue + 1
        vntValue = vntValue - 1
    Next
    ' Stop timer for "Slow" method
    oTimer.Quit1
    Debug.Print "Elapsed 1: " & oTimer.ElapsedTime1

    ' Start timer for "Fast" method
    oTimer.Start2
    ' Perform the "Fast" method
    For lngLoop = 0 To conRepeats
        lngValue = lngValue + 1
        lngValue = lngValue - 1
    Next
    ' Stop timer for "Fast" method
    oTimer.Quit2
    Debug.Print "Elapsed 2: " & oTimer.ElapsedTime2 & vbCrLf

    ' Add Time to list box
    lstTimes.AddItem mstrTestName & vbTab & _
                                      oTimer.Percent
End Sub
```

Avoid the Use of *Variant* Data Types

The `Variant` data type takes many bytes to store; therefore, it's much larger in memory than other data types. Also, it takes longer to read from and write to a `Variant` variable. For these reasons, you should always strive to use other data types before using the type `Variant`. In my tests using `Long` integers instead of `Variant` data types, the results were that the `Long` integers were accessed over 55 percent faster than the `Variant` data types.

Integer Versus *Long* Data Types

The results for whether to use an `Integer` or a `Long` were very inconclusive. In most instances, `Integer` and `Long` data types were both accessed quickly. An `Integer` is only two bytes in memory, whereas a `Long` is four bytes; therefore, an `Integer` should be slightly faster to access, but it's not as big a difference as accessing a `Variant`.

Byte Versus *Integer* Data Types

Going by the size of a data type does not always mean much. It would stand to reason that the smaller the data type, the faster it can be manipulated. This does not seem to be the case with the `Byte` data type. In fact, in my testing, I found that accessing a `Byte` data type was about 40 to 50 percent slower than accessing an `Integer` data type. This may be because a 32-bit operating system is used to dealing with two to four bytes at a time, and accessing just one byte may take extra time.

Fixed Strings Versus Dynamic Strings

Visual Basic creates most strings on-the-fly. This can result in a lot of overhead for sizing and resizing strings. In fact, if you test setting a value into a fixed string versus setting it into a dynamic string, the fixed string can be set about 40 percent faster. Because there's no overhead for reallocating memory, it makes sense that a fixed string can be written faster than a dynamic string.

Specific Object Types Versus Generic Object Types

If you're passing controls from a form to a generic routine that does something with these controls, it's much better to use the specific object type as opposed to a generic type such as `Control`. This means you should declare your arguments like this:

```
Private Sub SpecificPass(ctl As ComboBox)

End Sub
```

Avoid using an argument like the following:

```
Private Sub GenericPass(ctl As Control)

End Sub
```

This is faster because the compiler can resolve what the type of the control is at compile time, whereas the generic type has to be resolved at runtime. This takes extra time while the program is running and therefore makes it slower.

Procedure Call Versus In-line Code

Every time a function or procedure is called, some overhead is incurred. If you have a two-line function that's called from only three places, you might consider putting those two lines in the functions themselves and not making them a function. This can save some processing time. However, this can lead to some maintenance problems downstream. In the following example, a procedure is called to perform some calculation:

```
For lngLoop = 0 To conRepeats
   Call InlineCalc
Next
```

In the next example, the same code in the procedure is moved right into the loop:

```
For lngLoop = 0 To conRepeats
   intOp1 = 100
   intOp2 = 10
   intResult = intOp1 / intOp2
Next
```

Because you don't have the overhead of the procedure call, this code will execute faster.

Cached Properties Versus Not Cached

Retrieving values from properties is very slow. Avoid using properties in loops unless those properties are changing. Here's an example:

```
For intLoop1 = 0 To Screen.FontCount - 1
   For intLoop2 = 0 To Printer.FontCount - 1
      If Screen.Fonts(intLoop1) = Printer.Fonts(intLoop2) Then
         strGetFont = Screen.Fonts(intLoop1)
      End If
   Next intLoop2
Next intLoop1
```

The inner loop retrieves the value from the `Printer.FontCount` property every time through the outer loop. This value does not change, so you should move it outside both the loops. In addition, you reference `Screen.Fonts(intLoop1)` two times within the inner loop. Again, this value is not changing, so you should cache it to a local variable prior to entering the inner loop. Here's an example:

```
intPFonts = Printer.FontCount - 1
For intLoop1 = 0 To Screen.FontCount - 1
   strFont = Screen.Fonts(intLoop1)
   For intLoop2 = 0 To intPFonts
      If strFont = Printer.Fonts(intLoop2) Then
         strGetFont = strFont
      End If
   Next intLoop2
Next intLoop1
```

The reason for the speed difference has to do with how Visual Basic accesses properties attached to an object. The object name is stored in a *symbol table*, an internal structure that keeps track of the names of objects. Visual Basic generally uses a hashing algorithm to find the object in this symbol table. Once the object has been located, it uses this location to find the list of properties for this object in another table. Again, Visual Basic has to perform a hashing routine to figure out where that property is located. All of this hashing takes time—if you can eliminate it, you'll speed up your code.

Toggle *Boolean* Data Types Using the *Not* Operator

To toggle a variable between `True` and `False`, use the `Not` operator instead of an `If` statement. The `Not` operator performs a toggle on a `Boolean` data type, like this:

```
boolFlag = True
For lngLoop = 0 To conRepeats
   If boolFlag Then
      boolFlag = False
   Else
      boolFlag = True
   End If
Next
```

The following method is quicker than the preceding code:

```
boolFlag = Not boolFlag
```

This one is easy to understand, because you're dealing with one line of code versus five lines of code. Also, performing a `Not` operation results in a bitwise manipulation of the `Boolean` variable. This is a very quick operation compared to an assignment statement.

Be careful *not* to use the Not operator with any data type other than Boolean—especially when you're using numbers that are something other than True or False values (-1 and 0, respectively). Consider the following code:

```
Sub cmdBool_Click ()
   Dim intBool As Integer
   Dim intTemp As Integer



   intBool = True
   Print intBool       ' Prints -1
   Print Not intBool   ' Prints 0

   intTemp = 5
   Print intTemp       ' Prints 5
   Print Not intTemp   ' Prints -6
   If intTemp Then
      Print "intTemp is True"    ' Prints Here
   Else
      Print "intTemp is False"
   End If
End Sub
```

Notice that the Not operator performs bitwise manipulation. Therefore, manipulating 5 actually makes it -6.

Use *vbNullString* Instead of an Empty String

The constant vbNullString is much more efficient that setting a string variable equal to an empty string (""):

```
strValue = ""
```

Use the following line of code instead:

```
strValue = vbNullString
```

This is an optimization that's built into the compiler. Therefore, instead of having to reallocate memory for the string, you can use a specific constant to set the memory equal to a null pointer and mark the rest of the memory allocated for the string to "unused."

The *Len()* Function Versus an Empty String

Using the `Len()` function to check for an empty string is about 30 percent faster than using the <> or = sign:

```
If strTest <> "" Then
   ...
End If
```

The following code does the same thing but is more efficient:

```
If Len(strTest) Then
   ...
End If
```

This second code is faster because it doesn't take as much time to count the number of bytes that make up a string as it does to compare every character in one string against every character in another string. Even when the string is blank, the <> operator has to still do a comparison. In addition, the not equal (<>) sign is not a very efficient operator. Of course, I think you lose a little readability by using the `Len()` function.

Don't Compare Variables for Not Equal to Zero

If you're checking a numeric value against `0`, it's faster just to check the variable with an `If` statement:

```
If intTest <> 0 Then
   ...
End If
```

The following statement is equivalent to the first, but it runs faster (you will lose some readability, however):

```
If intTest Then
   ...
End If
```

Use *For...Each* Instead of *For...Next*

To loop through a collection of objects, use the `For...Each` construct instead of the `For...Next` looping construct:

```
For lngLoop = 0 To 10000
   For intLoop = 0 To Forms.Count - 1
```

```
        strName = Forms(intLoop).Name
    Next
Next
```

In my tests, the code using the `For...Each` construct runs at least twice as fast:

```
For lngLoop = 0 To 10000
    For Each oForm In Forms
        strName = oForm.Name
    Next
Next
```

This runs faster because the enumeration function keeps track of which object to retrieve when `For...Each` is used. However, when you access the collection using an index or a key value, a search must be performed through that collection every time you access it. This can take a while because searching through collections seems to be done sequentially.

With...End With

Using the `With...End With` construct is slightly faster than not using it. In Visual Basic 5, this construct seemed to be much faster than it does now in Visual Basic 6. Microsoft probably did some optimization underneath the hood. Here's a sample of the code where an object is declared of the type `Employee`, called `oEmp`. In the first routine, properties are set on the `Employee` object and then are retrieved back. In each line, the `Employee` object is referenced:

```
For lngLoop = 0 To conRepeats
    oEmp.EmpID = 1
    oEmp.FirstName = "Bill"
    oEmp.LastName = "Gates"
    oEmp.Salary = 100000
    strValue = oEmp.EmpID
    strValue = oEmp.FirstName
    strValue = oEmp.LastName
    strValue = oEmp.Salary
Next
```

In the next example, the `With...End With` construct is applied to the `oEmp` variable prior to going into the loop:

```
With oEmp
    For lngLoop = 0 To conRepeats
```

```
            .EmpID = 1
            .FirstName = "Bill"
            .LastName = "Gates"
            .Salary = 100000
            strValue = .EmpID
            strValue = .FirstName
            strValue = .LastName
            strValue = .Salary
        Next
    End With
```

You would think that because the code does not need to perform a lookup on the `oEmp` variable, it would be able to go directly to the location where the properties are in their symbol table. However, in these tests, there was only a slight increase in speed using `With...End With`.

Hide Controls When They're Loading

When you're loading any list-type controls, it's a good idea to turn off the redrawing of the control until it's fully populated with the data. On list boxes and combo boxes, there is no property to do this, so you need to set the `Visible` property to `False`. Here's an example:

```
lstItems.Visible = True
lstItems.Clear
For intLoop = 0 To 1000
   lstItems.AddItem "Loop " & intLoop
Next
```

In the next version, the `Visible` property is set to `False`, the list is loaded, and then the `Visible` property is set back to `True`:

```
lstItems.Visible = False
lstItems.Clear
For intLoop = 0 To 1000
   lstItems.AddItem "Loop " & intLoop
Next
lstItems.Visible = True
```

In my tests, this runs approximately 75 percent faster. Here's the reason for the speed difference: Every time an item is added to a list box, the visible portion of that list box has to be redrawn, and this takes a lot of time.

You can send a WM_SETREDRAW message to most list boxes and combo boxes with the SendMessage() API call. You pass a True or False value to tell the control to turn on or off its redraw functionality. You can then load the control and tell it to turn on its redraw capability.

Using *Move* Is Faster Than Setting *Left* and *Top* Properties

If you need to move a form or a control to a new location, make sure you always use the Move method instead of setting the Top and Left properties separately. Every time you set the Top property, it will move the form/control and then redraw the entire form/control. When you then set the Left property, it will also move the form/control and redraw the entire form/control. This cause two paint operations, and in a graphical environment, this can take awhile. Therefore, avoid code like the following:

```
For intLoop = 1 To 1500
   lblMove.Top = intLoop
   lblMove.Left = intLoop
Next
```

Instead, use the Move method, like this:

```
For intLoop = 1 To 1500
   lblMove.Move intLoop, intLoop
Next
```

Transaction Processing

If you're updating the values of several records inside a loop, you should place BeginTrans and CommitTrans around the loop. This can significantly speed up the update process. Therefore, you should avoid using code like this:

```
For lngLoop = 0 To 10
   oRS.MoveFirst
   Do Until oRS.EOF
      oRS!szLast_nm = "GATES"
      oRS.Update
      oRS.MoveNext
   Loop
Next
```

Instead, use code like this:

```
For lngLoop = 0 To 10
   oRS.MoveFirst
   oConn.BeginTrans
   Do Until oRS.EOF
      oRS!szLast_nm = "GATES"
      oRS.Update
      oRS.MoveNext
   Loop
   oConn.CommitTrans
Next
```

The second example is faster because the values are typically cached by either the client or the database engine instead of written directly to the table. Then, when you commit the data, it's written as a batch very quickly to the database.

Use SQL Instead of ADO Objects

Instead of using the ADO objects, you should use SQL directly because it's faster. For example, suppose you have code that updates a single column, like this:

```
For lngLoop = 0 To 10
   oRS.MoveFirst
   Do Until oRS.EOF
      oRS!szLast_nm = "GATES"
      oRS.Update
      oRS.MoveNext
   Loop
Next
```

You should change this code to use SQL instead. Here's an example:

```
strSQL = "UPDATE tblEmployeesRollback "
strSQL = strSQL & "SET szLast_nm = 'GATES'"

For lngLoop = 0 To 10
   oConn.Execute strSQL
Next
```

This is faster because every time you perform the `Update` method on the ADO object, it has to gather the data in the buffer area for the recordset, convert it to a SQL statement (`INSERT` or `UPDATE`), and then send the SQL to the back end. You therefore eliminate the gathering and converting to SQL steps by writing the UPDATE statement yourself. In addition, you don't have to bring the data back to the client each time you move through the loop. Instead, you just send the SQL down the server to be executed. This way, no data comes back to the client across the network. This is much faster because there's reduced network traffic.

In general, you should strive to use SQL whenever possible. For example, if you find yourself writing a loop in Visual Basic just to calculate a sum, average, count, minimum, or maximum, you should change the code to use the SQL aggregate function—`Sum()`, `Avg()`, `Count()`, `Min()`, or `Max()`—instead.

Forward Only Versus Keyset

When you're opening a recordset, it's always advisable to use a forward-only recordset instead of any other cursor type. A forward-only recordset will open about 25 percent faster against a Jet database and over 85 percent faster against a database server. Therefore, you should avoid opening an ADO recordset with the following:

```
oRS.Open strSQL, _
         oConn, _
         adOpenKeyset, _
         adLockPessimistic
```

Instead, you should use the following recordset type:

```
oRS.Open strSQL, _
         oConn, _
         adOpenForwardOnly, _
         adLockReadOnly
```

Of course this means you need to use SQL to perform any updates, because a forward-only recordset can't be updated with most drivers. However, as mentioned earlier, using SQL is much faster anyway.

The biggest reason this is so much faster has to do with what happens when you open a keyset type. First, ADO has to run the SQL string. Next, it queries the information about each of the columns returned. ADO retrieves the size and data type of each column as well as the column type. ADO also has to retrieve the list of primary key field(s) from the result set. Next, it loops through the resultset and grabs the values of the primary key fields to create bookmarks. It then goes back to the top of the resultset and starts reading the bookmarks to grab each row of data.

When you use a forward-only cursor, ADO doesn't need to know the column type—it just needs the data type and size. Also, it doesn't need to retrieve any bookmarks; it just goes through the resultset of data one time as opposed to two times.

Forward Only Versus Dynamic

A forward-only recordset is faster to open than a dynamic recordset. A dynamic recordset is the worst performing of any of the recordset types, so you should always avoid this type of cursor. A dynamic cursor takes so much time to open because it has to request a lock on every row it reads. It also maintains those locks until every page is read from the resultset. This takes a lot of extra time, and it also drags down the performance of your database server.

Keyset Versus Dynamic

A keyset is slightly better than a dynamic recordset in terms of getting the initial recordset built. Therefore, if you must use a fully scrollable recordset, use a keyset type.

Use an Image Control Instead of a Picture Control

The picture control has more overhead than the image control; therefore, you should always use the image control when you just need to display a graphic. Use the picture control when you need to contain other controls or align the picture either to the top or bottom. You should also use the picture control when you need to use some graphic methods. Using the image control optimizes both for speed and size.

Set the *ClipControls* Property to *False*

Clipping refers to the process Windows performs to determine what part of a control it needs to repaint after you move a form to become visible. By setting the `ClipControls` property to `False`, you can significantly reduce the time it takes forms to repaint, because only the area covered is repainted, not the entire form. The default is `True`, so you'll need to explicitly change this one. If you're using graphic methods, however, you may not be able to do this. This property applies to forms, frames, and picture controls.

Set the *AutoRedraw* Property to *True*

If `AutoRedraw` is set to `True`, Visual Basic will keep a bitmap of the form in memory. It uses this bitmap to redraw the form after it's revealed from another window covering it. This consumes a lot of memory at runtime, so you need to be careful with this one. If you're not using any graphic methods, you should set `AutoRedraw` to `False`. Most business applications can set `AutoRedraw` to `False`. This property applies to forms and picture controls.

Size Optimization Tricks

In addition to speeding up your application, you may also want to cut the size of your EXE file. This makes the application easier to distribute and faster to load. It also keeps the memory at runtime to a minimum, which can help your application run faster. Of course, by optimizing for size, you may sometimes find you have some maintenance issues. Let's first take a look at some sizing issues and then you can decide for yourself.

USE A CONTROL'S "DEFAULT" PROPERTY

In versions of Visual Basic prior to Visual Basic 5, if you eliminated a control's default property (such as `Text` or `Caption`), you would see about a 10 to 15 percent speed increase. For example,

```
lblZip.Caption = "Zip Code"
```

would be slower than

```
lblZip = "Zip Code"
```

However, with the new compiler in Visual Basic 5 and 6, this is no longer true. Both ways are equivalent now.

On the Compile tab of the Project, Properties menu, you are able to compile to Native code. You are also allowed to set an option to optimize for speed or size.

Get Rid of Unused *Dim* Statements

Suppose you wrote a function in which you use five local variables, but after a couple revisions of this function, you use only three. In this case, you should make sure you eliminate the unused `Dim` statements, because these take up memory at runtime. You can buy third-party tools to help you look for this type of problem.

Get Rid of Unused *Declare* Statements

When you use the `Declare` statement for a Windows API call, some additional overhead is added to your executable file. You should make sure you've only added those API calls that you actually use in your project. Eliminate any that are not used.

Eliminate Dead Code

Be sure to remove any functions and procedures you're no longer using. If you delete a control, be sure to remove any event procedures that are tied to that control. I make sure I never use an underscore character in the name of a procedure. This way, when I look in the General Declarations area of my forms, if I see a procedure with an underscore, I know it's a dead event procedure that's no longer tied to a particular control.

Comments Do *Not* Increase Size

Comments are stripped out in the final EXE file, so use them as much as you want.

Compile to p-code Instead of Native EXE

If you compile your application to p-code instead of using a native code executable, you'll find that the p-code version is about 20 percent smaller than the same native code executable. Of course, a native code executable will run a little faster, so it's up to you which is more important—size or speed.

Summary

There's sometimes a tradeoff between the size and speed of an application. Therefore, try to keep in mind some of these optimization tricks as you're programming. They can help your program achieve its optimum performance.

Review Questions

1. True or False? `Variant` data types are more efficient than `Long` data types.
2. Which constant should you assign to a string variable to set it equal to nothing?
3. Which cursor type is the most efficient?
4. Which cursor type is the least efficient?
5. True or False? Comments increase the size of your code.

Package and Deployment Wizard

AFTER YOU'VE COMPLETED WRITING AN APPLICATION, you now need to distribute it to your users. You can use the Package and Deployment Wizard to help you with this process. This chapter shows you how to create an installation program for your application.

Chapter Objectives

- Learn to pack up your application
- Learn to deploy your application
- Learn about dependency files

Sample Project File: Any Project

What's a Setup?

You need a program to help you make a setup for your program because most applications built with Windows are too large to fit on one disk. In addition, a lot of DLLs and OCX files typically need to be distributed with your EXE file. Most of these DLLs and OCXs need to be registered, and this is something you don't want the user to do. As a result, you need the help of a wizard.

The Package and Deployment Wizard (or *P&D Wizard*) supplied with Visual Basic 6 assists in the creation of distribution disks for your application. Creating setup programs for Windows applications is almost a full-time job in itself. The P&D Wizard can perform the following tasks for you:

- Create one or many compressed cabinet (CAB) files with all of the files you need to distribute CAB files. This will be described later in this chapter.
- Figure out how to fit the files on the distribution media type (floppy, CD-ROM, Network shared directory, or Web deployment).
- Create dependency files that tell other applications which files your component uses.

Getting Ready to Distribute

Prior to using the P&D Wizard, you should make sure your application is complete, functional, fully debugged, and tested. Then, and only then, are you ready to distribute your application to other users. You must also compile your application into an EXE file so that it's ready to be distributed.

Steps for Creating Distribution Media

No matter which tool you use to create a distribution of your application, you'll always go through certain steps. The P&D Wizard automates many of these steps for you.

Step 1: Create Your Application

You need to compile your application into an EXE file that can then be packed along with all the other files needed in order for your users to run your program.

Step 2: Decide on a Distribution Media

Windows applications are typically packaged on CD-ROM media—CD-ROMs hold a lot of data, and Windows applications tend to be quite large. You may choose to distribute your application on floppy disks, from a network shared drive, or even across the Internet.

Step 3: Figure Out Which Files Need to Be Distributed

Figuring out which files need to be distributed with your EXE file can be a daunting process. Luckily, the P&D Wizard greatly automates this process for you. The P&D Wizard relies on *dependency files* to figure out which files you need. A dependency file is simply an INI-style text file that describes a list of files needed to work with a DLL or OCX file. The main dependency file for Visual Basic applications is VB6DEP.INI. You can create your own dependency files for any components (DLLs or OCXs) that you create using the P&D Wizard.

Step 4: Determine Where the Files Will Reside on the User's Machine

You install the files in your setup program on the user's machine in basically two different locations:

- The folder where your application is installed
- In the \Windows\System or \Windows\System32 folder

Your program and setup files are generally installed in the folder underneath the Program Files folder or your own folder you create off the root drive. Of course, that is just a suggested location—the user can change this location when he or she installs the program. Any general-purpose DLLs or OCXs are usually installed in the \Windows\System on Win95/98 or in the \WINNT\System32 folder on Windows NT.

Step 5: Compress Your Files

You need to take all the files to be distributed and compress them into a smaller format so that they're easier to distribute. Usually, you'll use the P&D Wizard to accomplish this step. Some setup programs compress each file into an individually compressed file. The P&D Wizard creates one or more CAB files for you, depending on the media type you've chosen.

Step 6: Get It Out There!

Once you've created the media, you're now ready to get it into the hands of your users. You simply need to copy the files to floppy disks, place them on a shared network drive, burn them into a CD-ROM, or publish them to an Internet/intranet site. Once again, the P&D Wizard can help you with any of these tasks.

Visual Basic Runtime Files

Let's now look at the files that need to be distributed with your EXE file, besides any specific DLLs and/or OCXs that make up your applications. The Visual Basic programming language uses a lot of its own internal functions that reside in their own DLLs. The following is a list of each of the files you need to distribute along with your application. Don't worry about having to remember this list, because the P&D Wizard will automatically include these files in the cabinet files it builds:

- Msvbvm60.dll (the main Visual Basic runtime DLL)
- Stdole2.tlb
- Oleaut32.dll
- Olepro32.dll
- Comcat.dll
- Asyncfilt.dll
- Ctl3d32.dll

Of course if you include additional controls that are not a part of the Visual Basic runtime, you will need to include those files as well. The P&D Wizard will automatically include those additional files for you.

Setup Toolkit Files

The setup application that the P&D Wizard creates for you consists of a few more files you'll also need to include with your application's distribution disks. These files come from the Visual Basic Setup Toolkit that the P&D Wizard uses to help you distribute your application. Table 34.1 lists each of these files.

Table 34.1 Setup Files Needed for Distributing an Application

Filename	Description
Setup.exe	All setup programs for Windows actually run on the user's computer and just pull files from a CD-ROM, network drive, or floppies as needed. The Setup.exe file is a small program the user runs to preinstall certain files to his or her machine so that another setup program can take over the job of performing the main installation. For your Visual Basic applications, the file Setup1.exe performs the actual installation procedure. Setup.exe also copies the Visual Basic runtime DLLs to the user's machine so that Setup1.exe can run.
Setup1.exe	This is the main setup program that copies all the files for your application to the user's hard drive. This file is a Visual Basic application to which you have the source code. The source code for this application is located in your Visual Basic folder under the PDWizard folder.
Setup.lst	This text file is what the Setup.exe and Setup1.exe files use to determine which files are copied and where the installation process is to be completed.
Vb6stkit.dll	This DLL is used only by the Setup1.exe file. This is just a library of functions used during the setup process.
St6unst.exe	If the user decides to uninstall your application, he or she will run this executable. This file takes care of removing any components from the user's machine that are used only by your application.

Running the P&D Wizard

You can run the P&D Wizard in two ways: as a standalone application and as an add-in. To run the P&D Wizard as a standalone application, choose the Microsoft Visual Studio 6, Microsoft Visual Studio 6 Tools, Package & Deployment Wizard icon from your Programs folder on the Start menu. You also have the option of running the P&D Wizard as an add-in from the Add-Ins menu. If you run the wizard as an add-in, you'll only be able to create a setup package for the current project.

Once you start the P&D Wizard, you'll see the main screen, which starts you on the process of creating a package. You can select from three options, as shown in Figure 34.1. The first option is to create a package.

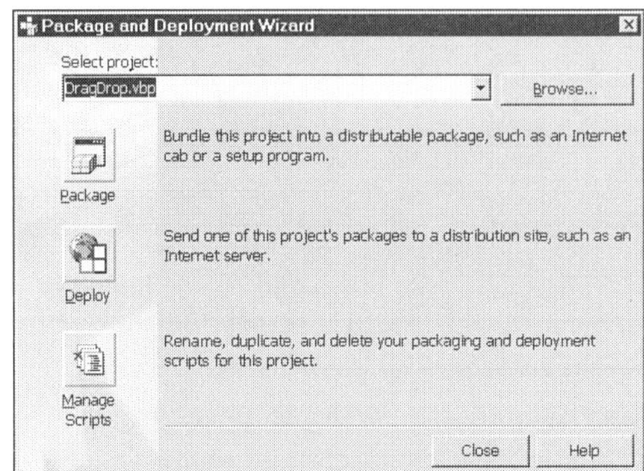

FIGURE 34.1 The Package and Deployment Wizard's main screen.

Creating a Package

A package consists of one or more cabinet (CAB) files. A *CAB file* is similar to a ZIP file in that multiple files are contained in the CAB file that will be uncompressed when the installation is performed. The package process gathers information from your VBP file to create the CAB file. Let's walk through the P&D Wizard to create a setup for the drag and drop application you built in Chapter 33, "Optimization."

From this screen, you select a project to run by clicking the combo box and selecting a project you have already built, by typing in the full path and filename of the VBP, or clicking the Browse button to select a VBP file. If you run the wizard as an add-in, the current project will be displayed, and you won't have the option of typing in the filename or clicking the Browse button. After you've specified the project, click the Package button.

Selecting a Package Type

After clicking the Package button, you'll be asked what type of package you want to create as shown in Figure 34.2. You have the option of selecting a standard setup package, an Internet package, or a dependency file. Here are some points to keep in mind:

- A standard setup package is used for any standalone applications your users will run on their desktops.
- An Internet package is used when you want to deploy an ActiveX control or DLL via the Internet or an intranet. These types of CAB files are full installations—the only difference is that there are no setup files. The browser will take care of the installation of the components automatically when the ActiveX component is used on an HTML page.

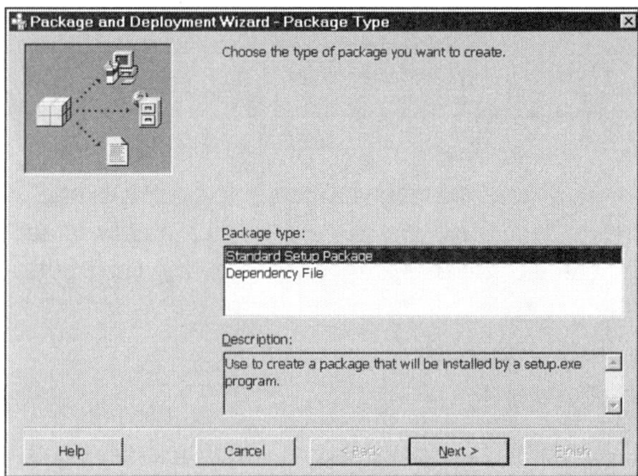

FIGURE 34.2
Selecting a package type.

Simply click the appropriate package type and then click the Next button to move to the next step. The discussion in this chapter uses a standard setup package as an example.

> **NOTE**
> **You'll only see the Internet package type if you've chosen an ActiveX component type of project.**

The only difference between an Internet package and a standard setup package is that the Internet package has two additional screens. One asks you whether you want to have the Visual Basic 6 runtime files downloaded automatically from the Microsoft Web site or included in your CAB file. The second screen asks whether your components are safe for scripting and installation.

Selecting a Folder for the Package

You'll now select a folder that's used to create the package that will eventually be placed onto distribution media. This folder is a temporary storage location until you build your final media. See Figure 34.3.

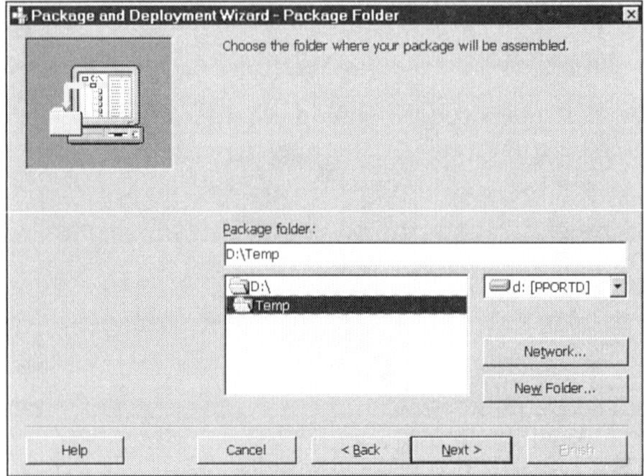

FIGURE 34.3 Specifying the package folder location.

Fill in the folder's name where you want to assemble your package. You can create the folder on a network drive, and you can even create a new folder from this screen. Once you've selected the package folder, click the Next button.

A List of Included Files

The next screen, see Figure 34.4, shows you a list of all the files that the P&D Wizard has determined are to be included with your package. You're allowed to add new files to this list, such as database files, INI files, and any help files. You have the option of removing files, but be careful not to remove any of the dependent files such as the Visual Basic 6 runtime files.

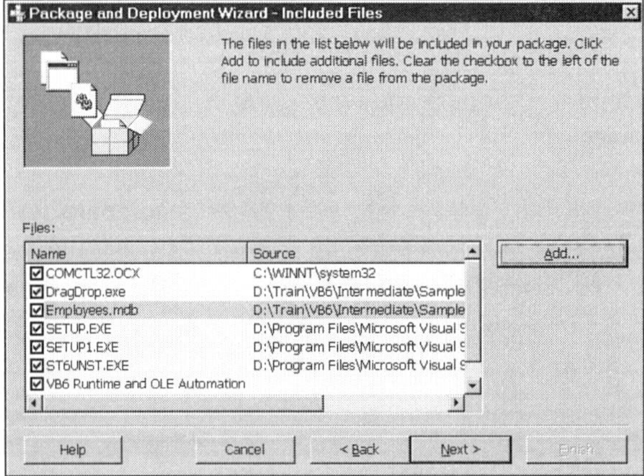

FIGURE 34.4 The list of included files.

On this screen, you add your database files, INI files, help files, graphic files, or any additional support files your application needs to run. Once you've added any additional files, click the Next button.

Cabinet File Options

On the screen shown in Figure 34.5, you choose whether you want to use a single CAB file or multiple CAB files. You might choose the single CAB file option if you're distributing your application on a CD-ROM, across the Internet, or from a shared network drive. If you're distributing via floppy disks, you need to choose the multiple CAB file option and specify the size of the disks you want to use.

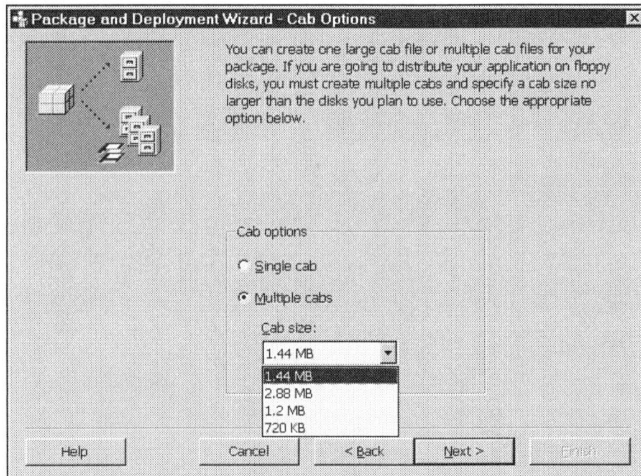

FIGURE 34.5
Selecting a CAB option.

Select the option you want to use and then click the Next button to continue with the P&D Wizard.

Installation Title

The Installation Title screen, shown in Figure 34.6, is where you type in a title to display on the initial installation screen the user sees when he or she runs the Setup.exe file. Pick a title that describes your application to the user.

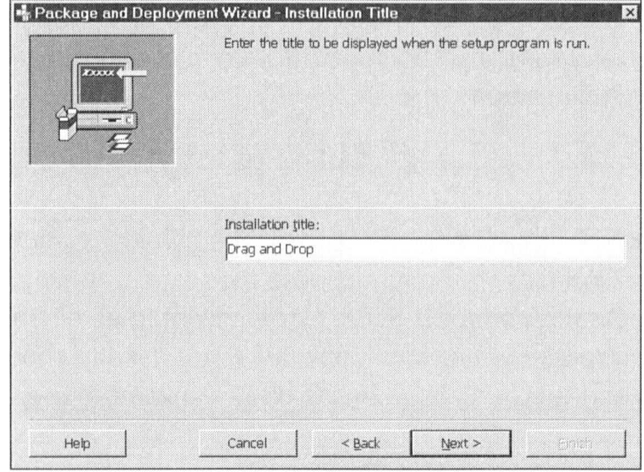

FIGURE 34.6 Specifying an installation title.

After you type in an installation title, click the Next command button.

Start Menu Options

Your application needs to appear in the user's Program menu. The Start Menu Items screen, shown in Figure 34.7, allows you to specify the location where you want your program to appear within this menu. You can set the name and as many subitems as you want.

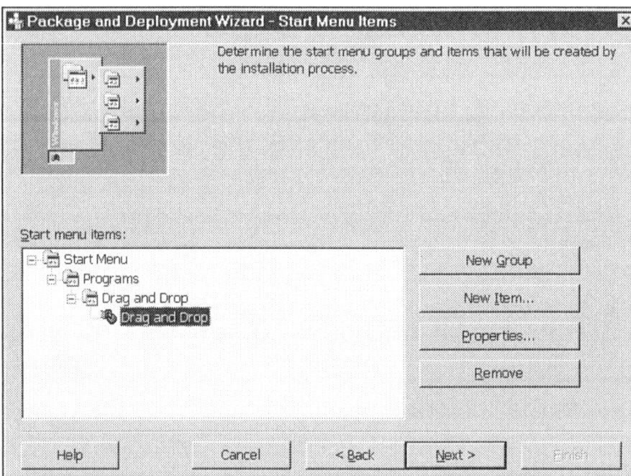

FIGURE 34.7 Specifying Start menu options.

Create as many groups and items on this screen as you need for your application. For example, if you have multiple EXE files to distribute, you can create new items under your main group. You can also set properties for each item, such as the path and name of an executable file to run when the user clicks a menu item.

Install Locations

The different components that make up your application each have a default installation target on the user's machine. For your application components, you can set the default installation location on the user's target machine as shown in Figure 34.8.

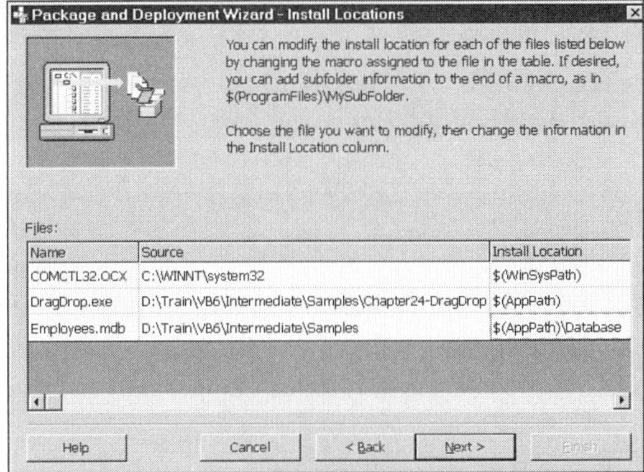

FIGURE 34.8
Setting install locations.

This screen is where you would modify the location of your database path. For example, you might change `$(AppPath)` to `$(AppPath)\Database` to create a folder under your main application for your database. `$(AppPath)` is a token that's resolved when the user chooses the location from the setup program. If the user chooses to install your program in a folder called D:\MyInstall, then you want to have the database folder under that folder.

Shared Files

On the Shared Files screen, shown in Figure 34.9, you choose any components you know are shared with other applications. This information is used by the Uninstall Wizard to determine whether the user will be prompted to remove this shared component when he or she uninstalls your application. If you know that no other application will use a certain file, then don't check that file's check box.

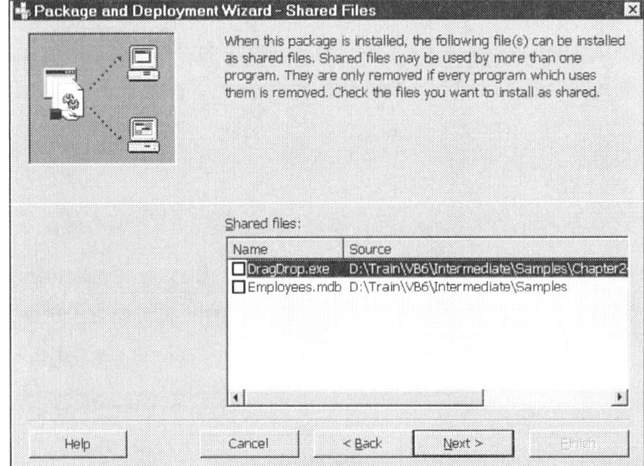

FIGURE 34.9
Specifying shared files.

Don't check any files you want to have automatically removed by the uninstall program. When you're finished with this screen, click the Next command button.

Saving a Script

When you're finished creating all the options for your package, you need to save this information in a script. This information is saved in a file with the same name as your VBP file but with the extension .PDM. Figure 34.10 shows the last screen in the P&D Wizard.

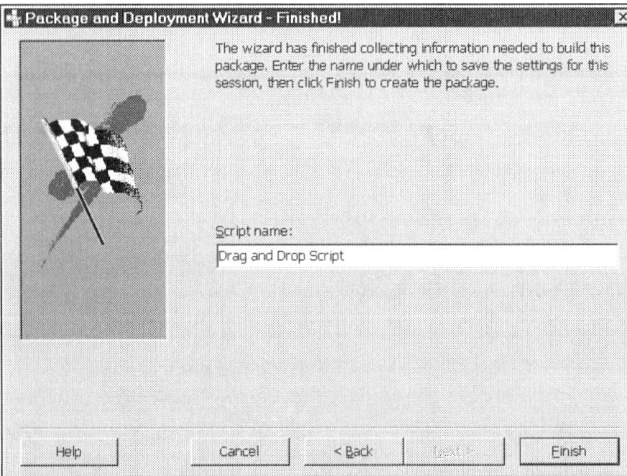

FIGURE 34.10
Saving script information.

Enter a descriptive script name and click the Finish button to have the P&D Wizard begin creating the CAB file(s) for your installation program.

When the P&D Wizard is finished creating the CAB files, it displays a report screen to you, as shown in Figure 34.11.

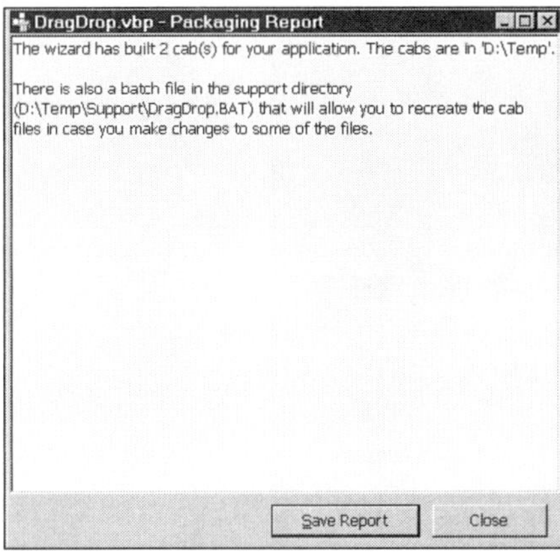

FIGURE 34.11 The Packaging Report screen.

This report file gives you information about what the P&D Wizard did for you. In the report shown in Figure 34.11, you can see that the P&D Wizard created two CAB files for the application located in the D:\Temp directory. It also created a BAT file that can be used to rerun the P&D Wizard in "silent mode." This is an unattended mode; therefore, if you make some minor changes to your EXE file or to any of the other files you've already added, you don't need to walk through all the steps in the wizard again. Of course, if you need to add new files, you will have to go through the wizard again.

Deployment Options in the P&D Wizard

After creating your package, you're now ready to deploy the installation package to a medium where your users can run it. This might be a CD-ROM, floppy disks, a network drive, or a Web server. This is where the second part of the P&D Wizard comes in. You'll now return to the main menu and select the Deployment button to start the deployment process.

Package to Deploy

The first screen of the deployment part of the P&D Wizard asks you to select a package to deploy (see Figure 34.12). Select the package you want to deploy from the combo box and click the Next command button.

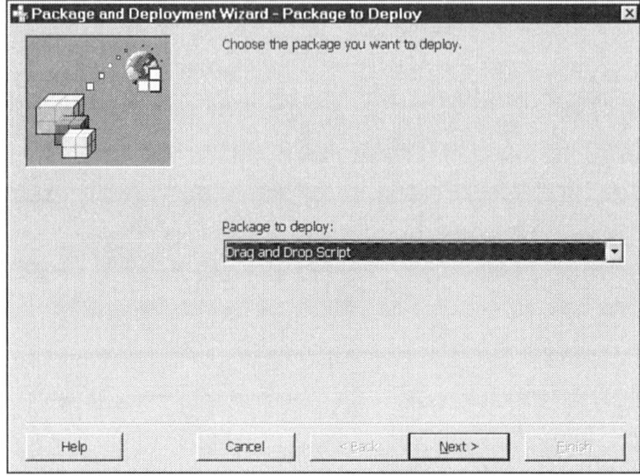

FIGURE 34.12 Selecting package to deploy.

Deployment Method

The next screen, shown in Figure 34.13, will allow you to choose the deployment method to use. Even if you've created multiple CAB files, you can still deploy over the Web, on a CD-ROM, or even on a shared network drive. If, on the other hand, you chose the Single Package option, you won't have the Floppy Disks option.

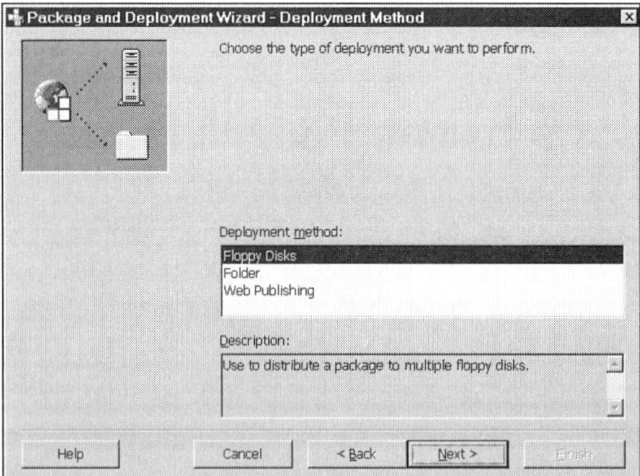

FIGURE 34.13 Selecting a deployment method.

Select the deployment method and click the Next command button.

Where to Deploy

Now you just need to select where you want to deploy the application (see Figure 34.14). If you choose the Floppy Disks option, you'll deploy to floppy disks. The P&D Wizard will prompt you for new disks as it copies the files to each one.

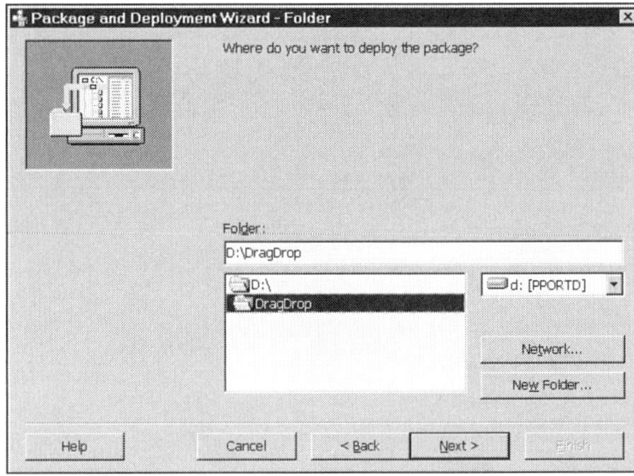

FIGURE 34.14
Specifying where to deploy.

Select a folder or create a new folder where you want to create the installation. Next, click the Next command button.

Ready to Deploy

After you've finished setting the deployment options, you need to save this series of steps in a script file as shown in Figure 34.15. This information is saved in the same PDM file as your package script. This script can then be used if you decide you need to repeat the deployment process.

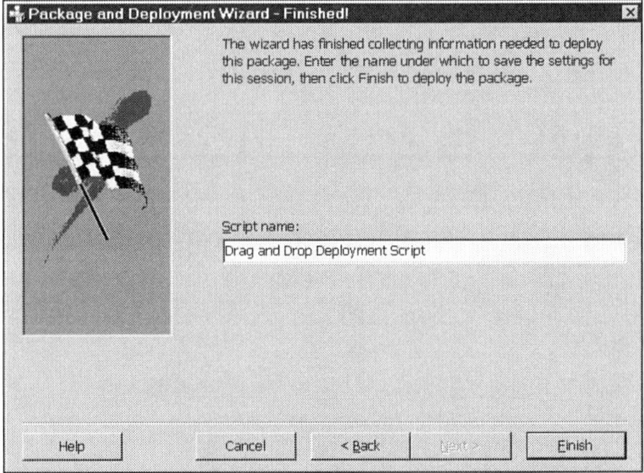

FIGURE 34.15
You're ready to deploy.

Once you are ready, click the Finish command button to have the files copied to the deployment folder or disks. Once the deployment process is complete, a report will be displayed that tells you the results of the deployment, as shown in Figure 34.16.

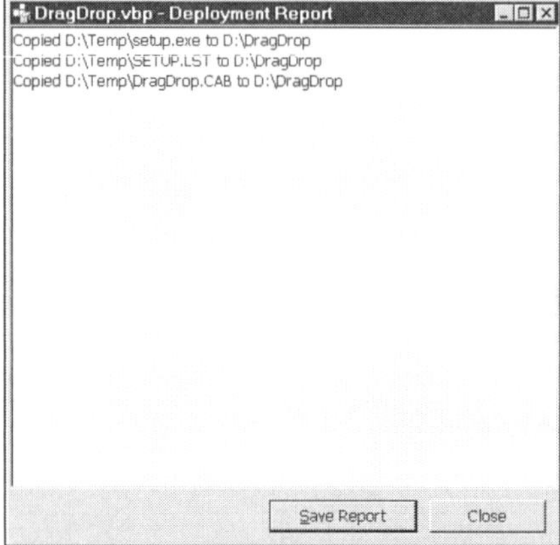

FIGURE 34.16 A deployment report.

What's a Dependency File?

A *dependency file* is a text file that closely resembles an INI file. It usually has a .DEP file extension and the same name as the component for which it contains dependency information. If you create any ActiveX components, you should generate a dependency file using the P&D Wizard. The P&D Wizard looks for this DEP file when you include your component in another project. It can then read this file to determine what other files need to be included in the setup of this application.

It's important that any dependency information is included with the components; otherwise, the application that uses these components might not run correctly because a file is not included that needs to be there. All the components included in the Visual Basic 6 package have dependency information in the vb6dep.ini file. The P&D Wizard will always check this file when it creates an installation.

What Can You Distribute from Visual Basic?

With all the different controls, DLLs, and graphics files that come with Visual Basic, it's sometimes hard to determine what you can and cannot distribute. Anything that comes with the Visual Basic development environment can be freely distributed. This even includes the source code in the Samples directory and in the Setup Toolkit.

If you purchase third-party controls from other vendors, you'll need to check with them as to whether their controls can be redistributed. Most of these controls are freely distributable, but a small percentage of them have runtime license fees. Be sure you determine your rights prior to purchasing the control or DLL.

The Setup Toolkit

If you want to see how the Setup1.exe program is written, check out the Setup1.vbp file in the \<Visual Basic Folder>\Wizards\PDWizard\Setup1 folder. Load up the Setup1.vbp file and look at the frmSetup1 form. In `Form_Load()` is where most of the processing takes place. You can also modify this code if you want to add your own special processing. For example, you might want to add your own logo to the main setup form. You could add a picture control to the frmSetup1 form and then add your logo to this control.

Testing Your Installation

After the installation disks are prepared, you should always test them out. You could use your machine, but unfortunately it won't have the same configuration your users have. Instead, you should use a machine that has never had a VB application installed on it. This way, you can ensure that all the appropriate DLL and custom control files are installed.

It's ideal to have a separate machine dedicated to just testing software installations. If you don't have this luxury, you can make a backup of an existing machine and then install a fresh copy of Win95 or WinNT on that machine. You want to make sure this machine has the same environment as what your users will have.

Steps for Testing Installations

There are some basic steps that you should always follow when you want to test your installation. It is very important that you test your installation program as thoroughly as you test your application. Let's review these steps now.

1. Install a fresh copy of Win95 or WinNT on a machine. You may also want to add applications that the users will have on their machines.

2. Immediately perform a back up of this configuration. You'll be performing tests many times, so making a backup allows you to restore files back to the "clean" machine faster than installing everything again. I recommend you buy one of the disk-imaging software packages on the market. These packages make a bit-by-bit copy of your hard disk and allow you to save that image to another location so that you can restore your hard drive in just a couple of minutes, as opposed to hours. (We use Drive Image at our shop for performing installations on test machines.)
3. Run your installation procedure.
4. If the installation process is successful, you should test every part of the application to see whether everything works correctly.
5. If something fails, try to identify the missing piece and then add that custom control, DLL, or ActiveX component to your setup file using the P&D Wizard.
6. Restore your machine back to a "clean" configuration.
7. Repeat steps 3 to 5 until your application works correctly.
8. I would also add that you should test your uninstall program as well. And after uninstalling, re-install the program to make sure it still works.

Summary

In this chapter, you learned to use the Package and Deployment Wizard to create distribution programs for your applications. This wizard performs most of the common tasks for creating distribution media. If you want to have more functionality, such as the ability to display "splash" screens, or need to customize INI files after the installation, you can modify the code in the Setup Toolkit. Also, several third-party installation utilities are on the market that are very customizable, but you purchase them at an additional cost.

Review Questions

1. What types of packages can you create with the P&D Wizard?
2. What's the name of the main Visual Basic 6 runtime DLL?
3. What are the two main locations where files are installed on a user's machine?
4. What's a dependency file?

Exercise

1. Create a setup from your Employee project.

Appendixes

A

VBA Programming Standards

PROGRAMMING STANDARDS ARE USED TO HELP PROGRAMMERS create a consistent structure, coding style, and logic of an application. Standards help a programmer create code that's easy to read, unambiguous, and easily maintained by other programmers in the organization. The standards included here are the ones currently used by Paul D. Sheriff and Associates, Inc. for the applications developed for its clients. Feel free to modify these to suit your organization's needs. This document is also included on the companion Web site for this book.

Reasons for Naming Conventions

There are many reasons programming standards are created. Most mainframe shops have had programming standards for years. Unfortunately, most PC programmers have forgotten or have never worked in a formal programming shop, and they often overlook this important step in application development.

Creating a programming standard does not limit your creativity, as most programmers seem to think. Instead, it helps you focus your creativity where it's really needed. You can concentrate on the program itself instead of having to always think about what name to give a variable. Think about the Windows environment (or even the Macintosh)—every program written for Windows has a consistent look and feel. This is why users like using Windows programs, because they don't have to learn everything about how a new program works—they already know how to use most of the new program's features. By using standards in your programming, you can also keep the programmer "look and feel" consistent. This means you spend less time figuring out what the variables are or how many indents a programmer used, and you can focus more on the logic of the program.

The use of standards can lead to reduced maintenance costs due to a consistent look and feel. This means you can move from one project to another very easily—even one someone else wrote—and immediately read and understand the code.

Environment Options

To start, you should make sure every programmer's Visual Basic environment is consistent, or if you are working alone, make sure that you at least set the following defaults. Visual Basic lets you set defaults for the development environment. Table A.1 shows the recommended values for some of those options. To set these values, select Tools, Options from the Visual Basic design menu.

Table A.1 Options to Set in Your Visual Basic Environment

Option	Value	Description
Editor Tab		
Tab Stops	`3`	Can be anything you want. I prefer `3`.
Require Variable Declaration	Checked	Requires you to declare all variables prior to usage by adding an Option Explicit statement to the beginning of every module.
General Tab		
Grid Units, Height Points	`60`	Can be anything but should be a multiple of `300` because that's the minimum height of a combo box. You should strive to make all controls a consistent size, and `300` is a good default height.
Grid Units, Width Points	`60`	(See preceding description.)
Environment Tab		
When a Program Starts...Prompt to Save Changes	Checked	Prompts you to save changes prior to testing the application. This is done to ensure no work is lost due to general protection faults (GPF) or other unexpected errors.

Option Explicit

Declaring all variables in your code saves programming time by reducing the number of bugs caused by typos and undeclared variables. For example, the following variables all look the same: `aUserNameTmp`, `sUserNameTmp`, and `sUserNameTemp`. If you don't set the `Option Explicit` statement at the top of every module, these different variable names could all have potentially different values. At runtime, you check the value of the `sUserNameTmp` variable when you really wanted to be checking the value of the variable `sUserNameTemp`. If you set the `Option Explicit` statement at the top of the module, the compiler will inform you of the typo. If you don't set the `Option Explicit`, the runtime engine will simply create another variable on-the-fly and assign a zero value to that variable. This can lead to a bug that's very hard to track down.

Custom Control Naming Conventions

An important part of any Visual Basic program is the controls placed on a form. All similar custom controls should have a common prefix. For example, text boxes should start with *txt*, and labels should start with *lbl*. Table A.2 shows the recommended control name prefixes for most of the controls in the Visual Basic environment. These prefixes are consistent with those documented in the *Visual Basic Programmers Guide*.

Table A.2 Custom Control Naming Conventions

Prefix	Control Type	Example
ani	Animation button	aniMailBox
cbo	Combo box	cboEnglish
chk	Check box	chkReadOnly
clp	Picture clip	clpToolbar
com	Communications	comFax
dat	Data control	datBiblio
dbc	Data-aware combo box	dbcStates
dbg	Data-aware grid	dbgLineItems
dbl	Data-aware list box	dblCustomers
dir	Directory list box	dirSource
dlg	Common dialog control	dlgFileOpen
drv	Drive list box	drvTarget
fil	File list box	filSource
fra	Frame	fraLanguage
frm	Form	frmEntry
gau	Gauge	gauStatus
gpb	Group pushbutton	gpbChannel
gra	Graph	graRevenue
grd	Grid	grdPrices
hsb	Horizontal scrollbar	hsbVolume
img	Image	imgIcon
iml	ImageList control	imlPictures

Prefix	Control Type	Example
key	Keyboard key state	keyCaps
lbl	Label	lblHelpMessage
lin	Line	linVertical
lst	List box	lstPolicyCodes
lsv	List view	lsvItems
mci	Multimedia control	mciVideo
mdi	MDI child form	mdiNote
mnu	Menu	mnuFileOpen
mpm	MAPI message	mpmSentMessage
mps	MAPI session	mpsSession
msk	Masked edit control	mskPhone
ole	OLE control	oleWorksheet
out	Outline control	outOrgChart
pbr	Progress bar	pbrCompleted
pic	Picture	picVGA
pnl	3D panel	pnlStatus
rpt	Report control	rptQtr1Earnings
rtb	Rich text box	rtbNotes
sbr	Status bar	sbrMDI
shp	Shape controls	shpCircle
sld	Slider	sldScore
spn	Spin control	spnPages
tab	Tab control	tabForm
tbr	Toolbar	tbrTools
tbs	TabStrip control	tbsForm
tmr	Timer	tmrAlarm
trv	Tree view	trvCustomers
txt	Text box	txtLastName
vsb	Vertical scrollbar	vsbRate

If you take care to name your controls with these common prefixes, when you're using a particular control in your source code, you'll be able to identify its type without having to refer back to the form. This can save you time when coding or maintaining your application.

Menu Naming Conventions

Just like custom controls, all the various menus you create should also use appropriate prefixes (see Table A.3). The prefix *mnu* should be used on all menus. This prefix should be followed by the caption of the menu. For each pull-down menu under the main menu item, use the first letter of top-level menu.

Table A.3 Naming Menus

Menu Caption Sequence	Menu Handler Name
`File`	mnuFile
`File.New`	mnuFNew
`File.Open`	mnuFOpen
`File.Send`	mnuFSend
`File.Send.Fax`	mnuFSFax
`File.Send.Email`	mnuFSEmail
`Help`	mnuHelp
`Help.About`	mnuHAbout

When this convention is used, all members of a particular menu group are listed next to each other in the Object drop-down list boxes (in the Code and Property windows). In addition, the menu control names clearly document the menu items to which they're attached.

Naming Conventions for Other Controls

For new controls not listed so far, try to come up with unique three-character prefixes. Note, however, that it's more important to be clear than to stick to a three-character convention.

For derivative controls, such as an enhanced list box, extend the preceding prefixes so that there's no confusion over which control is really being used. A lowercase abbreviation for the manufacturer could be added to the prefix. For example, a Crescent QuickPak Professional text box control could be named ctxtFirstName.

Third-party Controls

Each third-party control used in an application should be listed in the application's overview comment section, providing the prefix used for the control, the full name of the control, and the name of the software vendor (see Table A.4).

Table A.4 Third-party Control Naming Standards

Prefix	Control Type	Vendor
ctxt	Text box	Crescent
sscbo	Sheridan combo box	Sheridan

Variable/Object Naming

Variables are the building blocks of every application you create. As such, naming your variables is very important. When creating names for your variables, you need to make the purpose of the variable clear. The use of one-letter variable names should be avoided at all costs. This only leads to confusion when you look at the code at a later date.

The following list presents some standards you should follow when creating your variable names:

- Avoid one-letter variables.
- Make all variable names mixed case.
- Each word or abbreviation should be capitalized.
- Do not use the underscore character in a variable name.
- Use Hungarian notation (see the following section).
- Preface each variable name with the type of data it contains.
- Abbreviate variables only when absolutely necessary.

Hungarian Notation

Hungarian notation is a naming scheme for variables developed by a programmer who worked at Microsoft. Originally developed for C language programmers, it has now been successfully applied to many other languages. The use of Hungarian notation in a program gives a programmer a lot of information about a variable just by looking at the name. A variable that has been named using the Hungarian notation scheme tells a programmer the variable's scope (global, module, or local), what data type it contains (`Integer`, `Long`, and so on), and, of course, the purpose of that variable.

Hungarian notation is as valuable in Visual Basic as it is in the C language. Hungarian notation is widely used by Windows C language programmers and constantly referenced in Microsoft product documentation and in programming books. With all this attention on Hungarian notation, it seems this is a worthy standard that has stood the test of time, and it will probably be around for many years to come.

Visual Basic supplies type suffixes (`%`, `&`, `$`, and so on) to indicate a variable's data type. However, these suffixes are very cryptic to a new user of Visual Basic and also make source code difficult to read. Additionally, they do not explain what the variable will be used for or how it can be accessed. Table A.5 lists some examples of how you should create your variable names without using the suffixes.

Table A.5 Hungarian Notation Examples

Variable Name	Description
`intSend`	Represents a count of the number of messages sent
`boolSend`	A Boolean flag that defines the success of the last `Send` operation
`hWnd`	A handle to a window

In Table A.5, each of the variable names tell a programmer something very different because of the prefix added to each. This information is lost when the variable name is reduced to `Send&` or `Send%`.

NOTE
Do *not* use Hungarian notation on any properties or classes that will be exposed through an Automation Server to other applications. Keep these properties and class names generic so users can understand them.

Variable Data Type Prefixes

Table A.6 defines the standard variable data types in Visual Basic. These prefixes should be used when naming the variables in your program. Avoid the use of the Visual Basic suffixes (%, &, #, and so on) at all costs.

Table A.6 Variable Type Prefixes

Prefix	Data Type	Storage	Example
bool	`Boolean`	Two bytes	`boolPerform`
byt	`Byte`	One byte	`byteArray`
cur	`Currency`	Eight bytes	`curSales`
int	`Integer`	Two bytes	`intLoop`
dbl	`Double`	Eight bytes	`dblValue`
dt	`Date` and `Time`	Eight bytes	`dtEntered`
lng	`Long`	Four bytes	`lngEnv`
sgl	`Single`	Four bytes	`sglValue`
str	`String`	One byte per char	`strName`
vnt	`Variant`	Sixteen bytes plus one byte for each character in a string type	`vntAnything`
a	`Array`	Depends on size	`astrName`
typ	User-defined type	Depends on size	`typCustomer`
o or obj	`Objects`	Any object	`OConn`

Scope Prefixes

A variables scope refers to the locations within your application that a particular variable may be read or modified. For example, a local variable is one declared within a `Sub...End Sub` or `Function...End Function`. This variable may only be read or modified while code is executing within the `Sub...End Sub` statements. A module-level variable, on the other hand, may be read and modified from any procedure or function within the same module. Global or public variables may be referenced from any procedure or function within the same project. Table A.7 lists the common scope prefixes you should use.

Table A.7 Scope Prefixes

Prefix	Description
g	Global or public
m	Module- or form-level variable/object
st	Static variable

Local variables should not have a prefix. This will distinguish them as being local and not having a scope outside of the current procedure. Here are some examples of declaring variables:

```
Global gintLoop As Integer
Dim mstrName As String
Private pboolOpen As Boolean
```

Handles

When programming Windows using the Windows API, you're frequently dealing with handles to windows. You'll also find handles when dealing with the ODBC API. As such, you need a special prefix to identify handles. Use the prefix *h* to name a handle variable:

```
Dim hWnd As Long      ' Handle to a Window
Dim hEnv As Long      ' Handle to the ODBC environment space
Dim hdbc As Long      ' Handle to an ODBC data connection
```

User-defined Types

Declare user-defined types with the prefix *typ*. Variables that are dimmed of this particular type should also be referenced with a *typ* prefix. This will help distinguish the setting of elements in a user-defined type from the setting of properties in an object. Here's an example:

```
Type typCustomer
   strName As String
   strState As String * 2
   lngID as Long
End Type
```

When declaring an instance variable of a user-defined type, add a prefix to the variable name to reference the type:

```
Dim typCust as typCustomer
```

Class Naming

When creating your own user-defined classes, you need to be aware of who your target user will be for that class. If you'll be exposing that object and its properties through an Automation Server, you should not use Hungarian notation. Nonprogrammer types will not understand this type of notation.

It's recommended that you create `Property Get/Let/Set` procedures for every variable used within the class you want to give the user access to. Use Hungarian notation on all private data but do not use it on the `Property Get/Let/Set` procedures.

When naming your class modules, keep in mind that you need to give each public class a descriptive name that the user can understand. If you're creating an internal class that's only used within your program, use the prefix *cls* or maybe just *C* (see Table A.8).

Table A.8 Prefixes for Class Modules

Prefix	Description
cls or C	Only used for private classes
(none)	For any public classes that will be exposed through an OLE Server

Naming Constants

Constant names should use uppercase letters with an underscore (_) between the words. This will help distinguish your constants from the built-in constants in VBA. Also, be sure to always type your constants. If you do not type your constants, they will be of the type `Variant`. This means you're using up 16 bytes per constant. This is a big waste and should be avoided. Here are some examples of constant declarations:

```
Public Const TAB_ADDRESS As Integer = 0
Public Const TAB_PHONES As Integer = 1
```

Conditional Compile

For conditional compilation constants, use the prefix *cc*:

```
#If ccDEMO Then
   ' Perform some code here
#End If
```

Variant Data Type

If you know that a variable will always store data of a particular type, Visual Basic can handle that data more efficiently if you declare the variable of that type. For example, if you need to loop through an array, create an index of the type `Integer`, not `Variant`. In other words, avoid the use of `Variant` unless it's absolutely necessary.

Function and Procedure Naming

Here are some general guidelines to follow when naming your functions and procedures:

- Use mixed case, where each word in the procedure is capitalized.
- Preface all functions and procedures with a noun.
- Follow this noun with the action that will be performed on that noun.
- Do *not* use underscores in your function names—this makes it hard to determine which procedures are yours and which are Visual Basic event procedures.

Here are some examples of procedure names that should not be used because the verb comes first:

- `DisplayForm`
- `InitializeForm`
- `LoadStates`

Here are some examples of better procedure names:

- `FormShow`
- `FormInit`
- `cboStateLoad`

The difference is the noun, or *object*, is placed first. There are fewer ways to describe an object than there are for a verb to describe what will be done. For example, the verb *display* can be expressed a couple other ways, such as *show*, *draw*, or even *print*. However, a *form* is always a *form*, there's no other descriptor for it.

In object-oriented languages and even in VB, the object name is placed first and then the method or action you want to perform on that object. Objects are always nouns, and actions are verbs. You should follow this coding style when creating names for your procedures.

An additional benefit of this coding style is that when you use a cross-referencing tool or are looking in the Proc combo box, you'll see all functions that operate on a particular object grouped in one place.

Error Labels

Labels in a procedure should only be used for error handling. Otherwise, too many programmers would be tempted to use the `GoTo` statement. A `GoTo` statement can lead to many problems. Name your labels with the name of the procedure followed by the suffix *_EH*. Here's an example:

```
Private Sub cmdSave_Click()
    On Error GoTo cmdSave_Click_EH
    ...
    ...
cmdSave_Click_EH:
    ' Error handling here
End Sub
```

Commenting Your Code

Each procedure and function should begin with a brief comment describing the functional characteristics of the routine (what it does). This description should *not* describe the implementation details (how it does it), because these often change over time, resulting in unnecessary comment maintenance work or, worse yet, erroneous comments. The code itself and any necessary inline or local comments should describe the implementation.

Parameters passed to a routine should be described when their function is not obvious and when the routine expects the parameters to be in a specific range. Function return values and global variables that are changed by the routine (especially through reference parameters) must also be described at the beginning of each routine.

Each nontrivial variable declaration should include an inline comment describing the use of the variable being declared.

Variables, controls, and routines should be named clearly enough that inline commenting is only needed for complex or nonintuitive implementation details.

An overview description of the application, enumerating primary data objects, routines, algorithms, dialog boxes, database and file system dependencies, and so on should be included at the start of the BAS module that contains the project's Visual Basic generic constant declarations.

NOTE
The Project window inherently describes the list of files in a project, so this overview section only needs to provide information on the most important files and modules or the files the Project window doesn't list, such as initialization (INI) or database files.

Formatting Your Code

Because many programmers still use VGA displays, screen real estate must be conserved as much as possible while still allowing code formatting to reflect logic structure and nesting. Standard tab-based, block-nesting indentations should be three spaces. More than four spaces is unnecessary and can cause statements to be hidden or accidentally truncated. Less than two spaces does not sufficiently show logic nesting. The highest-level statements that follow the overview comment should be indented one tab, with each nested block indented an additional tab. Here's an example:

```
'*****************************************************
'* Procedure: FormCenter() - Center Form on the Screen
'* Author   : Paul D. Sheriff
'* Date     : Oct. 22, 1998
'* Revised  : Oct. 22, 1998
'*
'* Description:
'* Center Form on the Screen or MDI Main Form
'*
'* Syntax: Call FormCenter(frmFormName)
'*
'* Parameters:
'* <frm> frmFormName    => Form To Center
'***********************************************************
Sub FormCenter (frmFormName As Form)
   frmFormName.Left = (Screen.Width - frmFormName.Width) / 2
   frmFormName.Top = (Screen.Height - frmFormName.Height) / 2
End Sub
```

Operators

Always use the & operator when concatenating strings and the + operator when working with numerical values. Using + may cause problems when operating on two variants. Here's an example:

```
vntVar1 = "10.01"
vntVar2 = 11
vntResult = vntVar1 + vntVar2 ' vntResult =  21.01
vntResult = vntVar1 & vntVar2 ' vntResult = 10.0111
```

As you can see from this source code, the + and & operators create two different results when using the `Variant` data type. This is a good reason to always use the appropriate operator and avoid using a `Variant` data type.

Scope

Variables should always be defined with the smallest scope possible. Global variables can create enormously complex state machines and make the logic of an application extremely difficult to understand. Global variables also make the reuse and maintenance of your code much more difficult. Variables in Visual Basic can have the following scope, as detailed in Table A.9.

Table A.9 Scope of Variables

Scope	Variable Declared In:	Visibility
Procedure level	Event procedure, sub, function, or method	Visible in the procedure in which it's declared
Form level, Module level	Declarations section of a form or module (FRM, BAS, or CLS)	Visible in every procedure in the form or code module
Global/public level	Declarations section of a code module (BAS using `Global` keyword)	Always visible

In a Visual Basic application, only use global variables when there's no other convenient way to share data between forms. You should use a property on a form instead of using global variables.

Global Variables

If you must use global variables, it's good practice to declare all of them in a single module and group them by function. Give the module a meaningful name that indicates its purpose, such as GLOBAL.BAS.

With the exception of global variables, procedures and functions should only operate on objects that are passed to them. Global variables that are used in routines should be identified in the general comment area at the beginning of the routine. In addition, you should pass arguments to subs and functions using `ByVal`, unless you explicitly want to change the value of the passed argument.

Write modular code whenever possible. For example, if your application displays a dialog box, put all the controls and code required to perform the dialog box's task in a single form. This helps keep the application's code organized into useful components and minimizes its runtime overhead.

Summary

Programming standards can make the job of the maintenance programmer much easier. Because 90 percent of the time you'll be the maintenance programmer, you should try to follow some programming standards when designing your applications. Programming standards are absolutely essential in a multiprogrammer shop.

Database Standards

Database naming standards are used to help the DBA and the programmers who'll be using that database. By creating standards for the different objects you create in a database, each person using the database will know which type of object he or she is dealing with just by looking at the name of the object.

Database Naming Standards

In addition to programming standards, you may want to define some standards for naming the objects in your database. This will help you identify particular objects when you're reviewing your source code without having to look at a printed data dictionary. The following sections include some naming standards that can be used with the Microsoft Access database system, the Microsoft SQL Server database system, or any other database system you choose. Of course, some of these standards may need to be modified, depending on limitations of your particular database. If you use another database system, you may have to change, delete, or add more information for the types of objects used in that database system.

Database Naming Conventions

Name your database something that will make sense to you and your programmers. Try to avoid cryptic names with numbers, because these are not easily recognized by anyone who's not familiar with your application. Here are some examples of good database names:

- Customers
- Invoice
- GeneralLedger

Table Naming

Tables defined in a database should have a prefix assigned to them. For small applications, the prefix *tbl* has been used successfully by many programmers. Here are some examples of some table names for a project management system:

- tblProjects
- tblCustomers
- tblEmployees

For larger systems, such as an accounting application, you may want to group your tables by the subsystem in which the tables are modified directly by the application. Here are some examples of table names:

- empInfo
- empDesc
- glAccounts
- glPostings
- arPostings
- arReceipts
- rptList
- rptSelections
- rptSorts

Each table in this list has a prefix that identifies the subsystem where that table is most directly modified: *emp* relates to the Employee module, *gl* to the General Ledger module, *ar* to the Accounts Receivable module, and *rpt* to the reporting module. Once again, just by looking at the table name, you get a good idea of where that table is used. You don't need to refer to any printed documentation just to determine what the table is used for.

Obviously, there will be times when a table is used in more than one module. In that case, you need to make a decision about what the prefix should be. Either choose one of the modules or make a new prefix to identify tables that are used in more than one module. A good example of this is tables that hold validation codes such as states and types. You may want to use the prefix *val* for these types of tables—for example, valStates and valCustomerTypes.

Primary Key Definition

It's recommended you use an integer (`Long`) as your primary key for each table. This is a unique number that the user never sees; it's used internally to uniquely identify each row. This also cuts down on the amount of fields in your `WHERE` clause. Additionally, you can place this value in the `ItemData()` property of a list or combo box for quick retrieval of the full information from the table for the text portion of the list or combo box. From a performance standpoint, this is very efficient, because most database systems perform joins on integer types quicker than any other type.

If you use a `long` integer as your primary key, you always have the option of using the `IDENTITY`, `AutoNumber`, or `Sequence` numbers that will automatically generate an ID for you. This way, you don't have to remember to increment a number each time. However, some front-end applications don't allow you to always retrieve the value that was just generated, so you do need to weigh the usage based on your front-end application.

Common Columns

Each table in your system should contain columns that will allow you to track who made the last update and at what time and date that update was performed. The following field names are put into each of the tables in a database:

- sLastUpdate_id
- dtLastUpdate_dt
- iConcurrency_id

The last field can be used if you want to track multiuser access to this row yourself. This might be used in place of a timestamp field. If the database system you have does not support a timestamp feature, you could build your own incrementing field. Of course, this means you need to fill in this field and update it every time the table is modified.

System Tables

Often, you'll have tables that are used in multiple applications. Preface these table names with either *tbl* or *sys*. Here are some examples:

- tblTableIDs
- tblSystemVars
- tblStates
- sysValidations
- sysFlags

Temporary Tables

Sometimes you'll need to create some temporary tables (also called *work tables*) for use in your application. Preface all these tables with *wrk*. Temporary tables should always be created in a separate database if possible. This keeps clutter out of the main database. Additionally, on SQL Server, you can turn logging off on the database that holds the temporary tables. This will help speed up the database access and avoid out-of-log-space errors. In Access, this helps keep the size of the main database from growing and avoids a lot of compacting and possibly repairing.

Column Naming

Just as you name a variable with the data type that variable contains, you should do the same with the column names in your tables. By doing this, you don't need to refer to a printed data dictionary when looking at your source code. You'll be able to see a column name and determine what the data type is immediately. When defining columns to use in your tables, the following form is recommended:

```
<prefix><body>_<suffix>
```

Field Prefix

The *prefix* specifies the data type of the data stored in a column. The reasoning behind using a prefix to represent the column data type is that it provides useful information during programming. Many of the front-end development tools and data-aware controls in use today for the development of applications display the table's column name only, instead of the column name and data type. When the developer is mapping the column's data type to a Visual Basic, C, or a C++ data type, the column data type must be known in order to map the data correctly. If the programmer/developer constantly has to reference a secondary front-end tool to determine the data type of the column, much time will be wasted and possible errors will result due to incorrect data mapping between the database's data type and the Visual Basic data type.

Table B.1 lists the prefixes to be used in the SQL Server column naming convention. Also displayed in this table is the corresponding Visual Basic data type to be used in the event that a local copy of the SQL Server data is to be used during programming.

Table B.1 SQL Server Column Naming Standards

SQL Data Type	Description	Prefix	VB Data Type
Binary(n)		bin	*
Bit		bool	Boolean
Char(n)	Fixed-length character data from 1 to 255 bytes	s	String
DateTime		dt	Variant or String
Float		dbl	Double
Image		img	*
Int		l	Long
Money		mny	Currency
Real		sng	Single
SmallDateTime		sdt	Variant or String
SmallInt		I	Integer
SmallMoney		c	Currency
Text		txt	String
TimeStamp		ts	Variant or String
TinyInt		byt	Integer or Byte
VarBinary(n)		vb	*
VarChar(n)	Variable-length character data from 1 to 255 bytes	sz	String

** These large data types cannot be handled directly by a Visual Basic data type. Instead, they're handled through a custom control such as the image control for handling the SQL image data type.*

SQL Server and Access

Table B.2 lists the prefixes for each type of data that can be stored in a table in both SQL Server and Access databases.

Table B.2 SQL Server and Access Prefixes

Prefix	SQL Server	Access
bin	Binary(n)	N/A
bool	Bit	Yes/No
s	Char(n)	Text
cnt	N/A	Counter
dt	DateTime	Date/Time
dbl	Float	Double
img	Image	OLE Object
l	Int	Integer or Long
c	Money	Currency
sng	Real	Single
sdt	SmallDateTime	Date/Time
i	SmallInt	Integer
sm	SmallMoney	Currency
txt	Text	Memo
ts	TimeStamp	N/A
byt	TinyInt	Integer
vb	VarBinary(n)	N/A
sz	VarChar(n)	Text or Memo

Standard Suffixes

Many times, some standard suffixes are added to field names to help further identify the type of data a column contains. Some possible suffixes are listed in Table B.3.

Table B.3 Standard Suffixes

Suffix	Description
ad	Address
amt	Amount
cd	Code
desc	Description
dt	Date
fl	Flag
id	Identifier
nm	Name
qty	Quantity
tm	Time
txt	Text

Timestamp

A timestamp field should be contained in every table you create when using SQL Server. Some front-end engines can use this timestamp type when performing concurrency checking.

Index Naming

Indexes should begin with the prefix *idx*. This prefix should be followed by a name that identifies the field or fields contained within the index. Here are two examples:

- idxLastName
- idxCustID

Stored Procedure Naming

Stored procedures should begin with the prefix *proc* followed by a name that identifies the purpose of the stored procedure. Here are some examples:

- procGetCustomerID
- procCustomerInsert
- procGetNextID

TIP
It's recommended that you don't use the prefix *sp*, because this is used for the built-in SQL Server system procedures.

Trigger Naming

A trigger should begin with the prefix *trg*, followed by the name of the table (leaving off that table's prefix). It should then be followed by *del*, *ins*, or *updt* for the `Delete`, `Insert`, or `Update` trigger, respectively. Here are some examples:

- trgCustomers_del
- trgCustomers_ins
- trgCustomers_updt

View Naming

Views should begin with the prefix of *qry*. This matches the naming convention used in Microsoft Access databases. Here are some examples:

- qryCustomerShow
- qryCustomerInvoices

Default Naming

Defaults should begin with the prefix *def*:

- defState
- defCustType

Rule Naming

Rules should begin with the prefix *rul*:

- rulState
- rulCustType

Summary

Database standards can help make the jobs of DBAs and application programmers much easier. Using standards can help you identify column types in your Visual Basic program without having to look at the database. In addition, a DBA will be able to perform joins on like columns without having to lookup each column to see whether the data types are compatible.

Bibliography

THIS APPENDIX CONTAINS A LIST OF SOME recommended books and periodicals for reading.

Recommended Programming Books

Appleman, Daniel. *ActiveX Component Development with Visual Basic 5.0.* Ziff-Davis Press, 1997. ISBN 1-56276-287-7.

Appleman, Daniel. *Visual Basic Programmer's Guide to the Win32 API*. Ziff-Davis Press, 1996. ISBN 1-56276-287-7.

Jennings, Roger. *Database Developer's Guide with Visual Basic 5.0.* Sams Publishing, 1997. ISBN 0-672-30440-6.

Petzold, Charles. *Programming Windows, 2nd Edition.* Microsoft Press, 1990. ISBN 1-55615-264-7.

Spencer, Kenneth L. and Ken Miller. *Client/Server Programming with Microsoft Visual Basic.* Microsoft Press. ISBN 1-57231-232-7.

Vaugh, William R. *Hitchhiker's Guide to Visual Basic and SQL Server.* Microsoft Press. ISBN 1-57231-567-9.

Recommended Standards Books and Articles

Capucciati, Maria R. "Putting Your Best Face Forward: Designing an Effective User Interface." *Microsoft Systems Journal*. Microsoft Press, February, 1993.

McConnell, Steve. *Code Complete.* Microsoft Press, 1993. ISBN 1-55615-484-4.

Moncrief, Frank. "Master the Principles of User Interface Design." *BasicPro Magazine*. Fawcette Technical Publications, February/March, 1993.

Socha, John. "User Interface Design." *Visual Basic Insider's Technical Summit.* September, 1993.

The Windows Interface, An Application Design Guide. Microsoft Press, 1987, 1992.

ODBC References

Geiger, Kyle. *Inside ODBC.* Microsoft Press, 1995. ISBN 1-55615-815-7.

Microsoft ODBC 3.0 Programmer's Reference and SDK Guide. Microsoft Press, 1996. ISBN 1-57231-516-4.

Object-Oriented Programming References

For more information on object-oriented programming, OLE Automation, and the OLE 2.0 standard, consult the following texts:

Brockschmidt, Kraig. *Inside OLE 2.* Microsoft Press. ISBN 1-55615-618-9.

Coad, Peter and Edward Yourdon. *Object-Oriented Analysis.* Yourdon Press, 1991. ISBN 0-13-629981-4.

Meyer, Bertrand. *Object-Oriented Software Construction.* Prentice Hall, 1988. ISBN 0-13-629049-3.

Smalltalk V. Software from Digitalk. (Excellent tutorial for learning OOP.)

Taylor, David A., Ph.D. *Object-Oriented Technology: A Manager's Guide.* Addison-Wesley Publishing Company, 1990. ISBN 0-201-56358-4.

Wirfs-Brock, Rebecca, Brian Wilkerson, and Lauren Wiener. *Designing Object-Oriented Software.* Prentice Hall, 1990. ISBN 0-13-629825-7.

SQL and Database Books

Groff, James R. and Paul N. Weinberg. *LAN Times Guide to SQL.* Osborne McGraw-Hill. ISBN 0-07-882026-X.

Hernandez, Michael J. *Database Design for Mere Mortals.* Addison-Wesley Developers Press, 1997. ISBN 0-201-69471-9.

Periodicals and Conferences

The following sections list periodicals and conferences available for Visual Basic programmers.

Access/Office/Visual Basic Advisor Magazine

Advisor Publications

4010 Morena Blvd.

P.O. Box 17902

San Diego, CA 92177

(800) 336–6060

(619) 483–6400

Access/Visual Basic Advisor Conference

A conference designed for programmers interested in Visual Basic, Access, and SQL Server. Check the Web site for Advisor Publications for more details (`www.advisor.com`).

Visual Basic Developer

Pinnacle Publishing

P.O. Box 888

Kent, WA 98035–0888

(800) 788–1900

(206) 251–1900

`www.pinpub.com`

SQL Server Professional Newsletter

Pinnacle Publishing

P.O. Box 888

Kent, WA 98035–0888

(800) 788–1900

(206) 251–1900

`www.pinpub.com`

Visual Basic Programmer's Journal

Fawcette Technical Publications

280 Second Street, Suite 200

Los Altos, CA 94022–3603

(303) 541–0610 (customer service)

(800) 848–5523

(415) 917–7650

(415) 948–7332 (fax)

Visual Basic Insiders' Technical Summit (VBITS)

A conference for learning all about Visual Basic. There are several VBITS conferences each year. Check the Fawcette Web site for dates and locations (`www.devx.com`).

Windows NT Magazine

Duke Communications International, Inc.

P.O. Box 447

Loveland, CO 80539–0447

(800) 621–1544

(970) 663–4700

Products from PDSA

Besides the book you're currently enjoying, the following are other products from Paul D. Sheriff and Associates:

Video Training on Visual Basic Versions 3 through 6. (Available from Keystone Learning Systems.)

(800) 748–4838

`www.klscorp.com`

Video Training on Client/Server and Three-Tier Architecture. (Available from Keystone Learning Systems.)

Video Training on SQL Server 4.2 and SQL Server 6.x. (Available from Keystone Learning Systems.)

PDSA Consulting and Tools. (Available from Paul D. Sheriff and Associates.)

202 Fashion Lane Suite 223

Tustin, CA 92780

(888) 899–PDSA (toll free)

(714) 734–9792 (voice)

(714) 734–9793 (fax)

`Psheriff@pdsa.com` (email)

Visit the PDSA Web site at `http://www.pdsa.com`.

J

Answers to Review Questions

THIS APPENDIX PRESENTS THE ANSWERS TO THE REVIEW questions at the end of every chapter.

Chapter 1: Visual Basic Overview

Name the main object used in Visual Basic to build an application.

Answer: A form.

Name three types of applications you can build in Visual Basic.

Answer: Standard EXE, ActiveX EXE, ActiveX DLL, ActiveX control, IIS application, DHTML application, ActiveX document EXE, ActiveX document DLL, Data Project, and add-in.

List the three steps to creating a Visual Basic application.

Answer: Create the interface, set properties, write code.

What's the biggest advantage to graphical operating systems?

Answer: Small user learning curve and standard interface.

What's the big difference between Windows 3.*x* and Windows 95 or Windows NT?

Answer: Windows 3.*x* is a 16-bit operating environment, whereas Windows 95 and Windows NT are 32-bit operating systems.

Name three different parts of a window.

Answer: Any three of the following is acceptable: title bar, minimize button, maximize button, close button, and system menu.

Give some examples of events.

Answer: `Click`, `KeyPress`, `MouseDown`, `MouseUp`, and `DoubleClick`.

Chapter 2: Getting Started

What's a form?

Answer: A location to build a user interface.

What's a property?

Answer: Data that describes the characteristics or behavior of a particular object.

Which property displays the form maximized when it's displayed?

Answer: The `WindowState` property.

Which property changes the title bar of a form?

Answer: The `Caption` property.

Chapter 3: Controls

Which control is used to display information to the user but doesn't allow the user to change it?

Answer: A label.

Which control is used to retrieve typed input from the user?

Answer: A text box and sometimes a combo box.

Which control allows the user to select only one of a group of choices?

Answer: An option button.

Which control allows the user to select one or more of a group of choices?

Answer: A check box.

Chapter 4: Lists and Menus

Which control displays many items to the user?

Answer: A list box.

Which control displays just one item to the user?

Answer: A combo box.

How can you sort the items in a list or combo box?

Answer: Set the `Sorted` property to `True`.

How do you make a letter on a menu item underlined?

Answer: Place and ampersand (&) in front of the letter of the menu `Caption` property.

Chapter 5: Events Happen

What's the default event for a command button?

Answer: `Click`.

What's the default event for a text box?

Answer: `Change`.

What's the default event for an option button?

Answer: `Click`.

How do you bring up a code window for a particular control?

Answer: Double-click the control. Right-click the control and select View Code.

Chapter 6: Variables

Name four of the different data types supported by Visual Basic.

Answer: `String`, `Double`, `Single`, `Byte`, `Integer`, `Long`, `Currency`, `Date`, and `Variant`.

Declare three local variables using the three types you listed for the previous question. (Be sure to use the naming standards.)

Answer:

```
Dim strName As String
Dim lngValue As Long
Dim intValue As Integer
Dim dblValue As Double
Dim sngValue As Single
Dim vntValue As Variant
Dim curValue As Currency
Dim bytValue As Byte
Dim dtValue As Date
```

What will the following code display on a form?

```
Dim vntString
vntString = "100"
vntString = vntString + 50
Print vntString
```

Answer: 150.

Chapter 7: Arrays, Types, and Constants

What will the following code produce?

```
Dim aintValues() As Integer

ReDim aintValues(1)
aintValues(0) = 10
Print aintValues(0)
```

Answer: 10.

What will the following code produce?

```
ReDim aintValues(2)
aintValues(1) = 20
Print aintValues(0)
```

Answer: 0.

What will the following code produce?

```
Print aintValues(1)
```

Answer: 20.

Declare a constant named `conValue` that holds the value 1.

Answer:

```
Const conValue As Integer = 1
```

Write a statement that adds 10 to the constant you created for the previous question and put the result in a variable called `intValue`.

Answer:

```
intValue = conValue + 10
```

Chapter 8: Conditional Logic and Looping

Write an `If` statement that checks to see whether one number is greater than another and, if it is, displays a message box stating "Number 1 is greater than Number 2."

Answer:

```
If Number1 > Number2 Then
   MsgBox "Number 1 is greater than Number 2"
End If
```

Write a `Do...Loop` that loops from 10 to 1. Print each value on the form.

Answer:

```
intLoop 10
Do While intLoop > 0
   Print intLoop
   intLoop = intLoop - 1
Loop
```

Write a `For...Next` loop that loops from 1 to 100 and only prints the value 50 when the loop variable becomes 50.

Answer:

```
For intLoop = 1 To 100
   If intLoop = 50 Then
      Print intLoop
   End If
Next
```

Chapter 9: Procedures and Functions

True or false? You may use a letter or underscore as the first character for a procedure name.

Answer: True.

What's the file extension used for code modules?

Answer: BAS.

True or false? Global variables are declared in the declarations section of code modules or forms.

Answer: False. They need to be declared in BAS modules.

In the following code:

```
Dim intTemp As Integer
Dim strName As String
intTemp = 5
strName = "Bill"
Call Proc1(intTemp, strName)
Me.Print intTemp
Me.Print strName
Sub Proc1(intParm As Integer, strValue As String)
   intParm = 10
   strValue = "Hi There"
End Sub
```

For `Me.Print intTemp`, what is displayed?

Answer: 10.

For `Me.Print strName`, what is displayed?

Answer: "Hi There".

In the following code:

```
Dim intTemp As Integer
Dim strName As String

intTemp = 5
strName = "Bill"
Call Proc1(intTemp, ByVal strName)
Me.Print intTemp
Me.Print strName
Sub Proc1(ByVal intParm As Integer, strValue As String)
   intParm = 10
   strValue = "Hi There"
End Sub
```

For `Me.Print intTemp`, what is displayed?

Answer: 5.

For `Me.Print strName`, what is displayed?

Answer: "Hi There".

Chapter 10: Built-in Visual Basic Functions

What's the function that determines whether one string is contained within another string?

Answer: `Instr()`.

What's the function that returns the current system date and time?

Answer: `Now()`.

What's the function that returns only the current system date as a string?

Answer: `Date$()`.

What function allows you to add days, months, quarters, and so on from a date?

Answer: `DateAdd()`.

Chapter 11: Dialog Boxes

True or false? Once a modal dialog box is displayed, a user may also use other parts of the same application.

Answer: False.

True or false? The `InputBox()` function allows several values to be input.

Answer: False.

What's the name of the method that's invoked on a common dialog control to make the Save As dialog box to appear?

Answer: `ShowSave`.

Write the code that displays a form called frmModal modally.

Answer:

```
frmModal.Show vbModal
```

Chapter 12: The ADO Data Control

Which property do you click to bring up the property pages for a data control?

Answer: Double-click (`Custom`) or the ellipsis (...).

What two properties must you set on each text box to have the data control automatically fill in field information?

Answer: `DataSource` and `DataField`.

Which control would you use if you had to display multiple columns?

Answer: `DataGrid`.

Chapter 13: Data Control Programming

Which event do you use to perform data validation?

Answer: `WillChangeRecord()`.

Which event reports back errors from the data control to your form?

Answer: The `Error` event.

Which property can you use to report the current record position?

Answer: `AbsolutePosition`.

Which method do you use to search for a particular record in a recordset?

Answer: `Find`.

Chapter 14: Additional Data Control Topics

Which property do you set a data control to for populating the list portion of a data-bound combo or list box?

Answer: `RowSource`.

Which property do you set with a field name to populate the list portion of a data-bound combo or list box?

Answer: `ListField`.

Which property does the **`BoundColumn`** property match to—**`DataSource`** or `RowSource`?

Answer: `RowSource`.

What does the **`MatchEntry`** property do?

Answer: Performs drill-down matching as the user types.

Chapter 15: Multiple Document Interface

How many MDI parents are allowed in a Visual Basic program?

Answer: One.

How do you make a form an MDI child form?

Answer: Set the `MDIChild` property to `True`.

Can a child form be displayed modally?

Answer: No.

Where should you create pop-up menus?

Answer: On the main MDI form.

Chapter 16: The Debugger

What are the three modes in Visual Basic?

Answer: Design, Break, and Run.

Which key marks a line as a breakpoint?

Answer: F9.

Which statement prints values from the Immediate window when the application is in Break mode?

Answer: `Print` or `?`.

Which statement allows printing to the Immediate window from within the application?

Answer: `Debug.Print`.

Which statement causes Visual Basic to halt execution of your program?

Answer: `Stop`.

Chapter 17: Error Handling

Write an error statement that will cause Visual Basic to jump to a label named `FormLoad_EH`.

Answer:

```
On Error Goto FormLoad_EH
```

Which statement causes execution to continue at the line following the one the error occurred on?

Answer: `Resume Next`.

Which object/property returns a string describing the error that just occurred?

Answer: `Err.Description`.

Write the statement that turns error handling off.

Answer: `On Error Goto 0`.

Chapter 18: IDE and Editor Tips and Tricks

What's the hot key to bring up the Find window?

Answer: Ctrl+F.

What's the hotkey to bring up the Replace window?

Answer: Ctrl+H.

Which property sets the tab order of controls on a form?

Answer: `TabIndex`.

Why would you use a bookmark?

Answer: To move quickly to another location in your source code.

What's an add-in?

Answer: A program that will extend the functionality of the Visual Basic environment.

Chapter 19: Object-based Programming

What is *polymorphism*?

Answer: The ability for classes to use the same message names but produce different results.

What does *instantiate* mean?

Answer: Create a new instance of a class.

Chapter 20: Creating Class Modules

How do you expose `Private` variables from a class?

Answer: Using `Property Get/Let` statements.

How do you create a default property?

Answer: Set the Procedure ID in the Tools, Procedure Attributes dialog box to (Default).

How do you create a method?

Answer: Use `Public Sub` or `Public Function in the class module`.

Chapter 21: System Objects

Name three generic object types.

Answer: Form, Control, MDIForm, and Object.

Describe the function of the `New` keyword.

Answer: Creates a new instance of a class.

Which type of object is more efficient to use—generic or specific?

Answer: Specific.

Why?

Answer: The reference is compiled; it does not need to be determined at runtime.

Chapter 22: Collections

What are the built-in collections in Visual Basic?

Answer: `Forms`, `Controls`, and `Printers`.

How might collections help you in developing your application?

Answer: They allow you to store groups of objects and iterate over them as a group.

List the properties of the `Collection` object.

Answer: `Count`.

What are the methods of the `Collection` object?

Answer: `Add`, `Item`, and `Remove`.

Why should you build a class that encapsulates the `Collection` object?

Answer: To avoid having different object types in the same collection.

Chapter 23: Tips and Tricks

Which event do you use to restrict user input in text boxes?

Answer: `KeyPress`.

Which function do you use to force uppercase letters?

Answer: `UCase$()`.

What's the problem with the `LostFocus()` event?

Answer: Deadly embrace can lock up the user.

What does the `CausesValidation` property do?

Answer: Allows the user to click another control without firing the `Validate` event on the previous control when this property is set to `False`.

Which function would you use to display a currency value?

Answer: `FormatCurrency()`.

Which function would you use to display a date value?

Answer: `FormatDateTime()`.

Chapter 24: ActiveX Data Objects

Do you need a `Connection` object to establish a connection?

Answer: No, you can pass a connection string to a `Recordset` object.

Name two different types of cursors that ADO supports.

Answer: Forward only, dynamic, static, and keyset.

What are the properties of the ADO `Error` object?

Answer: `Description`, `NativeError`, `Number`, `Source`, and `SQLState`.

Why would you use a `Command` object?

Answer: To pass in parameters and receive output parameters from a stored procedure, to reexecute a query, to execute the same query on different connections, or to create prepared statements.

Chapter 25: Data Entry with ADO Objects

What do you use the `ItemData` property for?

Answer: Storing a long integer (generally as a primary key for a table).

How do you delete a row using ADO?

Answer: Use the `Delete` method.

Chapter 26: Wizards

True or false? The Data Form Wizard creates only one type of data entry form.

Answer: False.

True or false? The Application Wizard generates a complete application for you.

Answer: False. It creates a template from which you can finish creating an application.

Chapter 27: Visual Database Tools

True or false? The data environment can only be used at design time.

Answer: False.

Write code that opens a data environment connection at runtime.

Answer: `denvEmployees.cnEmp.Open`.

What's a `Command` object?

Answer: A reusable object that allows you to open a resultset or execute a SQL action query.

Will the Data View window show you queries in an Access MDB file?

Answer: No.

Can you modify the objects in an Access MDB file with the Data View window?

Answer: No.

Chapter 28: Using the Windows API

Which function can be used to search for a string in a combo or list box?

Answer: `SendMessage()`.

Which DLL contains the function to determine the Windows platform you're running on?

Answer: Kernel32.dll.

Which function returns the Windows System directory?

Answer: `GetSystemDirectory()`.

Chapter 29: Storing User Information

How do you create an INI file?

Answer: Use a text editor such as Notepad.

Which function retrieves data from an INI file?

Answer: `GetPrivateProfileString()`.

What type of database is the System Registry?

Answer: Hierarchical.

Which built-in function gets data from the Registry?

Answer: `GetSetting()`.

Which built-in function writes data into the Registry?

Answer: `SaveSetting()`.

If you had to store data for multiple users to get at, which location would you use (INI or Registry)?

Answer: INI.

Chapter 30: ActiveX Controls: Part 1

Which control would you use to store a repository of images?

Answer: ImageList.

Which control lets you display status messages to the user?

Answer: Status bar.

Which control gives you a hierarchical view of data using pictures and text?

Answer: ImageCombo.

Chapter 31: ActiveX Controls: Part 2

Which control can you use to select a date?

Answer: DateTimePicker.

Which tab control is easier to use—TabStrip or SSTab?

Answer: SSTab.

Chapter 32: Drag and Drop

Which property sets the icon to use for the dragging operation?

Answer: `DragIcon`.

Which property do you set to make the drag operation automatic?

Answer: `DragMode`.

Which event is fired when a control is dragged over another one?

Answer: `DragOver`.

What are the three "states" the `DragOver()` event can receive?

Answer: `vbLeave`, `vbEnter`, and `vbOver`.

Chapter 33: Optimization

True or false? `Variant` data types are more efficient than `Long` data types.

Answer: False.

Which constant should you assign to a string variable to set it equal to nothing?

Answer: `vbNullString`.

Which cursor type is the most efficient?

Answer: Forward only.

Which cursor type is the least efficient?

Answer: Dynamic.

True or false? Comments increase the size of your code.

Answer: False.

Chapter 34: Package and Deployment Wizard

Which types of packages can you create with the P&D Wizard?

Answer: Standard, Internet, and dependency file.

What's the name of the main Visual Basic 6 runtime DLL?

Answer: Msvbvm60.dll.

What are the two main locations where files are installed on a user's machine?

Answer: Program Files\<*your path*> and Windows\System or \Winnt\System32.

What's a dependency file?

Answer: A file that lists all the other files a certain component needs in order to run.

E

Sample Code Installation Instructions

THIS APPENDIX PRESENTS HOW TO INSTALL and use the code examples for this book.

Getting the Latest Service Pack

Before you do too much in Visual Basic 6, make sure you've downloaded the latest Visual Studio Service Pack from the Microsoft Web site. A good place to start to get the latest Service Pack is `www.microsoft.com/vbasic`. This usually points you to the latest Service Pack for Visual Studio 6.

Installation Instructions

To install the examples for each of the chapters, create a new folder on your hard drive. Download `CODE.EXE` from the companion Web site (`http://www.mcp.com/product_support`) to that folder. After it's on your hard drive, double-click `CODE.EXE` to extract it. Under this new folder on your hard drive, you'll find several folders, each one relating to those chapters in the book that have examples. Each folder is labeled with the chapter number and a short description of what the examples relate to. There's usually only one VBP file within each folder for all the examples, so you should be able to load that VBP file with Visual Basic 6 Professional or Enterprise Edition.

Sample Access Database

A Microsoft Access database called Employees.mdb can also be found in this folder. This database contains the tables necessary to run most of the examples in this book.

Upsizing the Database

You can upsize the Employees.mdb file to SQL Server using the Microsoft Access Upsizing Wizard or by using the scripts contained in the Scripts folder.

You can also upsize this database to Oracle or any ODBC-compliant database with the same scripts; however, you might need to modify the scripts somewhat for your particular database. I've tried to keep the SQL statements as generic as possible, but they're optimized for SQL Server because that's the system I use most often.

Load the scripts in the following order:

- Table.sql   Creates the tables for the employee system
- Insert.sql   Adds the data to the tables
- Index.sql   Adds some indexes to the tables

This assumes you've already created a database in your server to hold these tables.

Index

Symbols

A

B

C

D

E

F

G

H

I-J

K

L

M

N

S

T

U

V

X-Z

Other Related Titles

Doing Objects in Visual Basic 6
1-56276-577-9
Deborah Kurata
$49.99 US/$71.95 CAN

Using Visual Basic 6
0-7897-1633-X
Bob Reselman, Richard Peasley, and Wayne Pruchniak
$29.99 US/$42.95 CAN

The Waite Group's Visual Basic 6 Database How-To
1-57169-152-9
Eric Winemiller
$39.99 US/$56.95 CAN

The Waite Group's Visual Basic 6 Client/Server How-To
1-57169-154-5
Noel Jerke
$49.99 US/$71.95 CAN

Sams Teach Yourself Internet Programming with Visual Basic 6 in 21 Days
0-672-31459-2
Peter Aitken
$29.99 US/$42.95 CAN

Sams Teach Yourself Database Programming with Visual Basic 6 in 21 Days
0-672-31308-1
Curtis Smith and Michael Amundsen
$45.00 US/$64.95 CAN

The Waite Group's Visual Basic 6 How-To
1-57169-153-7
Eric Brierley
$39.99 US/$57.95 CAN

Database Access with Visual Basic
1-56276-567-1
Jeffrey McManus
$39.99 US/$56.95 CAN

MTS Programming with Visual Basic 6
0-672-31425-8
Scot Hillier
$29.99 US/$42.95 CAN

Building Enterprise Solutions with Visual Studio 6
0-672-31489-4
G.A. Sullivan
$49.99 US/$71.95 CAN

www.quecorp.com

Special Edition Using Visual Basic 6
0-7897-1542-2
Brian Siler and Jeff Spotts
$39.99 US/$57.95 CAN

Dan Appleman's Visual Basic Programming Guide to Win32 API
0-672-31590-4
Dan Appleman
$59.99 US/$85.95 CAN

Roger Jennings' Database Developer's Guide with Visual Basic 6
0-672-31063-5
Roger Jennings
$59.99 US/$85.95 CAN

The Waite Group's Visual Basic Source Code Library
0-672-31387-1
Brian Shea
$34.99 US/$50.95 CAN

All prices are subject to change.